The Economic Development
of Western Civilization

Books by Shepard B. Clough

MAKING FASCISTS (*with Herbert W. Schneider*)

HISTORY OF THE FLEMISH MOVEMENT IN BELGIUM

FRANCE, 1789–1939. A STUDY IN NATIONAL ECONOMICS

AN ECONOMIC HISTORY OF EUROPE (*with Charles W. Cole*)

A CENTURY OF AMERICAN LIFE INSURANCE

THE RISE AND FALL OF CIVILIZATION

L'HISTOIRE ECONOMIQUE DES ETATS-UNIS

THE AMERICAN WAY: THE ECONOMIC BASIS OF OUR CIVILIZATION

THE ECONOMIC DEVELOPMENT OF WESTERN CIVILIZATION

The Economic Development of Western Civilization

by Shepard B. Clough

PROFESSOR OF HISTORY
COLUMBIA UNIVERSITY

McGRAW-HILL BOOK COMPANY, INC.

New York   Toronto   London

1959

THE ECONOMIC DEVELOPMENT OF WESTERN CIVILIZATION

II

THE MAPLE PRESS COMPANY, YORK, PA.

To My Students

Preface

It will hardly come as an astounding revelation to my readers that I, as a professional historian, hold man's greatest heritage to be knowledge of the past, nor will they be greatly surprised to learn that I believe all current human behavior to be conditioned by "man's experience through time." It is, indeed, my firm conviction that "the wisdom of the ages" is man's choicest possession.

If I am correct in my estimate of the place of history in life, then it follows that historians have a weighty responsibility to discharge for their fellow men. It is their task to select, record, and interpret from myriads of experiences those which are the most useful in helping men to decide what kind of a world they want and in guiding mankind in its eternal quest for that world. Of necessity this assignment requires the study both of detailed events and of exceedingly broad movements.

In the present work, I have labored long and conscientiously to understand and to present a *part* of human experience which will have meaning in the human struggle for the attainment of higher levels of civilization. In other words, it has been my intention to show the relationship of economic activity to the human drama as it has unfolded through time. In addition, I have tried to meet one of the major criticisms of economic historians, so cogently pointed out by one of my masters, the late Wesley C. Mitchell, that we have been guilty of amassing data without plan or reason and that we have made little effort to establish what the necessary relationships among those data are.[1] Specif-

[1] Wesley C. Mitchell, "The Role of Money in Economic History," *The Tasks of Economic History*, a supplement to *The Journal of Economic History*, December, 1944, pp. 61–67.

ically, I have endeavored to organize economic data around the central theme of economic growth and to relate that theme to human strivings for civilization. I have done this for that part of the world known as Western Culture, especially Europe and North America.

Inasmuch as the preface of a scholarly book is the one place where the author may speak familiarly with his readers, it is not improper that I should confess to them my trepidation regarding the product of my efforts which they hold in their hands. I fear that critics may complain that I have undertaken too huge a task, that specialists may contend that I have not given enough space to some hobby of theirs, and that reviewers may argue that I should have written another kind of book from the one in these covers. These are the usual foibles of men who are dedicated to the proposition that knowledge to be "sound" must be stereotyped; they have to be borne with patience and fortitude by the would-be innovator. At all events, I am of the opinion that both scholar and student should resist allowing education to become so strait-jacketed by tradition that it loses all relevance to the world about us.

I should also confide to my readers that I, like all conscientious scholars, have a fear regarding the possible appearance of errors in my work and that, like most of my kind, I have taken extreme precautions to avoid them. Not only have I spent some seven years in writing this book and over a quarter of a century in the study of economic history, but I have imposed on my friends and colleagues to help protect me from slips. Fortunately I had the expert criticism of Professor Thomas C. Cochran of the entire manuscript and that of Professor A. P. Usher of a large part of the European sections. Furthermore, Elias Bickerman read those parts having to do with Ancient history, John H. Mundy, those dealing with the Middle Ages, and Garrett Mattingly, those covering the first three centuries of Modern Times. To all of these experts I am grateful, and I hereby exonerate them from all blame for those frailties of expression or of interpretation which they did not catch or which I was obstinate enough to retain in spite of their warnings.

Shepard B. Clough

Contents

List of Illustrations

List of Maps

PART ONE

Economic

Growth

CHAPTER 1

To the Reader

The Subject and Purpose of This Book

At the outset of any scientific research it is essential both for clarity of thought and for effective analysis that the investigator state as precisely and as cogently as possible what subject is under inquiry and why the study is being made. For fuller comprehension, the reader should have this information from the beginning. Therefore, let me explain my purpose and state as explicitly as I can what phase of man's experience on this earth I have sought to elucidate in this book.

Basically my purpose here is to make the kind of a contribution to knowledge which will aid mankind in attaining a higher level of civilization. I believe that to a very large degree man holds his fate in his own hands—that with sufficient knowledge of human behavior he can formulate and apply policies which will allow him to make more rapid progress than would otherwise be the case toward those earthly goals which he sets for himself.

By level of civilization I mean, as I have tried to show in my study, *The Rise and Fall of Civilization:*[1] (1) the achieving of universally acclaimed distinction in such esthetic and intellectual pursuits as architecture, painting, literature, sculpture, music, philosophy, and science; (2) the attaining of leisure in which to enjoy esthetic experiences; (3) the

[1] New York: McGraw-Hill, 1951; second printing, New York: Columbia University Press, 1957, p. 5.

3

creating of such a control over social environment that people will conduct themselves according to known and just rules for the welfare of all; and (4) the establishing of such a mastery of physical environment that people will attain freedom from want. The greater the extent to which a society produces esthetic and intellectual works of high merit, provides security for its members, and establishes material well-being for all, the more civilized that society is; conversely, the less a society realizes either qualitatively or quantitatively any of these tenets of civilization, the less civilized it is. Essentially this concept of civilization is that which extends throughout those parts of the world which lie in the tradition of Western Europe, that is, Western Europe itself, the Americas, Australia, New Zealand, South Africa, and the Philippines.

If this, then, is the purpose of our study, let us look at the specific object of our investigation—the historical growth of the economy of Western culture. Economic growth has been chosen because it is my firm conviction that economic well-being is a necessary condition for attaining high levels of civilization. It not only accounts for one of the essential elements of our definition of civilization—freedom from want—but it provides an economic surplus which allows people to devote their attention to the arts. Economic well-being makes possible leisure in which to enjoy esthetic creations; and it tends to reduce tensions among men, allowing them to lead better-ordered lives. Furthermore, economic growth has been accompanied by the expansion of commerce over large areas, and commerce has made possible an exchange of ideas and a competitive spirit among men for the attainment of higher levels of civilization. Commerce also has given us tools for communication and analysis, for the earliest known forms of writing came from the making of business records, the first systems of numerical notations stemmed from business transactions, and much of early mathematics, like geometry, was derived from measuring materials in exchange. Lastly, economic surplus has been responsible for the development of cities, and cities have been centers of civilizing activity. Most of the generally accepted achievements of high merit in science, engineering, sculpture, music, architecture, painting, and literature have been produced in cities or by people who received the impetus for their accomplishments in urban centers. So strong is the correspondence between peaks of civilization and the end of long periods of economic development in a given culture that economic growth and material well-being may be considered to be a "necessary cause" of high levels of civilization.

As to method, it should be noted that the historical approach has been employed because it provides, I believe, the most penetrating insights into the problem before us. From the study of actual human experience through time one can establish what the relationship among events has been and what analogies there may be among similar but never identical situations, which can be used with profit in the formation of private and public policies. Only in history, recognized as the study of the totality of human activity, is it possible to arrive at a synthesis of economic, social, political, intellectual, psychological, and geographical aspects of life in the dimension of time. And only in historical study are we able to understand the universality, intensity, and duration of various aspects of human behavior.

Finally, we have decided to include within our purview all the area of what we shall call Western European culture. We have done this because cultures are those segments of humankind in which behavior is most fundamentally distinguishable. In fact, a culture is defined as a society which has a body of learnable and transmissible knowledge the basic parts of which are homogeneous enough and firmly enough established to affect similarly and sharply the behavior of a large number of persons. People within a culture have similar ideologies which are recognized to be the ends of human endeavor, similar institutions or organizations for attaining these ends, and similar patterns or styles of thought and action. In brief, individuals constitute a culture if they have comparable views regarding the ends for which both individuals and the group should strive, employ in the aggregate similar methods of production, distribution, and use, have developed homogeneous tastes and techniques in creative activity, and are in relationships which are controlled by similar types of social, political, economic, and religious institutions.[2]

By such criteria as these, it is possible to distinguish such cultures as the Egyptian, Greek, Roman, Medieval European, Chinese, Russian-Soviet, Eskimo, Indian, and Western European. The mere mention of such divisions of humankind emphasizes the basic differences among cultures and the necessity of understanding them. In our age, states or coalitions of states tend to be coterminous with cultures; thus government, that is, the wielding of authority over the vast majority of the community, is added to the other attributes of culture. Indeed, the "culture state" seems to be on the way of superseding or altering the position of the national state; and tensions among these culture groups appear to indicate that future wars may be wars between cultures and hence true crusades instead of wars among national groups.

Although the role played by cultures in determining human behavior makes cultures important as objects of study, other reasons exist for

[2] Institutions may be defined as organized systems of practices and rules regarding a value or series of values and the machinery developed to regulate the practices and to administer the rules.

concentrating our efforts upon them. For example, the study of cultures tends to focus attention upon the acquired features of societal existence and hence upon those aspects of life which are subject to human control. Also such study leads to an interest in how patterns of behavior come into being, how they are diffused geographically, and how they change through time. And these three segments of a culture's history—creation, diffusion, and change—are fundamental to the giving of direction to human development. These are the three main phases of a culture's life around which we shall organize our material.

Concerning Western European Culture

Among known cultures, that of Western Europe has been the most dynamic. Its rate of change has been greater than that of any culture in recorded history. Its people have achieved a higher level of civilization, as already defined, than any other group in all the pages of history. It has established ideologies, styles of behavior, and techniques of performing tasks which have been diffused to such an extent that they are completely dominant in a large portion of the globe and are highly influential in other cultures.

One of the important keys to understanding the superior position of Western European culture is to be found in its major ideologies. For the most part, and especially since the eleventh century, the West has expressed a desire for economic betterment. No great portion of the culture has ever held high the ascetic ideal, that is, abasement of the flesh for the elevation of the soul. Rather, the peoples of the West have desired to control nature so that they would not be the victims of nature's whims, that they might increase their material comforts, and obtain economic surplus allowing them to devote time to activities other than the production of physical necessities.

Also in the West there has been a long-standing recognition of the desirability of rules of social conduct—of laws—to which people should conform and an antipathy for *ad hoc* or "after the fact" rules of behavior. Here the contributions from the Roman and Hebraic-Greek traditions have been strong, for the West acquired from them, respectively, certain legal concepts and the morality of the Christian religion. Moreover, the West has sought to prevent the settlement of individual or of group differences by force. Even though it has failed to prevent war, its ideology in this regard is clear.

Throughout its history Western culture has desired to understand the world, and this desire has given rise to an abundance of expository and analytical literature. Although in the early Middle Ages explanations of the universe were based mainly upon intuitive knowledge—upon revelation and logic—by the twelfth century emphasis was being placed upon cognition by empirical means and upon the testing of such knowledge to ascertain whether or not the senses were being deluded. Knowledge obtained through the senses and subsequently verified by a variety of methods has been the great distinguishing triumph of the West. It is the basis of science, that is, the discovery of necessary relationships among events.

The West has also had a love of beauty—an admiration for all the arts. For the most part its accepted artistic goal has been to achieve a kind of naturalism—to portray, explain, or glorify the object or theme treated in generally understandable terms.[3] The more specific styles of artistic expression have usually, at least since the Late Middle Ages, spread throughout Western culture so that the West has had similar patterns of art at various periods of time and has acknowledged and enjoyed the same great works in spite of local jealousies and rivalries. Thus, throughout the West, Gothic architecture, Renaissance sculpture, eighteenth-century music, and impressionistic painting are regarded as belonging to a common cultural tradition.

Much the same statement can be made about techniques (specific ways of performing tasks) and about modern technology (attitudes toward and physical equipment for producing goods and services). Indeed, similarities in ideologies, the proximity of various regions of Western culture, and the facility of communication among the people of the West have permitted a rapid diffusion of many physical things and modes of behavior within the culture.

This has been true of capitalism, classical economic theory, textile machinery, and more recently, styles of dress. The homogeneous character of Western culture has been fostered also by a multiplicity of institutions, that is, by organized efforts to regulate the behavior of a large part of mankind in such a way that it has form and meaning.

Yet complete homogeneity does not exist in Western culture. Its subcultures show particular and characteristic deviations from the basic ideologies, styles, and institutions. These subcultures are distinguished particularly by differences in language, literature, and political and historical traditions. Frequently they are organized as political states and as such have acquired an extensive sway over humankind. When the people of these states became imbued with the doctrine of nationalism—an intense love and even a supreme loyalty and devotion to the national state —there developed a basis for rivalry and hostility among the subcultures.

[3] Such exceptions to this generalization as surrealist painting come to mind, but they are not numerous enough to alter the rule.

PRESENT EXTENT OF WESTERN CULTURE
The Area of Western Culture.

Unfortunately this kind of rivalry has been sharp and has led to wars within Western culture—wars which can be regarded as civil conflicts.

Real as such divisive factors as national states have been and are, Western culture has a unity when one compares it with Chinese culture, Indian culture, or Russian culture. Furthermore, differences in most aspects of human behavior are greater between socioeconomic groups within a subculture than they are between subcultures. Thus intellectuals from France, Germany, England, and the United States have more homogeneity in their behavior and more common interests than, let us say, an intellectual in France and a French manual laborer. At all events, Western culture is homogeneous enough so that it may be regarded as constituting a useful unit of study, particularly if one seeks to comprehend basic socioeconomic behavior.

Concerning Economics, Economic History, and Economic Growth

Before proceeding with our historical study of the economic development of Western culture, let us stop briefly to become oriented in some of the fundamental concepts of economics, economic history, and economic growth. These concepts will provide an organizing structure for the material to be found in subsequent chapters.

Economics is a study of goods and services which have exchange value. It deals essentially with the following questions:

1. What goods and services are produced, in what quantities, in what places, with what regularity, and why?

2. By the use of what natural and human resources, with what productive arts, and by means of what savings are these goods and services produced?

3. By what economic organizations—families, guilds, companies, partnerships, or corporations—are they produced?

4. For whose eventual use are these goods and services produced?

If these are the central issues of economics, it follows perforce that they are the major subjects of economic history. Yet between the two disciplines there is a difference of emphasis. Economics is concerned primarily with the "here and now," and only secondarily with the past. It is, therefore, interested in analyses which will throw light upon current problems and will assist in policy formation. By contrast, economic history is concerned with the problem of becoming—with development—and hence places more emphasis upon processes, long-term trends, and factors of change. Of all the subjects to which it has devoted its talents and on which it has thrown most light that of economic growth stands out as predominant.[4]

By economic growth is meant essentially an increase in goods and services available for human use. One may speak of the economic growth of a political or territorial unit, like the economic growth of France or of Vermont, or of any other segment of mankind, like the economic growth of Western culture. The implications of economic growth vary, however, within the chosen division of mankind as the supply of goods and services increases not only in absolute, aggregate terms but also in proportion to the population. Therefore, economic growth usually signifies, and this will be our usage, not only an increase in the total supply of goods and services within a selected unit of mankind, but more significantly an increase in goods and services per capita of the population.[5]

In recent times, goods and services produced have come to be expressed in terms of national income or of net national product. These

[4] By antithesis, the study of economic growth includes economic decline.

[5] Some students prefer to employ the formula of goods and services per occupied person. The issue involved here is that theoretically, at least, a growing economy could have a great many unemployed young persons or a declining economy could have a great proportion of unemployed old persons with the result that goods and services per capita of the total population might not reflect accurately the productive potential of the economy. Thus the supply of goods and services per capita of the employed emphasizes the more strictly economic side of society and minimizes the demographic and social side.

measures are national because nation-states are the chief gatherers of the necessary statistical data. These data include wages and other compensation of employees, net income of unincorporated business, net interest received from private bonds, mortgages, and other loans, net rents of persons, including self-occupied homes, and net corporate earnings.[6] Unfortunately, reliable national income statistics do not exist for many years in the past, nor do many states have adequate statistical information from which to derive them.[7] Yet national income figures may be employed for making estimates that are accurate enough to show trends and to make international comparisons.[8]

For times preceding those covered by national income figures, that is, for those prior to anywhere from 1870 to 1918, there are statistics regarding national outputs of certain products like iron, steel, and coal, of freight carried on public carriers, bills discounted by national banks, and the volume of foreign trade. For earlier periods, it is possible to arrive at some idea of expansion from port transactions, the development of individual businesses, the number of inventions made, the introduction of new techniques, and the rise in real wages as derived from price-wage statistical time series. For still more remote times, general impressions may be had from a variety of written and archaeological records. For example, some notion of economic growth may be derived from very long-range increases of population, for more people could not be housed, fed, and clothed if there were not an increase in production. Some idea of development may also be gained from the growth of cities, on the theory that urban centers grow in size in direct proportion to the increase in production. And a notion of economic progress may be obtained from improvements in the standard of living of the people as reflected in better clothes, better food or food supply, better houses, and the production of great buildings and works of art.

A consideration of the factors of economic growth may be organized along the lines of the essential questions of economics—why goods and services are produced, with what natural and human resources, with what productive arts, and by means of what savings. Here the task of

[6] For a fuller statement, see Simon Kuznets, *National Income and Its Composition, 1919–1938*, vols. I and II (New York: National Bureau of Economic Research, 1941), and U.S. Department of Commerce, *Survey of Current Business*, Supplement, July, 1947.

[7] The margin of error for a country like France has been said to be as much as 20 per cent.

[8] See Simon Kuznets, *National Income—A Summary of Findings* (New York: National Bureau of Economic Research, 1946), part II; Colin Clark, *Conditions of Economic Progress*, 3d ed. (New York: St. Martin's Press, 1957); and *National and Per Capita Incomes, Seventy Countries* (New York: United Nations, 1949).

analysis becomes intricate, for not only are multiple variables involved but also many combinations of these variables. From the first, however, it will be helpful to bear in mind that economic growth will be sustained only if production is in excess of consumption per capita of the population and if the use or investment of that excess provides still greater production for greater consumption.

Why goods and services are produced depends up to a point upon physiological requirements, that is, upon the desire either to maintain one's own life and health or that of persons for whom one accepts some responsibility, like children, parents, or friends. To meet these basic requirements it is necessary in most climates and conditions to store goods against future emergencies like nongrowing seasons of the year, droughts, or destructive plagues; hence in most societies, even primitive ones, surpluses are produced although they may not be used in such a fashion as to produce still more goods. Beyond the satisfying of bodily needs, men may produce goods to meet some culturally inspired desire such as tools, an amulet, an opera house, a steel factory, or a four-car garage. Here the range is obviously very great and depends not only upon the ideologies which a culture has built up but upon the productive potential of the society. In any case there is much evidence to indicate that only those cultures which do not have the means of increasing their material well-being minimize the desirability of wealth and establish as determinant ideologies religion, physical asceticism, and indolence.

If the acquisition of material things constitutes an important goal in a culture, then the attainment of the goal will depend upon a great range of other factors. Among these the availability of natural resources per capita of the population plays a very significant role. Land, plant life, and animal life have been throughout history the most extensively and universally used resources. In fact, economic growth in the known past was first marked in those places where land was extremely fertile, as in the Nile, Tigris and Euphrates, and Indus River valleys. Subsequently development was great in areas which could draw upon the resources of other areas by trade, as in the case of Greece. Still later man began to dip into what has been called "nature's capital"—to exploit, often ruthlessly, inorganic substances stored up in the earth's crust over eons of time. In all cases, however, the actual exploitation of nature has depended very largely upon techniques. Coal, iron, uranium, and even wheat were not natural resources in an economic sense until man wanted them and had enough knowledge of the productive arts to obtain and use them. Only when desire for goods is accompanied by ability to get them do the bounties of the earth take on great significance for economic growth.

Of crucial importance, also, has been the directing of human resources to the production of goods and services. The larger the proportion of a population which devotes its energies to the productive process and the harder it works, the larger the quantity of goods and services which it can expect to turn out. Furthermore, the greater the proportion of natural resources to the population, the greater will be the chances of producing surpluses which can be invested for the production of still more goods. Populations in the past have outstripped a society's productive potential, and they may well do so again in spite of modern man's seemingly inexhaustible ingenuity in finding ways to turn into useful goods what only yesterday was worthless rubble. Obviously economic growth cannot go on indefinitely until people are packed on the earth's crust like sardines in a box.

A knowledge of the productive arts is an essential factor in economic growth, for they determine very largely the amount of human input that has to go into a unit of output. So important are techniques, indeed, that the theory has been advanced that they lead in effecting all economic and social change and that all other aspects of life have to adjust themselves to such alterations in the ways of performing tasks.[9] Although this theory overstates its case, it points to a crucial force in economic growth, to the entire question of "leads" and "lags" in change, and to the process of adjustment.

New techniques may originate within a society (indigenous or autonomous origin) or may be obtained from others (adaptive origin). In the former case, they usually come about as the result of some socially felt need, the gradual accretion of a great number of related details, and the putting together of these details in such a manner that a new process comes into being. In the latter case, they may be borrowed voluntarily or may be imposed by a more advanced culture upon a more backward one. The process of diffusion usually takes place first in those underdeveloped areas which are culturally close to an advanced one and where an exchange of goods and ideas is already taking place. Subsequently it involves more backward districts as the developed areas seek more raw materials and foodstuffs. What techniques and institutions are diffused is determined by what is demanded by the two parties and by the adaptability of what is transposed to the recipient's existing productive processes and knowledge. Simple things facilitating the production of basic goods and services, like transportation, usually precede the complex and the luxurious, and those requiring little capital ordinarily go ahead of those demanding a great amount.

This brings us to the role of savings in economic growth. Inasmuch as

[9] See William F. Ogburn, *Social Change* (New York: Viking, 1952).

greater production is obtained chiefly from better methods and better equipment, expansion requires excesses out of current production for developing those methods or for providing that equipment. Thus instead of devoting all its energy to producing goods for immediate consumption, a society that would grow economically must devote some of its energy to making capital or producers' goods. Such savings may be voluntary, or they may be forced.[10] But whatever their nature, savings are facilitated if the economy has a recognized, nonperishable measure of value for exchange, like gold, for accumulating savings, has institutions for safeguarding these stores, and has mechanisms for combining the savings of many persons, for creating credit, and for making investments.

The actual organization of business enterprise next becomes an important element in the analysis. Here much depends upon a division of labor, that is, upon the extent to which producers specialize on those things which they can turn out with less human input by doing only part of a job then they could if each did the entire task himself, as, for example, in the manufacture of automobiles. A division of labor necessitates a development of commerce, and those societies today which have the largest incomes per capita have a relatively larger proportion of their labor force in commerce and transport than do backward areas.

Finally, there are three other important factors of economic growth. The first of these is entrepreneurial leadership. Whether or not leadership is talented will depend upon its methods of recruitment (by merit, family ties, or force), upon training, and upon motivation. The second is that purchasing power should be divided equally enough so that there will be an effective demand for goods on the part of the masses, for a sustained demand will encourage entrepreneurs to risk their capital and their resources in the production of more goods. Thirdly, the functioning of any economy will depend upon general conditions conducive to orderly operations. Thus, periods of peace, social harmony, and political stability permit a greater devotion of energies to the economic process than do periods of strife.

To determine in the abstract the strategic importance of each of these factors in economic growth under all conditions is impossible. Change may originate in any segment of the economy, but its "trigger" effect will depend upon a myriad of other factors, especially upon the extent of

---

[10] Savings are said to be forced when they are not effected willingly. Thus they are forced when money is inflated, for someone, in our society the state, has spent to obtain goods beyond the ability to pay for them in the usual medium of exchange. Similarly savings are forced when an entrepreneur borrows money to build a factory and is subsequently unable to pay off his loan. His creditors have involuntarily come into the possession of capital goods.

rigidities throughout the society. Actually, the analyst is faced with the task of trying to determine what extends the range of opportunities for alternative decisions regarding the use of human and natural resources. Indeed, the range of opportunities for alternative decisions may be the key to understanding societal change.

Having considered the fundamental elements of economic growth, we come to the question, for whose eventual use are goods and services produced. Here a distinction must be made at once between capital or producers' goods—things which are capable of being used to produce more goods—and consumers' goods—things which individuals use up at a rapid rate in the process of living.[11] Also one must distinguish between goods which are designed to destroy what man has made, as in the case of war matériel, and those which are intended to add to the accumulation of the ages.

In a rapidly expanding economy, a larger part of national income goes into producers' goods than in a stable or declining economy, as has already been suggested. What happens is that people forego the joys of present consumption for future gain. In a growing economy they are willing to do this, because with expansion their standard of living rises, and being satisfied with some improvement, they do not demand for immediate use all that is economically possible. In a sense they get their cake and eat it too. Also, it is essential, as we have previously seen, that economic benefits do not go only to a very small group in society, be it a religious organization, members of a political hierarchy, or a social class, for the basic economic wants of a few are soon met and when they are, expenditures tend to be for luxuries rather than capital goods. A wide distribution of purchasing power has the effect of sustaining demand and of encouraging expansion.

The way the ownership of goods is held also has a bearing upon economic growth. Here the goal is to get enough concentration to obtain maximum efficiency of operation, but not so much that a group will have enough power to extort unreasonable sacrifices from others. Apparently some form of competition is desirable to prevent any one group from attaining a position that it can abuse. Finally, too great a concentration of ownership of goods may prevent the creation of incentives to work effectively, whether these incentives are wages, the attainment of status in society, or the sheer personal joy of creating something.

Desirable as economic growth may be, it cannot be expected to continue indefinitely, to infinity. It creates certain counterforces which tend

---

[11] The difference between the two is not always sharp. There is a twilight zone between the two types, illustrated by the "jeep," which may be used for pleasure and for plowing.

to curb it. In the past the most important of these retardative factors
have been:

1. The development of such large populations that income per capita
is reduced, and hence savings and investment are made more difficult.

2. The exhaustion of natural resources.

3. The directing of so large a proportion of the energies of society to
noneconomic endeavor, such as the building of opera houses, the construction of pyramids, or the establishment of country clubs, that total
production declines.

4. The destruction of productive capacity by war.

In no case in history has there been a straight-line progression of economic expansion; no society has attained and maintained economic
primacy permanently.

For the effective presentation of human activity through time, the
historian has used the device of dividing the past into periods, much as
the dramatist divides his play into acts and scenes. As a rule, periods of
history are marked off by what are considered to have been fundamental
changes in ideologies, institutions, and technologies. Thus the Ancient
period is said to have begun with the appearance of written records some
5000 years B.C. and to have continued to the disintegration of the Roman
Empire in the fifth century A.D. The Medieval period began with the
"fall" of Rome and lasted until the close of the fifteenth century with the
coming of the Renaissance and the discoveries of new worlds overseas;
and the Modern period commenced then and continued until the present.

Each of these time spans is further divided into many subordinate
periods, even though the characteristics of these smaller periods do not
apply equally to all parts of the culture. The dominant characteristics
usually indicate the "leads" in changes which are taking place in the
most dynamic parts of a culture and, by the same token, show where
"lags" are. The traditional periods of the economic history of Western
culture are:

1. The later Middle Ages, from the twelfth to the fifteenth century, in
which there was much over-all economic progress.

2. The sixteenth to the eighteenth centuries, which were characterized
by expansion overseas and economic growth in Europe itself.

3. The Industrial Revolution, which took place primarily from 1750
to 1870.

4. The deepening of industrial capitalism and the diffusion of the industrial system, from 1870 to 1914.

5. Strains and stresses in the economy of Western culture, from 1914
to the present.

In the following pages we shall endeavor to find the beginnings of those ideologies, institutions, and techniques which first gave Western culture its economic characteristics, a search which will lead us to scrutinize our heritage from the ancient past. Then for the time span since the twelfth century we shall endeavor to explain economic growth in all its many manifestations. Throughout our study, however, we shall endeavor to keep before our readers the relationship between material well-being and levels of civilization.

PART TWO

The Ancient and
Medieval Worlds

CHAPTER 2

Economic Achievements in the Ancient World

Inheritance versus Invention and Discovery

So impressed are modern men in Western culture with their own achievements that they seldom recognize the importance of their cultural heritage. They stand entranced by such notable accomplishments in their own time as the development of airplanes which exceed the speed of sound, the splitting of the atom, and the extension of life expectancy at birth by some 20 per cent in one generation. Even in their moments of contemplation, their minds are actively at work in the search for even more grandiose ways to extend control over their social and physical environment. In some instances Western man has become so impressed with his own achievements that he has displayed symptoms of a paranoid condition of superiority—a condition perhaps best relieved by shock therapy.

For the mental health of the Western world a consideration of the tremendous accomplishments of the past is definitely indicated as a specific. A realization that many early achievements, given the existing level of knowledge, were as great as anything seen in our time might give modern man a becoming degree of modesty, if not what we in Western culture consider to be socially desirable humility. In any case, Western man would do well to realize that knowledge both of the physical world and of society has been an accumulative process from which he is the chief beneficiary; and that all of his wonderful achievements would not be possible if it were not for this rich legacy. It is probably not too much to say that no important technique for producing goods, either agricultural or industrial, that no solution of mathematical or engineering problems, and that no important information regarding our earth has ever been permanently lost. Western man has, indeed, been able to build upon a very rich inheritance from the past.

Furthermore, Western man would also do well to consider the experience of man through time—to learn how progress has been made in the period of some 5,000 years for which we have written and relatively abundant archaeological records. If experience is indeed the best teacher, it can well be that modern man may learn to build even better than his forebears and to avoid some of the pitfalls which have brought other cultures to their doom.

The Beginnings of Man's Long Climb Upward

At the beginning of man's long climb up the scale of civilization, Homo sapiens was very close to the animal both in his knowledge of the world about him and in his way of life. In fact, if one assumes, in conformity with current evolutionary theory, that man is descended from some of the higher forms of animal life, the gap between man and animals must at one time have been very small. And if one has had any experience in trying to tame or train even the most advanced animals, one can imagine how uncivilized early man really was.

Although archaeologists, who specialize in the study of primitive man and his cultures, have relatively little evidence on the subject, they believe that remains which have been unearthed and that the behavior of the most primitive people now extant indicate that the first men on earth had practically no tools, could not control fire well enough to have it always available, followed animal traits in their relations with their fellowmen, and were primarily food gatherers rather than food producers. They picked berries, harvested nuts, and foraged for tubers, the eggs of birds and reptiles, and the seeds of plants, which came to be called grains. They did some hunting, clothed themselves, if at all, in skins, and sought shelter in caves, thickets, or trees. They had no surplus to allow leisure for pursuits other than the satisfying of bodily needs. Indeed, it is probable that, much like hibernating animals, they had to rely on their own fat rather than on stores of food to get them through the unproductive seasons of the year.

Obviously primitive man's greatest problem was to secure freedom from want, that is, so to extend his control over his physical environment that he could diminish the threat of imminent starvation. This meant, first, better tools and weapons and, secondly, the growing of foodstuffs rather than merely gathering them. Both of these things were crucial to economic advance, but to materials used in tools and weapons has gone the honor of furnishing names for the early ages of history. Thus we have the Paleolithic Age, in which tools and weapons were made of crude, chipped stone; the Neolithic Age, when polished stone was used; the Age of Copper, when copper tools and weapons prevailed; and so on through the Age of Bronze and the Age of Iron.

The dates for these various ages cannot be fixed with finality for all the world, for there seem to have been parallel developments in many places and different people advanced at different rates. Indeed, throughout the world today it is possible to find man at nearly every level of civilization. In the district which stretches from the eastern Mediterranean to the Persian Gulf, whence most of the heritage of Western European culture came, the Paleolithic Age extended from the early days of man's appearance on earth down to about 10,000 years ago; the Neolithic, from 8000 B.C. to the fifth millennium B.C.; the Age of Copper, from the fifth through the fourth millenniums B.C.; the Age of Bronze, from the end of the fourth millennium to the end of the second; and the Iron Age lasted through the first millennium B.C.

That the Paleolithic Age was the longest of these periods indicates how difficult it was for man to effect basic changes in his way of life—how difficult it was for man to take some of what seem to us very elementary steps forward. In fact, it is striking to the historian how rarely in the past just the right human talents, social drives, proper materials, and other factors came together with such a timing and in such proportions as to break through "resistance points" of advance. It is amazing to us how long it took man to find his way by the stars, to conquer oceans, to develop numerical notations, to grow annual crops, or to get energy from wind, waterfalls, or steam.

However difficult Paleolithic man found his problems, archaeological evidence shows that slowly but surely he solved some of them. He began to control fire and developed ways of producing it at will. His first crude weapons and tools, which were chipped from some hard stone, like flint, were gradually improved in quantity and workmanship, and they came to be differentiated for different tasks. In the course of time man added bones and ivory to the materials which he used for tools and weapons and he stored food in horns and skins. Still later he devised hooks and lines for catching fish, domesticated the dog so that he would have some help in the chase, employed rotary motion for drilling, utilized the principle of the lever and fulcrum for moving heavy objects, and invented the bow and arrow, the first composite mechanism of which we know. It is probable, too, that Paleolithic man had some means of transporting himself on water, whether it was on a crude raft, a log canoe, or a kayak. He did not have yet, however, the principle of the wheel and when he moved by land, as he frequently did in search of food because of droughts or "overpopulation," he carried his few belongings on his back, dragged them on poles, or pulled them on sledges.

Apparently primitive man, especially in those climates and areas where nature was not so bountiful as to provide steady sustenance and moderate temperatures, established a very definite ideology about economics —he had a most intense desire to avoid want. In the religions of people who lived under conditions of uncertain food supply, there are almost always found prayers, spells, rites, and incantations to the totem beseeching assistance in the hunt or aid to the supplicant in his efforts to overcome some economic trouble.

The universality of such practices, the doctrine that "gods help them who help themselves," and the very logic of a precarious food supply suggest that Paleolithic man was not averse to altering his ways, if change would make him more certain of the morrow. Finally, conditions became propitious for reform. Sometime between 10000 and 8000 B.C., as the northern ice sheets of the last glacial period were receding, the steppes and tundras of Europe were transformed into temperate forests and the prairies south of the Mediterranean and of Hither Asia were converted into deserts with oases and fertile river basins. As a result food gathering and hunting in these southern areas was poor, and the men who went to them had to find a new solution to their problem of food supply. This they did by domesticating grains and by taming animals, in short by raising their own food and thereby creating for the first time settled agriculture. Here was one of the major technological revolutions of all time, for only in settled societies is man able fully to meet Western culture's criteria of civilization. At least no nomadic society has ever done so.

With the beginning of settled agriculture man entered the Neolithic or New Stone Age. Tools were now improved by polishing, were given finer edges, and were further differentiated. The hoe and the sickle appeared, for they were needed in the cultivation and harvesting of grains. The earthen pot was shaped by hand for storing grain; other pots were developed because grains, unlike meat, could not be cooked over an open fire on a spit but had to be contained in some sort of vessel. Fermentation was discovered (and probably encouraged). Clothes came to be made out of animal and vegetable fibers, because hides were too

Primitive Spinning. One of the earliest techniques that required a composite mechanism had to do with the making of cloth. On this Athenian vase of the sixth century B.C., the process of turning wool into loose bands is shown by the major figure on the right. The central figure is spinning. The left hand holds the distaff with the loose wool while the right hand twirls and drops a heavy weight to which the thread is attached and so twists and draws out the fiber. The author has seen this same method employed in recent years in as sophisticated a place as modern Delphi. On the left of the vase two women are folding and packaging finished material. (*From the collection of the Metropolitan Museum of Art, New York. Fletcher Fund, 1931. Reproduced with permission.*)

warm in summer and not in large supply; the use of fibers led to the invention of the spinning stick and the loom. Bodily decoration gave evidence of a greater concern for esthetics.

Undoubtedly the most important of the cultivated grains were related to our wheat and barley and were selected from the seeds which food

Primitive Weaving. On the same vase that was represented in the preceding figure, a primitive loom is portrayed. The threads of the warp run vertically rather than horizontally as on more highly developed looms, as shown in the figure on page 263. The operator on the right is passing a spindle with the woof thread between the threads of the warp. The operator on the left is presumably dividing the threads of the warp to permit the passing of the spindle. Material is being made at the center of the loom at about waist height.

gatherers had been gleaning from mountains and marshes. In certain places Neolithic man had rice, millet, Indian corn, yams, manioc, and squash. Besides the dog, he numbered goats, sheep, cattle, and pigs among his animals.

Important as was the agricultural revolution of the Neolithic Age, it could not produce much of a surplus or effect much of a division of labor. Foodstuffs were too perishable to be stored for long. Tools were too elementary to provide much of a division of labor, since individuals could for the most part shape what they themselves needed. Transportation was too inadequate to make distant trade feasible; and man had not yet learned to make use of either animal or inorganic energy.

The Technological Revolution of the Age of Copper

Important as was the advent of settled agriculture in man's march forward toward higher levels of civilization, men of the Age of Copper between 5000 and 3000 B.C. were to witness still further changes which were to revolutionize man's economic existence. The most important of these innovations were:

1. The development of a technology of smelting and of working copper and later tin and lead.

2. The growth of trade and the perfecting of instruments of exchange, the most important of which was money.

3. The effecting of a greater division of labor than had ever been realized before.

4. The founding of more and larger settlements.

These innovations were introduced primarily in that great heartland of civilization from which Western culture was to inherit so much—the area bounded by the Sahara and the Atlantic on the west, by the Himalayas on the east, by the Causasus and Hindu Kush Mountains on the north, and by the heat of the torrid zone on the south.

That this area should have pushed through the points of resistance to economic progress, while so many other areas failed to do so, is one of the great facts of history. Among the reasons for the advance were the following: This region had unproductive seasons so that surpluses had to be provided for a portion of every year. It possessed extremely fertile land in oases and in great river valleys. It was protected against invaders by mountains and deserts. It had rivers for transporting goods over long distances, and access to seas navigable for relatively crude boats. Moreover, the necessity of controlling the waters of rivers for agricultural use may well have required a social organization that would make people obey rules for the general good of all. Periodic floods and long voyages meant that men had to acquire knowledge of the seasons and of the heavens so that they would plant at the right time and so that they could traverse safely trackless deserts, high mountain passes, and wastes of seas.

Conducive as such general conditions were to the changes which took place, it must be remembered that the geographic and climatic characteristics of the area had existed for a long time before any alterations in the economy were effected and that other more immediate and specific innovations must of necessity loom large in any explanation of what took place. Of these innovations the development of copper metallurgy was exceptionally significant. It set off a chain of technological changes in the fifteen hundred years before 3000 B.C. which may be considered to have had more far-reaching consequences than any subsequently arrived at up to the seventeenth century A.D.

Probably the first copper was found in its relatively pure state as a glistening metal in rocks or in the residue of some exceptionally hot fire which had been built on copper ore. But whatever the occasion for man's discovery of it, we know that Chalcolithic man, that is, man of the Age of Copper, was by about 4000 B.C. smelting it with charcoal in furnaces, heating it in crucibles, and pouring it into molds. He thus had a metal for tools and weapons which was far superior to stone, for it was lighter and less fragile, took a sharper edge, and could be more easily shaped to produce a greater variety of products. Of especial importance was the fact that men were acquiring knowledge about and skills in metallurgy which were applicable with minor variations to a great number of metals. Thus they were laying an essential foundation for the use of materials which were more efficient and more durable than anything known hitherto, and tapping large sources of supplies—those which had been stored up over eons of time in the earth's crust. Without these advances neither the high machine speeds of today nor the large amount of energy from inorganic materials, which we now take for granted, would be possible.

In addition to metallurgy, however, the Age of Copper witnessed the development of other techniques of the greatest moment. Pottery, which had previously been shaped by hand and fired for greater durability, began to be made on the potter's wheel and to be baked in special kilns.[1] The wheel, which is essential for the transmission of mechanical power and for the reduction of friction in land transportation, began to be used

---

[1] This invention seems to have appeared first in Hither Asia before 3000 B.C., to have reached Egypt by 2700 B.C., and the Indus River valley by about 2500 B.C.

Ancient Harness for Horses. On this Athenian amphora of the sixth century B.C. is portrayed a full front view of a quadriga (four horses harnessed to a light chariot). The ancient harness was quite inefficient, being so designed that when the horse pulled a heavy load the breastplate would slip up on the animal's throat and might cut off his breath. Horses were used to pull only light loads and were in general much smaller than our modern draft animals. (*From the collection of the Metropolitan Museum of Art, New York. Rogers Fund, 1905. Reproduced with permission.*)

on the cart.[2] Furthermore, bricks fired in kilns date from 2500 B.C. in India. Wooden plows appeared in Egypt and in Mesopotamia about

---

[2] Wheeled vehicles appeared in Sumer about 3500 B.C., in the Mesopotamian Valley generally by 3000 B.C., in India before 2500 B.C., in Egypt by 1600 B.C., and in China and Sweden by 1000 B.C. Incidentally, the Mayan, Incan, and Aztec cultures never made economic use of the wheel.

Egyptian Chariot. This wooden chariot is from the XVIII Dynasty, which means the period between 1800 and 1354 B.C. It was then that the horse was introduced to Egypt by the Hyksos. The "harness" for the horses suggests an adaptation to the horse of the ox yoke. Inasmuch as the withers of the horse, that is, the hump on the back where the shoulder bones meet, is less pronounced than on the ox, the horse yoke did not have much to rest against. The horse needed a collar which would rest upon its shoulders, but this was a relatively late development. (*Archaeological Museum, Florence.*)

3000 B.C.; oxen began to be used as draft animals, which meant that manure could be husbanded for specific use.[3] Carrying by water became more efficient because of the use of the sail (circa 3000 B.C.), which was one of the first instances of the employment of inorganic power for economic purposes, the construction of larger boats, and improvements in methods of steering.[4]

The combined effect of these innovations was greatly to increase economic activity. Smelting and working copper, turning pottery on the wheel, making kiln-fired brick, and constructing plows and wheels required skilled craftsmen who became specialists in their trades and who exchanged their products for agricultural goods. Better tools and agricul-

[3] Camels, asses, and horses were used primarily as pack and riding animals. Horses were much smaller then than they are now and, many scholars believe, were fitted with collars, adapted from the ox yoke, which tended to choke them when they pulled heavy loads, the collar pulling on their windpipes rather than on their shoulders.

[4] At this time the oar or oars used for steering were fixed on one or both sides of the stern of the ship. The hinged rudder, installed directly astern, was to come much later.

Model of Egyptian Yacht. This model of an Egyptian vessel from Thebes of circa 2000 B.C. illustrates many of the problems that were involved in early water carrying. The ship was so designed that it had a small hold. Its elevated portions, fore and aft, allowed it to be rocked to get it off bars and to facilitate getting it on and off landings. The paddlers constituted a good deal of the "pay load," although there is a short mast for a sail. The steering apparatus is not a hinged rudder but consists of two steering oars lashed to posts. (*From the collection of the Metropolitan Museum of Art, New York. Rogers Fund and Contribution of Edward S. Harkness. Reproduced with permission.*)

tural techniques meant an increase in the output of foodstuffs per worker on the land, and hence the accumulation of surpluses which could be used in securing such amenities as earthen jars or copper sickles through channels of trade. And new techniques of transportation at one and the same time made possible and reflected an extension of commerce.

Thus, a division of labor, which is the *sine qua non* of high output per capita, was taking place. Surpluses of different areas were being exchanged so that economies which were deficient in certain products had their outputs complemented by goods coming from afar.[5] And commerce was leading to a diffusion of knowledge which of itself tended to extend the vision and the imagination to new horizons. Withal, the range of opportunities for alternative decisions regarding the employment of human energies and other resources in economic activity was greatly extended.

[5] For example, the copper used in Egypt came mostly from the Sinai Peninsula; that employed in Mesopotamia came at first from Oman on the Persian Gulf. Furthermore, Mesopotamia obtained lead and silver from the Taurus Mountains of Asia Minor. Finally, finished goods seem to have been traded in this period between such centers as Sumer on the Lower Tigris and Euphrates Rivers and Egypt.

Change in the Age of Bronze

Change in the Age of Bronze, unlike that in the Age of Copper, cannot be traced directly to a metallurgical innovation despite the fact that the new period was named after such an advance. To be sure, bronze, a mixture of copper and tin, provided a harder and more durable metal for tools and weapons, but it was not so much better than copper that it could do more than accelerate developments already initiated. The economic revolution of the Bronze Age was effected primarily by the invention of money, which, I am prepared to argue, was one of the most important inventions of all time in that it greatly facilitated the exchange of goods and thus a division of labor, by the development of systems of writing and of numerical notation which made possible the recording and the transmission of data and ideas, and by the rise of cities and the great river-valley empires which established rules of conduct or laws for more orderly relations among men. Let us look at each of these developments in turn.

Economists usually define money as a medium of exchange, a measure of value, and a store of wealth. With the growth of trade it was essential to have some such instrument, for when one produces for unknown buyers, one cannot be certain that the purchasers will have goods to exchange which are really wanted in the market. Money is acceptable,

Roman Coin. This illustration is a denarius of of T. Carisius of 48 B.C. The profile of the Roman is clearly delineated. Profiles were used because they could be well rendered. Note the hammer and tongs on the reverse side of the coin. This particular piece has been mutilated by clipping the edges. Yet it was imperfectly cast in the first place. The denarius is the ancestor of the penny, the symbol for which today is d. (*From the Moneys of the World Collection of the Chase Manhattan Bank of New York. Used with permission.*)

however, in any market, because it is exchangeable for anything that is for sale. This is particularly true if money has the confidence of all, and early money had this confidence, for it consisted of pieces of metals, like gold, silver, and copper, which in themselves were in universal demand. Moreover, money permitted the amassing of wealth and the borrowing from many sources for the financing of large-scale enterprises, like distant trading expeditions, the construction of large buildings, and the execution of drainage and irrigation works.[6]

With the increasing use of money, banking came into being and with it the practice of charging interest. The former innovation meant that there were businessmen who specialized in the safekeeping of funds, in the accumulation of moneys from diverse savers, and in the lending of sums to those who would engage in business enterprise. Interest taking meant the creation of an incentive to hold savings in money and this practice made mobile wealth available for those who would pay to use others' savings in the hope of making a profit. Here were added features of the monetary system which were almost as important to economic growth as money itself.

The second group of advances of the Age of Bronze, as has already been noted, was the development of writing, the establishment of numerical notations, and methods of obtaining knowledge, all of which seem, from the archaeological information that we have, to have stemmed from economic activity. The earliest forms of writing and of numbers were developed in the keeping of records of business transactions. Temple priests, for example, became engaged in such numerous and complicated operations that they could not possibly retain the details in their heads and made such long-term contracts that, the span of life being what it is, others than themselves had to know about the commitments made.[7] Also, in business agreements quantities had perforce to be employed; this gave rise to the use of agreed-upon weights and measures.[8]

---

[6] Incidentally the metallic content of coins was not guaranteed by states until about 700 B.C.

[7] The earliest forms of writing were pictograms. Then came in turn hieroglyphs, which are conventional signs for things; ideograms, which are symbols for ideas; phonograms, which gave sound values to ideas and things; and finally in the nineteenth century B.C. the alphabet.

[8] In Sumer there was developed the place system in numerical notations, that is, the value of the number was determined by the respective relationship of symbols as, for example, when 1 and 2 are placed together they represent 12. Sumer had both the decimal system and the sexagesimal system. The latter lingers in the English currency system of pence, shillings, and pounds and in the English measure of feet and yards.

Then in the acquiring of knowledge, men of the Bronze Age effected a particularly significant revolution. Undoubtedly primitive man had come to know certain things simply by trial and error as, for example, in shooting fish with bow and arrow to aim over the fish. They did not known *why* it was necessary to do this, but experience showed that it was, and this *rule of thumb* was good enough for the purpose of getting fish. Strictly empirical knowledge was not, however, good enough for the task of solving more complicated problems, and men began to ask *why* it was necessary to aim over the fish in order to hit it. This search for the necessary and sufficient conditions always to produce the same or similar results was a veritable transformation in man's attitude toward the world about him. With it mankind was creating the essence of science—the ordering of demonstrable or observable data to explain a sequence of events—and thereby was laying the very foundation for mastery over his social and physical environment.

Evidence of the advances made can be illustrated from arithmetic, where the multiplication table was developed, and from geometry, where proofs were sought to explain why given conditions always gave the same answers. From such beginnings it eventually became possible to construct large buildings with accuracy. The Great Pyramid of Cheops (2420–2270 B.C.), for instance, contains 2,300 blocks of stone, some of which weigh 350 tons, has a base of 777¾ feet on each side, and has less than an inch of error in either length or level. Also celestial observation led to a development of astronomy, which permitted the accurate measuring of time, the seasons, and points of the compass. Accordingly sundials for regularizing human activity were invented and a calendar of 365 days was created.

All these revolutionary innovations of the Bronze Age made possible a greater division of labor, a greater output of goods and services per operative, the concentration of economic surpluses in different localities, and finally the establishment of cities. The first urban centers of which we have knowledge came into being somewhat prior to 2500 B.C. in the three great river valleys of the Nile, the Tigris and Euphrates, and the Indus, and a little later along the Yellow River in China. The largest may have had populations of some forty thousand, which is small by modern standards, but which was enormous compared with the size of agricultural villages of earlier times.

The same economic growth which made cities possible also led to the formation of great empire civilizations, such as those of Sumer, Babylonia, Assyria, Egypt, Mycenae, Phoenicia, and Crete. Social and economic relations in them came to be regulated by rules of conduct, known as laws, such as the Code of Hammurabi in Babylonia sometime around

1750 B.C., and by the creation of political powers which could make subjects adhere to their edicts. Most of these civilizations made important strides forward in architecture, that of Egypt especially expressing great refinement with its fluted columns, its colonnades, and its pleasing proportions. Sculpture became more naturalistic, especially in Mycenae; paintings in tombs displayed a search for perspective and the use of bright if monotonous colors. Music became more refined with the use of the heptatonic (seven-note) scale and the construction of better instruments, such as the flute, the harp, and the lyre.

In spite of the progress realized in the Ages of Copper and of Bronze, all the leading economies showed signs of decay by the end of the second millennium B.C. Inasmuch as the tools and weapons made of the new metals were expensive, many persons did not possess them; those who did had a great advantage in production and thereby were able to effect a considerable concentration of wealth and power. Eventually there developed a very wealthy class of kings, lords, or priests and a very poor class of slaves, serfs, tenants, or freemen. The demands of the former upon the latter were very great and these demands came to be sanctioned by custom and laws and enforced by mercenaries.

Because of the distinction in classes, the rich became separated from actual production and took very little interest in it. They bent no energy to the solution of technical problems, for they knew very little about them and cared less, nor did they plow back part of their surplus into capital goods, for they had no real reason to do so. They were largely content with spending such surplus as they had upon luxuries, such as tombs and temples, personal adornment, and pleasures of the flesh. In the very process of becoming civilized, they turned so much of their energies away from economic activity that they contributed to economic decay.

The poor, on the other hand, did next to nothing to increase production by developing new techniques or by improving their organization of work, because they had no leisure in which to experiment on new methods, no resources for such experiments, and no incentive to turn out more goods. They knew all too well that whatever increase they might produce would be taken away from them in one way or another.

Consequently, during the Bronze Age itself little progress was realized in the techniques of production, save for the development of clear glass in Egypt and for improvements in the ship. What economic progress there was came chiefly by the diffusion of techniques within and among the main centers of civilization, by the concentration of wealth in larger enterprises, by trade, and by the establishment of peace among warring lords.

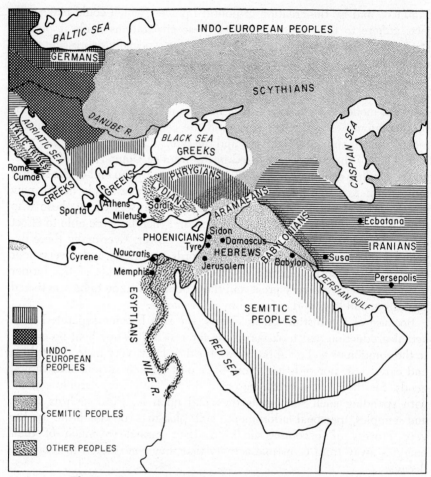

The Dominant Areas of the Copper, Bronze, and Iron Ages.

Then, to make matters worse, other peoples borrowed the production and war techniques of the leading economies. This fact led to the growth of economic rivals, to contests of strength among the great, and to intermittent raids on the centers of wealth by peoples on the frontiers. Indeed, the destruction of war and the political and social disorders which accompanied it were primary causes of decline. In fact, the Age of Bronze was to end with a series of wars and of mass migrations of warring peoples—the "Peoples of the Sea"—who came from what are now the Balkans and the Black Sea regions into more civilized societies. Hence the Iron Age was inaugurated by economic decline and by a cultural dark age.

The Dominant Areas of the Copper, Bronze, and Iron Ages.

The Age of Iron and the Supremacy of Greece

With the coming of the Age of Iron at about the beginning of the first millennium B.C. the center of economic life was to shift from the early river-valley cultures to Greece—the first great civilization upon the European continent. This event was of great import for Western culture, for it was from Greece that the West was to receive many of its richest legacies.

Undoubtedly the greatest technological event of the Bronze Age was the discovery of iron; in a very real sense, this one achievement compensated largely, in the broad perspective of the past, for the two millen-

Primitive Forge. The black-figure painting shown on this Attic vase of the sixth century B.C. pictures the kind of forge which was used in the metallurgical industry of Ancient Greece. Similar forges were found in many other cultures. The metal was worked into a "bloom," that is, a molten mass in the fire at the base of the forge. The upright furnace provided a draft for the charcoal fire. The fuel was put in from above. Note the tongs and hammers above the workers. (*London, British Museum, Greek Vase B 507. Adapted from photograph. Courtesy of the Trustees.*)

niums of relative technical stagnation. The earliest use of iron is still shrouded in mystery, but there is evidence that a tribe in the Armenian mountains was employing iron even before 2000 B.C. At all events iron tools and weapons began to be widely used in Palestine, Syria, and Greece by 1100 B.C. and thence spread to other lands.

The development of iron metallurgy and the use of iron products constituted in itself an economic revolution. Unlike copper and tin, iron ore is quite abundant in nature and widely distributed, so that iron tools and weapons were relatively cheap in terms of human input and came within the reach of nearly everyone. At last even rather poor people could avail themselves of equipment that was in most respects as good as that of the well-to-do. Iron was in Ancient Times, as it is today, a plebian metal and it had a democratizing effect, at least from an economic point of view.

A long list of old tools, including shovels, spades, forks, mattocks, axes, and scythes, were now made of iron, and new tools made their appearance, such as pickaxes for road work and sheep shears for cutting the wool which had previously been plucked from the poor animals. In gen-

Primitive Metalworking. After the metal had been "smelted," as shown in the preceding figure, it then had to be hammered to drive out impurities. This hammering was a tedious task and was not made lighter until the invention of a hydraulic hammer and, better, a steam hammer. So laborious was metalworking, in fact, that it is not unreasonable to suppose that all of Greece had no more iron at its disposal than is contained in one modern ladle, as pictured in the figure on page 378. Note the products of the smith: a saw, knives, hammers, weapons, and a pitcher. (*From T. Schreiber, Atlas of Classical Antiquities, ed. by W. C. F. Anderson, London: Macmillan, 1895, Pl. LXIX, Fig. 6. Reproduced by permission.*)

eral, therefore, agricultural workers were able to increase their production, particularly in those areas like European Greece where an exaggerated concentration of wealth had not taken place and where socio-economic rigidities had not become established. As farmers built up bartering or purchasing power, they were able to demand more industrial goods from specialized craftsmen—from ironworkers, potters, weavers, and carpenters.

The demand for craft goods had, in turn, an impact upon industrial techniques. By 500 B.C. carpenters had such new tools as the iron saw and, by 50 B.C., augers and planes. In addition, existing tools previously made of copper or of bronze, like chisels, drills, hammers, and adzes, were now made of iron. Smiths, who in the working of iron had to spend long hours hammering iron into desired shapes, because it could not be heated sufficiently hot by ancient methods to make it liquid enough to be cast in molds, soon invented hinged tongs better to hold their blooms while they worked them and developed a great variety of specialized

The Quern for Making Flour. Primitive peoples made flour by pounding the grain, as with the mortar and pestle, and by grinding it between two heavy stones. For a long time grinding was performed with querns. These consisted of a lower stone the top part of which was shaped like a cone. On this stone was placed another which had been so hollowed out that its excavated parts constituted two inverted cones. The upper stone was raised slightly from the lower by means of a spindle (set in the white space of the stone) that in turn fitted into a crosspiece what went through the upper stone. Such an arrangement reduced the danger of pieces of stone being nicked off in operation of the mill. Grain was placed in the upper part of the top stone, which thus served as a hopper, and was ground as it worked its way down between the stones. (*From V. G. Childe, Antiquity, vol. 17, p. 20, Fig. 1, 1943. Reproduced by permission.*)

hammers. Shortly after 200 B.C. they built special anvils for making nails and blocks for drawing wire. Masons, too, had better tools; most importantly, they developed the pulley (eighth century B.C.), which allowed the construction of cranes and blocks and tackles. Thus building was made more efficient; it became possible to drill tunnels and to construct aqueducts.

The Quern Driven by Horse. The quern in this drawing is exceptionally large. The upper stone is being rotated by a horse which has been hitched to a wooden frame attached to the stone. The flour would fall into a trough at the base of the stone and be collected by the workman. This picture is from a Roman sarcophagus of the second century A.D. (*From A. G. Drachmann, Archaeol.-Kunsthistoriske Meddelelser, vol. 1, p. 143, Fig. 9, 1932–5, Copenhagen, Det Kongelige Danske Videnskabernes Selskab. Reproduced by permission.*)

Furthermore, iron made possible improvements in various types of machines that did not stand up well when made of wood or the more fragile copper. Among these mechanisms was the water-raising wheel for irrigation and drainage; this consisted of a wheel fitted with pots or with chains holding pots that, as it turned, dipped water at the bottom of its arc and dumped it at the top. Because of its great resistance to friction, iron made new machines possible. Indeed, one of the most notable mechanical devices of the Iron Age was the rotary quern for grinding grain into flour. It consisted of two circular stones, the upper one of which turned on an iron pivot protruding from the center of the lower, which crushed the grain between them. By the fifth century B.C. this mechanism was being turned by animals hitched to a lever attached to the upper stone, which was the first use of animal power save for draft purposes. Once the principle of using nonhuman energy in industry became established, it was possible to conceive of employing inorganic sources of energy for power. It is not strange, indeed, that the water wheel, developed sometime after 100 B.C., was first applied to the grinding of grain and continued to be used almost exclusively for this purpose well into the Middle Ages.

Lastly, in the Iron Age, more attention was given by the educated in society to economic matters and one begins to get written descriptions of various kinds of mechanical devices. Archimedes (287–212 B.C.), one of the greatest mathematicians of all time, described the theory of the lever and thereby laid the foundation for theoretical mechanics, albeit that building on his work was slight until the end of the Middle Ages. He also wrote about the screw pump, which he may have invented, and he developed many military devices, especially the launching of stones by the elastic power of twisted ropes. Hero of Alexandria (circa 50 B.C.) described a number of gadgets, many of which were mere toys, such as pumps, the syringe, a fire engine, devices for adjusting the wick on a lamp, a windmill arranged to drive a bellows of an organ, and a contraption moved by the expansive power of steam. The Roman Vitruvius in about 1 A.D. wrote a famous book on architecture and mechanics, nearly all of which had been borrowed from the Greeks, which discloses that Rome had knowledge of all the principles thus far mentioned, as well as a solution to the problem of the transmission of power by gears. Then in the allied field of mathematics Euclid published his *Elements* of geometry in about 300 B.C., Apollonius of Perga (247–205 B.C.) prepared his geometry of cones, and Hipparchus (160–125 B.C.) invented plane and spherical trigonometry.

The developments mentioned here meant not only that men in the Iron Age experienced economic growth through their ability to increase individual production, but also that there was an ever greater division of labor than there had been in the Age of Copper. Indeed, the demand for iron tools and weapons was so great and the techniques of iron-mongering so specialized that ironworkers, among others, could concentrate upon the production of goods for unknown buyers. Finally, there was an enlargement of productive enterprises, for we find establishments employing twenty or even a hundred workers, and a thousand were at work in the Laureion silver mines of Athens.

As has already been stated, the area which profited most fully in an economic sense from the new methods of production was mainland Greece, in spite of the fact that the area is about the size of the State of New York and that only 20 per cent of its surface can be cultivated. Greece produced specialized agricultural products, like olive oil and wine, which could be grown on its hilly land and sold them in foreign markets which were easily reached by sea. Subsequently she also turned out specialized industrial goods, such as iron tools and weapons, pots, and works of art, for which there was a foreign demand. By exporting such goods, Greece was able to pay for the foodstuffs and raw materials which it lacked. In this exchange she benefited, for then, as is generally the case, industrial products required the expenditure per unit of value of less human energy than did raw materials and foodstuffs. Moreover, the home market, at least in Athens, tended to grow because of a fair degree of economic equality and the absence for a long time of the subordination of labor by force to a slave status and hence to something approaching an existence level.

Undoubtedly the wealth built up by great cities like Athens and Corinth provided much of the surplus which allowed human energies to be devoted to the arts, to philosophical speculation, and to technological improvements. Both in material and intellectual achievement and in their socioeconomic organization, the Greeks met in high degree the various conditions prescribed by Western culture's concept of civilization.

Why the Greeks did so well, or how any society achieves a high level of civilization, is one of the great problems of history. In this regard it is not without significance that the height of Greek civilization came at the conclusion of or shortly after the period of greatest economic growth, that is, between 600 and 400 B.C. Furthermore the Greeks built upon the excellent art forms of Mycenae, developed rules of justice because of comparative economic equality, had a social system that allowed men of talent to assume positions of leadership, and for a long time avoided stultifying rigidities.

Unfortunately this happy state of affairs was not to endure indefinitely, for Greece, like other societies which have attained positions of economic and cultural primacy, generated destructive forces within itself. Its superior agricultural and industrial techniques were diffused to other lands in the process of trade and colonization, particularly to the eastern Aegean and Mediterranean Seas, to Sicily, to Magna Graecia in southern Italy, and to the Black Sea area. Eventually these regions produced both for themselves and for Greek markets abroad the very goods that had previously been furnished by Greece itself. This development meant a decline in production in Greece, difficulties in getting sufficient food supplies from foreign lands, unemployment, a fall in real wages, and the development of rigidities, of which slavery was an outstanding example. Cheap labor meant that the internal market for goods declined and there was less incentive than there had been earlier to adopt laborsaving devices or to apply animal or inorganic power to machines.

Moreover, Greece was badgered by serious political problems that ate away its strength. For one thing, Greece never achieved political integration, but remained divided into city-states, which reduced the size of its domestic market, mitigated against an extension of the division of labor, and led to rivalries which resulted in intermittent wars. Finally, Greece was invaded by people on her northern frontiers and by Persians, and the ensuing wars were extremely devastating. Even though Alexander the Great was able to conquer most of the known world between 334 and 324 B.C., his efforts did little to revive a society that was on the way down.

The Rise and Fall of the Hellenistic East and of Rome

By the last half of the fourth century B.C., economic primacy and the center of civilization were moving away from Greece proper to Hellenized cities of the eastern Aegean and eastern Mediterranean Seas. Here Greek treatises on husbandry were widely read and Greek practices imitated; here, too, olive oil, one of Greece's main export products, was produced in such quantities that it captured Greek markets. Moreover, cities in Asia Minor and on the Black Sea became important sources of iron tools and weapons. Cotton cloth, first known to the Greeks in the fourth century, was made in Egypt and Phoenicia. Parchments and papyrus sheets on which to write were made, respectively, by Pergamum and Egypt. The curing of fish, long practiced by the Greeks, was adopted by others; and luxuries, which had long been supplied by Greece, began to come primarily from the Hellenized East. Trade also flourished in the economically developing regions, as is evidenced by the use of larger ships, some of which reached 5,000 tons burden, by the construction of lighthouses, like the famous one at Alexandria, and by the greatly increased use of money in exchange.

Undoubtedly Greece profited briefly in the third century B.C. from this general economic activity, but the revival was not enough to allow her to regain her former position. Throughout the Hellenistic period, from 338 to 30 B.C., the highest levels of economic prosperity and of civilization were attained in such places as Ephesus, Pergamum, Rhodes, Antioch, and especially Alexandria. Nearly all those who described new techniques at the end of the Iron Age, to whom reference has already been made, were from non-Greek cities—Archimedes was from Syracuse, Hero, from Alexandria, and Vitruvius, from Rome. Much of the sculpture of antiquity which has come down to us was from the Hellenistic East, such works as the "Dying Gaul" from Pergamum, "Laocoön" and the "Victory of Samothrace" from Rhodes, and the "Venus of Milo" from the Alexandrian school. Alexandria with its library of some 500,000 rolls, its medical school, and its observatory was the honored successor of Athens as the intellectual center of the world. It was thence that much of the knowledge of antiquity, even that of Greece, was transmitted to the West.

By the second century B.C., the Hellenistic East, in its turn, began to show signs of economic stagnation; in the first century B.C., it was manifestly on the decline. Here the age-old concept that the monarch owned the land and could collect dues from whoever worked it had the same effect as earlier—the exploitation of workers of the soil to a point where they had little incentive to increase production. Moreover, kings and their favorites got control of the more important industrial and commercial establishments and in their management of them made profits which were used for the owners' pleasure and culture rather than for the extension of economic activity through investment. Furthermore, a rise in population meant pressure upon the productive system, low wages, and low purchasing power on the part of the masses. Social disorders were numerous and wars between parts of Alexander's former empire were frequent. Finally, Rome entered the scene, sometimes upon the invitation of a wealthy group which wanted help, and once there used its position of power to its own economic benefit. Indeed, the chief aspect of the political history of the last part of the pre-Christian era was the absorption of the Hellenistic East by the Roman Empire.

Rome profited, as had the Hellenistic cities, from the various agricultural, industrial, and commercial techniques which it acquired from Greece or inherited from an earlier civilization of north central Italy—the Etruscan culture. Thus, in the formative period of Roman history from about the beginning of the first millennium B.C. to 270 B.C., an economic surplus was developed from greater agricultural output, from the manufacture of such goods as pottery at Arretium, the modern Arezzo, of spears, javelins, swords, picks, scythes, and chisels at Puteoli, the modern Pozzuoli, of the ubiquitous pots and pans at Capua, and from trade and the division of labor. Rome itself produced practically no new productive techniques, but it did organize well. It built numerous roads and ports which facilitated commerce, and it constructed great aqueducts for irrigating the land. In this period, too, the lower classes were given full citizenship, could participate in the most important political decisions, and could aspire to the highest offices of the state. Many of them owned their own land or small shops and hence had an incentive to increase output.

In the next period of Roman history, from 270 B.C. to 14 A.D., Rome extended its sway over Carthage, Macedonia, Syria, Greece, Egypt, all of Italy, southern Gaul, and some of Spain. This great empire the Romans administered politically to their economic advantage. Not only did the conquered lands have to pay tribute to Rome in one way or another, but they took Rome's specialized products in return for foodstuffs and raw materials—grain from Sicily, North Africa, and Egypt, copper, silver, lead, tin, wool, and hides from Gaul and Spain, salt fish from the Black Sea, and wool and dyestuffs from Asia Minor. Roman cities grew greatly in size as a result of this activity, Rome having a population of between 650,000 and 1,200,000 in the Augustan Age (31 B.C. to 14 A.D.); and urbanization gave a further fillip to economic development. With the formation of cities, Romans devoted more of their attention to the arts, particularly architecture, sculpture, and letters. In fact, the height of Roman civilization was probably reached at the end of the Augustan Age and in the first century A.D. at the time of or just after the economic activity of Rome had reached its peak. In this respect the experience of Greece was repeated.

Once again, as in the case of previous economies, Rome developed forces that led to its undoing. Land became concentrated in great estates, the latifundia, whose owners lived in luxury in cities and whose workers got so little for their labor that they had no incentive to increase output. Techniques were exported and used to produce in conquered lands what had been obtained from Roman cities—a development that was particularly marked in Gaul. Social tensions increased in urban agglomerations as employment declined, and even the policy of providing "bread and circuses" to keep the people quiet proved to be only a temporary expedient. Parts of the empire found their production impaired by overcropping, as in North Africa, and could not make necessary deliveries of grain; other areas revolted and refused to continue the payment of tribute. Wealthy Romans invested less capital in producers' goods, but spent their surplus on luxury products for themselves. Many large land-owners tried to make their estates self-sufficient and thereby they injured trade and the division of labor. Finally, Rome was attacked by "bar-barians" on the frontiers, by people who had already learned Roman economic techniques and ways of warfare. At last, in 476 A.D. one of these attacks resulted in the "fall" of Rome itself, but the fall was in essence the collapse of a fragile and empty shell.

In antiquity a pattern of economic growth and of economic decline was established, which was repeated several times. The Ancient world's experience contained many lessons of importance, but none was more significant than how to maintain economic development over long time spans. How the successors of the ancients tried to solve this problem will be the theme of the remaining chapters of this work.

CHAPTER 3

The Agrarian Economy of
the Middle Ages

The Middle Ages: The Formative Period of Western Culture

The term Middle Ages was coined in the Renaissance when Western Europeans were rediscovering the glories of Greece and of Rome. Their choice of an appellation for the years that stretched from the fall of Rome to the close of the fifteenth century had something derogatory about it. The coiners of the term were of the opinion that they were emerging from a millenium in which civilization had been at a low ebb, that they were leaving behind them a dark age, and that they were experiencing a great cultural revival. Subsequently in the Enlightenment of the eighteenth century their characterization of the Middle Ages received further confirmation, for writers like Voltaire condemned what they believed to be the dominant aspect of the Middle Ages—the superstition and irrationality of its religion and the poor taste of its people for things esthetic. Even the great architecture of the Middle Ages was dubbed Gothic, as though there were something barbarian and decadent about it.

The expression Middle Ages was, however, a gross misnomer for the thousand years after Rome was invaded by the peoples on its frontiers. It was not a time of waiting for a new and glorious future but rather the long formative period of Western culture, comparable in many respects

45

to the formative periods of the civilizations of both Greece and Rome. It was the childhood and perhaps even the period of puberty of the West. It was the time when some of the basic ideologies of Western European culture were being established, when attitudes regarding economics, society, politics, and philosophy were being formed, and when many of the institutions of Modern Times had their beginnings. The Middle Ages comprised, therefore, a period not to be scorned, but a period to be studied if one is to understand much that is fundamental to the Western world.

The Renaissance writers who coined the phrase, the Middle Ages, and their successors who confirmed and added to their concept did a further disservice to a comprehension of the era by lumping all the thousand years together and by applying their characterizations with little discrimination among times and places. In fact, most modern European languages even today use the singular Middle Age instead of the plural Middle Ages, thus implying that this was a static period with little social change. Indeed, in many histories of the Medieval world generalizations regarding life, work, and thought are presented as though they were equally valid for all of Western Europe during an entire millennium.

The Middle Ages did not, however, constitute a single unit. There were several acts to the drama, several scenes to each act, and several "off-stage" performances accompanying the main show. For at least the economic history of the Middle Ages, it is possible to discern four major periods: the first, from the fifth to the eleventh century, when a manorial economy was being established and when extensive trade over large areas was slight; the second, from the twelfth century through the thirteenth, when there was a revival of trade, an expansion of industry, a renaissance in arts and letters, and the beginning of a breakdown of manorialism; the third, in the fourteenth and early fifteenth century, when wars and the Black Death ravaged particularly France and England and when there were signs of economic stagnation; and the fourth, the latter part of the fifteenth century, when there occurred a Renaissance—particularly in Italy and the Low Countries—and also a new activity in commerce, and Portuguese and Spanish explorations and discoveries overseas. Even this periodization is, however, based upon the most typical aspects of what was taking place and does not mean that the same changes were taking place everywhere, for they were not.

Clearly one must beware of those hoary generalizations which are applied to all the Middle Ages and to all Western Europe. For the Medieval period we can subscribe to Voltaire's aphorism that "all generalizations are false, even this one." Fortunately the aphorism has an escape clause, of which we shall take advantage.

The economy of the Middle Ages is usually characterized as having been essentially agrarian—an agrarianism based upon the relatively self-sufficient manor and employing crude agricultural techniques. To an extent all this was true, but one should not lose sight of the fact that all economies, except very local ones, prior to the nineteenth century were predominantly agricultural, that the self-sufficient agricultural estate had appeared in the late Roman period, and that remnants of the manorial system were to remain far into Modern Times. Moreover, within the Middle Ages there were many changes in manorial life. Many varieties of agricultural enterprise existed. Improvements were made in agricultural techniques; and after the twelfth century there was a trend toward farming for a profit—toward capitalistic agriculture. Undoubtedly the changes which took place resulted in output per agricultural worker that was in general higher than it had been in the Ancient period. If there was a dark age for agriculture in the West, it was most marked at the time of the Germanic invasions when settled agriculture was disrupted.

Frequently the Middle Ages are characterized as having had little trading over a large area. To some extent this generalization is also correct, especially in the eighth and ninth centuries when the manor was largely self-sufficient, when political conditions made travel uncertain, and when Western Europe's commercial activity on the Mediterranean was severely reduced. Yet even in these centuries there were cities, like Venice, that lived almost exclusively from trade. The Scandinavians carried on trade through Russia with the Byzantine Empire. And certain products necessary to life, like salt, were distributed throughout the West. Later on, in the twelfth and thirteenth centuries, trade actually staged a great revival, and though it fell off in the fourteenth century, it was on the way to recovery in the fifteenth century.

In a similar fashion, medieval industry is frequently represented as having been organized into guilds, whose members charged a fair price for their goods, and as having been conducted on most primitive lines. To be sure there were guilds, but they varied so greatly in time and place that it is difficult to generalize about them except to say that they endeavored to regulate the production of goods and to monopolize the local market. Moreover, from the thirteenth century onward, particularly in large towns and in expanding branches of industry, there was a tendency for guilds to evolve in such a fashion that master craftsmen's shops produced for more than the local market and employed for wages workers who had little chance of becoming guildsmen. Moreover, some industries were never organized along typical guild lines, and by the twelfth century, some manufacturing was conducted in fairly large units, as, for example, the silk industry at Lucca and the woolen industry in Flanders. Nor were the medieval craftsmen's techniques so very backward. They included all that the Ancient world had used and many new things besides. When one compares the summary of ancient techniques by Vitruvius with the writings of Leonardo da Vinci at the end of the Middle Ages, one finds a world of difference, particularly in the field of mechanics.

As regards the overriding ideologies of the Middle Ages, many of which loom large in Western culture, it is correctly stated that they stemmed mostly from the accepted Christian religion and that man's main concern was to get into heaven where he would find his true reward for having lived in conformity with Christian principles. It is true, too, that he was told that avarice was a cardinal sin, that the accumulation of wealth implied avarice, and that the Bible bluntly stated that it was more difficult for a rich man to get into heaven than it was for a camel to pass through the eye of a needle.

Yet, in spite of all this, ideologies which stemmed from the flesh rather than from religious teachings were not unknown. Wealth is, after all, a relative matter and it was possible to rationalize the possession of it by the use to which it was put. Indeed, St. Augustine thought that wealth was excellent if employed for the common good. The Church itself sought riches and indulged in some very sharp practices, like the collection of relics in such abundance that there was enough wood of the "true cross" to build a fire, and like the sale of indulgences on such a scale that there was a "real estate boom" in Purgatory. The Franciscan order, established in the thirteenth century by the humble St. Francis, who would do no harm to man or beast, became wealthy in the generation after its founder's death. The Benedictine order preached the virtue of orderly work, and the Cistercians organized large farms which they operated in part to satisfy market demand. Lords and bishops were often given to ostentatious displays of material well-being.

From the twelfth century onward burghers managed in one way or another to find excuses for circumventing the Church's rules against taking interest and making profits. To be sure, the slogan of the medieval man was not "get rich quickly," perhaps because it was so difficult to do so, but neither was it, with few exceptions, to glorify the soul by abasing the flesh in poverty nor to renounce completely this world for the next. Here, as in so many phases of medieval life, there were contradictions between theory and practice. At least toward the end of the Middle Ages the trend toward investing surplus for individual gain, which is the basic ideology of the capitalist system, was being generally accepted. Here was an attitude that was to become dominant in Western culture.

Another cliché regarding the Middle Ages is that society was organized on a hierarchial basis in which every man was born into a given station from which it was difficult, if not impossible, to emerge. Such a generalization implies great social rigidity and the lack of opportunity for those of low birth and high talents to achieve an elevated status in society. This contention embodies some truth, especially with the firm establishment of feudalism by the ninth century and by the creation of guilds by the twelfth century, yet here again there is need for qualification. Although there was much less social mobility then than there is, for example, in present-day America, some mobility did exist. It was possible for the lowly born to achieve status within the Church or in monastic orders, for them to rise in the service of lay lords, and later, when trade became more general, for them to acquire status through wealth. In fact, it was the growing power of men of wealth—the bourgeois—that was to overthrow the basic hierarchical structure of the Middle Ages. It is difficult to say why the medieval bourgeois maintained their economic creativity so much longer than their predecessors in the Ancient world, but the range of opportunities open to them proved to be great and they managed in one way or another to play along with those in political power so that they were not squeezed to death.

It is also frequently stated that the Middle Ages were characterized by the universality of culture, the universality of the Latin language, and the lack of political centralization. There is much truth to all these allegations, for basic Christian doctrines were universal. Much of the literature, like the Arthurian cycle and the *Romance of the Rose,* available to the few who could read, was enjoyed throughout the West. Gothic architecture was the standard from the twelfth century to the Renaissance. Latin was the universal language of the Church and of scholars, and there was no general political power that embraced large parts of the West. Yet, when this has been said and emphasized, one must add the usual qualifications. Within Christian philosophy different schools of thought developed, and the very debates on religious issues led to questioning of the faith and ultimately to heresies. Even some of the propositions of St. Thomas Aquinas, today the very symbol of Catholic conservatism, were condemned after his death by the Archbishops of Paris and Canterbury; and Dante's *De Monarchia* was put on the *Index* in the sixteenth century.

Literature, too, in spite of its early universal character, began to be written in vernacular languages and to be more characteristic of the places of its origin. Latin, particularly toward the end of our period when "humanists" tried to purify it, gave way to national tongues. Thus, in the Middle Ages two important steps were taken which were to contribute much to the rise of nationalities—the literary use of national languages and the creation of national literatures. Eventually, too, Gothic architecture gave way to a revival of Greek and Roman forms. Last but not least, as feudalism waned, one feudal lord began to extend his sway over others, so that even in the political sphere the dream of a universal empire, attempted by Charlemagne in 800 A.D. and again by the German Otto in 962 when the new Roman Empire (which was called the Holy Roman Empire in the twelfth century) was founded, was not to become a reality.

Our main concern here is not, however, with religion, with art, or with politics, but rather with economic and social history, to which we must return. What we have been attempting to do is to show that the Middle Ages were not so completedly static nor from the twelfth century onward, at least, not so backward—not so dark—as has so often been maintained. Furthermore, we have aimed to indicate that traditional generalizations about the Middle Ages must be examined critically. Finally, we have suggested that many basic ideologies toward material well-being of the modern Western world had their beginnings in the Middle Ages, and that along with them there appeared in formative fashion some of our fundamental economic institutions.

The Establishment of the Manorial System

We begin our more detailed consideration of the economic history of the Middle Ages with an analysis of agriculture, not because in this segment of life were to be found the chief factors of economic growth, but rather because, as has already been said, agriculture was almost the sole economic activity of man in the early part of the Medieval period. Although few trustworthy statistics are available regarding the population of Medieval Europe and although we lack quantitative data regarding the distribution of the poplation by occupations, what evidence we have indicates that at the beginning of the fourteenth century between 80 and 90 per cent of the people of France were making their living directly from the land, and probably this proportion was approximately the same in other countries. Incidentally, this occupational concentration in agriculture was not to be much reduced for the whole of Western Europe until the nineteenth century.

In the study of medieval agriculture it is almost essential to begin with the organization of the manor, for this institution gave life on the land its dominant characteristics. In brief, the manor was a large estate, where the land was owned by a lord, where the common people were attached to the land which they had a right to work, and where these serfs paid the lord for the use of land and for protection in stipulated amounts of goods and services, and later in money.

The concentration of land in large estates was nothing new. Great estates had been formed in the the Italian peninsula during the period of Rome's expansion, in part, as a result of land grants to important personages and, in part, from inheritances, purchases, marriages, and seizures of a political nature. Large estates existed also in Gaul well before the Romans came to give the "barbarians" a model to follow. Furthermore, on the great holdings both in Italy and in Gaul a portion of the land was set aside for the use of the owner and the rest was divided into numerous plots to be worked by the rank and file of society—the *coloni*. Only a few districts, notably those that were very mountainous or those that were swampy or very heavily forested, escaped this development. And what was more, the Roman estate or Gallic *villa* pattern of agricultural life remained intact throughout the German invasions and well into the Medieval period.

As time went on, however, and as commerce diminished almost to a standstill, a change came over the large estates. Even in late Roman times, as we have seen, there had been a tendency for the estate to become self-sufficient, and this trend was accentuated particularly in the eighth and ninth centuries. As the estate produced mostly for its own needs, both its economic arrangements and social relations became more rigid.

One aspect of this growing rigidity was the institution of feudalism. In essence, feudalism was a system whereby all lay members of society owed allegiance to someone above until the supreme authority of the king or emperor was reached. Thus the serf owed allegiance to his lord, the lesser lords, like knights, to some superior lord, possibly a count or baron, and the highest-ranking lords to the highest potentate.

This infeudating of society resulted from a whole series of complicated factors. With little economic expansion, or commerce, or money, and with a considerable amount of disorder, the common people wanted above all else land and protection. Emperors, kings, and other politically ambitious personages, for their part, wanted power in order to be able to enforce their wills on others, to maintain order, and to live well. In order to raise armies for defense or to perform certain other public services, it came about that some of these political leaders invoked the time-honored dodge of claiming title to all land and of making grants to those who would perform for them certain specified services, such as furnishing soldiers in case of need. The recipients of large holdings, in turn, made smaller grants to those who would do the hard work in field and forest, but made them on condition that these grantees would perform certain services and deliver certain goods in payment. Other leaders, however, simply established local governments in response to need for order and in the absence of any other strong authority. At all events, princes got the means of establishing an armed force to maintain order; the lords got a labor supply for their holdings; and the lower classes got land for their own use.

To make these arrangements as binding as possible, one had to swear not only to be loyal to one's superior, but one had in essence to recognize that it was impossible to free oneself from one's obligations. All society thus became bound together by an intricate system of contracts, the sanctity of which was recognized by custom and supported by force. The lower classes were not slaves in the sense that they could be bought and sold,[1] but they were serfs who were not free to leave the land nor to break their ties to their lords. On the other hand, the upper classes were not free to effect changes in the arrangements with their underlings and in addition had to assume a certain responsibility for their serfs in times of famine, plagues, and wars. Kings and emperors, although in origin heirs to Constantine and Charlemagne, were little more than lords who had established their domination over other lords and had to rest content with a rather ephemeral political existence.

By the twelfth century this system had come into full flower. At that time many estates were 10,000 acres in size, although the very large ones of important lords, of bishoprics, or of monastic orders ran well over this figure. Inasmuch as these great estates had been built up of smaller holdings through marriages, gifts, inheritances, conquests, and mortmain, the holders of them usually owed allegiance to several superiors. It sometimes happened that these superiors were rivals, and when this was the case the raising of fighting forces through land-tenure obligations could not be relied upon to produce the desired results. Furthermore, the lands comprising the very large estates might be separated from one another by miles of intervening estates, a condition which precluded the possibility of operating the estate as a whole. The effective productive agricultural unit was the manor.

Description of the Manor

Although manors differed from one another according to variations in terrain, fertility of the soil, and the kind of crops grown, it is possible to present a composite picture of them. In the center of the manor was the

---

[1] There were cases, however, in which serfs were sold along with the land. Some household workers were also slaves. See the study on this subject by Charles Ver-linden of the University of Ghent.

Medieval Village with Open Fields. This small walled village is typical of many of the Middle Ages. The town itself is composed mostly of persons engaged in agriculture. They reside together and have their barns within the walls. Protection is provided by a thin wall and a water moat. Egress is by bridges and gates on three sides. At the center of the village is a small square, where open-air markets are held. Probably one of the buildings on it is an inn with a tavern. Nearby is the church. The buildings are of mortar, supported by timbers in the "half timber" manner. The land is cut up into strips worked by individual peasants. What looks like a large field seems to be a meadow along a brook and was probably too wet to cultivate. No common woodland appears in the picture, although there may have been one at a distance. In low lands, however, forests were very limited.

manorial village, dominated by a castle, manor house, or monastery, built for protection upon a height, or in flat country with a large moat around it. Attached to it were barns for livestock and for storing grain and hay and other buildings for housing the lord's bakery, smithy, and winery, brewery, or cider press, according to the local drink of the people.[2] Nearby the castle was the church, the size and general importance of which depended upon the wealth of the community and upon whether or not the manor belonged to a lay or religious lord.

Clustering around the manor house and church, but in a more exposed position, were the dwellings of the serfs. These were usually built of

[2] Fermented drinks were customary because by rule of thumb the people had learned that their water supply might not be sanitary. As a rule, wine was preferred to other drinks, but because grapes could not be grown in the colder climates, recourse was had to cider, beer, or ale.

stone or of wood and mortar, had tile, wood, or thatched roofs, and had few windows, because glass was dear and parchment let in little light. They were often designed, as is frequently the case even to the present, so that livestock in stalls or pens on the ground floor would provide some warmth in winter for the living quarters upstairs, unless, indeed, animals were taken directly into the household. Attached to these houses there was usually a garden, with an outhouse located hard by.

Then somewhere within the village there was a well or a fountain where people fetched their water. The streets were sometimes paved with stone blocks, but they were more frequently simply made of packed dirt and gravel, which became quagmires in the rainy seasons and dust bowls in the dry ones. There was also the lord's gristmill, located along a stream, if there were one that could turn a water wheel, or in an advantageous place to catch the wind, if the millstones were run by a windmill. Finally, around the whole there might be a stone wall with heavy gates of wood reinforced with iron, which were closed at night to keep out marauders.

Outside the village was the manor's forest, pasture, meadows, and arable land. The forest belonged to the lord, but peasants had the right to get their firewood there and sometimes to cut wood for buildings. The pasture or "commons" was opened to the livestock of all, but the number of head which any one person might turn into it was limited, because a too numerous herd in the possession of one peasant would mean that there would not be enough feed for the livestock of others. The meadows were also common to all, and there peasants might cut hay which would help get their livestock through the winter months.

The arable land was, of course, the most important part of the manor's existence, for it was the source of most of the people's food supply. Usually the arable land was divided into two or three large fields, which in turn were partitioned into small strips. Some of the strips were set aside for the exclusive use of the lord and constituted his demesne where he grew food for his household and household workers. Others were divided among those serfs who had a contractual right to land and varied in size, depending upon the fertility of the soil, from 5 to 20 acres, which was supposed to be enough to sustain a peasant family. Because typically one of the large fields was allowed to remain fallow each year, that is, was not cultivated but grazed, so that it might recover some of its fertility, the strips of both the lord and the peasants were scattered among these fields. Finally, the strips of one individual in each of the fields might be dispersed in order that each holding might be of equal fertility.

The holdings of a peasant had great stability and still give to the cultivated land in some parts of Europe a patch quilt character. This rigidity resulted from the fact that although peasant holdings could usually be inherited on the making of certain payments, they could not be sold nor could they, as a rule, be consolidated by marriage. Nor was there much incentive toward larger peasant holdings, for without markets in which to sell surplus products, except in times of famine, the chief purpose for having more land was to increase one's supply of consumers' goods. So what economic differences there were among peasants with land usually came about through harder work, better planning, thrift, and good luck and were manifested by better houses, better clothes, a better table, and more livestock. Investment for more than a modicum of greater production was, therefore, almost unknown among peasants and for that matter among lords.

Some serfs, as has already been suggested, were not fortunate enough to have any land other than garden plots to cultivate, and this class was filled by the younger children of peasants for whom there was no inheritance. Some of these people were cottagers or cotters and worked on the lord's land or on the land of well-to-do peasants in return for payments in kind. Others were the lord's servants, who could sometimes be sold. Some were shepherds or herdsmen; others were artisans who worked in the lord's mill, smithy, or ale or winehouse. A select few were employed by the lord as overseers, the chief of whom was the seneschal or bailiff, whose office came to be hereditary.

The entire structure of society, based as it was on an inflexible landholding system, was a rigid one; and this rigidity was maintained both by the lack of economic opportunity and by restrictions imposed by the lord on the individual activity of peasants. Since it was, indeed, in the lord's interest to perpetuate a system that supplied him with a satisfactory existence and that maintained relatively friendly relations among his serfs, he was at no loss to find ways to control affairs to suit his ends. Thus the lord established various claims upon the peasants and their lands, and when these did not suffice he sat in court over issues at stake and rendered decisions which favored the kind of world which he wanted.

In the course of time there came into being under this system a number of "dues," some of which were very burdensome, which the peasant owed the lord for the use of land. Among the most important of these were week work, boon work, and deliveries in kind. Thus the ordinary serf might have to work for his lord from one to five days a week, three days out of six being the most common. Inasmuch, however, as the rule was that each holding should provide week work, the serf might send a grown son to fulfill his obligation, but he might have to furnish at the same time a team of oxen or a cart and so was temporarily deprived of the use of his capital equipment. In planting and harvesting seasons, the serf was required to give additional services to his master, but this boon work was measured in tasks to be performed rather than by time. Thus the peasant might have to plow part of the demesne, or cut grain on one of the lord's strips, or thresh a given quantity of grain. Furthermore, the serf had to deliver to his lord some of the produce of his own land, maybe fish or honey, or a lamb in the spring, a pig in the late fall, a duck at Christmas, and eggs at Easter. If the manor was owned by a monastery or if the lord had many workers in his shops, deliveries in kind consisted more of basic foodstuffs.

In addition to fulfilling these regular requirements, the serf was subject to additional payments upon special occasions. When he gave a daughter in marriage, he had to make a payment in goods or money, although this exaction, known as *formariage*, was levied in France as a rule only when the daughter was wedded to a man from another estate. When the lord was in great need, as for example when he was at war, the serf had to pay a tallage or taille, an unspecified amount determined arbitrarily by the lord and hence subject to considerable abuse. The peasant was also subject to the *champart*, a part of his field crop, a survival of the Roman public tax, that theoretically went to the territorial prince but which was often simply confiscated by the serf's immediate superior. For the use of the lord's gristmill, drink-making equipment, and bakery, he had to pay fees, called banalities, which consisted of a part of whatever was being processed. Upon his death, a serf's heir or heirs had to deliver their best animal or some other object of value to the lord (heriot) and if a serf died without direct heirs, the lord got all his property (mortmain). Last but not least, the peasant had a pay a tithe to the Church, which was in theory at least a tenth of his annual produce.

The lot of the serf was thus not very brilliant and that of freemen was not much better. Even they had to provide week work, boon work, and deliveries in kind to the lord. In fact, they were free only in the sense that they were not subject to servile restrictions and that they could leave the land if they wished. What made the situation of the tillers of the soil particularly burdensome, at least from our modern point of view, was the practical impossibility for them to improve their condition. They could run away and join bands of vagrants who roamed the forests, but such a life, even if one were a Robin Hood, was a precarious one and not for the masses.

One should not, however, represent the life of the serfs as utterly miserable. They did get land to work and they got help from the lord in times of famine and other misfortunes. They also had time for play, which must have been very robust, if one can judge from the literary

accounts and pictorial representations of their fun. Their greatest difficulty, especially as regards economic growth, was that they were in a box
which was kept tightly shut by convention—by the various contractual
and customary bonds which we have described.

Production on the Manor

The chief natural resources in agricultural production are fertile land,
water, warmth, and sunshine; accordingly upon these ingredients de-
pends in large part the output of the individual farm worker. Western
Europe was particularly well endowed with these factors of farm production. As can easily be grasped from the accompanying map, Western
Europe had large plains of fertile land, such as the Po Valley in Italy,
the plain between the Pyrenees and the Massif Central, that from the
Massif Central to the Vosges, Ardennes, and Jura Mountains, and the
Rhone Valley in France, the flat land of the Low Countries, and the
Rhine Valley, the Danube Valley, and the great rolling stretches in Germany and Austria. Here was a vast area, quite different from the limited
arable land found in mountain valleys, coastal plains, or plateaus of
central Italy or of Greece or from the narrow strips of productive land
along the Tigris and Euphrates or Nile Rivers.[3] Furthermore, the natural
fertility of much of this land was enhanced by the fact that it had not
been exhaustively cultivated over centuries, but had been fairly recently
reclaimed from forests, marshes, and heaths.

Also Western Europe was blessed, as it still is, with plenty of rainfall
and a temperate climate, and although droughts and too much rain were
not unknown, they were usually relatively local in character. Sufficient
rainfall in the growing seasons meant that seed germinated quickly and
thus diminished the chances of erosion, that crops were lush, and that
pasture grass, except in mountain areas and in the colder regions, was
available to feed livestock out of doors for large portions of the year.[4] In
general, European climatic conditions were almost perfect for growing
the grains which constituted the staple food and for the husbandry of
those animals which were most important to human consumption—cattle,
sheep, pigs, and hens. The chief drawback was that winters were longer in
Western Europe than in the Mediterranean regions, but wood for fuel
was plentiful, grains could be stored and meat cured for the unproductive months, and after the fireplace and chimney, which reached Northern

[3] The fertile land along the Nile south of the Delta averaged only 12 miles in
width in Ancient Times.
[4] In some parts of Europe one sees even today few large barns for the storage of
hay or for the stabling of animals in the winter.

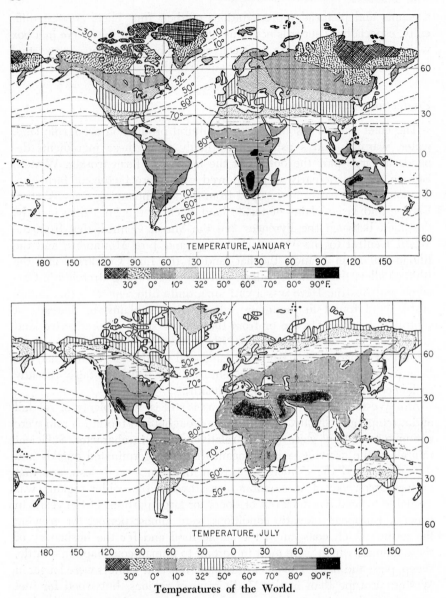

Temperatures of the World.

Europe in the twelfth century, replaced the brazier, it was possible to protect oneself indoors from the cold without being suffocated by smoke.

Output does not depend only on available natural resources, as we have previously indicated, but also upon a knowledge of the productive arts—upon techniques and technology. In this respect the farmers of the

0   1   3.9 7.8 11.8 15.7 19.6 29.5 39.3 59.0 78.7 INCHES

The Mean Annual Precipitation of Europe.

The Topography of Europe.

The Topography of the Chief Areas of Western Culture.

OVER 12,000 FT.

6000 - 12,000

3000 - 6000

1000 - 3000

0 - 1000

BELOW SEA LEVEL

Middle Ages knew about all the ancient methods of cultivation and had all the ancient tools. In their borrowing from their predecessors they simply adapted what had already been developed to a new environment. In the main medieval agriculture did not make great technological progress; given the rigidity of the landowning system and limited markets up to the twelfth century, great changes were hardly to have been expected. Yet the Middle Ages did witness the development of a harness for the horse (between the tenth and twelfth centuries) that did not choke the animal when it pulled. It also saw improvements in the plow—the introduction of the coulter up front to cut the sod, an iron plowshare that could dig into heavy soils, a moldboard that turned over the earth instead of just scratching it, and wheels that steadied the implement, made the plowing of a straight furrow much easier, and lessened the labor of the plowman. In fact, by the thirteenth century the modern walking plow had assumed its general form, although it was not yet made of the more durable steel. Lastly, the Middle Ages made progress in threshing, which is one of the more arduous of farm tasks. Up to the eleventh century grains, beans, and peas had been separated from their stalks, shells, and hulls by beating them with straight sticks or by driving animal-drawn sledges or rollers over them. But at that time the hinged flail came into use. If handled with dexterity, this was a great labor-saving device; if used inexpertly, it might crack the operator in the back of the head.

One of the greatest technological handicaps under which medieval agriculture labored was ignorance of how to maintain the fertility of the soil. Although medieval farmers had some manure and used it on the land, the pasturing of animals out of doors for large portions of the year meant that no great accumulation of the precious stuff was available for arable land. In fact, Western European farmers had less manure at their disposal than did agriculturalists in the Mediterranean regions, where cattle were, and still are, kept in stables the year round because of the lack of pasture in the dry summer months. Moreover, tillers of the soil in the Middle Ages did not know about the advantages of rotating crops, particularly with root vegetables, in order to reduce soil exhaustion; hence, as has been mentioned above, they grazed from one-half to one-third of the land each year so that its fertility might be maintained—a practice which obviously curtailed the amount of land per operative. Nevertheless, a rule of thumb prescribed shifts from wheat to barley to peas or beans, and it was from this swapping around that crop rotation of the modern kind was to be developed in the eighteenth century.

Withal, yields were very low by modern standards, probably being for wheat somewhere in the neighborhood of 4 bushels to each bushel of seed sown, although this was certainly exceeded on the alluvial soil of the Netherlands, as compared with some 14 bushels today. Animals were also small: even as late as 1710 sheep sold at the Smithfield Fair in England averaged only 28 pounds and beef cattle 370 pounds; whereas at modern slaughter-houses they would run 135 and 1,800 pounds, respectively. Under the common pasture system, improvements in breeds were difficult and took place mainly in areas where cattle were isolated and feed was so scarce that it had to be husbanded carefully for only the best animals, as on the islands of Guernsey and Jersey and in the lowlands of Holstein and Friesland. Under most circumstances fodder was in short enough supply so that the fall was a time for slaughtering, except those animals which were kept for breeding or for work or those, like chickens and cows, which produced all winter.

From a study of medieval agricultural technology, one reaches the inevitable conclusion that little progress was made and that little was realized very slowly. Nothing was done to relieve the farmer's back of the really heavy tasks. No one made two spears grow where only one had grown before, and little was done to control breeding in order to improve livestock. Whatever increase in output there may have been per worker was owing primarily to the bringing of more land into cultivation. Here lay the possibilities of increasing production and here lay also the roots for a decline of the manorial system.

Economic Expansion and the Decline of the Manor

One of the chief forces that upset the rigid manorial system, which has been described above, was a growth in population. From the middle of the tenth century to the famines and the Black Death of the early fourteenth century, there was a considerable natural increase of population in Western Europe. Neither the amount of this rise nor the reasons for it are particularly precise. It may be that numbers doubled, but it is fairly certain that they rose by 50 per cent. It is probable, too, that the cessation of pillages by Saracens, Norsemen, and Hungarians by the tenth century, the more orderly conduct of agricultural life, and some increase in production made possible a secular trend toward an excess of births over deaths.

A second important force in the decline of the manor was the revival of commerce and the growth of towns. In the eleventh century there was renewed activity in Western European trade in the Mediterranean, in the North and Baltic Seas, and along the land routes which joined the riverain countries of these two areas. With the revival of commerce on a larger scale, towns came into existence, and with the towns, there appeared industries which produced goods for unknown buyers in far-off lands. With trade of this kind, money reappeared in greater volume than formerly and economic relations came to be expressed more and more in terms of money prices instead of in goods, services, and land.

Thirdly, the rapid decline in population in the fourteenth century created a temporary labor shortage that had an effect upon the manorial system, particularly in England. And finally, the increased use of money and the consolidation of political power in the hands of kings with some authority led to a shift from armies composed of knights who owed military service to their lords to armies composed of soldiers paid with moneys raised by taxation.

Most of these factors operated together to undermine feudalism and the medieval manor, so that it is quite arbitrarily that we consider first the effect of the increase in population. As might be expected in an agricultural system that had little flexibility in production, there was a limit to the number of stomachs which could be filled on the manors. So as population grew, the excess, usually the younger sons, simply had to go elsewhere. Some of them took off on conquering expeditions, like that of the Norman adventurers in Sicily at the end of the eleventh century, or William the Conqueror's invasion of England in 1066; or on the Crusades to the Holy Land. Of more importance to the decline of the manorial system was the fact that others, in the twelfth and thirteenth centuries particularly, went to the towns to participate in the growth of commerce and industry and that still more moved to unsettled lands where a different form of agricultural organization was created. Both the opportunities for and better terms of employment in these new outlets for population made manorial arrangements seem particularly burdensome and in the long run proved them to be untenable.

In the next chapter we shall see in more detail what the condition of town workers was; here it is sufficient to state that these men were free and that they had a chance to improve their economic status by hard work and enterprise. For the present, we shall concentrate our attention upon the opening of new lands to cultivation. This movement becomes visible by the twelfth century, when recently founded religious orders, like the Cistercians, and enterprising lords took advantage of the available labor supply created by the increase in population to found new farms on land that had not yet been brought into cultivation, whether by clearing forests, by draining marshes, or by seizing territories beyond the frontiers.

So anxious were protagonists of the new agricultural settlements to attract labor that they indulged in current forms of advertising, which painted a rosy picture of the conditions on their lands; what was of still greater importance, they offered favorable terms of employment to those who would come to work for them. Thus on the new agricultural units freedom was granted to any serf who would stay on the job for a year and a day[5] and there, in fact, serfdom hardly existed. Here there was seldom any oath of fealty to the lord; there was no labor service comparable to week work and boon work; and there were no requirements like mortmain, heriot, and *formariage*. Inasmuch as the workers got by perpetual and inheritable contracts the right to cultivate a stipulated amount of land or the right to given quantities of goods produced, they were required to make certain payments to the owners of the land, whether lords or religious orders. Some of these dues were held over from the earlier manorial system, like tallage, the necessity of performing military service, and banalities, but these were all less arbitrary and less burdensome than they had been formerly and the last-named was actually rent for the use of capital equipment. The chief payment under the new arrangements was *le cens*, which was usually a fixed amount of money and was essentially what we today would call rent. Because this payment was a stipulated amount in a long-term contract, the burden of it was reduced as prices went up, which they were to do over the next centuries, for with rising prices the sums represented fewer goods.

As these fundamental changes in the relationship of lords to peasants were taking place—changes which were in the direction of establishing monetary relations between owners and workers—lords began to alter their attitudes toward agricultural enterprise. They were less interested than formerly in simply securing goods for their own consumption and more in getting goods for sale in the market in return for money or in receiving money payments for the use of their land. Their ends might be attained by dividing the land into strips or into unified farms and then of receiving salable products or *le cens* from the landholders, a system described by the German term *Landherrschaft*. But they also might manage the farm enterprise themselves and try thereby to produce not only enough to support their workers but also an extra amount for the market, a system known as *Gutsherrschaft*. Small, unified farms with the peasant living on the land were found, for example, on the reclaimed land of the Low Countries; whereas large estates farmed as units predominated on the conquered land east of the Elbe, a characteristic of this area which was to be maintained until after World War II.[6]

One further aspect of the inroads being made into the old manorialism

---

[5] A lord did not usually, however, extend this rule to apply to his own serfs, for he did not want to destroy existing manorial arrangements so long as they were of some advantage to him.

[6] The lands of Cistercian monasteries were also farmed as large units on the *Gutsherrschaft* principle.

was visible in the laws and customs of the new agricultural villages. In some places they received charters from their lords which were copied from those that had previously been granted to commercial towns. Hence the *hôtes*, literally the guests, who came to settle in the new agricultural villages had a status something like that of the burgesses in the commercial towns, had the right to nominate a mayor, and had some administrative autonomy. Of especial importance was the fact that the harsh seneschals or bailiffs of the manorial system were no longer present, for if peasants were treated as badly as they had been, they would simply pack off and the lord would be left with no labor. The new management had to have some semblance of being reasonable in order to be successful.

The territories into which this new organization of agriculture spread were of various kinds. In France from the Loire to the Meuse were to be found the new agricultural villages of which we have been speaking, and south of the Loire, *bastides*, or estates developed by lords. In Spain, lands taken by Christians from Moslems were colonized along military lines. In Italy, where feudalism was never very firmly established, changes took place as Saracens were driven out and as the civil wars of the tenth century came to an end. In the Low Countries, lands settled in the new manner were largely those reclaimed from the sea, the so-called polders, by building levees or dikes to keep the rivers within bounds and in some places to keep out the sea. The practice of building dikes was so successful that Flemings and Netherlanders were called upon to carry their arts to the lower reaches of the Elbe, and thence to settle Mecklenburg and Brandenburg. Indeed, Flemish colonists went to Thuringia, Saxony, Lausitz, and Bohemia. By the end of the twelfth century Mecklenburg was completely settled and by the end of the thirteenth so, too, was Brandenburg. Then the Teutonic Knights, from 1230 onward, pushed into East Prussia, Livonia, and Lithuania, establishing the system of *Gutsherrschaft*, while Bavarians and Rhinelanders spread out to Bohemia, Moravia, Silesia, the Tyrol, and even to the frontiers of Hungary.

With the extension of an agricultural system where large farms were operated by lords to produce goods for the market or where single farms were rented for money to individuals who lived on them instead of in villages, there developed some specialization in production—some division of agricultural labor. Thus from the twelfth century the Cistercian monasteries in England concentrated upon the production of wool; peasants and lords in the Bordeaux region of France specialized in wines; and lords east of the Elbe applied themselves to the growing of grain. In each of these cases, as in many others, much of the produce was sold in distant markets.

This new kind of farming was eminently successful compared to the

old manorial system. There custom-bound practices provided little surplus that could be sold, and lords whose lands were thus encumbered
eventually sought ways to free their estates from peasant claims. For
their part, serfs were anxious to improve their lot, which seemed to them
much worse than that of workers in towns or under the new agricultural
arrangements. Accordingly serfs were often freed for a monetary consideration. Many of their dues were commuted to money payments, and the
rules of heriot, *formariage*, and mortmain were lightened. Demesne lands
were sometimes sold to capitalists but more frequently were rented to
free peasants for money or for a share of the crop. Crop sharing, or the
métayer system as it came to be called in France, became particularly
popular in southern France and in central Italy, where it is still practiced.
When labor was in very short supply, as it was in England after the
Black Death in the fourteenth century, these arrangements were particularly advantageous to the peasants, for lords had to attract peasants to
their lands.

In these ways, and logically enough, actual serfdom in the feudal
sense and also manorialism broke down most completely and most
rapidly in those places where trade and industry were most highly developed. Thus in Lombardy, Tuscany, northern France, and Flanders
they were definitely on the way out by the middle of the twelfth century;
whereas in England they did not show signs of decay until the end of
the thirteenth century, and in isolated places were not very much altered
until later. Furthermore, periods of rising prices, now that agriculture
was at least partially geared to a price system, meant an additional pressure for change. Inasmuch as price rises were marked in the twelfth and
thirteenth centuries, after the Black Death in the fourteenth century,
from the early sixteenth century to the middle of the sixteenth century,
and from about 1720 to 1819, these were periods of alterations in the
agricultural system of Europe.

Despite the decline of the early manorial system, connected as it was
with feudalism, and of the growth of capitalist farming for profit through
money rents or through the sale of goods in the market, various remnants
of the earlier arrangements were projected into Modern Times. Lords
still had nominal title to the land, except where it had been sold clear
of all restrictions, and these titles gave the lords certain rights. As we
have already seen, they could collect rents and some services from their
peasants. They exercised justice over their people. They collected banalities, and where changes had been slight, they might have some rights of
heriot, mortmain, and *formariage*. The Church still collected tithes from
the peasants and the growing political states began levying taxes upon
them. Peasants had little voice in public affairs and many of them were

confronted with problems of trying to farm widely scattered strips with time-honored techniques. So with the beginning of Modern Times, there were agricultural reforms to be effected before all agriculturalists were freed of all obligations to overlords and could operate with entire liberty in a money economy. But changes there had been, and the trend was clear. Agriculture was on the way to becoming a capitalist enterprise in which profits could be made and a surplus could be invested for the making of still more profit.

CHAPTER 4

The Fall and Rise of
Medieval Commerce

Economic Decline to the Eleventh Century

In recent years many economic historians of the Middle Ages have
been inclined to represent commerce as the touchstone of medieval economic activity.[1] Their fundamental contention has been that the lack of
trade from the early Middle Ages to the eleventh century accounted for
economic stagnation in this period; hence the revival of commerce in the
twelfth and thirteenth centuries was largely responsible for the economic
growth which took place within this two-hundred-year span. Persuasive
as their arguments and data are, the position taken here is that numerous
factors, of which commerce was only one, interacted in such a way as
to have an accumulative effect of decline in the first half of the Middle
Ages and of revival and growth in the second half. Indeed, even the facts
presented by those who stress the overwhelming role of commerce suggest that the simplest explanation should be eschewed for the more complex one, that what was important in causing a decline and then a growth
was the result of many factors working upon one another.

That there was a decline of commerce in Western Europe in the first
half millennium of the Middle Ages is uncontestable. It is evidenced by

[1] For example, see the work by the great Belgian medievalist Henri Pirenne, *Economic and Social History of Medieval Europe* (New York: Harcourt, Brace, 1937).

the falling into disrepair of Roman roads, by the decline of towns, and by the lack of archaeological evidence in the form of goods or coins of any wide exchange of products. This lack of trade may be regarded, however, in part as an effect of economic decline rather than a main cause of it. As we have already seen, commerce within the Roman Empire had fallen off drastically before the Goth Odoacer replaced the last Roman emperor in 476 A.D., because Rome's production of exports was insufficient to offset imports, because internal disorders connected with the weakening power of the state made the transport of goods precarious, and because the tax-collecting system and public financial burdens had induced landowners to create self-sufficient estates.

To a large extent similar conditions existed in Britain, Gaul, and Spain. To these areas the loss of Rome as a market was a severe blow. Moreover, it was accompanied by a series of in-migrations, usually known as the "barbarian invasions," which were reminiscent of the migrations of the Peoples of the Sea at the beginning of the first millennium B.C. In the third century A.D., Franks crossed the Rhine barrier and pillaged as far as Spain before they came to a halt. Then the West Goths, after sacking Rome in 410, moved into Gaul and Spain. Vandals from Eastern Germany drove through the same countries to North Africa, whence they attacked Rome in 455. Huns raided Gaul and Italy in the middle of the fifth century and then vanished in Eastern Europe. East Goths migrated to Italy (489–493) and were ultimately absorbed there. Finally, Jutes, Angles, and Saxons from northeastern Germany invaded Britain. Burgundians came into southeastern Gaul; and more Franks came into Gaul in the fifth and sixth centuries. Even though these peoples may have been much less barbarous than they have traditionally been represented, their movements did upset the established system and with it commercial intercourse.

Moreover, no sooner had the barbarian invasions come to an end than Western Europe was threatened by a new and perhaps even more disturbing force from the outside—by the Moslems. In the sixth century an Arabian camel driver, known in history as Mohammed, claimed that he was the true prophet of God and shortly acquired a band of faithful followers. His religious sect grew by leaps and bounds and in the seventh century, fired by religious zeal, embarked upon conquests to win the world to its persuasion. Within a hundred years after their prophet's death Moslems had created a vast empire which stretched from the western bounds of India through Persia and Arabia and across the north of Africa. In the seventh and eighth centuries they overran Spain and, unsuccessfully, attempted an invasion of France. They occupied the Balearic Islands, Corsica, Sardinia, Sicily, and certain ports of southern

Italy. In 846 they raided Rome. In the tenth century, they had a military outpost at Garde-Freinet, a short distance inland on the French Riviera, whence they preyed on pilgrims and merchants taking the land route between France and Italy. This encirclement of Southern Europe by Moslems was made even more complete by their intermittent raids along the coast, such as their pillaging of Pisa in 935 and 1004, their destruction of Barcelona in 985, and their incursions into the Gulf of Lyons and into the Bay of Genoa.

As a climax, Western European life was disrupted by invasions of marauding Hungarians in the tenth century and of pillaging Normans in both the tenth and eleventh centuries. Under these circumstances what little trade had been maintained between Gaul and the Mediterranean was still further reduced. The lack of accounts of merchants traveling these routes from the south to the north and the absence of Arabic coins found in trading centers on them offer strong evidence of what was taking place. Towns that had lived on Mediterranean commerce were no longer important, and their decline was felt far inland. Fairs were now almost entirely of a local character, only that of St. Denis on the outskirts of Paris attracting buyers and sellers from a distance. The creation of an economy based on land was hereby given a new reason for being.

The decline of commerce and the growth of the manorial system had, in turn, a decided impact upon industry. With little opportunity for selling surpluses in distant markets and with the chief demand for industrial goods being on the large estates, industry came to be almost as exclusively manorial as agriculture itself. Here the people raised their own sheep for wool and raised their own flax for linen, spun these fibers into thread, wove the thread into cloth, and fulled and dyed their finished product. Nor was this work in textiles done by specialists in workshops. Rather it was carried on as a domestic enterprise by peasant women, children, and men in their spare time, especially in the winter months when work in the fields was slack. Furthermore, peasants could do most of the rough carpentry work which they needed, could process nearly all their own food, and could make their own clothes and some few of them their own shoes. Even the few things which they could not produce for themselves, largely because they lacked equipment, were for the most part furnished by the lord's mill, winery or alehouse, and smithy. In fact, about the only goods obtained through commerce were salt, iron, glassware, and pottery. Yet, the relatively wide distribution of salt in the sea and in mines, the many outcroppings of iron ore, and the prevalence of clay suitable for pots resulted in many small establishments which produced for nearby markets. Hence, it is not surprising that industrial techniques changed little during the first half of the Middle

Ages—that the great medieval inventions came after the eleventh century.

Nor is it strange that the concentration of economic life on the manor should have had repercussions on the use of money, credit institutions, and attitudes toward the accumulation of wealth. With the localization of economic activity on the manor, money ceased to be an important store of wealth and was used primarily as a medium of exchange for the few purchases peasants had to make. Even lords had no great accumulation of mobile wealth, and when in desperate financial need, as in times of wars and famines, had to have recourse to borrowing. Evidence of the decline in the use of money for other than small transactions is to be found in the coinage system established by Charlemagne. By the ninth century, the gold solidus of the Roman Empire had become so rare that a new money had to be brought into being. This money was based upon silver, obtained largely from older coins and from the melting down of silverware, rather than upon the dearer gold. Its basic measure was the pound (livre, libra) weighing 491 grams, which was divided into 20 shillings (sous, solidi), each of which was, in turn, divided into 12 pence (deniers, denarii). The significant thing about these measures was, however, that only pence and halfpence coins were ever issued, pounds and shillings being used only for bookkeeping purposes. This system, adopted in all the territories under Charlemagne's rule, was for the times satisfactory, since it provided the small change needed for purchases. Incidentally, these divisions of money lasted in most European countries until the French Revolutionary and Napoleonic period and persist even to this day in Great Britain and in certain parts of the British Commonwealth.

In spite of Charlemagne's efforts to establish a usable money for his empire and of the continued employment of his pound, shilling, and pence system, a state of anarchy befell money after the dissolution of the Carolingian Empire and the collapse of public administration in the monarchies which were created from its remnants. Feudal princes were quick to assume the privilege of striking coins, and kings frequently bestowed the right of minting on churches. As a consequence there were soon throughout Western Europe almost as many different pennies as there were fiefs; and to make matters worse the pennies were of varying degrees of fineness and weight. In the beginning of the eleventh century, a mark, probably of Scandinavian origin and weighing only 218 grams, was introduced into the Germanies, but it did not help stabilize money, for it was issued in varying weights by German princes.

Furthermore, those who had the right to mint were given to "calling the money down," that is, calling it in, issuing new coins of less value in their stead, and paying those who had brought in their coins penny for penny in the debased money. This was a very profitable operation and recourse was had to it with great frequency. For example, in the thirty-two-year reign of one German prince this act of prestidigitation was performed on the average of three times a year. Moreover, so much copper was ultimately mixed with silver, if indeed any silver was used at all, that coins soon turned black and were dubbed "nigri denarii." Finally, existing techniques of minting by hammering out pieces of metal and then stamping them with a die hit by a hammer were unable to achieve standard weights, sizes, and shapes. The differences in coins which resulted from the use of such methods invited both counterfeiting and such common practices as clipping edges and "sweating" silver coins, that is, shaking them in a leather bag until a certain amount of dust could be recovered. Little wonder that coins were looked upon with suspicion, were tested with the teeth for hardness before being accepted, and were sometimes weighed to check on tampering. If commerce had been thriving, such money would have been intolerable. Indeed when trade revived, monetary reform was the order of the day.

With all the rest of economic decay in the first half of the Middle Ages, there was also a decline in the use of credit and the adoption of a hostile attitude toward it. Churches and monasteries now had the chief accumulations of gold and silver, for one of the ways for the faithful to express their piety was to bestow their riches upon those institutions which held the keys to eternal salvation. Most of this wealth was in relics, ornaments, and adornments of various kinds, but it could be rendered mobile by melting it down and minting it. Recourse to such extremities was not rare, for when lords were in dire need of funds they borrowed from churches and monasteries. As can readily be imagined, they pledged repayment in the only wealth at their command—in revenues from their lands. If these revenues, or part of them, went to reduce the principal of their debt, their pledge was called a "live gage" (*vif gage*); but if they were pledged to the creditor without reducing the principal, the contract was called a "dead gage," or mortgage.

Invariably these debts were incurred to acquire consumers' goods rather than to purchase capital equipment for the purpose of producing still more goods. Inasmuch as this was the case, the religious lenders could hardly take advantage of the misery of the people to exact heavy tribute for the use of their savings. Thus it came about that the Church did not lend at interest or usury, as it was then called—a term which acquired all the discreditable overtones that it bears even to the present day. In time the Church supported its practice of not taking interest with the doctrine that money was in itself unproductive, that it was, in fact, "sterile." With such arguments it was able by the ninth century to forbid the laity to take interest and to reserve to ecclesiastical courts jurisdiction over questions involving usury. If these steps had not been taken, spend-thrift lords and princes would undoubtedly have borrowed much more than they did for purposes of ostentation. Moreover, heavy consumption debts would have resulted either in such a rapid change of or concentration in ownership that society based upon land, feudal loyalty, and manorial production would have been upset. Indeed, changes in the practice of borrowing for investment, in the taking of interest, and in the Church's attitude toward it came only with economic expansion and the need of capital for the conduct of business.

From all the evidence which has thus far been presented, the economy of most of Western Europe in the first half of the Middle Ages can be characterized as having been first in a state of decline and then of stagnation—as having evolved a socioeconomic system based on land in which rigidities prevailed and the "range of opportunities for alternative decisions" was extraordinarily limited. There were, however, two parts of Europe which did not conform to the pattern thus far laid out: they were certain Italian cities of the Adriatic and in the southern part of the peninsula, on the one hand, and specific ports of the Baltic and North Seas, on the other. In them long-distance commerce was being carried on when it was almost nonexistent in the West; and accordingly in them there was not such an extensive decline in business and business institutions as there was where manoralism was triumphant.

The focus of the trade of both these areas was Byzantium or Constantinople, a fact which requires a word of explanation. As is well known, the Straits of the Bosphorus had for centuries been the location of trading centers because of its situation at the juncture of transportation routes between the Black Sea, with all its great tributaries, and the Aegean and Mediterranean Seas with their vast littorals. During Roman times Byzantium rose to great importance. At the end of the third century A.D., when Diocletian divided the empire into two parts, he chose this most important center of commerce as his capital in the East. Then in the fourth century, when conditions in Italy were particularly disturbed, Constantine moved his capital from Rome to Byzantium and rechristened the city in honor of himself. Although barbarians subsequently made inroads into the Eastern Roman Empire,[2] they never upset the applecart as they did in the West. When they attained to the emperorship, they maintained authority, the dignity of their office, and their frontiers. Moreover, Moslem attackers who laid seige to Constantinople in 719 were turned back and were never able to dominate either the Aegean

[2] They defeated the Emperor of the East at the Battle of Constantinople in 378.

or the Adriatic Sea. As a matter of fact, many Italian towns—Naples, Gaëta, Amalfi, Salerno, Bari, and above all Venice—continued a rather tenuous recognition of the Emperor of the East until the eleventh century.

Throughout all this period the economy of Byzantium continued to be vigorous. In the eighth century, Constantinople had a population of a million people and was thus by far the largest city of the known world. Furnishing this great agglomeration of people with the basic necessities of life was in itself a major enterprise and required the tapping of supplies over a vast area. But what was more, many people in Constantinople possessed enough wealth to indulge in luxuries and semiluxuries, ranging all the way from elegant churches, like St. Sophia, down the scale to fine clothes and trinkets. The resulting active demand for industrial products kept the local craft shops and bazaars busy and attracted goods from far and wide. Indeed, Constantinople was a great entrepôt for such Eastern products as silks, spices, dyes, and perfumes and for such European goods as furs, amber, timber, and iron. Money was used in this trade and was free from gross tampering; credit practices, inherited from Rome, were maintained; and neither interest taking nor other forms of profit making were frowned upon.

So great was economic activity at Constantinople, so strong was its commercial magnetism, that it is not strange that Europeans were drawn into its orbit. Those most completely affected were Venetians at the head of the Adriatic Sea. Their city had been established at the time of the barbarian invasions when people of the mainland in need of protection sought refuge on the sandy lagoons off the coast. As time went on Venetians, having no other source of livelihood except fishing, turned to shipping and commerce. In both they were eminently successful.

At an early date Venetian merchants were trading with Constantinople and were finding this business particularly lucrative. There was always a good market for the silks, spices, and other luxuries which they brought back in exchange for their exports of timber and iron, both of which were in short supply in the Eastern Empire. Gradually they accumulated wealth, an important fleet, and enough power so that they became virtually autonomous in the eighth century and formed an independent republic in the ninth—a republic which lasted until 1797. When the Moslems threatened to extend their sway, it was in the interest of the Venetians to repel them, and they collaborated with Byzantium in doing so. By the beginning of the twelfth century they had rid the Adriatic of Dalmatian pirates and had control of the eastern coast of that sea. And in the eleventh century they stopped Norman expansion eastward and by so doing eliminated the competition of the rival ports of Naples, Gaëta, Salerno, and above all, Amalfi.

Meanwhile, Venetian traders became so important to the Eastern Empire that they were exempted from paying certain import duties (992), were allowed to establish numerous trading stations (*fondachi*) in many Eastern ports, and in 1082 were given the extraordinary privilege of not paying any commercial taxes—a privilege that citizens of the Empire did not enjoy. Furthermore, Venetians were not above trading with the infidel Moslems and established commercial relations with Egypt, Syria, and North Africa. In this trade they added to their standard articles of export Slavs from Dalmatia and the Black Sea, hence the word slave. Striking evidence of these trading connections is to be found in the facts that in the ninth century Venetians brought home from Alexandria relics of their patron saint St. Mark, and that in the eleventh century they built their great cathedral along Byzantine architectural lines.

Because of the commercial activity of Venice, with which all of its population was in one way or another connected, there was never any question there of establishing serfdom or of adopting a hostile attitude toward profit making. Interest was taken in one way or another; money was lent for investment rather than consumption. Fairly advanced forms of business organization were employed, like multiple partnerships and the *commenda* (collegantia), and literacy among laymen, which was then an indication of the scope of economic activity, was extensive, for otherwise it would have been impossible for merchants to keep their complicated accounts or to receive written reports from their agents.

To some extent, conditions resembling those in Venice existed in other Italian towns that traded with the East, especially Bari and for a time Amalfi. Moreover, Venetian commerce eastward was bound to have repercussions westward. At the end of the ninth century, the district around Verona and many places in the Po Valley were trading with the Queen of the Adriatic; in the tenth century, Pavia, Treviso, Vicenza, Ravenna, Ancona, and many other places had been affected. Certainly by the eleventh century, German products were coming through the Brenner Pass in the Alps and Eastern products were making their way northward in return. In Venice itself there began to be signs of manufacturing, especially luxuries like glass, playing cards, silk, and chessmen, that had hitherto been imported for far-flung European customers. Finally, certain other cities like Pisa and Genoa began to awake to the facts of economic life and to indicate a desire to break into the Venetian commercial act. Thus, from the principal Western trading center of the first half of the Middle Ages there radiated an idea and a practice which were to lead to a revival of commerce and to economic change throughout the West.

In addition to the economic ferment that grew from Venetian trade with the East, there was also, as has previously been stated, another area of economic activity in the first half of the Middle Ages—that in the Baltic and North Seas. Here the Northmen developed ships and seafaring ability which carried them far and wide. Not only did they reach Iceland, the British Isles, and the French and Netherlandish coasts, but even got to America about 1000 A.D. Most of their early excursions were of a raiding character, but in the course of time these people turned from robbery to trade—in the minds of some wags an easy transition. In the tenth century Hamburg on the Elbe, Thiel on the Waal, and London were all frequented by them. In the same century they established themselves in Normandy, whence their descendants, the Normans, conquered England and Sicily in the eleventh century. As was logical, they established commercial relations between their old settlements and the new and in time this trade attained proportions which were to have an impact upon the settled ways of economic life.

While the Northmen, or Norsemen, or Vikings, as they were also called, were thus building up an area of commerce in one direction, Swedes were active in another. From the Baltic they penetrated Russia and worked their way down the Dnieper River to the Black Sea—a route that in Ancient Times had been followed by Greek traders seeking Baltic amber. From the middle of the ninth century they established fortified trading posts, called *gorods* in Russian, along this artery of commerce and in these places they accumulated honey, furs, and females for Moslem harems. Each year a trading fleet left Kiev in the spring for the Black Sea and thence sailed on to its final destination at Constantinople. At the same time, other traders went down the Volga to the Caspian Sea and exchanged goods with Jewish and Arab merchants from the Moslem Caliphate of Bagdad. How important trade to these two centers was is difficult to estimate, but we do know that it must have been fairly large, for from the ninth century that with Byzantium was regulated by treaties and the Russians, as the Northern merchants were called, had a special quarter in Constantinople assigned to them. Moreover, it was through these commercial contacts with the East that Russia got its writing with Greek letters, its Byzantine style of art and architecture, and the Eastern form of Christianity.

The merchandise which came back from the two markets in the East and which consisted primarily of spices, was concentrated in the Gulf of Bothnia for here the two trade routes converged. Thence the goods were distributed throughout the Baltic, but there was a western entrepôt on the island of Gothland, where Eastern products were available to Northmen for sale in their sphere of interest. Eventually, however, the flow of Eastern goods through these places declined, for costs of transportation via the arduous Russian routes were much higher than those via Venice and after the twelfth century via the Straits of Gibraltar. Yet, while this trade lasted, it kept alive a desire for profits and familiarity with business practices. It provided a basis for greater economic activity at a later date.

Revival of Economic Activity in the Twelfth and Thirteenth Centuries

Although trade over long distances existed in the Adriatic and in the North and Baltic Seas during the first half of the Middle Ages, most of Western Europe's economy was moribund, based as it was on a rigid land tenure system and upon production for immediate consumption. By the end of the eleventh century, however, there were many signs of economic growth and in the twelfth and thirteenth centuries a revival took place which was to break the older rigidities and greatly extend the range of economic opportunities. Many forces, such as the growth in population, the rise of towns, greater industrial production, and more extensive trade, initiated this change. To attribute to any one of them the ultimate cause of what took place is to raise the problem of whether the hen, the egg, or the rooster came first to the poultry kingdom. The fact is that they all came together and one would have been meaningless without the others.

We have already seen how the growth in population affected agriculture—how the inability of the manor to feed more mouths led to the establishment of new farms on recently reclaimed or conquered lands and to a flow of people to the towns. Certainly, the expansion of agricultural enterprise created a demand for industrial goods: these colonists, like all others both before and after them, were in need of capital equipment in order to make themselves self-supporting; and for a time they even had to buy consumption goods in the market. Thus there was pressure on the means of production for such producers' goods as tools, plows, builders' hardware, and textile equipment and for such consumers' products as cloth and shoes. This pressure was reflected in an increased and geographically concentrated output of these very things.

Another factor of change had its origins largely in political conditions. Moslem and Norman invasions which lasted from the eighth to the eleventh century, atrocious cavalry raids of Hungarians at the beginning of the tenth century, and struggles among rival lords led feudal princes to build great fortified castles or burgs, frequently on the site of some earlier

LAND ROUTES (BY NAVIGABLE RIVERS ALSO)
+ + + + THE SILK ROUTE
- - - - ROUTE OF MARCO POLO, 1271–1295
· · · · · ROUTE OF WILLIAM OF RUBRUCK
• • • • ROUTE OF JOHN OF PIANO CARPINI
x x x x x x MONGOL BALTIC TRADE ROUTE
———— SEA ROUTES OF THE GENOESE
△△△△△△ SEA ROUTES OF THE HANSEATIC LEAGUE
———— SEA ROUTES OF VENETIANS
- · - · SEA ROUTES (FOLLOWED BY ARABS
         AND CHINESE)

AREAS OF RELATIVELY
DENSE POPULATION

AREAS OF MODERATE
SIZED POPULATION

Medieval Trade Routes.

town. In these fortresses there was a garrison of knights and a kind of donjon for the special security of the lord. As trade revived, itinerant merchants came to seek shelter at night and protection in time of need in these places and while there did a certain amount of business with the local people.

In the course of time, trade became so great that there was not enough room in the old feudal or monastic town for merchants and they had to establish themselves outside the burg, that is, in the *faubourg*. The inhabitants of the *faubourg* came to be known as *poorters* (Dutch) or portmen (English), for they were living in land *ports* of trade. Eventually, however, they became so numerous that they completely surrounded the old burg and themselves built a wall around their district for protection, thus creating a new burg. Accordingly, they came to be known as burghers, burgesses, or bourgeois, and because they were engaged in business instead of in agriculture, these terms came to mean men of affairs.

The concentration of merchants in towns and the new requirements of agriculturalists for tools and of lords for weapons created an active demand in towns for labor. By the eleventh century there was a definite drift of surplus manorial population to these new centers of production. Such a development was particularly marked in Flanders where cloth-making moved from the countryside to the towns. Here merchants were prepared to supply wool, fuller's earth, dyer's soap, and dyes to textile workers and to take finished products for sale elsewhere. Gradually weaving passed from the part-time occupation of women to the full-time job of men. In Italy, silk, which had been introduced from the East, moved into cities, as in the case of Lucca; and fustians, mixtures of linen and wool, began to be produced in places like Milan and Florence. Even the making of finished iron and copper products became concentrated in cities in spite of the locational disadvantage of having to bring in both iron and fuel.

As these changes took place, townsfolk began to acquire a legal status which made a deep inroad into the seignorial regime. In the first place, since these people did not hold land from the lord, they were under no obligation to him on that score. Secondly, for the conduct of their affairs they needed to be able to come and go as they pleased and hence to be free of attachment to the land. And thirdly, they required a government which would be less arbitrary than that of the lords and that would provide services which would further their own interests.

Certain things townsmen demanded, and gradually they were able to get their demands recognized as valid. Although most workers came of unfree parents, once they were off the land and were getting nothing from the lord, they were freed from paying anything to him. Thus by the late eleventh century the rule became established that if a serf remained a year and a day in a town, he was free. As the Germans said, *Stadtluft macht man frei.*

Furthermore, the sheer need of regulating affairs among the merchants led, by the early eleventh century, to the creation of a *jus mercatorum,* the beginnings of a commercial law, and to the establishment of merchant courts, called piepowder in England, where traders with their feet still dusty from the road (*pieds poudreux*) could get a fair judgment of their differences. By the twelfth century, these embryonic judicial bodies were becoming regularized by the formation of local town courts of aldermen whose members were chosen from among rich merchants. Also the need for defense measures required a governmental organization to manage the construction of walls, the raising of armed forces, and the building of markets. These things all necessitated the expenditure of funds and hence the establishment of a tax system. By the eleventh century, councils of burgesses were being elected to perform the various functions of government and thus to create an organization distinct from that of the lords. Some seigneurs, particularly ecclesiastical princes, looked askance at this turn of affairs and frequently offered considerable resistance to it. Yet, most of the lay lords realized that the towns indirectly increased their well-being by permitting the collection of tolls and the manipulation of money, and many ecclesiastical princes gave way to bourgeois demands when their position was weakened by disputes between the Papacy and the Holy Roman Empire.

During the twelfth century, the laws and government of the *faubourgs* were extended to the old burgs and thus all townspeople, except the clergy, had the same status. Accordingly a new estate or class, the third estate, came into being and took its place alongside the previously existing estates of clergy and nobility. Only later were country folk accepted as members of the third estate, but when they were taken in, they were made to accept an inferior political position.

The Development of Long-distance Commerce

Clearly the growth of towns and the breakdown of rigidities within them, the development of industry, the expansion of agriculture, and the growth of population all formed part of a pattern which was changing economic life. But certainly the revival of trade between distant parts of Europe was an important factor in, as well as a reflector of what was taking place.

In the late eleventh century, commercial expansion was apparent in many places, but it was particularly pronounced in northern Italy and in the Low Countries. Mediterranean commerce, which had been so rudely interrupted by the Moslems, except for that carried on by Venice and a few south Italian cities, began to show signs of life. Toward the end of the tenth century, Pisa and Genoa decided, first, that they ought to get into the trade which had made Venice so prosperous, and secondly, that it was their mission to wage a holy war against the Mohammedan intruders. When they began to put these thoughts into action, Dame Fortune deserted them. Nevertheless, they persisted in their efforts and finally their luck changed. In 1015, they were able to establish themselves on the island of Sardinia. In 1052, they destroyed the Moslem arsenal at Palermo in Sicily, and in 1087, they seized the Moslem city of Mehdia in North Africa. It was in celebration of this great victory that Pisans began the construction of their famous cathedral and it was with the booty taken from Islam that they decorated it.

Their successes against the followers of Mohammed were continued by crusades to the Holy Land. In 1097, the Genoese sent a fleet to support members of the First Crusade in their siege of Antioch and for their services got the privilege of establishing the first of many *fondachi* or trading centers in the eastern Mediterranean. Subsequently, all the Crusades were water borne, and by carrying and provisioning men fired with religious zeal, Genoese, Pisans, Venetians, and Marseillais reaped a rich harvest. Even Barcelona grew wealthy by capturing Moslems on crusades in Spain and selling them to Christian buyers.

Some idea of the profit-making motives connected with these enterprises is well illustrated by events of the Fourth Crusade (1204). Venetian shippers were engaged to transport the would-be liberators of the Holy Land to Palestine, but the pilgrims were unable to pay the price of the carriers, so the shippers took command of the entire expedition and diverted it to Constantinople, where they had so long plied their trade. The city was seized and sacked, and both Venetians and pilgrims brought back great amounts of booty. Among the rest was the famous Roman statue of gilded horses which to this day stands over the entrance to St. Mark's Cathedral.

By such exploits Western Europeans got control of the Mediterranean and began rapidly to develop trade upon it. Crusaders were free and easy in dispensing trading privileges in their ephemeral states and Europeans soon had *fondachi* throughout the eastern Mediterranean and the Aegean. The Byzantine Empire was no longer strong enough to keep them out. The Turks, who easily wrested the Holy Land from the Crusaders in the twelfth century, found it to their advantage to do business with the Christians. Besides they had no fleets with which to contest mastery of the seas until the fifteenth century. Thus, Europeans had even larger supplies of Oriental goods than ever before to distribute at home and soon trade in these products was being carried on far inland. Ports like Marseilles, Montpellier, Narbonne, and Barcelona developed trade into their hinterlands. Pisa began to share its prosperity with Lucca, Florence, and Siena. Genoa developed its commerce with Piedmont, with Savoy via the Mont Cenis Pass, and with the Rhone Valley. And Venice strengthened its ties with Germany via the Brenner, the Septimer, and the Saint Bernard Passes, and in the thirteenth century, via the Saint Gothard by the construction of the first suspension bridge in Europe.

While these changes were taking place in the Mediterranean littorals and their hinterlands, commerce was also being built up in the North and Baltic Seas on the foundations already established by the Norsemen and Swedes. Here Flanders was the unquestioned leader and the port of Bruges on the Zwyn River became the great trading port of the region —the "Venice of the North." Through it came English wool for Flemish looms, Bourgneuf "bay salt" from the Bay of Biscay, wines from Bourdeaux and La Rochelle, and fish and grain from the Baltic. Then, beginning in 1314, Venetians and Genoese sent annually organized fleets to the city via the Straits of Gibraltar. Bruges thus became the entrepôt for silks, rice, figs, dyestuffs, alum, cotton, spices, and other Mediterranean luxuries. Paradoxically enough, it was the coming of Italian ships with their deep draught which led to the development of the deeper ports of Damme and then of Sluys at the mouth of the Zwyn and it was competition from these places more than the silting up of the river that was responsible for the ultimate decline of Bruges.

In the north as in the south, the hinterland of North Sea ports was affected by the growth of trade. On the Rhine, Cologne and Mainz, in the Meuse Valley as far as Verdun, and on the Scheldt and its tributaries, Ghent, Antwerp, and even Tournai developed active trade. Then in the Baltic, commercial towns were established, largely to supply the agricultural colonists of eastern Germany with the many things which they needed and to serve as entrepôts for trade with the North Sea. Thus Lübeck was founded in 1158 on the banks of the Trave. Wisby was begun in 1160 on the island of Gothland; and Stralsund, Danzig, and Riga came into being in the early thirteenth century.

Development of Transportation, Fairs, and Hanses

As can easily be imagined, the extension of commerce in the twelfth and thirteenth centuries was accompanied by important improvements in transportation. Nor is it surprising that the most dramatic changes occurred in seafaring, for the bulk of goods moved by water. By the twelfth century, Mediterranean seamen were using astronomical tables especially prepared for their needs. By the thirteenth century, they were employing a primitive compass, probably derived from China, had the astrolabe for finding latitude by astronomy, and were beginning to make accurate maps—the *portulani*[3]—based upon actual observations rather than upon fancy. Most significant of all, however, was the invention in the thirteenth century of the rudder to replace steering oars. This instrument, located directly astern, gave much better control of a vessel than had been possible earlier, for steering oars were difficult to manage in heavy seas. Moreover, it made possible closer sailing into the wind and construction of larger vessels. Galleys, in which oarsmen and supplies for them occupied much of the pay space, became obsolete. The larger ships which were built could no longer be pulled up on beaches for repairs nor could they find refuge in many of the small ports that had formerly been in use. Because they required deeper and better-protected harbors and because such places were few in number, shipping came to be more concentrated than in the past. This centralization, in turn, led to the construction of better port facilities with cranes, docks, and warehouses.

Important as such innovations in shipping were, inland transportation also improved. Between the tenth and twelfth centuries, the horse collar and iron horseshoes were developed and their use diffused, which greatly increased the effectiveness of the horse as a draft animal. Also the lowly wheelbarrow was invented in the thirteenth century and although it was used mostly on farms, it was employed in towns for short hauls of light loads. Old roads were rebuilt and new ones laid out, usually at the expense of merchants or of burgesses of the towns. Bridges were built at such a rate that this industry experienced a veritable boom. Canals began to be dug in Lombardy in the twelfth century, the *Naviglio Grande* which was constructed between 1197 and 1257 from Milan to the Ticino River being 31 miles in length. In the thirteenth century, the Low Countries started their network of man-made inland waterways which revolutionized their methods of transportation. Although locks were not invented until the fourteenth century, water levels were maintained by the construction of dams over which barges were drawn by means of winches.

[3] In the early Middle Ages map making had fallen to a low level, for cartographers in the absence of knowledge gave free rein to their imaginations. They represented the earth as a flat circle with Jerusalem in the center, with the east at the top where the Garden of Eden was supposed to be. There were three almost shapeless lumps representing Africa, Europe, and Asia surrounding the Mediterranean Sea. Because a perfectly straight Nile bisected the Don River, they formed a "T." Hence the maps are referred to as "T in O" maps.

Some effort was also made to remove man-made obstacles to trade. Territorial princes began to realize how valuable trade was to their lands and took steps to protect it. They conducted campaigns against "robber barons" (*Raubritter*) and by the thirteenth century had driven them to remote places. They even sold or otherwise abolished some of their tolls, although enough were left to constitute an obnoxious abuse down to the nineteenth century. The right of wreckage, whereby a lord could claim anything that the sea cast up upon his shores and which encouraged putting lights in the wrong places to cause disasters, was abolished or regulated by agreements. And arrangements were made to guarantee foreign merchants freedom from arrest for the debts of their fellow countrymen.

To facilitate merchandising, lords encouraged the establishment of great fairs within their territories. These institutions should be distinguished from the local, weekly retail markets which frequently went under the name of fairs, for the great fairs were meeting places of merchants coming from distant parts with wares which they sold at wholesale to buyers from both far and near. The great fairs began to appear in the eleventh century and prospered until the end of the thirteenth— in the period when distant trade was of a peripatetic nature. In fact, they declined when merchants began to establish fixed places of business in centers like Bruges, and they never developed in cities like Venice where merchandising had always been sedentary.

The most important of the great wholesale fairs came into being along the land routes traveled by merchants coming from the two main economic centers of Europe: the Low Countries and Northern Italy. They reached their fullest flowering where the two currents of trade met, that is, in Champagne in northern France.

An individual fair was established by act of the territorial prince in whose lands it was situated and this act of creation usually granted to merchants highly cherished privileges. For example, those who went to the fair traveled under a "safe conduct" of the prince, were exempted from reprisals for crimes committed or debts contracted outside the fair, and were not subject to escheat, that is, to the lord's right to claim their property in the case of their death. Moreover, lawsuits or acts of execution against merchants were suspended during the "peace of the Fair" and above all the canonical prohibition of usury was temporarily set aside.

A fair was held as a rule only once, or at most twice a year, but various towns in Champagne managed to organize a series of these trading sessions which covered nearly the entire year. Because of concentration of wholesale trading marts it was practical for merchants coming from different parts of Europe to have permanent residences in several of the fair towns. At the fair of Troyes, for example, the Germans had their own "house," and traders from Montpellier, Barcelona, Valencia, Rouen, Auvergne, Burgundy, and Geneva had their own stalls or inns. At Provins there were special lodgings for Lombard, English, and German merchants; and the same was the case at the fairs of Bar-sur-Aube and Lagny. In the wake of merchants, students and travelers went to France and became well versed in French culture. This fact accounts in large part for the spread of French Gothic and French literature throughout Europe in the twelfth and thirteenth centuries.

As trade over large areas became important, merchants began to form associations for security and for advancing their mutual interests. By the eleventh century these bodies, known variously as merchant guilds, hanses, *charités*, or *compagnies* were in evidence throughout Europe. Their main goal was to become powerful enough so that they could establish monopolies and get special privileges in the towns where they operated. In addition, they created rigorous rules of conduct for their members and made entry into their closed circle much sought after and difficult of attainment. When members of a merchant guild embarked upon a trip, they formed small armed caravans for protection under the command of a "captain." Sometimes, they bought and transported merchandise in common and divided the profits according to each man's investment.

In the course of time, these hanses or guilds began to specialize in certain kinds of activity in given regions, the Paris Hanse of Water Merchants, for example, limiting its operations to transportation on the Seine between Paris and Rouen, and the London Hanse of Flanders, to trade in cloth and wool between Flemish towns and London. Also wholesale merchandising became more sedentary, because the need of convoying land shipments decreased, wealthy merchants wanted to avoid weary travel, and other ways were worked out for selling and buying. Merchants began to operate through agents, partners, or factors in far-off places, like Bruges, Lübeck, Venice, or London. They also began to have enough confidence in one another so that it was possible to do business on the basis of samples, which was the foundation for those bourses or produce exchanges which were to be so important in Modern Times. Finally, by the end of the thirteenth century, a considerable division of labor had developed among merchants, some specializing in just one product, like wool or woolen cloth, and almost all making a sharp distinction between trade and transportation.

With these new developments, the concept of trading associations was never lost sight of, even though merchant guilds as such became less important in town life as rich merchants got political power into their own hands. Association was still the rule in maritime trade and here merchants frequently banded together to form "companies of merchant adventurers" for exploiting certain markets. In these companies, merchants shared the expenses of shipping and warehousing but traded for their individual profit in goods which they themselves owned. Association also took the form of leagues, or hanses, of towns for furthering their common interests.

The most important of these leagues of towns was the Hanseatic League. It began when Lübeck, seeking protection for its merchants in the half-conquered territories in which they operated, made a treaty of friendship and free trade with Hamburg (1230). Subsequently nearly all the shipping towns in the North and Baltic Seas from Cologne northward became joined in the pact and thus constituted a potent force. At its height the Hanseatic League had one of the largest *kontors* or trading centers at Bruges, was established in the Steelyard at London where it enjoyed special privileges, reached out to Novogorod in Russia, and traded deep into continental Germany via the Rhine, Weser, Elbe, and Oder Rivers. It was the agency that took Prussian wheat, Russian furs, and Baltic timber, tar, and salted herring to the West and that brought back woolens, hardware, salt, and Oriental luxuries to its customers.

Although cities of the Hanseatic League enjoyed a prosperity unequaled by any other part of Germany, trade along the Rhine and in the southern part of the country was by no means insignificant. Here association was largely among individual merchants rather than among towns and they managed to set up trading posts in the great commercial centers, like the *Fondaco dei Tedeschi* at Venice. Only in the Late Middle Ages, however, did south Germany reach its medieval economic heights, for only then did the salt works at Salzkammergut and Luneburg come into large production and only then, too, did the mines of Bohemia and of the Tyrol become important.

The area of greatest commercial revival in the twelfth and thirteenth centuries was along an axis that ran from Italy to the Baltic. Here goods of various kinds and of widely distant origins moved in some quantity. Here trade organizations were the most advanced. Here the manorial system broke down most completely. And here, as we shall see in the next two chapters, the most important developments took place in industry, in the use of money, and in business organization.

CHAPTER 5

The Revival of Industry
and Business Institutions

Industrial Growth in the Twelfth and Thirteenth Centuries

Hardly less impressive than the commercial revival which we have been discussing was the revival in the twelfth and thirteenth centuries of industrial production. In fact, these two segments of Europe's economy went forward *pari passu;* and it is scarcely conceivable that this should not have been the case. Because of the heavy costs of transportation, much of the trade by land was in goods of high value per weight that could not be produced locally, like fine woolen textiles, silks, metal wares, glass, clocks, and spices; except for spices, they were products in which considerable value had been added by "manufacturing." Even trade by sea was in goods that had been or were destined to undergo some processing, as in the case of salt, wool and woolens, and even grain, timber, wine, and dried or salted fish.

Secondly, the growth of towns, attributable in part to the concentration of industry in them, created a new demand for industrial goods. Although population data are scarce before the fourteenth century, we know that Venice, Genoa, Milan, and Florence each had populations of around a hundred thousand by 1450, and that Florence, at least, had had only about half that number in the thirteenth century, and again only half of that in the twelfth century. Ghent and Bruges had populations of about fifty thousand in the middle of the fourteenth century; Paris perhaps eighty thousand at the beginning of the fourteenth century. In 1450 Nuremberg had about twenty thousand; Brussels, some forty thousand; Louvain, twenty-five thousand; and Strasburg, twenty-six thousand. The mere building of dwellings to accommodate these people, the clothing and the feeding of them, and the equipping of their places of work required for the times a tremendous industrial effort.

Thirdly, foreign wars, such as the expeditions into eastern Germany, the struggles with the Moslems for control of the Mediterranean and of Spain, and the Crusades created a new and concentrated demand for military equipment. The agricultural expansion at home and the agricultural colonization beyond the frontiers of Western Europe necessitated the production of all kinds of farm equipment. Finally, increased transportation and the general needs of commerce required a greater output of harnesses, horseshoes, carts, wagons, and ships.

With this greater industrial production, it is not surprising that there was a concentration of production in certain parts of Europe and that there was some division of labor. It was not mere coincidence that the greatest industrial growth in the second half of the Middle Ages was located in the major areas of trade and of town development—in northern Italy, in Flanders, and in northern France. Nor is it to be wondered at that most of the advance in industrial techniques was realized in these same places, and from the twelfth century onward, and that the acquisition of new methods of production in these main centers proved to be a powerful factor in perpetuating their industrial preeminence.

In the course of economic history those industries which have pioneered in progress from primitive to more advanced techniques have been, at least until recently, connected with the production of food, clothing, and weapons, in part, because of the universality of demand for these things and, in part, because of a general familiarity with the fundamental processes upon which new techniques have been based.[1] This was certainly true in the Middle Ages. In the production of food we have already referred to the development of the plow for use on the heavy soils of Europe, to the invention of the collar which made the horse a useful draft animal, and to the use of iron shoes for both horses and cattle. To this list should now be added water and windmills for grinding grain. Although the water wheel was not new, its use was greatly extended from the tenth century onward, while the European windmill, perhaps adapted from Oriental predecessors, appeared in the

[1] A qualification is introduced to this generalization because in our times very advanced economies have imposed other industries on backward areas in their search for such raw materials as oil.

twelfth century. At least by the end of the Medieval period, wherever grain was ground in large quantities, as near the towns of the Low Countries, northern France, Italy, and England, gristmills were always in evidence. By 1086, so it is said, England had over five thousand mills, most of which were water driven. If each mill did the work of a hundred men per day, as has been estimated was the case, then there was available on the average the work equivalent of one man to every four or five members of the population. For the first time on any appreciable scale the industrial capacity of man was being increased by the inorganic forces of nature. This was a fact of the greatest moment, because it was this kind of power which was to account in very large part for the enormous economic growth in Western culture after 1800.

In the textile industry progress was also marked in the second half of the Middle Ages, particularly in Flanders and northern Italy. Here there was early specialization, a great development of trade, and the invention of new techniques. In Flanders, there had been an important production of woolens from early in the Medieval period and Charlemagne had made gifts of them to foreign potentates whom he was trying to impress. In the tenth century Norsemen traded in them; and in the eleventh and twelfth centuries itinerant merchants used them as one of their staples of trade, notably at the fairs of Champagne, for "no other woolens equaled them in texture, finish, or color." In the thirteenth century Hanse towns bought Flemish stuffs for sale throughout the Baltic and even to Russia. Italian merchants purchased them for their Eastern trade; and the two famous woolen guilds at Florence, the Arte di Calimala and the Arte della Lana, bought them for final finishing and dyeing.

Gradually Flemish production of woolen textiles reached a point where locally grown wool was insufficient to meet the demand of spinners and English wool began to be imported in large quantities. By the twelfth century Flanders was already heavily specialized in textiles and the industry was becoming firmly established in the neighboring districts of northern France—in towns like Amiens, Beauvais, Châlons-sur-Marne, and Provins.

At the other end of the axis of long-distance trade, in northern Italy, the development of woolen textiles was comparable to that of Flanders. Here Florence was the outstanding center, although Milan, Padua, and Verona were also important. Like Flanders, the City of Flowers early became famous for its stuffs, having good customers among Churchmen and lay nobles and among Pisan merchants who sold to the East. In the course of time the members of its woolen guilds acquired capital and they seem to have reinvested much of their earnings in their businesses. So successful were they that at the beginning of the fourteenth century

Florence was producing annually a thousand pieces of cloth which were worth about a million gold florins and was giving employment to some 30,000 of its 100,000 people. It was, indeed, woolen textiles from which came much of the wealth that permitted the formation of the great Florentine banks and that made possible the great artistic achievements of the Renaissance.

In addition to woolen textiles, the second half of the Middle Ages witnessed the rise of the silk industry and in a lesser degree that of cotton. Silk had been known in China as early as the third millennium B.C., but only reached Constantinople, probably through the efforts of Christian missionaries, in the sixth century and Greece in the seventh century. Subsequently the techniques of silk manufacturing, like many other Eastern processes, were brought by merchants from northern Italy to their cities of origin, for they wanted the profit in producing as well as in merchandising articles for which there was a great demand.

Efforts to introduce the silk industry into Italy met almost at once with considerable success. By the second half of the ninth century, silk was being mixed with wool at Lucca and shortly silks were being produced in half a dozen places. In 1272 the process of reeling the fine silk thread from cocoons was mechanized at Bologna and this invention gave the West a great advantage over the East. Cities began to foster the industry by granting it subsidies and attempted to force landowners to plant mulberry trees. Lucca was particularly successful in its efforts, but so, too, were many other cities, particularly Venice. In the early fifteenth century, it is said, the Queen of the Adriatic had 25,000 workers engaged in the trade.

The cotton textile industry was, like silk, also introduced into the West from the East. It was brought to Spain by Arab Moslems, and the Spaniards learned the techniques of production from their conquerors. Barcelona became the first center for cotton cloth, but by the fourteenth century the industry had reached Milan and Venice and subsequently made its way northward. If raw cotton had been more plentiful or more easily grown in Europe, this textile would have had a brilliant success, for it had the great advantage over wool of not being itchy in the heat of summer. As it was, cotton textiles only came into their own when cotton could be produced cheaply on the virgin soils of the New World.

As textile industries expanded and production became concentrated in cities, technological improvements were realized that accounted for still further growth. The most important of these advances was in spinning. Up to the thirteenth century such short fibers as wool, cotton, and flax were made into thread by hand-feeding them onto a twirling stick or spindle or falling weight that twisted them to the desired fineness. These threads were then run onto bobbins by use of a quilling wheel. This instrument consisted of a large wheel, rotated by giving the spokes a push with the fingers, which was connected by a belt to a small wheel to which was affixed the bobbin that turned very rapidly. By 1298 the quilling wheel had undergone slight alterations which permitted spinning and winding to be combined on one machine and into one operation. In other words, the spinning wheel had come into being. In the fourteenth century the rotary crank was applied to the large wheel and was turned by a pedal worked by the spinner. Here was an invention of the first magnitude, for the task of spinning was reduced almost by one-half. Finally, in the sixteenth century, if not before, a "flyer" or fork was placed over the spindle in order to wind the thread evenly on the bobbin. This machine was so successful that it remained virtually unaltered until the eighteenth century.

In other phases of textile production, improvements were also made, although none was quite so dramatic as in spinning. Weaving was advanced by the construction of better shuttles, heddles, and reeds, and the draw loom was introduced from the East which permitted the making of patterns, like damasks. In the fulling of cloth, that is, the beating of it in water to shrink it in order to increase its density and durability, technological progress was marked. Fulling had been done by beating the cloth with sticks and was a most arduous and wet task. In the twelfth century it began to be done by machines which worked on the triphammer principle. Great wooden plungers were rigged up so that they would be lifted by a peg in a shaft turned by a water wheel, and let fall when the peg reached the top of its arc. Furthermore, new dyes were brought into use, some of them coming from finds in the glass industry, and Florentines pioneered in making dyes fast, particularly by the use of alum.

In the last half of the Middle Ages there was also expansion in the production of tools and weapons. The greater use of machines, like water wheels, created a demand for rapidly moving parts made of metal; the expansion of agriculture meant a greater need for metal tools and builder's hardware; and wars against the Moslems, the Crusades, conquests in Eastern Europe, and internecine troubles of various kinds resulted in an increased market for instruments of destruction and of defense. Then with the introduction of gunpowder from China, where, incidentally, it had been used mainly for fireworks, there was a demand for a new arsenal of weapons.

Although there was less concentration in the metallurgical industry than there was in textiles because of the location of production near the many outcroppings of ore, increased production was marked in the foothills of the Alps in northern Italy, in the Walloon part of the Low Countries, and at Hildesheim and Nuremberg in Germany. It was in these places, too, that the most important technological changes in the metal trades occurred. In them was developed in the late twelfth century a bellows with a valve which closed when the instrument was collapsed, thus forcing all the air out of the spout. When in the thirteenth century water wheels were used to run this type of bellows, a strong enough blast was produced to liquefy iron. Thus many of the impurities were removed from iron which previously had been hammered out of the spongy mass which had been obtained from less intense fires; what was more, liquid iron could be cast into various forms that earlier had been unattainable, like iron vessels, iron pipes, and even iron cannon.[2]

Inasmuch as cast iron is brittle and cannot be used for many purposes involving stress, as for example swords and cutting tools, a large amount of iron still had to be hammered or "wrought." To aid in the performance of this task, heavy beam hammers were by the twelfth century put into use. They were allowed to rest on a fulcrum, were raised by filling buckets attached to their lighter ends with water, and were allowed to fall with a striking force by dumping the buckets. Then, in the fourteenth century, trip hammers, activated by water wheels, as in the fulling machines, were applied to forging and made the task of hammering much more rapid. Moreover, a wire-drawing machine was developed in Nuremberg in 1350. Rolling mills were used in Germany in the fifteenth century. Rolling both reduced the amount of forging that had to be done and produced sheets of metal for making breastplates and wagon tires.

In spite of the almost revolutionary advances in metallurgy, textiles, and grain grinding, no technological innovations of the Middle Ages were of more importance in the general, if not in the economic, history of Europe than those made in printing and papermaking. Although there is strong evidence that the idea of printing was borrowed from China, where printing from wooden blocks was practiced in the sixth century A.D. and from movable wooden characters in the eleventh century, specific printing techniques in the West differed enough from those in the East to suggest that they were not merely imported from abroad. What appears to have been a fairly autonomous development in Europe led to the use of wooden blocks in printing the elaborate capital letters which ornamented manuscript books in the late twelfth century and then in the late thirteenth century in printing entire pages. The first use of the latter

---

[2] Many early cannon were, however, made of brass or wood, strengthened by iron hoops.

technique was at Ravenna, Italy, which had been in close relations with Constantinople and to which may have come Eastern printing technology. In any case, printing from wooden blocks was a great improvement over hand writing and by the fifteenth century was in common use at Brussels, Ulm, Venice, and several other places.

The task of carving separate blocks for each page of a volume was, of course, enormous, so it was logical that there should have been a search for a method whereby type once carved could be used over and over again. Finally, the quest for such a process resulted in the making of printing blocks for individual letters, the assembling of this type to reproduce whatever text was to be printed, and after the printing had been completed the "knocking down" of the type for reuse. This use of "movable type" was attempted at a number of places—at Limoges in 1381, at Antwerp in 1417, at Haarlem in 1435, and at Avignon in 1444, but it was Gutenberg at Mainz who in the 1440s brought the technique to a point of successful operation and it is to him that the credit for the invention is usually given.

Movable type was received with enthusiasm in printing establishments all over Europe and not being hampered by guild restrictions was widely adopted. By 1500 books were being produced in large quantities compared with earlier times and were being sold at low enough prices to be within the reach of vast numbers of people. Movable type "democratized" learning, just as iron had democratized metal tools in the Iron Age. It was one of the most important inventions of all times.

Perhaps movable type would not have had the effect that it did if it had not been accompanied by the development of a cheap material on which to print. Parchments made of hides, or "sheepskins," as they are still called by college students whose diplomas are sometimes printed on them, were expensive; papyrus, the ancient writing material of the Egyptians, was not available in Europe. The answer to the prayer of printers was paper.

The techniques of papermaking, even more than those of printing, were borrowed from the East. They were practiced in China as early as 100 A.D. and gradually made their way westward along trade routes dominated by Moslems, having appeared in Bagdad in 793, in Egypt in 900, in Sicily in 1109, in Spain in 1150, in southern France in 1189, in Italy in the thirteenth century, and in Germany in the fourteenth century.

The process of papermaking as introduced into Europe consisted of beating some fibrous material like linen rags, which had been softened by water, into a pulp, spreading the resulting mass in a thin layer on screens, which allowed the surplus water to drain off, and then pressing the substance on the screens into dry sheets.[3] The most laborious task involved in papermaking was the beating of the fibers to pulp and it was to perform this work that Medieval Europe in the beginning of the fifteenth century made its greatest contribution to the industry. What was done was simply to rig up trip hammers—the third application of this device which we have cited—and to run them by water wheels. The hammers did the work of beating, much as in fulling and in forging iron. This development greatly reduced the cost of papermaking and also increased production to a point where there was a demand for a cheaper raw material. This was found later in cotton fibers and much later still in wood pulp.

Finally, the printing trade needed more efficient presses. Although the screw press, similar to the "letter presses" seen in offices only a generation ago, was in use, it was slow acting. Improvements were now made in it by changing the screw so that it would close the press with fewer turns.

Among other technological advances in the Middle Ages, the most important stemmed from clockmaking. Both the fine craftsmanship and intricate gearing systems developed in this trade were of great value in the further development of mechanical contrivances of all kinds. Ever since the Bronze Age, time had been measured by hourglasses or water clocks, which worked on the principle of the amount of sand or water which flowed through a small aperture. Eventually, Moslems devised water clocks which would produce at stipulated intervals a mechanical puppet show, much as cuckoos appear at the end of every hour in our cuckoo clocks. Apparently, out of these mechanical accompaniments to the timekeeper itself came the inspiration for mechanical clocks.

By the thirteenth century European clockmakers were attempting to build mechanical timepieces and had come to grips with the principal difficulty in doing so—that of controlling and regulating the speed at which gears turned. Finally, they found a solution to their problem by the invention of an escapement that permitted a strategically placed gear to turn just so far and no farther per second and to control the escapement by a balance wheel. Just when these two inventions were first made is not clear, but they appeared in the famous Dover Castle Clock in England in 1344 and shortly thereafter were found in numerous places. At the end of the Middle Ages there was a real clock-building boom, every town believing that it was not up-to-date unless a clock adorned the steeple of the local church, the town hall, or the castle.

Still another industry in which notable advances were realized in the

[3] Watermarks are obtained by designs placed on or in the screens. The fine lines of the screens can be seen in the paper upon which these words are printed by holding it up to the light.

TORCHIO
PER STAMPAR I LIBRI.

Printing Press of the Seventeenth Century. On this screw press only one sheet of paper could be printed at a time. The pressure was provided by the screw, turned by the worker. The bedplate with the type was rolled under the screw by turning the handle which the worker has in his left hand. A bedplate not in use is at *N*. At *EE* are probably cases of type. Ink was put on with the leather-covered instruments at *M*. (*From Vittorio Zonca, Il Nuovo Teatro, 1656.*)

Middle Ages was glassmaking. Here the standard practice was to place a molten mass of silicon at the end of a hollow tube and to "blow" the glass until it was of the required thickness and to shape it by cutting and by bending it with forceps. At Murano near Venice and at Limoges in France, craftsmen achieved great skill in this technique and made their products famous throughout all Europe. In the tenth century they learned how to color glass, which made possible the stained glass windows that were to beautify high-vaulted Gothic cathedrals, like those of Chartres and of Paris. By the thirteenth century crystal glass was being made which was so clear that is was used for artificial jewels and so transparent that it was employed in the first eyeglasses of which we know. Then, in the fifteenth century, Murano craftsmen began to blow glass into cylinders which when cut and flattened made windowpanes up to twenty square inches. Thus, it was technically no longer necessary to set small pieces of glass in lead frames in order to let in light, although window glass did not become cheap enough for the common man until it began to be rolled in the sixteenth century. Finally, Venetians began to coat glass with lead to make a mirror and later substituted mercury for lead in order to get a better reflection.

In the closely allied pottery industry, the Middle Ages also made technical progress. Although pots were still turned on the potter's wheel in the time-honored way, the use of better clays and better glaze resulted in the manufacture of what were essentially new products. Thus, in Italy, the adoption of colors that had been employed in the glass trade led to the making of Majolica ware and to the production of the terra-cotta statues and friezes which were made famous by the Della Robbia family.

Still another flourishing trade of the second half of the Middle Ages was building. It was then that housing was constructed on a large scale in the growing towns and that most of the great architectural monuments which today attract admirers from all over the world were erected. With this great activity, it was only natural that stonecutters, masons, and carpenters should have advanced their arts. Quarrying was improved with better chisels and in the fourteenth century by the use of blasting powder. Masons made new uses of pulleys, derricks, and scaffolding. And workers in wood developed the mechanical saw for cutting logs into boards and timbers in the twelfth century,[4] the carpenter's plane in

---

[4] This was the so-called up-and-down saw. Previously logs had been tilted up in the air on a fulcrum and a workman on the ground and another on top of the log laboriously pulled a long saw back and forth. The new invention was a saw worked up and down by a crank run by a water wheel. Circular saws were an eighteenth-century invention.

the fourteenth century, the brace and bit to replace the bow drill, water wheels to run grindstones, bolts and nuts to hold carriages together, and the wood-working lathe run by crank and treadle.[5]

Simultaneously great progress was also made in architecture and in the plastic arts for the adornment of great buildings. In both the Romanesque style and in the later Gothic, efforts to achieve height, size, and impressiveness created problems of stress hitherto unknown in the West. Gradually solutions to all of them were found, chiefly by the juxtaposition of arches and the use of flying buttresses. So expert did architects become that they were able to construct vaulted roofs out of masonry instead of wood, and one of them, Brunelleschi, was able to build the great dome of Santa Maria del Fiore at Florence without erecting a temporary support during the construction (1461). In sculpture, a development of techniques and craftsmanship led to the creation of some of the most famous masterpieces of all times, like the figures on the facade of the cathedral at Chartres, the doors of the Baptistry at Florence, and the works of Michelangelo. In painting, efforts to achieve movement, color, perspective, and realism led to the great masterpieces of the Renaissance in the Low Countries and in Italy.[6]

Hardly an industry of any importance, hardly any aspect of life was without some change in the second half of the Middle Ages. In mining, pumps were improved in the urgent task of getting water out of the diggings—improvements which were to lead ultimately to the invention of the steam engine. In lighting there was the invention of the wax and tallow candle, which was much more efficient than the old oil lamps without chimneys. In distillation, methods were found in the twelfth century to get alcohol from wine, which was to provide the world with a new and powerful stimulant. In warfare, wheels were put under cannon to take care of the recoil and to give artillery more mobility; mortars were developed to lob balls over walls; and incendiary projectiles were made more effective. And as by-products of dyeing and glassmaking, discoveries were made of the industrially important nitric, sulfuric, and hydrochloric acids.

Organization of Urban Industry

As medieval cities grew under the stimulus of commerce, political power came to reside in the hands of rich merchants. This was particu-

---

[5] Wood-working lathes had previously been turned by pulling down a flexible pole and using its recoil to rotate a spindle around which a cord, attached to the pole, had been wound.

[6] The first work devoted entirely to perspective was by the painter Piero della Francesca (1416?–1492).

larly true in the north where lords did not move into towns until the sixteenth century and so were not on the spot for the exercise of authority. It was also generally true in the Mediterranean littorals, for even if the lords lived in town, they usually engaged in trade and so had interests similar to those of the merchants.[7] Accordingly the economic organization of town life and the economic policies of cities reflected the interests of rich wholesale traders.

The class character of regulations was particularly clear as those affected the provisioning of towns with food and drink. Since the city fathers were exclusively consumers of foodstuffs, they wanted adequate and steady supplies at reasonable, if not at low prices. To achieve their ends they forced on both peasants and retail food merchants all kinds of restrictive rules and these people had to submit to them because they depended on cities for markets. By the late twelfth century, among the rules imposed on them were prohibitions on middlemen, more exactly, on "regrating," that is, on buying goods for resale, on "forestalling," that is, buying goods before they reached the towns, and on "engrossing," that is, hoarding goods as a protection against rising prices or shortages in supply. Moreover, all food commodities had to be publicly exposed and for a certain period of the day sold only to burgesses. Butchers could not hide meat in their cellars; bakers could not store more grain than was normally needed for their own ovens. All traders in food were subject to rigid inspection, and defrauders were severely punished by having their goods confiscated, by fines, or by being banished from their trade or even from the city itself. Finally, maximum prices were sometimes established and "quality inflation," that is, selling inferior goods at the maxima, was rigidly repressed.

While such rigid restrictions were placed upon the food trades, no such strict rules were applied to the wholesale business in foods in long-distance trade, for some of the rich merchants were engaged in this activity and they did not want to do anything to curb their opportunities for making a profit. All that they required was that foreign suppliers sell through one of them, that is, through an official (licensed) broker or Unterkäufer, and that these same foreigners should not engage in retailing in competition with peasants. Local burgesses, who bought grain, fish, and wine at wholesale, were not subject to the same limitations. They might sell at retail and reap the profits derived therefrom.

Town policies regarding the food trade constituted a pattern which came to be applied to all retail trade and to local retail industry. So far

---

[7] In Tuscany and neighboring regions, these city-dwelling lords gave expression to their egos by building great towers, each trying to surpass the other. Such structures may still be seen in such places as Bologna, Perugia, and above all San Gimigniano.

as industrial goods were concerned, the rich merchants who dominated town life wanted again steady supplies of quality merchandise, fair prices, and peaceful industrial relations. Artisans, the chief producers of industrial goods for the local market, wanted reliable outlets for their products, just as the peasants did, and were willing to accept certain restrictions on their activities in order to get them. Thus, a kind of "deal" was made whereby town fathers granted a monopoly of business in the city to individual trades, sometimes even for the payment of fees, and in return demanded that artisans submit to the Church's principle of a just price (*justum pretium*) and to a variety of regulations which would guarantee a high standard of product.

To these ends regrating, forestalling, and engrossing were forbidden here, as they were in the food trade. Woolen cloth had to be "all wool and a yard wide." Night work was generally outlawed for fear that it would lead to inferior workmanship. Artisans had to work in shops facing the street, as they still do in many European trades, and to keep their goods continually in sight for public scrutiny. Craftsmen could not practice more than one trade in the belief that a "Jack-of-all-trades" is a master of none.

Nor did such rules constitute merely a paper program. They were strictly enforced. Artisans who broke the rules were severely punished by fines and suspensions; in the case of repeated infractions, they might be subjected to the ignominy of having their shoddy goods exposed before their shops for all to see. Still worse, the artisan might be read out of his guild and hence prevented from practicing his trade. Although these rules did not entirely prevent cheats from such artifices as giving short measure, stealing customers' raw materials, or skimping work in general, they had considerable efficacy in maintaining honesty, quality, and fair prices.

The organizations among artisans which provided a means for maintaining monopolies, for enforcing rules of production, and for regulating supply were the craft guilds. The origins of these institutions have been the subject of long dispute among scholars, some believing them to be found in the collegia of the Roman Empire and others in workshops of the lord. Still others, including the present author, believe that they simply grew up to meet the needs of the times. At all events, by the end of the eleventh century artisans were forming fraternities (*fraternitates*) along lines determined by the goods produced for retail sale and were using merchant guilds or religious societies for their models. Before long these bodies were in evidence all over Europe and were being called craft guilds (*métier* or *jurandes* in French, *arte* in Italian, and *Amt*, *Innung*, or *Zunft* in German). Thus there were guilds of tailors, bakers, cobblers, cabinetmakers, blacksmiths, and boatmen. Each had a monopoly for the production and retail sale of its special products in the town —a monopoly sanctioned by public authority—and each was subject to the type of restrictions already mentioned.

Craft guilds gradually developed an elaborate organization of their own for the control of their monopoly. In order to regulate the amount of production and the quality of goods, they created an elaborate procedure for training labor and for limiting the labor supply. Thus to become a master craftsman and a full-fledged member of the guild who could produce goods in his own shop for direct sale to retail customers, it was necessary for a young man to serve as an apprentice to a guild master for a period, on the average, of seven years. During this time the master craftsman had at his disposal a worker, but in return he had to house, clothe, and feed his charge.

At the end of the apprenticeship, the trainee was supposed to be well skilled in his trade and to be ready to practice it as a wageworker, or as he was then called, a journeyman, a word derived from the French *journée,* meaning day. The journeymen worked for guild masters, but in some crafts and in some countries it was usual for them to travel around from place to place and from master to master to learn various regional "tricks of the trade." Journeymen masons often went on a *tour* of this kind to work on whatever large building was going up and to see the masterpieces of the building art, like the great cathedrals and public buildings. Even today, it is not unusual for French chefs to make a *tour de France* in order to learn how to prepare all the more famous regional dishes.

Eventually the journeyman might become a master craftsman. This step required qualifications other than skill in his craft and the production of a "masterpiece" which would give the guild wardens proof of his ability. The aspirant had to have enough capital to set up shop and to convince the guild that he would be able to pay his membership and other guild fees. He had to be married, for it was necessary to have someone keep house for him and his apprentices. And he had to be of good character and standing in the community, so that the guild could be reasonably sure that he would obey the regulations governing the trade. If he could meet all these requirements, he was taken into the craft and allowed to share in the monopoly of the market—to sell *good* goods at a fair price. If he could not, he remained a journeyman or turned to some other kind of work.

Furthermore, craft guilds built up detailed rules regarding production methods and selling procedures. Such measures were presumably designed to assure quality products, but inasmuch as guild members were jealous of one another and feared that some individual would get rich at the expense of others, these regulations aimed also to maintain economic equality among masters. Thus, all members of an organized craft were required to use the same techniques and were forbidden to introduce new methods unless approved by the guild. All masters had to work the same number of hours and have the same amount of equipment, because if one worked little and others much, or if some had few tools and others many, differences in wealth would soon appear. Finally, all were forbidden to advertise their wares, even not being permitted to sneeze to attract the attention of passers-by to their wares; all were prevented from selling to other than citizens of the town; and all were subject to price restrictions.

Naturally enough this standard pattern of urban industrial production for the retail market, with all its built-in rigidities, could not be and was not applied everywhere and in all trades with the same degree of thoroughness. In some cities rich merchants tried to suppress guilds, for fear that they would get so powerful that they would demand a voice in public affairs or even take over town governments. Such efforts were made, usually without success, at Rouen in 1189, at Brussels in 1240, and in practically all Flemish cities at some time during the fourteenth century. Moreover, the craft guild system never was applied to industrial workers in the countryside nor to those producing for wholesale trade. Moreover, where economic activity, particularly commerce, was intense, the rigidities of the guild system could not be maintained, if, in fact, they ever came into being.

In spite of all regulations which have been mentioned above, economic inequalities did grow up among guild masters, especially where opportunities for expansion were great. The rich enlarged their shops, took on more apprentices and journeymen than the poorer masters, and what was particularly significant, made it practically impossible for journeymen to become guild masters. More and more they endeavored to reserve their part of the monopoly to their sons, or to their sons-in-law, or to other close relatives by demanding impossible tests of aspirants or by requiring extraordinarily high membership fees. Thus, the rich guildsmen became in fact industrial employers, hiring workers for money wages and producing for profit.

Evidence of such changes begins to be ample by the first part of the fourteenth century. In nearly all cities of any importance a distinction began to be made between the major and minor crafts, the major ones being where the transformation just described had taken or was taking place. In London there were the very wealthy livery companies which were far above the ordinary guilds in privileges and power. In Paris there

were the Six Corps des Marchands. In Lucca there was the all-important
Arte della Seta, and in Florence, the famous Arte di Calimala and the
Arte della Lana. These last two organizations, like most of the others,
kept the guild monopoly intact and used the word guild in their names,
but neither was operated in the traditional guild manner. The few members of these bodies bought large quantities of raw material outside the
town, thus breaking the rule against forestalling. They had the material
worked up by artisans who were paid by the piece, contracted the job
out to a master at a fixed-upon price, or took masters in as partners. They
did the fulling and dyeing with machines that only a few could afford,
thus violating restrictions on numbers of workers and equality of equipment; and they sold their finished products at wholesale to middlemen,
thus breaking the rule of selling only directly to customers. The rich
guildsmen even changed the organization of production, for instead of
turning out everything in shops facing streets, they had some spinning,
weaving, and knitting done in the homes of workers under what was
called the domestic system and some done in fairly large establishments
to which workers came, as in the modern factory system. In both cases,
however, employers always kept title to the material being processed,
whether is was raw wool or semifinished cloth, and more and more
frequently they owned the means of production that the workers used.[8]

Under these conditions the status of workers was considerably altered.
No longer could workmen look forward to membership in the guilds,
unless they were fortunate enough to marry the "boss's daughter," or to
having their own shop and apprentices. With the new dispensation, those
who toiled were dependent upon wages for their existence. If there was
no work because of the poor organization of supplies or because goods
were not selling, their employers would drop them with little thought of
the suffering which might be caused. If there was work, hours were long,
being usually from dawn to dusk; wages were low, being just enough
to provide a miserable standard of living; and working conditions were
not good, even if one remained at home, because of poor light and little
heat.

What proportion of the working class in the large cities had evolved
to these conditions, it is difficult to say, but the numbers were not insignificant. At the beginning of the fourteenth century 10 per cent of the
entire population of Ghent is said to have been engaged in spinning or
weaving, and half the craftsmen at Ypres to have been engaged in the
manufacture of cloth. These proportions indicate clearly that masters
must have been few and workers many. At all events, wageworkers were
numerous enough so that they organized and agitated for the improve-

[8] In the domestic system, workers usually owned their spinning wheels and looms.

ment of their lot. Journeymen began first to form loose groups, called *compagnonnages* or *Gesellenverbände,* to find work for their members and later to defend their interests in their relations with the masters. Urban wageworkers in the late thirteenth and fourteenth centuries initiated attacks upon the political monopoly of the commercial patriciate and made out of these efforts a real social movement. The revolt of the Ciompi at Florence (1378–1382), which was led by clothworkers, was of this character and so were the uprisings in many Rhenish, Flemish, English, and French cities.

As can readily be imagined, labor agitation of this nature was suppressed with vigor. Masters conspired to boycott workers who had disturbed the peace and cities formed leagues to prevent agitators from getting work within their walls. Finally, legislation of the budding political states shows efforts to contain labor. Both the English Statute of Laborers of 1350 and the French Royal Ordinance of 1351 aimed to prevent workers from conspiring to better their lot and set maximum wages which they could receive. Thus was established a line of action which was to remain essentially intact until the end of the eighteenth century.

CHAPTER 6

Money, Credit, and
Business Organization

The Development of Money and Credit

In the various phases of industrial expansion which we have been describing, the one common characteristic was an increase in the use of money as a medium of exchange. This was true in agriculture, in commerce, in industry, and in the employment of labor. Little wonder, then, that businessmen wanted money which was respected and which would be accepted over large areas. They wanted a money that was not being so continuously debased that debtors could always count on paying off their obligations in cheap money.

Under the circumstances, it is not surprising that monetary reform was the order of the day in the great commercial centers of the thirteenth century, nor that the lead was taken by the greatest of all such centers —by Venice. The first move toward a hard-money policy was made in 1192 when a new coin, called the grossus or groat, was struck. The issuers of this piece of money took cognizance of the fall in the value of older coins and established the value of their coin at two grams of silver, which was approximately twelve times that of the existing penny. Thus came into being a shilling or sou which, as we have seen, had been only a bookkeeping measure in Charlemagne's system. The groat proved to be just what creditor businessmen wanted and became so popular that all

Lombard and Tuscan political jurisdictions struck similar coins of their own.

Beyond the Alps, efforts to create stable and standard moneys were inspired not only by rich merchants and bankers but also by monarchs who were endeavoring to establish their authority at the expense of rival lords. They saw in monetary reform a way to help commerce and, at the same time, by a kind of reversal of Gresham's law, a method by which they could drive the cheap money of the lords out of circulation.[1] Once this had been accomplished, lords would be deprived of an important source of income both from ordinary minting and from debasing the coinage, or, as we would say nowdays, from inflation. Thus, in England the sterling coin was struck at the end of the twelfth century. In 1266 the French king, Louis IX, impressed by the great success of the Venetian groat, established the gros tournois (groat of Tours)—a coin that was joined a little later by the more valuable gros parisis (groat of Paris). These pieces, all twelve times the value of some penny, were favorably received by tradesmen and were adopted or imitated in Flanders, in the northern Netherlands, and in Germany, where they were known as Groschen.

Important as was the introduction of groats and shillings in their various forms, they did not entirely meet the needs of commerce, for any large sum in them was bulky and heavy and consequently hard to transport. Hence merchants requested the use of gold coins which would be per value only a fraction of the weight of silver. Eventually their demands were heeded and gold began once more to be minted in Europe. The first of the new gold coins was struck by Frederick II, Holy Roman Emperor, whose brilliant Sicilian court was a center of art and learning. His gold augustales, struck in 1231, were because of their design and sharply etched lines the numismatic masterpieces of the Middle Ages.

The gold coins of Frederick II did not have, however, a wide circulation and were not adopted outside of Sicily. It remained for northern Italy with its relatively great volume of commerce to make gold popular. In 1252 Florence began to strike its gold florins, so-called because they had the floral emblem of the city, the lily, stamped on them. Shortly afterwards Genoa began to issue its gold ducats, from the Italian *duca*, meaning duke, and in 1284 Venice followed the example of its commer-

[1] This law, as stated by Sir Thomas Gresham in the sixteenth century, was that cheap money drives dear money out of circulation. In the short run, dear money is hoarded or goes into hiding if there is a chance of turning it later into a stable money at a favorable rate of exchange, or into goods at advantageous prices. In the long run, however, cheap or unstable moneys go out of use because they do not serve the true purposes of money.

Florins and Ducats. It has been explained in the text that great commercial centers needed money in which traders could have confidence. Thus Florence created the florin (top) and Venice the ducat. The lily of Florence on the florin is of excellent design. The ducat shows Christ with a Doge against the sea, whence came Venice's wealth. (*From the Moneys of the World Collection of the Chase Manhattan Bank of New York. Used with permission.*)

cial competitor. Then Northern Europe fell into line, France issuing gold coins based on the gros tournois in the thirteenth century and Flanders and England following suit in the fourteenth. Inasmuch as these coins were equal in value to twenty silver groats or shillings, they were, in fact, pounds and thus gave reality to another of Charlemagne's bookkeeping fictions. Because they had considerable value and stability, they constituted a real blow to the minting activities of lesser territorial princes whose moneys could not compete with them. The future was clearly with moneys issued and guaranteed by centralized states.

Important to economic growth as were improvements in the coinage systems of Western Europe in the thirteenth century, the parallel development of credit instruments was of even greater significance for the long run. Such instruments provided ways for transferring debits and credits without the handling of money, the essential devices for borrowing funds on a large scale, and the means for businessmen to express their trust in one another, which is the basis of all transactions.

Of all the instruments of exchange the most significant was undoubtedly the bill of exchange.[2] In its simplest form, it was both an acknowledgment by a buyer that he had received goods from a certain person for a stipulated sum and also a promise that he would pay the seller for them in a given amount at a specified place and subsequent time. Thus a bill of exchange written by a Fleming at Bruges for purchases made from a Venetian would read as follows:

---

[2] Its name comes from *bulla*, originally meaning seal and then by implication any document, and the fact that it almost always involved an exchange operation from one currency to another.

I, Hans Olbrechts, have accepted goods from you, Giovanni Cipolla, at Troyes, September 1, 1353, to the value of 1,000 gros tournois and I promise to pay you in Venice 1,100 ducats by June 1, 1354.

(Signed) *Hans Olbrechts*

As can be readily seen, the Venetian merchant was hereby extending credit to the Flemish buyer—was actually financing the latter's commercial operations by allowing him time to sell his goods before paying for them. Payment of interest on the loan was concealed in the difference between the two sums mentioned.

This simple form of the bill of exchange was subsequently supplemented by the draft, in which three persons were involved instead of two. It was an order on the part of the buyer, Olbrechts, to use the case already cited, ordering someone owing him money, let say in Venice, to pay by a given date the seller of the goods, Cipolla, what was due him. Therefore, this document would read:

I, Hans Olbrechts, have accepted goods from you at Troyes, September 1, 1353, to the value of 1,000 gross tournois and I hereby direct Giuseppe Bellini to pay you, Giovanni Cipolla, 1,100 ducats in Venice by June 1, 1354.

(Signed) *Hans Olbrechts*

Thus, not only was Cipolla extending credit to Olbrechts, but Olbrechts had already extended credit to Bellini. What was important here was that the network of credit relations in one document was being extended.

Finally, toward the end of the Middle Ages an addition was made to the draft which greatly added to its usefulness. If, in the case above, the third person, Bellini, agreed to make payment as specified by writing "accepted" on the face of the document, the draft became an *acceptance*. If Bellini was a responsible businessman of good standing, the acceptance might be used by Cipolla as security with which to raise funds. He might even take it to a banker and for a fee (later known as a discount) get his money at once. He had thus more opportunity to step out of his role as lender, if he was himself in need of funds.

Closely related to this document was the *lettre de foire*, or fair letter, which was developed at the fairs of Champagne. If a merchant, Dupont, wanted to buy some silk goods from Lucchese, but was short of funds, he might ask Lucchese to trust him until the next fair. If Lucchese was willing, Dupont wrote a *lettre de foire* in which he acknowledged purchase of the goods and agreed to pay Lucchese a given sum, including interest, at the next fair. If Lucchese was, on the other hand, reluctant to extend the desired credit, both he and Dupont might go to a mutual acquaintance, perhaps a local money-changer, who would be asked to guarantee that Dupont would make the payment. If he agreed, the *lettre de foire* was so written. However, it might be that Lucchese could not wait for his money, in which case the money-changer might lend the necessary funds to Dupont and the *lettre de foire* would be written so that the sum which Dupont paid back had a hidden interest charge in it. This was, in essence, a straight banking operation.

All of the credit instruments put together constituted means whereby those with initiative and courage would get credit for the conduct of their business. A lot of water had, indeed, passed over the dam since the time when most loans had been made by monasteries to lords for the purchase of consumers' goods. With the new instruments of credit, loans were of a business character; they were meant to be self-liquidating, that is, if the transaction as envisaged was carried out, the borrower would have the wherewithal to meet his obligation. Furthermore, most credit consisted of what today would be called commercial loans, for they were aimed to move goods and to be paid back in short periods of time. They were not usually made to finance capital equipment which could be amortized only over long periods. Lastly, the new instruments provided ways for the easy transfer of funds and most importantly for hiding interest charges. A charge for the use of borrowed funds was essential both to encourage savings and to permit investment.

Other Banking Services

In addition to instruments of credit, there developed other practices which we associate with banking services. At the end of each Champagne fair there was a period in which buyers and sellers came together to settle their accounts by clearing debits and credits among themselves without the use of money except to arrive at final balances. Thus, to take a simple case, if Olbrechts sold to Cipolla, and Cipolla sold goods of equal value to Dupont, then Dupont to Lucchese, and finally Lucchese to Olbrechts, the accounts of all four could be cleared in a face-to-face gathering of the principals by a mere canceling of claims. Such a practice, which on another scale is accomplished today in America through our checking system, greatly simplified the whole problem of payments.

Then, as has already been mentioned, money-changing became common: the many different kinds of coins necessitated exchange operations in nearly every transaction between merchants at any distance removed from one another; furthermore, so many of the coins in use were of such uncertain and changing value that persons with a detailed knowledge of them were needed to determine their worth. The first money-changers were merchants who engaged in exchange as a side line to their commercial activities, but as their exchange business grew, it usually proved to be more profitable than buying and selling goods; hence they tended to specialize in the buying and selling of coins. Since some of them accumulated considerable wealth in the exercise of their trade, they had money to lend against such promises to pay as were contained in *lettres de foire*, drafts, and acceptances. When this happened, they had become in effect bankers. Although some of them were Jews, whose religion did not proscribe interest taking, and some where natives of the places in which they operated, most of them were of Italian origin and were known in the north as Lombards.[3] Even to this day the numerous Lombard Streets which one encounters in cities throughout Western Europe indicate where these people plied their trade in the Middle Ages.

In the Lombard Streets, money-changers were not the only ones, however, who were performing some service connected with money. There were the goldsmiths, usually natives of the city in which they did business and generally members of a guild. They came to specialize in safe-keeping valuables for others in the safes or strongboxes which they had for protecting their own wares—a very important service in those days of uncertain law and order. Both goldsmithing and safekeeping were profitable and eventually goldsmiths acquired funds that they could lend to others. In fact, they even lent money given them for safekeeping on the theory and experience that they needed to have on hand only enough to meet the expected, current demand of depositors. This practice led them, at least by the seventeenth century, to the issuing of "promises to pay," that is, "goldsmiths' notes," which, like modern banknotes, circulated from person to person. These "promises to pay," which could be paid by using the desposits of customers, came actually to exceed the amount of money on deposit. When this happened credit had been actually created by issuing paper—a very major discovery. But we are getting ahead of our story.

Still farther down our hypothetical Lombard Street, or at least around the corner from it in a little less respectable position, was to be found the pawnbroker.[4] To him came those who had some piece of personal property that they were willing to leave as security for a cash loan with the understanding that they could get their property out of "hock"—the place where it was kept—by paying back the loan plus interest.

[3] The role of Jews in medieval banking has usually been overstated. Although Jews were important here, recent scholarship has shown that, whereas their practice of taking interest was general, Christians took interest on such a scale that their competitors had little advantage in this regard.

[4] The three gold balls hung over pawnshops today as a symbol of the kind of business transacted came into use in the Late Middle Ages. The origin of this symbol is not clear. Some say that it was taken from the Medici coat of arms, which had six balls, but this is not certain.

Still farther on were the scriveners or notaries who drew up public and legal documents for those who could not write. In the practice of their trade they came to know a lot about everybody's business and this knowledge gave them an opportunity to make deals for a quick profit to themselves. In time, they, too, had money to lend at a price to those who had a good proposition but not enough cash with which to execute it.

Somewhere along the street there were rich merchants who made another type of loan known as a "rent." This particular type of operation developed from the fact that the rich for speculative purposes bought lands in expanding towns and built houses on them to rent to others. Sometimes these building speculators overreached themselves financially and had to borrow. Instead of borrowing on mortgage, they agreed to pay the person who lent to them specified sums at stipulated periods for as long as the lender lived. The amounts which the lenders received on these loans, which were very much like modern annuities, were known as "rents" and the recipients, *rentiers*, that is, people living off investments, which is the present-day meaning of the term.

Although there were cases of the untimely decease of *rentiers* because those paying the rents thought they had paid enough and took the appropriate action necessary to cancel their obligation, a similar kind of loan had a vogue in municipal and later in national finance. In order to raise funds, towns contracted to pay a lender at periodic intervals a "rent" on a loan for as long as the lender lived (a rent on one life) or as long as he and a named heir lived (a rent on two lives). These rents became so extensive that cities sometimes assigned the adminstration of certain of their revenues to these *rentiers*. In 1164, for example, Genoa handed over some of its income for a period of eleven years to a society of lenders (*monte*) for sums that had been advanced. Then in the thirteenth century it consolidated its debt by selling rents, and finally it permitted these rents to be sold to third parties. It was to administer this kind of business and the city revenues pledged against rents that the first deposit bank in Europe, that is, a bank to receive deposits and to use them as a reserve against the loans it made, came into existence at Barcelona in 1401 and that the famous Bank of Saint George (Cassa di San Giorgio) was founded at Genoa in 1407.

Still other types of loans were created in connection with maritime construction and sea-borne commerce. In these trades the demand for capital was great, for both the building of vessels and the purchase of cargo and supplies entailed large outlays. Furthermore, in them there was either feast or famine, for although successful voyages paid off handsomely, the danger of total loss from shipwreck or pirates was ever present. What was wanted, therefore, was not only a way of borrowing capital, but also a method of dispersing risks. To a degree these needs were met by the bottomry contract, the respondentia loan, and the sea loan. The first of these was a loan for financing the construction of a ship and was secured by the vessel itself; the second was for financing trade and was secured by the cargo; and the third was for financing a voyage and was attractive because it permitted sharing in the profits. If all went well, these loans provided much-needed funds and paid lenders good returns. If disaster overcame a ship or its cargo, the loss was spread among both owners and lenders.

It was from these loans, especially the last, that underwriting developed. An enterpriser would draw up a description of a voyage which he contemplated and would invite others to join him in putting up part of the capital and in sharing in the profits. This they were to do by writing their names under his. If several "underwrote" the venture, both the risks and the earnings were shared, so that failure would not fall heavily on one person. Seldom was it that several voyages failed at once, as in the instance of Antonio's ventures in *The Merchant of Venice*. Sharing risks, which, as we shall see in more detail later, is the main principle in insurance, had so many advantages that it was extended in the seventeenth century to cover losses from fire and in the eighteenth, hardships resulting from the early death of an insured person, that is, to life insurance.

In all these developments the borrower always gave the lender some consideration in one form or another for the use of capital. This premium on accumulated mobile wealth was crucial for the growth of the capitalist system and for economic growth under free enterprise. Although the Church fathers maintained a more or less fictitious opposition to the taking of interest in the later Middle Ages, all signs pointed to their losing the battle. Territorial princes gave permits for the establishment of "loan tables" in the commercial towns. The Papacy made use of bankers, upon the payment of fees or other charges, for the collection of Peter's pence, the transfer of moneys to and from Rome, and for the general management of Church finances; and abbots, now not having funds to lend, borrowed from bankers when they wanted to purchase land or erect an extraordinarily expensive building. Moreover, no objections were made to some interest-taking methods, like that in "rents," on the ground that the lender ran a real risk of loss. Finally, it was clear from business practices that society, in general, condoned charging interest and that the Church would have to adjust its teaching to the world as it was.

Just what interest rates were in the later Middle Ages has been the subject of much discussion, and generalizations about them have varied widely because the great diversity of risks actually resulted in many different rates. For strictly business loans to persons with good credit ratings, the interest charge was around 5 per cent per annum; but the risks might be so great or the borrower so little known or so unreliable that the rate would go up to 12 or 15 per cent. Rates on loans to public authorities, like towns and monarchs, were usually high because their record of repayment was not good. Bankers might make loans to a king or a prince on condition that he would expel their competitors from his territories, usually Jewish bankers, and then the rate would be low; but if they made a loan to a princess to ransom her captive spouse, or to a town to cover the expenses of war, or to a monastery to buy a piece of the "true cross," the rate might go to 50 or even to 100 per cent. At all events, rates were high enough to make banking a very profitable business, and many great families, like the Bardi, Peruzzi, and Medici became wealthy by it. Also, the risks were great and, as we shall see, two of the houses named above went under by overextending their loans.

Business Organization

As business grew in volume, it was quite natural that the organization for the conduct of affairs became diversified. It was hardly to have been expected that the single owner-manager type of business enterprise, as found in the craft guilds, would be adequate for large undertakings. Thus, with the revival of business and the need for more working capital, partnerships, the favorite way for medieval businessmen to pool their resources, became more common. Frequently there were multiple partners, as in the case of the Bardi bank, where there were fifteen, and usually all participated actively in the enterprise. In the course of time, however, partnerships developed in which some of the partners were just investors (sleeping partners) and others were the active managers— an arrangement known as the commenda. Then, there were the merchant adventurers who pooled expenses on a trading voyage, but traded their own merchandise for their own account. Finally, in Genoa in the thirteenth century, there were cases where investors were allowed to buy *loca*, that is, shares, in the construction of a ship, very much as they were later to buy them in joint-stock companies, but that was a development of a later period.

The growing complexity of business operations made necessary, in turn, elaborate records and better bookkeeping methods. The first requirement here was for businessmen to know reading, writing, and arithmetic; and in point of fact burgesses created the first nonreligious schools in Western Europe expressly for teaching these subjects to their children. In the twelfth century city fathers began to shift the burden of these schools onto the taxpayers by making them municipal institutions and began also to have textbooks prepared in the various national languages to supplant the books in Latin which had hitherto been adapted from monastic schools. Indeed, record keeping was one of the important ways by which spoken vulgar tongues of Western Europe came to be put down in written form and became literary languages. It is not at all strange that the dialects of the great commercial centers should have achieved the status of national languages; that the early masterpieces of national literatures, like Dante's *Divine Comedy*, should have been written in them; that the dialect of the London area should have become standard English; that the language of the Île-de-France and of the Champagne fairs should have become French; or that the dialect of Tuscany and especially of Florence should have become Italian.

Not only, however, did businessmen need to know how to read and write a popular language, but they also needed an efficient method for doing their figuring. Roman numerals, then in use, were exceptionally awkward to handle, as the reader can easily see for himself by trying to add MXL and CCVIII, or better by attempting to multiply or divide them. Thus it was with enthusiasm that Western Europeans adopted Arabic numerals, which Arabs borrowed from India. In the twelfth century, the use of these numerical symbols spread like wildfire throughout the business world; and the use of Roman numerals came eventually in our time to be limited to tombstones and academic buildings.

Finally, businessmen needed a better system of bookkeeping than had previously been in use—a system that would give them a clearer idea of their credit and debit position both in general and in relation to specific persons. The answer to their need for such a method of accounting was double-entry bookkeeping, invented at the beginning of the fourteenth century and first described in detail by a Venetian, Lucas Pacioli in his *Summa de arithmetica, geometrica, proportioni, et proportionalita* (1494). This method involved three sets of books: a daybook in which all transactions were written down in chronological order as they took place, a journal in which transactions were analyzed as credits and debits under such headings as cash on hand, accounts receivable, accounts payable, and goods in stock, and a ledger in which transactions were posted both as debits and credits by individuals. Under this system the two sides of the ledger always had to balance, inasmuch as every item was both a debit and a credit and its totals had to agree with those of the journal. Men of affairs could thus ascertain whether or not their debits were larger than their credits, if their inventories were moving or frozen, if they were short of cash, or if they were extending too much credit. The books did not tell them, however, what their costs in certain classes of transactions and in specific goods were or what the running inventories were. Not until the twentieth century when cost accounting was developed were these kinds of information possible. Only with cost accounting, however, were any notable advances made in the medieval system of bookkeeping.

Town Economic Policies and Economic Stagnation

In spite of all the improvements in the conduct of business which we have been describing, there were two particularly disturbing elements on the economic scene toward the end of the Middle Ages. One was the adoption by towns, and also by some kings, of restrictive economic policies. The second was an actual slowing down of economic growth in the fourteenth century and the beginning of a period of economic stagnation.

The restrictive policies of towns and monarchies began when guilds acquired political power and came to take a share in the determination of city affairs. These newcomers to the political scene were bent upon exercising to the full their monopolistic positions both at the expense of merchants who brought goods to the city and of producers in the immediate vicinity of the town. In their little world it seemed to be to their advantage to keep out all competing goods and to raise prices to what the traffic would bear. Accordingly in towns where guilds had power, taxes on products from the outside were raised to prohibitive levels and "foreign" workers were rigidly kept out.

Under the pretext of some exclusive right, perhaps extorted from a territorial prince for a bribe or by revolt, producers were prevented from opening up shops outside of the town boundaries, or from selling, except at fair time, any commodities that had not been produced within the walls. In 1314, Ghent, for example, forbade the sale within the city of any cloth that had been made within a radius of 3 miles of the town limits. In such widely dispersed places as Flanders and Florence, women spinners were required to sell the product of their labors to merchants in the towns. And in the former, legislation against rich manufacturers who produced for export became so hostile that in the middle of the fourteenth century the business of these people fell off and many Flemish weavers migrated to Florence.

In a similar way, town particularism hampered large-scale commerce, for the guilds wanted all the business, wholesale as well as retail, for themselves. They harried wholesale merchants by adopting the "staple right" whereby traders passing through their towns were required to unpack their wares and offer them for sale to the burgesses, even though they might have wanted to sell them elsewhere and though there was no opportunity for selling them where they were stopped. In some places, too, boatmen's guilds claimed the exclusive right of towing all boats within their jurisdiction and even of transferring cargoes to their own barges. Fortunately, such policies were not everywhere pursued with the same vigor, especially in southern Germany, where capitalist industry was just beginning, in most of Italy, where the rich manufacturers wanted to trade outside and could compete with foreign products, and in England, where royal authority curbed the extreme protectionism of the towns.

Indeed, in places like England, where the territorial prince had considerable power, there began to appear policies which were designed not just for towns but for the entire realm. They were, in fact, embryonic state economic policies. The first indications of such measures were found in England, where in the early fourteenth century Edward II attempted to prevent the importation of foreign cloth, except for the use of the nobility. In 1331 Edward III tried to get Flemish weavers to come to England to build up the infant cloth industry and thus process at home the raw wool which had been going to Flanders. In 1381 the first of the English "navigation acts" was attempted by requiring goods in trade with England to be carried in English ships. Although this measure was unsuccessful, it was indicative of things to come. Then, in 1463 foreigners were forbidden to export raw wool from England and in 1464 Continental cloth was prevented from being imported.

Quite logically such steps brought on retaliatory acts from the Low Countries. The Duke of Burgundy (1419–1467) prohibited the importation of English cloth in regular trade-war fashion. Furthermore, he used the infant-industry argument to create a fleet which would compete successfully with Hanseatic shippers. He subsidized the fishing industry, which was growing rapidly, in part, because of the invention of the herring cask in 1380, and he got a portion of the Hanse's trade in this great staple. He assisted Antwerp in its development as a port and thereby began the growth of a shipping center which was to take the place of Bruges and, in fact, to become the trading center of the Western World in the late fifteenth century.

These examples of territorial economic policies, which when adopted by national states in early modern times were to be lumped together under the term of mercantilism, might be expanded many fold, but it is of no point to do so. What is important, however, is to realize that these restrictive measures coincided with a halt in the economic expansion of the West. Indeed, signs of economic stagnation were numerous in many places by the early fourteenth century, although all of Europe was not affected in the same degree. By then agricultural expansion to unclaimed lands either at home or on the periphery of Western Europe had virtually come to an end. Business at the Champagne fairs had fallen off and was not at once replaced by commerce at the important ports, like Bruges, and in 1343 a number of large Italian banking houses, like the Bardi and Peruzzi, collapsed.

The reasons for the failure of Western Europe's economy to maintain its earlier rate of growth are extremely complex. To some extent the trouble may have been owing to the diversion of capital from economic enterprise to noneconomically productive activity such as the building of great cathedrals, like those of northern France, southern England, and northern Italy, or the patronage of the arts, as in the cases of Frederick II in Sicily and of the rich merchants of Florence. In some degree, the difficulty may have stemmed from the lack of new industries with mass markets or from high enough wages to keep up the buying power of the lower classes. In some measures it may have been owing to the restrictive policies of guilds and of towns.

Whatever the causes of slackening economic growth, it was accompanied by a series of calamities of dramatic proportions. The first of these disasters was the terrible famine of 1315 to 1317, when the usually reliable European weather was extraordinarily unfavorable for the growing of crops. In the town of Ypres alone, 10 per cent of the population disappeared under its impact. Then three years after this scourge came the Black Death, probably the bubonic plague. Of all the epidemics in European history, it was definitely the worst. It is estimated that before it had run its course (1350), it had carried off more than a third of the population.

To these scourges there should be added those of a man-made character. There were social upheavals, to which reference has already been made—the struggle of guildsmen and rich manufacturers against merchant oligarchies in towns. There were uprisings by peasants in their efforts to better conditions granted by manorial lords, like the *Jacqueries* of the Île-de-France in 1357, the Flemish revolts of 1323 to 1328, and the English insurrection of 1381. There were civil wars in Italy and political anarchy in Germany. There were wars between the Kings of France and the Counts of Flanders from 1302 to 1320. But worst of all, there was the Hundred Years' War from the middle of the fourteenth century to the middle of the fifteenth between France and England. It upset the economy of all of France and laid waste a large part of the kingdom, so that there were whole regions "where there was no longer to be heard a cock crowing or a hen clucking." Little wonder that Western European economy seemed to have reached its technological and resource zenith. What it needed was a new opportunity to expand. Fortunately it got it with a return to more peaceful conditions followed by the expansion of Europe overseas in the sixteenth century.

PART THREE

The Economic Expansion of
Western Culture—1500 to 1800

CHAPTER 7

European Discoveries
and Expansion—1500 to 1700

Characteristics of Europe's Economy in Early Modern Times

In order better to tell their stories, historians have established the end of the fifteenth century and the beginning of the sixteenth as the turning point between Medieval and Modern Times. Although Europeans who awoke on the morning of January 1, 1500, certainly noticed no great difference from January 1, 1499, and were totally unaware of arising in a new historical era, changes took place in the course of European history within the designated time span which were important enough to justify historians in their seemingly arbitrary periodization. These changes were (1) the development of humanism, (2) the growth of science as a method of attaining knowledge, (3) the Protestant Revolt, (4) forward steps in the rise of national states and of nationalism, (5) geographical discoveries overseas, and (6) the beginning of the economic exploitation by Europe of the newly found lands. Each one of these changes had an effect on economic growth in Western culture and hence each requires consideration here.

Humanism was an intellectual movement which had as its center of interest the ancient classics and largely through them a concern with things of this world, including humankind. It represented a definite trend away from theology and scholastic philosophy and toward physical, social, and political interests. It was apparent in painting by a shift from religious subjects to scenes of the flesh (and frequently in the flesh), in literature, by a spate of translations of Roman and Greek classics into modern languages and by stories of this world, like Boccaccio's *Decameron* and Erasmus' *Praise of Folly*, and in architecture, by greater emphasis on lay buildings—palaces of lordly and worldly princes and public structures, like the Palazzo dei Medici in Florence, the Louvre in Paris, and the Rathaus in Bremen. With such changes came a more openly acknowledged interest in material well-being and a greater desire for wealth in order to procure those things which humanists held in high esteem. Although people might still be told that it was more difficult for a rich man to get into heaven than for a camel to pass through the eye of a needle, more and more appeared willing to take their chances on this score. Indeed, without wealth how could men create or enjoy those very things in the arts which the humanists were maintaining were the true marks of civilized people—were the real things worth living for?

The second of the big changes that mark the break from the Medieval to the Modern period was the development of science. For a long time men had been accepting statements by the Church Fathers or other great authorities, like Aristotle, as true, and by using those statements as premises had gone on with formal logic to draw conclusions from them. Obviously results obtained were frequently in direct contradiction with what could be observed by the senses in nature and were of little use to the men who were concerned with material things—architects, engineers, or mathematicians. Clearly, men dealing with this world needed knowledge based on actual observations, upon regularities derived from controlled experiments, and wherever possible upon mathematical verification. They needed "science," which comes from the Latin word *scire*, to know. They had to be able to identify events in sequence, to analyze interrelationships among these events, and to discover why and how they occurred in a given order. Once man had taken this attitude toward the real world, he was on his way toward mastery over his physical environment. This very mastery—the mastery of space by better means of transportation, victory over temporary shortages in food supplies, triumph over disease, and the turning to human use of vast quantities of animate and inanimate resources from quinine to coal—became in the mind of Western man another mark of civilization. Here again, economic growth, which was part and parcel of man's domination over his environment, came to be considered a necessity in the process of becoming more civilized.

The Protestant Revolt, for its part, contributed to the new turn in

Western culture by breaking the authority or "universality" of the Roman Catholic Church. For the study of economic history this was not without importance, since the Church's injunctions against taking interest and against the accumulation of wealth were further challenged and what remained of the Church's preachments regarding poverty as a virtue was attacked. In fact, some of the new religious sects, like the Calvinists, proclaimed the desirability of practicing thrift, or what in economic terms would be called saving for investment, in order to increase material well-being. Although Protestant behavior in matters economic differed but little from that of the Catholic, as is witnessed by the fact that economic progress was registered with apparently little distinction in both Protestant and Catholic countries, the Protestant ethic probably made it easier for the Protestant man of affairs than for the Catholic to bring his conscience into accord with his efforts to accumulate wealth. Furthermore, ethics rather than Catholic theology, that is, behavior of individuals in conformity with what was acknowledged to be the welfare of society rather than the dictates of the Church regarding the faithful observance of the sacraments, became a greater concern in Western culture than it had been earlier.

Still another aspect of the changes which were clearly being advanced in the century that marked the division between Medieval and Modern Times was the formation of dynastic states along more national lines. In brief, the national state is a political entity that embraces all the people of a nationality, that is, people who usually speak the same language or clearly related dialects and/or are drawn together by common historical traditions or by similar literatures, music, and art. In this development away from governments by lay or clerical princes in those territories in which they could claim supreme authority and toward governments where people at least thought that they were bound together by common ties, the governed expressed some willingness to be joined together politically. This recognition of the doctrine of consent was eventually to contribute to the development of popular government, to a highly emotional loyalty on the part of the people to their nationality, and to policies for the strengthening of the nation-state. Although common economic interests, such as a desire for better police protection, standard business law, the abolition of local barriers to trade, and standardized weights, measures, and money, played some role in the formation of nationalities, national economic legislation tended to knit people together into some semblance of an economic unit, frequently at the expense of other national states.

Indeed, national states were to become divisive forces in Western culture and eventually to engage in wars which threatened to bring that culture to destruction. It is possible, but by no means certain, that a threat of attack from outside the culture or a common desire to perpetuate the culture may in our day bring national states into a working arrangement of some kind which will keep them from destroying themselves.

Lastly, the end of the fifteenth and the sixteenth century can be considered a turning point in the history of Western culture, for it was then that Europeans made what were probably the greatest geographical discoveries of all times and began a movement known as the expansion of Europe overseas which was to bring Western culture to large portions of the globe and which was to have a profound effect upon Europe itself. Within a generation Western Europeans brought within their ken more than half of the land mass of the world—Africa, India, the Far East, North America, and South America—and they developed practical routes for getting to the shores of each. They proved, what had long been believed, that the earth was round, and they were thereby able to explain empirically how by sailing westward one came to Eastern ports, the phenomenon of night and day, and the change of the seasons. Man had at a stroke found answers to problems pertinent to his control over the physical world and discovered an undreamed-of quantity of land to settle and of resources to exploit.

Western Europeans were not slow to take advantage of their new opportunities. Not only did they bring in so many new products and such great quantities of well-known goods from the lands which they discovered that the imports had a veritably revolutionary effect, but they also picked up such quaint ideas about how man lived in a state of nature that these notions were to have a profound effect upon political thought and practice at home. Furthermore, they inaugurated a migratory movement, especially to the Western Hemisphere, which was to make prior migrations, such as those of the "People of the Sea" at the beginning of the first millennium B.C. and of the "barbarians" who came into the Roman Empire in the fourth and fifth centuries A.D., look like toy models. In fact, they began a process which was to carry Western culture to territories a hundred times greater than Western Europe—to an area that by the middle of the twentieth century was to have greater industrial and agricultural production and a much higher output per capita than the heartland of Western culture itself.

So great was economic progress and material well-being to become in one part of this overseas area, i.e., the English-speaking section of North America, that this very region was to become one of the most important centers of Western culture. Finally, with the expansion of Europe overseas, Western Europeans inaugurated a process whereby Western culture, especially in its economic aspects, was to a greater or less extent to be borrowed by or foisted upon every other culture of the entire globe until it might appear that the whole world was destined to be Europeanized.

Indeed, the diffusion of Western culture's economy to other parts of the world and shifts in the centers of leadership in Western culture resulting from unequal rates of economic growth are basic aspects of our present study.

Preparation for the Great Discoveries

The great discoveries of the late fifteenth and sixteenth centuries, which were so profoundly to change the course of economic history, were in actuality the culmination of a long process of acquiring geographical knowledge and of developing shipping techniques for the mastery of the seas. They provide an excellent example of how the accretion of knowledge and innovations in technology increase the range of opportunities for alternative decisions.

As we have previously seen, late medieval mariners had the compass for giving them direction; the astrolabe, which helped them to establish their positions in latitude, especially if they could go ashore to get an accurate sighting; and astronomical tables, which were of some assistance in guiding them across trackless wastes of water. They had fine maps, the *portulani*, of those coasts which were much frequented by sailing men and good techniques of cartography. And they had ships, especially the caravel and the galleon,[1] steered by rudders and propelled in part by the inanimate power of wind, which regularly made the hazardous voyages, even to English Channel ports.

With all this equipment, however, sailors would not have been so anxious to probe the unknown seas if their curiosities had not been aroused by snatches of geographical knowledge about far-off lands and by theories regarding the shape of the earth. Many were clearly intrigued by the proposition that the earth was round, which was by no means a new idea in the fifteenth century nor one that was entertained only by the lunatic fringe. As far back as the sixth century B.C. Pythagoras had contended that the earth was round. Both Plato and Aristotle supported this contention in the fourth century B.C. Eratosthenes of Alexandria had in the third century B.C. very ingeniously and with considerable precision

---

[1] The caravel was a ship of about fifty tons, with three and later four masts, which carried lateen sails and had a castle at the stern. The galleon, similar to the Portuguese *naus*, was considerably larger, broader of beam, and more seaworthy than the caravel, and usually had castles fore and aft.

calculated the circumference of the earth;[2] and Claudius Ptolemy of Alexandria (second century A.D.) incorporated the idea in his summary of ancient geography which was passed on to the Christian world and was much in vogue in the fifteenth century. Indeed, Ptolemy made the thought of voyaging westward in order to get to the eastern lands in China especially tempting by underestimating the earth's circumference and by overestimating the extent to which Asia protruded eastward toward Europe. Many fifteenth century geographers, like Pierre d'Ailly in his *Imago Mundi* (1410), argued cogently that the world was round; many practical seamen, of whom Columbus was only one, read and were convinced by such scholars. Indeed, Columbus wrote in the margin of his copy of d'Ailly's book opposite the argument regarding the sphericity of the earth, "Yea, verily, the earth is round."

In the second place, late Medieval Europe had from time to time been set agog by tall tales of far-off places, of lands of great wealth, and of heathen waiting to be brought under the banners of Christ. Sometime after the Fourth Crusade, the legend of Prester John came into being and was subsequently revived at irregular intervals. Usually Prester John was represented as a Christian who had created a Christian kingdom in some barbarian land and was waiting (this went on for three centuries) succor from the West. Somewhat later, vague reports trickled back to Rome from missionaries sent out to the Mongols of great lands awaiting the true word of God. Then there were the travels of Marco Polo of Venice—a man who spent the best years of his life, from 1271 to 1295, in China. As luck would have it, Marco was captured by the Genoese after his return and slapped into jail. There he had a cellmate by the name of Rusticiano of Pisa [Rusticello], who had done some work as a ghost writer and who apparently had that sixth sense that allows one to tell when a tale will find a market. In any case, after hearing Marco relate his adventures, he convinced his much-traveled friend that they should collaborate on a book that would tell of the East. The resulting work was a best seller. So successful was it, in fact, that imitators who had never traveled beyond their garden gates tried to outdo Marco in fanciful accounts of far-off places and thereby simply built up in the popular mind a belief in great riches somewhere in the unknown awaiting the audacious.

But if there were theories to be tested about the world, more or less

[2] Having learned that on the day of the summer solstice, there was no angle of the sun at noon at Syene, near the Tropic of Cancer, Eratosthenes measured the angle of the sun at noon on the same day at Alexandria. This gave him the arc of a segment of the earth's circumference, the length of which was the known distance between Alexandria and Syene. His error resulted from the fact that the measurement of the distance from Alexandria to Syene was inexact.

wild tales about people to be saved, and extravagant estimates of wealth to be had for the taking, there was close at hand evidence of Eastern products which brought good profits in trade. In fact, spices were being so widely used in such quantities to liven the taste of both food and drink that there seemed to be no question about profits if one could only get supplies. Venice, however, was the only European power which seemed able to secure deliveries, for it had made the necessary arrangements in the thirteenth century with the Arabs who had dominated the Red Sea area and later with the Ottoman Turks who captured Contsantinople in 1453 and Egypt in 1517. Although Venice had not taken undue advantage of its monopoly, if one may judge from the fact that the prices of spices in Europe did not go up after 1453, it was doing so well that many European traders wanted to break into the field. Since the Eastern trade routes were closed against intruders, the only possible way of horning in on Venetian profits was to find an entirely new route to India or to the Spice Islands of the South Seas.

For these various reasons, "for God, for gold, and for glory" (or curiosity), Europeans began to push out into the unknown Atlantic. As early as the thirteenth century two Genoese brothers, Ugolino and Vadion Vilvaldo, attempted (circa 1291), when Venice was sewing up the spice route through the Red Sea, to find a route to India via Gibraltar. Then in 1312 another Genoese, Lanzarote Mallocello, discovered one of the Canary Islands, which still bears his Christian name. Anonymous explorers found the Madeira Islands (1330) and the Azores, or what appears to have been the Azores on contemporary maps (1351); and Catalan, Majorcan, and Italian sailors probed along the African coast.

The first organized effort at exploration, however, was attempted by Prince Henry the Navigator of Portugal (1394–1460). His imagination fired by a campaign led by his father King John I in 1415 across the Straits of Gibralter and by the consequent seizure of Ceuta (1415), he decided that African conquests offered great chances of profit and vast numbers to be saved for Christ. Accordingly he established at Sagres in the southwest of Portugal a school of navigation to which he brought seamen, navigators, and geographers. He founded colonies in the Madeiras and Azores, which turned out to be profitable, and then pushed his men southward along the coast of Africa. By 1434, the much-feared Cape Bojador had been rounded. In the 1440s, Cape Verde was passed; and in 1457 the Cape Verde Islands were discovered, and being uninhabited, settled. In the meantime, enough gold was found, enough fanciful tales of a Christian kingdom, now located in Abyssinia, were related, and enough natives were brought back as slaves to whet the appetite of Portuguese and other European adventurers for further exploration.

For a time after the death of Prince Henry exploring activity of the Portuguese declined,[3] but it was eventually revived by Prince John, who became King John II. He guessed that the way to India lay around Africa and once of this mind relentlessly pushed his quest for the golden route. In 1487 one of his men got to India via the Red Sea and wrote from Cairo that the place to trade in India was Calicut on the Malabar Coast. In the same year, Bartholomeu Dias, under orders to round Africa, if possible, got far enough into the Indian Ocean to be sure of his great find—that Africa could be rounded. Then, in 1498, Vasco da Gama went all the way to Calicut and returned not only with the good news that India could be reached by an all-water route, but also with spices which are said to have brought a profit that paid the entire cost of his voyage sixty times over.

While these discoveries were being made, another great find was in the making—that of the lands of the Western Hemisphere by Christopher Columbus. This man, who in his lifetime acknowledged himself a Genoese, made seamanship his profession and voyaged widely, certainly making the trip to England via Gibraltar and perhaps to Iceland. These experiences undoubtedly nourished his *Wanderlust*, as did also his marriage to the daughter of a wealthy Portuguese who held grants of land in the Madeiras. At all events, although a man of little formal education, Columbus read widely of the *Travels of Marco Polo*, the stories of Prester John, the concept of the sphericity of the world, and the tale that in the Atlantic there was a great island, Antilia—a myth that may possibly have come from a Norse legend. Following Ptolemy, Columbus believed the earth to be much smaller than it is; following Marco Polo, he thought that Japan extended far into the Pacific; and following a Florentine scientist, Paolo dal Pozzo Toscanelli, who wrote a Lisbon priest that he believed one could get to Asia by sailing westward, Columbus believed that China could be reached by striking directly across the Atlantic.

In the course of time he developed an ambition to undertake such a voyage westward and sought support from King John II of Portugal. But John, who was heavily committed to the route around Africa, refused, and Columbus then turned to Spain for aid. For seven years he pleaded his suit in vain, but finally after Spain had driven the Moors from their last stronghold of Granada and was free for other enterprises, his pleas were heard and assistance was granted. Somehow the necessary funds were raised, largely by borrowing and certainly not by Isabella's pawn-

---

[3] In 1469 the Portuguese government did, however, give a trade monopoly in Africa to Fernão Gomes on condition that he would continue explorations there. He kept his bargain and got nearly to the Congo River, but his work lacked the drive of that of Prince Henry.

ing her jewels. A fleet manned by a crew of 120 was fitted out at the little port of Palos; in the late summer of 1492 the voyage was begun, and on October 12 the historic landfall was made at San Salvador in the Bahamas. Although Columbus thought that he had accomplished the amazing feat of reaching the Far East by sailing westward, he had, in fact, made a much more significant find—he had discovered a new world throughout which Western culture was to spread and to which economic primacy was to fall in the twentieth century.

Upon his homeward journey Columbus encountered bad weather off Portugal and sought refuge in the Tagus River near Lisbon. Apparently this circumstance gave the discoverer an opportunity, which he could not resist, to boast of his exploits to King John who had so cavalierly refused his services a scant decade earlier. With real braggadocio Columbus told the Portuguese monarch of all his doings and of his discoveries, whereupon King John blithely laid claim to them on the ground of prior discovery. In consternation Columbus sent a messenger overland to Madrid to warn his sponsors of a trick, and they rushed a delegate to Pope Alexander VI, himself a Spaniard by birth, at Rome with a request to support their cause. Thus it was that the Pope issued the famous bull establishing the Papal Line of Demarcation around the world, granting to Portugal the unknown lands in the eastern half of the globe and to Spain those in the western half. Portugal, furious at this turn of events, threatened to go to war if the Papal decision was allowed to stand. Fortunately, the principals had recourse to negotiations which led to the signing of the Treaty of Tordesillas (1494) and thereby to the establishment of a new demarcation line, which was more favorable to Portugal, 370 leagues west of the Cape Verde Islands, or at about the 46th meridian west longitude. This settled matters between the rival claimants, but late-comers to exploration, like Francis I of France, could well ask, and did, to see "Adam's will wherein he divided the world between Spain and Portugal."

Hard upon the voyages of Columbus and Da Gama, there were other explorations too numerous even to be listed here. Columbus made three more voyages before his death in 1506 and never gave up the idea that he had found a westward route to the Malay Peninsula. Pedro Alvarès Cabral, sailing for Portugal, set off for India in 1500 but took such a westerly route in order to get full advantage of the trade winds of the South Atlantic that he struck the Brazilian coast, which he realized lay according to the terms of the Treaty of Tordesillas in the Portuguese sphere of influence. Amerigo Vespucci, a Florentine, took part in the Portuguese expedition of 1501–1502, which followed up Cabral's discovery of Brazil, and came to the conclusion that inasmuch as the new finds did not resemble any of the descriptions of the Far East known to him what must be involved was the discovery of a *Mundus Novus*— a contention which resulted in this New World being named after him.[4]

Then Ferdinand Magellan, a Portuguese who went over to the service of Spain because he failed to win promotion at home, sailed (1519) westward in order to claim the Moluccas for Spain and to avoid entirely Portugal's half of the earth. He got around South America by passing through the straits which bear his name, sailed up the west coast of the Americas for an unknown distance, and then struck out across the Pacific, which he, like most others of his day, thought to be narrow. Here trouble began, for provisions of both food and water were drastically inadequate for the months at sea. Nevertheless, the fleet reached the Philippines, which Magellan claimed for Spain and where the leader lost his life, and then dropped down to the Moluccas. Here, one of the three remaining ships, the *Vittoria*, was loaded with spices and took off for home through the Indian Ocean. Although badgered by further food shortages, the vessel reached Sanlúcar, Spain, in 1522 with eighteen survivors. In spite of the terrible losses the voyage was considered a great success. Spain claimed the Philippines and the Moluccas, although it sold the latter to Portugal for the princely sum of 350,000 gold ducats (Treaty of Saragossa, 1529). The profit on the cargo of spices that got back is said to have exceeded the cost of the entire expedition. At last the world had definite proof that the earth was round.

The Formation and Early Exploitation of Overseas Empires

As soon as claims to the newly discovered parts of the world had been staked, the claimants made a mad rush to get what economic benefits they could from their finds. Not only was there a desire to recoup the heavy costs of exploration, but there was an almost unnatural lust in the haste with which the pioneers expected to get rich. Here was an interesting commentary both on the motives behind exploration and on the prevailing ideologies in the Western world.

The Portuguese, for their part, knew that they had a good thing in the spice trade to Europe via the Cape of Good Hope and vigorously set about making the best of it. First, they sought complete mastery of the

---

[4] The letters which Vespucci wrote to friends on this subject became justly famous. They led a second-rate German geographer, Martin Waldseemüller, to propose that the new land mass be called America, for he thought that Vespucci was its discoverer. In 1541, the much more important geographer, Gerardus Mercator, prepared a map in which *America* was used for both continents in the Western Hemisphere, and this name stuck.

Indian Ocean in order to prevent supplies of Eastern products from going to their competitors, the Venetians. This mastery they obtained when Francisco d'Almeida, in one of the most decisive battles of Modern Times —that of Diú in 1509—defeated a combined Arabic and Egyptian fleet, some of whose ships, incidentally, had Venetian artillery and Venetian gunners aboard in order to protect the Republic's spice trade to the last.

Secondly, the Portuguese launched a plan, devised by Alfonso d'Albuquerque, their greatest colonial leader, to establish land bases for trade throughout the area of their operations. Thus they took Goa, which became the center of Portuguese power in the East, Malacca, the control point for spices, and Muscat and Ormuz, which dominated the Persian Gulf. Then their men pushed through to the Moluccas in 1512, thus being the first to discover the Pacific, coasted Formosa, and established contact with Java and Siam. In 1542 they visited Japan and in 1557 established a settlement at Macao, which was to be the oldest European possession in China.

In this great eastern empire, the Portuguese had no thought of settling their own people, even in sparsely populated regions, or of developing an economy based upon the principles of productivity and economic growth. The Italian model of imperialism was so firmly fixed in their minds and the opportunities of the East were so propitious that their one aim was to profit from trade—of buying cheaply and of selling dear. For the long term, this was a grave error, for it was not a difficult task for stronger powers to push the Portuguese out of their trading centers. For their part, natives were as willing to sell to representatives of one nationality as to those of another.

Then the Portuguese rulers made another serious mistake by declaring trade with the East a royal monopoly, contending that all the benefits should accrue to those who had financed the discoveries. As time was to show, Portuguese kings were unable to rise to the great entrepreneurial challenge. Not only were their losses great and their costs of administration heavy, but they could not prevent sailors and ship captains from trading on their own accounts or from ignominiously cheating them. Worst of all, they did not even try to distribute their Oriental products in Europe. They left this business to others, especially to the Dutch and Italians, who picked up cargoes at Lisbon and took them to various distribution points, notably to Antwerp. It was chiefly this trade that made the city on the Scheldt for a brief while the leading financial center of Western Europe. In the end Portuguese kings sold off their monopoly to the highest bidder, and when Portugal became a part of Spain (1580– 1640), others, especially the Dutch, went directly to the East instead of to Lisbon for their spices, and Spain exploited the resources of its little neighbor for its own advantage. By then the height of Portuguese economic power had been passed.

The other part of Portugal's overseas empire, Brazil, like all the New World, presented a different problem from that of the East. Here, inasmuch as there was no existing trade to take over, recourse had to be had to other means of realizing a profit on sums sunk in exploration. The first inclination was to hunt for the accumulations of gold and silver which rumor had it existed in large quantities. Only when the possibilities of finding treasure petered out, was serious attention given to settlement and production.

By 1532 Brazil had a small settlement and the land had begun to be parceled out in *capitánias* or holdings from the crown, each capitaincy stretching 150 miles along the coast and indefinitely into the interior. Gradually the capitaincies were settled with white people, Negroes, and Indians, who cultivated sugar cane, cut brazilwood, and mined gold. Very shrewd economic forecasters of the time might well have guessed that this kind of exploitation was in the long run to pay off better than one-sided trade in luxuries.

The lands which the Spanish discovered in the New World were like Portugal's Brazil in that they had no developed trade which could be directed toward Europe and in that they were entirely unknown quantities. Hence the first task to be accomplished was exploring the new lands, which, given their size, was a formidable undertaking. The second task was to conquer the Indians, if conquest is not too ambitious a word for what was involved. These assignments fell to the lot of the adventurous *conquistadores*. Motivated by dreams of gold, hopes of glory, visions of God, and at least in one case by a desire to bathe in a fountain of youth, these intrepid pioneers had within a half-century spread out on the west coast of the Americas from Chile to the Rouge River in Oregon, on the east coast from Florida to the Argentine, and in the interior from Arizona and the northern boundary of Mississippi, over all Central America, and to what were to become the major centers of South America. Nor were the comings and goings of these men fruitless. To a remarkable degree their searching brought them the very kind of rewards which they desired.

The first great success of the *conquistadores* was realized by Hernando Cortés in Mexico. When this hardy landed on the coasts of Mexico and heard stories of the great wealth of the Aztec Indians, he promptly burned his ships so that his men would not take off and struck boldly overland to reap his harvest. When he reached his destination, he found a people with a fairly high degree of civilization and fabulous stores of gold and silver, but a people who had never discovered iron, which impaired their fighting effectiveness, and who offered up human sacrifices in such numbers to their gods that a revolt against the ruling minority was always smoldering—a situation of which he hoped to take advantage. He discovered also that the Aztecs' chief city, located on the present site of Mexico City, was built on an island in a lake and was connected to the mainland by an aqueduct and causeway—a situation which proved to be vulnerable to the Spaniards. Finally, Cortés encountered a friendly people who made the great mistake of inviting the *conquistador* and his men into the town.

Once inside the city precincts, Cortés displayed a degree of perfidy that has become legendary. He took the emperor captive, expecting to start a revolt among the people against their leader, but on the contrary so aroused the populace that they turned on him and drove him to the mainland. There he calmly cut the city's water supply and the causeway over which its food came and in essence waited for hunger to do its work. When the people were sufficiently weakened, he took the city (1521) and sacked it. His most important haul was the Aztecs' store of precious metals—an amount that did honor to the most fantastic dreams of his ilk.

The second great success story of the *conquistadores* was that of Francisco Pizarro. He had served under Balboa at the Isthmus of Panama and in the hard school of Balboa's murderer and successor, Pedrarias. Like many others he heard the tall tales of high civilization and wealth of the Incas of Peru and like many before him was impatient to get at them. Finally, in 1532 he was able to realize his hopes. He penetrated the Incan empire with a small band of followers and immediately began a plot to get political power. He found a situation in which two brothers were disputing the succession to the throne, and by posing as arbiter between the two and then using the successful one as a puppet, he got the hold over the people which he wanted. When ultimately the natives turned against him, he defeated them without much trouble, for they, like the Aztecs, had not yet acquired iron and steel. It is said that Pizarro offered to let the emperor ransom himself by filling a room 22 by 17 feet 9 feet deep with gold ornaments. Once the treasure had been delivered, the Spaniard murdered the "ransomed" man in cold blood. When this take was melted down, it was found to be worth some five million dollars.

Although these were the most famous exploits of the *conquistadores*, they were not the only ones of their kind. The civilized inhabitants of Guatemala and Mayans of Yucatan were both subjected to the yoke of Spain; the Chibchas in the highlands of Columbia near Bogotá, famous for their fabled *El Dorado*, a man who according to legend was every year plated with gold and thrown in the lake, were conquered and robbed; and Venezuela and Chile were overrun. Then, when no more treasures remained to be seized and the conquering of more people seemed futile, the Spaniards turned to mining. They discovered a real mountain of silver at Potosí, Peru, and went to work on it with vigor, as is attested by the fact that the roaring mining town of Potosí had 120,000 inhabitants in 1580 and was thus the largest city in the Americas. They also found fabulously rich mines at Zacatecas and Guanajuto in Mexico and lesser diggings in a hundred other places.

Although conquering, robbing, and mining were the chief economic activities of the Spaniards in the Americas during the sixteenth century, some interest was shown in agriculture. Spanish lords and gentlemen received large grants of territory and many of the grantees took off for the New World to make their fortunes off the land. They were largely responsible for the introduction into the Western Hemisphere of a host of domesticated plants and animals, in which America was extremely poor. The *conquistadores* introduced the horse, which gave them great mobility and thus one of their most distinct advantages over the Indians, while their successors brought in cattle, sheep, goats, chickens, and pigs. They also introduced into America sugar cane, wheat, barley, rice, rye, coffee, cotton, a number of garden vegetables, and fruits. They were the first to send back to Europe most of the things that America gave to the Old World—tobacco, chocolate, the "Irish" potato, Indian corn, quinine, the tomato, and the turkey. They were largely responsible, because of their success in cultivation, for the initial increase in the use of sugar, rice, and coffee in the Old World. And they were chiefly accountable for the introduction of Negroes as slaves into the New World.[5] But the importance of permanent settlements in Spanish America in the sixteenth century should not be exaggerated, for in 1600 precious metals constituted 90 per cent of the Old World's imports from the New and in 1700 the total Spanish population of the New World was only 150,000. Economic growth was largely a thing of the future.

While the Spanish and Portuguese were thus instituting the process by which their brand of Western culture was to become dominant in the Western Hemisphere from Mexico southward, and while the Portuguese in their exploitation of Eastern trade were beginning to make European economic life and European ways felt by Eastern cultures, the other great colonizing peoples—the English, the Dutch, and the

---

[5] Indians could not be enslaved in Spanish America. They were, however, exploited in one way or another. By the *repartimiento* system Spaniards were given the right to all or part of an Indian's labor and by *encomienda,* the right to collect tribute, reminiscent of feudal dues, from Indians in given districts.

French—who were eventually to do so much in spreading Western culture to non-European parts of the world, were also taking part in the expansionist movement. Their late start put them under a severe handicap, for by the time their first explorers set sail the routes to the East around Africa had been preempted by the Portuguese; the area of exploration for a way to Cathay via the South Atlantic had been monopolized by Spain; and the Treaty of Tordesillas had divided the whole undiscovered world between the two Iberian states. Although the opportunities for discovery, conquest, and glory thus seemed extraordinarily limited, the late-comers concentrated their efforts at first upon finding new routes to the Far East chiefly either via a Northeast passage around Scandinavia and Russia or a Northwest passage through or around the land mass of North America. Their efforts in the former direction bore little fruit, but those in the latter area took them to that part of the New World which was to become the wealthiest area of the entire planet. Furthermore, their failure to find new routes to the East led these powers to encroach upon Portugal's pathway around Africa, and to struggle among themselves for primacy in the colonial world.

In the French case the process of discovery was an excellent example of the accumulative effect of knowledge, each successive explorer building upon the foundations laid by his predecessor. Here, the chain of explorations began with Jacques Cartier, an experienced mariner from the Breton town of St. Malo, who reached and claimed for France the Gaspé Basin in 1534. The next year he sailed up the St. Lawrence in the hope of getting through to China. When he saw water breaking in the river, he believed—or so it is said; the story is probably apocryphal—that he had succeeded and exclaimed *"La Chine!"*, thus giving a name to the rapids above Montreal which has stuck to them even to the present day (Lachine Rapids). Then Samuel de Champlain carried on where Cartier left off, founding a settlement at Quebec (1608) and exploring the Lake Champlain region and all the Great Lakes, which he claimed for France. Subsequently, a priest named Marquette and a trader, Joliet, went part way down the Mississippi and they were followed later by Robert Cavelier de la Salle who reached the Gulf of Mexico and claimed all the land drained by the great Father of Waters and its tributaries for his King—*Le Roi Soleil*—Louis XIV. Thus the French carved out for themselves an empire which consisted of the heartland of America and Canada.

The English in their search for a route to China sent out an Italian, Giovanni Caboto, more commonly known as John Cabot, in 1496. He explored some of the coast of North America, thus giving England a claim to what was to become the Atlantic coast line of most of the United

States. Then his son Sebastian, Martin Frobisher, Henry Hudson, and William Baffin one after another tried in vain to push around North America, discovering and claiming Newfoundland, Hudson Bay, and Baffin Bay, which were to give the English a hold from which they could contest the Canadian territory with the French. Finally, the Dutch, for their part, got a foothold at New York, thanks to the explorations of Henry Hudson (1609), who went up the Hudson River as far as what is now Albany.

These discoveries of the French, English, and Dutch were definitely disappointing, for they did not open up a golden gateway to the East, nor very promising lands as areas of settlement. The French could not at first cope with the cold and could get very little out of Canada except fish and furs. The English failed in their efforts to settle Newfoundland in 1582; and Sir Walter Raleigh was unsuccessful in his attempts to establish a colony at Roanoke, Virginia. Even the Virginia Company's settlement on the James River, the Plymouth Colony, and the Massachusetts Bay Colony were at best only struggling outposts in the wilderness for some years after their founding. Indeed, advocates of permanent colonization and settlement, like the unsuppressible Richard Hakluyt at the end of the sixteenth century, seemed to be barking up the wrong tree. Even the Dutch colony at New Amsterdam was insignificant compared with what the Portuguese had in the East.

The French, English, and Dutch were not, however, content to admit defeat. From the first they had coveted Portuguese and Spanish colonial wealth and had speculated on how they might encroach upon it. Needless to say, cerebration on the problem led them to identical conclusions, for the range of possibilities was extremely limited. First, they agreed that they might do well to trade in Latin America, second, that there would be profit in plundering Spanish galleons on their homeward voyages, third, that they themselves could go to the Far East via known routes and get the spices which the Portuguese were selling to them at such a profit, and fourth, that they should take some of the less well-defended and apparently fertile lands in Central and South America and bring them rapidly into production of things, like sugar, that Europeans wanted. They tried all four of these solutions.

The story of what they did may be begun with the efforts of John Hawkins, an Englishman, to develop trade in slaves between the Guinea Coast and Spanish Caribbean colonies—and, of course, to bring back from the New World gold, silver, or merchandise in exchange for his human cargoes. Unfortunately the Spaniards did not like his plan, and when they caught him at Vera Cruz, they fired on his ships with such effectiveness that the poor man was just able to escape with his skin back to England. Inasmuch as peaceful trade seemed to be impossible, recourse was had to the next possibility—privateering. This profession fitted the personality and spirits of one of Hawkin's men, Francis Drake, to a T and he set out to harass the Spaniards in the West Indies. After a successful turn at this sport, he sailed around South America, up the coast of California, across the Pacific to the East Indies, through the Indian Ocean, around Africa, and thence back to England (1580). Plundering as he went, Drake sailed into port loaded with loot, much to the delight of Good Queen Bess, who promptly joined in his good fortune by helping herself to a share of the booty. Subsequently other Elizabethan sea dogs took off on similar junkets, one of the most famous being that of Thomas Cavendish who held up Spanish galleons along the Spanish Main and also tried his luck in the Pacific.

Robbery on the high seas was, however, a precarious business at best and in this case contributed toward bringing on retaliations, of which the Armada of 1588 was the most famous. Consequently, some among the late-comers wanted to try the third possibility of getting into the pioneers' colonial jackpot—going directly to the source of Portugal's spice supplies in the East. Thus would they get all the profit that was to be had from this trade.

That the Dutch should have been the first to have had recourse to this stratagem has a historical explanation. Netherlanders had obtained the lion's share of the carrying trade of spices from Lisbon to Antwerp and had made a very good thing out of the practice. The Netherlands, however, rose in revolt against Spain in 1566, and although the southern provinces were subdued, the northern provinces established their independence (1579). The upshot of this situation was that the Dutch cut shipping to Antwerp, while the Spanish, for their part, prohibited the Dutch from going to Lisbon to pick up Eastern products.[6] Thus excluded from a very profitable business, the Dutch had every incentive to go directly to the East for what they had previously obtained in Portugal.

Nor were the Netherlanders entirely unfamiliar with the routes which the Portuguese had laid out to India and the Spice Islands, for many of them had sailed on Portuguese vessels and one of them, Jan Huyghen van Linschoten, had published a well-known and fairly detailed account of his voyage. Therefore, it was with the expectation of success, if the Spaniards could be avoided, that a fleet set out under Cornelis van Houtman which reached Java in 1595 and thus proved that the Dutch could go to the source of spices as well as anyone else. This voyage was followed by a veritable flotilla of twenty-two ships that put out in 1598 to test whether the route around Africa or that around South America was

[6] It will be recalled that Portugal became part of Spain in 1580.

the more feasible, thirteen ships heading for the Cape of Good Hope and nine for the Straits of Magellan. Since only one of the latter got back, the African route was decided to be the better of the two and was developed earnestly by merchantmen of the Dutch East India Company (founded 1602). One of this Company's greatest colonial administrators, Jan Pieterzoen Coen, gained the upper hand in Batavia, Java, and the Moluccas; one of its great explorers, Abel Janszoon Tasman, discovered Tasmania and New Zealand and proved Australia to be an island. Their successors drove the Portuguese from Malacca (1641) and Ceylon (1658). The Dutch established a contact with Japan, which was the main relationship which this country had with Western culture until the coming of Commodore Perry in 1854, and they founded a successful colony (1652) at the Cape of Good Hope, near the present city of Capetown, as the supply station for ships in the Indian trade.

Dutch inroads on Eastern commerce proved to be extremely profitable, and as a result the small nation of the Netherlands became the wealthiest state per capita in Western Europe during the seventeenth century. It did not, however, have everything its own way and was early confronted by competition from the English and the French. The former did, in fact, charter their East India Company two years before the Dutch did theirs and shortly thereafter sent merchantmen to the East for spices. At first the Dutch were not particularly hostile to the newcomers, for they appeared to be useful in subduing the Portuguese. But when the English attempted to establish themselves in the Spice Islands, the Dutch uttered a very emphatic "no" and were able to uphold their injunction with force. So the English turned their attention to trade with India and the Persian Gulf, getting a foothold at Surat in 1609, founding a station at Madras in 1639, securing Bombay in 1661, and establishing themselves at Calcutta in 1690. The French, for their part, planted small colonies on Madagascar and Réunion (1642), got footholds in Senegal and Guinea, where they could trade in slaves, and through their East India Company (1664) established posts at Surat and Pondichéry in India, where they conducted a promising trade.

By the end of the seventeenth century trade in cotton, cotton textiles, and other Indian and Persian products was proving to be even more profitable than trade in spices, so the fact that the Dutch had excluded the English and the French from the Spice Islands was not of primary importance to the newcomers. Nevertheless, they waged war on the Dutch either together or singly from the middle of the seventeenth century to the end of the War of Spanish Succession in 1713. The small Netherlandish state could not stand this kind of attrition and it had to reconcile itself to limiting its activities. Its holdings in the East remained important, however, for they included Ceylon, Sumatra, the Celebes, the Moluccas, part of Borneo, New Guinea, the Malay Peninsula, and Java, where coffee growing became important. And in Africa it still had its colony at the Cape of Good Hope.

With the elimination of the Dutch from the real contest for power in the East, the struggle became one between the English and French. Although these two peoples had been sparring at each other for some time, the struggle became particularly bitter after 1707, for then the collapse of the Mogul Empire in India left a vacuum into which both contenders rushed—and in their haste to extend their dominions they came headlong into conflict with one another. In the wars which ensued, waged under the leadership of two brilliant generals, Joseph François Dupleix and Robert Clive, the English emerged the victors at the conclusion of the Seven Years' War (Treaty of Paris, 1763). Henceforth the French were to remain in their few stations as traders rather than as colonizers. It was the English who would try to implant Western culture's economic practices and ideologies in India.

While these various tests of strength were going on in the Far East, still other attempts were being made by the colonial late-comers to profit from overseas expansion. For one thing they all seized lands in the Caribbean area in the hope of producing goods which would supplement what was grown at home and in the expectation of trading with or of preying on Spaniards. Thus the Dutch took Curaçao and Dutch Guiana or Surinam; the English occupied St. Christopher or St. Kitts,[7] Bermuda, the Barbados, Jamaica, the Bahamas, some of the Virgin group, and still others of less renown; and the French seized Martinique, Guadeloupe, the western half of Santo Domingo (now Haiti), and a number of lesser places. In most of these areas attempts were made to grow tobacco, but frequent oversupply of the market and consequent falls in price led eventually to less specialization—to the growing of rice, coffee, indigo, cotton, cocoa, and sugar. The last of these came to be the most important of all. It came to satisfy the sweet tooth of Europe that previously had had to rely upon honey, and it provided the ingredient of an entirely new alcoholic beverage—rum—that was to have wondrous effects on trade and upon man.

Also, the French, Dutch, and English made more or less serious attempts to settle their lands in North America, but progress was very slow. In 1663 French Canada had only some three thousand French inhabitants and in 1763 but about eighty thousand, and New Orleans was in 1722 only a struggling village of five hundred. The Dutch colony of New

[7] The French had part of the island until 1713 when they surrendered it to the English.

European Discoveries and Expansion to 1763.

British possessions
French   "
Portuguese possessions
Dutch   "
Spanish possessions

Amsterdam, which was captured by the English in one of the many wars between these two peoples (1664) and rechristened New York, had only fourteen thousand inhabitants in 1760. And all the original thirteen English colonies along the Atlantic seaboard had a population of but 275,000 in 1700 and seemed destined to be hemmed in by the claims of the French in the north and west. The future, based upon production, was, however, theirs. And the French threat was removed at the time of the French and Indian War, or, as it was called in Europe, by the Seven Years' War (1763), when France ceded Canada to England and Louisiana to Spain in compensation for that country's loss of Florida to England.[8]

By the middle of the eighteenth century, therefore, Western European culture had been carried to both North and South America and it looked as though is would eventually become dominant throughout the New World. It had come in contact with the cultures of the East and bade fair to drag them into its economic orbit. What the economic impact of Europe on the rest of the world and of the rest of the world on Europe would be remains to be seen.

[8] Florida was returned to Spain in 1783.

CHAPTER 8

Economic Consequences of
European Overseas Expansion

A General Statement

Of all the major movements which mark the transition of Europe from the Middle Ages to Modern Times none was more pregnant with change than the expansion of Europe overseas. The impact of Europe on cultures beyond the seas and the influence of these cultures on Europe contributed much to giving the world the cultural configuration which it has today. Yet in spite of its importance, expansion has been studied less and understood less than such other great developments of the sixteenth century as the Protestant Revolt, the rise of national states, and the development of capitalism and its institutions. The ramifications of the movement were so wide, its results often so subtle, and its action so intertwined with other forces that its complete significance has proved elusive. In the few pages at our disposal here, all that we can hope to do is to make clear the outstanding economic aspects of European expansion.

Undoubtedly the most important consequence of this movement was its marked impetus to economic growth. Overseas areas constituted a vast new market for all kinds of things from the motherlands, as is always the case in colonial undertakings, and the overseas areas gave the Old World supplies of goods that were to create entirely new industries. Secondly, the expansion of Europe led to the importation of so much

140

gold and silver bullion into Europe that the prices of goods, based as they were on these metals, rose enormously. This price rise had a stimulating effect on business enterprise, but caused considerable social tension, particularly between lords of the land and those peasants who had long-term contracts with their overlords and whose obligations were fixed in money. Thirdly, the overseas movement tended to effect a shift in the center of commerce and subsequently of economic activity generally from the Mediterranean Sea area to the Atlantic seaboard—a shift that has been glorified with the rubric "Commercial Revolution." Fourthly, colonialism led to fundamental changes in business organization, for large-scale overseas enterprises required greater sums than could be provided by former institutions. In fact, European expansion is largely responsible for the coming into being of the stock company. Fifthly, from increased trade and an increased division of labor stemmed an ever greater use of money as a medium of exchange, and this increase led to important developments in banking practices. Lastly, the overseas movement contributed to changes in political, social, and to some extent, economic ideologies which were to become integral parts of Western culture.

American Treasure and the European Price Revolution

The story of the economic impact of expansion on the Old World begins with a consideration of bullion imports and the rise in prices, for these developments came first in point of time and had effects which were pertinent to most of the other changes. They had a bearing upon the increased use of money, on banking, on debtor-creditor relationships, on savings and investments, and on economic growth generally.

References which have already been made to the hauls of bullion made by Cortés in Mexico and Pizarro in Peru and to the high production of such mines as that of Potosí have suggested that vast amounts of gold and silver were brought to Europe following the discoveries. Spanish America was the largest source of shipments and for that area careful studies give us an excellent idea of the sums sent through official channels to Spain and the dates of the shipments.

To these totals should be added about 10 per cent for smuggling, an undetermined sum brought in by the Portuguese from Africa, and the production of the newly opened silver mines of Germany and Austria, like those of Joachimsthal, and of the gold mines of Salzburg and elsewhere, in order to get a complete picture of the increase in Europe's supply of precious metals in the first century of Modern Times. If such a computation is effected, if allowances are made for the exportation of

Table 1. Spanish Imports of Fine Gold and Silver from America

(In grams)

Period	Silver	Gold
1503–1510		4,965,180
1511–1520		9,153,220
1521–1530	148,739	4,889,050
1531–1540	86,193,876	14,466,360
1541–1550	177,573,164	24,957,130
1551–1560	303,121,174	42,620,080
1561–1570	942,858,792	11,530,940
1571–1580	1,118,591,954	9,429,140
1581–1590	2,103,027,689	12,101,650
1591–1600	2,707,626,528	19,451,420
1601–1610	2,213,631,245	11,764,090
1611–1620	2,192,255,993	8,855,940
1621–1630	2,145,339,043	3,889,760
1631–1640	1,396,759,594	1,240,400
1641–1650	1,056,430,966	1,549,390
1651–1660	443,256,546	469,430
Total	16,886,815,303	181,333,180

SOURCE: Earl J. Hamilton, *American Treasure and the Price Revolution in Spain* (Cambridge, Mass.: Harvard University Press, 1934).

certain amounts of gold and silver to the East in payment for goods, and if the usual estimate of the Old World's store of bullion in 1500 is used, one will find that Europe's holdings of gold and silver more than tripled from 1500 to 1650. Furthermore, if a study of the area distribution of the newly acquired treasure is made, it will be seen that despite Spain's efforts to keep the gold and silver within its boundaries, precious metals went to all parts of Western Europe in payment for the difference between Spanish merchandise imports and its exports, that is, for the settlement of Spain's deficits in foreign trade.

As American bullion came to be exchanged for goods, it began to lose value in terms of actual merchandise, that is, prices began to go up. This was because (1) supplies of gold and silver increased much more rapidly than the stock of goods, (2) the rate of circulation of money was accelerated with the boom in commercial transactions,[1] and (3) individuals, fearing shortages of goods or higher prices, used their free balances for immediate instead of future purchases.

[1] See p. 144, n. 3.

From recent, intensive studies of the price rise of the sixteenth century and the first half of the seventeenth,[2] it is clear that prices rose at different rates in different countries, that prices of some goods rose more rapidly than those of others, and that the prices of goods went up faster than that of services as expressed in money wages. Prices went up first, as one would expect, in Spain where American bullion was first thrown into the market and then increased in other countries almost in direct proportion to the extent of their participation in the new trade along the Atlantic seacoast. Prices, as expressed in gold and silver, stopped rising first in Spain as a reaction to the decline in the influx of bullion, to the fall in trade, and to the resulting deceleration in the rate of circulation of money, and then declined in other parts of the world.

Furthermore, historical studies show that prices of staples produced locally for local consumption increased less rapidly than prices of goods produced for distant markets—that, for example, the rise in the price of wheat was less than that of luxury woolen cloth, that of beer inferior to that of hemp and tar used in shipping, and that of meat to that of tools and weapons. Finally, the statistical time series in these studies show dramatically the lag in the rise in wages behind prices and suggest how wageworkers, who were mostly in industry, were caught in a wage-price squeeze.

The entire phenomena of the price rise affected the lives of contemporaries so deeply that it was the object of much comment and some serious study. Men of the times, in spite of their realization of what was taking place, were, however, at a loss to explain why it was occurring. Apparently it was not until 1568, when a French political philosopher, Jean Bodin, penned his *Reply to the Paradoxes of M. Malestroit*, that anything was published which approached a satisfactory explanation of the price rise. Bodin was first in Modern Times to express the fundamental principles of the quantity theory of money; that is, if the quantity of money in circulation is increased without a comparable increase in the supply of goods, prices tend to react upward. It remained for later students to point out that an increase in the rate of circulation of money had

[2] See especially the work of the International Scientific Committee for the Study of Prices. Among its publications are Earl J. Hamilton, *American Treasure and the Price Revolution in Spain, 1501–1650* (Cambridge, Mass.: Harvard University Press, 1934); Henri Hauser (Ed.), *Recherches et documents sur l'histoire des prix en France de 1500 à 1800* (Paris: Les Presses Modernes, 1936); M. J. Elsas, *Umriss einer Geschichte der Preise und Löhne in Deutschland* (Leyden: Sijthoff, 1936); Sir William Beveridge, *Prices and Wages in England from the Twelfth to the Ninteenth Century* (London: Longmans, 1939); and N. W. Posthumus, *Nederlandsche Prijsgeschiedenis* (Leyden: Brill, 1943).

the same effect on prices as an increase in the volume of money,[3] and for still more recent scholars to stress that the course of prices is also conditioned by the rate with which people use their free balances for the present purchase of goods. Nevertheless, Bodin, it should be said to his credit, hit upon a general proposition that within broad tolerances has been shown time and time again in history to have had general validity.

Contemporaries also recognized that the price rise favored debtors and penalized creditors. It was clear to all that debtors had to produce less than formerly to meet their money obligations, for they got more money per unit of what they produced. Thus a peasant whose various dues to his lord had been commuted to money payments found that his payments were much lighter at the end of the sixteenth century than had been those of his grandfather in 1500, because he had to grow only 3 bushels of wheat to realize the same amount of money that his forebear had gained with 10 bushels. Contrariwise, it was obvious that creditors were being paid off in money which bought only a fraction of the goods which it had previously commanded. Thus a lord who received money dues established in the late fifteenth century could only buy a third or a fourth of the amount of goods with the same sum in 1650.

This situation led many lords to seek a revision of their arrangements with their peasants.[4] This was difficult to do if the peasant stood on his legal rights, but all too often the peasant lacked adequate legal advice or political power for a real defense. Thus lords were frequently able to change the terms of peasant payments and even in some cases to substitute a short-term lease of from five to fifteen years for the inheritable contract. In nearly all cases they were able to increase traditional dues that were not for specific amounts, as with heriot and relief, or to take undue advantage of practices, like that of *mainmorte* [mortmain]. As can readily be imagined acts of this kind frequently led to troubles between lords and peasants which became so inextricably mixed with the religious sentiment of the sixteenth century that some of Protestantism has the appearance of a social movement.

In England, special circumstances created a particularly tense situation and a whole series of special social and economic problems. Here the price of wool went up with such amazing rapidity that the prospect of profits enticed many large landowners to go into sheep raising. They

---

[3] If the rate of circulation per annum doubles, let us say, then the effect is the same, according to the theory, as doubling the amount of money, for each unit of money accounts for double the volume of transactions.

[4] It also helps to explain why so many lords were willing to strike boldly overseas in search of fame and fortune.

were convinced that they could get far more purchasing power from their land in this way than they could by continuing to receive the much-depreciated (in real value) dues from peasants. However, to conduct the new type of agricultural undertaking successfully, it was necessary to have large pastures enclosed by fences and hedges, and to get the large pastures it was necessary to get rid of the peasants and their rights to work small plots. This the land-hungry lords did by depriving their people of traditional privileges, like the right to turn out their livestock in the common fields, or by raising fees or leases to prohibitive levels.

By these and similar devices, it is estimated that in the sixteenth century about 5 per cent of the Midlands, where enclosures were the heaviest, was enclosed and that in a few counties the percentage ran as high as 10. It was so great that many of the people forced off the land were unable to find other employment and became public charges or beggars. Indeed, the increase in pauperism was so large in Elizabethan England that a system of poor relief provided by parishes came into being and begging was condemned as both a national calamity and a social nuisance. Moreover, enclosures went so far that government circles in London feared for the food supply of both the city and the entire nation and enacted legislation, like that limiting the size of flocks and prohibiting the conversion of arable to pasture, to stop it.[5] Lastly, enclosures contributed to outbreaks and revolts, often in connection with religious and social movements, like Kett's Rebellion in 1549 and the agitation of the "Diggers" and "Levellers" in the seventeenth century.

In addition to the tensions thus caused in agriculture by the rise in prices, there were also troubles in industry between employers and employees. As a result, both apprentices and journeymen tried to get better terms from guild masters. Workers in the domestic system agitated for higher rates for their spinning and weaving, and laborers in large central shops demanded higher wages. In some places there were strikes and in others, riots. So severe, in fact, did labor troubles become that both France and England took legal steps to suppress them by forbidding strikes and by establishing maximum wage rates.[6] Obviously the decline in the real purchasing power of wages was understood, even if the policies adopted to deal with it left much to be desired.

That aspect of the rise of prices at a more rapid rate than wages which, however, contemporaries did not understand was what has come to be known as "profit inflation." Briefly this was that with prices rising and wages lagging behind, profits tended to be larger, that is, they were "in-

[5] The latter was repeated in 1593.

[6] See the Elizabethan Statute of Apprentices (1563) and the French decree of Villers-Cotterêts (1539).

flated," especially in those enterprises where wages constituted a high percentage of the total costs of production. Such a situation, at least in theory, increases the incentives of business entrepreneurs to augment their investments in capital equipment so that they can make more profit. In this way "profit inflation" is supposed to favor economic growth. Economic expansion depends, however, on so many factors of which the desire to increase profits is only one that "profit inflation" does not operate automatically in accordance with the theory. In Portugal and Spain, for example, conditions favorable to the making of larger profits seem to have had a limited influence on economic development, except in the case of investments in colonial enterprise and in sheep raising.[7] Its effect in industry was slight, partly because of a limitation of natural resources, a general unwillingness to save for investment, and an attitude, especially on the part of the nobility, that participation in industrial activity was degrading.

In the Netherlands, also, new investments were largely in colonial enterprises, like the East India Company, and in agriculture, where production was increased by new techniques that foreshadowed the "agricultural revolution" of the eighteenth century, but there was some investment in industry for the processing of colonial products, like chocolate, coffee, and spices, and for the production of ships and ship supplies. In France, the difference between prices and wages in the sixteenth and seventeenth century seems to have had but slight general effect upon commerce, industry, or agriculture. Nevertheless, the French took advantage of special situations to expand economic activity, as in the case of the slave trade, the refining of cane sugar, and the development of certain luxuries, like silk and glass.

"Profit inflation" undoubtedly had its greatest and clearest impact in England. In agriculture, production on large farms, even of wool that required little labor, was increased to take advantage of the opportunity to earn large profits. In commerce, new investments were made, as we have seen, in all kinds of enterprises from Drake's privateering to the establishment of overseas trading companies. And in industry, investments were placed in a whole list of trades, often at the instigation of

---

[7] The Mesta, a country-wide organization of sheep herders—a kind of national guild—had a strong position in this phase of agriculture and also in politics. With the extraordinary rise in wool prices, the Mesta increased output, having at its peak control of perhaps three million sheep. The organization arranged the migration of sheep from the coastal areas, where the animals were wintered, to the mountains, where they grazed in summer; it controlled pastures, and it secured favorable laws for the sale and export of wool. Unfortunately, however, the success of the Mesta resulted in overgrazing large areas, which led to soil erosion and to the turning of much of the Castilian highlands into veritable agricultural wastes.

Elizabeth's economic "brain truster," Lord Burghley. Many of these would undoubtedly not have been made, or they would not have been made in the same volume, if the likelihood of profits had not been good. Thus much new capital appeared in iron mining, in saltpeter and alum production, in brewing, in shipbuilding, and in coal mining, especially in the Newcastle area. In all these trades production increased remarkably and in all of them new techniques, which required capital outlay, were employed. In fact, so great were the changes that more and more they are now regarded as having constituted an early English industrial revolution.[8]

The Growth of Commerce and the "Commercial Revolution"

With all the changes in agriculture and industry which occurred in the sixteenth century, clearly that branch of economic activity which experienced greatest growth was commerce. Just what the magnitude of that development was is impossible to state with precision, for reliable statistical information on trade is sadly lacking for this early period. From the movement of ships in the major parts, from a few cases where tax and customs returns are available, and from information regarding shipbuilding, we know that the expansion was very great. When one considers that Spain and Portugal received more gold and silver from overseas between 1500 and 1650 than was in existence in Europe at the former date and that much of this treasure went from the states of the Iberian Peninsula to other parts of Europe in payment for goods, one gets some conception of the extension of European commerce. To say that its total volume doubled within the first century of Modern Times would be a conservative statement.

Whatever the growth of European commerce may have been, it is clear that the greatest expansion was realized along the Atlantic littoral from Gibraltar to Hamburg and from Land's End in England to Newcastle-on-the-Tyne. Here were to be found the colonizing nations which were putting royal treasure and income from taxes into overseas explorations and colonial expansion. Here were the merchants who sought products for fitting out expeditions and for trading with natives the world over. Here were the places where colonial goods from the far corners of the world were marketed. And here, too, were the best ports of Europe, conveniently located for using the new routes around Africa and across the Atlantic.

[8] See John U. Nef, "The Progress of Technology and the Growth of Large Scale Industry in Great Britain, 1540–1640," *The Economic History Review*, vol. 5, no. 1, pp. 9–18, 1934.

Under the circumstances it is little wonder that places like Cadiz, Lisbon, Bordeaux, Rouen, Antwerp, Amsterdam, Bristol, and London grew by leaps and bounds. It is said that Lisbon's port on the Tagus River was, at its height in the 1540s, literally choked with ships and that Antwerp at its peak in the 1560s witnessed the passing up and down the Scheldt of 500 ships a day. Nor is it astonishing that in the thirty-year period prior to 1618, the number of English ships is said to have doubled and that in the middle of the seventeenth century the Dutch had a merchant marine estimated at four times the size of that of all Italy, of Spain, and of Portugal combined.

So drastic was the shift in the center of international commerce from the Mediterranean to the Atlantic and especially to the North Sea ports that it has traditionally been called in the annals of European history the "Commercial Revolution of the Sixteenth Century." It was, indeed, one of the great locational changes of history, quite comparable to the transfer of the center of economic activity in Ancient Times from Greece to Rome, in the Medieval period from Rome to Byzantium, and in the twentieth century from Western Europe to the English-speaking part of North America. It meant that henceforth for some three hundred and fifty years important economic advances were to be recorded primarily within a 500-mile radius of Belgium. Here the most important economic innovations were to be realized, the greatest economic growth was to be attained, and the highest incomes per capita of the population were to be reached. It was this economic well-being that made possible Western Europe's political and cultural leadership in Western culture.

Important as the "Commercial Revolution" was, the impression should not be left that commerce elsewhere suddenly disappeared. Although the center of trade left the Mediterranean, commerce on the Middle Sea continued in considerable volume. All the leading commercial states of the seventeenth century—the Dutch, the English, and the French—had trading companies that exploited the possibilities of the Levant, and for a time they did reasonably well. Moreover, Venice did not collapse like a punctured balloon, although its business was hurt when the Portuguese got control of the Indian Ocean, when the Ottoman Turks, who overran Egypt in 1517, became difficult in the bargains which they tried to drive, and when, one might add, the Portuguese refused an offer to sell all their spices to Venice (1521). The Queen of the Adriatic continued to have an important banking business, to ship in the Mediterranean, and to carry on commerce through the Alpine passes with Germany. Indeed, it had enough vigor to play an important part in all the many coalitions to stave off the extension of Turkish power westward in the Mediterranean, especially that which defeated the Turks at the Battle of Lepanto in 1571 and that which gave Venice the Peloponnesus of Greece (Treaty of Carlowitz, 1699). The "decline" of Venice was a gradual and genteel one, befitting a lady of high station. And so, too, were the "declines" of Barcelona, Genoa, and Marseilles, if, indeed, in the case of the last it is appropriate to speak of a decline.

The failure of Mediterranean trade to grow at the same rate as that of the coastal areas of the English Channel and the North Sea meant that those regions whose economy was based on commercial intercourse with the Mediterranean tended to stagnate. This was particularly true of south German cities, like Augsburg, Munich, and Nuremberg, and to some extent, of Swiss cities like Geneva. Even on the other side of Germany, in the Baltic Sea area, normal commercial activity seems to have been affected adversely. Here the Dutch began to supplant Mediterranean suppliers of spices and other Eastern products and to take the place of Hanseatic traders in bringing to the West both grain from Danzig and shipbuilding timber from Scandinavia. Then the herring, which for centuries had spawned in the Baltic, for some strange reason shifted their grounds to the North Sea during the sixteenth century. This was an important loss to the economy of the Baltic and a real gain for the Dutch, for herring was one of the few fish that was salted and pickled on a commercial scale for the large market created by Catholic rules against eating meat on Fridays and other days of abstinence.

Expansion and Business Organization

With the growth of commerce and of industry stimulated by the expansion of Europe overseas, business was confronted with problems of entirely new magnitudes. First and foremost, it was faced with raising amounts of capital which seldom if ever had been amassed for completely new undertakings. For example, as late as the beginning of the seventeenth century it took upwards of half a million dollars at 1955 prices to send a fleet of four ships totaling 1,400 tons to the Far East with a cargo. Then secondly, it was obvious that the newly proffered business opportunities, lucrative as they might be if they succeeded, entailed far more risk than the usual entrepreneurial venture. The English East India Company, for example, lost about one out of every four ships which it sent out in the first years of its existence.

In the case of Portugal, the pioneer in the new trade, problems of financing and risk taking were partly met by declaring trade with the Indies a monopoly of the royal houses—a stand based on the fact that the rulers had financed the discoveries—for the monarch's revenues were supposedly adequate to provide capital and to sustain temporary losses.

In the long run, however, this solution was not successful, for Portuguese kings showed themselves inept as businessmen and did not have large enough resources at their disposal. They made the great mistake of not organizing the distribution of spices within Western Europe for their own profit; they gave too great concessions in return for loans, as for example, an almost exclusive right for a time to the Italian house of Affaitadi to buy spices at Lisbon for sale in Antwerp. They lacked the resources to outfit large flotillas and/or to fight the French, Dutch, and the English, and they were unable to safeguard their interests after union with Spain (1580).

The Spaniards endeavored to meet the exigencies of the new situation by erecting a mixed system of government and private enterprise. The state furnished the galleons to escort privately owned vessels which yearly made the trip as a fleet to the New World and back. This system seems to have worked well until Spain became so weakened by foreign wars that the government could not keep up its part of the arrangements. In the end, foreigners were able to break into the trade monopoly by smuggling and through the Asiento agreement and to operate successfully because of the lower prices which they could quote to the colonials.[9] From the early eighteenth century onward, Spain's trading position worsened rapidly and in the early nineteenth century its colonies in Latin America, except for Cuba, became independent.

The English, Dutch, and French worked out still other arrangements to exploit the possibilities of overseas trade. Here royal houses played but minor roles. The Tudors probably did not have the personal means to engage in trade on a large scale; the Stuarts in the seventeenth century were no better off, for the rise in prices increased the costs of government, higher taxes made the rulers unpopular, and the unpopularity involved them in a struggle for power. The Dutch, for their part, had no royal house, their form of government being republican. The French kings were so taken up in foreign conflicts or in questions of royal succession before Louis XIV, who reigned from 1643 to 1715, none of them was in a position to turn his own fortune or that of the state toward commercial enterprise. Thus the main burden of organizing for the exploitation of overseas trade fell upon private entrepreneurs.

As we have already seen, late medieval experience furnished some

---

[9] The first inroad into the monopoly occurred when the Spanish sold the right to bring slaves to Spanish America to the Portuguese. This Asiento was surrendered briefly to the French in 1701, but the French lost it to the English at the Peace of Utrecht in 1713. In addition to the slave trade, the English had permission to send one ship a year, the *navio de permiso,* to the New World and this offered a splendid opportunity for smuggling.

hints as to what methods businessmen might employ to solve some of their problems. From the Mediterranean, enterprisers had the example of multiple partnerships in which all the partners were active in management, of the commenda in which some of the partners were merely investors and hence were known as sleeping partners, of loans secured by cargo or ship, that is, the respondentia loan and bottomry contract, respectively, and of sea loans in which the lender advanced money to a shipper with the understanding that he would get a relatively large return if the voyage succeeded. Furthermore, sixteenth-century businessmen could profit from studying the case of those medieval traders who had banded together to get special commercial privileges from territorial princes and who shared common expenses of warehouses, hotels, and protection while traveling.

From medieval practice, therefore, as well as from common sense, it was clear that capital requirements for the new commercial enterprises could be provided in two ways: either by bringing capitalists together in the same enterprise as active operators or by bringing them together in undertakings in which they were strictly investors with no managerial responsibilities. When recourse was had to the former arrangement, the resulting form of business organization was the regulated company, as in the case of the English Merchant Adventurers, the Eastland Company, the Levant Company, and the Muscovy Company. In each instance, merchants got monopoly rights to trade in certain areas; they pooled their resources to buy or hire ships, and they elected officials who laid down the main lines of every program. But merchants in these companies actually traded on their own, as in the Spanish case. With their own funds they bought goods which they wanted to take to foreign markets; they did their own selling, and they bought up foreign products for their home customers. They simply shared certain expenses to keep capital requirements of the individual to a minimum and to distribute risks of loss.

The regulated company had its drawbacks, for competition among members for business abroad was keen and the allocation of blame if a voyage failed led inevitably to animosities, recriminations, and dissolutions. Therefore, from the beginning of the seventeenth century, the alternative form of organization—combining the capital of investors rather than combining active tradesmen—became more common. Here the practice was for an entrepreneur or group of entrepreneurs who wanted to launch a specified business to issue shares of stock and to offer them to the investing public at a given price. Let us suppose that the English entrepreneur in a colonial trading venture estimated that the capital need of his project would be £100,000. To raise this sum a thousand shares at £100 par value would be issued. The organizers would buy some of the shares, perhaps enough to keep control of the offices and policy-making bodies, each share having one vote, and sell the rest.

What investors had, then, was part ownership of a tangible business—of the actual property that the money might be spent for. If the business prospered and its property increased in value, they got not only a share in the earnings which might be distributed in the form of dividends, but also they profited by the fact that their stock would go up in price. If the business failed and was liquidated, the most that they could lose was the amount of their investment. Moreover, they could not be held liable for the company's debts to the extent of all their property, as would be the case if they were active managers.

This joint-stock arrangement was one of the most important inventions in business organization of all time. Its greatest advantage was that it could tap the savings of very large numbers who had liquid capital at their disposal and thus could bring together the sums that were needed for large enterprise. It furnished the public a way of putting its capital to work, even in small amounts, without involving the investors in complicated tasks; it limited investors' liability; and it permitted the stockholder to get cash when needed by the simple expedient of selling some or all of his holdings. Lastly, the joint form of business organization had the advantage of not coming to an end upon the death of any one of the owners, as did individually owned businesses. Those who inherited the shares of the deceased owners simply became the new owners, and the business went forward as though nothing had happened. This allowed very long-range planning and gave continuity to policies. In brief, the joint-stock company had so many advantageous features that the wonder is it was not developed much earlier.

The first joint-stock ventures of which we know were attempted by the English for overseas trade in the middle of the sixteenth century, as in the case of the Guinea or African Company and Drake's voyage of 1577–1580.[10] Not until the establishment and success of the English East India Company, chartered December 31, 1600, did this form of business actually come into its own. This new concern was launched, interestingly enough, by men who had had experience with a regulated company—the Levant Company—and the first minutes of the Company were kept in the books of the Levant enterprise. For the first voyage of the East India

[10] Queen Elizabeth was one of the purchasers of shares in this venture, which explains why she was able to share in the profits, as we have seen above. She was so delighted when her investment paid off that she knighted Drake on the quarter-deck of his ship. The privateer became Sir Francis on the spot.

Company the founders sold shares amounting to 68,000 pounds to some two hundred investors, then when the ships got back to port, they divided both profits *and* capital among the stockholders. Obviously such temporary arrangements made planning difficult and the raising of sufficient funds both uncertain and expensive;[11] so, as the Company's ventures became more regular, a permanent capital was established and a permanent organization created (1657).

The East India Company was granted by its charter the privilege of being the only English concern which could trade in the East Indies. In addition it was charged with setting up its authority in places where it was to operate and in administering these areas. In brief, in return for a trade monopoly the Company was given the task of performing all the acts of government in those regions under its jurisdiction. That this arrangement was, at first, favorable to the Company there can be no doubt, for profits were high, the voyage of 1612 paying 220 per cent on the investment. Nevertheless, there was another side to the ledger. The defense of the monopoly was expensive,[12] administrative costs in the East were high, and waging war caused heavy losses. Nevertheless, the Company went forward, even emerging from the long war with the French (1756–1763) with its trading position strengthened. In fact, it was not until free-trade ideas became well established that the Company lost its trade monopoly (1833). Not until it appeared incapable of meeting modern colonial requirements in the Sepoy Rebellion of 1857 did it lose its function of colonial administrator.

Almost as old in the history of joint-stock companies as the English East India Company was the Dutch East India Company, chartered March 20, 1602. Like its English counterpart, this concern grew out of multiple partnerships organized, much like the English regulated companies, and out of temporary joint-stock companies, created for individual voyages to open routes to the source of spices in the East. Moreover, the charter of the Dutch Company was similar in many respects to that of the English. It provided that the Company should have a monopoly of trade in all the territory between the Cape of Good Hope and the Straits of Magellan. It bestowed upon the Company the right to exercise in this region all the privileges, prerogatives, and powers usually held by sovereign states—to seize and defend territories within its sphere of action, to make peace, to levy taxes, to administer justice, and to make local laws.

---

[11] Amounts needed for financing rose rapidly. For the third voyage, 1,629,040 pounds were raised.

[12] In 1628 a rival group was granted the monopoly of trade in the East in return for a loan to the government of 2 million pounds. The original company was soon able to merge with these newcomers and to continue on its way.

Moreover, in addition to these delegated powers, the Company had the assurance of the support of the Netherlandish government in case of trouble, for the same persons who controlled the Company directed the affairs of state.[13]

Similar, however, as were the Dutch and English East India Companies in origin and charter, they differed fundamentally in structure and administration. Whereas the management of the English Company was controlled by stockholders, who elected a board of directors and officers, the Dutch concern was run by political appointees. Thus, the general policies of the Company were laid down by a board of seventeen directors who were chosen from six local "chambers" on the basis of their importance. Thus there were eight directors from the chamber of Amsterdam, four from Zealand, and one or two each from Rotterdam, Delft, Hoorn, and Enkhuizen. The members of these local chambers, which conducted the local business of the Company, were selected by the Estates General of the various provinces. Even when fleets were fitted out, this political and decentralized character of the Company was maintained, each local chamber being charged with getting certain supplies and each assuming a proportion of the cost, again in proportion to its importance.

With this organization the Company achieved remarkable success. It took the spice trade away from the Portuguese and defended it successfully against both the English and the French. And when the spice business fell off, it found substitutes in coffee, tea, and cocoa. From 1605 to 1614 the Company paid dividends which fluctuated from 3 per cent to 75 per cent of the par value of its stock and during its entire existence, until its dissolution at the end of the eighteenth century, it averaged dividends, so it is said, of 18 per cent.

With the excellent profits records made by both the English and Dutch East India Companies in their early years, it seems strange that the French did not rush immediately into competition with them. Not until 1664, however, did the French East India Company come into being, and then it was established largely through the initiative of Louis XIV's remarkable minister for economic affairs, Colbert. It was he who convinced a group of private entrepreneurs that France should go after the lucrative Indies trade, and it was his support that made the project feasible. He gave the organizers of the Company a charter with privileges and prerogatives similar to those of the Dutch and English Companies; he awarded them the assets of the French colony of Madagascar, and when the French investing public failed to take up but half of the

---

[13] In return, certain of the Company's profits and a portion of the value of captured Spanish and Portuguese ships went to the government.

8,200,000 livres of stock, it was he who got the King to give the concern the 4,000,000 livres lacking.

Unlike the English and Dutch East India Companies, the French Company did not have at first a good record of earnings. During the first twenty years its losses were heavy, in part because of the Dutch War (1672–1678), but the Company was reorganized and kept doggedly on. It established trading posts, notably at Surat and Pondichéry, got into the importation of textiles, including cottons, traded with Siam and China, and in spite of many vicissitudes made progress. In the middle of the eighteenth century, it had reached a point of importance and power at which it could contest under the leadership of its most brilliant colonial, Joseph François Dupleix, control of India with the English Company, which was at the time directed by one of its greatest leaders, Robert Clive. Although the attempt failed and the French Company henceforth declined until it vanished in the French Revolution, it might have been successful with greater support from the motherland.

In any case, the three great East India Companies thoroughly established the joint-stock form of business organization for colonial enterprise. It was employed in the Dutch West India Company (founded 1621), in the French West India Company (1664), and in such English enterprises as the Virginia Company, the Massachusetts Bay Company, and the Hudson's Bay Company. By the end of the seventeenth century, indeed, the joint-stock company had become so seasoned and its advantages so generally recognized that it was being used in domestic business undertakings like banking, mining, and even manufacturing; in fact, wherever the needs for capital were great.[14]

As joint-stock companies grew in number and in capital, the floating of issues of stock and the trading of existing shares became big business, so big, in fact, that a new occupation came into being—that of stock-broking. In the pursuit of their trade brokers assembled first at places where men of wealth congregated, as at commodity exchanges, like the Royal Exchange in London (1571), the Amsterdam Bourse (1611), or at coffeehouses, but eventually they founded exchanges exclusively for trading in shares, like the London Stock Exchange (1773). Here the business of stock trading gradually took form, including the practice of speculating on rises or falls in the price of stock. With the earnings of companies fluctuating widely and with many new concerns being established to undertake uncertain projects, like trying to find a Northwest Passage to China, "booms" and "busts" were frequent. The most

[14] Among the first of the joint-stock companies for domestic enterprise in England were the Mineral and Battery Works Company and the Mines Royal Company for silver and copper mining.

remarkable of all such incidents was the South Sea Bubble which burst in 1720. It was of such proportions and injured so many people that it put the joint-stock form of business organization under a cloud from which it did not entirely emerge until a century later.

Cultural Consequences of European Overseas Expansion

So widespread were the effects of expansion of Europe overseas that hardly a single phase of European culture was left untouched by it. Nevertheless, it would be a mistake to consider all of the new trends in Europe's economic development as primarily the result of expansion. Thus, although colonial markets added greatly to trade, home markets far exceeded those of overseas areas, and hence the two should be treated together when consideration is given to the pressure which demand placed upon the means of production—to what is commonly called the Industrial Revolution. Similarly, the development of a money economy, of capitalism, and of capitalist institutions, accelerated as it was by colonial commerce and the importation of bullion from overseas, needs to be studied in the context of Europe's total experience and not simply as a phase of overseas expansion. Also, in spite of the fact that colonial trade contributed greatly to the rise of those cities which were to give Western civilization most of its styles of art, its social classes, its leading ideologies, and its patterns of government, it would be a mistake to discuss the rise of cities in terms of expansion alone.

Although such topics must be left for later pages, two subjects should be introduced here as consequences of the expansion of Europe. The first is the effect on European life of new products from overseas; the second is the impact of expansion on the European mind.

The introduction of cocoa from the New World in the sixteenth century, the importation of tea from the East in the seventeenth century, and greater supplies of coffee from the Near East, from Java, and later from the New World had an almost revolutionary effect upon the European's breakfast menu and upon his social habits. Henceforth, one or the other of these beverages was to oust wine in the early morning or to supplement the other usual breakfast drink, milk, especially in cities. Moreover, these new drinks led to the establishment of entirely new places for people to congregate for social intercourse—to the founding of coffeehouses or cafés and of tea rooms and chocolate shops. They became, to a greater extent than had ever been beer halls and wine taverns, social centers, writers' and artists' clubs, political forums, reading clubs, and even business offices. They were an entirely new institution for the dissemination of news and for the exchange of ideas.

Another product which was important to European life because of new supplies from overseas was sugar. This sweetening, much cheaper than honey, had much to do in making coffee, tea, and chocolate popular and had a revolutionary effect on cooking. It made possible and certainly more available to all economic classes a long list of pastries; it allowed the fabrication of a completely new line of sweet alcoholic drinks, the cordials and the liqueurs of the present day; and it permitted the expansion of the candy trade to unheard-of proportions.

America also gave the Old World tobacco and thereby provided Europeans who used it comfort, snob prestige, and nose and throat irritation. This weed was introduced into Spain in 1558, and somewhat later by Jean Nicot, whence the word nicotine, into France, and by Sir Walter Raleigh into England. In spite of considerable opposition to its use (Benjamin Franklin once said that if God had intended that man smoke he would have turned up his nose to provide an adequate draft), tobacco became ever more popular. The typical country squire of the seventeenth century is invariably pictured with a long-stemmed clay pipe in his hands. And the effete dandy of the same period is represented as preening himself with a pinch of snuff, belittling his social inferiors with a snap of his little snuffbox, and as astounding the uninitiate with a prodigious number of sneezes.

Among new food products introduced into Europe from America, the most important was undoubtedly the potato. This lowly tuber has the supreme advantage of being one of the few vegetables that one can eat day after day without fatiguing the taste buds and of providing more calories per acre than any other easily cultivated crop. Introduced into Spain in the sixteenth century, it encountered considerable hostility. It is said that as late as the eighteenth century Louis XV of France wore a potato flower in his buttonhole to show that it was not poisonous! Yet the potato made progress, and became a standard article of diet throughout Western Europe and an absolutely essential one in some regions, like Ireland.

Furthermore, the New World gave the Old three other staple foods, codfish, Indian corn or maize, and the tomato. Although the cod had been known in Europe before the sixteenth century, catches off the Newfoundland and New England coasts became so large and the dried and salted fish so well preserved that the fish could be marketed at remarkably low prices. Thus it became a regular part of the diet of the poor and to some extent took the place of herring on days of abstinence. For its part, maize became widely grown because of its large yield per acre as a grain for livestock, but entered human diets only in a few districts, like the Piedmont in Italy and Rumania. And tomatoes eventually became widely used to give flavor to numerous bland products, like pastes.

Among luxury food products, the Old World got the turkey from the

New and the guinea hen from Africa, which added variety to the poultry menu and as semiluxuries came to be traditional meats on very festive occasions. Among medicines, Europe received several herbs, but quinine or Jesuits' bark for relieving fevers from Peru and opium for diminishing pain were of the greatest value. Among industrial raw products, it got a number of dyes, of which indigo was the most famous, and eventually large supplies of cotton which were to revolutionize the textile trade.

The expansion of Europe overseas resulted, also, in the introduction of or greater supplies of many finished goods which the well-to-do acquired for comfort or for prestige. There were silks which went into elegant clothes, rugs, carpets, and hangings to cover bare floors and walls; fine porcelain (chinaware) to supplement that of Europe or to supplant the more common earthenware, and new perfumes to gratify the olfactory sense—and if one can believe our present advertisements, to entice the unwary male. There were cotton textiles from India and Persia, which gave rise to a style demand at the end of the seventeenth and beginning of the eighteenth century that seemed insatiable. And there were products from China, such as embroideries, fans, umbrellas, screens, porcelains, and the Sedan chair,[15] in such number that an entirely new style was created—the *chinoiserie* of the eighteenth century.

As these material things from realms beyond the seas were making their mark on Europe, knowledge, imagined or real, of these same regions was having an impact on European ideologies and attitudes. When Thomas More (1477–1535) penned his *Utopia* and Francis Bacon (1561–1626) wrote his *New Atlantis*, they not only placed their dream worlds overseas, but furnished them with what they imagined were some of the characteristics of life among American natives, including a much greater equality in wealth than existed in their Europe. Montaigne (1553–1592), Montesquieu (1689–1755), Voltaire (1694–1778), and Jean Jacques Rousseau (1712–1778) used the example of the "noble savage" to criticize many of Europe's man-made institutions and to plead for their obliteration; Thomas Hobbes (1588–1678), on the contrary, argued that life among savages was violent and that to emerge from a state of nature it was necessary to erect governments with power to maintain order. Expansion overseas became also a literary theme, the greatest of modern epics, the *Lusiads* by the Portuguese Luiz Vaz de Camoëns (1524–1580), singing of the voyage of Vasco da Gama.

In addition to imaginative and fanciful treatments of overseas lands, there were also factual accounts which tried to provide Europe with an accurate body of geographical knowledge. There was the Catholic mis-

---

[15] So-called because it was introduced at Sedan, France.

sionary and staunch defender of the natives in Latin America, Bartolomé de Las Casas (1476–1566), whose *Brief Account of the Destruction of the West Indies* (1554) and *History of the Indies*, not published until the nineteenth century, are justly famous. There were the French explorers, Jacques Cartier (1491–1557), who wrote a *Brief Account of the Voyage Made to the Islands*, and Samuel de Champlain (1567–1635), who published several books of his explorations in the Great Lakes. There was Richard Hakluyt (1553–1616), who began the great collection known as *The Principal Navigations, Voyages, Traffiques, and Discoveries of the English Nation*, that was continued after his death by Samuel Purchas. And there was Gerardus Mercator (1512–1594), who constructed the most accurate and up-to-date maps of the sixteenth century and who invented the Mercator projection for showing the round world and its parts on flat surfaces.

In general, it is safe to say that contact with distant civilizations made Europe more firmly impressed than ever with knowledge arrived at by observation and by verification—with efforts to explain, without recourse to the supernatural, why one event in a given series followed another. Furthermore, this contact made Europe more conscious of its own faults and desirous, as if to prove that it was superior to all the rest, of a society where people lived according to known and just laws, where is was possible to create and enjoy works of art of a universally recognized high order, and where there was economic security for all. In fact, relations with the rest of the world tended to make Europe formulate its concept of civilization.

CHAPTER 9

Science, Technology, and the
Early Industrial Revolution—1500 to 1700

Science and Technology in Western Culture

Of all the remarkable aspects of Western culture, none is more distinctive than Western knowledge of and control over physical things. Developments within the last 450 years have permitted the West nearly to triple its members' expectation of life at birth. They have made available for human use a variety of materials, whether located deep in the earth's crust or high in the heavens, that hitherto had been deemed of no importance. They have allowed the West to eliminate famines, to move mountains, to conquer distances, and to learn many of the innermost secrets of nature. All these things Western man has accomplished chiefly because of his science and his technology, crucial advances in which were made in the sixteenth and seventeenth centuries.

The essence of the new science was, as has already been mentioned, the acquiring of knowledge based upon accurate observation, upon the quantification of observations, and upon the verification of the data thus obtained by the use of mathematics and by repetition of the experiment or observation. This science was, furthermore, a system of knowledge in which related events were established as having taken place, in which events were arranged in a necessary sequence, that is, a sequence without which the events could not have taken place, and in which relation-

160

ships between two events or among all in the sequence, both of a qualitative and quantitative character, were accurately determined. Henceforth Western man was not satisfied with trial-and-error methods, with rules of thumb, or with supernatural explanations of what had happened, at least as regards material things. He wanted to have verifiable answers to what, why, when, where, and how an event had taken place and to be able to repeat or to observe again for his own satisfaction the event or events in question.

The essence of the new technology, on the other hand, was the development of ways of performing tasks by machines driven by energy from nonhuman sources and of ways of rendering materials, especially those of an inorganic nature, useful to humankind. Western man obtained from machines moved by mechanical power or chemical or physical reactions the services of a number of "slaves," which allowed him greatly to increase his output in terms of his own input of energy. Furthermore, the new technology enabled him to increase the supply of available materials by finding ways of rendering useful what was abundant in nature. Thus coal came into use as a source of energy to supplement wood. Iron and steel were developed as building materials to supplant wood and to strengthen masonry. Hydroelectric power was perfected to reduce the use of coal, and the fission of uranium bids fair to become a partial substitute for coal. Rayon and acrylic fibers are taking the place of silk and to some extent also of cotton and wool, and plastics have found a use in places where steel, wood, or rubber were once employed. It may have been that the new technology stressed quantity rather than luxury production, but it permitted a tripling of the population of Western Europe from the early eighteenth century onward and perhaps a quintupling of the goods available for human consumption per capita of the population.

The development of this technology and of the new science was long acoming. Both had roots in the Middle Ages, and deeper roots reaching back into the remote past of mankind. Medieval man had displayed an intense desire to know about all kinds of things, and although scholastic philosophers had endeavored to obtain knowledge by deduction from premises derived from such authorities as St. Augustine, the Bible, Plato, and Aristotle, their very curiosity, disputations, and doubts led to a search for other methods for finding the "truth." Men of the Middle Ages had also displayed an interest in techniques and, as we have already seen, improved such contrivances as the water wheel, the windmill, and the horse collar and developed new ways of transforming common and abundant materials into useful products, like sand into glass and iron ore by means of blast furnaces into cast iron.

From such beginnings, from the accumulation of much detail, and from an intensified interest in things of this world, there was realized in the sixteenth and seventeenth centuries a new synthesis in both science and technology. In science this synthesis was brought about by a galaxy of intellectual giants. Among them was Francis Bacon (1561-1626), who made an appeal for direct observation and the use of inductive rather than deductive logic. There was Nicholas Copernicus (1473-1543), who advanced the theory that the earth revolved around the sun rather than the sun around the earth, which was a direct attack upon authority— a theory which was refined by Johann Kepler (1571-1630). There was Galileo Galilei (1564-1642), who carried on a number of experiments which allowed him to determine the rate of acceleration of falling bodies, to establish the isochronism of the pendulum, that is, that a pendulum makes its swings in regular intervals of time irrespective of the length of the arcs described, and to state that the trajectory of a cannon ball is a parabola. There was William Gilbert (1540-1603), who experimented with magnets and laid a foundation for electricity. There was William Harvey (1578-1657), who through painstaking research learned that the heart was a muscular pump and that blood circulated throughout the body. There was René Descartes (1596-1650), who believed that the physical world operated mechanically and who urged the use of mathematics to describe its movements. And there was Isaac Newton (1642-1727), who by his development of calculus, his statement of the laws of gravitation, and his enunciation of the laws of motion contributed much to the realization of Descartes' dream—establishing a conception of the world as a great machine.

In the short space of two centuries new methods of seeking knowledge and a new attitude toward the world came into being. This "scientific revolution," as historians have come to call it, was among the greatest changes in the intellectual life of man.

To what extent the scientific revolution and the new synthesis in technology, or the "technological revolution," were related and acted upon each other, it is difficult to say. What is clear, however, is that both movements emphasized experimentation, exact observation, and mathematical expression of findings. Moreover, in both science and technology men manifested an intellectual courage without parallel. No problem seemed to be so difficult that it was automatically relegated to the category of the impossible and thus discarded. Men of the new science and of the new technology had confidence in their methods and were willing to tackle everything from explaining the entire cosmos to making water run "uphill." There is no doubt but what scientists made use of new techniques, like that of lens grinding which made possible the telescope, for their observations and their experiments. And there is no question but what scientists gave expression to ideas, like that of using steam to force water up a spout, which were picked up by engineers. Not yet, however, were men of science concerned with solving technological problems, nor did mechanical technicians rely on men of science for overcoming their difficulties. Only much later did "pure science" and "applied science" begin to cooperate closely.

The technological revolution of the sixteenth and seventeenth centuries is to be further characterized by the fact that the widest and deepest industrial changes resulting from it seem to have been realized in England and Scotland, thus effecting a locational shift in the center of industrial activity to the north. Indeed, England seems to have experienced, as we have seen, an "industrial revolution" from approximately 1540 to 1640 which laid the foundation for an even greater "industrial revolution" in that country in the eighteenth and early nineteenth centuries. Furthermore, the new technological methods of production stressed the output of staple goods for mass consumption. This was of great moment, for it launched much of our present concern with economic growth and it helped to establish the basic ideology in Western culture that all people should be free from want and should partake of economic well-being. Moreover, businessmen came to learn that production for mass consumption offered greater possibilities for making profits than luxury production for a select few, for the wants of the many are less quickly satisfied than those of a restricted elite. Thus there came about a concern for the purchasing power of the masses, for continuing investments in producers' goods to turn out products within the price range of large numbers, for effecting a division of labor and of adopting laborsaving devices, and for developing cheap materials to take the place of expensive ones. This emphasis upon quantity rather than upon luxuries was in keeping with Christian conceptions of welfare, with democratic ideas of well-being for all, and with capitalism's apparent need for expansion.

Coal and the First Industrial Revolution in England

Without any question one of the most crucial innovations in the technological revolution of the sixteenth and seventeenth centuries was the use of coal as a major source of heat energy. Although coal had been known for centuries in China and had been the object of some commerce toward the end of the Middle Ages from Newcastle-upon-Tyne, from Nottingham, and from Liége in what was to become Belgium, coal was never used systematically and upon a relatively large scale in industry until the second half of the sixteenth century. Then, as is always the case with all major innovations, a number of factors came together in England in fortuitous proportions and timing to result in the widespread use of this combustible.[1]

Perhaps the most impelling of all the conditions conducive to the use of coal were (1) the need for a cheap fuel to take the place of wood and (2) the presence of coal near the surface where it could easily be mined and near water transportation that allowed its being moved at low cost. The need for heat energy in England was extraordinarily great. The relatively cold climate required the heating of living and working quarters for a large portion of the year. Here the people drank beer or distilled liquors, the manufacture of which required heat. Here it was necessary to have many windows to light up interiors enough to permit close work, and the manufacture of glass took a great amount of fuel. Here salt could not be obtained by the sun's evaporation of water from sea brine, so water had to be gotten rid of by artificial heat. Here there had recently been a considerable development of alum production, of gunpowder manufacture, and of smelting, all of which required charcoal, and of shipbuilding, which took a great amount of lumber.

Under such demand the price of charcoal soared and that of ship-building timbers increased elevenfold from 1500 to 1640. In most Continental countries, like France and Italy, for example, a local shortage of wood simply drove lumbermen or charcoal burners farther into the mountains for supplies that were often floated down streams to market. In England, the almost complete absence of uninhabited forests precluded such a solution to the problem of the shortage of wood; whereas the importation of lumber except for quality use, like Baltic and later American timber for shipbuilding, was not feasible because of transportation costs. Coal was an obvious answer to England's fuel problem. At no other place in Europe was this substitute source of heat so readily available as there.

Still another important factor in the use of coal in industry in England was a greater economic expansion than in any other place in Europe from the middle of the sixteenth century to the middle of the seventeenth. The absence of devastating warfare at home allowed resources to be turned into productive activity. Between 1540 and 1640, population rose from three million to six million; and this 100 per cent increase put pressure upon the means of production to meet mass needs. And a number of new industries expanded very rapidly, like iron smelting by blast furnaces, the number of furnaces increasing from 3 to between 100 and 150 in this century.

[1] John U. Nef, *The Rise of the British Coal Industry*, 2 vols. (London: Routledge, 1932).

On the other hand, most of the Continental countries were torn by dynastic and religious wars from 1540 to 1640. Spain failed, in part, to make essential investments in industry because of the diversion of resources to wars against the Turks, the French, and the rebellious inhabitants of the Low Countries. The Spanish Netherlands suffered from the Spaniards' crusade against it and from the subsequent cutting off of its commerce from the sea. The production of cloth at Hondschoote, for example, fell from 80,000 pieces a year for the period 1560–1569 to 8,000 pieces for the period 1646–1649; the population of Antwerp declined from 100,000 in 1577 to some 30,000 in 1650. Italy suffered a relative setback with the shift of the center of commerce from the Mediterranean to the Atlantic. France was torn by the Wars of Religion, and the Germanies were wasted by the Thirty Years' War (1618–1648). The Northern Netherlands was the country with the best chance of rivaling England's development, but it turned its energies heavily in the direction of commerce and to industries without a mass market appeal, like shipbuilding, and besides it had no known resources of coal.

Still another reason for England's rapid industrial development from 1540 to 1640 was the relation between prices and wages. Henry VIII devalued in 1536 and 1539, which caused a price rise, it should be noted, before the influx of metals from the New World began on a large scale. These devaluations had the effect of raising prices, but as was usual, wages did not go up at the same rate. Thus because commodity prices were up, real wages down, and costs of production in terms of prices low, the opportunity to make large profits encouraged entrepreneurs to undertake new business ventures. Apparently this situation gave a shot-in-the-arm to English economic activity, but was not protracted enough drastically to impair the purchasing power of the masses. Prices of goods consumed by the lower classes did not go up so fast as those consumed by the rich, probably because of technological improvements in the manufacture of staples that kept costs down. Moreover, from 1600 to 1640 wages increased as fast as prices of consumers' goods, those of miners even advancing at a more rapid rate than prices.[2]

Furthermore, England's break with the Roman Catholic Church had some relevance to the country's economic expansion from 1540 to 1640. As we have previously seen, the Protestant Revolt did not cause a sudden change in attitude toward the accumulation of wealth or toward the approval of such capitalistic practices as the taking of interest; Catholic businessmen had for long been trying to get rich, and Protestant

[2] John U. Nef, *Naissance de la civilisation industrielle* (Paris, 1954), pp. 122ff. Also by the same author, "Prices and Industrial Capitalism in France and England," *The Economic History Review*, vol. 7, no. 2, pp. 180–181, 1937.

theorists did not adopt doctrines favorable to interest charges until after 1650. But the Reformation did have the effect of adding at least a few economically unemployed holy men and women to the labor force and hence of making them more productive. The seizure of Church lands and their sale or gift to laymen meant a greater economic development of these properties. Indeed, many of the new mining enterprises were on lands previously owned by the Church or religious orders, which had never shown any signs of exploiting them on a large scale, and many of the large entrepreneurial investments in coal mining were made precisely by the new owners of former Church lands. Finally, the Protestants, by stressing the desire to create a heaven on earth and thus of establishing a greater degree of economic well-being among the lower classes than had existed previously gave a fillip to the production of consumers' goods for the masses.

Also new investments in England seem to have been directed into industries designed for quantity production, whereas on the Continent such placements of capital were made especially in luxury trades. Thus, in France there was a development of the silk industry, in the Netherlands of faience, and in the Germanies of silver mining, with production for the masses being carried on in traditional ways. In England, on the other hand, the greatest advances were made in such industries as glassmaking, brewing, salt refining, sugar refining, soapmaking, and the production of alum and gunpowder. Each of these industries adopted coal as its chief source of heat energy and thus gave an impetus to the use of a great resource that had been stored up over eons of time. The only major fuel-using industry that still relied on charcoal was iron metallurgy which, for technical reasons that were not resolved until the eighteenth century, could not employ coal.

New Techniques in Mining and Metallurgy

The beginning of the use of coal on a fairly large scale in England at the middle of the sixteenth century had important consequences for future economic developments. Not only did coal provide man with an abundant source of heat energy, but it led to larger production units. It accustomed businessmen, because of the high cost of coal-using equipment, to make larger investments in industrial undertakings. It resulted in organizing larger bodies of labor and of effecting a division of labor, and it gave an impetus to the development of new techniques of production in the use of heat energy and in mining.

Another important source of technological change in the sixteenth century was the production of silver in Central Europe. During most of the Middle Ages, the greater part of this metal had been obtained from lead ores along the Rhine in the Germanies, in Bohemia, in Hungary, and in the eastern Alps. By the fifteenth century supplies from these sources had been greatly reduced because of the exhaustion of the mines, but the demand for silver was increasing because of the need for making payments in precious metals for Eastern goods and because of the need for a greater volume of coins. Under the circumstances recourse was had to copper ores that contained silver, even though the recovery of silver was somewhat difficult. Silver had been separated from lead simply by heating the ore to the melting point of lead and then letting this metal flow off. Such a simple method of refining could not be used in the case of copper ore, so lead was mixed with it in order to absorb the silver and then the silver was subsequently separated from the lead. Thanks to this process carried on in the famous *Saigerhütte*, the production of silver and copper in Central Europe increased some five times from 1460 to 1540.

The mining of copper and silver ore and the mining of coal led to the driving of deep shafts, to the development of greater power-driven pumps to get water out of the diggings, to new hoisting techniques, to new power-driven machinery for crushing the ore, and to new smelting processes. Quite logically, therefore, some of the most remarkable feats in mining engineering in the sixteenth and early seventeenth centuries occurred in England and Central Europe and the leading work of the period on mining and metallurgy, *De Re Metallica* (1556), was by a German, Georg Bauer, who is better known by his Latinized name of Agricola.

Indeed, efforts to remove water from mines accounted for many important developments in machinery during the sixteenth century. Inasmuch as suction pumps, the best-known pump at the time, can raise water only some 34 feet and mines ran down to 600 feet, the suction pump was employed only with the greatest difficulty. Agricola describes, however, a system in which suction pumps were arranged in series, one above the other, and all were worked by an intricate arrangement of levers driven by a water wheel. Such a mechanism was awkward, subject to frequent breakdowns, and not very efficient, so the search went on for better methods of getting water out of the mines. Chains of pots, like those used in ancient times for irrigation, were tried, but they could not cope with large flows. Force pumps, in which a plunger forces water up a pipe, were introduced, but they broke frequently because of the high pressure on the sides of the pipe at the base of the column of water. Then balls of horsehair attached to a chain and drawn up through a pipe with its bottom end in a sump, that is, in water, were employed

Pumping Machinery. One of the most serious of early mining problems was to keep the diggings free of water. Pails on endless chains were used and later, as this picture shows, a series of vacuum pumps. They were activated by a series of levers, raised and lowered by a "crank and shaft" arrangement. The shaft was turned by a waterwheel. (*From Agricola, De Re Metallica.*)

with some success. Also Archimedes' screws, repeated several times, were used, but they, too, were not very satisfactory because of the heights involved. Finally, the problem of raising water, made still more imperative by the need of better water supplies for the rapidly growing towns and cities, led to the suggestion by Baptista Porta in 1560 of filling a pipe with steam, of condensing the steam to create a vacuum in the pipe, and then of letting air pressure force water up the pipe to an outlet. It led, also, to a project by Solomon de Gaus in 1615 for a steam-driven fountain which was to operate much as a steam kettle with a long spout and a tight-fitting lid does when it throws water from the spout. Here were two principles which were to contribute very directly toward experiments that led to the invention of the steam engine in the eighteenth century.

Another important problem in mining is hoisting. For this work many ingenious devices were employed such as the horse whim, whereby a chain to which was attached a bucket was wound around a drum that was revolved by the draft of horses. This machine involved heavy equipment and such novel gadgets as the friction brake to control the speed at which the bucket was lowered. Hoisting also led to an intricate device in which a water wheel 36 feet in diameter with two sets of buckets could be run forwards or backwards by a workman who controlled the flow of water to the wheel.

Once ore or minerals were on the surface of the ground, there were the problems of crushing, loading, and transporting. Carrying was greatly facilitated by the development of crude railways, which were usually just planks laid on the ground along which carts were run, and by the use of water carrying whenever possible, even if this meant the digging of new canals, dredging rivers, building locks, or constructing docks. Many of the first "railways" ran from pit heads to nearby rivers, as from St. Etienne in France to the Loire, and many of the early coal mines in England were opened near the sea to get advantage of water transportation. Loading was done more and more by chutes and hoists; crushing or stamping ore was increasingly accomplished by water-driven trip hammers. Even Branca's proposal for an impulse steam turbine (1629) was portrayed as activating hammers for crushing.

Mining also involved engineering feats of shoring and of retaining-wall construction requiring great ingenuity and audacity. One of the most curious engineering accomplishments of the time was to be found at Culross, Scotland. Here Sir George Bruce, having acquired lands confiscated from the Church, discovered that he possessed rich veins of coal which ran under the sea. To exploit this treasure he built a pit head on the shore at a point that was under water at high tide, but completely

A Mine Winch. To raise loads from mines was still another serious problem in the sixteenth century. In this picture a load is being lifted by means of a chain wound around a winch. The winch is run by a horse-drawn sweep above ground and the power is transmitted to the shaft by a system of gears. Note the braking device on the large wooden drum. (*From Agricola, De Re Metallica.*)

Sixteenth-century Forge. There was considerable advance made in the technique of ironworking between the sixth century B.C. and the sixteenth century A.D. At the latter date a stronger draft was furnished by a taller chimney and by the use of large accordion bellows made of leather and worked by a water wheel. The smith is forming his bloom, however, much as at an earlier date. The tongs are the same and little change has taken place in the hammer and anvil. The smith in the foreground is probably shaping the product by hammering and is tempering the metal by dowsing it in water. (*From Agricola, De Re Metallica, 1556.*)

Sixteenth-century Blast Furnace. The blast furnace was a rather tall furnace in which a hot fire was provided by charcoal and a strong draft induced by a high chimney and bellows. The furnace was charged from the top with charcoal and ore, piles of which lie in the right foreground. Mallets for breaking up the large pieces lie in the center foreground. In the left foreground is the ever-present anvil. Metal formed at the base of the furnace and was drawn off from the impurities which were either burned or came out as slag. (*From Agricola, De Re Metallica, 1556.*)

above the water-mark at low tide. To protect the pit head at high tide he built a retaining wall; then he constructed a dock so that barges could be loaded directly from the mine at high tide, and finally he installed elaborate pumping machinery to keep the whole from being flooded.

The story is told that when James I was taken by Sir George to visit this mine the party went underground at low tide when the encroachment of the sea was not easily foreseen. After having spent some time inspecting the shafts and galleries, the party emerged at high tide. When James I, who was not notable for physical courage, saw the sea all about, he began to cry treason. Sir George had to do some fast explaining to quiet his king.

While mining gave a stimulus to the use of machinery, to the adoption of mechanical power, and to remarkable achievements in engineering, innovations in the ferrous metal industry were being introduced on a scale which was to revolutionize methods of production and cheapen iron articles to a point where they would be within the reach of all. Here the crucial change was the widespread use of the blast furnace, which, as we have previously seen, was invented in the fourteenth century. No longer was it necessary to forge iron at great labor and with considerable waste of metal. It was now possible to separate the metal from most impurities by heating the ore to the melting point of iron and then letting it run off, much as in the case of silver smelting. This technique of smelting iron became firmly established in the period under discussion in the southeast of England, in the Midlands, in the Bishopric of Liége, and in Sweden. In these places, also, molten iron right from the furnaces was cast for a number of purposes, such as the making of anchors, nails, chimney plaques, and kettles, or was run through rolling mills to make sheets for iron stoves and the like. These articles became exceedingly cheap by comparison with what they had been and were henceforth objects of mass consumption, but their price was to fall even more in the eighteenth century when technical difficulties that had prevented the use of coal in smelting were solved and this cheaper fuel to a large extent replaced charcoal. Then began that close affiliation between coal and iron that was to play such an important role in the subsequent development and location of industry.

Advances in Mechanical Techniques

Important as were the extended use of coal and the smelting of iron and silver in effecting changes in industry during the sixteenth and seventeenth centuries, other innovations were made which also tended to increase production for mass consumption. These consisted primarily in the development of power from falling water and the wind and from the application of this power to an ever greater number of machines that could accomplish tasks which had previously been performed by man.

Evidence of the search for mechanical power and of mechanical contrivances is to be found in the writings of all the great mechanical engineers of the day. Perhaps the most noteworthy confirmation of the trends of the age in mechanics is to be found in the *Notebooks* of Leonardo da Vinci (1452–1579)—painter, sculptor, anatomist, military planner, engineer, and genius extraordinary. During his lifetime Leonardo filled over 5,000 pages with drawings of his conception of things, most of which he explained in "mirror writing," that is, in writing that could be read only when reflected in a mirror, so that unscrupulous pryers into his affairs would be discouraged. Even though the *Notebooks* were published only well after Leonardo's death, they were early read by many persons and had a considerable influence upon succeeding generations of technicians.

Support, also, of the drive to make fuller use of water power and of machines is to be found in the work of Georg Agricola to which reference has already been made in connection with mining, in Agostino Ramelli's *Le Diverse e Artificiose Macchine* (1588), in which many of Leonardo's suggestions are developed, and in Zonca's (1568–1602) *Novo Teatro di Macchine e Edifici* (1607), in which special attention is given to propelling such heavy machines as the fulling mill by power from water wheels.

In this period little improvement seems to have been made in the design of the water wheel, although Leonardo made suggestions which were preliminary to the invention of the water turbine in the nineteenth century. What was of particular significance were the ingenious uses to which the "overshot wheel" was put.[3] From Agricola and Zonca, one can get some idea of the many purposes to which water power was put for want of any other satisfactory source of great power and one can get also some notion of the difficulties of using the water wheel to meet so many industrial needs. Moreover, it should be remembered that power from water depended upon an abundant and steady flow of falling water and hence was available in only certain places and even in them frequently for only limited seasons of the year. Water power was thus employed primarily in hilly or mountainous country and in industries in which the materials to be processed, like grain, could be transported

---

[3] The "overshot wheel" was one in which water fell on the wheel at the top. The weight of the water, as well as the force with which the water hit the wheel, turned the wheel. In the "undershot wheel" water hit the blades at the bottom of the wheel. Hence the force of the water was all-important.

NVOVO THEATRO

MOLINO TERAGNO D'ACQVA.

Grist Mill Driven by Water. Advance in the milling of flour can be seen here by comparing this scene with that of the quern. Here is mechanical power at work. Energy is provided by falling water, admitted into a sluice at the gate *C*. The speed of the water turns a simple paddle wheel. The rotary power is conveyed by shafts and gears to the millstones. Grain is dumped in the hopper and falls down between the revolving stones, which have been cut with grooves on their contiguous surfaces. The flour is scooped out of the bin by the miller on the steps and is then bagged. (*From Vittorio Zonca, Il Nuovo Teatro, 1656.*)

Windmills for Grinding Grain. Power for grinding was furnished by wind as well as by water. The two mills shown in the foreground are post mills, that is, they rest on posts. The whole mill has to be turned so that the arms will face into the wind. This construction limited the size of the mill and made the entire apparatus subject to accidents. An improved type was the turret mill, seen in the background, in which just the top turned so that the arms would face into the wind. This permitted the building of more durable structures out of masonry. Note the manner of transporting grain on the human back, on pack animal, and on carts. See also the millstones in the left foreground.

with comparative ease to the source of power and the finished products then be carried at relatively low cost to market.

The windmill had greater mobility than the water wheel, yet areas where strong and steady winds prevail are relatively few and even in them calms occur often enough to make the windmill unreliable as a source of readily available power. Furthermore, the traditional windmill had certain technical weaknesses which limited its effectiveness in industry. The so-called post mill was actually set upon a post so that the mill could be turned in order that its arms could be made to face into the wind. Such an arrangement restricted the size of the mill and had such other defects as making the mill hard to turn, getting out of level, and having a foundation that had to be repaired often. To overcome some of these difficulties Leonardo proposed attaching the arms of the mill to a turret atop the main mill that could be turned independently of the rest as need be. This proposal was worked out in detail by Ramelli

and was actually put into practice by Dutch engineers in the late sixteenth century. It greatly improved the efficiency of the windmill, but
wind as a source of power still left much to be desired.[4]

Although neither the windmill nor the water wheel was satisfactory
enough as a source of mechanical power to discourage men from seeking an alternative source in steam, these two devices were used so widely
that engineers came to devote much attention to problems of transmission of power. Da Vinci, for example, described shafts, pulleys, and belts.
He probably invented the roller chain drive and improved the block
chain drive and sprockets. He designed conical, spiral, and graduated
gears, roller bearings to reduce friction, and universal joints. He made
one roasting spit run with weights, as in contemporary clocks, and another which was activated by a propeller placed in a chimney to catch
the rising hot air. He made steel springs to provide power and got regularity into some of his apparatus by employing the pendulum. A society
which gave birth to all these devices was one that was using a considerable amount of power and carrying it to machines.

In this period of the "early industrial revolution" important inventions
were also made on machines that turned out goods, although changes
in this field were not so dramatic as those which were to be realized in
the eighteenth and nineteenth centuries. In spinning, Da Vinci proposed
the "flyer" which allowed spinning and quilling, that is, the twisting of
fibers into thread and the reeling of the finished thread on a bobbin at
the same time. This important step in making spinning fully automatic
was put into operation about 1530 by Johann Jürgen, whose spinning
wheel also had the treadle-and-crank arrangement so that the hands of
the operator would be entirely freed of the task of propelling. Leonardo
also designed power-driven silk reeling and twisting machines and a gig
mill, improved by Zonca, for raising the nap on cloth.

Another important contribution to the machinery of the textile industry
was the ribbon loom. It was so designed that the movements of the
weaver in making one ribbon were automatically transmitted to the
making of other ribbons. This apparatus appeared in Leyden in 1621
and by the end of the seventeenth century was in general use. As can
easily be imagined, the ribbon loom was an intricate piece of machinery
and a step in the attempts which were made to render weaving automatic. Then there was the all-important invention of a knitting machine
or stocking frame by the Reverend William Lee (1589) that permitted
making 1,000 or 1,500 stitches per minute compared with 100 stitches by
a fast hand knitter. Indeed, this invention threw such a fright into pro-

[4] The fantail which would keep the arms of the mill always facing into the wind
was invented in 1750.

fessional hand knitters that Lee became extremely unpopular in his
native England and fled to France in hope of finding a more friendly
environment for himself and his machine.

Considerable progress was also made in the sixteenth and seventeenth
centuries in the clock industry, which produced, as we have previously
seen, precise workmanship that was essential for the development of
industrial machinery. Although public tower clocks had become common

The Stocking Frame. One of the most important of the early advances made in the
textile industry in Modern Times was the stocking frame. It performed the intricate
operation of knitting. As pointed out in the text, an operator could make many
more times as many stitches on the frame than he could by hand. The stocking
frame gave a fillip to the putting-out system. (*Reproduced with permission of
Textile World.*)

by the end of the Middle Ages, there was a demand for small, portable timepieces. These were made possible by the use of the coil spring, an invention attributed to Peter Henlein of Nuremberg in the last decade of the fifteenth century. The first clocks powered by springs did not, however, keep good time, for whereas the existing foliot balance and verge escapement had proved satisfactory when the mechanism of the clock was subjected to the constant force of weights, they were not adequate to control the variable force of an expanding spring.

Before a solution to this problem had been found, a new and urgent need for accurate timekeepers had come into being because of long-distance navigation of mariners in longitudinal directions. Navigators were for their own safety forced to establish their longitudinal positions with accuracy. Inasmuch as the determination of a point in longitude consists fundamentally of comparing the time where one is, established by "shooting the sun," with the time at some fixed point, let us say at Greenwich, it is essential to have an accurate timepiece in order to know exactly the time at Greenwich.[5]

After Galileo had discovered that a pendulum makes its swings in constant intervals of time irrespective of the length of the arc, he tried to employ the pendulum in a clock to be used at sea. Such a clock was partly built by Galileo's son (1642), and Huygens in the Netherlands built pendulum clocks for use on ships (1657, 1661). The great trouble with this principle was that the arc of the pendulum could not be controlled because of the motion of seagoing vessels. The use of a coil spring seemed to offer better prospects of getting an accurate navigational timepiece and a return to it was eventually made. The uneven force of the spring was finally compensated for by the use of a balance wheel and hairspring, invented by the Englishman Hooke in 1658, the anchor escapement by Clement in 1680, and the deadbeat escapement by Graham in 1715; moreover, satisfactory methods for controlling the effects of temperature changes were developed by the Frenchman Le Roy in the middle of the eighteenth century.

In both agriculture and industry any number of other devices were invented or proposed which were eventually to play a role in the mechanizing of production. In sixteenth-century Italy Giovanni Cavallina invented a seed drill, the first important composite agricultural machine since the plow; which spread seed much more evenly than sowing by hand and which placed it under the soil where it could germinate quickly. In the cultivation of vineyards small plows, drawn by horses, were used to tear out weeds; in effect these were the immediate forerunners of the

---

[5] Astronomical observations to determine the time at Greenwich had to be too precise to be depended upon. They were then not practical.

horse-drawn cultivator. And in the cultivation of the much-prized tulip in the Netherlands, much was learned of the use of fertilizers and of rotating crops which was to stimulate experiments that led to the agricultural revolution of the eighteenth century.

A list of some of the things not yet mentioned, which were included in Da Vinci's *Notebooks,* will give some idea of the ramifications of efforts in the sixteenth and seventeenth centuries to control physical environment. Thus we find both taps and dies for cutting threads on nuts and bolts, a machine for making files automatically, a flying machine, parachutes, wheel lock pistols and muskets, breech-loading cannons, rifled firearms, a centrifugal pump, hydraulic press, dredges, locks for canals, plans for draining the Pontine Marshes near Rome, and a canal from the Atlantic to the Mediterranean. To be sure, some of Leonardo's conceptions could not be realized until centuries later because of the need of preliminary work, improved craftsmanship, or a social demand for the product, but he opened vistas which stirred the imagination of his successors.

Finally, the dissemination of information was greatly extended by the growth of printing—a means of communication which was especially important to the diffusion of technological information because of its ability to reproduce details with a minimum of error. Important printing establishments, like those of Plantijn in Antwerp, Kromberger in Spain, and Caxton in England, were founded throughout Western Europe and had a great financial success based, in part, on religious tracts connected with the Protestant Revolt and the Counter Reformation. In fact, this success allowed them to issue many works, notably the technical, which otherwise might have been too risky for publishers to undertake. For the most part, technological changes in printing came slowly after Gutenberg's great breakthrough, although new and famous type faces were developed, like italics by Aldus Manutius in Venice (1495–1515) and roman upper and lower case by Nicholas Jensen in France, and some improvements were made on the screw press to make operations faster. It was not, however, until the eighteenth century that presses were operated by compound levers and not until the nineteenth that typesetting machines were invented.

What the immediate impact of all these technological innovations was on actual production, it is difficult to say. What is clear is that machines increased the productive capacity of individual workmen and that although machine goods tended to be of inferior quality to the handmade, they were cheaper and appealed to the masses. Furthermore, machinery required larger investments and more intricate organization of business than previously; and the existing types of prime movers with their centralization of power required the concentration of production in a given place. Some concentration of production was actually realized. Jack of Newbury had, by way of example, in the first part of the sixteenth century a weaving factory of 200 looms and 600 workers. Capital required per mine in England rose from £100 under Elizabeth to several thousand under the Stuarts, and a London brewery under Charles I had a capital of £10,000. The trend toward capitalist enterprise on a large scale, which was to attain such extraordinary proportions in the twentieth century, was clearly in evidence by the end of the seventeenth century.

CHAPTER 10

Establishing the Capitalist System

Capitalism and Its Relation to Economic Growth

In the preceding chapters devoted to economic developments in the later Middle Ages, to the expansion of Europe overseas, to the extension of commerce, and to the growth of machine industry, we have been discussing many of the changes which in their totality were to result in the creation of an economic system known by the generic term of capitalism. As can readily be seen from the name of this economic system, capital played a large role in the new ordering of material things. Although in all previous economic systems capital, defined as an accumulation of surplus beyond what is necessary for meeting the short-run requirements of life, existed, it was mostly in the form of houses, roads, or public buildings rather than in equipment with which to produce more goods. Under capitalism, on the other hand, capital came from savings which were a substantial part of annual production and much of it was in the form of money and negotiable securities that were used to acquire machines and raw materials and to hire labor in an impersonal market for wages in order to produce those goods and services which its owners deemed would result in the producing of still more capital or profits. Thus the new capital had more mobility than the old; that is, it could be transferred more easily from place to place and from owner to owner largely because it had an "exchange value" resulting from acceptance of the idea of interest charges, and acceptance of this practice was possible because mobile capital was used more and more for making goods rather than for immediate consumption.

Furthermore under capitalism, the means of production came to be increasingly in the hands of the owners of capital instead of in the hands of workers; this allowed a planning of production on a larger scale than had been possible previously. This may have taken away from workers some of their motivation to produce, although it probably relieved them of many managerial headaches. Lastly, the development of the capitalist system meant that economic relations among men became more impersonal than they had been—that everything was regulated by a price system—and that one of the most important ideologies among men was the improvement of their material conditions. To recapitulate, capitalism came to be a system in which a relatively large amount of capital was mobile, transferable, and available at a price to anyone with good credit standing, in which capitalists hired labor for a wage in an impersonal market and sold what was produced for money, and in which the incentive to economic action was the desire for profits primarily for the improvement of one's standard of living.

The emphasis on individual well-being in this system and the desire for profits led at times to a disregard for the general welfare, even though there was nothing inherent in the system, as Karl Marx was to argue later, that was inevitably to result in the rich getting richer and the poor getting ever poorer. Under capitalism, indeed, mankind was to achieve greater economic growth and general economic well-being than had ever been attained previously under any other system. Capitalism seemed to work best when there was an expansion of economic activity and this expansion, it was found, could be realized not only from reaching out to encompass more and more of the population of the world and by supplying an ever greater variety of goods to society, but also eventually by increasing the purchasing power of the masses so that their demands would provide new opportunities for investment.

In the development of industry in England in the century from 1540 to 1640, there was a tendency toward mass production for mass consumption, as in the case of beer, and it was this very production that necessitated investments of capital in machines and factories and the hiring of labor for wages on a scale never before seen. In the expansion of Europe overseas, also, large investments were made in the hope of realizing profits in trading ventures, in colonizing activities, and in raids on native stores of bullion in the New World. In supplying society with a greater variety of goods, like window glass, gunpowder, and cast iron from home manufactures, or like cotton, spices, fish, and lumber from overseas, new opportunities were created for the use of capital in capitalist ways.

Such uses brought into being or strengthened in the sixteenth and seventeenth centuries certain economic institutions and practices that were essential for the proper functioning of the system. One of these institutions was money, that is, as we have already seen, a generally accepted measure of value, a medium of exchange, and a store of wealth. Without money it would be extremely difficult, if not impossible, to effect savings, to have mobile capital, to invest as one would in time and space, to lend or to borrow for interest, to hire labor for wages, or to have impersonal economic relations regulated by a price system. With the vast quantities of gold and silver brought in from the New World and with new supplies of silver from the mines of Bohemia, Tyrol, and Hungary, Western Europe got large amounts of those very metals which were used in coin money. Then, in addition, credit instruments, like bills of exchange and various "promises to pay the bearer on demand," came to perform more of the functions of money and thus to extend the use of a medium of exchange in economic relations.

Then with the development of capitalism a new fillip was given to banking. Bankers were primarily the ones to whom fell the task of amassing the savings of many persons in order to have quantities of capital large enough for financing vast undertakings. Banks were the chief lenders to those enterprisers who would attempt to produce more goods and services for profit. Banks did much of the transferring of debits and credits between individuals who had accounts with them (giro banking) and of transmitting funds over long distances. Also from safekeeping services which bankers performed for the wealthy, banks developed two practices which were extremely important to the growth of the capitalist system. The first was that they would lend out at interest moneys deposited with them, for they soon came to realize that all depositors would not be likely to withdraw all of their deposits out of the bank at the same time. The second was that they could issue "promises to pay the bearer on demand" which circulated like money. In the first instance, banks were able to put idle funds of depositors to work without the direct knowledge of the principals, and in the second case, they were able to *create* money, which was one of the major discoveries of Modern Times.

Finally, the capitalist system altered traditional forms of business organization. As the need for greater amounts of capital became real, the tendency was for individual entrepreneurs to band together in one way or another. This was done, as we have seen in an earlier chapter, by the formation of multiple partnerships, of companies of merchant adventurers who shared expenses but traded as private individuals, of sociétés en commandite in which some of the investors were sleeping partners with no responsibility for management, and of joint-stock companies in which many investors bought shares representing the value of the enterprise and received a pro rata portion of any earnings paid out.

With the development of mechanisms for effecting savings and making investments—two of the essential factors in economic growth—there was a greater use of money than hitherto and the creation of an extensive and delicate price system. These institutions made possible a greater exchange of goods and division of labor, which were two other important factors in economic growth.

The Development of Money and Banking in Germany and the Low Countries

Although the various parts of the capitalist system—money, the price system, banking, the capitalist spirit, the making of investments for profit, and the impersonalization of economic relations—came about *pari passu*, banking was in a sense in the center of the new developments and epitomized the new ways of doing business. It was the most important means for bringing together savings for many persons and for making loans to enterprisers in both the fields of production and distribution. And banking was to become the principal agency for regulating the supply of money by the issue of banknotes and the extension of credit.

In the latter part of the Middle Ages, as we have already seen, banking become more important in economic life and various banking services, ranging all the way from pawnbroking to the making of large loans, became differentiated. In the first two centuries of Modern Times banking took new strides forward, assuming a particularly significant place in the economic life of those parts of Central and Western Europe where there were large-scale productive enterprises and extensive commercial undertakings. Augsburg in southern Germany, for example, became a banking center because some of the principal exploiters of silver mines were located there and because it was on the trade route between the Rhine and the Danube and between the Rhine and the overland trade routes with Italy. Antwerp became a second great center because it was the chief place for the distribution of spices in the west and north and for the export of textiles and metals from its hinterland to other places easily reached by ocean shipping. Amsterdam was a third center, being a successor to Antwerp in Eastern products after the Spaniards sacked the city (1585) and the Dutch had cut its shipping from the sea by controlling the lower reaches of the Scheldt. London was a fourth center because of the growth of industry for a mass market and the development of colonial and other ocean commerce. And there were minor centers of banking at Lyons, Geneva, Barcelona, and Paris because of trade with distant places.

Of all of the bankers of early Modern Times the Fuggers of Augsburg did undoubtedly the most business and were certainly the most picturesque. They were in their age what the Medici had been in theirs—and they illustrate well the way banking capital came into being and the kinds of business in which bankers engaged.

The first member of the Fugger banking clan of whom we have information was Hans, who came to Augsburg in 1380. He was a clothmaker and one of those individuals who in the era of guild production began to turn out products for more than the local market. He specialized at first in fustians, cloth made from linen and wool, but then turned to cottons made from raw materials brought from Venice. Apparently his wares enjoyed considerable favor, for upon his death he left a small fortune.

Hans's son, Jacob, continued in the cloth trade, and so did Jacob's sons, Ulrich, George, and Jacob, the latter becoming known as Jacob the Rich. They extended the family business to include woolens, silks, spices, and jewels. Their ventures prospered so that they were able to establish connections in Italy, the Netherlands, Silesia, Poland, and Hungary. By 1473 the Fuggers had members of the Habsburg family, the ruling house in Austria, as clients, and a little later they undertook to serve the Pope by transferring sums from Northern Europe to Rome. They adopted the best bookkeeping practices of their day and an excellent reporting system to keep abreast of events which affected business activity and to be informed of the credit standing of their customers.

Under the direction of Jacob the Rich (1459–1525) the Fugger fortunes flourished. He engaged heavily in silver mining, and incidentally in copper and lead production, and made investments in that mining equipment and mining machinery to which reference has already been made. His primary activity, however, was in accepting deposits, in lending them out at interest, and in transferring moneys over long distances. Many of his loans were for strictly business purposes, but more and more he was drawn into the practice of making political loans to emperors, kings, bishops, and towns. It is even said that Charles V used moneys borrowed from Jacob to influence electors of the Holy Roman Empire when he was chosen Emperor. For the time being, loans of this type did not backfire. Even though Jacob lived lavishly and engaged in such socially desirable enterprises as the building of the Fuggerei in Augsburg —a "garden city" for the poor—he left at his death what was undoubtedly the greatest personal fortune that had been amassed since Roman times.

Under his immediate successors, the capital of the Fuggers continued to grow, but so, too, did their political loans. The financial needs of Charles V seemed to have no end, for he required funds with which to fight the French, the Turks, and the Protestants and with which to fit out armed escorts for ships trading to the New World. His successor, Philip II of Spain, had almost as serious financial problems, because of his wars with the Netherlands, and accordingly kept turning to the Fuggers for help. In 1560 the Habsburgs owed the Fuggers some 4 million gold gulden, or twice the fortune left by Jacob the Rich. In subsequent years the Fuggers had to take heavy losses on account of their political loans, and although they managed to play an important role in banking for a while longer, they dropped from sight as great bankers in the seventeenth century.

The Fuggers were not, by any means, the only large bankers of the sixteenth century. At Augsburg alone there were the Welsers, who financed overseas commerce, the Hochstetters, who got into the Lisbon-Antwerp spice trade, the Rems, the Manlichs, the Meutings, the Adlers, and the Haugs. In fact, all the main commercial centers had banking families of a similar kind.

Banking activity at Antwerp was particularly vigorous because of the large amount of distant trade in the city. This commerce had grown exceptionally fast after the middle of the fifteenth century, as foreign merchants moved from Bruges to Antwerp because of the special privileges granted them and because of the better port facilities required by the larger vessels which were coming into use. In fact, Antwerp's location was especially good, for the Scheldt was deep, and because it was a river, it provided a great expanse of wharf facilities. Moreover, the city was situated far enough from the sea to be safe from casual marauders but not too far to make access difficult and it had access to a large hinterland via the Scheldt, its tributaries, and numerous canals.

In the early sixteenth century Antwerp came into its own, for it became the center in Western Europe for trade in spices and other luxuries from the East and in gold and silver from America. It also became the great entrepôt for Western and Northern European goods, like textiles, metal products, and ships' stores, which went to pay for Europe's imports. Finally, as a result of its commercial activity, Antwerp had a certain amount of industry, such as the making of glass, majolica ware, sugar refining, printing in such famous establishments as that of Plantijn, and even painting, if that may be classified as an industry, with such great masters as Quentijn Matsys and the Breughels.

With all the business that was located at Antwerp it was only logical that there should have been banking. All of the major bankers, like the

Fuggers, had important branches there; and there were large local firms and many minor operators and merchants who engaged in the business of borrowing and lending. Sometimes bankers and traders combined their resources to buy up large quantities of pepper in Lisbon, as was done by the Italian house of Affaitadi in 1552; sometimes they made large loans to the King of Portugal with the understanding that spices would subsequently be sent to them. They also financed smaller undertakings by lending on bills of exchange; they transferred credits between distant places; they "cashed" drafts; they lent to cities for public works; and they made loans to kings and queens in order to get favors or to take advantage of high interest rates which were offered them.

For many years Antwerp was a thriving place, but eventually it fell victim to religious strife. When Philip II of Spain tried to keep his Netherlandish provinces from becoming Protestant, he unleashed a war that was long, bitter, and destructive. Antwerp was partially ruined and what was worst the Dutch were able to get control of the lower Scheldt and thus cut the city's access to the sea. As the latter condition persisted, Antwerp fell as rapidly as it had risen; it did not recover from second-rate status until the nineteenth century when once again it became an important port.

With the fall of Antwerp, London and Amsterdam rose to prominence in the economic life of Europe. The former, with a good port well inland, had a thriving trade in wool and textiles and in those articles of mass production previously discussed. The latter rose to prosperity largely on the strength of the fact that it became Antwerp's direct successor as the European center of Eastern trade and had the added advantage of trading directly with the East instead of through Portugal or Spain. Like Antwerp, too, Amsterdam developed a certain number of industries of which the most important were shipbuilding, textiles, faience, and food processing, as in the case of herring.

Because of its great importance in trade, Amsterdam became a great money mart and a pioneer in banking practices. In 1609 it took a crucial step forward with the founding of the Bank of Amsterdam, an institution designed to put order into the confused monetary, banking, and payment conditions of the country. In these fields, indeed, there was almost anarchy, because the wars with Spain had led to the debasing of the many coins (there were, for example, fourteen different mints) and the influx of foreign merchants and bankers from Antwerp had introduced into the country a wide range of moneys and a new set of faces with varied credit standings. Under the existing circumstances, money-changers had a field day, but they gouged their customers to such a point that the business community rose up in wrath. At this point the city fathers decided that they would have to bring some order out of the chaos. Their method of doing so was the founding of the Bank. To the new institution they relegated by legislation a considerable amount of business, for they required that all bills of exchange over six hundred florins be payable only at the Bank and they suppressed many of the private money-changers, thus forcing people with moneys to change to come to the official institution.

Strangely enough the Bank of Amsterdam was not supposed to perform one of the major functions of banking—it was not supposed to make loans, although it did eventually lend to the city of Amsterdam itself, to the East India Company, and to the municipal pawnshop. Its main activity was the one for which it had been organized, that is, to bring order into the exchange of coins, to facilitate the transfer of funds, and to accept the deposits of customers. In pursuing these lines of business the Bank rapidly became one of the most important banking establishments in Europe. It controlled the minting of coins by providing the mints with gold and silver for making standard coins and by withdrawing debased money from circulation. It changed moneys at official rates and by honest weight, and it transferred on the order of depositors sums to the account of creditors by effecting changes on its own books—a giro banking operation. This latter service was so great a boon in the making of payments that the practice of withdrawing deposits from the bank fell into disuse. If a depositor wanted cash, he simply sold his "claim to money in the bank," or bank money, to another person, and there was always a market for this kind of money (it even sold at a premium) because of its convenience and the demands of those who did not have deposit accounts with the Bank.

The efficient services rendered by the Bank of Amsterdam contributed their share toward making Amsterdam the financial center of the world. Traders from all corners of the globe cleared their accounts here. Here was the greatest mart for gold and silver, in part, because after the middle of the seventeenth century both metals could be exported without serious difficulty. Here capital might be borrowed from private bankers at reasonable rates, if the loan was to be used in legitimate commercial activity. Here, too, were to be found businessmen from all over Northern Europe to learn Dutch banking practices for the purpose of introducing them at home.

Money and Banking in England and France

The next important development in the field of money and banking was taken by one of the direct offshoots of the Bank of Amsterdam—the

Bank of Stockholm. This step was the issuing of bank notes. Whereas in Amsterdam depositors sold their receipts for what they had deposited in order to facilitate the making of payments, in Stockholm the Bank itself issued promises to pay (1661) which circulated for the making of payments. These promises to pay—these notes of the bank—were printed instead of handwritten, so they were standardized, except for the serial number and date and the fact that they were issued in various denominations. They carried the following text:

The bearer of this note of credit has a claim upon the Bank of Stockholm under number (such-and-such) for the sum of (denomination inserted here) copper money, this is hereby certified by us the undersigned, Commissioners of the Bank and Accountants, and also verified through the seal of the Bank hereto affixed. Given in the Bank of Stockholm, Year (such-and-such). (Amount in numerals)

(Signatures)   Seal.

Such pieces of paper were especially useful in Sweden where coins were copper and extremely heavy, the largest, of 10 dollars, weighing 43 pounds and more common ones as much as 7 pounds. But they had a greater significance than being convenient—they permitted the Bank of Stockholm to issue more money than was on deposit, that is, to extend credit or to create money. This was an excellent thing so long as people had confidence in the notes—a confidence based on the Bank's ability to make its promise good—for it allowed an expansion or contraction in the supply of money according to the needs of the business community. In fact the issue of bank notes was one of the major inventions of Modern Times.

Important as was the role of the Bank of Stockholm in the development of bank notes, undoubtedly the real success in the use of this instrument should be attributed to the English. In Britain, as elsewhere, merchants and public scriveners engaged in receiving moneys for safekeeping, in lending, and in transferring sums from place to place. Frequently these people might have so much coin on hand that they would take it to the Royal Mint in order to get the protection of the latter's vaults. This practice worked after a fashion until 1640 when Charles I suddenly refused to release the deposits of the merchants at the Mint until they had granted him a loan. This kind of a holdup antagonized the merchants who henceforth entrusted their extra coin to goldsmiths, for these people also had strongboxes and vaults.

Goldsmiths had already been doing some lending and other banking business, as we have seen, and now with the new amounts left with them, they had an opportunity to expand their operations. They began to lend

Money of the Seventeenth and Eighteenth Centuries. The first piece shown above is an early English check, or order on Mr. Morris to pay a certain sum. The second piece is a John Law bank note. The third is one of the famous "pieces of eight," the Spanish milled dollar. It circulated widely in the American colonies. (*From the Moneys of the World Collection of the Chase Manhattan Bank of New York. Used with permission.*)

out at interest sums deposited with them on the assumption that all depositors would not want their money at the same time. This lending of other people's money proved so profitable that the goldsmiths began to encourage merchants to make deposits with them by paying interest on such sums, higher rates being paid for long-term than for short-term deposits. Unlike the Bank of Amsterdam, they allowed their depositors to withdraw their funds, but like the Dutch institution they permitted depositors to transfer sums from one to another by bookkeeping transactions, to write orders to pay a certain sum to a certain person, as in the modern check, and to sell their deposit slips, that is, to sell their claim to "bank money." From this last practice came the issuing of paper money in England.

The most important of the early forms of paper currency were the goldsmiths' notes. These notes were given to depositors in place of coin at the time of the withdrawal of funds, were issued in various denominations, and were essentially goldsmiths' promises to pay the bearer on demand a certain amount of coin. In the course of time these notes took the place of receipts for deposits, for they were more convenient, and assumed an important position as a medium of exchange. Soon the imaginative goldsmiths realized that they could issue notes up to a large percentage of deposits, as well as lend a large portion of the deposits, and that they could thus increase the amount of money upon which they could collect interest. In fact, from experience they learned that a coin or bullion reserve of 20 to 30 per cent of their notes in circulation was sufficient to meet the calls of their depositors for cash.

For a time all went well with these operations, but eventually goldsmiths began to make political loans—loans to the Crown—and the kings' credit turned out to be poor. In 1672 the British monarch issued a "Stop of the Exchequer," which meant a stop to the payment of his obligations to goldsmiths. This action forced many goldsmiths to close their doors and destroyed public confidence in goldsmiths' banks and in goldsmiths' notes. Obviously a new solution to the banking situation had to be found.

For some time the possibility of creating a bank along the lines of the Bank of Amsterdam had been debated, and now the possibility seemed to have become a necessity. Only the Whigs appeared to fear the establishment of a strong public bank on the ground that it might lend money to the King and thus strengthen his position, but their hesitation was removed with the change of ruling monarch as a result of the "Glorious Revolution" of 1688–1689, which ended the reign of the Stuarts and brought the less autocratic William and Mary to the throne. Accordingly, the Whigs changed position and the Bank of England was brought into being in 1694.

The fundamental plan for the Bank was worked out by a Scot, William Patterson. His proposition was that a group of private financiers would lend the government 1,200,000 pounds at 8 per cent in return for a charter, granted by Parliament, which would confer on them the right to accept deposits, buy and sell precious metals, borrow, lend, and transfer funds, discount bills of exchange, and *issue bank notes*. This plan was approved by Parliament, and the Bank finally began operations. At first the new institution encountered considerable opposition. The Tories disliked it because they regarded it as a Whig scheme and even tried to scuttle the Bank by offering the government a loan of 2,000,000 pounds for approval of a bank with land as reserve. Their plan failed, but the Bank of England loaned the 2,000,000 pounds promised by its rivals. Then the goldsmiths opposed the Bank for the obvious reason that it would encroach on their operations. They tried to drive the Bank out of business by buying up the Bank's bank notes and demanding at once payment in bullion or coin. This "run" on the Bank might have worked, but the Bank refused payment to the raiders and its action was sustained by the government.

Although private bankers continued to do business in England, the Bank of England was for a long time the only joint-stock bank in the land and the only bank that enjoyed the right of issuing bank notes. It engaged successfully, moreover, in all kinds of banking operations, although most of its business was in short-term loans to finance commerce, except for sizable loans to the East India Company and the South Sea Company. It weathered two serious financial storms in the early eighteenth century, once in 1720 when the South Sea Bubble burst and once again in 1745 when the young Pretender marched on London and people suddenly decided that they wanted hard money instead of bank notes. After that the Bank, its prestige increased by the strength which it had shown in the crises, gained wide support. It attracted deposits from all sides, including smaller banks, and it lent money to banks when they were short of funds, thus giving stability to the money market, to financial institutions generally, and hence to business itself.

One of the many reasons which explain the greater economic development of England than of France in the eighteenth century was the fact that Great Britain had a superior banking system. Although the French were fully cognizant of the importance of a large, stable, "central," joint-stock bank, a great banking fiasco put joint-stock banking under a cloud for a long time. The fiasco in question is connected with the name of John Law. This personage was a Scot who had a firm belief that money greased the wheels of economics. He came to France with a proposition that he be given a charter for a bank patterned after the Bank of England, and his request was granted. He opened the doors of his establishment in 1716, began to accept deposits, to transfer funds, make loans, accept bills of exchange, discount promissory notes, and most significantly of all, to issue bank notes. Unlike the Bank of England, which pursued cautious policies, the Law Bank went overboard in issuing bank notes and in investing in wild speculations. Furthermore, from its very beginnings the Bank was on shaky ground, for only one-fourth of its capital was paid in and much of this was in the form of government securities of dubious value. Then bank notes were issued in such volume that the whole experience provided a classic example of overissue. In fact, notes in the amount of 148,560,000 livres were issued in the first two and a half years and 2,696,000,000 livres worth of notes were outstanding in May, 1720. In 1718 the Bank became a royal institution with the King as sole stockholder and heavy investments were made in government securities. Finally, the Bank made large loans to a colonial trading company that Law founded—the Mississippi Company—and when this concern failed to make appreciable earnings, the prices of the Bank's stock and of the Mississippi stock stopped rising. Suddenly people lost confidence in Law's schemes and in the Bank's notes. Prices in the paper money went up, a run on the Bank began, and the joint-stock banking venture collapsed disastrously.

So horrendous was this entire experience that the French remained extraordinarily gun-shy of large banks, of paper money, and of stock companies throughout the eighteenth century and in some respects well into the nineteenth. Banking was carried on in France by private bankers who operated without the aid of a central institution that would take their deposits and make them loans when necessary in order to give flexibility to credit and stability to business. Not until 1776 was such a bank created by Turgot, the King's chief Minister, who was deeply interested in economic matters. Although the word bank was discreetly omitted from the title of the new institution, it being called Caisse d'Escompte, the Caisse operated much like the Bank of England. At long last France was on the way toward acquiring a sound banking structure, but again it ran athwart political considerations. The Caisse was forced to overinvest in government securities and collapsed during the French Revolution.

Money, Instruments of Credit, and the Price System

Important as banking was, one should not lose sight of the fact that the very *raison d'être* of banks was to amass savings and to put them to work and that these savings were in the form of money, which we have indicated several times to be a measure of value, a means of exchange, and a store of wealth. In many ways money should be regarded as the basic institution of the growing capitalist system, for without it the other characteristics of the new order would have been impossible. It was not that money was in and of itself new, but that it came to permeate all economic aspects of life and to regulate more fully relations among men. It was by means of a greater use of money that savings came to be effected more easily, that they were amassed more readily, and that they were invested more efficaciously. It was by a greater use of money that the owners of capital goods were able to bring together necessary materials, to hire labor for wages in an impersonal market, that is, without assuming responsibility for employees' welfare, and to sell finished products in an uncertain market in hopes of making profits, that is, of acquiring more capital. It was the extensive use of money that gave rise to an elaborate price system covering all scarce goods and services which were exchanged. And it was through money that changes in amounts of savings, investments, credit, and prices came to affect business activity, that is, to create business fluctuations or business cycles.

Considerable attention has already been given to money in the sixteenth century. We have seen that the European stock of those precious metals, gold and silver, used in coins increased three times from 1500 to 1650 and that this augmentation contributed to a greater use of money. The supply of "money" increased, however, much more than this because of the development of credit instruments which had the same economic characteristics as coins. Among the most important of these devices were the bills of exchange. They were, indeed, much like our modern checks and were widely used in distant trade, although in local transactions they were used sparingly, as is the check even today on the Continent. By being "discounted" by banks, bills of exchange served as a basis for loans, for the bank that paid the ultimate payee of the bill before its due date for a consideration was actually lending money at interest. And bills served as media of exchange, for once they had been accepted, we would now say endorsed, by a bank or merchant of good standing, they might circulate like coins.

Furthermore, the supply of money was increased by bank notes. Banks realized that they could issue "promises to pay" with deposits placed with them as reserves in a proportion of 1 to 5, that is, with a 20 per cent reserve. Just how greatly the money supply was increased by this practice and by other credit instruments before the beginning of the eighteenth century, it is very difficult to say, but it is possible that by 1700 somewhere in the neighborhood of a third of all payments were made by these kinds of money and that the increase from 1500 was somewhat in the same proportion as that of bullion. In other words, the total supply of money from 1500 to 1700 may have increased as much as six times.

As has been suggested earlier, the great advance in the use of money meant facilitating the exchange of goods and services. With a greater exchange of goods and services, the price system developed, for the exchange value of all goods and services came to be expressed in money terms. In fact, long-term studies of prices show how product after product and service after service came to have a price tag placed on it. Then, with prices placed on everything, these prices became more sensitive to changed conditions of supply and demand and to the supply and demand of money, that is, prices varied more easily than before. Greater variations began to appear between classes of goods and services, as, for example, between what was paid for consumers' goods and what was paid for services, between prices of imports and prices of exports, and between prices of industrial goods and prices of agricultural products. These changes in the "terms of trade," as they are called, meant at least temporary maladjustments and frequently serious social tensions. Furthermore, there were seasonal fluctuations in the prices of some goods, especially agricultural products, for supplies were greater at harvest time than at other periods of the year and the costs of and legal restrictions on transportation and storage made difficult a steady flow of goods to all markets throughout the year. Also, farm prices fluctuated with weather cycles and regionally with local conditions, a series of bad years pushing the prices up and a number of good ones pulling prices down. Lastly, prices fluctuated in response to changes in the total supply of money relative to supplies of goods and services.

A detailed account of all these types of price changes from 1500 to 1700 would require more space than can be devoted to the subject here, important as such a discussion might be to explain conditions attractive for the investment of new capital in enterprise, for stimulating technical improvements in production, and for encouraging entrepreneurial activity. It is important to remember, however, that European prices doubled or tripled from 1500 to 1640, as has been discussed in an earlier chapter. It should also be realized that prices reacted generally downward from about 1640 to the decade of the 1720s, probably because of a less rapid rate of increase in the supply of money and because of greater quantities of goods and services relative to the supply of money coming into the market. Then from the 1720s to about 1819 prices moved upward once again, because of increased supplies of bullion, especially from Brazil, and a rise in demand resulting from an increase in population, colonial settlements overseas, and war, with exceptional heights being reached during the general upheaval of the French Revolution.

Although it is usually said that the capitalist system has functioned most smoothly during periods of upward secular price changes, qualifications to this generalization must be made. At least, economic growth took place under both long-term rises and falls in prices. As we have previously seen, when prices rose, wages lagged behind and this condition of "profit inflation" had some tendency to encourage investments in productive enterprise. On the other hand, when prices fell over a long period of time, the purchasing power of savings increased so that when the savings were invested they created more capital goods than they would have at the time saved. Furthermore, with declining prices producers had an incentive to improve their methods in order to lower costs and the less efficient were often forced out of business, leaving the field to the more efficient. Price changes were clearly not the prime determinants of economic growth.

Public Finance, Insurance, Bourses, Bubbles

As more and more of the economic relations among human beings came to be expressed in terms of money, many older institutions became outmoded and many new ones were brought into being to meet the exigencies of a money economy. In no phase of life was this more apparent than in public finance. No longer were payments in kind, in services, or in military support sufficient for kings and lesser lords to perform the functions of government. Wars could no longer be fought with armies composed of feudal knights and untrained peasants. They were fought by professional mercenaries who knew how to use the new firearms and the new tactics which were coming into being, and obviously the mercenaries had to be paid and provided with expensive matériel. Navies, too, became more costly with the development of specialized fighting ships with heavy artillery on board, and with larger numbers of ships in fleets. The Spanish Armada that sailed against England in 1588 was composed of 130 ships and 30,000 men; the Christian fleet that fought the Turks at the Battle of Lepanto in 1571 consisted of 250 galleys. Then costs of government went up as kings attempted to extend their sway over larger areas, to establish statewide administrative and legal systems, and to develop their economies by subsidies to entrepreneurs.

Under these circumstances changes in governmental revenue systems were the order of the day. Many of the old dues dating from feudal times were commuted to money payments and rates were raised or new taxes levied on the consumption of products, like salt, wine, and beer, on outward signs of wealth, like doors and windows, on supposed incomes, on the heads of citizens (poll taxes), and on imported goods, especially luxuries, like silks and cotton prints, which cut into the business of local producers.

In spite of such changes, however, tax revenues failed to meet the costs of government, especially those arising from war, and governments resorted more and more to borrowing. Sometimes they combined tax reforms with loans, farming out certain taxes, notably those on consumer's goods, in order to get payments at once. Sometimes they granted privileges, like the right to establish a bank, in return for loans. Sometimes they had recourse to "forced loans," when other methods failed. And sometimes they tried to raise funds by making government loans attractive investments. This required keeping the government's credit good and interest rates high and/or by offering the public securities that had special advantages. One such type was the *rente* or the annuity, which was particularly popular in France. This kind of security had been used in late Medieval Times, as we have previously seen, to finance real estate and housing enterprises, but was now adopted on a larger scale. The *rente* consisted of a pledge on the part of the borrower to pay the lender in return for his moneys annual amounts for a given number of years, or for the life of the lender, or even in perpetuity, thus providing, if everything went well, a steady source of income to the lender. Then a variation on the theme of the annuity was developed which had a considerable vogue. This was the tontine, devised by Lorenzo Tonti, financial adviser to the French First Minister, Cardinal Mazarin, in the middle of the seventeenth century. According to his scheme, annuities would be bought by a "class" or age group of subscribers whose living members would receive a high rate of interest on the amount paid in by *all* members of the class until only a few members of the class remained alive, but the principal would be retired by the death of the subscribers. Thus those who lived longest stood a chance of getting large payments, while those who died early would get little, and their heirs would get nothing. People who entered into such an arrangement were, in effect, betting on their own longevity.

One of the early difficulties encountered with both annuities and tontines was that investors could buy an annuity on the life of a second person. Accordingly shrewd financiers bought annuities on the lives of persons for whom the expectation of life was long. Thus they sought out young girls, on the theory that females live longer than males, in good health, who had had all of the serious disease of the time, like smallpox, diphtheria, measles, and mumps. Inasmuch as such a selection had not been envisaged by the founders of the tontines in their estimates of mortality rates, costs of the scheme turned out to be much higher than had been anticipated. Yet the sale of *rentes* and annuities have remained important down to the present, and the abuses to which they were subjected have been gradually curbed. The element of chance in them attracted those with sporting penchants, and the investment features proved popular with those who wanted to make financial provision for their last years.

With the sale of these various types of government securities, public debts came into being. To be sure princes had created debts from time immemorial, but in their cases it had been understood, at least in theory, that they would pay off their obligations. With the new public debts, there was no expectation that all securities would ever be completely retired. At most it was hoped that high-cost securities for short terms (the floating debt) might be replaced by low-cost obligations of long duration (consolidated debt). Just what the consequences of creating such debts were to be, contemporaries in the sixteenth and seventeenth centuries were not entirely sure. Some felt that the debts would impair the credit of governments and bring rack and ruin to the economies involved. Others thought that the debts would make little difference in economic activity or in government credit, if the states were able to meet their interest payments regularly. In actuality the effect of public debts depended very largely upon the purpose for which they were used. If they went into investments in productive enterprise, especially for goods of mass consumption, they contributed to economic growth. Unfortunately much of the sums obtained was used for conspicuous consumption, like that at the Court of Versailles, and thus stimulated luxury industries which had little impact upon raising national income per inhabitant. Other amounts went into war and war matériel that in and of themselves are destructive, although they may have been necessary for protection, and large sums were employed for the administrative business of government, which was notoriously inefficient.

Another institution which developed with the spread of an economy based upon the tenets of capitalism was insurance. As more and more goods and services became subject to monetary valuation and as the loss of property or of life caused greater hardships on individuals, it was quite logical that people should attempt to minimize the economic results of misfortune by sharing risks—by the device of paying premiums to a central fund from which they were to receive agreed-upon amounts in case of stipulated losses. Marine insurance, which had existed in the late Middle Ages, became more highly developed and specialized, especially in England. There a group of marine underwriters assumed the habit of foregathering after the Glorious Revolution of 1688–1689 at a coffeehouse run by Edward Lloyd, and there they adopted the practice whereby several of them underwrote part of a risk on a ship, a practice which allowed them to handle very large policies. To assist them Lloyd began publishing *News* pertaining to shipping matters—a publication that became known as *Lloyd's List* in 1734 and in 1760 as Lloyd's *Register of Shipping*. Even to this day Lloyd's is a loose association of underwriters doing business together and insuring parts of a given risk.

Fire insurance, likewise, became organized in the first two centuries of Modern Times on the generally accepted principles of sharing risks. It appeared in Germany in the sixteenth century in the form of mutual-aid societies for rebuilding those properties of its members which were destroyed by fire. It developed in England after the Great Fire in London in 1666. One of the first companies there was the Fire Office, founded by a famous writer on economic subjects, Nicholas Barbon, which insured 5,650 buildings from 1686 to 1693. In England, too, there were fire mutual-aid societies, like the Hand-in-Hand Society and the Amicable Contributions for Insuring against Fire. In 1706 a company was founded that was absorbed by still another organization to form the Sun Fire Office in 1709, a company that is in existence today.

Life insurance probably had its beginnings in marine insurance, when the life of a skipper was insured along with the cargo, in the sale of annuities which provided experience with mortality rates, and to a lesser extent, in bets placed by various individuals that a given prominent person would die before a certain date—a practice, incidentally, which had to be forbidden by law because of the number of murders to which it led. For satisfactory operation, life insurance required a knowledge of laws of probability, which were worked out by Blaise Pascal in the seventeenth century, and of mortality rates, that is, rates at which people at different ages and in reasonably good health would die, information which was developed from empirical data in the seventeenth century. In the last years of that century life contracts began to be written, sometimes in conjunction with the sale of tontines. Then in the eighteenth century stable companies were formed to sell life insurance—companies that did a sizable business, especially in Scotland and England.

Still another institution of the growing capitalist system was the bourse or the exchange. Clearly as more and more goods came to be sold for money, as government securities and the shares of stock companies became more numerous, and as insurance began to be more widely practiced, merchants and other men of affairs needed places to congregate for the transaction of business. To be sure in certain trading centers of the Middle Ages, there had been essentially the equivalent of bourses, such as the Rialto at Venice and the Beurs at Bruges, but in the sixteenth century such marts became more common and more highly developed. Antwerp opened its famous New Bourse in 1531. Sir Thomas Gresham, having observed the Antwerp establishment, built an exchange in London (1571) as a private venture, an enterprise which was a direct forerunner of the Royal Exchange. The Amsterdam Bourse was opened in a new building in 1611, and bourses were established in other cities, like Lyons and Geneva. In part the bourses served as commodity exchanges, for merchants bought and sold there on the basis of samples and made contracts for future delivery. In part they were money markets where men could borrow and lend. In part they were security exchanges where businessmen could buy and sell stocks and bonds. And in part they were underwriting offices, for in them underwriters plied their trade.

As can easily be imagined, the presence of so many men with money, engaged in operations that almost always involved a certain financial risk, frequently led to wildcat speculative schemes and sometimes to downright frauds. At Antwerp a mania developed for betting on all kinds of events, whether a given ship loaded with pepper would arrive safely in port, whether or not a given person would die before a stipulated time, whether or not the price of wool would go beyond a given point, or which one of two sparrows on a branch would first take flight. Some of these wagers had a direct connection with business, as in the case of a man who bet that a certain cargo of pepper would arrive in port, if he had an interest in the cargo or if he had a stock of pepper on hand the price of which would go down if the available supply of pepper were increased. Under such circumstances individuals would recoup some of their losses by placing their wagers in such a manner that by winning them they would cover some of the losses sustained if the ship did not arrive or if the supply of pepper were increased enough to bring the price of the spice down. On the other hand, many of these wagers were matters of sheer chance and could easily lead to crime.

One way to get rich on the exchanges was by taking advantage of fluctuations in prices. A person might buy a certain product in hope that the price of it would go up, sell "short," that is, sell what he did not then possess in hope that prices would go down before he had to deliver the product, or buy for future delivery in order to have goods at prices of which he was sure. One might also engage in arbitrage operations, that is, if the price of wool were much lower in London than in Antwerp, including costs of transportation and handling, one would buy in the London market and deliver in Antwerp.

If one wanted to get rich quickly, one might try to manipulate prices. This could be done by cornering the supply of a given product like wool, that is, by "cornering the market," and then by forcing users of the product to pay exorbitant prices because they had to have wool in their business. Prices might also be raised by spreading false rumors, or advantage might be taken of existing prices if one had advance information of events, like the loss of a ship of pepper or the declaration of war, which would affect business. Or prices might be manipulated by appealing to the gambling elements in society.

One of the earliest and most extraordinary speculative manias occurred in the Netherlands in the 1630s. Tulips had been introduced into Holland from the East and from Mediterranean Europe in the late sixteenth century and had met with much favor among the merchant classes. After the wars with Spain were practically over and people had more time to devote to the peaceful art of gardening, the prices of tulips began to go up. In 1633 a great rush to buy tulip bulbs began, for everyone thought that it would be possible to get rich from the cultivation of these tubers. For a time prices continued to rise, and as they did people began to go mad. They pawned their jewelry, mortgaged their homes, and sold productive enterprises in order to buy bulbs. Under this buying pressure prices of tulips soared, one much-prized type, a black tulip, going to several times its original value. In time a point was reached where there were few buyers at the prices demanded, sales fell drastically, and panic overcame the masses. The collapse came in 1637, bringing ruin to the uncanny greedy and a rich harvest for the canny few.

Then in the second decade of the eighteenth century there was a great wave of speculation, this time centered in France and England. In France the movement was connected with the name of John Law, who has already been discussed as the founder of a central bank which so overextended the issue of bank notes that the French lost confidence in his paper. In addition to the bank, Law attempted other ambitious projects. The first of these was the Company of the West, more commonly known as the Mississippi Company, which was founded in 1717, a year after the opening of the bank. The plan for this institution was actually devised by others than Law in order to mop up floating debt obligations of the state by selling stocks in a company which eventually would profit from privileges granted it by the government. From the outset, the Company was given the exclusive right of trading with Louisiana, of developing mining interests there, and of importing a certain number of slaves. Then a year later it was granted a monopoly of the beaver trade in Canada. With these privileges in hand, the Company looked like a good investment and its stocks sold well from the very first. Its initial popularity went to the heads of its sponsors, however, and they began immediately to expand the scope of the enterprise. In 1718 they bought the tobacco monopoly in France. In 1719, when the name of the Company was changed to Company of the Indies, they took over other French trading companies—the French East India Company, the Guinea Company, the Company of Santo Domingo, the China Company, and the African Company; and they even got the privilege of collecting those taxes which were farmed out, of minting coins, and of managing the public debt. Thus through the Company and the Bank, Law controlled the major part of France's trade with the East and with the Western Hemisphere, France's central banking, France's public finance, and had golden opportunities to make profit from the exploitation of a rich colony, of the beaver trade, and of the slave trade, to say nothing of tobacco and tax farming.

This extraordinary concentration was made possible by a simple but ingenious financial scheme. Capital of the Company was raised by selling shares for government securities or for notes of the Bank. In the case of government securities the Company received interest payments which it could use to finance its productive efforts and by absorbing these obligations strengthened the credit standing of the bonds which also formed part of the investment portfolio of the Bank. In the case of payment in bank notes, the position of the Bank was improved, because with the Company holding large amounts of the notes the danger of a run on the Bank was reduced.

The success of the first sale of shares in the Company is to be accounted for in large part by the fact that government securities were selling at a large discount and holders of them felt that shares in the Company might be of more value in the long run. In the longer run, however, it was necessary for the Company to show earnings in order to keep the confidence of investors. This might have been possible if Law had pursued more cautious policies and if the stock of the Company had not become the object of a speculative mania. The French, particularly Parisians, and to some extent foreigners, too, got the notion that Law was a financial wizard and that his enterprises had the touch of Midas. They began to bid up the prices of Company shares until a raging "bull market" in "Mississippi" stock developed. This was facilitated by the fact that the shares were transferable from person to person, that is, were made out to the "bearer" rather than to a specified person and further by the fact that Paris already had an active money market. By December, 1719 Company stock with a par value of 1,000 livres was selling at 10,000 livres, and Law was selling more and more shares—"watering his stock," as market operators were to call it in a later day.[1]

In January, 1720, when the Company and the Bank merged, people actually rioted in the Rue Quincampoix in their efforts to buy stock.

[1] The expression, "watering stock," came from a drover's trick of letting his cattle drink their fill immediately before a sale so that they would weigh more than if they were empty.

Once again individuals liquidated their possessions in order to get title to a part of Law's enterprises. Under such pressure, prices of shares kept climbing, but they finally reached "resistance points" beyond which buyers would not go. Some large speculators realized that the earnings of the Bank and the Company would have to be fabulous indeed in order to pay dividends on the stock equal to a reasonable rate of interest at the prices for which they were acquiring shares. Hence some of these investors began to sell blocks of their holdings, and these sales aroused the fears of others regarding the success of the Company's operations. Sales then came in volume, and prices of shares began to sag. Law tried to stop the avalanche of selling by forbidding speculation in the Rue Quincampoix and by throwing much of his personal fortune into the breach. But his efforts were of no avail. By July the "Mississippi Bubble" had burst ignominiously.

Although many gullible and greedy, but otherwise innocent, persons lost their fortunes in the collapse of this scheme, it did wipe out some of the government debt built up during the War of the Spanish Succession (1701–1713). More significantly, the Law debacle discredited joint-stock banking and the joint-stock form of business organization. The corporate form went practically out of use both for banks and for other forms of economic activity, much to the detriment of French economic growth.

While these events were taking place in France, England was also having a paroxysm of speculation. The insanity in England began during the War of Spanish Succession. At that time France received from its ally, Spain, the right to the slave trade in Spanish America, the Asiento, which had previously been held by the Portuguese, and incidentally developed a certain amount of trade with Spain's colonies overseas. This turn of affairs the English did not relish and founded in 1710 a joint-stock company entitled the Governor and Company of Merchants of Great Britain Trading to the South Seas and Other Parts of America and for the Encouragement of Fishing. This was the full name of the South Sea Company.

This organization, like Law's in 1717, sold stock to raise capital and took government securities in payment for the shares. This operation permitted the funding of a portion of the government debt, that is, of taking short-term obligations off the market, and gave the Company a source of revenue that could be used for developing actual trade and for paying dividends. The Company might not have amounted to very much had it not received a most extraordinary windfall in 1713 as a result of the Treaty of Utrecht. In this settlement of the war, England instead of France got the Asiento privilege, which allowed it to sell 4,800 slaves a year in South America and to send a ship a year, the permission ship, to trade in the Spanish colonies of the New World. These concessions were bestowed upon the South Sea Company.

The Company's operations became exceptionally profitable, so profitable, in fact, that the price of South Sea stock went up. Thereupon the managers of the Company became emboldened and decided to take a leaf out of John Law's book. In 1719 they took over a government loan in a manner to make everyone who was a party to the transaction extremely happy. By their action the government effected a reduction in the rate of interest which it had been paying and received a bonus as well. In exchange for their bonds, bondholders got South Sea stock, which was going up in price, and the Company realized a sizable profit on the deal. This entire operation was so successful that the Company soon agreed to take over the entire public debt of England, save for the loans made the government by the Bank of England and the East India Company. The favorable issue of this gigantic undertaking hinged upon the rise in price of South Sea Company stock, so that holders of government bonds would exchange their bonds for stocks. The price of the stock did go up, but too fast and too high. Englishmen acted as though deranged in their efforts to acquire South Sea shares. They bid up the prices of the stock from £129 at the end of January, 1720 to £1,050 on June 24, 1720. This extraordinary rise carried the entire list of stocks into a raging bull market, East India shares, for example, going from £200 to £440 in the first half of 1720. Worse, the wave of speculation brought into being a host of "bucket operators" who founded all manner of fly-by-night concerns in order to get into the stock-selling act. Some of these phonies were of the most brazen kind, like a company for improving the art, lately found out, of making soap, a company for making gold out of sea water, another for bringing fire from hell, and still another for "purposes which shall henceforth be disclosed."

The South Sea Company objected strenuously to this kind of competition and got a bill through Parliament—the Bubble Act (1720)—which forbade the founding of stock companies without an act of the legislature. Also at the urging of the Company the government dissolved many of the harum-scarum concerns referred to above. In spite of such measures the prices of the shares of the remaining companies continued to soar, although their earnings did not warrant the increases. Even the crash in France did not bring investors to their senses. Finally, when the South Sea Company won a suit against four companies which were misusing their charters and thereby aired some of the worst abuses to which the corporate form was being subjected, speculators began to run for cover. In August the fall of prices began, South Sea stock going to £120 in December and the shares of other concerns falling precipitously, some of them, indeed, vanishing with the companies themselves.

The crash was a resounding one. In the cleaning up afterwards widespread corruption was uncovered in government and in politics generally, especially on the part of Whigs. Nevertheless, it was a Whig, Sir Robert Walpole, who did most of the hard work of putting things aright. He thereby won such a reputation that he was able to rule for twenty years as prime minister and to establish, incidentally, many of the practices of responsible ministerial government. He was able, moreover, to save for government bondholders about 60 per cent of their investment and he was succeessful in salvaging enough of the South Sea Company to keep the organization in business, eventually, however, with government securities as its only assets.

In England, as in France, the madness of 1720 threw a cloud over joint-stock organizations. The Bubble Act remained on the books until 1825, so that stock companies could be formed only with the consent of Parliament. In spite of this restriction, the English made greater use of the joint-stock form than did the French, and this fact proved to be an important asset in the industrial expansion of England in the late eighteenth and early nineteenth centuries—in what has come to be known as the English Industrial Revolution.

CHAPTER 11

Mercantilism—The Dominant
Economic Theory of Early Modern Times

The Theory of Mercantilism

In every society, that is, in all groups of people living together who are so closely bound that there is a common desire to perpetuate the group, some at least rudimentary ideas exist concerning how economic affairs of the group shall be conducted. As the economy of a society becomes more complex and more highly developed, these elementary ideas become elaborated until they constitute a body of doctrines and are then glorified by the term "economic theory." Economic theory invariably reflects the environment from which it emanates and hence varies from place to place and in any one place at different times as the milieu itself changes. Moreover, theory inevitably conditions the economic practices and policies of a society, since, indeed, it is for this purpose that it is created. In almost all cases, too, economic theory is closely related to the question of economic growth, for its design is to explain how to attain specified economic goals, including improvement in material well-being, or to provide a rationalization for the lack of growth by deprecating material things and lauding existing conditions and even poverty.

In the first two and a half centuries of early Modern Times, economic theory was particularly influenced by five major developments: (1) great economic growth, (2) an enormous increase in the use of money, (3) the expansion of trade over long distances, (4) the acquisition of colonies overseas, and (5) the rise of national states. Accordingly theory aimed to explain how growth was attained and what the roles of money, of commerce, of production, and of colonies were in effecting that growth. Especially characteristic of the theory, however, was that it sought as its primary goal not the direct welfare of the individual but the economic strengthening of the state so that centralized control would be furthered and military power increased. Improvement of the economic status of the individual was a real, but a secondary consideration in the theory of the times.

To all the economic theory from 1500 until well into the eighteenth century has been given the generic term *mercantilism*. This lumping is unfortunate, for, as we shall see presently, both economic theory and practice varied widely from place to place and changed through time. Furthermore, mercantilism is a descriptively inaccurate term, because it implies that emphasis was put primarily on trade, whereas in reality stress was placed upon building the economy of the unitary state by all possible means. In brief, mercantilism in both theory and practice was economic state building.

Hence, the state intervened in all phases of economic life, primarily by means of regulations to attain its desired ends. In and of itself, this was nothing new, but the lengths to which it now went constituted a veritable innovation. The state engaged in an extensive amount of economic planning and also in a tremendous amount of control over private economic activity. Eventually, much of that state econmic planning went awry, largely because it tried to keep alive uneconomic enterprises, because it curbed private initiative, because its red tape caused bitter hatred of the system, and because it engendered national rivalries which led to wars and the loss of the very purpose of the planning. In the eighteenth century mercantilism came under attack by those who believed that greater economic growth would be attained if the state regulated the economy less and left it to the interplay of "natural law" and that the economy of the state would be stronger if more attention were given to the welfare of the individual. The doctrines of *laisser faire* and of economic individualism were direct attacks upon mercantilism and mark the beginning of its end.

The Mercantilism of Portugal and Spain

The use of political authority to regulate and direct economic activity had been resorted to on an important scale in Europe of the later Middle

Ages. Towns adopted measures for encouraging and controlling production by the guilds within their walls and, in those places where business with distant places developed, for aiding larger-scale enterprises to get needed supplies, to have an adequate labor force, and to maintain lines of communication with foreign customers. Furthermore, towns adopted rules for provisioning their citizens with food in order to avoid shortages that might be caused by bad crops and by forbidding export to areas where prices of those goods which were needed at home were very high. Lastly, with the development in the fifteenth and sixteenth centuries of warfare in which fighting was done by mercenaries, silver and gold were hoarded in veritable war chests in order to have the wherewithal to hire soldiers in time of need.

Inasmuch as the conditions which gave rise to these various economic policies of the towns of the Middle Ages continued well into Modern Times, it is not surprising that the general tenor of the policies continued too. Guilds, for example, were not completely abolished in France until the French Revolution and hence exerted considerable influence on the government to maintain their monopolies, to restrain producers of different but competing goods, and to keep up the quality of products placed on the market. Manufacturers and traders sought governmental aid in furthering their endeavors, particularly in the newly discovered lands overseas. Famines remained a danger because of the poor means of internal transportation and hence led to a continuing of rules regarding provisions. And, as wars were fought on ever larger scales and as war matériel became more expensive, governments had to have larger sums at their disposals for emergencies.

As national states achieved territorial unification by some lord extending his sway over other lords among whom he was *primus inter pares,* state economic theory and state economic practices began to take more definite form. This development was clearly evident in the case of Portugal. This small state, as we have seen, achieved territorial unification early and supported the efforts of several of its princes to explore the unknown areas of the South Atlantic. With the discovery of an all-water route to India the Portuguese acquired almost overnight a most lucrative trade. Immediately the royal house claimed the exclusive right to this trade on the ground that it had financed the explorations and was the only agency in Portugal capable of exploiting the newly found riches. Accordingly it instituted a number of regulations to keep out interlopers and it conducted its commercial affairs with the idea of reaping a profit. This profit was to be measured by the amount of bullion that it amassed in its coffers, and bullion was to be obtained by having what came to be known as a favorable balance of trade, that is, exporting goods to a greater value than was paid for what was imported.

By its practices during the heyday of its commerce with the East, Portugal established certain principles which were basic to mercantilist doctrine. The first of these was that colonies were to be exploited for the exclusive benefit of the mother country; the second was that all trade was to be regulated so that the metropolitan country would have an excess of exports over imports; the third was that national wealth was to be measured by the amount of bullion that a state had within its borders and therefore that precious metals should be accumulated at all costs.

These three principles became still more firmly entrenched in mercantilist theory by Spanish practice. Like Portugal, Spain herself was anxious to reap all the benefits of trade with her colonies which, as we have seen, proved to be rich in precious metals, the very stuff of national wealth, and so declared all commerce with the Spanish New World a national monopoly. In order to keep out foreigners trade was controlled by the Casa de Contratación, which ruled that all commerce between Spain and the Spanish colonies pass through specified ports in America, of which Porto Bello and Vera Cruz were the most important, and through a single port in Spain—Cadiz to 1503, Seville from 1503 to 1717, and then Cadiz once more. Licenses were required of all those who would go to the New World and these were not granted to foreigners, nor for that matter to Spanish Jews, Moors, or converts. Ships going to and from the New World were made to sail in fleets to keep out interlopers and to ward off pirates. And the greatest pains were taken to prevent the gold and silver brought to Spain from leaking out to other states in payment for imports.

Spain was successful in acquiring large supplies of bullion, but the chief effect of them upon the economy of Spain was to make prices go up. Gold and silver did little to stimulate the productivity of the country nor could they be relied upon to purchase the sinews of war when they were most needed. Indeed, when Spain became involved in disastrous foreign conflicts, it did not have and it could not buy what was needed for victory. By the Treaty of Münster (1648), the Dutch were given the privilege of trading with the West Indies and by the Treaty of Utrecht (1713), as previously explained, the English were given a monopoly of the slave trade to the Spanish colonies and the right to send a ship a year to Porto Bello. Mercantilism as practiced by the Spaniards did not lead to great economic development nor toward material well-being. Few important Spanish economic theorists seemed to realize that production of goods and not hoards of gold were essential to national economic strength and to national defense.

The Mercantilism of the Netherlands

With the economic decline of Spain, first the Netherlands and then England rose to positions of economic primacy in Western Europe, and France followed close behind them. The economic situations in which these states found themselves were profoundly different from those in which Spain and Portugal had been and accordingly the economic policies which they followed and the economic theories that they spun diverged from those of their Iberian predecessors.

As we have already seen, the great economic growth of the Netherlands was based fundamentally on trade. Not only had the Low Countries developed a thriving commerce in exchanging local products and those of neighboring lands and seas for Baltic goods, but they had also reaped a rich harvest in bringing spices and other Eastern products from Lisbon to the west and north of Europe. Then, as has been stated above, when Spain tried to suppress Calvinism in its Netherlandish possessions in a long war that split the country into the southern (Belgian) provinces and the northern (Dutch) provinces, Dutch shippers, having been shut out of Lisbon, went directly to the East for the goods that had brought them such great profits in the past. There they carved out for themselves a colonial empire large enough to satisfy the hopes of the most imaginative burghers.

Because the Netherlands was a very small country with relatively little industrial activity and because its great prosperity had been achieved by trade, it was quite logical that cerebration concerning the basis of national wealth should have led to commerce and that state economic policies should have been concerned primarily with the exchange of goods. It was not a sheer accident that one of the greatest of Netherlandish legal minds should have argued for a *mare liberum* against the English contention of territorial waters and that the Dutch bent every effort to defend their commerce by force when it was attacked by jealous rivals in the seventeenth and eighteenth centuries. Thus Dutch mercantilism was characterized more than that of other peoples by its aim to facilitate trade. The Netherlands, unlike most contemporaries, levied almost no customs duties on imports, for it realized that multilateral international trade was in its interests, that tariffs hurt this trade, and that duties levied on imports tended to increase the price of goods in exchange and would thus be a disadvantage to the nation. This was a far cry from the usual high protectionism of mercantilism, yet it was practiced until the 1770s, by which time the peak of Dutch trading supremacy had passed.

Similarly, Dutch policy regarding the amassing of bullion differed fundamentally from that of Portugal or that of Spain. Although individual Dutch traders wanted to make money profits, Dutch statesmen and theorists recognized that the mere hoarding of bullion within the nation served no constructive economic purpose, except as a reserve behind credit instruments. They saw that the export of bullion was necessary to acquire goods that could be sold at a profit for still more bullion and hence permitted virtual free trade in precious metals. Thus bullionism was minimized in Dutch mercantilism in the interest of aiding commerce.

The Dutch, however, like the Portuguese and the Spanish wanted to keep the benefits of Eastern trade exclusively for themselves. To this end as we have seen, they established a trading company, the Dutch East India Company, to which was given a monopoly of this trade and the task of defending, administering, and exploiting the colonial empire. In other areas than the East, the Dutch also used the device of the trading company, as in the case of the Dutch West India Company and the Boards of Directors of Levant Commerce and Navigation, but in these places the Dutch were willing to forego attempts at monopoly and to compete with others as best they could. When the trading position of the Dutch began to decline relative to the English, it was not because of an inability to render services at low cost, but rather because of insufficient military force to withstand all the attacks that were directed against the Low Countries. From the middle of the sixteenth century onward the Dutch had to meet the onslaughts of the English, French, and Portuguese. They had to leave Brazil in 1661, New Netherland in 1667, and Ceylon and the Cape Colony during the Napoleonic Wars. In the Far East their trade fell off, for although they maintained their hold on the East Indian possessions, the narrow policies of the East India Company led to the disintegration of the organization and to its final dissolution in 1798. By the end of the seventeenth century, Dutch commerce had suffered an enormous decline relative to that of its leading rivals, although its gross volume held up fairly well. Dutch economic supremacy, built on trading goods produced by others, lasted little more than a century.

English Mercantilism: A Stress on Production and Trade

Portugal, Spain, and the Netherlands did not stress in their theory of economic state building the production of either agricultural or industrial goods. This was left to England and France, which ascended the scale of economic importance upon the decline of Dutch power. These two states had great productive potential and because they lacked, at least at first, such trading opportunities as the Portuguese and Dutch enjoyed or found no Indians whom they could rob of hoards of bullion, as had the Spaniards, they set great store on production. To be sure, they recognized the desirability of a favorable balance of trade and the role that colonies might play in developing commerce, but their mercantilism was always tempered with the notion expressed by Adam Smith in his *Wealth of Nations,* published in 1776:

The annual labor of every nation is the fund which originally supplies it with all the necessaries and conveniences of life which it annually consumes, and which consists always either in the immediate produce of that labor or in what is purchased with that produce from other nations.

Evidence of the significance given to production as the basis of national wealth was apparent in England in the sixteenth century. Then, William Cecil, later Lord Burghley, Secretary of State and Lord Treasurer in the reign of Elizabeth, resorted to all manner of expedients to foster industry. He encouraged the manufacture of munitions and ammunition so that England would literally be more powerful. He gave monopolies by letters patent, which were at the origin of the patent system, to those who would undertake the mining of sulfur and saltpeter. He paid foreign workers in the metallurgical trades to come to England in order to teach their arts to local workers. He tried to preserve the forests along the sea coasts in order to guarantee a supply of timber for shipbuilding; and he encouraged the cultivation of flax and hemp and the making of canvas so that English carriers would have these much-needed products. And he even insisted that Protestant England eat fish on Friday so that the fishing industry, the training ground of sailors, would not be impaired. He made labor almost obligatory by the Statute of Artificers of 1563 and he endeavored to make business conditions so attractive to entrepreneurs that they would make capital investments.

In the seventeenth century, in spite of political disputes and revolution, the English continued to emphasize production in their plans for attaining national economic grandeur. With the Whigs, who generally were representative of business interests, becoming more powerful in politics, English economic rules became more and more positive in their direction of developing both output and trade. Guild regulations regarding the production of goods gradually waned; industrialists became freer to introduce new techniques of manufacture and to produce poorer goods in order to give more people products at lower prices. And a protective tariff was erected to preserve the English market for English producers.

Also, in this century, however, the English placed great importance on the expansion of commerce, for the wealth that the Portuguese and the Dutch had obtained through trade could not be ignored. This point is clearly made by economic writers of the time, like Roger Coke, whose *Discourse on Trade* (1670) had a great vogue, and Sir William Temple, whose brilliant pen and vantage point as English ambassador to the Netherlands were well used in the cause of lauding trade. So impressed did the English finally become with the importance of commerce in their economic state building that they fought the Dutch on several occasions in order to reduce competition from their rival; they founded overseas trading companies, like the English East India Company, and they enacted the famous Navigation Acts of 1651, 1660, 1663, and 1673.

These last-named laws indicate the lengths and the detail to which the English were willing to go to get more business for their nationals. The acts provided that no goods produced in Asia, Africa, or America could be brought into England except in English ships or in the ships of an English colony (save for Indian goods), captained by an Englishman, and manned by an English crew. They stipulated further that goods produced in Europe had to be brought to England in English ships or in the vessels of the country in which goods were produced or in ships of the ports which were the usual outlet of these goods. They required that colonial produce from Portuguese and Spanish possessions had to be brought in from Portugal or Spain, which was a direct blow at the Dutch carrying business. They required that vessels in the English coasting trade be captained by Englishmen. They imposed heavier customs duties on goods brought to England in foreign vessel than in English ships. They "enumerated" certain articles, like sugar, tobacco, cotton, indigo, ginger, and dye-woods (the list was subsequently extended), which had to be sent from an English colony only to England or to another English colony. They stipulated that most foreign goods (wine was an exception) imported by English colonies had to be imported from English ports in English ships. And they placed special duties on some goods shipped from one English colony to another, like sugar from Barbados to New England for the making of rum. Here was a program worthy of the most exclusive system of the Portuguese or Spaniards for reserving markets, getting shipping, and making England the center of the entrepôt or warehousing trade of the world.

The end of commerce was not considered to be, however, as it had been in Portugal and Spain, the piling up of precious metals. In the many controversies over the English East India Company's practice of exporting silver with which to get goods which could be sold for more bullion than was exported, the argument seemed to favor the getting of more goods. As early as 1621, Thomas Mun, a director of the Company, published a pamphlet entitled *A Discourse of Trade from England into the East Indies*, which was followed shortly by his more famous *England's*

Treasure by Forraign Trade or the Ballance of Our Trade is the Rule of Our Treasure. Here he argued so convincingly for the use of bullion to further trade instead of simply piling it up within the state that he won a large portion of his countrymen to his way of thinking. Sir William Petty in his *Political Arithmetic* (1690), for example, contended that the real sources of wealth in any state were not gold and silver but land and labor. Nicholas Barbon in his *Discourse on Trade* (1690) and his *Discourse Concerning Making the Money Lighter* (1696) tried to show how a useful stock of goods could serve a country better than a store of bullion. And Sir Joshiah Child, Governor of the East India Company, maintained in *A Discourse on Trade* (1696) that the mere supply of gold and silver within a state was of no importance, but that it was essential to have low interest rates so that enterprisers would borrow capital for developing their activities. Even Charles Davenant, inspector general of imports and exports and an ardent Tory, insisted, in his *Discourses on the Publick Revenues and Trade of England* (1698), that the real value of money consists in its being a medium of exchange and therefore that it should be allowed to serve its appointed function. In the light of such arguments it is not strange that in 1663 England adopted what amounted to almost free trade in gold and silver.

In its commercial policy England endeavored in many ways to increase its productive capacity. It obtained in the Methuen Treaty with Portugal in 1702 an outlet for English woolens in return for Portuguese wines, and the English East India Company exported woolen goods at a loss in order to pacify woolen manufacturers who complained of the importation of calico prints. The Treaty of Utrecht, as we have seen, contained the important Asiento agreement which gave England an increased market for its goods in Spanish America. Export bounties were paid on goods that England had in large supply and on which prices were low, a policy that found expression in the Corn Law of 1689 which provided for the payment of subsidies to those who sent grain abroad when prices were below specified levels. In 1721 the Calico Act forbade the importation of calicoes on the ground that these cheap and stylish fabrics from the Orient were ruining the woolen industry, yet unlike their French contemporaries, the English permitted production of these stuffs at home, the Manchester Act of 1735 being very explicit on the point.

Throughout the eighteenth century England continued to protect its industry with high customs duties, to reserve its colonial market for its own industrial goods, and to direct colonial trade to its shores so that it would have a good supply of raw materials for the entrepôt trade. Such measures contributed to England's economic growth and to the technological changes which constituted the Industrial Revolution. Under them England's foreign trade quadrupled in value from 1700 to 1789 and its industry, especially the cotton textile and metallurgical branches of it, grew by leaps and bounds.

In spite of this economic development there were Englishmen who writhed under governmental rules and regulations pertaining to trade and to some industries. Sir Josiah Child, to whom we have already referred, is alleged to have claimed that the economic laws of England were nonsensical, having been enacted by country gentlemen who were not even capable of administering their own estates. Bernard de Mandeville, a Netherlandish physician living in England, likened a national economy, in his *Fable of the Bees* (1714–1719), to a hive that prospered most when left entirely alone to operate on the *natural* principle of self-interest. And David Hume, the philosopher, attacked nearly all the sacred cows of mercantilist doctrine in essays published in 1752 and 1753. In his view, money was fundamentally a means of facilitating exchange and was to be regarded as national wealth only in so far as it could be used to grease the wheels of trade. In his opinion the term "favorable balance of trade" was a misnomer, for if it led to the accumulation of bullion within a country and prices went up, the high prices would discourage foreigners from buying in that country, exports would decline faster than imports, and bullion would flow to other areas, thus reestablishing a more equitable distribution of bullion and a closer real balance between exports and imports. That is, Hume considered that the amassing of bullion in extraordinary quantities in any one country was impossible because the price mechanism would cause precious metals to flow to those places where goods were cheap in terms of gold and silver. Hume also held that trade is of benefit to all those who are parties to a transaction, for through trade goods are moved about in such a way that each buyer ultimately gets what he desires. This being the case, he favored measures which would raise the general level of multilateral trade among nations, for doing so would be of benefit to England.

The greatest of all critics of the mercantile system was, however, Adam Smith, whose *Wealth of Nations* (1776) marked the true break between mercantilist and laisser faire theory. Smith, like Hume, attacked all the dogmas of traditional mercantilism—bullionism, favorable balance of trade, tariffs, colonial regulations, and shipping monopolies. As we have seen, he believed that the wealth of a nation was to be measured by the fund of goods that it had and that this fund depended upon the goods and services which a state could produce or obtain in trade with what it had produced. He thought, also, that this fund could be increased if there were a greater division of labor among producers, that is, if each one produced those things which he could make most cheaply and from the sale of which he could obtain the wherewithal to buy the other things that he needed, instead of each trying to turn out goods to meet all his requirements. This principle of specialization in the production of those things in which one had comparative advantages (advantages comparable or superior to those of others who were making the same products) should be, according to Smith, applied on an international scale in order to get the best possible utilization of world resources and talents. If this doctrine were followed, not only England's economy, but that of the entire globe would be improved. To attain this goal, it would obviously be necessary for nations to allow their economies to function without governmental interference—for production and commerce to be free of all man-made impediments and encouragements that would disturb a market-determined division of labor. Eventually the English came to agree with the main tenets of Smith's doctrine, but this day did not arrive until the second quarter of the nineteenth century when England's productive advantages were so great that the economy had little to fear from foreign competition.

French Mercantilism

The economic position of France during the two and a half centuries with which we are concerned here was more analogous to that of England than to that of Portugal, Spain, or the Netherlands. France had neither routes to the Far East that provided from the beginning a remunerative carrying trade nor overseas possessions with stores of precious metals in the hands of natives which could be seized. To be sure, the concept of bullionism played a role for a time in France, as it did in England, and so, too, did the idea of a favorable balance of trade. In fact, a royal ordinance of 1540, frequently reiterated thereafter, forbade the export of bullion as contributing to the "impoverishment of our subjects," and there was legislation to suppress the importation of luxuries, for "by their purchase great sums are drawn from our kingdom by foreigners." Yet, very early the French realized that economic well-being and national economic strength depended primarily on producing goods and services and that the concept of a favorable balance of trade was important not so much as a means of accumulating bullion as for indicating the competitive vigor of a nation's productive establishment. In the sixteenth century, accordingly, the French government offered subsidies, tax exemptions, grants of monopolies, loans, and letters patent to develop such industries as glass making, sugar refining, tapestry weaving, and woolen, silk, and linen textile manufacturing. Sully, Minister to Henry IV, stated in an oft-quoted passage that "feeding the flocks and working the land are the two sources of French nourishment—the real mines and treasures of Peru"; and Richelieu, Minister from 1624–1642, did his best to establish trading companies and to construct a merchant marine.

Moreover, early French theorists expressed opinions which were in line with the economic practices already mentioned. Jean Bodin (1520–1596), as we have seen earlier, criticized the amassing of precious metals as a national economic policy on the ground that by so doing the chief result was an increase in prices, while he stressed the importance of production in judging the economic strength of a nation. Barthelémy de Laffemas (1545–1611), Controller General of Commerce, recognized the usefulness of a supply of gold and silver for the conduct of state business and the desirability of having a favorable balance of trade, but he saw that the possession of funds and an excess of exports over imports depended on production. Of a similar mind was Antoine de Monchrétien (1576–1621), for he argued, "it is not the abundance of gold and silver, the quantity of pearls and diamonds, which makes states rich and opulent, but rather the things necessary for life. . . . " Therefore he urged state economic development of agriculture, industry, and commerce, the acquisition of colonies, and an international division of labor.

Important as were these early economic theories and state practices of the French, the climax of French mercantilism was reached during the ministry of Jean Baptiste Colbert (1619–1683). Colbert, the son of a cloth merchant of Rheims, became economic adviser to Louis XIV, France's great "sun king." For economic theory Colbert had little stomach, but in practical economic matters he had the greatest interest and enthusiasm. Like many of his French predecessors, he was a staunch believer in productivity. Regarding bullionism, he said that it was a "narrow and little principle, but that great things could be accomplished in its name." To obtain bullion it was necessary to build up the entire productive capacity of the state—and to this end Colbert actually devoted his entire career.

Colbert believed that foreigners would buy French products if the goods turned out were of high quality. To foster manufacturing he gave subsidies to industries, carried the policy of creating royal manufactories much further than it had been pushed previously, and did his best to introduce new industries. That there might be a sufficient labor supply he forbade the emigration of skilled French workers; he encouraged boys to marry before they were twenty and exempted families of ten or more from paying taxes, if none were priest or nun; and he conducted a severe campaign against begging, charity, and general indolence. In order to insure that French products be of high quality, he issued detailed specifications for goods and for the methods by which they were to be produced, an edict concerning the dyeing of cloth having, for example, 371 articles. He built roads, bridges, and canals in order to improve France's transportation system; he tried to make France a customs union and although he failed, he paved the way for a reform that was realized during the French Revolution.

So far as foreign trade was concerned, Colbert believed that there was a given quantity of it and that if France were to increase her share, she

The English Fleet Trying to Aid the Besieged Protestant City of La Rochelle, France, in 1627. The English at this time had a hundred ships, 5,000 men, and a hundred horses, which gives some indication of the economic magnitude of warfare that could be carried on overseas. The French were able to prevent the English from relieving La Rochelle. (*From Edwin De Turck Bechtel, Jacques Callot, George Braziller, Inc., New York, 1955. Courtesy of the publishers.*)

would have to take something from others, and that the quickest way to get it would be to take it by force. "Commerce," he wrote in 1669, "is carried on by 20,000 vessels and that number cannot be increased. Each nation strives to have its fair share and to get ahead of the others. The Dutch now fight this war [of commerce] with 15,000 to 16,000 vessels . . . the English with 3,000 to 4,000 . . . and the French with 500 to

MAP OF THE "FIVE BIG FARMS" BEFORE 1664

•••••• Tariff of Normandy, Picardie, Poitou, Berry and Bourbonnais
– – – – Tariff of Bourgogne
x x x x x Tariff of Champagne
o o o o o Tariff of Anjou
▬▬▬▬ Tariff of The Loire

French Customs Barriers in the Seventeenth Century.

600. The last two countries can improve their commerce only by increasing the number of their vessels and can increase the number only . . . by paring away from the 15,000 to 16,000 Dutch ships." He, therefore, approved of Louis XIV's first war on the Netherlands and gloated over the fact that in 1669 "this state is prosperous not only in itself, but also in the condition of want which it has created in neighboring states. Extreme poverty appears everywhere. Only Holland still resists." In 1664 he adopted for the area of the "Five Great Farms," which was most of the center of France, relatively low tariffs in the hope that "free trade" would give France more commerce, but he reverted to high protective

tariffs upon the loud laments of producers who feared foreign competition. He founded the French East India Company, which he hoped would wrest Indian trade from the Dutch and the English. He tried to secure colonies and to exploit those that France already had. In his efforts to colonize Canada he ordered soldiers there to marry and he sent out women in order that they might be able to. Prior to dispatching one of his colonizing cargoes he sent this characteristic message to his agents: "We prepare one hundred and fifty girls, mares, horses, and sheep [to send to you]."

Unfortunately for France, Colbert's efforts to develop the national economy were not crowned with unqualified success. He placed a great deal of emphasis upon the luxury trades and this was probably a mistake, for great economies have always given a relatively large place to goods of mass consumption. Also his economic planning suffered much from Louis XIV's wars of glory and of conquest. The treasury could not stand the burden of large military establishments and of aid to industry and to commerce, nor were the energies of the French people sufficient to carry on grandiose economic enterprises and war simultaneously. Although French commerce grew and the French merchant marine increased in size during Colbert's rule, the events of the seventeenth century indicated clearly that the future of France's economy was in production rather than the development of a great foreign commerce, like the Dutch, or the exploitation of colonies, like the Spanish.

In the eighteenth century, France continued for long to practice "Colbertism," that is, its own brand of mercantilism. It maintained high protective tariffs, encouraged exports, and most characteristically of all, tried to bring the new industrial techniques which were being developed in England to France so that its productive position would be maintained. Nevertheless, in France, as in England, several economic theorists raised their voices against so much government intervention in business affairs. In the first place, there were the so-called neomercantilists, among whom the most important were John Law, François Mélon, and François Véron de Fortbonnais. The distinctive features of their doctrine was the belief that since money was the lifeblood of business activity, there should be a large enough supply of it, in coin or in paper, so that there would be a greater exchange of goods and hence a greater division of labor. Sound as this view may have been in an economy where commerce was still curbed by the limited use of a medium of exchange, it received a hard blow with the fiasco of the Law System.

A greater future lay in the doctrines of those who concentrated their energies in making direct attacks upon government economic rules and regulations. One of the earliest of such critics in France was Pierre de

Pesant de Boisguilbert (1646–1714). He believed that there were natural laws of economics applicable in all times and climes and that they should be allowed to take their course without interference from political bodies. If this were done, French manufacturing would be relieved of restricting regulations, commerce would grow, and agriculture would be improved. A healthy equilibrium in international trade would also be created and simultaneously a more vital French national economy. Another in this group was Richard Cantillon, an Irishman in the banking business in Paris, who attacked the concept of the favorable balance of trade on much the same grounds as Hume and added the idea that there are cycles of national economic primacy which are created by economic laws and that to fly in the face of these laws is both foolhardy and useless. Also Vincent Gournay (1712–1759), intendant of commerce and usually classed with the next group of which we shall speak, should be included here because of his activity in having the works of English writers critical of government intervention in economic affairs translated into French.

The hardest blows delivered at mercantilism, however, were those of the Physiocrats—literally those who believed in the rule of nature. The founder of this school was physician to Madame de Pompadour, François Quesnay (1694–1774). He had become profoundly impressed by Isaac Newton's attempts to explain the physical universe in terms of natural laws and by Harvey's theory of the circulation of the blood, whose marvels he had witnessed in his most famous patient. Like so many others of his age, Quesnay argued that if there were natural, eternal, and immutable laws which governed the physical universe, there must also be similar laws which operate in the social, economic, and political worlds and that social scientists, like physical scientists, ought to be able to discover these laws by the use of reason—by sitting down, by keeping cool, calm, and collected, and by *thinking*.

By the use of the method which he proposed for all, Dr. Quesnay set about the discovery of natural laws in economics. His finds were first published in articles in the famous *Encyclopédie*, but his system was more amply described in his *Tableau économique* (1758). Dr. Quesnay "discovered," or thought that he had, that agriculture is the fundamental source of wealth—the source of what he called the net product. Industry simply combined things, and commerce moved them around. Obviously goods and wealth did circulate, on the analogy of the circulation of the blood, among the agricultural, industrial, and commercial segments of the economy, and this circulation was determined and regulated by natural laws. This being the case, and nature being assumed to be good, it followed that no man or man-made institution, like government, should interfere with nature's handiwork. Hence all governmental and guild restrictions on commerce, all rules pertaining to the production of goods, and all limitations on agriculture should be done away with. Man should adopt the policy of *laisser passer, laisser faire*—nature should be allowed to operate freely.

Although there were those who thought that it was perfectly "natural" for man to intervene in economic affairs to prevent himself, for example, from starving to death, or to get out of the way in case of a natural avalanche, Physiocratic ideas, especially those having to do with government regulations, had a considerable following. Popularity was given to this philosophy by such important figures as Dupont de Némours (1739–1817), Mercier de la Rivière (1720–1793), and Robert Jacques Turgot (1727–1781), Chief Minister of France from 1774 to 1776. During his term of office, Turgot abolished many of the old regulations pertaining to the commerce of grain and tried to get rid of the guilds, although he was removed from office before the latter reform was completely carried out. Thus in France as well as in England, traditional mercantilist theory came in for severe attacks and even mercantilist practice was slightly mitigated. In France, however, the doctrine of free trade was to have less success in subsequent public policy, for France was not to have the strong competitive position in production which the English acquired through the Industrial Revolution.

In most other European lands, French Colbertism was followed more or less closely, and in them it had much the same evolution that is had in France itself. It was introduced into Russia by Peter the Great (reigned 1689–1725) and was applied with energy by Catherine the Great (reigned 1762–1796). In the German states, it was preached by a group of writers, known as Cameralists, and was practiced by most states, especially by Prussia, where Frederick William the Great Elector and Frederick the Great endeavored to develop industry. Then, in the latter half of the eighteenth century, its basic principles came to be attacked by those who read English and French criticism and by local adepts of Physiocratism. The application of laisser faire theories to domestic economic affairs and of free-trade principles to foreign trade was, however, retarded because of traditionalism and the rapid advances made by England in manufacturing.

Mercantilism and the Colonial Scene

Inasmuch as colonies played such an important role in European economic development during the period when mercantilist thought was dominant, it was only logical that economic state-building theories should have special relevance to the policies which were followed in overseas possessions. In the first place, mercantilism regarded the acquisition of colonies as highly desirable, for the Portuguese and Spanish cases, to say nothing of the Venetian and Genoese, provided clear evidence of the wealth that was to be gained from them. In the second place, mercantilists took the position, getting their ideas in part from the Venetians and Genoese, that their colonies existed exclusively for them and for their material benefit. This was the famous "colonial compact," or *pacte colonial*, as the French called it. From it were derived nearly all the details of mercantilist colonial theory—that trade between the homeland and its colonies should be reserved to the motherland, that this commerce should be carried in ships of the state or of the colonies concerned, that the colonies should buy whatever they could from the production of the homeland, that they should not produce for sale or for distant commerce what could be bought from the metropolitan state, and that they should produce and sell only what the mother country wanted.

Within the broad framework of the colonial compact the policies of the different colonial powers varied to meet different conditions both at home and abroad. In general, one set of principles was applied in cases where colonial production was developed to a point that provided articles for trade and a second set dealt with actual settlement by Europeans and with economic development. The first category had to do mainly with the East, for a time with Spanish America, and in the seventeenth and eighteenth centuries with all America. The second concerned primarily the Americas, especially the West Indies and English North America.

In the case of the East, when the Portuguese found a new route to the source of supply of goods that had been coming to Europe for a long time as a virtual monopoly of the Venetians and Genoese, nothing was more natural than that they should establish a monopoly of trade over the new routes for themselves. Their problems were, first, to get sufficient supplies in the East by establishing bases and some control over the natives and, secondly, to prevent foreigners from learning of their secret routes and from breaking into the trade. The East was organized by Albuquerque, as we have seen, but keeping foreigners out was a more difficult and persistent matter, especially for a country with fewer than two million people.

The monopoly of the Portuguese in Eastern trade was, in fact, broken by the Dutch, who not only learned of the all-water route to the East, but established their sway over Sumatra, Java, the Moluccas, parts of New Guinea and Borneo, the lower part of the Malay Peninsula, which they lost to the English in 1824, and Ceylon, which they also lost to the

English (1796). Moreover, the Dutch entered into trading relations with China to 1661 and with Japan from 1638 to 1854, and they founded a way station at the Cape of Good Hope, which they actually settled. For the administration of the Eastern trade they used the device of a joint-stock company with monopolistic privileges rather than a royal monopoly. Like their predecessors, however, the Dutch were concerned almost exclusively with trade rather than with settlement and economic development. Accordingly, they established trading stations and tried to get goods into them for trade. When they wanted a given product, they began by paying high prices for it, but when supplies became large, they cut prices to the bone. This practice was followed both in the case of coffee, which the Dutch introduced into Java in 1700, and of sugar, which they had brought in somewhat earlier. In the case of some of the spices their policies were similar, but they sometimes went so far as to destroy plantations to prevent a contraband trade that threatened to develop as a result of the low prices which they were paying and the high prices which they charged in Europe. In essence, the Dutch were not seriously concerned with the economic development and welfare of their colonies, but rather in commerce in easily obtained goods that would give large returns.

The Dutch, again like the Portuguese, were faced with encroachments by states which had greater productive capacity at home and greater military and naval potential, namely, France and England. These powers were not successful in breaking the Dutch hold on the East Indies, but they did get established in India for what turned out to be the more profitable trade in Indian cotton goods and tea. Both these nations endeavored to create national monopolies of trade by using the system of private monopolistic companies, like the English East India Company (1600) and the French East India Company (1664). Like the Dutch, both were primarily interested in commerce rather than settlement and economic development. However, their attempts to get the lion's share of the trade brought them into a conflict that reduced French holdings in the East to a few minor ports (1763).

In the Western Hemisphere, mercantilist policies at first resembled those applied in the East, for the Spaniards' find of gold and silver stores provided articles of value for trade and the *conquistadores'* demands for supplies from home to allow them to rob the Indians more effectively created a market for Spanish goods. Thus Spain developed strict regulations so that it could reap all the benefits of trade. Not only did it require that all trade pass through control ports in Spain and America, as we have seen, but also that ships in the trade sail in fleets and that all foreigners should be kept out of colonial trade—a rule that broke down because of the need for slaves and the force of foreign powers. Although Spaniards introduced many European plants and animals into the New World, they did little to exploit the riches of their lands, except in the case of silver mining. They kept enterprising people like the Jews and Moors out of their colonies and granted land in large amounts to nobles and to missionaries, who had little stomach for the production of goods for commerce.

To be sure, eventually sugar and tobacco were grown in large quantities in Cuba, Haiti, and Santo Domingo, cattle were raised in the La Plata region, sheep in Peru, and indigo and cochineal for dyes in more tropical climes, but the economic life of all these regions was made miserable by Spanish rules pertaining to trade. For example, goods from what is now Argentina had for a long time to be transported over the Andes to Peru and thence northward and, along with all west coast products, across the Isthmus of Panama and then on to Spain. Worse perhaps, the Philippines were allowed to send only one ship a year to Mexico (Acapulco) for fear that too much silver would leak out in the China trade. This limitation on shipping not only restricted Spanish commerce in the Far East, but it hurt trade with Mexico. It meant that supplies in the Philippines ran dangerously low, that space on the one ship was very dear, and the transportation of goods unnecessarily costly. Even in the West Indies and Central America the fleets sailed only twice a year, with the result that sugar and tobacco piled up, costs of warehousing were high, and shortages of European goods were periodic. Small wonder that colonial Spaniards traded with foreign smugglers to get rid of their produce and to secure the goods they needed at lower prices than they paid to their countrymen. New Englanders carried on a brisk trade with the Spanish West Indies; the Dutch broke through the Spanish colonial blockade so successfully that they had for a time what amounted to a monopoly of the Spanish cocoa trade. And when the English obtained the Asiento in 1713, they accomplished little more than getting legal recognition for what they had for a long time been doing illegally.

Only in the eighteenth century, when Spanish power was insufficient to maintain its colonial trade intact, did the Spaniards liberalize their regulations. By about 1740 individual vessels, called registered ships, were authorized to go to the colonies and to trade in any port. In 1764 a regular semimonthly mail service was established between Spain and the West Indies and La Plata. In 1765, trade was opened to all Spaniards; in 1775, they could trade in many ports in South America and after 1789 to all in Mexico. In 1778 the system of having all ships sent in fleets was abolished. These more liberal policies resulted in a considerable increase in the trade of Spanish America, but Spain was not to reap the full benefit from it, for in the early part of the nineteenth century, most of her American colonies were to fight for and to win their independence from a motherland that had given little serious consideration to their economic welfare.

The history of Portuguese policy in Brazil was not unlike the policies pursued by Spain in America. The Portuguese made grants to nobles of large estates, *capitánias*, which were fiefs of the Crown and which usually comprised 150 miles of coast line and an indefinite extension inland. The actual cultivation of the soil got under way slowly, but sugar was introduced in the sixteenth century and ultimately became a commercial crop for which the home demand was great—a crop which, incidentally, led to the bringing of the first Negro slaves to the New World. In the late seventeenth century the Portuguese began to push inland from the coast, for gold was found in the Minas Geraes districts in such quantities that in the eighteenth century Brazil accounted for nearly 80 per cent of the world's production; diamonds were also discovered in such supply that Brazil was the main source of these stones until South African mines came into production in the late nineteenth century.

For a long time Portugal paid little attention to its American colony, although it endeavored, true to the principles of the "colonial compact," to reserve all of the trade with Brazil to itself. With the loss of their Eastern commerce and with the finding of gold and diamonds, however, the Portuguese began to take more interest in their possession, raising it in 1645 to the status of a principality with the eldest son of the King as Prince of Brazil, attempting to establish a monopoly of trade in gold, and making diamond mining a monopoly of the Crown. Because of their inferior military power, they were unable to keep out foreigners. The Dutch established themselves in Guiana, whence they traded with the colonists, and so threatened the entire possession that these interlopers had to be bought off with trading privileges in 1661. Finally, Portugal proved too small a power to hold Brazil. The colony declared its independence in 1822.

The Dutch in the New World pursued policies which were similar to those which they adopted in the East. Inasmuch as they were primarily a trading people, they acquired colonies largely for the purpose of carrying on commerce with the natives or of having bases whence they could conduct a smuggling business with the colonies of other powers. Netherlanders did not emigrate to any of their colonies in large numbers and they showed relatively little enthusiasm for developing colonial agriculture. To be sure, sugar was grown in their West Indian islands, especially Curaçao, and grain was produced on the manors of the great patroons of Nieuw Amsterdam, but the main activity of the Dutch in the West

Indies was trading with Spanish colonists, to whom they brought slaves, and in Nieuw Amsterdam, it was commerce with the Indians from whom they got furs in return for rum and supplies. They endeavored to give a monopoly of trade to the Dutch West India Company, which had some success from 1621 to 1648, but the nature of their commerce was more suitable for individual initiative than for the action of a large company. Unfortunately, Dutch citizens frequently pushed their enterprise rather far with the result that the Netherlands was dragged into trouble with foreign powers—trouble that was augmented by rivalries within Europe. They had to leave Brazil, and they were forced out of Nieuw Amsterdam (1664) and out of a part of Guiana (1803) by the English. What remained to them was of little significance and the position of primacy which they had enjoyed in American trade gradually fell to the English and Americans.

So far as the French were concerned, they early realized how important colonies might be to their economy and, as we have seen, claimed Louisiana and Canada as a result of exploration and grabbed some of the less firmly held West Indian islands from Spain, notably Martinique, Guadeloupe, and Haiti. From the first, the French pursued colonial policies in the New World which conformed strictly to the basic principles of the colonial compact—that colonies existed exclusively for the benefit of the motherland and that trade should be reserved to French nationals. As in the East, so in the Western Hemisphere, the French attempted to control and develop their holdings by the creation of monopolistic companies. In the West, however, these companies did not have great success: The monopoly of the French West India Company was withdrawn after five years and the Company was liquidated between 1672 and 1674; the Canada Company and its successor, the Company of New France, had but brief existences, the latter passing from the scene in 1664. The necessity of developing production, the large capital investments required, and the lack of French emigration (there were only 7,000 white inhabitants of the French West Indies in 1642 and 3,000 in Canada in 1663) were greater handicaps than proprietary rule could cope with. From the third quarter of the seventeenth century onward, French holdings in the New World were governed as royal colonies, with the backing of the state at every turn.

In the course of time, the French were successful in getting production under way, particularly in the West Indies. Tobacco was grown there with success in the first half of the seventeenth century, and sugar, introduced in about 1640, became such an important commercial crop that the French islands became the veritable sugar bowl of France and of a large part of Europe as well. Then in Acadia, or Nova Scotia, as the

English called it, a thriving fishing trade developed; in Canada, fur traders and to some extent lumbermen did a lively business. Even in Louisiana prospects were promising, with the establishment of a settlement in the Mississippi Delta in 1699 and the founding of New Orleans in 1713. In 1787, French trade with the New World was five times greater than its commerce with the East and was a little more than one-fifth of all French commerce.

Unfortunately for France, national rivalries for colonial trade were so acute that many of its overseas possessions were lost in the eighteenth century. The French had to surrender Acadia to the English in 1713 (they had obtained it in 1667). They ceded Louisiana to their ally Spain in compensation for the loss of Florida after the Seven Years' War (1763), and although Napoleon got it back in 1800, it was sold in 1803 to the United States. The French gave up Canada to the English also in 1763, retaining only two small islands off the coast, St. Pierre and Miquelon, and they lost Haiti during the Napoleonic period to native revolutionaries. They fell victim to the animosities engendered by the very policies of colonial mercantilism.

English colonial policy in the New World conformed, like that of other European nations, to the ideas contained in the colonial compact. As we have already seen, the Navigation Act of 1651 and subsequent measures reserved shipping between England and the colonies to English and colonial ships and required that many articles be exported exclusively to England and certain others be imported only from England. Furthermore, England paid bounties to stimulate production in the colonies of those goods which it lacked, like tar, pitch, hemp, masts, yards, and flax (1704), indigo (1749), potash (1751), and silk (1770).

In two important respects, however, English experience in the New World differed from that of its predecessors and profoundly influenced its colonial policy. First, Englishmen went to the colonies of North America as permanent settlers in fairly large numbers; the population of the thirteen colonies was two million in 1776. Secondly, these people in the New World, especially those of New England and the Middle Atlantic states, developed the production of many goods to which they were accustomed in the homeland rather than strictly "colonial" products. Not only did they consider themselves to be the equals of Englishmen at home and deserving of treatment equivalent to that of their fellow men in the old country, but they undertook the development of an economy that was to make them in certain respects commercial rivals of the English. Therefore, when the English took steps to preserve the trading or manufacturing interests of some of their compatriots, the colonists felt sorely injured.

One of the fields in which the Americans had great success from early in their history was shipbuilding, for they had timbers for masts that were unequalled in the Old World and vast supplies of oak for frames and planking. In fact, on the eve of the American Revolution one-third of all ships flying the English flag had been built in America. Success in shipbuilding led directly to shipping, and American carriers, particularly those from New England, built up a lively shipping business, a flourishing fishing fleet off the coasts of Massachusetts and Maine, and a thriving whaling industry throughout the Atlantic Ocean. In their carrying business, the Americans developed a trade in fish from New England and flour from the Middle Atlantic states to the West Indies,

Table 2. Commerce of American Continental Colonies with England

(Annual averages, in thousands of pounds sterling, current value)

	Exports to England			Imports from England		
	1701–1710	1731–1740	1761–1770	1701–1710	1731–1740	1761–1770
New England	37	64	113	86	197	358
New York	10	16	62	28	92	349
Pennsylvania	12	14	35	9	52	295
Maryland-Virginia	205	394	468	128	207	491
Carolinas	14	177	330	22	94	262
Georgia			36		3	40

where these products were exchanged for sugar and molasses. The latter were brought back for refining and for the making of rum; then sugar and rum were carried to England, where they were sold so that manufactured goods could be paid for, or to Africa where they were swapped for Negroes for resale in the colonies. Moreover, American shippers carried tobacco and cotton from Virginia, South Carolina, and Georgia directly to England and brought back supplies for these colonies, but if they could not get a good return cargo, they simply sold their ship in England at a handsome profit and returned to begin all over again.

In all trade, except that to India, colonial vessels were treated as English ships, with all the same rights, privileges, and prerogatives, and they might even import wine as they would, for England had none for sale, and export flour freely, for England had at that time an abundant supply of the staff of life. But colonial shipping was hurt, especially that of New England, when the English West Indian planting interests decided Americans should not go to Spanish or French West Indian islands for sugar and molasses. Indeed, English sugar refining interests got in the Molasses Act of 1733 a heavy duty levied on *all* sugar and molasses going to the colonies on the ground that colonial sugar refining and rummaking were hurting their business. In a similar way, many infant industries in the colonies were injured by legislation to protect the colonial market for English manufacturers. Thus the Woolens Act of 1699 forbade the transportation of wool, yarn, or woolen textiles from one colony to another. The Hat Act of 1731 forbade the export of hats (mainly beaver hats which were then much in style) from one colony to another and a hat-maker from having more than two apprentices. The Iron Act of 1750 prevented the manufacture of iron and steel goods in America, although it permitted the free export of pig iron to England, and several laws prohibited colonies from aiding their own industries by means of subsidies.

Table 3. English Combined Imports and Exports

(Annual averages, in thousands of pounds sterling, current value)

	1701–1710	1731–1740	1761–1770
American continental	556	1,313	2,843
British West Indies	942	1,781	3,406
India	582	1,179	2,516
Ireland	579	1,045	2,850
Total Empire	2,802	5,751	12,651
Total Europe	7,673	10,555	11,740
Grand total	11,069	18,919	25,930

For a time many of these rules were not rigidly enforced; manufacturing developed in both New England and the Middle Atlantic colonies, while trade grew apace between England and the colonies.

However, after the Seven Years' War, or the French and Indian War as it was called in America, the English took the position that the colonies should pay a part of the costs of the conflict that was waged for their protection and should not interfere with English economic development. Consequently new taxes were levied and the older restrictions on colonial trade and manufacturing were enforced with some degree of rigidity. Thus the Stamp Act of 1765 required stamps on many documents in order to provide more revenue; the Sugar Act of 1764 reduced the rates contained in the Molasses Act, but these new rates were actually collected; and the Townshend Act of 1767 placed rates on several articles that were imported into the colonies. Such measures led to a great deal of bitterness, although it is clear that Americans profited by being members of the empire. In fact, one of the reasons why Scotland wanted to be united with England (1707) was to get the same privileges enjoyed by American shippers. Moreover, American commerce suffered after the Revolution because American ships no longer had the trading rights of English ships. Nevertheless, England lost what was to become the greatest economy of the world by a narrow policy that was derived directly from the colonial compact. Half a century later she repealed the Navigation Acts (1849) and gave her remaining colonies a greater degree of equality of treatment so far as economic development was concerned.

PART FOUR

*Rapid Economic Growth and Locational Shifts
in Western Culture's Economy—1800 to 1914*

CHAPTER 12

The Setting of the Industrial Revolution

The Industrial Revolution: A Revised View

In historical study, as in all branches of knowledge, views of certain periods or of certain developments sometimes become established in a wave of exaggerated statement and must subsequently be revised in the light of more sober judgment, more thorough analysis, and more abundant data. Thus it has been with the Industrial Revolution.

Time was when this great movement was considered to have been a very sudden transition in the production of industrial goods from handicraft to machine methods. This rapid change was conceived as having resulted from the invention of a few mechanical devices, especially textile machines and the steam engine—and that these inventions leaped full-blown from the heads of geniuses, all of whom were English. Also, this earlier view gave the impression that England was rapidly covered with factories, that these factories were inhuman places where women and small children worked to exhaustion, that England soon became an island of factory hands as well as of shopkeepers, and that the "Revolution" came to an end sometime in the early nineteenth century.

In the course of time this conception of the Industrial Revolution, based as it was on a tendency to intensify the dramatic elements of a period of rapid change, came to be tempered by a more judicial appraisal of what took place, by a fuller knowledge of events, and by a more complete understanding of technological change. Now economic historians recognize that the process of mechanizing industrial production was a slow one in that it depended upon the accretion of many mechanical details and upon a multitude of other contributing forces working over a long period of time. They are in general agreement that the new machines and methods of production would never have come into being if it had not been for the contributions of Ancient Times to mechanics, for the work of such men as Leonardo da Vinci, for the mechanical experimenters, Continental as well as English, of the seventeenth century, for the development of big markets, and for the growth of large savings and investments made possible through money and other instruments of exchange and credit. Furthermore, modern historians contend that the Industrial Revolution has no real conclusion—that the basic principle of the Revolution, making goods by using machines moved by energy from nonhuman sources, has continued to dominate industrial production up to the present time.

In addition to stressing the many antecedents and the long-continuing aspect of the Industrial Revolution, recent economic historians have tended to emphasize the fact that with the Revolution man was able for the first time in history to use on a large scale the inanimate resources of the earth which had been created over eons of time both for constructing things and for obtaining energy for both heat and motion. In a short period of time man freed himself from reliance primarily on the products of photosynthesis—on growing plants and animals—for satisfying his material wants, except for foodstuffs, and he thereby made available for humankind resources which were many fold more abundant than what had been previously available.

Then, too, historians now recognize that the Industrial Revolution did not have exclusively deleterious results for workers. Although working conditions in many of the early factories were certainly abominable, it is now generally thought that they were little worse than what they had been in the putting-out system or even among some farm laborers. Industrialization seems from an early date to have led to higher real wages among industrial workers and to have resulted in an increase in national income per capita of the population.

Finally, modern scholars of the Industrial Revolution stress that areas other than England met most of the conditions necessary for the mechanization of industrial production, that those regions soon borrowed from the heartland of industrialization the ingredients which they lacked, and that from an early date, these same districts made important contributions of their own to industrial techniques. In fact, the diffusion of industrialization from its points of origin, together with the process of adapting it to undeveloped regions, constitutes one of the most important aspects of the entire subject. Obviously more people have been borrowers of industrialization than direct contributors to it.

In short, then, the new look which has been given the Industrial Revolution emphasizes the point that not only was the productive capacity of the individual worker in industry greatly increased but the earth's crust was made to disgorge its treasures on an entirely new scale. It stresses the fact that a multitude of forces was at work creating an environment conducive to change and that the inventions of machines were only one of these factors. And it regards industrialization not as having been extraordinarily debasing to workers, but as having contributed to the economic well-being of industrialized peoples and to their political and military power vis-à-vis the other peoples of the earth. Indeed, most students of recent history would agree that the dominant position in the world of those in the area of Western culture is to be accounted for primarily by the productive capacity of individuals of the West.

The Desire for Material Betterment; Savings and Investments

However much economic historians may have altered their descriptions and analyses of the Industrial Revolution, they have all agreed that here was a movement entailing extraordinary economic growth. At no previous time of equal length in all human history had there been such a rapid increase in the production of goods per capita of the working force. Inasmuch as we are here confronted with the problem of economic growth, we are concerned with the same kind of factors which we have seen contribute to economic development at other periods of time, namely, with the strengthening of ideologies for material improvement, with a growth in savings and investments, with an increase in effective market demand, and with innovations in the productive arts.

Evidence of a greater desire for economic improvement was to be found on every hand. New men of wealth, dubbed "bourgeois" because, as we have seen in the growth of towns, those with recently acquired riches lived in the bourgs, were attaining higher prestige in society. Although Molière could poke fun at these late arrivals on the top rungs of the economic ladder, the fact was that their positions of economic power gave them a considerable amount of authority in all walks of life. In the Netherlands, the chief patrons of the arts came from among the new men of wealth; from the late seventeenth century the chief subject matter of Dutch artists was scenes from bourgeois life, if not the bourgeois themselves. In England the Whig party, which drew its strength from the middle class, dominated the political life of the country from the ministry of Robert Walpole until near the end of the century.

In France, practically all the philosophers of the Age of Reason, like Voltaire, Jean Jacques Rousseau, and Diderot, came from the bourgeois class and in a subtle way preached the wisdom of material improvement. They argued that there were laws of society, just as there were of the physical universe, and they proceeded to tell mankind what they were. One of these laws was that man wanted to be happy, which is the traditional position of the hedonist. A second was that man had natural "rights," of which life, liberty, and property were the most fundamental. And a third was that in order to enjoy the good life, to be happy, man had to have wealth which he could accumulate and use, unfettered by tradition or man-made law. Here were the expression of an ideology, a means of attaining it, and an attack upon privilege.

A desire for material improvement came not only from such reasoning or from the observation that bourgeois were assuming a more important position in public life, but also from the fact that almost the only way for a commoner to rise in a society dominated by a nobility that inherited its position was by acquiring wealth. It was only with money that titles of nobility could be acquired for themselves; and only with large dowries that they could marry off their daughters into the caste above.

That the ideology for material well-being was becoming more firmly established is evidenced by efforts to abolish laws and destroy traditions that prevented some persons from engaging in the more lucrative trades. Thus gradually nobles freed themselves from rules which forbade them from engaging in certain kinds of manufacturing and trade on danger of losing their titles. Artisans sought to break into the monopolies of others, which led to a weakening of guilds. And entrepreneurs tried to sell to an ever larger market in order to increase their earnings, which brought on the tariff unification of national states and the abolition of governmental grants of special privileges.

Then, too, the desire for material improvement was intensified by the development of special groups which formed because their members were thrown together in their efforts to better their lot. One of the most important of these groups was composed of those who left the countryside and went to live in cities, for they would not have made the change if they had not been highly motivated to acquire riches of this earth. Another group of the same kind was composed of those who broke their ties with their homelands and set out for wild and poorly known colonies overseas. Indeed, one of the reasons why the ideology for material betterment has been so strong in American life has been because the act of migration meant an autoselection of those who were urgently bent upon improving their economic status. How important the urban movement was can be gathered from the fact that the population of London increased from 674,000 in 1700 to 900,000 in 1801, that of Manchester from some 5,000 to 100,000 in the same period, that of Paris from an unknown size to 650,000 before the Revolution, and that of Bordeaux from 43,000 in 1688 to 109,000 in 1790. The importance of the second group can be envisaged when it is recalled that the population of the thirteen American Colonies increased from 434,000 in 1715 to 4,000,000 in 1790 and that all English emigrants from 1700 to 1800 are estimated to have numbered a million.

Finally, it seems that the desire for economic well-being grew *pari passu* with opportunities for economic growth, as had been the case so frequently in the past. Thus, as industrialization offered ever-greater opportunities for getting a larger supply of this world's goods per capita, everybody wanted more. Here was a two-way action in which the ideology for economic improvement contributed to economic development, and economic development fostered a desire for material betterment.

One of the branches of economic activity in which this reciprocal play of forces was most visible was savings and investment. In their desire to get on in the world, many people showed a willingness, if not even an anxiety, to put aside some of their earnings in order to invest in producers' goods that would make them still better off in the future. In some quarters, as among Calvinists in many lands and as among the colonists in America, leaders preached vigorously the virtues of thrift. To those who were not accustomed to the amenities of life, a small improvement in their standard of living gave so much satisfaction that they were able to save income above a minimum of increased expenditures. In his quotations from and comments upon the diary of Samual Walker of Rotherham, T. S. Ashton has given us an example of this phenomenon from an early stage of capital accumulation in industry:[1]

"1741. In or about October or November of the same year, Saml. and Aaron Walker built an Air Furnace in the old nailer's smithy, on the backside of Saml. Walker's cottage at Grenoside, making some small additions thereto, and another little hutt or two, slating with sods etc., with a small Garth walled in: and after rebuilding the chimney or stacks once, and the furnace once or more, began to proceed a little, Saml. Walker teaching the school at Grenoside, and Aaron Walker making nails and mowing and shearing, etc., part of his time.

"1743. Aaron Walker now began to be pretty much imploy'd, and had 4 shillings a week to live upon. . . .

"1745. This year Saml. Walker, finding business increase, was obliged to

[1] T. S. Ashton, *The Industrial Revolution 1760–1830* (London: Oxford University Press, 1948), pp. 95–97.

give up his school, and built himself a house at the end of the old cottage, then thought he was fixed for life; then we allowed ourselves ten shillings a week each for wages to maintain our families."

At this time the value of the concern was put at £400. But in the following year £100 was added by Jonathan Walker (a brother of Samuel and Aaron), £50 by John Crawshaw (who had previously been employed "as much as we could, at 12 pence per day"), and £50 by Samuel himself. Thus equipped, the partners set up at Masborough first a casting house and then, in 1748, a steel furnace. The story that Samuel Walker rose to fortune by stealing from Huntsman the secret of crucible steel has no foundation: it was not by such methods, but by unremitting labour, thrift and integrity that success was achieved. Year after year some addition, great or small, was made to the plant. In 1754 a warehouse was built, and a keel—characteristically called *The Industry*—was put on the river. Four years later the partners dug "a navigable cut" and "improved the road for Holmes to Masbro' and lanes towards Tinsley —Gloria Deo;" and in 1764 they added to their establishment "a large shop for frying pan makers." It was not, apparently, until 1757, when the stock had reached £7,500, that the Walkers allowed themselves a dividend—of £140; and throughout, the proportion of the profit that was distributed remained small. Thus is came about that by 1774 the capital had reached £62,500. Profits on the manufacture of guns during the American War, ploughed back as they were, had, by 1782, raised the figure to £128,000. In this year Samuel Walker died, but the policy laid down by him was continued by his heirs, and in 1812 the assets of Samuel Walker & Co. were estimated at £299,015, and those of a sister concern, Walker and Booth, at a further £55,556.

In addition to the financing of economic growth with the capital of those who found saving easy because their increased earnings greatly exceeded what they were accustomed to spend on living and besides the plowing of business profits back into plant, economic development was also furthered by capital amassed by banks through deposits and earnings on loans. Then, there was capital acquired from land rents that went especially into certain types of undertakings, like coal mining in England, that were closely connected with land ownership. Capital amassed in commerce often went into productive equipment, as in certain branches of the putting-out system. There was capital, too, accumulated from small investors through the sale of shares. And there was capital gathered together through the collection of taxes, some of which got into the hands of investors in sizable amounts because it was paid out to the holders of large blocks of state bonds.[2]

The reasons that induced the owners of these accumulations to invest

[2] This was true, at least in the case of England, where the public debt mounted to 861 million pounds in 1815, which has been established to have been 8 per cent of the money income of the country. In the case of France, amounts of the tax leases to farmers almost doubled from 1726 to 1786.

their moneys in large amounts in industrial enterprises are extremely complicated. In the last analysis, the chief reason was that high profits were to be expected from industrial undertakings. A secular rise in prices from at least the middle of the eighteenth century onward gave a certain buoyancy to economic activity; and machines seemed to make possible a dramatic reduction in costs of production without bringing down prices.

Whatever the reasons for investments in industry may have been, however, it is clear that capital for investment was becoming more abundant and that it could be had cheaply if governments did not bid up interest rates by their own borrowing. In the case of England the legal rate was lowered, following market conditions, from 10 to 8 per cent in 1625, to 6 per cent in 1651, to 5 per cent in 1714, and to 3 per cent on "consols," on the consolidated debt of the kingdom, in 1757. In businesses with good credit ratings interest charges seem to have followed a somewhat parallel course, 5 per cent having been common at the beginning of the eighteenth century and 3 per cent in 1756. It is undoubtedly safe to conclude with T. S. Ashton:[3]

The deep mines, solidly built factories, well-constructed canals, and substantial houses of the industrial revolution were the products of relatively cheap capital.

Market Demand; Labor Supply

Although savings and investments are considered by many students of the Industrial Revolution to have been the most strategic factors in breaking down the rigidities of traditional methods of industrial production, the fact remains that people were motivated to save and to invest because they expected thereby to better their material conditions. Furthermore, it is clear that their expectations depended in large part upon an increase in the effective demand for certain goods—upon a market in which there was both a growing desire for goods and a growing ability to pay current prices for them.

The reasons for an expansion of demand were numerous. In the first place, population increased in all the countries of Western Europe. In France the number of inhabitants has been established to have gone up from 20,000,000 in 1700 to 26,000,000 in 1789; in Austria to have increased from 20,000,000 in 1700 to 27,000,000 in 1800; and in England and Wales to have gone up from but 5,500,000 in 1700, to 6,500,000 in 1750, to nearly 9,000,000 in 1801, when the first census was taken, and to 13,750,000 in 1831. For all of Great Britain the population was 11,000,000 in 1801 and

[3] *Op. cit.*, p. 11. Similar conditions do not seem to have prevailed in France.

16,500,000 in 1831. Although from about 1740 to 1830 the birth rate appears to have remained fairly steady, there was a reduction in mortality rates. In England, it went from 35.8 for the decade 1730–1740 to 21 for the decade 1811–1821, owing mostly to the installation of closed sewerage systems, the development of better water supplies for cities, better medicine and surgery, improvements in hospital care, and perhaps better food supplies.

These increases of population meant that, given stable patterns of consumption, the need for goods increased. In all countries named above, prices went up, reacting to the greater demand and the larger supply of precious metals coming especially from Brazil. In fact, prices rose in France from an index of 100 in the period 1726–1741 to 164 in the years 1785–1789 and in England from 100 in the 1750s to 130 for the years 1790–1795. At the same time, an increased pressure of population on food supply was to be noted and thus on the ownership of land and upon methods of agricultural production. This explains, in part, why there should have been a new enclosure movement in England and tensions between peasants and manorial lords in France, which was one of the factors that contributed to the course of events during the French Revolution of 1789.

The growth of population appears to have had a very direct effect upon the textile trades, especially cotton, and upon building, for each individual had to have his own clothing and bedding and each expected to have a family of his own with its own separate living quarters. The market for cotton textiles was, in addition, increased by a style demand, especially for cotton prints in the "Persian" and "Indian" manner, for interior decoration, for calicoes in ladies' wear, and for cotton sheets that began to replace linen on the beds of gentry.

As Daniel Defoe wrote in 1708:[4]

We saw our persons of quality dressed in Indian Carpets, which, but a few years before, their chambermaids would have thought too ordinary for them; the chintzes were advanced from lying on their floors to their backs, from the foot cloth to the petticoat, and even the Queen herself at that time was pleased to appear in China and Japan, I mean China silks and calicoes. Nor was this all, but it crept into our houses, our closets and bedchambers; curtains, cushions, chairs, and, at last, beds themselves were nothing but calicoes or Indian stuffs.

The market for housing can be seen by a study of the growth of cities in the eighteenth century and by a survey of building in many of the villages. In England, completely new rural communities came into being

---

[4] Defoe, *Weekly Review*, January, 1708.

to take care of peasants forced off their holdings by enclosures and in France and the Low Countries new houses were constructed upon land that was being reclaimed from forest and sea to grow the food needed by the greater numbers of people.

The building of houses created a new market for builders' hardware, iron and steel tools, and construction equipment, thus giving a fillip to the iron and steel industries. This stimulus was fortified by a wave of canal and road building that meant a great demand for picks and shovels, for stone drills and sledges, wheelbarrows, and equipment for canal locks. Finally, the struggle between England and France for colonial possessions and domination of the seas, the American Revolution, the French Revolutionary Wars, and the Napoleonic conflicts meant an enormous increase in demand for munitions, ammunition, and naval fittings.

Another important consideration regarding the development of the market was that demand came to be concentrated on fewer producers. The urban dweller had a larger choice of persons to whom he might go to satisfy his wants and he tended to go to those who sold at lowest prices. Moreover, managers of big undertakings, like those in charge of the construction of a canal or the fitting out of a ship, and officers in quartermasters' corps preferred to deal with a few suppliers rather than with a multitude. This fact, and the great improvement in transportation owing to canal, road, and port construction, made possible a greater specialization of production by regions and by plants than had ever been possible before. During the Industrial Revolution in England the cotton textile industry became concentrated in Lancashire, iron production in the west Midlands, and salt refining along the coasts from Durham to Cheshire.

From overseas markets there came also an increased demand for goods, a greater specialization in products, and from the very nature of foreign trade an ever greater concentration of orders on a few merchants and from them, in turn, on a few producers. The tonnage moving through English ports increased, for example, over six times from 1700 to 1800 and the value of French trade, which on the eve of the French Revolution was about the same as the English, is said to have gone up from 215,000,000 livres in 1716 to 1,153,000,000 livres in 1787.[5] Thus the pressure of foreign demand on producers per capita in England was exceptionally great, for, as we have seen, the population of France was at this time nearly three times that of England and Wales. Some idea of the impact of foreign commerce on industrial production can be gleaned

[5] Arnould, *De la balance du commerce* (Paris, 1791). An increase of some four times if adjustments are made for price changes.

from the accompanying table, which indicates for the eighteenth and early nineteenth centuries a tendency for foreign trade to "lead" or grow faster than industrial production. In fact for this period, the generalization is frequently made that commercial growth came before the development of new techniques of industrial production, although the reciprocal relations between commerce and industry were obviously very great.

Table 4. Total British Overseas Trade and Industrial Production, 1700–1933
(1913 = 100)

Years	Total overseas trade	Industrial production	Index of relationship
1700–1709	0.5	1.3	38.5
1710–1719	0.6	1.4	42.9
1720–1729	0.8	1.6	50.0
1730–1739	0.9	1.7	52.9
1740–1749	0.9	1.7	52.9
1750–1759	1.0	2.0	50.0
1760–1769	1.3	2.0	65.0
1770–1779	1.4	2.4	58.3
1780–1789	1.5	3.1	48.4
1790–1799	2.4	4.3	55.8
1800–1809	3.4	5.9	57.6
1810–1819	4.3	7.2	59.7
1820–1829	5.3	10.0	53.0
1830–1839	7.5	14.7	51.0
1840–1849	11.2	20.2	55.4
1850–1859	19.0	28.3	67.1
1860–1869	27.3	36.1	75.6
1870–1879	41.4	48.1	86.1
1880–1889	55.3	58.1	92.2
1890–1899	67.1	68.1	98.5
1900–1909	80.8	80.3	100.6
1910–1913	94.8	91.8	103.3
1914–1918	74.3	88.4	84.0
1918–1926	85.1	81.9	103.9
1927–1929	103.1	100.8	102.3
1930–1933	86.2	94.1	91.6

SOURCE: Werner Schlote, *British Overseas Trade* (Oxford: Blackwell, 1952), p. 51.

The impact of increases in foreign commerce on industry was particularly great because of the great concentration of trade in certain goods. Thus in Great Britain in the years 1814–1817, the first for which pertinent records are available, 78 per cent of all English home-produced exports were finished goods, and of these about 75 per cent were textiles and 8 per cent metal products, especially those made from iron. In the years

1814–1845, 70.4 per cent of net imports, that is, imports excluding re-exports, were raw materials, and of this amount about half was destined for textile processing. In France, this kind of concentration on goods that were in mass demand and could be turned out in greater quantity by the aid of machines was less great, for the French specialized in the exportation of luxuries, art products, foods, and wines; yet even there the growth of textiles was marked and was to become more so as the nineteenth century advanced. From early in this process of industrialization, European states, which were to be in the vanguard of economic development, were to make goods for mass markets, were to import raw materials and foodstuffs, and were to process raw materials so that they could export finished products. It was in this manner that the industrial states of Western Europe came to be known as the workshop of the world.

The Labor Force

In any consideration of the great complex of factors which combined with a timing and in proportions that were propitious for effecting changes in industrial techniques, serious attention must be given to the labor force. It was necessary to have workers who were willing to be employed for money wages, who were capable of operating the new machines, and who were numerous enough to meet the demand of employers.

Until recently, historians of the Industrial Revolution were of the opinion that England was particularly forward in this regard. They pointed to the fact that the peasants, who had been forced off the land by enclosures, were now without land by which to maintain themselves and were so desperate for work that they would have made a pact with the devil himself. It was, indeed, thought that a large labor force was waiting at the very doors of the factories for employment at low wages.

This view has now been boldly challenged. Although English landlords were engaged in depriving peasants of those holdings which they had for long had the right to farm and thereby took away from large numbers of the agricultural class their customary means of making a living, it is now realized that most of those who were pushed off their holdings did not flock immediately to industrial cities, but sought agricultural employment on the enclosed farms, on reclaimed lands, and on canal and road-building projects.

Furthermore, recognition is now given to the fact that in the early history of the Industrial Revolution in all parts of the Western cultural area no great difficulty was experienced in finding an adequate supply of labor, irrespective of whether land reforms pushed peasants off the land or, as in France, attached peasants more firmly to their holdings. In Lancashire, Alsace, or New England, industry attracted workers from rural districts, in spite of overcrowding in cities, long hours of work in unsanitary factories, and wages that were far from munificent, but in general a little higher than what had been earned on farms. The reasons for labor's having been attracted to industry were, first, that life in the city was thought to be more glamorous than on the land, secondly, that work in urban areas was more readily available and less seasonal than that in rural districts, and thirdly, that nearly all members of a family could be employed in industry for money wages—for visible income. This last point was of particular significance, for women and children had been notoriously "underemployed" on the farms, in the sense that they earned very little, whereas in certain industries, as in textiles, they found ready employment because of their dexterity in the performance of delicate tasks. Therefore the total "take-home" pay of a family must have seemed very large to many workers, even though it may not have been capable of buying the same "list of goods" as farm income. People seemed to be willing to give up light and air, the great outdoors, and farm-fresh products in return for a little more finery, the pleasures of the "crowd," and the "cultural" opportunities of the cities.[6]

In some respects and within obvious limits the presence of a large labor force that was nearly destitute would have been a drawback rather than an advantage in the process of industrialization, for the extremely poor cannot save to invest nor can they buy goods which are placed on the market. If there had not been a growing demand, those who did have surplus for investment would have found little incentive for placing it in productive enterprise. On the other hand, some shortage of labor in the face of growing demand seems to have encouraged the adoption of new ways of doing things—the introduction of more machines. Indeed, in the United States where there has traditionally been a dearth of labor, the major characteristic of inventions has been devices to take the place of labor or to make labor more efficient, as is evidenced by the cotton gin, the assembly line, and "automation."

In every discussion of the supply of workers in the Industrial Revolution, one must take into consideration another aspect of the question, that labor was becoming much more mobile than it had been for centuries. With the breakdown of feudalism and the manorial system, workers in Western Europe were no longer legally bound to the soil, but were free to seek their fortunes where they pleased. With the adoption of the

---

[6] J. D. Chambers, "Enclosure and Labor Supply in the Industrial Revolution," *The Economic History Review*, ser. 2, vol. 5, no. 3, pp. 319ff., 1953.

same machines in many places, techniques were standardized enough so that a worker could easily adapt himself to the requirements of employment in many places, and with improvements in transportation, especially by water, workers could travel at relatively low cost to seek jobs in distant places. Indeed, with the Industrial Revolution one of the greatest "movements of population" of all times took place, with people moving to cities chiefly within the same linguistic area, across the Atlantic to the New World, and in North America from the Eastern seaboard to the sites of mineral deposits, water power, and transportation centers further inland.

Although it is now thought that the enclosure movement gave England and Scotland no marked advantage over other lands in the matter of sheer numbers of workers available for employment, these two countries seem to have had a jump on all others in that their workers were freer than those anywhere except in the American Colonies from the confining restrictions of guild regulations. In fact, in England most of the guilds in those industries in which mechanization was the most pronounced, that is, in the textile and metallurgical trades, had long since relaxed their rules, so that many workers could attain the full development of their potentialities and experiment with new methods of production.

Moreover, in England and in America payment on a piece basis, especially in the putting-out system, provided an incentive for workers to introduce improvements in their operations so that they could earn more. On the Continent, on the other hand, labor's range of opportunities was much more limited, for guilds continued in existence, for a long time successfully maintained opposition to new industries (cotton prints were not permitted in France until 1759), and curbed the development of the putting-out system.

Furthermore, England seems to have had some advantage in industrialization through having a relatively large body of moderately well-trained workers to run the new machines. Inasmuch as England and Scotland had thriving textile and metallurigical trades before the advent of machines and inasmuch as the first machines employed skills that were very close to those used in handicraft production, there were many workers who could move without delay into the operation of machines. In this connection, one should take note of the fact that in the spread of machine technology, those techniques which moved most rapidly and most easily to new areas were those which were close to handicraft techniques, in part because they could be used by workers with their handicraft skills. This was especially noticeable in the field of textiles, the new machines being the first of English inventions to be adopted by France, the first to make important headway in the United States, particularly in New England, and the first to be taken in by underdeveloped areas, such as Italy in the second round of industrial diffusion, especially after the middle of the nineteenth century, and in India, in the third round, especially after 1900.

But the greatest advantage which the United Kingdom possessed in the matter of labor was a goodly supply of workers at the most advanced technical levels. From the very outset of the Industrial Revolution a premium was placed upon men who could construct the new machines, repair them when they broke down, and make such complicated preparations for their use as setting warps in intricate patterns on mechanical looms.

Apparently the supply of labor with the highest skills was greatest where interest in investigation was most intense, where primary education was most widely developed, and where mechanical contrivances were widely enough developed to provide opportunities for advanced training. Although the study of "natural philosophy" was being greatly expanded in the British Isles, on the Continent, and in America during the eighteenth century, although new schools were being established to give instruction to the children of the merchant classes, and although some new industrial techniques were developed in France as well as in England, the British were undoubtedly leaders in all these respects. The universities of Glasgow and Edinburgh had no peers in matters of scientific inquiry and experimentation in the late eighteenth century and it was more than mere chance that James Watt, a laboratory assistant at the former institution, should have become familiar with the expansive force of steam and the problems of its utilization as a prime mover in industry. The Scottish system of primary education was the best and most widely diffused of any in Western culture, and Nonconformist academies adopted curricula that for the age were heavily weighted toward practical affairs. Thus it was not an accident that many of the early inventors and mechanics were Scotsmen—that, for example, seven of Watt's eight assistants in the business of setting up steam engines were Scots. Finally, as we shall see in more detail later, England was the pioneer in the employment on a large scale of new machines and productive methods, and thus provided greater opportunities than any other region for training in the highest skills.

From very early in the Industrial Revolution, people in foreign lands realized that the English possessed industrial techniques which gave them a cost advantage, and foreigners expressed a burning desire to acquire the new methods of production for themselves. Ideas traveled with great speed, with the result that general notions about the new machines were soon known in France, the Austrian Netherlands, the

Rhineland, and America.[7] To get new machines actually constructed and set up for use in the lands of adoption was not, however, an easy task. Its successful accomplishment depended upon highly skilled workers, and they came to be actively sought after. The French offered large subsidies to anyone who could bring over English technicians, construct "English" machines, and put them to work. John Cockerill, the son of an English worker, built a great industry at Liége in Belgium for the construction of machines. Samuel Slater, who had been employed by Richard Arkwright, came to Rhode Island, where he went into partnership with local enterprisers to form the firm of Almy, Brown and Slater, and thus laid the foundation for a great textile machine industry. As late as the middle of the nineteenth century, the Amoskeag Mills at Manchester, New Hampshire, had a special recruiting policy in Scotland in order to get an adequate supply of highly trained technical men in their shops.[8] And the history of the introduction of machines in Germany and Italy is shot through with the names of foreigners who brought new techniques to these countries.

For their part, the English realized that they had knowledge and skills which were of such advantage that they should keep them to themselves. The extent of their concern is indicated by the following:[9]

. . . laws of 1774 and 1781 made it an offense to export tools or utensils used in manufacturing cotton and linen cloth, and to send abroad sketches, models, or specifications of textile machines. Similar regulations were applied to the secrets of the metallurgical trades in 1785 and 1786, and a general act of 1795 endeavored to prevent the leaking out of information about manufacturing techniques. Skilled workers were not allowed to go abroad after 1782; and if they did, they were to return within six months or lose their British citizenship and have their property confiscated. These British efforts to keep a national monopoly of their advanced techniques by a strict control were not completely abolished until 1843.

The Availability of Power and Industrial Raw Materials

Important as were the supply of skilled labor, the demand for goods, and the investment of much capital in the process of developing mechanized industry on a large scale, the availability of industrial raw materials

[7] The French Encyclopédie Méthodique, published at the end of the eighteenth century, had several volumes devoted to a remarkable set of plates portraying a great variety of industrial and agricultural machines that had just come into being.

[8] Daniel Creamer, "Recruiting Contract Laborers for the Amoskeag Mills," Journal of Economic History, vol. 1, no. 1, pp. 42–57, May, 1941.

[9] S. B. Clough and C. W. Cole, Economic History of Europe (Boston: Heath, 1947), p. 405.

played a role in determining the specific places in which industry would be located. In general, it may be said that in so far as the transportation of materials used in manufacturing constituted a large element of final costs, industry tended to settle at places where the bulkiest and hardest to move materials were found, especially if they were much bulkier and much harder to transport than the finished products made from them.

At the beginning of the Industrial Revolution one of the most important locational factors was water power, for no other source could produce mechanical power so cheaply. Water had to be used where it was found, for not until it could be used to generate electricity could it be "transported" to other locations. Consequently, most of the early cotton textile centers among the industrial countries were found along rivers in hilly regions, as in Lancashire in England, along the Merrimack River in New England, in the Vosges Mountains in France, and later on the southern slopes of the Alps in Italy.

Other industries responded to other locational factors, the iron-smithing industry being located near ore outcroppings in forests, salt refining being centered near salt mines or salt marshes which had abundant fuel at their disposal, sawmills in or near forests, and brickyards near clay-banks. Furthermore, inasmuch as water transportation was by far the cheapest form of carrying freight at the end of the eighteenth century, industries that involved the shipment of bulky and weighty products profited from being near good ports to take advantage of shipping by sea and from being located on an extensive inland waterway system in order to reach the largest possible source of supplies and extent of market. Those industries which required great skills, like watchmaking or machine-tool making, tended to be drawn to areas having specialized labor; those that depended upon style demand, like women's clothes, tended to settle near their markets both to be abreast of changes in demand and to have close contact with customers.

The exact force of the various factors determining location changed as new techniques made possible the generation of different kinds of power, the use of different raw materials, and new forms of transportation. Thus the invention of the steam engine gave a new mobility to the power plant and made the location of industry possible at any site where costs of transportation were low. The discovery of a method of smelting iron ore with coke took the smithing industry away from outcroppings of ore in forests and located it near coal mines, for the very good reason that some five tons of coal were used to smelt one ton of ore, and the finished product weighed much less than the ingredients which went into it. And the building of railways gave a flexibility to carrying that had never existed when main reliance was placed on water transportation.

England seemed to be particularly favored by Providence as regards those factors which were primary in determining the locations of industry in the second half of the eighteenth century. In the matter of raw materials it was especially blessed. It had, in the first place, large supplies of native-grown wool for the manufacture of a product that up until 1802 constituted Britain's most valuable export and for long thereafter remained one of the more important British items sold abroad. The large supply of native-grown wool, increased by the enclosing of land for pasture in the sixteenth century and the extension of sheep grazing in the Highlands of Scotland in the eighteenth, meant the existence of a kind of agriculture which could make profitable use of marginal land. It meant such a wide dispersion of raw material that household workers under the putting-out system could readily be supplied without high transport costs. And it contributed both to giving employment to "underemployed" women and children and to avoiding imports that would have given Britain a problem of settling foreign debts.

England also had large supplies of raw cotton at her disposal, for through military victories in India the British were able to get raw cotton from that source and subsequently to introduce cotton growing successfully in their American Colonies.[10] In the New World, commission merchants made the British desire for cotton widely known and after emphasis was taken from trying to grow long-staple fiber in the Sea Islands off the coast and placed on growing short staple on the mainland, and after the invention of the cotton gin in 1793, American supplies of cotton for British jennies were great.[11] In 1821, of the 1,305,000,000 pounds of raw cotton which Americans exported, 71 per cent went to Great Britain, 11.5 per cent to France, and 7.5 per cent to other countries.

In the matter of sources of energy, England was also well endowed. Although other countries, especially Alpine countries, had superior potential supplies of water power, England had many small streams that could turn the wheels of that day and had a reliable enough rainfall to keep the streams almost as full as the Alpine torrents which were fed by mountain snows. So far as coal was concerned, however, England had a great advantage. The early development of mines around Newcastle, which were on the very shores of the sea, the consequently cheap transportation of coal to numerous ports of which London was the most important, and the use of coal in industry placed England far ahead of

[10] Southern plantation owners found that cotton could be grown on their lands more profitably than tobacco, with its widely fluctuating prices. Moreover, shippers already engaged in bringing "colonial produce" to England discovered that cotton could provide very lucrative cargoes.

[11] As late as 1784 eight bags of American cotton were seized at Liverpool by customs officers on the ground that that much fiber could not have been grown in America.

other countries in the utilization of a product which was to assume enormous proportions as a factor in location. France's output of coal was low in the eighteenth century, although its main field in the North was opened between 1720 and 1734; German production was almost insignificant, the first mine in the Ruhr Basin going into operation only in 1841. In 1840, Great Britain produced 31,024,000 tons of coal, compared to 3,929,000 tons for Belgium, 3,091,000 for Prussia, and 3,003,000 for France.

So far as iron ore was concerned, although Great Britain was only moderately well supplied, the country had been a leader in the late eighteenth century both in the per capita use of iron products and in the development of a new technology in the smelting and refining of iron. In England, there were many outcroppings of iron ore, but in the northern and central sections and in the great valley of Scotland coal was in close proximity to the ore—and this proximity provided a glorious opportunity for experimenting with coal, which was already being used for domestic heating and for such industrial purposes as brewing and as a fuel for smelting iron. It was the eventual substitution of coke for charcoal which was to revolutionize the ferrous metal industry and to make iron products more plentiful and cheaper than ever before.

In relatively few others places were coal and iron found in quantity in such happy union. In the great Lorraine iron field, there was little known coal in the eighteenth century, and besides at that time only limited amounts of alluvial ores were smelted because the abundant minette ores could not be worked satisfactorily with charcoal. In the Ruhr coal field, there was no iron. And in the American Colonies, where blast furnaces sprang up in such quantity that in 1775 they actually outnumbered those of England and Wales, vast supplies of timber made possible the working of deposits in New Jersey and the Adirondacks of New York. Only as the industry moved into Pennsylvania was coal used as a fuel, following examples out of Britain. Most smelting was carried on at forges wherever there were outcroppings of ore, water power to work the bellows, and forests to provide fuel, as in the Walloon parts of the Austrian Netherlands, in the Rhineland, in Lorraine, in Sweden, on the nothern slopes of the Massif Central in France, and on the southern slopes of the Alps.

Transportation

In the matter of ocean carrying England was also very well off. At the end of the eighteenth century it was estimated that out of a total of 4,026,000 net tons of shipping for all of Western culture, Britain had 6,856,000 tons to 250,000 for France and 970,000 for America. Her great

DI MACHINE, ET EDIFICII.
PORTE PER SOSTENNER L'AQVA D'ALCVN FIVME PER
BISOGNO DELLA NAVIGATION ET ALTRO.
Tauola I

Seventeenth-century Gate Lock. Economic growth required that there be a greater division of labor and a greater division of labor demanded cheaper transportation. The use of the lock made possible cheaper transportation inland. This picture shows the boats apparently being raised. They have come into the lock from downstream through the gate C. As the gate B is opened, with C closed, water rushes into the lock from upstream. When the lock is full the boats will continue up the stream. Note that the boats are small and probably two of them are for short hauls. Note, too, that the gates are opened and closed by winches. Gate locks served also as dams, on gently flowing streams. (*From Vittorio Zonca, Il Nuovo Teatro, 1656.*)

RIVERS ——————   CANALIZED RIVERS ==========   CANALS - - - - - - -

The Canal Era of the Early Nineteenth Century in the United States.

overseas trade meant that she had a vast organization both for selling her merchandise and for tapping the resources of the earth. Moreover, the Navigation law which required that certain materials should be brought to England in English ships meant the development of an entrepôt trade which made England mistress of certain supplies. Liverpool, for example, came to be the center for trade in cotton, and this fact was of immense significance in keeping Lancashire mills supplied in times of shortages, as during the Napoleonic Wars.

Furthermore, the English recognized early the importance of improving their inland waterway system. Indeed, Adam Smith in an oft-quoted passage in his *Wealth of Nations* stated:[12]

As by means of water-carriage, a more extensive market is opened to every sort of industry than what land-carriage alone can afford it, so it is upon the

[12] Bk. I, chap. 3.

RIVERS ——————   CANALIZED RIVERS ==========   CANALS ----------

Major Waterways of Western Europe.

sea coast, and along the banks of navigable rivers, that industry of every kind begins to subdivide and improve itself.

In the light of such opinion as this, it is not strange that the English began early to render their rivers more navigable and to build canals. Much of this pioneer work is associated with the name of James Brindley (1716–1772), an illiterate millwright. One of his first important accomplishments (1761) was building a canal for the Duke of Bridgewater from the Duke's coal mines to Manchester—a waterway that at one place was carried high in the air by an aqueduct. Subsequently Brindley joined Liverpool and the Mersey River with Manchester and built the Grand Trunk Canal, which joined the Midlands and North of England and had an outlet to the sea. Thus was launched a canal-building mania which provided Britain with one of the best inland waterway systems of the time and which, incidentally, gave a fillip to the joint-stock company, for canal entrepreneurs almost always employed the joint-stock form of business organization.

Perhaps the country to be most thoroughly infected by the English canal-building bug was the United States. There the major transportation problems of the times were to render the many rivers which flowed in parallel lines into the sea more navigable so that deeper hinterlands could be tapped, to augment coastwise traffic, and to connect some of the major rivers with good ports. Thus, one of the first canals was on the Connecticut River in order to circumvent the falls at South Hadley (1794); another was the Middlesex Canal between the Merrimack River and Boston (1804); a third connected Charleston with the Santee River (1800). Only later were attempts made to construct canals westward, the most famous and most successful of all being the Erie Canal, opened in 1825, and the Ohio Canal that joined Cleveland on the Great Lakes with the Ohio River. Of the Erie's chief rivals, the canal from Harrisburg to Pittsburgh was only a moderate success because it had to make use of a railroad portage at the Allegheny divide. The Chesapeake and Ohio Canal, which aimed to reach the Ohio River, never got beyond Cumberland, Maryland. By the time it was constructed, steam railways were offering such stern competition that canal building waned and all but disappeared.

In France, there was relatively little canal building in the eighteenth century. Indeed, the government had such serious financial problems to face that it could not take on anything else and private companies showed little interest in such undertakings, for capital requirements were very great and all sorts of internal tariff barriers and tolls curbed domestic traffic. In the seventeenth century Colbert had shown an interest in canal construction and had actually built the famous Languedoc Canal that joined the Atlantic Ocean with the Mediterranean Sea via the Garonne River. Relatively little else, however, was done either to make swift-flowing rivers, like the Rhone, navigable or to build canals until after the Napoleonic period. Then a wave of canal construction got under way, which led to the joining of Paris with Lyons via the Burgundy Canal, to the connecting of the Rhine with the Rhone, and to the construction of lateral canals on the Garonne and the Loire.

Other areas pursued various policies in the matter of water transportation. Germany had several navigable rivers which stretched far inland, but they all ran parallel to each other so that there was no natural network of water traffic, and river shipping was interrupted by innumerable tolls and tariffs. Here little effort was made to connect the rivers except for the Elbe and Oder and not until French occupation were customs barriers reduced in number. In the Low Countries new construction was marked in the early nineteenth century and much the same can be said of northern Italy.

Although the carrying of bulky cargo was much cheaper on water than on land (in fact, a ton of goods could then be carried across the ocean for what it cost to travel 30 miles on land), land transportation was almost always involved to some extent in bringing goods to a given location for processing or in carrying finished products to consumers. Thus good roads were absolutely essential for economic progress, because a horse could draw over an ordinary dirt road five times what it could carry on its back and could pull two or three times on a good road what it could on a poor one.

In the matter of roads, England also had some advantage, for a great wave of road building took place in the country in the eighteenth century. In order to reduce costs of road construction below those occasioned by the laying of cobblestones, two Scotsmen, Thomas Telford (1757–1834) and John McAdam (1756–1836), developed a system for creating a firm roadbed of fairly large rocks by covering these rocks with smaller stones, and by binding the whole together with gravel or slag. The road thus had a firm foundation that could take heavy traffic. It was crowned so that water was drained off it and flanked by ditches that prevented it from being washed away. The methods of Telford and McAdam, which are the basis for all modern road building, although asphalt and concrete have been substituted for clay and gravel on the surface, were extensively used by turnpike companies which built toll roads as investments.

The English example of road building was followed in the American Colonies, much as was the canal-building mania. In the New World the need for road construction was obviously very great, for settlement inland necessitated building absolutely new means of communication, since before the coming of the white man there were only Indian trails, which were hardly more than footpaths. Thus dirt roads were constructed by towns and villages, "turnpikes" were constructed by joint-stock companies between more important towns, and "post roads" were built by the government to hasten postal service between the chief centers. The Federal government even proposed to build arteries leading to the West, of which the Cumberland Road, or National Turnpike as it was also called, was the most important. This effort failed, however, because those who did not profit directly from the road were not willing to pay taxes for its construction. For a time road building was left primarily to the states.

Road building in France, Italy, and the Austrian Low Countries was less active in the eighteenth century than in England and America, in part, because they had networks of Roman roads. Here attention was given mainly to repairs and improvements of existing systems, although the French founded the famous School of Bridge and Road Building for training civil engineers. So far as the Germanies were concerned, they had few Roman roads and did little to unite their many ports with good roads until the nineteenth century. Here as on the Continent generally, improved transportation facilities did not precede industrialization—they came as part of the introduction of machines at a later date.

CHAPTER 13

The Mechanization of Industry

New Techniques of the Industrial Revolution

The intricate interconnections among the various branches of human activity constitute one of the most baffling objects of study for social scientists. Investigators want to know what role economic phenomena play in the creation of social institutions and in the formation of interest groups. They want to know how social institutions and interest groups make their weights felt in political life, how political action influences the minds of men, how ideas and ideologies react on economic behavior, and so on in endless variations. It is unreal to isolate one part of the exceedingly complex pattern of life in society and then to attribute all change to it. It is more in accordance with what has actually happened through time to recognize that "multiple factors" in various parts of the total scene account for great movements in society.

Thus in the study of the Industrial Revolution, mechanical inventions, chemical discoveries, and the development of new techniques may be so separated from the environment whence they sprang as to make their appearance seem completely artificial—to make them seem to be the brain children of a few notable geniuses. Moreover, their adoption may be made to appear as though they were in the vanguard of change and as though other parts of societal life, like ideologies, political practices, and social groupings, "lagged" behind and adjusted to them. As a matter of fact, however, most new ways of turning out goods have come about

259

as the answer to well-defined and recognized needs, as if to confirm the old adage that "necessity is the mother of invention" and as if, indeed, new techniques "lagged" behind a social need for them. Furthermore the factors which contributed toward bringing forth new techniques were not only numerous but they came together for the first time in all history in just the right proportions and in just the right relationships to produce new mechanical contrivances. Here is striking evidence of the importance of the doctrine of necessary concomittances, which is opposed to the traditional manner of thought that assumes a prior cause and subsequent effect, as in the simple syllogism.

The necessary and sufficient forces which were at work together in the environment which produced mechanized industry seem to have been, as we endeavored to show in the last chapter, (1) a desire for material betterment, (2) a considerable knowledge of mechanics, hydraulics, and metallurgy, (3) capital for investment, (4) a demand for more goods, (5) raw materials in sufficient and concentrated supply to be worked on a large scale, (6) methods of transportation to make possible the accumulation of supplies and to carry finished goods to market, and (7) workers who were willing to work for a daily wage and who were able to adapt themselves to new ways of doing things. Furthermore, we have tried to demonstrate that these conditions for industrial advance were most adequately present in Great Britain, although to a greater or less extent they existed in many places in Western culture, so that, in fact, mechanized industrial production diffused fairly rapidly, once its advantages had become recognized.

Mechanization of the Textile Industry

In the early phase of the Industrial Revolution, the most far-reaching inventions were made in the textile, ferrous metal, and power-machine industries. The demand for the products of all these phases of production was great; all had the possibility of producing rich rewards for successful entrepreneurs, and all at the handicraft stage required extraordinary amounts of human energy and procedures which were extremely boring and repetitious. Moreover, technical changes in these industries had a profound effect upon subsequent industrial developments. Those in the textile trades did much to show the advantages to be derived from a division of labor, to establish production on a factory basis, and to turn out standardized goods for an unknown market. Improvements in the manufacture of ferrous metals and the consequent lowering of the price of iron made available a building material which was essential for the construction of machines that could withstand the wear and tear of rapid operation under heavy load. And the development of power plants, using inanimate materials that were in large supply, made possible the driving of machines which were concentrated in factories and the propelling of carriers that furnished safer, more adequate, and cheaper transportation.

Which branch of industry should be regarded as the pioneer in change is somewhat arbitrary, for innovations were visible at about the same time in various trades. However, inasmuch as some of the first of the more dramatic aspects of mechanization took place in the textile industry, especially in the making of cotton cloth, it has become traditional to begin the account of the Industrial Revolution with this industry.

That some of the first important changes in techniques in the eighteenth century should have taken place in this trade is not surprising. In the first place, textile techniques were already at such a point of development that only a few minor alterations had to be effected to render both spinning and weaving semiautomatic and to make the application of mechanical power to these operations practicable. Secondly, inasmuch as many persons were familiar with existing textile techniques because of the widespread practice of spinning and weaving, the inventive talents of very large numbers were brought to bear on solving fundamental problems of cloth manufacture. Thirdly, cloth was in great demand, for everyone used it and some, like the inhabitants of large cities and pioneers overseas, did not produce their own because of more pressing demands upon their time. Fourthly, the cotton branch of the textile industry was free of guild restrictions on the use of new methods to reduce costs of production. Lastly, since workers in the putting-out system were paid piece rates, they had an incentive to adopt new ways of production.

In the textile industry, the real bottlenecks of production were in spinning and weaving, for the fulling of woolens had been mechanized, cottons could be printed expeditiously with woodblocks on flat presses, and the hand operations of carding (straightening out such fibers as cotton) and combing (mixing short fibers in a fluffy mass so that they can be twisted) consumed little time. In spinning, the problems were that an operator had to "draw out" the fiber into a loose strand, then twist this strand by use of a spinning wheel which was run by a foot pedal, and finally wind the finished thread onto a bobbin. This process was slow, tedious, expensive, and ill paid. What was needed was a method of production which would mechanically perform some or all of these operations.

In weaving, the main difficulty was "throwing" the shuttle through the strands of thread that constituted the warp and then of "beating" the thread left by the shuttle so that it would come compactly against the previous thread thrown. In the case of one weaver working alone, the width of a piece of cloth was determined by the distance to which he could reach to his right to throw the shuttle and then to his left to throw it back again; or in the case of two weavers working together, one at each side of the loom, by the distance that the shuttle would travel with one throw. In any case, the pace of these operations was slow, for the throws were fatiguing and between every throw the weaver had to pull the beater.

Because spinning and weaving were light enough to be practiced by anyone, even children, and because both tasks could be performed in odd moments of the day and in seasons when other work was slack, entire households, especially in country districts, became engaged in them.

Hargreaves's Spinning Jenny. In the model shown above one may see the upright spindles which gave the rovings the twist. The carriage on top of the machine through which the threads went could be pulled backward and pushed forward, thus drawing out the thread to give it fineness. Mechanical power could be easily substituted for the man-operated crank. (*Reproduced with permission of Textile World.*)

Hand Loom. This wooden hand loom of the early nineteenth century was used in Maine. The photograph shows the threads of the warp strung through the string heddles. By operating the pedals the heddles may be raised and lowered so that a shed is obtained between the alternate threads of the warp. Through this shed the shuttle passes with the thread which constitutes the woof. The beater, upon which the hand of the operator may be discerned, is pulled back toward the operator and pushes the thread of the woof back to make the material firm. (*Reproduced with permission of Textile World.*)

Then, as the market demand for textiles increased and trade in them became profitable, certain merchants tried to employ this widely dispersed labor force for their own interests, that is, they took raw materials to the workers, sometimes provided them with looms and spinning wheels, paid the workers by the piece for their efforts, and marketed the finished products.

With the "merchant-employer" or "putting-out" system, the stimuli to

Arkwright's Carding Machine. The fine metal pins that are sticking up on the rollers, which turned in opposite directions, carded wool, that is, made it fluffy and ready for spinning. (*Reproduced with permission of Textile World.*)

portant steps toward the development of power-driven machines in the textile industry was the water frame, patented by Richard Arkwright in 1769. Arkwright, although a barber by trade, was familiar with the process of making cloth and had a keen eye for opportunities for earning an extra penny. Possibly he knew of a plan for a power-driven spinning frame which had been developed by a certain Thomas Highs or Hayes, but at all events after a series of law-suits he began in 1785 to produce water frames for spinners. His enterprises flourished to such a degree that he was able to brag that his fortune would be enough to pay off the national debt of Britain.

Hard on Arkwright's invention came a large cluster of other technical innovations in the making of cloth—a cluster which provides a classic example of how pressures for change bring forth inventive responses and how major developments in technology result from an accumulation of many details. In spinning, Samuel Crompton, the son of a yeoman farmer and a spinner and tinkerer by trade, produced the "mule," which was a cross between the roller and spindle method of making thread—a machine that made such excellent thread that curious spinners bored holes in the inventor's shop in order to peep in on the secret device. About 1782 a machine was invented to make rovings at low cost, which was a significant step forward because both "mules" and "jennies" used rovings rather than the loosely carded fiber. Furthermore, Richard Roberts, a maker of machines, patented in 1825 the "self-actor," which provided for the automatic motion of the carriage in order to draw threads; John Thorpe of Rhode Island, the center of the textile machine industry in the New World, substituted (1828) for the flyer with hooks on it a flanged annular ring on a C-shaped traveler, which facilitated the winding of the thread on a bobbin and kept the thread under perfect tension.

In the application of mechanical power to weaving, the crucial invention was the "power loom," which was patented in 1785 by Edmund Cartwright. This young man, unlike his contemporary contributors of new techniques, was an Oxford-trained classicist and clergyman. He became interested in mechanics through stories which he heard from his parishioners and applied himself to the devising of an automatic power loom that could keep pace with the expected abundance of yarn from Arkwright's frames. Cartwright's fertile mind soon solved some of the major problems involved in producing the desired machine and before the end of the century his power loom was being widely adopted. In addition, the weaving branch of textile manufacture got a loom which was capable of weaving figures and other designs in cloth—a loom that was the invention of the Frenchman Vaucanson and that was subsequently improved by Jacquard (1801). Finally, metal looms began to be made in 1803 and in the same year steam power was for the first time applied to the process of weaving.

In other phases of clothmaking technical improvements were realized that contributed to the general movement of increasing output per unit of human input. Thus in carding, Richard Arkwright developed (1775) the "crank and comb," probably after the designs of others, which turned the carded fiber out in the form of a strand that could then easily be made into rovings. The French chemist, Berthollet, developed a method of bleaching with chlorine which came to supplant the usual and more cumbersome practice of exposing cloth to the sun in order to make it white. Thomas Bell invented a cylindrical press (1783) for printing cloth, which embodied a principle that was eventually to be introduced into the printing of books (1790). And John Mercer developed a method of processing cotton that gave this fiber a silky feel—"mercerized cotton."

As these various inventions increased the production of cotton goods, the demand for raw cotton grew by leaps and bounds. Here, however, a real bottleneck existed, for picking seeds from the bolls was a slow and laborious task, one man being able to clean only from 1 to 6 pounds of cotton per day. Some advance in overcoming this difficulty was made with the invention of the rolling mill, which would clean up to 25 pounds per day, but this device could only be used on long-staple cotton and long staple could be grown successfully only in a few parts of the region that supplied most of Europe's cotton—the Southern states of the United States.

A successful solution to the problem of picking seeds from cotton was finally found by the American Eli Whitney, a professional tinkerer and inventor, in 1793. His cotton gin, which consisted of circular saws with dull teeth that pulled cotton fiber through a comb so fine that the seeds remained behind, was capable, if manned by three men, of cleaning some 50 pounds of cotton a day. Inasmuch as this machine worked best on short-staple cotton and short-staple cotton could be grown in the upland Piedmont region of the American South, it was a great boon to that region's economy. It permitted the extension of cotton culture at the very time when a money crop was being sought to accompany tobacco. The gin was largely responsible for the increase of the cotton crop in the United States from 1,500,000 pounds in 1790 to 85,000,000 pounds in 1810,[1] and incidentally for the extension of the plantation system and of Negro slavery. It thus contributed much to the tensions which developed between the Northern and Southern states, which led finally to the War between the States.

These various inventions in the textile trades came by the end of the eighteenth century in England and by the conclusion of the first half of the nineteenth century in Belgium, France, Germany, and the North-eastern states of the United States to have a visible effect upon the character of industry. In the first place, the expense of the machines was such that only men of wealth could acquire them, which meant that the means of production were gradually to become the property of investors instead of workers—one of the hallmarks of the capitalist system. Sec-

---

[1] Incidentally, cottonseed oil began to be used for lighting (1818) and cottonseed cake as a feed for livestock (1821).

ondly, the machines were heavy enough so that they had to be housed in well-constructed and sometimes especially built establishments, which meant that they were actually concentrated in buildings that came to be known as factories. Thirdly, this concentration of production was accentuated by the fact that mechanized power, at first water and then steam, could not be provided economically unless it worked many machines at once. And fourthly, the use of power and large supplies of raw materials coming from overseas meant that the location of plants had to be in hills where there was water power, at places where the raw material could be brought by water, and/or where coal could be delivered at low cost. Thus the adoption of machines tended to destroy the merchant-employer or putting-out system, to create a factory system, and to locate the cotton textile industry at such places as Lancashire or Derbyshire in England, on the banks of the Clyde in Scotland, around Rouen, Lille, and Mulhouse in France, at Ghent in Belgium, in the Rhineland near Krefeld in Germany, and along such rivers as the Merrimac in New England.

Of all the cotton textile centers of the world, Britain was by far the most important because of its leadership in the new techniques. In the first half of the nineteenth century, Great Britain consistently took more than half of all American exports of cotton, and usually more than half the American crop was sent abroad. By the beginning of the nineteenth century British cotton textile exports were of greater value than its exports of any other product and in 1841 nearly twice as many workers were employed in the English cotton textile trade as in all the metal trades, ranging from the smelting of iron ore to the making of clocks.

The economic gains which fell to England as a result of the advances in the technology of making cotton cloth were the envy of other nations of Western culture and of manufacturers of other types of textiles. Some countries, notably France, sent industrial spies to England to learn the new techniques and gave subsidies to manufacturers who adopted the new machines or who employed English workers, skilled in the new ways of production, while certain political entities, like the Northern states of the United States, gave bounties to those who would improve local methods of spinning and weaving. Some entrepreneurs, like Thomas Cockerill at Seraing in the Belgian Netherlands, and like Samuel Slater in Rhode Island, made fortunes in producing machines patterned after those of England.

Producers of other kinds of textiles, for their part, showed evidence of a desire to lower costs by the use of power-driven machines and by developing new sources of raw materials. The jenny was used for spinning wool as early as 1773, although it was not widely adopted for this purpose until after 1785; the power loom was employed in the woolen trade in the first half of the nineteenth century; and wool was brought from Australia to the English market after 1818, one-half of all the wool that was woven in England coming from down under by 1850. Concomitantly, there was a shift in location of the British woolen industry from the southwest to Yorkshire, which gave the industry water power from the Yorkshire hills and cheap transportation through the ports of Liverpool and Hull and along the Liverpool-to-Leeds Canal and the River Humber. Similarly, in the United States the woolen textile trade tended to be located where there were port facilities and/or water power, as at Fall River and Lowell, Massachusetts, and in the Mohawk Valley of New York State. In France and Germany, mechanization of the woolen industry occurred mainly after 1850, and by that time the steam engine had been developed to a point where it could provide necessary power efficiently and where it was being used to make cheap inland transportation possible. Accordingly, in these countries the woolen trade remained to a large extent in traditional centers of production in order to take advantage of the supply of skilled workers, as at Rheims, Sedan, Elbeuf, Roubaix, and Carcassonne in France and at Aachen and Berlin in Germany.

In the manufacture of silk, mechanization also went on apace. Here the Jacquard loom, driven by mechanical power, came into general use and the ordinary loom for plain cloth began to be employed by 1844, especially at the great silk manufacturing center of Lyons in France. In the linen industry, the first successful spinning machine was patented in 1814 and the power loom began to be used extensively about 1840. In knitting, an improvement was made with the invention of the circular knitting machine by the Englishman Brunet and of the latch needle (1863), which made the application of power to knitting both possible and profitable. Then in sewing, there was the invention in 1846 of the sewing machine by the American Elias Howe—a device which was to change profoundly the needle trades and to put the manufacture of clothing into factories.

Ferrous Metallurgy and Machine Tools

Important as were the new techniques in the textile trades in awakening the imaginations of businessmen to the advantages of mechanizing industrial operations, in using power from inorganic sources to drive machines, and in concentrating production in factories, changes in the production of textiles were of no greater moment for the long-range effect upon industry than were those innovations which appeared in the refining of ferrous ores, in the making of steel, and in the transformation of these materials into useful objects. Because of improvements in these trades, Western culture, which had a complete monopoly of the new techniques, acquired a new "building material." Without these materials economic growth would have encountered an almost insurmountable obstacle.

In the refining of iron ore, the location of smelting has been determined by the relative costs of bringing ore and fuel together, for the raw ingredients in this process are bulky and cheap in respect to the finished product. In general the tendency has been for smelting to be settled near supplies of fuel, for per ton of ore several tons of fuel have been needed. Consequently, prior to the nineteenth century, when charcoal was the fuel used in the iron trade, smelting was usually carried on in forests as close to ore outcroppings as possible. If woodlands were depleted of good charcoaling wood and if prices of charcoal rose to be inordinately high, the industry migrated to new sites, as in the case of England where ironworking went from Sussex and Kent to Shropshire, the Midlands, and south Yorkshire between the sixteenth and eighteenth centuries. Such moves were expensive; and then in the late eighteenth century were not certain of finding any area where charcoaling wood was plentiful. Obviously a substitute fuel for charcoal was needed to release the industry from its strait jacket.

Experiments to find a fuel to take the place of wood had become numerous in the seventeenth century and invariably these experiments involved the use of coal. In its raw state, coal was not very satisfactory for working iron, because it did not provide a hot enough fire to permit the metal to run out of the blast furnaces into pigs, it had so much sulfur in it that it could not be used for casting because of resulting flaws, and it could not be used for making the almost pure malleable iron, known as wrought iron, for it rendered this product too brittle. What was required was some way to purify coal so that it would produce a hotter fire and would not contaminate the iron.

Credit for overcoming the deficiencies of coal must go to a Quaker ironmaster of Shropshire, Abraham Darby of Coalbrookdale. It was he who first reduced coal to coke by burning off its coal gas and other impurities in an oven, much as wood was reduced to charcoal, and who used the resulting fuel in smelting. Partly because the coal which he employed, that is, Shropshire clod coal, made good coke and partly because his blast furnace was high and his blowing equipment extraordinarily powerful, his process proved successful (1709). Subsequently coke fires were made hotter by the invention of piston air pumps (1761), which gave a stronger blast than bellows, and by the use of a blast of hot air instead of coal—a change that was developed by J. B. Neilson in Glasgow in 1828.

Yet the use of coke in smelting was adopted with less speed than might have been imagined, although it was taken up more rapidly in England than in France or the United States. As late as 1846, some three-fifths of the pig iron produced in France was smelted with charcoal and in the United States not until 1855 did pig iron produced with coke surpass that smelted with charcoal, for wood was in relatively abundant supply.

Soon many other improvements were made in the production of iron goods. Coke was used to make cast iron, as in the case of pots and cannon, to heat pig iron before it was hammered to get malleable wrought iron, and to heat wrought iron prior to running it through grooved rollers (slitting mill) that turned it into rods. Furthermore, the making of wrought iron was accelerated by the discovery (1784), almost simultaneously, of puddling by Peter Onions, an ironmaster, and Henry Cort, an Admiralty contractor. These men found that if pig iron was heated in a reverberatory furnace out of direct contact with fuel and if the molten mass were stirred or "puddled," many of the impurities would be burned off, thus rendering the usual amount of hammering unnecessary. Then, too, the production of wrought iron was facilitated by the invention by Isaac Watt in the 1780s of the steam hammer, which could deliver 150 blows a minute of a weight amounting to 120 pounds, and by Henry Cort's development of a rolling mill that not only pressed out some of the carbon contained in the iron but had the advantage of producing iron sheets that could be used in boilers, as ship's plates, and armor.

The use of coke on a large scale in processing pig iron accounts in part for the transfer of the ferrous metal-working industries to the proximity of coal. In the case of England the shift was clear, particularly in the making of builders' hardware, like nails. In Belgium an important ferrous metals industry developed around Liége and in the province of Hainaut, where there was plenty of coal and to which iron ore could be easily and cheaply brought by water. In France an iron industry was created under governmental encouragement and bounties near coal at Le Creusot—an industry, incidentally, based upon techniques brought to France from England by industrial spies and by English ironmasters like William Wilkinson. In the United States, there was a trend toward the concentration of the industry in the Pittsburgh area of Pennsylvania to take advantage of supplies of coal. And in the Germanies, by the 1840s the industry began to be located in the two main coal fields of the country, in the Ruhr Valley and in Upper Silesia. All of these areas employed the new techniques which had been so largely developed in England, but it took them a long time to overcome the advantage which the technological headstart had given the English. In 1865, for example, more than half of all the world's annual production of pig iron was accounted for by the United Kingdom.

In the making of steel, which was to be one of the most important branches of the ferrous metal industry, England also achieved an early position of primacy because of the development of superior techniques. There, toward the middle of the eighteenth century, Benjamin Huntsman, a clockmaker, mechanic, and general tinkerer, joined a multitude of experimenters who were trying to make a better grade of steel for watch springs. In his work he heated wrought iron in a crucible and added specific amounts of carbon in the form of pure glass in order to give his product the degree of hardness and ductility desired. This process was satisfactory for the immediate purpose for which it was designed, but steel produced by it was expensive because of the necessity of first making wrought iron and then of using a high-cost method for getting the requisite amount of carbon back into the iron.

The need for steel was, however, ever more pressing, for it was the only known metal which could stand the strains and stresses of the increased speeds at which machines were operated and of the heavier tasks that the new devices were called upon to perform. Cast iron was too brittle for railroad rails, drive shafts, and tires for wheels; wrought iron was too soft and pliable for a host of products ranging from nails to bridge beams. Yet the relatively high price of steel drastically limited its use—and this limitation threatened to hamper the growth of machine industry.

Under these circumstances ironmasters and trained chemists began an earnest search for a way to make cheaper wrought iron and hence cheaper steel. Thus it was that William Kelley, an American blacksmith from Kentucky, demonstrated in 1851 a method, which incidentally he did not develop to the point of practical application, whereby pig iron could be made into wrought iron without hammering, and that Sir Henry Bessemer, son of a French refugee living in England, made practical a similar manner of making wrought iron and patented the crucial step in his procedure (1856).

The Bessemer process consisted of driving a powerful blast of air *through* a molten mass of pig iron so that such an intense heat would be produced that carbon and other impurities would burn off and a nearly pure iron would result. This was a big improvement over puddling in a reverberatory furnace, for in that system the fire was in a compartment of the furnace separated from the molten iron and carbon was burned out of the iron by the heated gases passing over it—a very slow process indeed.

The methods employed by Bessemer, in spite of all their promise, were not a great success at the outset. Ironmasters who made the heavy capital investments necessary to acquire the essential equipment frequently complained that the regulation of the blast was extremely difficult—that if they left it on too long it oxidized the iron so that it would not forge and if they did not leave it on long enough, too much carbon remained in the iron. Moreover, they claimed that no matter what they did the Bessemer process would not reduce their pig iron to wrought iron. In view of such complaints Bessemer went to work to try to find reasons for the difficulties encountered. So far as the length of the blast was concerned, he argued that from experience with the color of the flame from the blast one could determine approximately when to turn off the air and stop the action. So far as the failure of his method to reduce certain pigs was concerned, he had to admit that he had originally experimented with particularly good quality Swedish pig iron and that pigs made from ores with a phosphoric content could not be treated by his process. This was a severe blow to many of the ironmasters of Staffordshire and the Midlands of England and of Lorraine in France, where ores contained large amounts of phosphorus.

The advantages to be derived from a cheaper method of making wrought iron, and thus of steel, were so great and phosphoric ores were so abundant in many of the established metallurgical centers that experimenters were spurred on to surmount the shortcomings of the Bessemer process. They soon succeeded in perfecting a method of making steel directly after the "blow" had produced almost pure iron by simply adding to the still-molten mass an iron with a sufficient amount of carbon to produce the desired quality of steel. Then in 1866, Sir William Siemens, an Englishman of German birth, and two French brothers, Emile and Pierre Martin, developed an altogether new method for the industry —a method which became known as the Siemens-Martin process. This new procedure consisted of pouring molten metal into a shallow pan-like container—the "open hearth"—and then playing a mixture of gas and air upon it in order to burn off carbon and other impurities. Although this process was much slower than that devised by Bessemer, taking between seven and eight hours as compared with half an hour, it had several distinct advantages. It permitted the use of scrap iron. It could handle a greater range of ores, including those with a low phosphoric content; it yielded some 10 per cent more of the metal input; and most important of all, it allowed testing for carbon content so that a more accurate control could be exercised in the production of steel of desired hardness and ductility.

Then, hardly had the Siemens-Martin process become a proved success than two English chemists, Thomas and Gilchrist, developed (1878) a method for satisfactorily smelting phosphoric ores. These men simply lined their furnace with magnesium limestone, which served to absorb the phosphorus, thus permitting the refining to go on in the desired manner. Although in time the limestone lining of the furnace would become saturated with phosphorus and would have to be replaced, it could be broken up and sold as fertilizer.

Finally, other metallurgical chemists found that various qualities could be given steel by alloying it with other metals—manganese to give it greater ductility, tungsten to make it hard, and chromium to prevent it from oxidizing. Obviously here was science serving as the handmaiden of industry.

All these technological changes had an enormous effect upon economic growth and upon the nature and location of the ferrous metals industry. They made possible a great reduction in the price of steel—it fell by 50 per cent from 1856 to 1870—and thus made this metal available for a host of uses for which iron itself was not suitable. Furthermore, they came to the conclusion that coke was the absolutely essential fuel in refining iron; hence the industry was freed from forests and limited supplies of wood. The new techniques also determined that for a long time to come iron ore would be brought for refining to the proximity of coal deposits because of the larger requirements of coal per ton of ore. And finally, these men made possible the exploitation on a large scale of the hitherto little-used phosphoric ores of Lorraine and Luxembourg which are the greatest deposits of Western Europe and one of the most important of the world. The new techniques go far to explain why such great centers of the steel industry came to be located in the Ruhr Valley of Germany and in the Pittsburgh area of Pennsylvania and why the nexus of ore-coal relations came into being in the Lorraine-Ruhr area and in the Northern Minnesota–Pennsylvania–Ohio regions.

Dramatic as was the development of techniques in the refining of iron ore, it was scarcely more striking or more essential for the mechanization of industrial production than improvements in the methods for fashioning iron and steel into desired shapes. If industry had continued to rely upon the hammer and the anvil, upon files, clumsy molds, and man-driven drills and lathes, it would not have been able to make strong, long-lasting machines to perform industrial tasks accurately and efficiently.

Pressures for bettering the technology of metal working began to make themselves felt almost as soon as iron and steel came into greater supply and industry indicated a need for sturdier machines. As early as 1774, John Wilkinson, a man of inventive mind and business genius—a kind of Arkwright of the metal industry—patented a drill for boring cannon which was of the utmost importance, for not only did it greatly improve this weapon and lead to more general use of firearms with rifled bores, but it permitted the making of accurate cylinders, so essential to the proper functioning of the steam engine.[2] Henry Cort, as we have already seen, patented the rolling mill in 1783, which made possible low-cost boiler plate and armor. Henry Maudslay invented (1797) his slide rest, which moved by an accurate screw device on an all-metal lathe—a contribution to metalworking that greatly facilitated the accurate cutting of metal and that made possible such automatic devices as the screw-making machine. Thomas Gifford and S. Guppy developed nail-making machines in 1790 and 1796. The intrepid John Wilkinson launched an iron boat in 1787 and manufactured cast-iron pipe to carry water 40 miles to Paris. In 1837, Crawford "galvanized" iron, that is, he covered it with a coat of zinc to keep it from rusting—a process that was a forerunner of "tinning iron" (1879), which made possible the tin can.

These various inventions were the product of tinkerers and humble craftsmen who added detail to detail until they had something new— they were not for the most part the work of scientists who were hunting for "necessary sequences" to obtain definite ends or to test various hypotheses in their laboratories. In general, these inventions answered real social needs, for they made possible a more extensive use of iron and steel, more efficient machines, standardization of types, and interchangeable parts—a development to which Eli Whitney in America made an especial contribution. Finally, they did much to further the division of labor in the machine industry and to the concentration of production in factories. John Wilkinson himself applied many of these inventions so successfully that he became in his day a veritable iron magnate. The Cockerill Company used many of them in its great machine shops at Liége, Belgium, and the German industrialist Borsig had such a large establishment for them that he employed 1,200 men by 1847.

The Need for Power—the Steam Engine

In few historical movements have the interrelationships of various developments been so striking as in the Industrial Revolution. As the story is told, it seems as though each new machine came into being when the need for it was great—that machine answered machine in a great contrapuntal symphony that gave rise to the most remarkable industrial advances of all time. Concomitant developments were indeed extraordinary, one set of conditions giving an impetus to the search for new tech-

[2] The drill was soon improved by a German, Breithaupt, who constructed a horizontal cylinder-boring machine in 1807 at Cassel.

niques throughout a given trade or industry. Of all these concomitances, none is more striking than the invention of the steam engine—a device which was essential for driving the heavy machines which were coming into being and which had much greater locational mobility than the water wheel. It was, indeed, to free machines from the limitations imposed by the low "horsepower" of treadmills, by the fickleness of windmills, and by the arbitrary locations at waterfalls required by the water wheel.

The idea that motion could be obtained from steam had been known to the ancients, for evidence exists to show that Hero of Alexandria made a reaction sphere. Little attention was paid, however, to the properties of steam nor were any serious efforts made to make use of steam until the seventeenth century. It was then that Solomon de Caus (1576–1630), an industrious experimenter, discovered that if a tank filled with steam were closed and if the steam were then condensed a partial vacuum could be created. It was then that Branca (1629) designed a turbine driven by steam. It was then, too, that experiments which were being pushed to improve pumps in order to remove water from mines led to the use of steam.

The first important step in the employment of steam for pumping appears on limited evidence to have been taken by Edward Somerset, later Marquis of Worcester, about 1663. At least in that year the Marquis and his heirs were given a monopoly of a "water commanding" engine for ninety-nine years—a contraption that seems to have been capable of raising water about 100 feet. We know of a certainty, however, that subsequently Thomas Savery, a British army officer, either made improvements upon the Marquis's device or came independently to design a very similar "atmospheric engine." This machine consisted of a tank connected to a pipe that ran down into water and to another that ran upward. Following the principle laid down by Caus, a vacuum was created in the tank by condensing steam which had been introduced into it. Then when the valve of the pipe running down to water was opened, air pressure forced water up into the tank; and this water was, in turn, forced out of the tank and up the other pipe by steam pressure.

Although this machine had some utility for light work, it was not very practical for the most urgent pumping task of the times, the heavy job of pumping water out of mines. It had to be located within a relatively few feet of the level of the water to be pumped, it had to use higher pressures than existing equipment could stand; and its action was slow and inefficient. Consequently the search for better pumps went on, and very shortly considerable success was attained by a combination of principles already known. This new synthesis, the most crucial in the development of the steam engine, was effected by Thomas Newcomen, an ironmonger of Dartmouth, England, about 1708. The novelty of his work was that he used steam to work a piston within a cylinder in order to get an up-and-down motion. The piston was attached to a beam resting on a fulcrum, which was connected in turn with a regular atmos-

Savery's Final Steam Engine. This was really an "atmospheric" engine. With valves A and B both closed, the steam was admitted to the spherical chambers. This steam was condensed by running water over the sphere from the reservoir C. When a vacuum had thus been created, valve A was opened and atmospheric pressure drove water into the chamber. Valve A was then closed and valve B opened. Steam under pressure was then admitted to the chamber and water was blown up the vertical pipe. (*From A. Wolf, A History of Science, Technology and Philosophy in the Sixteenth and Seventeenth Century, London: George Allen & Unwin Ltd., 1935. Courtesy of the publishers.*)

The ENGINE for Raising Water (with a power made) by Fire

REFERENCES
—

1 The Fire Mouth under the Boyler with a Lid or Door.

2 The Boyler, Content 13 Hogfheads.

3 A Brafs Cylinder to Rarifie and Condenfe the Steam.

4 The Great Bars that Support the Houfe and Engine.

5 The Great Ballanc'd Beam that works the whole Engine.

6 A Lead Cyftern fill'd by the Mafter Pipe.

7 Very ftrong Chains fixed to Pifton and the Plugg and both Arches.

8 The Little Arch of the Great Ballanc'd Beam that moves the Sliding Beam.

9 The Sliding Beam mov'd by the little Arch of the Great Beam.

By courtesy of the Science Museum, Kensington

Newcomen's Steam Engine. The nine "references," which form part of the design of this illustration, explain the operation of the engine. It should be added that within the cylinder 3 there was a piston. It was forced upward by the introduction of steam below it. This steam was condensed, creating a vacuum below the piston, so that when a valve at the top was opened to let in air atmospheric pressure was enough to push the piston back into place. The beam activated a water pump. (*By courtesy of the Science Museum, Kensington.*)

pheric water pump. From the accompanying diagram it can be seen that, by letting steam into the cylinder under the piston, the piston is driven upward. Then by condensing the steam to create a vacuum and by opening a valve at the top of the cylinder, air pressure will force the piston downward to its original position. In this way it was possible to pump water more cheaply than by any other method; hence the engine was a success for over fifty years. In time improvements were made on the original design, valves being opened and closed automatically by a mechanism attached to the beam, and a safety value, invented by Henry Beighton of Newcastle in 1717, was placed on steam boilers to reduce the danger of blowing them to bits by too high pressures.

Quite logically, the Newcomen engine attracted considerable attention among businessmen, mining engineers, and even professors of "natural philosophy," and experiments were conducted with it both for the purpose of explaining important principles and of improving it. It was not extraordinary that professors at the University of Glasgow, where instruction in natural phenomena was emphasized, should have used a model of the engine in the course of their lectures. Nor was it out of the ordinary that an instrument maker by the name of James Watt (1736–1819), who had a shop on the premises of the University, should have been called upon to repair and set up a Newcomen model for demonstration purposes.

While at his task, Watt made what in retrospect seems to have been a very elementary observation—that the chief defect of the Newcomen engine, that which made it particularly inefficient in the use of fuel, arose from the alternate injection and condensation of steam in the cylinder. Clearly, in order to prevent steam from condensing, at least in part, before the piston reached the top of its stroke, the cylinder had to be warm; conversely, on the return of the piston to its starting position at the bottom, the cylinder had to be cold in order to condense the steam. This meant an enormous waste of energy. Therefore, Watt began a search for a method by which this difficulty could be overcome. He hit upon it in 1765. His solution consisted of using a separate condenser which could be kept permanently cool, while the cylinder remained always hot. This single alteration increased the efficiency of the engine four times.

Important as this improvement was, however, the engine had to be further developed before it could have any significant impact upon the evolution of industry. This development proved to be exceedingly demanding in capital, technical skills, and entrepreneurial talent. John Roebuck, Watt's first financial supporter, was so heavily drained of funds that he sold out his share of the patent, which had been taken out in 1769, to Matthew Boulton, a well-to-do businessman of Birmingham. In many ways, this was a fortunate occurrence, for Watt now had access not only to greater supplies of funds, but also in moving the scene of his investigations from Glasgow to Birmingham, he became established nearer to ironworks and machinists who were able to produce the parts which he needed and closer to the potential market for his product. In fact, his first engines were used primarily for pumping water to turn water wheels which ran bellows at ironworks and for pumping water out of iron mines. They were not, however, used immediately for pumping water out of coal mines, which can be explained by the fact that the engines at the beginning were leased rather than sold and that the royalty paid for their use was based upon the savings effected in fuel and that the cost of fuel was not great for coal mine operators.

Undoubtedly James Watt would have gone down in history as one of the great inventors of all time if he had made no other contribution to the atmospheric engine than that already described, but he saw great possibilities in the power of steam as a prime mover and he went on to realize them, encouraged as both he and Boulton were by Parliament's extension of their patent from 1775 to 1800. One of Watt's most pressing desires was to get rotary motion from his engine, but he was stymied for some time because patent rights kept him from using the "crank and shaft" system—a method employed for getting rotary motion on spinning wheels and today illustrated by the mechanism on the sides of steam locomotives. In 1781, however, he attained his desired goal with his "sun and planet" system—a device which consisted of putting geared teeth in the shaft that was driven up and down by the beam and by having these geared teeth engage a small geared wheel on the down stroke and running free on the up stroke. In 1782, he patented the double-acting rotative engine, in which steam and vacuum were used alternately at each end of the cylinder, and he adopted the principles of the expansive power of steam by stopping the flow of steam before the piston had completed its stroke, relying upon expansion to finish the job. In 1784 he introduced "parallel motion," whereby the piston rod was attached to the beam in such a manner as to let it move in a straight line; he added the throttle valve to regulate the flow of steam, and in 1788 he put a governor on the engine to give it greater regularity and smoothness of operation.

After a long, hard struggle filled with discouragement and reverses, the partnership of Boulton and Watt began about 1786 to prosper. By 1800 it had built and set up some five hundred engines both at home and abroad. These engines were still used chiefly for pumping water, even in the Paris waterworks, but they were also employed in iron mills, in textile factories, in breweries, and in a host of minor trades. In 1807 Robert Fulton propelled his *Clermont* on the Hudson River with a steam engine and as early as 1814 Robert Stephenson constructed a successful steam locomotive. The future of the steam engine was thus amply assured. Improved as it was by three important French inventions—the tubular boiler of Seguin in 1817, the pressure gauge of Bourdon in 1849, and the injector of Gifford in 1858 for getting water into a boiler that was under pressure—the steam engine was employed ever more widely. In 1850, Great Britain had 71,000 horsepower of steam in the cotton industry to 11,000 horsepower of water, and 54,000 horsepower of steam in other branches of the textile trades to 13,000 horsepower of water. In 1847, France had 5,000 steam engines with a total horsepower of 60,000, and in 1846, Prussia had some 22,000 horsepower of steam, 14,000 of which were in the mining and metallurgical industries. Clearly the age of steam had come.

Mechanization of Other Industries

Although the invention of the steam engine, the development of cheaper methods of making iron and steel, and the finding of ways for making cloth by machines were most crucial in bringing about the mechanization of industry on a large scale and the concentrating of it in factories, many other changes in technique were realized which contributed to the Industrial Revolution. In all phases of production efforts were made to find ways for improving output while diminishing human input and for rendering useful the vast supplies of inorganic materials in the earth's crust without relying upon turning them into organic matter. More raw materials, more mechanical transformation of them, and more use of prime movers per employee were the aims in industrial change.

Although the steam engine was destined to be for long the most popular source of mechanical power, the water wheel continued to be important especially where falling water was abundant, the flow steady, and coal scarce, as in Scandinavia, the Alps, New England, and the Piedmont region of the Appalachian Mountains. Moreover, water power continued to be used to the extent that it was because the old type of flutter wheel came to be supplanted by a much more efficient manner for harnessing the force of falling water—by the water turbine, invented by the Frenchman Fourneyron in 1832. This turbine was particularly efficient in rendering useful large masses of water with slight fall or velocity, whereas the Pelton wheel was adapted for handling small flows at great speed. These two machines did much to keep alive the use of water power, even in those cases where factories had to be located at relatively inaccessible spots, until the development of electric power and high-voltage transmission made power from water more mobile.

Attempts to make the water wheel more effective were characteristic of the efforts of man to get machines to do work which had previously been performed by human hands. In lumbering and woodworking, for example, the circular saw, invented in Great Britain in 1777, was to revolutionize the use of wood. No longer was it necessary to employ hand-hewn timbers or to avoid using boards in construction because of the high cost and laborious task of sawing them with "up-and-down" saws worked by hand or water power. Henceforth they could be cut from logs with dispatch and accuracy. Furthermore, the band saw for sawing logs was invented in 1808, although it was little used until the end of the century. The rotary planer was patented in 1793; the Blanchard lathe, which turned pieces of wood against cutting disks in such a fashion that irregularly shaped objects, like ax handles and shoe lasts, could be produced, was invented in 1820.

In the paper industry, a dramatic step toward more rapid production was taken by the Frenchman Louis Robert, who invented (1799) a machine to make paper in a continuous strip. It actually took the wet ground rag pulp from the tank in which it lay, spread it on a fine wire screen, pressed out the water, dried the paper, and wound the final product on a roll. The sugar industry was improved by employing better evaporating equipment and the steam engine for running grinders; whereas the use of beets as a source of sugar during the Napoleonic period, when the Continent was blockaded from West Indian supplies, laid the basis for an industry that was to make great progress after 1830.

Boulton, Watt's partner, developed a power-driven machine for stamping coins. Warfare was made more "mechanical" by the invention of the breech-loading and percussion lock guns (about 1807), the development of the revolver (1836), the rifling of cannon to give a projectile a twisting motion for greater accuracy, the invention of the machine gun by R. J. Gatling, an American, in 1862, and the development of the needle gun (1866) in which the charge was set off when the needle pierced the shell. Gunpowder was produced by a new mechanized process, devised by the French during the French Revolution, in which the various ingredients were pulverized and mixed by putting brass balls in a barrel and rolling the whole instead of by use of mortar and pestle.

Furthermore, the mechanization of communications was inaugurated with the independent discovery of the electric telegraph by Samuel Morse in America and by Cooke and Wheatstone in England (1837). More rapid water transport was forecast by the invention of the screw propeller (1836). The turret lathe was patented in 1845. Compressed air began to be used in mining and the coal disk cutter came into being in 1852.

Remarkable as all these changes in the field of mechanics were, they were hardly more significant in the process of industrial development than the application of chemistry to industry. Progress in chemistry in the late eighteenth and early nineteenth century was little less than phenomenal. Although by the middle of the seventeenth century alchemists had become acquainted with most common metals, their alloys and salts, and although they knew about a few acids and the major alkalis, chemists had by the nineteenth century reached a point in their knowledge where they could explain chemical phenomena or attain desired results for industrial production. Henry Cavendish discovered the chemical composition of water (1784). A. Lavoisier found the nature of combustion. J. Dalton proposed the atomic theory (1803), indicating that all properties had fixed amounts of elements; Joseph Gay-Lussac described the elementary composition of organic matter (1811); and D. Mendeléyev (born 1834) classified the elements.

With such work going on it is not to be wondered at that practically minded chemists began to make contributions to industry. Thus, Dr. John Roebuck of Birmingham (1718–1784) improved the making of sulfuric acid, which is basic to industrial chemistry. Claude Louis Berthollet developed prussic acid (hydrocyanic acid), used chlorine for bleaching and discovered that potassium chlorate could be used in gunpowder in place of saltpeter. Nicholas Le Blanc discovered (1789) a way of making soda, the basic industrial alkali, from sea water.

The effects of all these changes in mechanics and chemistry both upon economic development and upon society were enormous, yet they were only the beginning of a movement which has continued at an accelerated pace down to the present day. The new techniques made possible an increase in units of output per unit of human input beyond the wildest dreams of man. This fact made feasible a great increase in population, which per capita had available more of this world's material goods than had ever before been the case. And those peoples who had mechanical weapons attained very suddenly so superior a power position in the world that they could exercise their wills with great abandon over a large part of the humankind of other cultures. Yet these changes were not without drawbacks. Conditions of work in the early factories left much to be desired. Living in industrial towns was a far cry from the bucolic existence of the countryside, or so it seemed to many of the Romantic poets of the first part of the nineteenth century, although people themselves seemed to be perfectly willing to leave the country for the "glamor" of the city. Finally, the larger number of people meant a speeding up of the rate at which inorganic raw materials, which by their very nature were limited, would be used up. Indeed, one of the pressing problems became a search for new supplies of raw materials, both inorganic and organic, at home and abroad, and a quest for abundant materials in nature which could be used as substitutes for those that were becoming exhausted.

CHAPTER 14

The Agricultural Revolution
and its Aftermath

The Nature of Changes in Agriculture from 1750 to 1900

In the periods of history during which economic progress has been
particularly rapid, four characteristic developments have always occurred. Labor-multiplying techniques, more commonly called laborsaving devices, have come into use. Labor has been better organized,
usually by dividing jobs in such a way that an individual worker spe-
cializes in performing some limited task. New amounts of capital have
been invested in producers' goods. And new sources of raw materials
have come to be exploited by and for the expanding economy.

In the hundred years between the invention of the spinning jenny and
the perfecting of the Siemens-Martin process of making steel when industry was undergoing extensive mechanization, agriculture was also
being profoundly altered by the introduction of new productive techniques, by changes in landholding, and by bringing new lands into cultivation, particularly in the expansion of the frontier westward in the
United States and Canada, in the *mise en valeur* of Australia and New
Zealand, and in the greater exploitation of the soils of the West Indies
and South America. Concomitantly there came to be greater specialization of agricultural production by regions within Western culture, greater
use of machinery, greater division of labor in performing agricultural

tasks, and greater investment of capital in soil and in farm equipment. Farming thus became more capitalistic in character. Goods were produced for an unknown and/or distant market rather than for producers' consumption. Farmers with large holdings provided investment capital and hired labor for wages, while those with small holdings were themselves both capitalists and laborers. Successful operations came to depend on the relationship of those prices which farmers received for their goods and those which they paid for what they purchased. If this relationship favored them, farmers accumulated capital. If it was against them, they had to borrow and thus became so indebted that sometimes control or even ownership of their enterprise passed to financial institutions.

In general, the new agriculture required relatively large landholding units in order that production be adequate to permit the amortization of invested capital. Consequently fairly large farms were formed where the value of production was not high per acre, as in the growing of grains and the raising of sheep and beef cattle in America and Australia, and where the new agriculture was first applied, as in England and Eastern Germany. In France, Belgium, and Western Germany, however, a contrary landholding movement got under way in answer to social and political forces. Inasmuch as in those places peasants who had a right to work plots of land got clear title of their holdings, a system of small holdings was constituted which made the adoption of the first of the new techniques difficult. Their owners had eventually to concentrate on raising those products which required large amounts of labor per unit and which permitted high value production per acre, such as dairy products, eggs, fresh fruits, and vegetables.

The most significant consequence of the new agriculture in the period from the middle of the eighteenth century to the end of the nineteenth was not, however, changes in the size of holdings but the increase in the output of foodstuffs in Western culture and the avoidance of famines by more reliable methods of production, better storage facilities, and better means of transportation. It was this better and more adequate food supply that in part made possible the great growth of Western culture's population and that was in part responsible for better nutrition and hence better health records than had ever before been achieved. The agricultural revolution, in short, contributed much to the economic progress of the last two centuries.

New Agricultural Techniques

To ascertain whence came the initial impulses for the improvement of agricultural techniques is extremely difficult. Perhaps the pressure of population, perhaps Western man's search for ways to make his work less burdensome, perhaps opportunities for making profits through sales, and certainly a combination of these and possibly other factors led to changes in methods of agricultural production. Advances in Western European farming had, to be sure, been going on for a long time. As we have already seen, toward the middle of the Medieval period land was reclaimed on a large scale in the Po Valley and the Netherlands. Traction and transportation were improved with the invention of the horse collar that rested on the shoulders of the animal, and the output of land was augmented by the introduction of new crops, like buckwheat and mulberry trees for the production of silk. From time to time thereafter, changes were effected in answer to some specific need, as in the case of the horse-drawn cultivator for working the soil around vines, the introduction of alfalfa and clovers in the seventeenth century in order to get better forage, and the propagation of some specially good breed of livestock, like the Merino sheep in Spain in the late seventeenth century. Finally, various regions specialized more and more in producing goods for an unknown market, as did England in the growing of wool for the Netherlandish textile trade, the Baltic area in the growing of grains for any famine area of the Baltic and North Sea coast, and Holland in developing tulip bulbs for a widely dispersed flower trade.

Until the late eighteenth century such changes were not, however, sufficiently numerous in time and place to have had a profound and general effect upon agriculture. For the most part, production was carried on in the time-honored way. Grains were the chief cultivated crop and they were raised typically in the three-field system whereby each field was left fallow every third year. Animals were turned out to pasture in the commons with the result that breeding was uncontrolled. And so little was known except in an empirical way about fertilizing that no systematic plan could be followed for enriching the soil.

In the eighteenth century, however, a definite breach was made in the bastion of tradition surrounding agriculture. As in the case of the Industrial Revolution, the initial stage on which the Agricultural Revolution made its appearance was in England. There various forces such as the demand for agricultural produce, the desire for gain, a knowledge of husbandry and of ways in which it had been improved elsewhere, adequate amounts of capital to permit experimentation, and the possibility of creating farms large enough to take advantage of new methods came together in just the right way and with the right timing to effect change.

The revolution which thus took place in agriculture is usually associated with the names of certain innovators who pioneered in the employment of new techniques. These men borrowed widely—they accumulated and consolidated details until they had in effect something new. Eventually they came to seek the sequences of those things which would give them desired results.

Among the earliest and most illustrious of these agricultural pioneers was Charles, Viscount Townshend (1674–1738). As he addressed himself to the problems of his large estate, he became impressed with the wastefulness of the practice of letting a portion of the arable lie fallow every year and he dedicated himself to a search for a method whereby fertility of the soil could be maintained even if all the soil were made to produce a crop every year. He experimented with various plants which could be rotated with grains and discovered that by growing clover, which captures nitrogen from the air and returns it to the soil, and by cultivating turnips, which loosened the soil, an idea obtained from the Netherlands, he could get a good return on a piece of land every year. He became such a staunch advocate of using turnips in his rotation system that he was given the nickname "Turnip" Townshend, and he was so successful that many were inspired to follow where he led. The most famous of his disciples was perhaps Coke of Holkam (1752–1842), who standardized a four-crop rotation on the lines suggested by Townshend, a practice which became known as the Norfolk system. Coke had so much success with it that the income on his estate was multiplied ten times within the span of forty years. This was a notable achievement even though it was abetted by a price rise and a favorable market.

A second hero of the English Agricultural Revolution was Jethro Tull (1674–1740), who became famous for innovations in field husbandry. On his father's estate in Berkshire, he experimented with sowing seeds in rows, instead of flinging them broadcast, and cultivating between the rows to keep out weeds, a procedure which, incidentally, provided a dust mulch conserving moisture in the soil. In order to get seeds sown as he wanted them to be, Tull devised a seed drill, the direct ancestor of modern planters, and in order to cultivate more easily between rows he developed a "horse hoe" or horse-drawn cultivator, which he had seen at work in the vineyards of Languedoc in France. To give publicity to his innovations, he wrote two famous books which had a great vogue, *Horse-Hoeing Husbandry* (1731) and *The Horse-Hoeing Husbandry, or, An Essay on the Principles of Tillage and Vegetation* (1733).

A third agricultural pioneer in England was Robert Bakewell (1725–1795), who began to manage his father's estate in Leicestershire in 1760. He experimented widely with new agricultural techniques and new crops, especially grasses, but he is best known for his efforts to improve breeds of sheep, horses, and cattle. Although the science of genetics had not yet developed, systematic knowledge was not needed to conclude that stock could be improved if animals having visibly desirable qualities were used for breeding purposes and if those with potently undesirable features were prevented from coming together in common pastures. Consequently Bakewell engaged in selective and controlled breeding in an empirical way and achieved considerable success. With sheep he endeavored to replace the rangy animal whose sole advantage was its ability to travel fast and far with a chunkier breed which would have more meat and wool—a breed that came to be known as the New Leicestershire. Similarly, he produced a better strain of beef cattle, the Dishley or New Leicestershire longhorns, and a bigger and stronger horse. At the South-field livestock fair, which was near his home, the average weight of sheep increased from 28 to 80 pounds and that of cattle from 370 to 800 pounds between 1710 and 1795. Most of this increase is to be attributed to the success which Bakewell had in breeding, although some of it may be accounted for by better feeds and stabling of animals.

A fourth prominent English agricultural reformer of the period was Arthur Young (1741–1820), who publicized the work of the innovators and carried on intensive propaganda in its behalf. His several books usually took the form of reports of agricultural procedures which he observed as he traveled about. Those like *Farmer's Tour through the East of England, Tour in Ireland,* and *Travels in France* were highly informative, even though his observations were strongly flavored by his faith in the new agriculture and by the physical comforts which he had enjoyed during the day on which he wrote. In 1784 he began publishing an agricultural review, the *Annals of Agriculture,* which became justly famous for the encouragement it gave to agricultural advances, and in 1793 Young was appointed secretary of the Board of Agriculture, which was the first governmental department devoted exclusively to agriculture.

The interest which the new agriculture generated was enormous, and for a time farming enjoyed a veritable style vogue. George III of England became known as "Farmer George" and contributed to Young's *Annals of Agriculture* under the pen name of Ralph Robinson. In France, not only did latter-day Physiocrats preach the virtues of the new agriculture, but many leaders in society played at farming. Marie Antoinette had a Swiss chalet in the Park at Versailles, Le Hameau; Catherine the Great of Russia, Lafayette, and George Washington exhibited an admiration for the homely virtues of farm life.

Other countries of Western European culture kept reasonably well informed of the success which the new agriculture was bringing to England and fairly well abreast of English procedures. The French, for their part, knew about what was going on across the Channel as is attested to by the inclusion in the famous plates of the *Encyclopédie* of detailed sketches of the new agricultural machines and by the success of the volumes written by Duhamel du Monceau between 1751 and 1760 on English agricultural methods. In Prussia, Albrecht Thaer not only published his *Introduction to the Knowledge of English Agriculture* (1798) and his *Principles of Rational Agriculture* (1809–1812) but also founded the first Prussian school of agriculture (1804). And in America, Jared Elliot in his *Essays on Field Husbandry*, published from 1748 to 1762, made known to his compatriots the work that was going on in England; and Thomas Jefferson gave publicity to English agricultural techniques.

Furthermore, non-English lands made important contributions of their own to the Agricultural Revolution. A Frenchman, Parmentier, did much to popularize the potato upon the Continent by writing a famous book on the nutritional and gastronomic virtues of the lowly tuber. A German chemist showed, as early as 1747, that sugar could be obtained from beets, a discovery which was in the course of the nineteenth century to have a profound impact upon the sugar plantations of the West Indies. Americans, for their part, did important work in the selection of seed, especially of short-staple cotton, tobacco, and corn. And the French contributed much to the improvement of livestock by means of their breeding stations, especially of the Merino sheep on the estate of Louis XVI at Rambouillet, and to the development of veterinary medicine with two schools, established in 1761 and 1765.

Further Application of Science and Mechanics to Agriculture

The search for new agricultural methods thus carried forward in the eighteenth century was continued in the nineteenth at an ever-accelerated pace. The objectives of the searchers' quest were then to maintain or to increase the fertility of the soil, to develop laborsaving machinery, to improve the quality of seeds and livestock, and to bring vast areas of virgin soil in overseas lands into cultivation.

So far as improving the fertility of the soil was concerned, enormous progress was made as a result of increased knowledge of the chemical composition of plants and therefore of those ingredients which were needed in the soil as food for plants. The pioneer in this work was a German chemist, Justus von Liebig, whose important discovery that plants consist chiefly of phosphorus, potassium, nitrogen, and water dates from the 1840s. Up to this time fertilizers had been applied to the soil in purely empirical ways, marl (a lime clay), wood ashes, soot, and manure being used however experience seemed to dictate. From Liebig's time onward it was possible by an analysis of the soil to determine what chemicals had to be added in order to get best plant growth.

This scientific advance led directly to the use of so-called commercial fertilizers. At first one of the chief sources of phosphates and nitrates was Peruvian guano, the droppings of birds, British imports of this material increasing from 1,700 tons in 1841 to 220,000 tons in 1847. Subsequently, phosphate rock was pulverized for farm use and sometimes was treated with sulfuric acid to make superphosphates; linings of Thomas-Gilchrist furnaces were broken up for sale to farmers after Lorraine ore began to be smelted on a large scale (post-1878). Later also nitrates began to be obtained from mines in Chile; and potash, that from time immemorial had been secured chiefly from wood ashes, began to be mined in various places, especially at Stassfurt, Germany (1861), and later in Alsace. Moreover, the growing practice of stall feeding to take advantage of cultivated forage crops resulted in the saving and controlled use of manure.

In the realm of farm machinery great progress was made, especially in America where labor was scarce, land abundant, and extensive agricul-

McCormick's Reaper. Power for this machine was provided by horses that were attached to the pole at the right of the illustration. The gears were driven by power from the wheel which supported the machine on the ground. The gears gave a reciprocating motion to the cutter bar. One may discern the pointed fingers of the bar. Sharp edges of triangularly shaped steel attached to a thin bar slipped back and forth through slots in the fingers. These "knives" cut the grain, which was gently pushed against the cutter bar by large arms which revolved like a reel. The grain, after being cut, fell on the canvas apron in the rear. (*From Lucy L. Wilson, Picture Study in Elementary Schools, The Macmillan Company, New York, 1902. Courtesy of the publishers.*)

ture was, with the opening of the Middle West, the order of the day. Here Cyrus H. McCormick and Obed Hussey developed successful reapers in the 1830s, using the principle of a cutter bar composed of double-edged knives moving in a reciprocating fashion through slotted fingers.[1] With the cutter bar, horse-drawn mowers for hay and reapers for grain began to replace the backbreaking scythe, especially where operations were large enough to warrant the investment and where labor was in short supply. These machines, along with the twine binder (1878) and the "combine" (combination reaper and thresher) of the 1880s, made possible "extensive agriculture," that is, farming large tracts with little labor, as opposed to "intensive agriculture," that is, much labor per unit of land and of product. It was, indeed, by extensive agriculture that the vast plains of the Americas and of Australia were put under cultivation and that the lowest costs of production were attained in grain growing.

Similarly, in the development of farm implements for tillage Americans made important contributions to mechanization. John Deere, a Vermont blacksmith who had gone "West" to Illinois, made plows with mold-boards constructed of sheet iron which scoured, that is, freed themselves of dirt, better than those made of cast iron (1838), and then made the still better all-steel plow (1847). Somewhat later James Oliver built a combination cast-iron and steel plow (1870) that had great popularity in the East, more than 175,000 having been in use by 1878. At this time, too, came sulky or riding plows which eliminated the drudgery of holding the plow and walking interminable miles in a dusty furrow. Then after the War between the States, when new lands were being rapidly brought into cultivation, disk and spring-tooth harrows were introduced, which had the advantage over the earlier spike-tooth type in that they did not break so easily or clog so readily and consequently did a superior job of pulverizing the soil. Finally, cultivators were improved by the use of steel and by the construction of sulky models (1856).

In addition to these horse-drawn implements, which were aimed at performing most of the work formerly done with scythe, spade, and hoe, threshing machines were improved to lessen the backbreaking use of the flail or to eliminate the rather repulsive practice of driving mules or horses hitched to rollers over the grain. Winnowing machines were perfected to remove the chaff from the grain and consequently to do away with the laborious job of throwing the grain and chaff into the air on a windy day in hope that the wind would take away the chaff and leave the grain behind. The first successful threshing and winnowing machine

---

[1] It should be noted, however, that a Scot named Bell had previously anticipated the work of McCormick and Hussey but employed the principle found today in barbers' clippers.

in America was invented by Hiram and John Pitts of Maine (1837). This contraption required a considerable amount of power, which was provided at the outset by horses pulling sweeps, but which subsequently was furnished by horses on treadmills, by water, and then by steam. It is estimated that by the use of this machine the productivity of man at this task was increased six times. Indeed, it has been said by authorities that by the use of all the devices here described, as well as of others like the seed broadcaster and the seed drill, the number of man-hours required per acre in wheat production in the United States was reduced from seventy-five prior to 1830 to thirteen in 1880 and that wheat production was increased some three to six times per man-hour.

Such dramatic achievements were made even more striking by improvements obtained through the use of better strains of seeds and better breeds of animals. Farmers came more and more to buy their seeds of seedmen; and seedmen, with more business on their hands, were able to search for varieties that would be hardy under extreme climatic conditions, to make selections of high-producing strains, and to experiment with cures for plant diseases. Agricultural botany flourished and its practitioners became ever more competent in their subject. After the Irish potato famine of 1845, for example, they made an earnest effort to find a type of potato which would be resistant to blight. By 1880 they were able to list 175 varieties and through careful record keeping to select strains which in the midst of diseased plants had remained healthy. Moreover, new varieties of vegetables were introduced; these not only tempted palates but also increased vitamin intake.

So far as livestock was concerned, more breeds came to be generally known and the better ones to be favored by farmers. Breed associations came into being, for breeders found from experience that they could get better prices if their animals possessed standardized characteristics—characteristics which altogether too often were those of color and shape rather than of productive ability. Regions which imported stock, and this was especially true of the United States, exercised care in the selection of animals for the very good reason that the investment being made was large and costs of transportation appreciable. It was not an accident that many of the early breeds in America came from England where selective breeding was most highly developed. From England came the Jersey, Aryshire, and Guernsey among dairy cattle, the Devon, Durham, and Hereford among beef cattle, the Clydesdale among horses (the Percheron came from Belgium), and among sheep, an English variety of Merino which was further developed in New England.

In all of this work both private and public organizations played important roles. The English created the famous experimental station at

Rothamsted and the United States began its network of stations in 1857. Government departments of agriculture became common, that in the United States dating from 1862 and the English Board of Agriculture being raised to the status of a ministry in the same year. Agricultural schools were founded in all the leading countries of Western culture. The Royal Agricultural College at Cirencester, England, was established in 1845. The French school at Grignon was set up during the July Monarchy, and the German institution at Hildesheim opened its doors in 1858. In the United States the first agricultural school was founded at Cleveland in 1855, but the greatest impetus to agricultural education came when, in 1862, Congress granted to each state from the public domain 30,000 acres for each senator and each representative in the House in order to promote "the liberal and practical education of the industrial classes." Furthermore, every nation had one or more agricultural societies for the dissemination of agricultural knowledge and for the defense of farmers' interests. Thus England had its Royal Agricultural Society, founded in 1840. France had its Société des Agriculteurs, Germany its Bund der Landwirte, and the United States its Patrons of Husbandry, more commonly known as the Grange (1867). Finally each nation had agricultural periodicals, agricultural fairs, and agricultural books with which the farmer could keep abreast of the numerous advances continually being made in the agricultural arts.

Still another important change that took place in the agriculture of Western culture in the nineteenth century was the bringing of vast tracts of virgin soil in the New World, South Africa, Australia, and New Zealand into cultivation. As it increased in volume and could be transported at low cost, produce from these regions entered into direct competition with Western European output. Western Europe was thus forced to protect its agriculture with high tariffs, to shift productive effort to crops in which a great amount of labor per unit was needed, or to allow farming to deteriorate.

The magnitude of settlement of new land staggers the imagination. In the United States, from 1860 to 1900, about one-quarter of the entire country passed into private hands. This was a land mass equal to the combined area of Great Britain, France, Germany, and Italy. Much of this land lay west of the Mississippi River and included some of the most fertile soil in the world, particularly the black and prairie soils which lie between the longitude of Memphis, Tennessee, and that of Bismarck, North Dakota. In disposing of these rich acres, the government of the United States offered, under the Homestead Act of 1862, to give 160 acres free to the head of any family if the family would reside on and cultivate the holding for five years, or to sell the land to the head of the family after six-months residence for the prevailing minimum price, which was about a dollar and twenty-five cents an acre. In addition, the government made large land grants to railway companies to foster rail construction into the West in order in turn to hasten settlement. And it made important grants of land to mining and timber companies to accelerate the exploitation of the nation's wealth.

In Upper Canada, later known as Ontario, the number of acres under cultivation quadrupled from 1842 to 1871 and with the building of the Canadian Pacific Railway by the government settlement was made in the Prairie provinces. With the introduction there of hard red wheats and durum, which were hardy in cold climates, production grew by leaps and bounds, the three provinces of Manitoba, Saskatchewan, and Alberta eventually accounting for 90 per cent of all the wheat grown in Canada.

In Australia, a territory the size of the United States, agricultural and grazing lands in use in 1882 amounted to 100 million acres, on which sheep and cattle did most of the work of getting fed by seeking wild grasses. In the Argentine, agricultural and grazing lands equal to about one-quarter of those of the United States were being exploited by the end of the nineteenth century.

Changes in European Landholding

With the bringing into cultivation of large tracts of virgin soil overseas which produced for distant and unknown consumers, with the development of new agricultural techniques which required fairly important capital investments and large holdings, with an increase in the consumer's reliance upon the market for the acquisition of goods to satisfy his wants, and with a growing belief in the equality of man, with its corollary that the few had no *natural* right to exploit the many, two profound but diametrically opposite changes in the landholding systems of Western culture took place. On the one hand, large estates tended to be formed where new agricultural techniques were adopted most rapidly, as in England, and where production on a large scale for a distant market predominated, as in Germany east of the Elbe and in the grazing and grain-growing regions of overseas lands mentioned above. On the other hand, small holdings predominated where peasants got title by political action to the land which they had had the right to work from time immemorial, as in France and in those regions dominated by France during the Revolution and the Napoleonic period, and in districts where dairy and poultry farming was or became general, as in the Eastern United States and Canada, in Denmark, and in the Netherlands. Moreover, whatever the size of the holding, everywhere in Western culture the old seignorial system was discarded and business transactions between farm workers and landlords came to be determined exclusively by money payments.

In England, as has already been said, the chief characteristic of land-holding change in the period under consideration was the formation of large estates. The rise of agricultural prices from the middle of the eighteenth century to after the fall of Napoleon and the development of a larger market for foodstuffs owing to the growth of population and the rise of cities made agricultural enterprise more enticing for those who aspired to greater gain. Furthermore, lords who were bent on supervising the growing of agricultural products found the old strip system to have many disadvantages: a field could not be drained or irrigated except with the consent of neighboring holders; land was wasted in roads; time was lost in going from field to field; disputes over boundaries were frequent; no winter crops could be grown because of the right of common pasture on the arable fields from August to February; and rules of cultivation were such that weeds from fallow land might sow their unwanted seeds on the fields of its neighbors.[2] Finally, English agricultural entrepreneurs recognized that to use the new machinery they had to have large fields to cultivate, because horse-drawn implements could not be maneuvered in small strips and because only large-scale production could pay off the costs of expensive equipment.[3]

For these various reasons the new movement to enclose fields got under way. In essence that involved consolidation into one holding of the many strips of land worked by many different holders in many different ways, and literally enclosing the field with a hedge or fence. Enclosing was almost always realized in the interest of and by lords who wanted to farm for profit. Consequently it forced the uprooted peasants to readjust to the new order of things as best they could. Some of them were settled on consolidated farms on parts of the estate; others became farm workers on the enclosed lands of the lords; still others, especially the younger members of peasant families, went to commercial or industrial towns to seek employment.

In spite of the disruption which enclosures caused peasants, lords were able to execute their designs without recourse to physical force. In the seventeenth century, indeed, peasants frequently consented to giving up their rights in return for compensation, but especially from 1760 to 1845, enclosures were effected by private acts of Parliament, that is, by political force against which peasants had no redress. In 1845, moreover, the

[2] See criticism of the open-field system by the Reverend John Lawrence, *A New System of Agriculture* (1726).

[3] On this subject consult Edward Lawrence, *The Duty of a Steward to his Lord* (1727) and the writings of "Turnip" Townshend.

General Enclosures Act provided that subsequent decisions regarding the consolidation of land should be made by special commissioners, for the number of bills for enclosure were becoming too numerous for Parliament to handle.

For their part peasants were indemnified for surrendering their rights to the land which they worked. Freeholders, who had paid small quit-rents to the lords to be free of other claims, were given the largest compensation. Copyholders, whose tenure was specified in a "copy" of the manorial roll and whose payments to the lord were not insignificant, got somewhat less; cotters, who held simply a cottage and perhaps a garden plot and who had rights on the common pasture, received still less; and tenants at will, who rented land from the lord at his pleasure, were sent off empty-handed.

How many peasants were displaced by the enclosure movement, it is impossible to say, but we do have a good estimate of the amount of land involved. From 1700 to 1845, that is, from before the Agricultural Revolution to the General Enclosures Act, 14 million acres or one-quarter of all the arable of England was brought together. In 1873, it is said, half the land of the country was held by 2,250 persons—a concentration that is apparent in Table 5.

Table 5. Division of Land in England

Class of owner	Average area held by each owner, in acres	Area held, in acres	Per cent of land held
Public bodies and wasteland		2,950,000	8.6
Cotters, less than 1 acre	0.21	150,000	0.4
Small proprietors, 1–100 acres	18	3,930,000	11.4
Lesser yeomen, 101–300 acres	169	4,140,000	12
Greater yeomen, 301–1,000 acres	498	4,780,000	13.9
Squires, 1,001–3,000	1,708	4,310,000	12.5
Great landowners, commoners having over 3,001 acres	6,597	8,490,000	24.6
Peers	14,320	5,720,000	16.6
Total		34,470,000	100

England thus acquired the large fields which could be cultivated with less labor and more machinery, but it remained to be seen whether or not English agriculture could stand competition from the virgin soils overseas.

Across the Channel in France, changes in landholding were, as has been suggested, very different from those which we have just described.

The evolution away from medieval agriculture had been slower there than it had been in England and the wealthier French nobles had been less concerned with the actual cultivation of the land than the English, for they tended to rely for their incomes on money payments, services, and the delivery of goods by their peasants rather than on the raising of produce. As prices rose in the eighteenth century (it is said that they went up some 63.7 per cent from the period 1721–1741 to the years 1785–1789),[4] nobles tried to increase their revenues by more scrupulously than ever collecting what was due them, by attempting to revise the terriers or copyholds so that the obligations of the peasants would be augmented, and by increasing the share paid them by the métayers or sharecroppers. Such efforts created bitternesses which were accentuated by the fact that many of the *philosophes* championed the cause of the peasants and certain nobles granted concessions that made general reform seem to be possible. Voltaire, for example, inveighed against seignorial justice in which the lord sat in judgment of cases in which he was a party at interest and against *mainmorte personnelle*, by which peasant heirs could not inherit the rights to the holding unless living on the holding itself.

In France, unlike England, pressure for the actual acquisition of land to cultivate came from peasants rather than from lords. Here peasant land hunger resulted from an increase in population, few opportunities for alternative employment, and an unequal distribution of land. In fact, it is estimated that whereas peasants constituted 90 per cent of the population they had the right to work for themselves only 30 per cent of the land. In one way or another, to be sure, they worked most of the noble lands, which constituted about 27 per cent of the total, clerical lands, which amounted to 15 per cent, and the land held by bourgeois, which was 27 per cent of the whole, but their wages or other remunerations were meager and they were generally discontented with their lot. In 1789, on the eve of the French Revolution, peasants wanted, as was made clear in their lists of grievances (the peasant *cahiers*), the abolition of the most arbitrary abuses under which they lived, the acquisition of more land, and clear title to the land which they had the right to work.

When Louis XVI called representatives of the three estates together in a national Estates General to find a solution to his pressing financial problems, members of the Third Estate, led by bourgeois, took the position that they were assembled to effect reforms and in the face of royal threats refused to disperse before reform was achieved. In the midst of the accompanying tension in which urban workers, particularly those of Paris, supported the Third Estate, a wave of mass hysteria, known as the

---

[4] C. E. Labrousse, *Esquisse du mouvement des prix et des revenues en France au XVIIIe siècle* (Paris: Dalloz, 1932).

Great Fear (*Grande Peur*) spread through the French countryside. In some strange manner rumors flew about that armed forces were coming to enforce harsh demands on the peasants, if not to slaughter them. To protect themselves against such dire, if false, threats, peasants began to attack noble châteaux and to burn manorial rolls (terriers) so that no records would exist to which new burdens could be added.

This agitation frightened noble delegates to what had been the Estates General but which had transformed itself into the National Constituent (Constitutional) Assembly in Paris. On the celebrated night of August 4, some of the nobles promised to surrender certain of their seignorial rights without receiving compensation and to give peasants clear title, free of all seignorial encumbrances, to their land upon payment of indemnities equal, as a rule, to the revenue which they would expect to get from a holding over a period of twenty years.

Although peasants at first rejoiced at these gestures, they were subsequently disgruntled because of the payments required and other reforms that were being realized by the urban leaders of the revolutionary movement. Only after further uprisings and when the urban revolution was threatened both by civil war and by attacks from abroad did peasants get clear title to their lands without the payment of any indemnity, for their support of the Revolution was absolutely necessary. As a result, a considerable portion of the agricultural land of France was destined to be in small holdings on which many of the horse-drawn implements were not practicable and from which such small incomes were derived as to mitigate against owners' making capital investments in farming.

This was not, however, the only reform of the French Revolution which contributed to a system of relatively small holdings in France. Early in the Revolution, the state seized the lands of the Church on the grounds that they belonged to the people, and with them as a reserve, issued money (the assignats) in order to pay the pressing bills of the government. Church lands were to be sold in part for assignats, which would then be retired, and in part for regular currencies, which would be used to pay the growing expenses of the state. Although the scheme did not work as planned, assignats being issued in such large quantities that they could not be retired and that their value declined in one of the great inflationary episodes of Modern Times, land was actually sold. Some of it went to speculators and to wealthy persons who bought large parcels, because the terms of purchase generally required large and immediate payments, but probably more than half of it went eventually into the hands of peasants. Similarly, the lands of the nobles who fled France during the Revolution, the so-called *émigrés*, were seized by the state and sold; and steps were taken, the *Ventôse* Decrees, which aimed to distribute among Revolutionary soldiers the property of the "suspects" —those suspected of being opposed to the Revolution—although not much land was disposed of under them. Of the land thus distributed, perhaps half was acquired by peasants and became divided into small holdings.

All subsequent efforts to undo the land reforms of the Revolution failed. The Napoleonic regime confirmed the Revolutionary disposition of Church lands by the Concordat of 1801 and it did nothing to return noble lands to their former owners. Even the *"milliard des émigrés,"* an indemnity paid to nobles in the Restoration (1825), did not result in the reconstitution by nobles families of large estates. Finally, the Code Napoléon is said to have worked toward a system of small holdings, for it specified that a father with one child should leave the child half his property; one with two children, two-thirds of his property; and one with three or more, three-fourths of his holdings. When reliable censuses of landholdings were taken in France, it was seen that France had, indeed, more small holdings than most countries, but there were still some farms of good size.

Table 6. Landholding in France

Size of holding, in in hectares	Number of holdings			
	1862	1882	1892	1908
Very small: less than 1		2,167,667	2,235,405	2,087,851
Small: 1–10	2,435,401	2,635,030	2,617,558	2,523,713
Medium: 10–40	636,309	727,222	711,118	745,862
Large: 40–100	154,167	142,088	105,391	118,497
Very large: over 100			33,280	29,541
Total		5,672,007	5,702,752	5,505,464

In Germany, the landholding situation became more complicated during the nineteenth century than in either England or France because various states pursued different policies in the matter of peasant and land reform. In a general way, it may be said, however, that in Prussia east of the Elbe and in Mechlenburg, large farms were created by lords from their estates, that in Hannover, Schleswig-Holstein, Westphalia, and Upper Bavaria, large peasant holdings predominated, and that in the west and southwest, along the Rhine, the Main, and Neckar Rivers, small holdings were the most usual.

The explanation for the differences in the various regions of Germany is to be found in the nature of the seignorial system in the three regions, the kind of agriculture best suited to the different soils and climates, and in the character of reforms which were effected. In Prussia east of the Elbe, the lords traditionally had overseen production on their own lands. They grew grain successfully and found a ready market for it in Western Europe, whence they imported a variety of products such as salt, textiles, and wine. Thus they came to farm for profit rather than to hold land on which they could collect seignorial dues in kind or money.

Table 7. Landholding in Germany

Area of tillage, 1907	Millions of hectares	Acreage of holdings, in per cent			
		Up to 12.5	12.5–50	50–250	Over 250
East of the Elbe	13.9	8.5	22.7	28.5	40.3
West of the Elbe	17.9	22.0	40.0	30.0	8.0

Under this system of *Gutsherrschaft*, that is, the production of goods, the labor services of peasants were of extreme importance to lords and they made every effort to maintain serfdom intact. That they were successful in their endeavor is attested to by the fact that their peasants were usually not free to leave the lord's estate, had to render him many services, even the menial ones (*Gesindedienst*), such as work in the lord's kitchen and stables, and had to swear to him an oath of allegiance.

In spite of the extreme subservience of peasants to lords, a movement for reform got under way in the Germanies. Peasants agitated for freedom from seignorial restrictions and Prussian leaders came to believe, after Napoleon's defeat of their country, that they should get peasant support for a war of liberation by making concessions to them. Thus the edicts (1807–1809) of Baron von Stein abolished serfdom, allowed peasants to leave the land, relieved them of *Gesindedienst,* and permitted them to buy land. At the same time, however, the lords saw to it that the process of reform gave them opportunities to create large holdings. Indeed, the Stein decrees stipulated that lords had the right to consolidate holdings in large fields, if peasants were given land elsewhere on the estate, and to seize tenures which dated from the second half of the eighteenth century. Similarly, the reforms of Hardenberg, especially the edict of 1811, decreed that those peasants whose right to work a parcel of land was considered heritable could receive clear title to two-thirds of their holdings, but only on condition that the other third be surrendered to their lords. This rule, which in 1816 was declared applicable only to those who could perform *Spanndienst*, that is, could yoke a pair of oxen, other peasants being required usually to surrender up to one-half of their holdings in order to become full proprietors of the rest, played into the hands of the lords, inasmuch as it permitted them to increase the amount of land which they could farm for profit.[5]

In the rest of Germany the seignorial regime was more analogous to that of France, with the richer lords relying on payments from their peasants in kind or money for their incomes rather than on the production of crops for market. This was the system of *Grundherrschaft*. Thus when reform began in Western Germany, lords were less able to hold onto their lands since they stood in a weaker position both politically and economically than their neighbors across the Elbe. In those areas which the French dominated completely at the time of the Revolution, as on the left bank of the Rhine, reforms of the French type were applied wholesale and small peasant proprietorships were created. Here feudalism was abolished (1798) and peasants were given clear title to their holdings without having to pay any indemnity. The property of the Church and the lands of *émigrés*, in this case nobles who opposed the Revolutionary or Napoleonic regimes, were seized and sold.

In the area between the Rhine and the Elbe, as in the Kingdom of Westphalia where French influence was still great but less complete than in the Rhineland, land reform of the Napoleonic period was characterized by the abolition of seignorial dues with compensation.[6] This forced those without enough land on which to make a living to sell out and permitted the richer peasants to form medium-sized holdings.

In other European countries, landholding reforms followed one of the three patterns experienced in Germany. In Denmark, serfdom was abolished in 1788 and peasants were given title to the lands which they had had the right to work, but they had to pay compensation to the lords. Consequently there were small holdings along with large estates until after 1899, when lands of the state, of the church, and of some very large proprietors began to be partitioned. In Belgium and the Netherlands, seignorial dues were abolished during the French period of domination (1795–1814). Peasants got title to their holdings, and they were given opportunities to buy properties of the Church and of *émigrés*. In these countries many of the scattered strips were consolidated in unitary farms, especially where the existence of canals made access to dispersed pieces of land particularly difficult.

In Austria, Joseph II abolished serfdom by a decree of 1781, thereby giving peasants freedom to move about as they would, to own land, and to marry whom they pleased. After the Revolution of 1848, Austrian

---

[5] The *Kossaten* and *Häuslern*, that is, the cotters, did not have their houses and garden plots granted to them until after 1850. Manors continued to be the administrative units in some legal respects until the reform of 1892

[6] In Saxony indemnity payments were made as late as 1907.

peasants were allowed to acquire land upon the payment of an indemnity. In Italy, although the King of Sardinia began peasant reforms in Savoy prior to the French Revolution, peasants were not freed from seignorial obligations until the French became masters of the land. Much of the arable here remained in large estates, the latifondia. Small holdings predominated in such mountainous districts as Liguria, the Abruzzi, and Molise, but there were some medium-sized farms where agriculture was highly commercial, especially in the Po Plain with its silk culture, rice growing, and cheese making. In Sicily and Naples lords usually attended to the raising of crops in the *Gutsherrschaft* manner of the region east of the Elbe, but they were prone to use their profits in conspicuous consumption rather than in capital investments on their lands. In the Papal States and Tuscany, the métayer system, or as it is called in Italian, the *mezzadria*, predominated and consequently large estates were general and little was done to improve the land. Chief evidence of agricultural advance was to be found on the large estates of the Po Plain, where young nobles like Cavour and capitalist farmers made farming pay and were thus encouraged to keep their holdings intact. Both took advantage of the opportunity to acquire more land when the holdings of the Church and of religious orders were sequestered and sold after unification of the country (1860).

Table 8. Landholding in Italy

Size of holding, in acres	Percentage of total units	Percentage of total average
Up to 5	83.3	17.4
5–25	13.6	24.2
25–125	2.6	23.3
125–250	0.3	9.1
250–1,250	0.1	17.3
Above 1,250	0.07	8.7

In Ireland, Spain, and Eastern European countries, large estates were general and reform was slow. In Ireland, except for Ulster, large holdings were owned mostly by absentee English landlords who had obtained their properties through conquest and who collected high rents from their tenants. Only in the face of strong opposition from members of secret societies, like the Molly Maguires, and of a 47 per cent decline in the population in the seventy years after the potato famine of 1846, did the English government endeavor to establish better conditions for tenants by the "three F's" in the laws of 1870 and 1881—fair rent, fixity of tenure, and freedom to sell leases. Not until 1903 did the British government create a fund to enable Irish peasants to buy land by making small annual payments.

In Spain, serfdom was abolished during the Napoleonic period, but although the Church and orders lost their lands, large estates have never been broken up, for the proposed reforms of the republic (1932) were arrested when this regime was overthrown in 1936. In Rumania, serfs were freed in 1864 and were given an opportunity to acquire land in proportion to the number of oxen which they could harness. The compensation which they had to pay the lords, however, was so great that few could make payments and the land remained in large estates, 37½ per cent of it being in holdings of 1,250 acres or more in 1905. In Hungary, serfs were freed in 1848, but they had to pay the lords such large indemnities that they did not acquire much land. Hungary was, therefore, a land of large estates and on them grain was grown so abundantly that in 1900 Hungary was the world's third largest exporter of wheat, ranking after the United States and Russia.

In the latter country, where serfdom had not reached its height until the end of the eighteenth century, peasant reform was not begun until about the middle of the nineteenth century. Then money payments, that is, quitrents, began to be substituted for seignorial dues. Serfs took violent action for reform, especially after Russia's defeat in the Crimean War, and landlords experienced such a shortage of labor that they were hiring some workers for wages and were beginning to think that the peasant system was uneconomical. In 1848, peasants were encouraged to buy land; between 1859 and 1866, 2 million serfs were freed on the estates of the Crown and an equal number on noble estates were emancipated by the edict of 1861. By the terms of this measure peasants not only were freed from seignorial dues but also, on the payment of an indemnity, they were given title to the land which previously they had had the right to work. Inasmuch as many peasants did not have savings with which to pay the sums required of them, the state provided funds in the form of state bonds immediately to compensate the lords for their loss of seignorial dues and allowed the peasants up to forty-nine years to make reimbursement for these advances.

Unfortunately this peasant reform did not work so well as had been anticipated. Landlords, already heavily in debt (40 per cent of their estates and 70 per cent of male serfs had been mortgaged prior to 1861), were short of working capital for farming on a capitalist basis and sharply falling agricultural prices in the period 1873–1896 made their situation still worse. Under the circumstances in which they found themselves, they dumped the bonds which they had received at low prices. These sales did not suffice to meet their needs, so they began to sell land to the richer peasants, the kulaks. In fact, they disposed of some 59 per cent of their lands before 1916.

Emancipated serfs, for their part, had great difficulty in making their payments to the state, especially because of the fall of agricultural prices which followed so soon on their having been freed. Moreover, because redemption payments seemed to be so burdensome, some peasants (15 per cent up to 1880) did not even try to obtain land. In order to rectify this situation, the purchase of land was made compulsory in 1881 and payments were simultaneously reduced by 27 per cent. Even so, many peasants were dissatisfied either because their payments were too heavy or because they had too little land. In addition, they suffered from periodic famines, like the one of 1891–1892. After Russia's defeat by Japan in 1905 and in the face of peasant agitation, some effort was made to meet these complaints. The state canceled all peasant emancipation payments. It built railways to aid the peasants in getting their produce to market, and encouraged the construction of storage facilities in order to provide more adequately for years of poor crops. Not until the Bolshevik Revolution of 1917, however, were attempts made on a large scale to satisfy peasants' hunger for land by the seizure of large estates.

Landholding in Areas of Western Culture outside Europe

In the great agricultural areas overseas which were settled by Europeans, the landholding problem was quite different from that in the Old World. In the new lands there was no firmly established seignorial system with its elaborate network of dues which were to be paid for the right to use the lands of the overlord, nor was there any shortage of land to meet the requirements of a discontented rural population. On the contrary, in most places there were vast unpopulated, or sparsely populated, territories where the major initial problems were (1) how to get people to settle on the land and (2) how the land should be divided among newcomers.

As a general rule, land in these territories in the period prior to the second quarter of the nineteenth century was originally granted to friends of the kings who had taken claim to it, to administrative officials, and to religious orders. These large grants were, as a rule, subsequently sold in order that the original grantee be able to realize something on his holdings. Sometimes these sales were in small lots to attract colonizers, sometimes in fairly large units to speculators who might subsequently sell them to actual farmers, and sometimes in large estates, if conditions of soil, climate, topography, and the market were such as to make large-scale operations feasible and profitable. As a rule, relatively large farms were created in these lands, and recourse was had to "extensive" rather than to "intensive" agriculture, that is, to the use of a large amount of land per worker and to practices that gave relatively low production per acre but high production per man-hour. Furthermore, extensive agriculture meant the use of cheap labor, as on the cotton plantations of the American South and the sugar plantations of Cuba, the adoption of a great amount of machinery, as on the wheat farms of the American Middle West and of Canada, or the raising of sheep and cattle on ranges where the animals did most of the work of feeding themselves, as on the ranges of America, Australia, and the Argentine.

In the United States the first grantees, like Lord Baltimore in Maryland, William Penn in Pennsylvania, John Mason in New Hampshire, and the Virginia Company, received large amounts of land. Subsequently these grantees disposed of parts of their tracts in order to have their lands settled. In the region from New England to Virginia the Colonies usually gave or sold land to yeoman farmers in amounts sufficient at the time to support a family, a fact which goes to explain the predominance even to the present day of the family-sized farm in this area. From Virginia southward, where cotton and tobacco culture thrived, buyers of land were capitalist farmers, and as a rule, they acquired large tracts.[7]

After the War of Independence, the United States sold public land in rather large units because the task of disposing of it in small parcels was very great. Indeed, many of the Founding Fathers, of whom George Washington was a good example, speculated in land by buying large tracts from the government and then selling it as opportunity permitted in small units. During the War between the States, however, the government adopted what was essentially a new policy in disposing of public lands. In large part to win the people of the Northwest to the Northern cause, the government passed the Homestead Act of 1862[8] which provided, as we have already seen, that 160 acres would be given free to any head of a family who resided on or cultivated for five years his holding upon the payment of a small registration fee; or this same person might buy his land after a residence of six months at the prevailing minimum, about one dollar and 25 cents an acre. In some areas, 160 acres constituted too small a farm to sustain a family and so "homesteaders" sometimes sold their lands, which gave others an opportunity to form

---

[7] In the mountainous parts of these territories, plantations could not be operated and so the land was sold in family-sized lots.

[8] The Preemption Act of 1841 had provided that heads of families who had settled on unsurveyed public lands of the frontier and who were actually squatters had the right to purchase their land at the minimum price when it was actually put on sale. This Act was repealed in 1891.

larger farms. Also it was possible for the farmer to get land under the Timber Culture Act (1873) by planting trees on part of it, under the Desert Land Act (1877) by irrigating it, or under the Timber and Stone Act (1878) by staking a claim for what was declared to be nonarable. Moreover, large amounts of public land went to interests which were later to sell great and even mammoth tracts to farmers. Thus the railroads got over 131 million acres from the Federal government and another 51 million acres from states as subsidies. The states received some 203 million acres from the Federal government to accelerate the making of public improvements and to support agricultural and technical schools under the College Land Grant Act of 1862. And some land was sold at public auction. Just what the landholding situation was, it is difficult to say, but according to the census of 1880 the average farm had 134 acres, whereas that of 1950 indicated an average of 200 acres. Two-thirds of the tracts reported in 1950 as farms were actually rural residences for town dwellers or rural laborers. Thus, producing farms had a much larger acreage than the national average. In 1880, most of the farms were worked by owners, only about one-quarter being operated by tenants.

In Australia land was granted freely in large tracts until 1831; then it was sold at auction; and after 1847 some of it was leased with an option to purchase. In general the unit holding was very large because much of the land was only suitable for grazing. In fact, tracts were so large that the problem of squatters in remote parts became a major issue. In Canada, the family farm was characteristic of the Maritime provinces, Quebec, and Ontario, although farms ran somewhat larger in Quebec than in the other eastern regions because the French had once had a seignorial system with large holdings that was not entirely obliterated until 1854. In the Prairie provinces, however, where some 90 per cent of all Canadian wheat came to be grown, land was sold in large units so that the average farm there is some 335.4 acres as compared with an average of less than 200 in the east. Then in Chile, 50 million of the 57 million acres of the country were owned by about 2,500 persons at the end of the nineteenth century, and concentration in the Argentine was probably as great.

The Impact of Overseas Competition on European Agriculture

Although the four major phases of the agricultural history of Western culture from the end of the eighteenth century to the close of the nineteenth were (1) the introduction of horse-drawn machinery, (2) the use of science in the treatment of the soil, in the selection and care of plants, and in the breeding of livestock, (3) the freeing of serfs in Europe with

the attendant formation of small holdings in France, Belgium, the Netherlands, and Western Germany and of large estates elsewhere, and (4) the
bringing into cultivation of vast areas overseas, there was still another
development of great importance—the impact of overseas competition
on European agriculture. From the early 1870s grains and meat, especially mutton and beef, began to come into Western Europe in large
quantities and at prices which European producers could not meet. Accordingly Europeans had to adjust their operations to produce those
things in which they could compete or they had to seek high protection
by means of tariffs, embargoes, and other restrictions on imports. If recourse was had to the first solution, experience came to show that they
could compete in those products which required a large amount of labor
per unit, like fresh vegetables, fresh fruit, poultry, dairy products, and
pork. If salvation was sought in protection, the price of such staples as
wheat remained far above the free-market level and hence resulted in
making the consumer pay a kind of subsidy to the farmer.

From at least 1817, Western European farmers had feared foreign
competition, for at that time France had imported grain from the Ukraine
at prices which were extremely low in order to meet shortages of famine
proportions. Then toward the middle of the nineteenth century farmers
became particularly apprehensive, for in 1846 England repealed its Corn
Laws, that is, its protection on grains. France again imported wheat from
Russia at low prices, and in the early 1860s most Western European
countries reduced their tariffs on agricultural products as part of a general European movement to lower rates. The realization of these fears
was postponed by the Crimean War (1853–1856), which closed the
Baltic and Black Sea to Russian grain, by the American Civil War (1861–
1864), which turned American energies to war, and by the brisk demand
for home-grown foods at relatively high prices because of the growth of
population, buoyant price levels, and comparatively high purchasing
power resulting from industrial expansion. In fact, the period from 1853
to 1873 was one of prosperity for European farmers.

Yet the threat of overseas competition was particularly great and it
began to be felt after 1873. A reduction in ocean freight rates occasioned
by the success of clipper ships and the appearance of iron tramp steamers
and a reduction in the cost of land carrying with the construction of
railways into the belts of extensive agriculture, like the American Middle
West, made transportation cheaper. Furthermore, the use of cheap labor
in Eastern Europe, the mechanization of wheat growing in America, and
the grazing of cattle on the vast ranges of wild grass permitted the importation of agricultural goods into Europe at derisory prices. The cost
of transporting grain from Chicago to New York went from 33 cents to

14 cents a bushel between 1870 and 1881, that of transatlantic shipping fell from 20 cents a bushel in 1874 to 2 cents in 1904, the opening of the Suez Canal in 1869 reduced rates from Australia to London, and refrigerator ships and cars made possible the handling of meat in the 1880s. Then to make matters worse for the European farmer, the general level of prices reacted downward beginning in 1873 and remained low until 1896—a period known as the "long depression in prices." In this period agricultural prices fell lower than industrial prices, which only added to the woes of the farmer. The great staples were particularly hard hit, the price of wheat for example dropping from a dollar and a half a bushel in 1871 to 86 cents in 1885, and for one day to 23 cents, whereas the price of meat declined by about 25 per cent from 1873 to 1896. Meanwhile grain exports from North America increased from an annual average of 5,500,000 bushels for the years 1851–1860 to 150,500,000 bushels in 1880. The United States raised its exports of chilled meat from 1,095 hundredweight in 1874 to 1,275,948 hundredweight in 1889. Australia brought its exports of wool to Britain up from 38,018,000 pounds in 1850 to 505,197,000 pounds in 1910. Finally, China and Japan undercut European silk producers so drastically that the end of the growing of the silkworm in Europe seemed imminent.

The plight of European farmers was, moreover, made even more disastrous as a result of a series of misfortunes. In the first place, a number of bad years with too little or too much rain hurt grain production; rinderpest destroyed cattle in the 1860s; sheep rot took a heavy toll of sheep in the late 1870s; phyloxera, a minute, green insect, raised havoc with the vineyards of France; and an epidemic disease destroyed silkworms. Under such circumstances it is not strange that in Great Britain 4,000,000 acres out of a total of 23,000,000 acres of arable went out of cultivation between 1867 and 1907, that the number of sheep in Germany declined from nearly 25,000,000 in 1873 to 10,866,772 in 1897, that French wine production fell from 1879 to 1889 by two-thirds, and that French raw silk production fell by one-third.

Nor is it to be wondered at that farmers cried for tariff protection, that they organized politically to get it, and that their efforts were by the late 1870s producing results. The French Société des Agriculteurs managed to push through the famous Méline tariff of 1892. In Germany, tariff rates were raised in 1879, 1885, and 1888 and the Bund der Landwirte got exceptionally high protection in the agricultural tariff of 1902. Italy raised its rates in 1878, 1887, and 1891 and tangled with the French in the famous tariff war from 1888 to 1899. And even in free-trade Great Britain there was serious agitation led by Joseph Chamberlain and his "Fair Traders" for protection. Yet neither here, nor in the Netherlands,

Denmark, or Finland was a return to high tariffs attempted. These free-trade nations pursued the policy of changing their agricultural production to lines in which they could compete.

Undoubtedly the most drastic and dramatic adjustments to overseas competition were made in Denmark. There, at the beginning of the agricultural depression when wheat prices began to slump, farmers followed the old adage of "Down corn, up horn" and turned from the growing of grain to the raising of livestock, especially cattle. When, however, meat prices also went down, they did not send their herds to slaughterhouses but increased their output of dairy products. Beginning in 1875 they formed cooperative creameries to handle milk and to produce butter and cheese. The invention of the De Laval cream separator helped in the mechanization of creamery work (1879) and the practice of pasteurization, which followed Louis Pasteur's famous paper on lactic fermentation in 1858, and the making of butter by the addition of lactic acid and of cheese by the use of special cultures, allowed them to produce more efficiently and to standardize their products. Their buttermilk they used to fatten pigs, which they could raise at low cost, and they added poultry as a sideline to take up the winter months when field work was light. For their products the Danes found a ready market—the English breakfast table which traditionally carried, along with porridge, bacon, eggs, cheese, and buttered toast. The value of Danish exports of these goods increased tenfold from the early 1880s to 1914.

To some extent the Netherlands followed the Danish example, and even in those countries which had tariff protection farmers made some alterations in production in the face of overseas competition. Gradually hogs took the place of sheep, the hog population of Germany rising from some 7 million in 1873 to over 22 million in 1907; the acreage given to the sugar beet in France nearly tripled from 1860 to 1914.[9] The acreage given to potatoes in Germany increased nearly 20 per cent from 1880 to 1912; the production of fresh vegetables grew impressively with the coming of rapid transportation. The bovine population, largely in dairying, grew steadily in both France and Germany. Moreover, the holders of large estates acquired more machinery in an effort to reduce costs, as was being done in America, the number of mowing machines quadrupling in France from 1862 to 1892 and increasing some twenty times in Germany from 1895 to 1907 when the process of mechanization was most rapid.

[9] The growing of sugar beets flourished after the middle of the century. Most countries gave subsidies to growers. The granting of bounties became so extensive that sugar-beat–growing nations signed the Brussels Convention in 1902 by which they agreed to stop paying export bounties and to punish by high tariffs those states which continued to give them.

Finally, better field and animal husbandry brought an improvement in yields per acre and in production per head of livestock. Thus European agriculture was prevented from going into eclipse. Only in England was there for the moment little effort to save the farms and by World War I England was producing less than 25 per cent of its food needs.

The period of low prices, especially for agricultural products, was one of great agricultural expansion in overseas lands, as we have seen, but in spite of this growth and the inroads made on European agriculture, these areas experienced considerable discontent among farmers. The grumbling was particularly marked in the United States where it took the form of agitation for better railway and shipping rates, demands for more liberal terms on which to get public land, and "campaigns for monkeying with the money," that is, for forcing prices up by inflationary policies. In Russia, the price decline made the emancipation payments more difficult, as we have seen, and led finally to the cancelation of peasant obligations. And in Canada it led to greater production on larger units. Finally, in 1896 a rise in agricultural prices saved the farmer from being crucified on a cross of depressed prices. During the experience of the Great Depression there had developed a greater division of labor in the world, the satisfying of a greater proportion of Europe's needs by imports, and an improvement in agricultural techniques.

CHAPTER 15

The Revolution in Commerce

Economic Progress and the Distribution of Goods

On preceding pages many instances have been encountered in which economic progress, defined as an increase in the supply of economic goods and services per capita of the population of a given area, was accompanied by a greater division of labor, but in no case was this characteristic of growth so marked as in the nineteenth century. Then there was a greater specialization of tasks among workers and also a more extraordinary specialization of production among various areas of the world than had ever before been witnessed in human history. And there was also an extraordinary growth of commerce, for individuals and whole regions became less economically self-sufficient than they had been, increased purchasing power permitted members of the economically lower classes to enjoy goods which had previously been beyond their reach, and interregional dependence brought new products into the market. In fact, the development of mechanized industry itself seems to have depended to a large extent on the growth of trade, for machine-made goods would not have been possible if large amounts of raw materials had not been amassed and the finished products disposed of through commercial channels.

In recent economic history an abundance of evidence exists to show that those economies which have experienced the greatest growth have had an exceptionally large proportion of their population engaged in exchanging goods rather than in the actual production of them. Thus, a comparison of the occupational distribution in the year 1931 of two countries like Britain and India, whose national incomes per capita were in the ratio of six to one, indicates that the former had a much higher percentage in the service trades than did the latter.

In like manner, in any given economy, as for example that of the United States, a greater concentration of the occupied population is to be found in trade, finance, and transport as economic progress is made.

Table 9. Distribution of the Working Force in 1931
(In per cent)

Occupation	Great Britain	India
Agriculture	6.1	70.5
Mining and manufacturing	38.0	17.15
Domestic service	8.1	2.7
Other	47.8	9.65

Table 10. Distribution of the Working Force in the United States
(In per cent)

Occupation	1850	1950
Agriculture	63.6	14.5
Forestry and fishing	0.4	
Mining	1.1	1.75
Manufacturing and mechanical industries	16.3	28.8
Construction		4.48
Transportation and communication	0.5	7.77
Trade	4.0	18.44
Professional services		.08
Finance and real estate	12.2	3.51
Educational, domestic, and personal services		9.23
Government not elsewhere classified		11.45

The increased division of labor, the accompanying dependence of the consumer on the market, and a growing tendency for various regions to specialize in the production of those goods in which they had a comparative advantage put pressure on agencies for the distribution of goods to improve their services: on transportation to better its methods of carrying, on communications to speed up the exchange of information, and on national states to change their commercial policies. The response to the new needs was remarkable. Retailing assumed a new place in the selling of goods and gave rise to new types of enterprises like the department store and the cooperative, while wholesaling became better organized and more important. In transportation great improvements were made in the older forms of carrying and new techniques came into being, like the steam locomotive, which provided at long last a cheap means of carrying heavy loads on land, and the steamboat, which made water carrying less expensive and more certain. Improved methods of communication resulted from the extension of postal services, from the invention of the telegraph, and the establishment of extensive telegraph lines, including cables across the Atlantic. Finally, in this period so much credence was placed in the virtues of freer trade, if not of free trade, that many man-made hindrances to commerce were abolished.

The Extension of the Market

The extent to which a division of labor took place and to which people became dependent on the market is difficult to measure with any degree of accuracy, but several indicators point clearly the direction in which the economy was moving. First, the growth of population and a great increase in urbanization meant that more people were perforce dependent on the market for most of their economic wants. From 1800 to 1870 the population of the United States increased from 5,300,000 to 38,500,000 and Europe's population just about doubled between 1800 and 1875. Moreover, the percentage of the population living in towns of 2,000 or more went up appreciably, being, for example, in England 51.3 per cent of the population in 1851, in France, 28.9 per cent in 1861, and in Germany, 35.8 per cent in 1867.

Table 11. Total World
Commerce
(In billions of dollars,
contemporary values)

Year	Amount
1840	2.8
1860	7.2
1880	14.8
1900	20.1
1913	40.4

Secondly, the amount of freight moving on canals and railways suggested a great increase in commerce and an extensive division of labor. For example, the number of tons of freight carried one kilometer on rivers and canals in France in 1847 was 1,760,000,000 tons; in 1875, it was 1,964,000,000 tons. Furthermore, in France the number of passengers carried one kilometer on railways in 1853 was 1,000,000,000; in 1875, it was 4,786,000,000 and the number of tons of freight hauled one kilometer rose from 1,000,000,000 in 1854 to 8,136,000,000 in 1875. In the United States, the railways carried 39,302,000,000 ton-miles in 1881.

Thirdly, the great expansion of international trade indicated a growing specialization of production by regions. As can be seen in Table 11, this trade among nations increased nearly seven times in the forty years from 1840 to 1880. Moreover, a very large part of this trade was accounted for by states in Western culture, which meant that here was to be found the greatest regional division of labor.[1]

Table 12. Distribution of World Trade
(In per cent)

Year	United Kingdom	United States	Germany	France
1840	32	8		10
1860	25	9		11
1880	23	10	9	11
1900	21	11	12	8

Railways and Waterways

Undoubtedly the most important new technique in the commercial revolution of the nineteenth century was the railway. It made possible the tapping of supplies in remote places. It carried bulk products cheaply to centers of population, and it had flexibility enough to reach the very maws of machines. Moreover, as we shall see later, the large amount of capital required for railway construction gave an enormous impetus to the joint-stock form of business organization and to such innovations as limited liability and preferred stock. Lastly, the vast volume of equipment which railways required spurred economic activity and also contributed much to business fluctuations because of the uneven rate of investment in railways.

The idea of applying the steam engine to transportation had found expression as early as 1769 in a cumbersome contraption for use on roads fashioned by a Frenchman, Nicolas Cugnot. Subsequently, the Englishman Richard Trevithick constructed locomotives (1801, 1808), but his machines were designed for hauling around coal mines and had limited use. Finally, George Stephenson brought steam locomotion to the point of practicability, his *Rocket* attaining the exceptional speed of 31 miles per hour on a line from Manchester to Liverpool in 1830.

[1] One should add that the great number of political divisions in western culture had a tendency to increase these percentages.

ONE HUNDRED YEARS OF
RAILWAYS

ROCKET Nº2 STEPHENSON 1833

2-2-2 EXPRESS ENGINE "LADY OF THE LAKE" 1862

2-4-0 EXPRESS ENGINE "PRECEDENT" 1874

2-2-2-2 COMPOUND EXPRESS ENGINE "QUEEN EMPRESS" 1893

4-4-0 EXPRESS ENGINE "PRECURSOR" 1904

STANDARD 4-6-0 EXPRESS LOCOMOTIVE "ROYAL SCOT" CLASS

The Development of the Railway Locomotive. The picture of Rocket No. 2 shows on the side of the boiler the cylinder of the steam engine of the time, which developed from the work of Watt. In this cylinder the piston is pushed back and forth by introducing steam at both ends of the cylinder and by having exhaust valves at both ends. The numbers under some of the models refer to the wheels of the engines. The first figure gives the number of the guide wheels in the front. The next figure indicates the number of drive wheels. And the last number shows the number of supporting wheels at the rear of the engine. (*Courtesy of British Railways.*)

Track Laying on the Union Pacific Railroad. Railway building was one of the greatest of new economic activities in Western culture in the middle decades of the nineteenth century. For the most part, material for the new track was brought to the operation along the track already built, and it was lifted by derricks from the supply train to flatcars. In this picture wooden ties were brought to the work by horse team, which means that they were being supplied from local sources. The covered wagons at the left may have had nothing to do with railway building and been put there by the artist to show the means of land transportation which was being replaced. Carrying by horse-drawn wagons to and from railways continued up to the early twenties. (*Courtesy of the Union Pacific Railroad.*)

In spite of Stephenson's achievements, however, many engineering problems had to be solved before railroads could play an important role in commerce. At first, for example, the flanged wheels which were used to keep the cars on the track crept up on top of the rails on curves and some time elapsed before it was discovered that the wheels should fit loosely on the rails and that they could be attached to swivel trucks under the cars. Then, at first, the draft in the firebox was insufficient to keep up the steam pressure when the locomotive was not in motion—a difficulty which was overcome by forcing steam up the smokestack to create a draft. At the outset, too, brakes were uncertain affairs, being pushed against the wheels, and were not made safe and easily applied or released until George Westinghouse perfected the vacuum air brake in 1886.[2] Furthermore, couplings were loose affairs which had so much play in them that when a train started the cars were yanked, particularly the last ones, so violently that passengers were toppled over backwards.

[2] This was an arrangement whereby the brakes were held off by air pressure and hence were applied when the pressure was relieved or when there was a leak in the system.

The building of roadbeds also presented serious engineering problems. Initially rails were sometimes laid on piles, but experience showed that rails had to rest on a resilient bed which came to be provided by wooden ties. Originally, too, cast-iron rails often cracked because of the brittleness of the metal, a defect that was overcome by the use of steel after the Bessemer and Siemens-Martin processes had made possible the sale of steel at low cost. And various widths of track—which gave occasion for a "'battle of gauges" in England in the 1840s—meant that passengers had to change trains when the one that they were on reached a stretch of track with a different gauge and that freight had to be transshipped from time to time.[3]

The construction of bridges and tunnels also created difficulties for early railway builders. Stone bridges did not stand up well under vibration and wooden bridges were subject to the action of weather and fire; hewing holes through the earth with hand drills was at best grueling labor. In time, however, bridges came to be made of iron and steel (the 1,595-foot long Brooklyn Bridge, of steel suspension construction, was completed in 1883); tunneling became easier with the invention of the compressed-air drill (in use in mining coal in 1849), which was used for the first time in railway tunnel construction on the Mont Cenis between Italy and France (1871).[4]

In addition to such technical difficulties, a certain amount of popular hostility toward railways existed in the early years of building. Not only did farmers along rights of way complain that the belching wood burners frightened their horses and scared their cows but all sorts of arguments were used against the new form of carrying. Some military men thought that the transportation of soldiers by rail would make the men so soft that they would not be able to fight. Some medical authorities feared that passengers would get lung trouble from the damp air of tunnels, and some moralists warned that dark passages would give uncouth males an irresistible opportunity to kiss the ladies and even advised the potential victims of such advances to place pins between their teeth whenever the train became dark.

Lastly, construction costs of railways were so high and earnings so uncertain that relatively few capitalists were willing in the early days to risk their fortunes in these kinds of enterprises. Nevertheless, there were intrepid souls, people like George Hudson, the "railway king of Eng-

---

[3] The standard gauge of 4 feet 8½ inches was hit upon in England in 1846, but the 7-foot gauge and narrow gauges were frequently used.

[4] There were also improvements made in surveying. In one of the early tunnels, gangs working from opposite sides of a mountain failed to meet! Ofttimes there were queer curves in the track at the center of the mountain to bring two tunnels together.

land," the Rothschilds on the Continent, and in America Cornelius Vanderbilt of the New York Central, John Murray Forbes of the Michigan Central, Jay Cooke, an erstwhile Philadelphia bank clerk, Jay Gould, a country store clerk, Jim Fisk, a Vermont peddler, and Daniel Drew, an upstate New York drover, who had faith in the future of rails, invested heavily in them, and profited mightily from them (or from the manipulation of railway stocks on stock exchanges). Yet, in most countries, private capital had to be supplemented by public grants in order to get the railways built. In France, over one-third of the cost of railway construction was borne by the state; in Belgium, the Germanies, and Russia the government provided over half the needed funds for the actual building and operating of the railways. In the United States railway construction was greatly advanced by grants of public lands to railway companies—grants that totaled some 183 million acres or an area three times the arable land of England.

Most of the first railways were built to unite coal mines with waterways or to join two populous centers where an already great amount of traffic existed. Thus among the early lines in England were the Stockton and Darlington (1825), which was designed to carry coal and was so successful from the outset that the price of coal at Darlington fell at once by more than half, and the Liverpool and Manchester line (1829) that was intended to carry cotton. In France, the first regular railway (inaugurated in 1832) was built to connect the coal and iron center of St. Etienne with Roanne on the Loire River, and the next lines were constructed to join Paris with such suburbs as St. Germain-en-Laye (1836) and Versailles (1837). In Germany, the first line ran from Nuremberg to Fürth (1835); in Belgium, from Brussels to Malines (1835); in Italy, from Turin to Moncalieri (1848); and in the United States, the section of the Baltimore and Ohio, from Baltimore to Elliott's Mills (1830).

As the advantages of railways became firmly established, railway building caught the imagination of businessmen, politicians, and the general public, and construction went forward at a rapid pace. Many of the early lines were short and eventually they had to be brought together by mergers in order to avoid reloading. In some countries, railways were laid out according to master plans; whereas in others they were built in a hit-or-miss fashion with all the attendant headaches of duplication of services and cutthroat competition. In England, where governmental planning was at a minimum, a "clearinghouse" for railways was established in 1842 and many lines were brought together in mergers by George Hudson from 1844 to 1847. In France, Michel Chevalier, economic adviser to Napoleon III, devised a scheme for five main lines radiating from Paris to the principal parts of France and a sixth to join

An American Express Train. The familiar "romance of railroading," which captured the imaginations of generations of boys (and their elders) and which lives on to some extent, is reflected in this excellent lithograph by Currier and Ives, made in 1866. In the background one may see a contemporary river steamer. (*Courtesy of the Association of American Railroads.*)

Bordeaux with Marseilles. In Belgium, the national plan was more or less determined by international traffic, with two transversal lines, one running through Brussels from the Netherlands and Antwerp to France and the other from Cologne, Germany, to Liége, Malines, and Brussels to Ostend for steamer connections to England. In Germany, the great design of Friedrick List, the most famous of all Continental national economists,[5] aimed to join the various parts of the country and especially to overcome the commercial provincialism that had resulted from the fact that rivers flowed in parallel lines to the North and Baltic Seas. In Russia, Sergius Witte, who worked his way up from station agent to Minister of Communications and Minister of Finance (1892–1903), built both strategic and economic lines toward the West and laid out the trans-Siberian line to Vladivostock. And in the United States and Canada railways were built from north to south to unite existing cities and then westward, more or less along wagon routes, in order to furnish connections between parts of the country that were not connected by natural waterways.[6]

[5] That is, of the school which aimed to develop the economy of the individual nation irrespective of the development of other nations.

[6] The first American transcontinental line was completed in 1869, when two crews, one working westward and another eastward met at Promontory Point, Utah. The Canadian Pacific, the first transcontinental line in Canada, was opened for traffic in the 1880s.

RAILWAYS
OF EUROPE
IN 1940

The Railway Age.

321

Some idea of the transportation revolution effected by railways can be had by reference to the accompanying map.

By the third quarter of the nineteenth century, railways had become so successful that canal building fell off and the future of inland shipping began to look dim except for bulky products of low value, like grains and ores, and then chiefly on easily maintained rivers and lakes.[7] Henceforth canal construction was limited mostly to the building of connections between inland waterway systems and between oceans to shorten routes. Thus a ship canal was constructed from Dortmund to Emden to facilitate getting products from the Ruhr to the sea; another canal was begun to connect the Rhine with the Danube via the Main. The Sault Ste. Marie Canal was built (1896) between Lake Superior and Lake Michigan to facilitate the shipping of iron ore from the Mesabi Range of Minnesota to the blast furnaces of Pittsburgh, Cleveland, and later Gary, Indiana. Of interocean connections the most famous were the Suez Canal, opened in 1869, which cut 4,000 miles off the haul from India to Western Europe,[8] the Kiel Canal, that was built across the Danish Peninsula to reduce the length of the route between the North and Baltic Seas, the Panama Canal, begun by a French company under the leadership of De Lesseps and completed by American interests in 1914, which shortened the water route from San Francisco to Liverpool by 5,666 miles, and the Corinth Canal across the Corinthian Isthmus in Greece (opened in 1893).

Shipping on navigable rivers continued to be important, particularly with the development of the steamboat, and was facilitated both by international conventions and by bold engineering undertakings. At the Congress of Vienna in 1815 a convention was signed to open international rivers to vessels of all countries. Agreements for the reduction of tolls not needed to maintain services were negotiated among the powers, and international commissions were created to regulate traffic on such important waterways as the Rhine (1831) and the Danube (1856). Many rivers were dredged and contained by levees or dikes in order to deepen

[7] Some strategically located canals, like the Erie, continued to prosper for a time. In 1860 this canal handled more tonnage than the New York Central, the Hudson River, and the Erie Railroads combined.

[8] The British government had been instrumental in constructing a railway across the Isthmus of Suez in 1854. The canal was, however, built by an international company. The work was directed by a French engineer, Ferdinand de Lesseps. Disraeli bought for Great Britain almost half the shares of the Suez Canal Company with capital lent the treasury by Baron Rothschild. Partly to insure the life line to India the British established a veiled protectorate over Egypt in 1882. The Suez Canal carried 20,275,120 net tons in 1912 and 33,446,014 in 1929, of which 65 per cent was British.

their draught. The Scheldt River below Antwerp and the Lower Mississippi had such high levees that ships actually passed above the surrounding country. These levees allowed Antwerp to become one of the major ports of Western Europe and permitted New Orleans to receive in 1843 tonnage which was twice that handled in New York. Finally, shipping on the North, Baltic, and Mediterranean Seas and on the Great Lakes grew rapidly and coastwise shipping flourished.

Ocean Shipping and International Trade

Important as railway and inland waterway transportation was in tapping resources over large land masses, in bringing various complementary products together for processing, and in carrying manufactured goods from industrial centers to widely dispersed consumers, ocean shipping was of extraordinary significance in the economic development of Western culture. It was a factor which fostered Europe's becoming the "workshop of the world," allowing that area to import raw materials and to export manufactured goods. Because the "terms of trade," that is, the relative prices for these two classes of goods, resulted in more value being added per unit of human input in manufactured goods than in raw materials and foodstuffs, intercontinental carrying was important in aiding Europe especially, among the industrial areas of Western culture, to attain a position of economic primacy in the world.

The growth of ocean shipping was made technically possible both by improvements in sailing vessels and by the development of the steamship after the middle of the nineteenth century. The design of sailing vessels was improved, enabling them to carry greater burdens or, as in the case of clipper ships, of transporting passengers and perishable freight of high value at increased speeds. Furthermore, sail carrying costs were kept low, for vast resources of timber in the New World permitted the construction of vessels at low cost and the use of iron (after 1832) and of steel (after 1879), which were in good supply in Great Britain, made possible the building of vessels of great durability cheaply.

Sailing vessels carried so well and at such low rates that they gave steamships stiff competition down to the late 1880s, but there were also technical reasons why steam did not establish its supremacy over wind at an earlier date. The first steamships required so much fuel that they could not bunker sufficient coal to carry them on long journeys and have space left for a payload (the American-built *Savannah* crossed the Atlantic in 1819 in twenty-nine days but used steam for only eighty hours of the passage, and not until 1838 was a crossing effected exclusively with steam). Furthermore, paddle wheels were easily damaged by

The Steamship *Hibernia* of the Cunard Line. This drawing of 1847 shows a combination sail and steam vessel. The inefficiency of the steam engine made it impossible to bunker enough fuel to get the vessel all the way across the Atlantic under steam. (*Courtesy of the Cunard Steamship Company.*)

storms, and wooden construction limited keels to 300 feet. Thus, while steamships were used successfully first on rivers, lakes, and inland seas for short hauls, they made little headway on the oceans.

Yet, the potentialities of steam propulsion were so great that inventors, engineers, and entrepreneurs strove to realize them. One of the greatest obstacles in their path to success was eliminated by the invention of the compound engine (1854), which led to the development of the triple and quadruple expansion engines—machines that reused steam two, three, or four times and saved so much fuel that they solved the problem of bunkering. Then, the screw propeller, invented in 1836 and first employed by the British Admiralty in 1843, permitted doing away with the vulnerable paddle wheel. Finally, iron and steel construction (the British East India Company began to acquire iron vessels in 1839) made possible such large vessels that there was ample room for steam equipment, fuel, and a cargo that would pay a good profit.[9]

As techniques of ocean carrying improved, shipping services on the

[9] Improvements in ship construction and in navigation were made continually. Ballast tanks were introduced to lessen rolling, ships were divided into watertight compartments, gyroscopic compasses which automatically controlled the rudder were adopted, and buoys and lights became more numerous and better regulated.

high seas became greatly extended. Hitherto most carriers had been traders, like the East India Company, and transported cargoes for others whenever it was convenient for them to do so. In the first half of the nineteenth century, however, shippers came to limit their activities to carrying and at the same time became differentiated according to the service which they provided. Some of them would go anywhere at any time there was a cargo and thus came to be known as running "tramp steamers." Others plied between stipulated ports but with no fixed schedules. And still others ran packets or liners, catered to passengers, and maintained regular schedules—services which were furnished primarily by great shipping companies, like the Cunard Company (1839), the French Compagnie des Messageries Maritimes (1851), and the American Collins Line, which reached its peak in the early 1850s. This division of labor in ocean carrying, together with technical improvements and an increased volume of business, permitted a considerable reduction in costs. In fact, charges of transporting grain from New York to Europe were cut in half from 1874 to 1884; charges from Odessa to the United Kingdom fell to one-sixth the former price just at the time when sail was giving way to steam.

Table 13. Shipping Tonnages, Sail and Steam
(In thousands of net tons)

Nation	1850		1880		1890	
	Sail	Steam	Sail	Steam	Sail	Steam
Great Britain	3,396	168	3,851	2,936	2,936	5,042
United States	1,540	45	1,206	146	749	197
France	674	13	641	277	444	499
Germany			965	215	709	723

As ocean shipping grew, the various nations of Western culture came to attach new importance to the possession of strong merchant marines. They recognized in them not only a way to seek out new markets for their wares, to exploit new sources of supplies, and perchance to obtain colonies, but also a means whereby the nation could effect important earnings and enhance its striking force by giving more mobility to its fighting forces. Consequently most states encouraged both shipbuilding and shipping. To be sure, the old type of navigation act that restricted carrying between the motherland and distant parts, including colonies, to ships of the homeland and that kept foreign vessels out of a nation's coastwise trade were done away with, by Britain in 1849 and 1854 and

France in 1866 and 1869,[10] but new methods of assisting shippers were substituted for the old. Thus lucrative mail contracts were given to carriers who built ships to specifications that made them useful as fighting ships in time of war, outright subsidies were paid to shipping companies and to shipbuilders, and government loans on easy credit terms were granted to those who would venture in ocean carrying. Great Britain, for example, awarded important mail contracts to the Cunard Line and to some other shippers at the time when the transition from sail to steam was taking place and carriers were reluctant to risk their capital in what appeared to be a somewhat uncertain enterprise. Later, when Germany won the "Blue Ribbon" of the North Atlantic, that is, had the fastest ship in service from Europe to New York, Britain loaned Cunard 2,600,-000 pounds at 2¾ per cent interest, which permitted the building of the *Lusitania* and the *Mauretania*, in order to regain the symbol of primacy. France, for its part, gave both mail contracts to shippers and direct subsidies to both shippers and shipbuilders (1881).[11] Germany, also, granted favorable mail contracts to its carriers, gave low railway rates on goods shipped abroad, subsidized its main lines, and after the Russian cholera epidemic of 1894 required emigrants from Russia and Austria to pass through quarantine stations maintained by the Hamburg-American Line and the North German Lloyd, which meant, in effect, that most of the emigrants sailed with these lines.

The assistance thus given by most of the Great Powers to their merchant marines had to some degree the desired effect, for the tonnage under their flags remained high. The United States, which gave its shippers little aid except for mail contracts, witnessed, on the other hand, a decline in the proportion of its foreign trade carried in its own bottoms from 66 per cent in 1860 to 10 per cent in 1914. Much of this fall was to be attributed to the lack of advantages in the building of steel vessels compared with those enjoyed when construction was of wood.

Shipping rivalries among nations were keen and competition among shipping companies was extraordinarily severe. So sharp did rivalry become, in fact, that individual companies made an effort to mitigate competitive practices of a cutthroat character by forming pools and com-

[10] The United States reserved coastwise shipping all through this period to vessels of American registry.

[11] The latter policy was not very successful, for at first the periods in which aid was given were deemed too short and later (1893) subsidies were based upon distance covered, which led to the construction of cheap sailing vessels that plied the waterways of the world more or less in ballast just to get the subvention. One company received more from the mileage subsidy than it did from freight. Hence, in 1902 subsidy arrangements were altered to favor steam construction and the actual carrying of goods.

bines. The first of these was among British carriers in the Calcutta trade (1875), but the most famous of all was the North Atlantic Shipping Conference (1908) which embraced the lines of various nations. By means of such associations, shippers endeavored to fix prices, to prevent rebates, and to compete for business by giving good service. National states condoned such practices, because the rates of members of the pool were but little if any higher than those of nonmembers and because excessive shipping competition could lead to extraordinarily heavy drains on public treasuries.

At all events, ocean carrying, together with shipping on railways and inland waterways, accounted for a rate of growth in international trade which may even have exceeded that of the actual production of goods.

Table 14. Foreign Trade per Capita

Country	Period	
	1851–1853 (Swiss franc of 1853)	1929 (U.S. dollar of 1929)
Denmark		266
Netherlands	387	243
Switzerland	406	228
Great Britain	268	219
France	101	103
Germany	83*	100
United States		79
Russia	19	5.7

* Zollverein

Furthermore, these exchanges among nations constituted an intricate network. Whereas earlier much of international commerce had been bilateral (trade between two countries), exchanges of goods now became characteristically multilateral (trade among many countries). By means of what appeared, from a historical point of view, to be an exceptionally well-developed multilateralism various economies got what they wanted and turned out what they could competitively best produce.

With the extension of multilateralism great economic inequalities developed as between industrialized and nonindustrialized regions, as can be seen from Table 15. The explanation for the great differences in national income per capita of the gainfully employed among the various nations is to be found, in part, in the fact that the costs of turning out industrial goods were reduced more than those of producing agricultural goods and, in part, in the fact that agricultural products were thrown on the international market from the 1870s onward, which tended to keep agricultural prices low.

Patterns of consumption in countries of Western culture changed so greatly after the beginning of the nineteenth century and were so different from those found in countries of Eastern culture that the international comparisons given here accentuate the material inferiority of the economically backward areas. These comparisons do, however, indicate

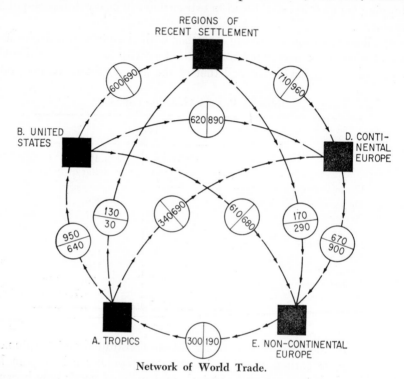

Network of World Trade.

greater well-being in those areas which were more heavily industrialized and which had an extensive division of labor than in the less industrialized.

With the development of multilateralism, exact balances among nations were never struck in the exchange of physical goods, because so many other items for which payments had to be made entered international accounts. Thus some nations performed shipping services, provided insurance, and did a banking business for others. Some received the expenditures of tourists, some, remittances from emigrants; some, earnings on investments, and some, cancellation of debts, which was actually a default. Thus the annual statement of foreign trade and pay-

Table 15. National Income per Person in Work
per Year
(In international units*)

Country	Period	Amounts
United States	1800	786
	1850	828
	1899–1908	1319
Great Britain	1860–1869	707
	1894–1903	842
Germany	1805	114
	1854	406
	1894–1903	820
France	1800–1812	248
	1850–1859	426
	1900–1909	597
Japan	1887	100
	1897	101
India	1867–1868	132†

* One international unit is what one dollar would
buy in the United States, on the average, in the
period 1925–1934.
† Estimated.
SOURCE: Colin Clark, *Conditions of Economic
Progress*, 2d ed. (London, Macmillan, 1951)

Table 16. Index of Wholesale Prices, United States
(1910–1914 = 100)

Year	All commodities	Farm products	Textiles
1865	185	148	266
1870	135	112	179
1875	118	99	141
1880	100	80	128
1885	85	72	105
1890	82	71	103
1895	71	62	79
1900	82	71	95
1905	88	79	96
1910	103	104	104

ments of an economically advanced country, such as Great Britain early
in the nineteenth century, indicated an excess of imports over exports,
but large earnings from investments overseas, from insurance, shipping,
banking, tourists, and emigrants were more than enough to cover such
deficits. In fact, the British balance of trade and payments usually showed

an excess of credits over debits and this excess made possible a growth of British investments overseas from early in the nineteenth century to World War I—an investment which was 1,302,000,000 pounds in 1885 and 3,763,000,000 pounds in 1913. Similarly, French foreign investments increased from 15,000,000,000 francs in 1880 to 45,000,000,000 francs in 1914.

These relations among economically advanced states and the more retarded ones, together with an ardent nationalism in the former, account in large part for the revival of imperialism, particularly after 1873. As we shall see in greater detail later, Western European nations came to believe that their economic interests would be furthered if they had political control over areas which could provide them with raw materials and markets for their goods and for their investment capital.

The balance sheet of a rapidly developing country like the United States indicated heavy borrowing abroad for investment, large immigrant remittances, which might be considered a cost of acquiring a labor force, payment on foreign borrowings, and an excess of exports over imports to get the wherewithal to make these payments to foreign creditors.[12] The international account of an economy having slow economic growth would show but little deficit for borrowed capital, heavy indebtedness for services, and some excess of exports over imports to pay for debts owed abroad.

Table 17. Balance of Trade and Payments

Item	Great Britain (in millions of pounds)	United States (in billions of dollars)
	1910	1896–1914
Merchandise	−159	+9.3
Investments	+187	−3.0
Services	+90	−7.2
Other	+35	+0.2
Unestimated		−0.3
Capital movement:		
Available for investment abroad	+153	+1.0

Although under certain circumstances an excess of imports over exports of physical goods might be economically justified, a belief that there was a special virtue in an excess of exports over imports persisted. This doctrine was particularly marked in those countries where the desire

[12] Foreign debt was also reduced by defaults or by declines in securities which were owned by foreigners. These items did not, however, appear in the balance sheets.

for material improvement was strong, where the realization that economic growth entailed industrialization was lively, and where the establishment of manufactures lagged behind that of other economies. It was
preached by many statesmen and by a group of national economists, like
Henry Charles Carey (1793–1879) in the United States,[13] Friedrich List
in Germany (1789–1846), and Paul Louis Cauwès (1843–1917) in
France. These theorists argued that to be economically strong and industrially powerful a nation must have a highly developed industry and
well-rounded production; hence, national economic policy should assist
economic growth with tariffs and subsidies.

The views of these men were opposed, however, by those who stressed
the advantages to be derived from a division of labor and who consequently advocated free trade among nations and the nonintervention of
the state in economic affairs at home. Most of these laisser-faire theorists
were at first to be found in Great Britain, which had such technological
advantages over other states that it had little to fear from foreign competition, especially in manufactures. There the doctrine of free trade
enunciated by Adam Smith in his *Wealth of Nations* (1776) was elaborated by a brilliant group of the "classical school of economics"—by
Thomas Malthus (1766–1812), David Ricardo (1772–1823), John Stuart
Mill (1803–1873), and Alfred Marshall (1842–1924). Subsequently the
free-trade faith was picked up and preached abroad by theorists like
Jean Baptiste Say (1767–1832) and Frédéric Bastiat (1801–1850) in
France. Even businessmen who were able to compete in the international
market, like the Manchester manufacturers, the Bordeaux wine growers,
and the cotton plantation owners of the American South, wanted low
tariffs either to be able to buy cheaply what they needed or to get tariff
concessions from other states so that they could sell more easily to them.

Already in the eighteenth century, as we have seen,[14] a current of
laisser faire was flowing, which in so far as international trade was concerned was exemplified in the Eden Treaty (1786) between France and
England—a trade agreement by which France lowered its rates on English textiles and Britain reduced its duties on French wines to the level
of those on Portuguese wines.[15] Hardly was the ink dry on this document,
however, than the French Revolution broke out (1789); this embroiled
France in foreign wars that were not brought to an end until Napoleon's

[13] Alexander Hamilton's *Report on Manufactures* (1791) had an impact on the
thinking of these men.

[14] See Chap. 11 above.

[15] Inasmuch as England's trade arrangements with Portugal, which were incorporated in the Methuen Treaty of 1702, gave Portugal favored treatment in wines,
Britain lowered its rates on Portuguese wines after the signing of the Eden Treaty,
so that the French did not get the equality of treatment which they had expected.

defeat at Waterloo in 1815. In these wars the French had extraordinary success upon the Continent, but they failed utterly in their efforts to bring the "island of shopkeepers," as Napoleon called Britain, to its knees by military action and their chances of doing so seemed slight after their disastrous naval defeat at Trafalgar in 1805. Thus it was that France tried to bend England to its will by economic warfare—by constructing a closed economic system, known as the Continental System, against the English.

The theory on which the Continental System rested was that England's economic well-being depended upon its export of manufactured goods and that if British exports to its principal market, the European continent, were cut off, industrialists would have to close their factories, workers would become discontented, and the government would sue for peace. In the meanwhile, France would be able to gobble up the markets closed to Britain. The increased demand for goods would stimulate French manufacturing, and growth of industry would augment France's military and political potential.

Almost immediately after France declared war on Great Britain (1793) the first stones of the foundation of the Continental System were laid. The Eden Treaty was annulled. A large number of English products were prohibited from entering the French market; in October, 1793, *all* British goods were proscribed, and in September of the same year a blow was aimed at English shipping by requiring that all goods brought to France be carried in French bottoms or in the vessels of the country in which the cargo was produced. As Barère, the great tribune of the Revolution, stated, "Let us declare a solemn navigation act and the Isle of Shopkeepers will be ruined. Carthage will thereby be destroyed."

These rules were subsequently intensified and extended, especially in times of particularly hostile relations between France and Great Britain. Thus the tariff of 1796 was very harsh and new navigation laws were so rigorous that made-in-England buttons on the skipper's jacket were enough to cause the French to declare that a cargo was of British origin and a ship's putting in at a British port was enough to outlaw the vessel and to render it subject to seizure.

For a moment it looked as though such measures might accomplish their desired end and French hopes soared when the Bank of England suspended gold payments (1797). But England did not succumb to the attacks upon its commerce. When warfare was renewed after a brief interlude of peace (1802–1803), Napoleon applied the blockade with vigor and extended it to nearly the entire Continent (Berlin Decrees of 1806 and the Milan Decree of 1807). The English, for their part, declared by Orders of Council of 1807 a blockade of all ports from which Englishmen were excluded, outlawed all ships that tried to run the blockade, and required neutrals to go to a British port before proceeding to the Continent, which was one of the reasons for the War of 1812 between the United States and Britain. Furthermore, the British encouraged their shippers to break through the blockade and were so successful in getting them to do so that English goods were found on the Contient in such large amounts that French quartermaster corps bought English shoes in Hamburg for the French soldiers for their march on Moscow (1811–1812). Moreover, French industry was unable to take full advantage of the market reserved to it, especially in such things as cotton textiles made from the raw cotton which had to be brought from overseas. This failure so aroused the ire of the satellites that they abetted the English efforts to break the blockade. Eventually leaks in the Continental System became so great that Napoleon had to recognize them. At the end he turned the various restrictions on trade into a money-raising device by selling licenses for the importation of British goods.

Upon the defeat of Napoleon, the Continental System came officially to a close, but by the tariff of 1814 France prohibited a long list of goods. It raised rates in 1816, and instituted high protection with the corn laws of 1819, following the poor crops of 1816–1817, high prices for food, and the first large-scale importation of Russian grain. Even French shipping was favored with a flag tax (*droit de pavillon*), which was a charge levied on foreign vessels bringing goods of third nations to France, a *droit de tonnage*, which was a special tax per ton on foreign ships, and a *droit d'entrepôt*, which was an extra charge on goods that had been warehoused in other than their country of origin before they arrived in France —a tax aimed at England's middleman position in overseas trade. In England, agriculturalists demanded protection and got it with the Corn Law of 1815, which was revised slightly downward in 1828 with the Duke of Wellington's sliding scale, while industrialists worked behind a tariff barrier and had the advantage of laws designed to prevent the exportation of industrial secrets and the migration of skilled workers. In the United States, high protection was instituted in 1816, partly as a result of sentiments aroused during the War of 1812 against the commercial policies of France and Britain.

Yet, in spite of an apparently universal policy of protection, cogent arguments for free trade were being spun and certain interests, particularly commercial ones, took a firm position for lowering tariff barriers. In fact, commercial men in London signed a petition for free trade in 1820 and William Huskisson, who was President of the Board of Trade, that is, Britain's department of commerce, from 1823 to 1827 worked arduously for the abolition of the worst impediments to trade. He did much to abolish the Navigation Acts, opened trade with British colonies to foreign goods (1822–1825),[16] wiped out absolute prohibitions and prohibitive rates on imports, replacing them with duties that did not exceed 30 per cent *ad valorem*, did away with prohibitions on the exportation of goods and with export bounties, and permitted the emigration of skilled workers (1824) and the exportation under license of industrial machines (1825).

The tariff reform movement was subsequently carried further by Robert Peel, who was Prime Minister from 1841 to 1846. As First Lord of the Treasury he instituted an income tax to furnish a substitute revenue for customs duties; then he cut the tariff (1842), allowed the exportation of machinery (1843), abolished the export duty on coal (1845), did away with the export duty on raw wool (1844), and most important of all, repealed the Corn Laws (1846) when agricultural prices soared, especially in Ireland, following the potato famine of 1845.[17] Furthermore, he continued a policy begun by his predecessors of negotiating free-trade or freer-trade commercial treaties with foreign states. Britain supported Latin American nations in their efforts to get independence, and supported the American Monroe Doctrine (1823) to keep foreign powers from "intervening" in the affairs of the states of the Western Hemisphere. It negotiated a trade agreement[18] with the youthful state of Greece (1837) and another with centuries-old Turkey (1838). Britain got trade concessions from Persia (1836, 1857). It "opened up" China by the Opium War of 1840–1842, fought the Crimean War to keep the Danube and the Black Sea area open to its commerce, and it won trade concessions from Japan in 1858.

Although free trade may have looked particularly good to Britain with its strong competitive position in industrial goods, most Continental countries continued protectionist policies during the first half of the nineteenth century. France maintained its rates at a high level during the July Monarchy—the so-called "Bourgeois Monarchy" from 1830 to 1848. The

[16] The imperial preference system remained in force, however, until 1860, that is, Britain charged lower rates on equivalent goods coming from its colonies than on goods coming from foreign countries and its colonies collected lower rates on goods of British origin than on goods of foreign make.

[17] Agriculturalists, in general, opposed the repeal of the Corn Laws, for they feared competition from low-cost producers. They did not suffer from overseas competition until the 1870s because of the costs of transportation. The most ardent advocates of the repeal of the Corn Laws were to be found in the Anti-Corn Law League, directed by two free-trade enthusiasts, Richard Cobden and John Bright. The Chartists, who wanted an extension of the suffrage, also supported repeal.

[18] Most of Britain's trade agreements in this period were with the less economically advanced countries with whom England's trade was growing. Britain's exports to Continental countries did not go up much from 1815 to 1837.

United Netherlands adopted protection (1821–1822).[19] Prussia, although it enacted a relatively low tariff in 1818, began in 1833 to bring many of the German states together into a tariff union (*Zollverein*) and thereafter raised its rates. Finally, the Kingdom of Sardinia, the most important of the Italian states, Russia, and Austria all had high customs duties.

By 1850, however, signs were abundant that ultraprotectionism was going to be modified. Not only was Britain moving toward free trade but many producers of raw materials and foodstuffs in several of the less economically developed countries, like the cotton interests of the American South, favored a reduction in tariff rates so that they could get manufactured goods more cheaply.[20] In fact, in the United States tariff rates were lowered steadily from 1833 to the War between the States. Some of the smaller nations began to reduce rates because much of their trade was perforce with other economies. The Netherlands virtually abolished customs duties from 1845 to 1877, Belgium greatly reduced its rates after 1851, and Sardinia did away with excessive forms of protection under the leadership of its great statesman Count Cavour.

The crowning event, however, in this movement toward lower tariffs was the Anglo-French commercial treaty of 1860. For some time advocates of free trade in France and Britain had been preaching the advantages of lower rates. Finally, Michel Chevalier and Richard Cobden exerted their influence with Napoleon III and Gladstone respectively, and persuaded the two powers to negotiate a commercial treaty. This document provided not only for low rates but also stipulated that each signatory would extend to the other "most-favored-nation treatment," that is, would grant the other the lowest rates extended to any other nation. Subsequently, both France and England negotiated a whole series of trade agreements which contained the "most-favored-nation clause" with other powers and usually introduced some reduction of rates in them. Thus, through a network of most-favored-nation clause treaties, the lowest rates which Western culture had ever known became generalized.[21]

Reaction against these low rates set in, however, with the extraordinary depression in European agriculture after 1873. With low prices, with such misfortunes as phyloxera, sheep rot, and poor harvests, and with an influx of agricultural goods from overseas, European farmers began to clamor for protection. Then in those lands where manufacturing had made little headway, industrialists demanded protection for infant in-

---

[19] Belgium, which was united with the northern Netherlands from 1815 to 1830, introduced a sliding-scale corn law and a navigation act (1844).

[20] Canada moderated its rules by trade agreements (1857).

[21] In this same period many of the measures to protect national shipping were abolished. Thus the French did away with their surtaxes on foreign shipping in 1866.

dustries.[22] In Europe customs duties began to move upward with the Austrian tariff of 1878 and continued to mount until World War I. In 1910 the average rates on all imports, including those on the free list, were computed on an ad valorem basis to have been as follows: France, 8 per cent; Germany, 8.4 per cent; Italy, 9.6 per cent; Spain, 13.4 per cent; Russia, 38.9 per cent; whereas the rates on just dutiable goods entering the United States were 38 per cent. Only the Netherlands, Finland, Turkey, and Great Britain continued to pursue free-trade policies.

As time went on states came to use various devices to keep out foreign goods when competition threatened. The French, for example, had two sets of rates, minimum and maximum, so that they could change their rates as they would and yet give minimum rates to those countries with whom they had most-favored-nation clause treaties and maximum rates to all others. Embargoes were resorted to in order to minimize foreign competition, sometimes under the guise of sanitary regulations, as when in 1885 Germany prohibited the entry of American pork, and sometimes to prevent one nation from "dumping" surplus products abroad at prices greatly below those charged at home. Sometimes, too, rates, were made to apply to goods so specified that the products of one country had a preferred position. Germany, which had most-favored-nation clause treaties with France and Switzerland, thus gave Swiss importations the advantage by granting low rates to cows raised at altitudes of 1,000 meters or above. Moreover to encourage exports, states gave subsidies, such as outright subventions at the time of exportation, subsidies on production, drawbacks, that is, payments to offset the duties levied on imported materials used in exports, and cheap transportation rates on national railways or shipping lines for carrying goods abroad. Finally, some nations which had colonies, especially France, Spain, and Portugal, adopted steep preferential rates,[23] although Great Britain and the Netherlands remained loyal to the principle of free trade in the administration of their empires.

One of the immediate consequences of protective commercial measures was the outbreak of tariff wars. Among the most acrimonious of these conflicts was that between France and Italy (1888–1899). Each nation believed that it had been particularly discriminated against in new commercial laws and consequently placed extra-heavy duties on the other's goods, used all imaginable obstructionist tactics, and even cracked down on loans from one nation to the other. Similarly, Russia and Germany

---

[22] In the United States, the North, which had most of the country's industry, dominated the political scene and got protection.

[23] Such preferential rates could not be applied to certain colonial areas because of international agreements. This was the case with the Belgian Congo and Morocco.

were involved in a tariff struggle from 1879 to 1894, France and Switzerland were in one from 1893 to 1895, and Germany and Canada, from 1897 to 1910.

Tariffs also aided the creation of monopolies and selling agreements, because high protection allowed the formation of cartels which could establish prices without fear of having them undermined by foreigners. Moreover, tariffs usually meant higher prices on the domestic market and antiquated production methods.[24]

Tariffs were defended by asserting that they allowed certain industries to become established, that they mitigated shocks from sudden influxes of goods, and that they were a means of planning for increasing the economic and military potential of a nation. Furthermore, advocates of tariffs claimed that the free movement of goods required the free movement of people so that populations of those areas with no comparative advantages in production could move to areas where there was work.[25] Finally, protectionists pointed out that tariffs in this era were not so high that international trade was stopped and that a kind of world-wide division of labor was created in spite of them.

Developments in Communications and Marketing

With a greater division of labor both in domestic economies and in the entire world and consequently with a greater dependence of the individual upon the market for goods to satisfy his needs, pressures were great to improve the means of communication and the methods of marketing. Business needed to know from day to day what prices were and to have the means of placing orders rapidly before conditions of trading varied. Sellers and buyers needed to have a market where staple goods could always be exchanged and where prices could be established through free negotiation. And both merchants and consumers needed places to which they could go to get the goods that they required.

Most important among improvements in communications from the end of the eighteenth century to the last quarter of the nineteenth were the extension of postal service, the invention and adoption of the electric telegraph, and the establishment of penny newspapers. Prior to 1800, letters were carried mostly by private enterprises, like the Turn and Taxis

[24] Within the larger economies, however, competition was often sufficient to prevent production from becoming moribund.

[25] Their opponents maintained, on the other hand, that the free movement of goods served as a substitute for the free movement of people. Such an argument might have some validity in a place with goods to sell, like Britain, but made less sense in a poor region, like southern Italy.

company in Germany and the early "express" companies in the United States. After 1800 national states began to create their own mail services and as they did so they introduced such reforms as standard rates for equal weights, low charges (the penny post was introduced into England in 1840), and adhesive stamps. Moreover, they greatly expanded postal services by opening post offices in every hamlet and they speeded carrying by entrusting the post to railways (England did so in 1838). How significant all these changes were can be imagined from the fact that the number of letters carried in France, for example, increased from 4 million in 1830 to 358 million in 1869.

Significant as such mass communications were for economic growth, speed of transmitting messages was often of extreme importance. Many a financial *coup* was made possible by advanced information about a crop failure, a military victory, or some other event that would have an impact on prices. Even before 1800 businessmen had used carrier pigeons to send information with dispatch, but such experiments were not very successful because the birds could not be trusted to fly to the right places. Then, they tried various types of semaphore systems to relay messages from place to place (the Chappe telegraph system, invented in 1793, was capable of transmitting messages from Strasbourg to Paris in 6½ minutes), but such devices were of little use in fog and rain or darkness.

In the quest for a sure and rapid method of communcation experiments were made with electric signals as early as 1753, but not until the 1830s did the German Weber, the Englishman Wheatstone, and the American Morse make progress with this method. Finally, Morse succeeded in transmitting by electricity a message from Baltimore to Washington (1844) and thus got credit for inventing the telegraph. Almost immediately railways strung wires along their rights of way in order more efficiently and surely to control traffic and those wires were soon used for sending private messages. In 1860 there were 126,140 kilometers of telegraph lines throughout the world on which 9 million messages were transmitted. In 1851 the first submarine cable was laid from Dover to Calais, and in 1866 the first transatlantic cable was put in operation. Then, at the end of the period at present under consideration, Alexander Graham Bell invented the telephone (1876) which was to facilitate communication still further, for it made the sender and receiver independent of "middlemen" and could be put at the beck and call of everyone.

Lastly, the diffusion of information important to business was speeded by the appearance of low-priced newspapers. Although daily journals of news had existed before 1800 (the first English daily dated from 1702), they were costly and were read primarily by the well-to-do in

A Telegraph Unit of the Northern Army Stringing Wire during the War between the States. The telegraph was adopted very rapidly and played a role during the War between the States. This picture illustrates how warfare is conditioned by technology. (*From the American Telephone and Telegraph Company collection.*)

Bell Telephone Box. The primitive character of the original telephone is well illustrated in this photograph. It was a self-contained instrument, the mouthpiece and telephone being the same. (*Courtesy of the Bell Telephone Laboratories.*)

coffeehouses and other public places. The cylindrical press, introduced into newspaper printing in 1812 by the *London Times,* reduced costs and the sale of advertising space provided a new source of revenue. By the middle of the nineteenth century the "penny" newspaper was well established and carried information useful to both the businessman and the consumer.

The craftsman who produced and sold goods in his own shop gradually disappeared, although in certain trades, like tailoring and shoemaking, the old form of organzation died slowly. And the peddler who carried a small quantity of a large number of items of light goods from needles and pins to pots and pans began to be inadequate to the task of distribution. In their stead came the retail store, the first of which seem to have been for dry goods (mercers' shops), for colonial products (spices and teas), and for a large assortment of wares (the general store). These establishments were fairly common by 1800, but became ever more numerous as the century wore on. From a small dry goods store came the first department store, La Belle Jardinière of Paris (1830); another department store of Paris, Le Bon Marché (1852), adopted the practice of charging fixed and marked prices; and the house of Potin, a Parisian grocery establishment, developed a reputation for excellent quality and great variety at fair prices.

With the appearance of such retail establishments based on the profit motive, there came into being also consumers' cooperatives, founded on the principle that consumers would furnish the capital necessary for an enterprise and distribute among themselves whatever profit there might be from their purchases. The outstanding pioneer organization of this nature was founded in 1844 by a group of workers at Rochdale, near Manchester, England. This society, which furnished a pattern for cooperatives all over the world, was organized on the joint-stock company plan, with capital being furnished by the sale of stock to an unlimited number of members. The "co-op" sold goods at regular market prices, but at the end of the year made a distribution among its members in proportion to the amount of goods purchased. The success of the Rochdale experiment was so great that many cooperatives were established throughout Western culture both for distributing goods and for producing them.[26]

The development of retail selling by those who did not produce their wares created a problem of getting supplies, for manufacturers were numerous and the demand for goods was uneven. Thus there came to be a need for the services of middlemen between retailers and producers— for the wholesaler. Previously, what wholesaling there was had been

[26] In 1929 consumers' cooperatives in Great Britain and Ireland had 6,168,984 members, or 10 per cent of the population, and did a business of 216,967,000 pounds.

done by merchants who brought goods to fairs, by traders, like the English East India Company, who sold their wares when they came into port,[27] and by specialists who had stalls in central halls, like the Blackwell Hall in London, the *Halles Centrales* in Paris, and the Washington Market in New York. Now wholesalers established warehouses in various areas where they kept stocks of goods, sent out "runners" or "drummers" to drum up trade among retailers, and so replenished the inventories of retailers.

[27] Often these sales were "by candle," that is, bids were accepted so long as a candle continued to burn.

CHAPTER 16

Revolutions in Investing, Business Organization, and Finance

Capital Investment and Economic Growth

The establishment of new means of transportation, of communication, and of distribution, the growth of machine industry organized in factories, and the development of a partially mechanized agriculture required an enormous investment of capital. Railways were notoriously expensive to get into operation because of the vast amount of land that had to be acquired, the need for extensive grading, the building of bridges and tunnels, the construction of terminals, and the purchase of rolling stock. In the English cotton-spinning industry, capital equipment per worker in handicraft production was about 5 pounds; whereas it was 118 pounds in factory production in 1892. Indeed, capital invested per gainfully occupied worker in Great Britain appears to have gone up some 50 per cent from 1865, when many of the large initial outlays had already been made, to 1913.[1] The crucial facts here were that savings, which permitted human energies to be diverted from the actual production of goods for immediate consumption, were being effected and that these savings were being used to create capital goods, which would

[1] In the same space of time, national income per gainfully occupied worker increased some 70 per cent. The capital invested per worker in Japan in 1913 was about one-seventh the amount invested per worker in France.

eventually make possible the turning out of still more goods. Just what the rate of saving or the rate of investment was in Western culture in the hundred years prior to 1875 is impossible to determine with accuracy. From what evidence we have, it would seem that capital formation in the United States was at the annual rate of about 20 per cent of national income in the 1870s and in the United Kingdom at about 17 per cent of national income in the 1860s.

Economists are generally of the opinion that such savings and investments are extremely important to economic growth,[2] but because they have recently placed so much emphasis on the role of investment perhaps the introduction of a caveat here is in order. Investment cannot be considered to be the *single* cause of economic growth, nor in and of itself to have made economic development possible. As has been frequently stated in preceding pages, change in economic life takes place as a result of many factors operating concomitantly. One scholar has been so bold as to estimate that only about 10 per cent of the economic growth in the United States during the eight decades prior to 1953 is to be attributed to the rise in the stock of tangible capital consisting of buildings, machines and other equipment, inventories, and foreign assets.[3] This estimate, if anywhere near actuality, indicates that a large proportion of economic growth depends upon ideologies, techniques, and organization of production, in short, upon "national efficiency."

Business Organization—the Corporate Form

One aspect of change that contributed greatly to "national efficiency" from the eighteenth century to the last quarter of the nineteenth was the growth in the size of economic enterprise. Industrial plants, railways, shipping companies, and department stores had to be large by comparison with earlier undertakings in order to exist at all. Inasmuch as optimum size was large, capital requirements were likewise very great. This being the case, the single owner-manager type of business no longer sufficed for large enterprises. It became necessary for many persons to be associated in order to get together adequate amounts of capital and to assemble necessary technical and managerial talents.

From the earliest days of the Industrial Revolution, partnerships were

[2] Colin Clark, *Conditions of Economic Progress*, 2d ed. (London: Macmillan, 1951), pp. 506ff.

[3] Solomon Fabricant, *Economic Progress and Economic Change*, Thirty-fourth Annual Report of the National Bureau of Economic Research (New York, May, 1954). From tangible capital are excluded consumers' equipment, military assets, land, and subsoil assets.

numerous. They came about, in some cases, because inventors then as now did not ordinarily have either the capital resources or the business acumen needed to exploit their finds. James Watt had to seek the assistance of Matthew Boulton to get his steam engine produced and marketed. Richard Arkwright, although probably more of an entrepreneur than an inventor, required capital aid from his wife and from Jedediah Strutt, whom he took on as a partner. And Edmund Cartwright had several partners in his efforts to launch his power loom.

In other cases, as we have previously seen, the resources of a single partner did not suffice for the task at hand and so multiple partnerships were formed. Some partners were chiefly investors and did not participate directly in the management of affairs. Such persons came to be known as "sleeping partners"; and their position received special recognition in the business form known as the société en commandite, for they were exempt from liability for debts of the concern. This type of company was recognized by the Code Napoléon (1802) and enjoyed particular favor on the Continent. Out of it grew the société en commandite sur actions (with shares), which, while retaining full liability of the partners who were active in management, gave an opportunity for relatively small investors to place their funds without incurring liability.

In England, however, the joint-stock company came to be developed more fully than the "sleeping partnership," and was, indeed, more adequate to meet the challenge of the times. The corporation was an excellent instrument for amassing large amounts of capital from numerous investors. It provided a way for investors to diversify their risks by placing their eggs in several baskets; and it had the advantage of "being perpetual," in the sense that it was independent of any one individual and could continue in operation despite changes in personnel at the top.

The joint-stock company had come into being, as we have seen, in the seventeenth century with the establishment of trading and colonizing ventures overseas, but then it went under a cloud following the mania of speculation in the second decade of the eighteenth century with the collapse of the Law system in France and the breaking of the South Sea Bubble (1720) in England. Indeed, joint-stock companies were not permitted in the two countries mentioned (by the Bubble Act of 1720 in England and by similar legislation in France) unless Parliament or the King granted the right by special act or charter. In France, the few such companies which actually came into being were suppressed by the revolutionaries from 1793 to 1795. Although the Code Napoléon allowed their creation, joint-stock companies had to be specially approved by the state and were so surrounded by a mass of red tape to prevent fraud that few entrepreneurs had recourse to them. In England, on the other hand, charters for the establishment of incorporated companies were given with increasing frequency as the eighteenth century progressed, especially for the building of turnpikes, canals, and bridges and in Scotland for the launching of insurance companies and even banks. Incorporated companies proved so successful and the need for more in order to take advantage of existing opportunities was so great that the Bubble Act was repealed in 1825 and incorporation by registration, if certain requirements were met, was permitted in 1844.

Hard upon this liberalization in England of the use of the joint-stock type of business organization many speculative companies were founded which soon went under, but such adverse experience was not sufficient to discredit the corporate form. On the contrary, it was used ever more extensively. And it became ever more effective, especially by the addition of limited liability and of the preference share. Limited liability meant that investors would not be liable for the debts of a corporation in which they owned stock—a privilege based on the assumption that stockholders were running considerable risk in letting others use their capital. Limited liability was applied to the stock of most types of businesses in England in 1855 and 1856 but was not granted to the stocks of incorporated banks until 1858 and to those of insurance companies until 1862.

The preference share, or preferred stock, as it is called in the United States, was stock which had a preferred position vis-à-vis common stock in that it received limited dividends before earnings were paid out on common stock and it had a prior claim on a company's assets in case of bankruptcy. It came into being from the fact that in launching certain types of businesses, such as factories and railways, more capital was frequently required than had been originally anticipated and sponsors of enterprises found that they could only get new investors to put money in their undertakings if they were able to offer additional securities that had a good chance of showing profits. So essential did the preference share seem to be for amassing capital to bring some enterprises to the productive stage that it was approved in a special case by the English Parliament in 1825 and given legal status in 1863.

The joint-stock company had so many advantages that it made headway in all parts of Western culture. As early as 1811 New York permitted the incorporation of companies engaged in certain types of manufacturing; both Connecticut (1817) and Massachusetts (1830) adopted the principle of limited liability; all states had some kind of law permitting incoporation by 1860. French legal restrictions were relaxed in 1867, and those of various German states were abolished after the founding of the Reich in 1870. So important did corporations become that to a marked degree economic progress was reflected in the number of joint-stock companies and in the amount of their capital. In 1844 England had 994 incorporated companies with capital of 345,000,000 pounds, in 1840 France had 260. In 1867 Italy had 291 with paid-in capital of 1,192,000,000 lire, and in 1870 Prussia had 276.

The increase in the use of the joint-stock form made necessary the establishment and expansion of stock exchanges—of marts where corporate securities could be readily bought and sold. There had to be places where new issues could be launched, where those with savings could place their funds, change their portfolios, or turn their holdings into cash. In London, stockbrokers who had been carrying on their activities at Jonathan's Coffee House moved first (1773) to the Stock Exchange Coffee House and in 1802 to the Stock Exchange. At the latter date the Exchange consisted of 500 brokers, but new members were accepted upon the payment of a small fee. Only later was membership restricted by charging aspirants large sums.

The French Bourse, which had been founded in 1724, was reorganized in 1816 with a membership of sixty persons and with a list of seven stocks. In the course of time, business expanded to a point where so many companies wanted a market for their securities and so many brokers

The New York Stock Exchange in 1853. The presiding officer receives bids which are recorded by the clerks at his sides and transmitted by one of them by wire to brokerage houses. (*Bettmann Archive.*)

(*agents de change*) wanted a place to operate that trading was permitted on the peristyle of the Bourse—an exchange that soon became known as the Coulisse. In 1889 trade in commodities was separated from trading in securities at the old Bourse, which became known as Le Parquet, and membership in this body was increased to seventy in 1898.

In New York brokers organized for business in 1792, but they did not found the New York Stock Exchange until 1817. Their business subsequently flourished so that in 1880 they bought and sold securities to the amount of 95,737,000,000 dollars. In Berlin, Amsterdam, Vienna, and Rome similar developments took place, either with existing exchanges growing and becoming specialized in the handling of securities or new institutions being created. In 1887 stocks listed on European and American exchanges had a market value of some two and a half billion dollars.

Important as joint-stock companies and stock exchanges were in furthering economic growth, they made possible practices which came in for a considerable amount of criticism. Investors were usually absentee owners who exercised little real control over management despite their power to select members of boards of directors, to voice their views at annual stockholders' meetings, and in extreme instances, to bring a minority stockholders' suit against the management. In general, stockholders showed such apathy toward their companies that management came to dominate affairs. In fact, a class of managers came into being whose members in the upper echelons frequently adopted a proprietary attitude toward the company which employed them. Sometimes these people, many of whom in this period were also investors in the companies for which they worked, used their power for their own benefit. They were in a position to give business to other concerns in which they may have had an interest, as was done in the case of the Union Pacific Railroad when its promoters let the actual construction contract at exorbitant prices to their own company, the Crédit Mobilier. Members of the management group could also speculate in the stock of their company, for they knew its value better than anyone else. They could unload their holdings if the stock was overvalued and threatened to go down, and they could "water stock" by issuing stock certificates to themselves at a nominal price.[4]

Still another criticism made of the corporate form was that it permitted the concentration of control of a large part of the economy in the hands of a few. This might be accomplished by a system of "interlocking directorates" in which some persons served as directors of several banks and

---

[4] *Poor's Manual*, a United States investment manual, estimated that in 1900 1,250,-000,000 of the 3,100,000,000 dollars' par value of stock in the hands of the public was water.

business concerns. Thus a small clique could determine the line of credit that businesses would get, could refuse credit to competitors, and could acquire so much power that it could determine the policies of governments and even overthrow regimes which were hostile to it. Prior to World War I directors of the Dresdner Bank in Germany sat on the boards of about two hundred corporations; American financiers like George F. Baker, President of the First National Bank of New York, and John Pierpont Morgan, the great investment banker, held so many directorships that it is difficult to see how they could have done much else than go to directors' meetings. The *deux cent familles* which controlled the Bank of France dominated in turn a large part of big business in France.

Concentration of control might also be effected by use of the "trust" —a procedure made famous by the Standard Oil Company. In 1879, when the Company did about 90 per cent of the petroleum business of the United States, holders of the majority stock of the various corporations composing Standard Oil placed their securities in the hands of trustees, receiving in return trust certificates. Thus the stockholders got a share of the earnings of the Company, had complete and permanent control of their concerns, and obtained greater freedom of action and greater privacy of operations than was possible in the ordinary corporation.

When this kind of trust arrangement was declared illegal (1890) in the United States and the term trust had become a synonym for large enterprise, other ways to extend control over businesses were found. In one of the new procedures, the organizers of a company limited the amount of voting stock issued and by owning a controlling interest in this small amount of stock dominated the affairs of the company. A second method involved securing proxies from a large enough number of stockholders to allow control of stockholders' meetings and election of their candidates to directorships. Still another device was that of the holding company, first sanctioned by law in the state of New Jersey in 1888, whereby a corporation was formed simply to own stock in several subsidiaries which actually produced goods or services. The United States Steel Company, founded in 1901, was essentially a holding company and was the first corporation to have a capitalization of a billion dollars. Finally, and least subtly, concentration of economic activity could be effected by the merger, which was simply the bringing together of two or more companies to form a new corporation. An indication of how mergers led to concentration is offered by such facts as the drop in the number of banks in England from 600 in 1824 to 250 in 1865, 55 in 1914, and 11 in

1937. In the United States in 1904 three hundred of the largest corporations had two-fifths of all the capital in manufacturing establishments.

In instances where concentration of ownership or control was not possible, competition among businesses could be mitigated in other ways. One of these was by means of the "pool," which appeared first in Europe in the first half of the nineteenth century. This consisted usually of a loose agreement to maintain prices and to limit business to established quotas. A more formal arrangement was the cartel, one of the first of which was the Rhenish-Westphalian Coal Syndicate (1893) in the Ruhr. By the terms of the cartel device independent companies agreed to maintain established prices, to abide by quotas on the amounts of their sales, which were based upon productive capacity and size of investment, and to pay into the cartel treasury fines if the terms of the cartel were broken. Cartels had a particular vogue in Germany, where law did not ban monopolistic practices, in France after 1884, when the law forbidding agreements on prices was abrogated, and in international trade, where three of the most famous organizations were the dynamite cartel of 1886, the railmakers' cartel of 1904, and the North Atlantic Shipping Conference of 1908.

In England and the United States not only the common law, but also popular sentiment was hostile to monopolistic practices. Pools and cartels were virtually outlawed, except in the case of the export trade and shipping and in railway carrying,[5] and a definite campaign was launched against most monopolistic devices. In America a series of Federal laws, like the Sherman Anti-trust Act of 1890, declared any combination in interstate commerce which was in "restraint of trade" to be illegal. What constituted "restraint of trade" had to be decided by the courts. This turned out to be a most difficult thing, especially when great combines were able to lower prices and evidence could be presented to show that many of the most efficient businesses were large ones.

To what extent antitrust legislation prevented wealth from becoming concentrated in a few hands and monopolistic practices from being indulged in is difficult to ascertain. About all that can be said is that businessmen contrived to try to reduce competition, that identical prices for standard products were often arrived at through trade association meetings without any provable collusion having taken place,[6] and that

[5] In the United States the Webb Act of 1918 allowed exporters to make cartel agreements. Railway pools were allowed by the Transportation Act of 1920.

[6] Among such bodies might be mentioned the Comité des Forges in France, that was something of a cartel, and the National Association of Manufacturers in the United States, which was founded in 1895.

the courts did not find an inevitable correlation between size of enterprise and objectionable practices.

The Price System and Money

Undoubtedly the assumption which lay behind much of the opposition to monopoly was that competition was necessary to keep prices low; and certainly the primary reason for the great concern with prices was that they came to regulate many of the relations among men, to determine the individual's ability to acquire goods and services, and to permit a division of labor. So important did prices become, indeed, that much attention was given to a study of how prices became established.

Since prices are expressed in money, it was obvious that both the supply of goods and the supply of money were major factors in determining the relationship between the two. It was also clear that, inasmuch as goods and money were held by individuals, their willingness to part with the one in order to have the other depended upon their respective desires for a long list of goods and services, upon their purchasing power, and upon their expectation of what prices would be in the future. It seemed reasonable, too, that prices would be influenced by the number of sellers (monopoly, duopoly, or oligopoly) and by the number of buyers (monopsony, duopsony, oligopsony), by the velocity at which money circulated (a rate determined by the amount of payments made divided by currency in circulation plus demand deposits in banks), by costs of production, and by the possibility of increasing or decreasing the supply of both goods and money.

In the hundred years prior to 1875, prices were relatively stable, that is, indices of wholesale prices fluctuated within a range of 100 to 200, except in France during the French Revolution and in America during the War of Independence, the War of 1812, and the War between the States. In France, as has been mentioned in connection with the discussion of landholding, in order to pay government debts, the revolutionaries issued assignats, treasury notes which were to be retired upon the sale of land. Once launched upon such a course, revolutionary leaders could not resist the temptation to continue issuing more paper; consequently assignats lost value steadily until in 1795 they were worth 5 per cent of par, or stated in another way, assignats had gone down in value 2,000 per cent. In 1797 the Directory repudiated the assignats as worthless and at the same time declared a "two-thirds bankruptcy," paying its creditors one-third of their claims in new bonds and two-thirds in *mandats territoriaux*, which were similar to the assignats and had no market value.

In the United States, high prices of the Revolution were to be accounted for primarily by the issue of Continental currency in large amounts without sufficient backing. Some of the "Continentals" were retired in 1780 at the ratio of 40 to 1 and the rest in 1790 at 100 to 1. With the War of 1812, prices of imported goods rose to about double what they had been in 1800 and prices of domestic articles went up some 50 per cent partly because of interference with foreign trade and partly because of domestic expansion. With the Civil War the wholesale price index for ninety-two articles was at 71 in 1860 but at 127 in 1865 (1913 = 100), owing to an increase in economic activity and to the issue of paper money which had no reserve—the so-called greenbacks.[7]

In spite of the relative stability of prices there were secular or long-term trends in price levels. Prices rose in the period 1721–1741 to 1819; then they reacted downward until about the middle of the nineteenth century. Thereafter they rose until 1873; they fell again until 1896, and they rose once more from 1896 to after World War I.

These long-term trends in prices, which contain within themselves changes of shorter duration that had to do with poor harvests or fluctuations in business activity, have usually been explained exclusively by consideration of money. It is very probable, however, that because of population growth and war, the demand for goods increased faster than supply from early in the eighteenth century to 1819, that supplies increased somewhat faster than effective demand in the period from 1819 to 1848, that with the enormous outlays of capital occasioned by the building of railways and the diversion of energies from productive activity during a whole series of wars stretching from the Revolution to 1848, through the Crimean War, the War of Italian Liberation, the Seven Weeks War, the American Civil War, and the Franco-Prussian War, supplies of goods fell off in relation to demand from 1848 to 1873. With the development of production on a large scale overseas and the growth of ocean shipping by which quantities of overseas products entered the European market, supplies of goods more than exceeded the volume and velocity of circulation of money from 1873 to 1896. These statements are, however, deduced from the manner in which prices behaved and so they may be said to be almost tautological.

At all events, to arrive at a full understanding of prices it is necessary to consider in more detail another factor in the equation—that of the volume of money, the velocity of its circulation, and the value of the metal or metals into which currency was convertible. As can readily be

---

[7] It should be added that Russia declared one metal ruble worth 3 rubles 60 kopecks of paper money in 1827. Austria declared an 80 per cent reduction in the value of its paper in 1811 and a 60 per cent reduction in 1816. In both instances, the value of the gold coins was brought down to the level of the paper money.

imagined, the volume of money in circulation increased rapidly from the end of the eighteenth century to the last quarter of the nineteenth, for the growth of commercial transactions required greater amounts in order to effect payments. In the case of the Bank of France, for example, the note circulation went up from 69,000,000 francs in 1816 (current values) to 251,000,000 in 1847, and to 2,300,000,000 in 1880. In addition, payments were also made in other negotiable instruments, which may be considered money, such as checks, bills of exchange, money orders, and letters of credit. In the English-speaking world, the check, which is in essence a bill of exchange payable upon demand, supplemented bank notes and coins to such an extent that in England it was used to make half the total value of payments and in the United States in the post-World War II period it has been employed to make some 80 per cent of the volume of payments.

Not only did the volume of money in Western culture increase at a rapid rate in the first three-quarters of the nineteenth century, but each unit of money assumed a bigger role in the making of payments, that is, the velocity of the circulation of money went up, especially money in the form of checks. The rate of turnover of bank deposits, calculated by dividing the volume of debits in a given space of time by the average amount of deposits outstanding in the period, appears to have risen in the United States from less than five before the Civil War to over twenty-five after World War I.

As money thus became more abundant and more efficient as a medium of exchange, it remained remarkably stable, as has been previously stated, as a measure of value, that is, prices fluctuated within narrow limits. This was accomplished, in part, by making money ultimately redeemable in gold and/or silver,[8] by varying the amount of bullion to be paid out as these metals commanded more or fewer goods, and by exercising some control over the supply of money, including both the volume and the velocity of circulation of money.

Throughout most of the nineteenth century a major consideration of the makers of monetary policy concerned the selection of a monetary standard—the kind and amount of metal or metals in which currency should be redeemed. In 1774 the English adopted to all intents and purposes a gold standard, for gold coin became the sole legal monetary standard at the rate then defined by mint ordinances, but in 1816 the government formally decreed gold to be the only standard of value at the rate of 113 grains of fine gold to the pound, with silver coins issued only as tokens having very little silver in them.

[8] Payments in bullion were suspended in a few emergencies, but redemption of paper bank notes in metal was generally adhered to.

Most countries, however, used at the time a bimetallic system. In 1791 the United States adopted a decimal system in place of the sexagesimal system of the pound and fixed the silver content of the dollar (a word derived from Thaler, which in turn came from the fact that much silver was mined in Joachimsthal in Bohemia in the sixteenth century) at 371.25 grains with a ratio of 15 grains of silver to 1 of gold. The French, for their part, decided in 1793 upon a decimal system of coinage, decreed in 1795 that the franc should contain 5 grams of silver 0.9 fine, and declared in 1803 that the ratio of silver to gold should be 15.58 to one. Other peoples of Western culture for the most part followed these examples.

Still other changes resulted in establishing monetary "unification" on a national basis and "national monetary sovereignty." Thus, in the reforms of the hundred years prior to 1875 a single unit of national currency replaced a number of regional moneys. How important this was can be realized from the fact that in the Revolution France's two major livres were abolished in favor of the franc. In 1850, twelve different Swiss currencies were reduced to one. Following Italian unification in 1860 several different monetary systems were fused; and in 1875 nine different currencies in Germany were replaced by the bimetallic mark. Furthermore, the earlier custom of letting foreign currencies circulate more or less freely at home was abolished, so that henceforth the state considered itself sovereign in respect to money and the control thereof. So firmly did this concept come to be rooted and so important to the economy did the managing of money become that the surrender of monetary sovereignty constitutes a major obstacle to European unity plans of the post-World War II era.

Whatever the final judgment of national economic policies, of which the monetary was only one, will be, the fact remains that those which had to do with metal standards operated with a fair degree of success and were not held to so rigidly that they could not be altered when conditions seemed to justify a change. Thus during the first half of the nineteenth century the bimetallic arrangements functioned well, for although gold increased somewhat in value no great difficulty was encountered except in the United States where in 1834 the mint ratio was changed to 16 of silver to 1 of gold. After 1850, however, fluctuations in the respective prices of gold and silver were great enough to have a serious effect on the established ratios and consequently on the use of metals in money, for the hoary doctrine of Sir Thomas Gresham that cheap money drives dear money from circulation operated with inflexible rigor. Changes were then made in the ratios and the metal content of currency units.

The supply of gold greatly increased following the discovery of gold in California and Australia in 1848 and 1849, the annual average world output of gold going up from 15,740,000 dollars for the period 1801–1850 to 121,210,000 dollars in the period 1851–1885. Under these circumstances gold lost value in terms of silver, with the result that gold began to flow to bimetallic countries driving silver out of circulation; silver began to flow to silver-standard countries like some of the German states and India. Commodity prices rose by 25 per cent from 1850 to 1866. At the latter date gold stopped losing value in terms of silver, although there was no reduction in production, which indicates the importance of other factors than the amount of precious metals in the price equation, and gold and silver returned to their former relationship of about 15½ to 1.

During the years when gold was cheap in relation to silver and the white metal was taking flight from countries with a bimetallic system, there was a danger that silver coins would entirely disappear from circulation. To prevent such an eventuality, most of the countries concerned simply reduced the fineness of silver pieces; the United States took such action in 1853 and most of the Continental countries west of Germany followed suit. Inasmuch as they did not act together, however, exchange rates were upset and silver fled from one country to another depending on how high it was valued. To bring some order out of the resulting chaos, Belgium proposed the formation of a monetary union whose members would have similar coinage systems and identical metal content of coins. This proposal led to the founding of the Latin Monetary Union in 1865; this had as members France, Belgium, Italy, and Switzerland, and after 1868 Greece, and Spain, Rumania, Finland, and several South American and Central American states collaborated with it. Efforts were made to get England and the Germanies to join the Union but England refused on the ground that she was not a bimetallic[9] country and Germany was not wanted by France after the Franco-Prussian War (1870).

While these attempts to put more order in the monetary systems of Western Europe were being made, events were working toward the adoption of a gold standard. In 1873 Nevada silver mines began to produce and shortly thereafter silver began to become cheaper in terms of gold, the ratio shifting from 22.10 to 1 in 1889 to 32.57 to 1 in 1893. Under these conditions it became the turn of gold to be driven out of circulation and for silver to be used widely in actual coins. In this instance, however, monetary experts were ready with a remedy for the new malaise—they simply advised going on a gold standard to maintain

[9] In 1857 a convention was held at Vienna among Central European countries to establish uniform currencies. The basic coin was to be the Thaler of 18.66 grams of silver. Inasmuch as gold coins were not given legal status, the members of the union were on a silver basis. Austria withdrew from the group in 1867.

the stability of prices. Thus Germany and Holland adopted the gold standard in 1871 and 1873; the Scandinavian Monetary Union, which included Denmark, Sweden, and after 1875 Norway, followed suit upon its formation in 1873. The Latin Monetary Union suspended the minting of silver coins except as tokens in 1874, thus adopting the "limping standard," taking gold as the real measure of value, with silver limping along behind.

Bimetallism was, indeed, in full retreat from 1873 onward, having almost no supporters at the International Monetary Conference at Cologne in 1881 or at Brussels in 1893. There were those, however, who attributed the downward march of prices to the use of gold as a measure of value and who advocated the "unlimited coinage of silver." Proponents of this idea were to be found, logically enough, among miners of silver and among representatives of debtor groups. They were particularly strong in the United States, where they had enough power to secure the passage of the Bland-Allison Act (1878), which required the Secretary of the Treasury to coin into dollars not less than 2 million nor more than 4 million dollars' worth of silver each month, and the Sherman Silver Purchase Act, which provided that the Secretary of the Treasury should buy 4,500,000 ounces of silver bullion each month and issue in payment for it legal tender known as the "Treasury Notes of 1890."[10]

With the depression of 1893, the demand for gold in payment of silver coins or certificates was so great that the gold reserve of the Treasury of the United States was threatened. This fact, plus the continued fall in prices, gave the advocates of the free coinage of silver an opportunity to push their cause. It was then that William Jennings Bryan, the Democratic candidate in the presidential campaign of 1898, advocated the unlimited coinage of silver at the ratio of 16 to 1. In an impassioned speech he promised that "Mankind would not be crucified upon a cross of gold."

Such flights of oratory were not sufficient, however, to carry the day; and the Republicans won the election with promises of a "full dinner pail" and their platform of sound money. By 1900 they had adopted gold as the legal standard, but contrary to Bryan's gloomy expectations prices did not go down. New supplies of gold were coming into the market as a result of a more adequate exploitation of South African deposits, the use after 1890 of the cyanide process of getting gold from ore,[11] and the opening of gold fields in the Klondike (Canada), in Alaska, and in

[10] Under the Bland-Allison Act 378,166,000 dollars' worth of silver or silver certificates (notes payable in silver) were issued. Under the Sherman Act 156,000,000 dollars' worth of silver bullion was acquired.

[11] This process recovered some 90 per cent of the gold in the ore as compared with 60 per cent from the mercury method.

Siberia. These new supplies plus the greater use of negotiable instruments, like checks, resulted in a larger supply of money. This fact, together with the extension of a demand for goods, tended to push prices upward in a secular trend that was to extend through World War I.

Banking

The actual provision of money was a function of the banking system and of national states. More and more, banks not only performed their traditional tasks of furnishing means for safeguarding funds, of accumulating the savings of many, and of making loans to entrepreneurs, but also they came to control credit and thus to influence the rate of business activity.

The most influential institutions in the formation of credit policies were the "central banks."[12] These were semipublic bodies which were less concerned with making a profit than with providing money to meet the needs of the commercial world and to give stability to the entire monetary and credit structure of an economy. They stood ready to extend credit to other banks which might be threatened with insolvency, particularly if their assets were good but not really marketable, and they were in a position to *create* money in order to have the wherewithal to lend. They have been likened to fire departments which try to prevent fires, send out fire engines to put out conflagrations once started, and make at their own volition an almost inexhaustible supply of extinguishing fluid.

Among the oldest of the central banks among the major powers were the Bank of England and the Bank of France. The Bank of England, which was granted a charter first in 1694, could issue bank notes that were essentially promises to pay, up to a total of 14 million pounds with first-class securities as backing, but for every bank note issued in excess of that sum the Bank had to increase its hoard of bullion by an equal amount. This method of controlling the note issue, known as the "currency principle," meant that the Bank could not increase the supply of money very entensively by the issue of bank notes,[13] but it soon discovered other means for overcoming the rigidities imposed on it by law. By encouraging the use of checks, it actually fostered another medium

---

[12] This particular term did not come into use until the early part of the twentieth century, although as we have seen, this type of bank had been in existence some time.

[13] The Bank was allowed in 1847, 1857, and 1866 to increase the number of bank notes in circulation beyond the limits prescribed to meet emergencies. In 1890 the Bank borrowed 2 million pounds in gold from the Bank of France to weather a temporary storm.

of exchange, as we have already seen, which greatly added to the volume of money in circulation. Furthermore, by extending or restricting credit to other banks, which were its chief clients, it could do much to regulate in turn the bank credit extended to business and thereby to control business activity and the need for money. Thus in times of great expansion, the Bank of England raised its discount rate (in the panic of 1866 it was pushed up to 10 per cent) and in times of depression the Bank reduced it (from 1894 to 1896 the rate stood at 2 per cent)[14] in hope of returning the economy to an even keel.

Furthermore, the credit situation in England could be influenced by the Bank's "open market" operations. If the Bank bought securities in the market, it provided the business community with more funds with which to do business; if it sold securities, it absorbed money and hence took away from the business community some of the media of exchange with which to operate.

In France the central bank, the Bank of France, was founded in 1800 by Napoleon. Its issue of bank notes was based upon a different principle from that of the Bank of England—it operated on the "banking principle" rather than on the "currency principle." This meant that instead of limiting the issue of notes to a low maximum and requiring the deposit of bullion as a reserve for notes issued over this ceiling that notes would be issued with commercial paper as the main reserve. Consequently as more commercial paper came to the Bank for discount (it did business both with other banks and directly with businessmen), the note issue could be increased, and when less came in, the note issue would be restricted. Such a system, although it required the maintenance of rather large reserves so that calls made on the Bank could always be met,[15] gave the French economy a large and yet flexible money supply. This was important inasmuch as checks, in spite of their convenience, never developed widely in France and businessmen discounted small bills. Yet, the Bank of France could regulate the supply of money by altering the discount rate, and because it dealt directly with businessmen as well as with banks and operated branches all over France, it could control credit by decisions to accept or to refuse commercial paper for discount.[16]

[14] This practice also had an effect upon foreign money markets. If the English rate was high, foreign gold went to London in search of profits; if it was low, English gold went into foreign investments in hope of getting better earnings.

Unfortunately the changes in the discount rate did not come early enough nor were they drastic enough to prevent business fluctuations. They were usually remedial rather than preventive.

[15] In 1847 they were half of the note issue.

[16] This was one of the reasons that the Bank of France did not have to change the discount rate so often nor so drastically as the Bank of England.

In most of the other countries of Western culture, central banks came into being which pursued policies similar to those of the Bank of England or of the Bank of France, or adopted procedures which were a compromise between these two. The Reichsbank in Germany is an example of the third group. Although it followed the banking principle of the French, did business directly with individuals as well as with banks, had many branches, and had to maintain a one-third reserve of metal or treasury bonds against its total issue of bank notes, it could exceed this limit if it paid a 5 per cent annual tax on the excess.

In the United States, however, central banking had a hard time of it. To be sure the First Bank of the United States acted as a central bank from 1791 to 1811, but its charter was not renewed, partly because of the conservative policies which it pursued and partly because state banks, supported by a basic "states' rights" sentiment, hoped that they would be the lucky recipients of lucrative government deposits. When Congress decided not to renew the charter of the First Bank, many banks were chartered by the states, their number increasing from 86 in 1811 to 246 in 1816. Unfortunately these banks overextended themselves and in 1814 all of them outside of New England were unable to pay out specie for their bank notes. Because of the crisis, the fact that the government was required to take state bank notes in payment of taxes and bonds, and the demand of the Treasury for a central bank, which would receive its funds on deposit and transfer them from place to place, Congress finally reached the decision to establish a new central institution. In 1816 it gave the Second Bank of the United States a charter for twenty years.

The course of the Second Bank was extremely stormy. At first it was grossly mismanaged, and subsequently, under the direction of Nicholas Biddle, it became a political football between those interests, especially in the West and South and in Eastern cities like New York, led by President Jackson, which favored states' rights, feared moneyed interests, or resented the leadership of Philadelphia, and Eastern interests, represented by Biddle, which desired stable money and "sound" banking policies. From this match of wits and power, President Jackson emerged the victor and consequently blocked a renewal of the Bank's charter (1832). Again banks chartered by states began to appear on every hand, especially in parts of the West which were so sparsely settled that it was alleged "wildcats were the only customers." The policies of many of these banks, now dubbed "wildcat banks," were, in fact, so wild that this term became synonymous with loose banking practices.

In the ensuing years banking suffered by the absence of a lending institution of last resort and by a laxity of state supervision. The government experimented with the so-called Independent Treasury System, whereby it placed its money in vaults in customs houses and mints, thus keeping capital idle and not providing for regional needs. Only with the coming of the War between the States, when more conservative business interests were in power, when the need for Federal governmental supervision of banking was more urgent than ever, and when the government wanted to sell more of its bonds, were important reforms effected.

When the South repudiated its debts to the North, the financial stringency was so severe that many Northern banks failed, especially in the Mississippi Valley. Furthermore, the fact that there were 12,000 different types of bank notes in circulation, many of which had been issued by bankrupt or discredited banks, made even those who usually favored cheap money realize that reform was needed. Consequently Congress passed the National Bank Act of 1863, which provided that every bank that accepted Federal regulation could deposit government bonds with the Treasury of the United States and issue bank notes with these bonds as security.[17] This privilege, heavy Federal taxes on the bank notes of state banks after 1865, and a decision to deposit government funds with national banks, curbed wildcat state banking.[18]

The National Bank Act remained in operation until 1913.[19] Although it was an improvement on what had existed before, it left much to be desired. The system of reserves tended to bring deposits of banks to New York, which forced the New York banks to maintain large liquid assets. As these assets were often lent at call on the New York Stock Exchange and as they fluctuated widely, they constituted an unnecessary element of instability. Furthermore, the concentration of reserves in New York meant that some parts of the country were poorly served when it came to financing great seasonal activities, like moving the wheat crop. Most important of all, however, the supply of bank notes under the National Bank Act arrangements did not expand and contract in unison with business needs, but with the amount of government bonds in the market and their market value.[20] Had it not been for the concomitant growth in

[17] At first bank notes could be issued in volume up to 90 per cent of the market value of the bonds, and not beyond a limit of 300 million dollars. In 1875 this limit was removed, but country banks were required to maintain a 15 per cent reserve against bank notes, whereas, for banks in reserve cities, the reserve requirement was 25 per cent.

[18] Furthermore, the National Bank Act provided a way for banks to use greenbacks, unsecured paper money in the amount of some 450 million dollars that had been issued to finance the war, for this currency could be used to buy government bonds. This fact tended to bring greenbacks up to par.

[19] When the Federal Reserve System was created.

[20] Banks did not retire their notes as a rule to meet seasonal demands, so there was little contraction. To hold low-interest government bonds against the day when more money would be needed was not profitable.

the use of checks and the elasticity which this practice gave the volume of money, stringencies would have been much greater than they were.

Crucial as central banking became in the world of finance, the business of receiving deposits from customers and of making loans was for the most part conducted by other types of banks—institutions which came to be differentiated both by the way they acquired funds and by the type of loans which they granted. Thus in "private banks" capital was provided mostly by rich owners or partners, whereas in joint-stock banks it was raised by the sale of stock. Savings banks were characterized by the fact that their deposits were in small amounts. Deposit banks were distinguished by the fact that they specialized in handling commercial deposits which could easily be "withdrawn" by the writing of checks; trust companies were set off because of their specialization in the administering of other peoples' property.

On the lending side, there were investment banks, which made long-term commitments to business enterprises and sometimes held large blocks of their stocks or bonds; there were also commercial banks making short-term, self-liquidating loans to businesses, mortgage banks lending on mortgages, and last, but by no means least, banks doing a mixed business.

At first most of the great banks were private banks, *les hautes banques,* as they were called in France, like the Rothschilds, the Barings, the Hopes of Amsterdam, the Bleichröders of Berlin, Mallet Frères in Paris, and Morgans of New York, but the trend was in favor of joint-stock institutions, for they provided a way of amassing great amounts of capital and a method of limiting an investor's liability. The Société Générale of Belgium, founded in 1822, was one of the first of such organizations and its success led to many imitators, such as the Crédit Lyonnais (1863) and the Société Générale (1864) in France, the Diskontogesellschaft (1851) in Germany, and Lloyds in England (1889).[21] In England and Germany, especially, and to some extent in all countries, there was a further tendency for banks to merge. The number of banks in England fell from 600 in 1824 to 55 in 1914, and to 11 in 1937, when five-sixths of the country's banking was done by the "big five"—Midland, Westminster, Lloyds, Barclays, and the National Provincial. In Germany the famous "D" banks—the Darmstadt Bank (1870), Diskontogesellschaft (1851), the Deutsche Bank (1870), and the Dresdner (1872)—were reduced in 1932 to the Danatbank (a fusion of the Darmstadter and Dresdner) and the Deutsche, which had absorbed the Diskontogesellschaft.

---

[21] England removed its prohibition on joint-stock banks in 1826, permitted their establishment without special act of Parliament in 1844, and extended to them limited liability by acts of 1859, 1862, and 1879.

With the trend toward joint-stock banking and toward mergers, there was also a drift toward mixed banking. With a few great banks, except in the United States where in most states bank branches were limited by law, it was inevitable that banks should amass funds in many ways and make many types of loans. Moreover, concentration on long-term investments had brought both grief and scandals in its wake. In England, Overend, Guerney, and Company went under in 1866 because it entered into promotion ventures which froze its assets. Baring Brothers, which had gone heavily into Argentinian bonds and found in 1890 that these securities could no longer be moved at a profit, was saved only by a committee of bankers, organized by the Bank of England, which gave Barings time to unload its holdings and an opportunity to reorganize as a joint-stock bank. In France, the Crédit Mobilier, a joint-stock institution organized by the Péreire Brothers in 1852, financed the building of railways, the establishment of the French Line, and the reconstruction of the Rue de Rivoli. It engaged in such questionable practices as paying dividends out of capital and foundered when money became tight in 1866 and there was no market for its assets. Finally, in America, Jay Cooke and Company failed (1873) because of being overextended in Northern Pacific Railway securities, which would not move.

On account of such experiences most of the great banks leaned toward commercial banking, yet their portfolios, that is, their list of investments, held substantial blocks of government bonds, large amounts of business securities, and some mortgages, in addition to very large holdings of discounted bills. Specialized banking persisted, however, with the continuance of such investment banks as the Banque de Paris et des Pays Bas (1872) in Paris and of mortgage banks, like the Crédit Foncier (1852) in France, and of savings banks. Such new "specialists" came into being as postal savings banks, whose main purpose was to encourage thrift, and the German innovation, the Schulze-Delitzsch Banks, which were cooperative credit societies to serve small businessmen, and the Raiffeisen-Hass group, which were made up of rural credit cooperatives to finance farming.

In the aggregate these various banks came to constitute a tremendous power in the economic world. In France, the Bank of France had such a powerful position and its stock was so closely held that it was said two hundred families could dictate to whom credit should be extended, even to the point of refusing loans to the government if it were in hands hostile to them.[22] In Germany, the Dresdner Bank claimed before World War I that its directors sat on the boards of more than two hundred corporations, thus participating in making policies for these businesses

[22] Francis Delaisi, La Banque de France aux mains des 200 Familles (Paris, 1936).

and determining the bank's line of credit to them. And in England, bank loans, especially for commercial activities, did much to determine the directions in which the economy expanded. So important did the part which banks played in the economies of the Western world become that some observers characterized the capitalism of the West from about 1870 to at least the great depression of the 1930s as finance capitalism.

Public Finance

With the increased use of money and with the extension and intensification of state activity the expenses of running governments became so great that changes had to be made in public finance systems. Existing tax structures were either inadequate in providing necessary revenues or had such undesirable economic effects that they had to be revised. The excess of expenditures over receipts was so large that every state had a large funded debt. Government spending became so great that it could stimulate business booms.

The extent of the demand on governments for funds is well illustrated by the French case where expenditures of the national state increased from 900,000,000 francs (current value) in the early 1830s to 5,067,-000,000 francs in 1913, or by that of England where expenditures rose some 370 per cent from 1850 to 1913 and amounted to about 20 per cent of national income. Some idea of the nature of expenditures may be gathered from Germany, where federal, state, and local branches of government allocated in the fiscal year 1913–1914 31.9 per cent of outlays to the military, 19.3 to education, 8.6 to highways, 8.6 to debt service, 7.7 to welfare, 3.7 to police, and the remainder to a host of other services.

To raise funds to meet the new demands central governments relied primarily on customs receipts, excise and stamp taxes, and borrowing; local governments had recourse to property taxes and licenses on business. In Great Britain of the early nineteenth century two-thirds of the tax revenue of the royal treasury came from customs and excises, whereas local governments got some 95 per cent of their revenue from taxes on property.

In many countries, expenditures exceeded receipts because existing tax rates could not be pushed up fast or far enough to meet growing needs, and spending jumped suddenly beyond all reason because of such events as war. Borrowing became the order of the day, accordingly, and public debts grew alarmingly. That of France, for example, more than doubled from 1848 to 1871. In that country exceptional expenditures became so important that a double budget system was adopted (1881), one for ordinary receipts and expenditures and the other budget for extraordinary (non-recurring) receipts and expenditures—a practice that was followed by many other countries.

The desirability of balancing governmental budgets, at least for recurring expenditures, was so generally recognized that tax reforms were steadily sought. In general demands for tax changes were conditioned by such social and political considerations as a desire to make all citizens contribute a share to the public purse without losing the votes of any one group, to distribute the tax burden according to ability to pay, and to make assessments on actual wealth and not on arbitrarily determined amounts or upon sums arrived at by bargaining. Furthermore, there was a general tendency to favor, at least in theory, direct taxes (property, income, or inheritance taxes), which would be paid by the person taxed, instead of indirect taxes (excises, customs duties, and licenses), which could be passed on by the taxpayer to others. In Great Britain an income tax was instituted in 1799 under the stress of war, but it was subsequently abolished, only to be reestablished in 1841. It was made "progressive," that is, heavier according to the size of the income, in 1909. This impost was so remunerative that it provided two-thirds of the national government's income by the post-World War I period. The United States adopted an income tax during the Civil War, but dropped it in 1872, when needs for revenue were less urgent, and reintroduced it only in 1913 following the adoption of an amendment to the Constitution that settled the question of the tax's legality. Prussia adopted an income tax (1851, 1891) and a progressive tax on property (1893); the German Reich instituted an income tax in 1913 and France, in 1917. An inheritance tax was experimented with in Britain during the French Revolutionary and Napoleonic Wars, was reintroduced in 1853, and extended in 1894 and 1909. A similar tax was levied in Germany in 1906, was used temporarily in the United States from 1862 to 1870 and from 1894 to 1902, and was made a fixture after World War I. France, for its part, was slow to effect tax reforms but came to rely heavily on indirect taxes and permitted taxes to be levied on the "apparent value" of things.

Business Cycles

Despite increases in economic well-being resulting from the mechanization of industry, the development of production in new lands, the extension of commerce, and the division of labor, modern capitalism had its flaws. One of the most important weaknesses of the new system was that it seemed to generate within itself forces which led to business booms and to business depressions. Fluctuations in business activity were, in essence, nothing new, but prior to the nineteenth century they appeared to have been caused mainly by forces that were not strictly economic, like weather and war.

In the nineteenth century, however, things changed. According to the late Wesley C. Mitchell, one of the great analysts of the business cycle, the new fluctuations had four phases, each of which was characterized by forces that led to the next phase. These may be described as follows:

1. *Expansion.* Expansion comes on the heels of *revival.* It is characterized by an increase in production, a higher level of employment, higher wages, bigger profits, and greater consumption of goods. Prices rise and businessmen are optimistic about the future. More capital is invested in plants and equipment.

2. *Recession.* As expansion gathers momentum by the interaction of the forces listed above, it reaches a point where the economy is handling as much volume as it can profitably. Costs of production increase. Management becomes less efficient; interest rates are up, and prices reach a level so high that some buyers put off purchases. Plant expansion is curtailed and the makers of producers' goods begin to suffer. As these manufacturers close their plants, purchasing power is reduced and workers are laid off. Similar conditions soon appear in other industries. Banks begin to worry about the loans which they have made and start to call them in.

3. *Contraction.* Pessimism now sets in among businessmen. Prices go down; production declines; profits are reduced; bank loans shrink; and unemployment becomes more general.

4. *Revival.* With the contraction of business, less money is needed to conduct affairs and interest rates go down. Management tries to cut waste and to reduce costs. Prices become so low that certain groups, especially those on fixed salaries, begin to buy. Retailers start to build up their inventories. Factories improve their organization and begin to renew their equipment. Bankruptcies become fewer. Prices are more stable and show a slight inclination to rise, and confidence begins to return. Before long the economy enters the phase of expansion and the experience begins to repeat itself.

Business fluctuations showed many variations in detail from this basic pattern. Some of them were short and "mild"; others were long and "deep." In every one some segments of the economy developed against the general downward trend. In general, it may be said that periods of prosperity were longer and periods of depression were shorter in times of secularly rising prices, as from at least 1801 to 1820, from 1850 to 1873, and from 1896 to the end of World War I, and that the reverse was true in times of secularly falling prices as from 1820 to 1850 and from 1873 to 1896, this last period being known as the Great Depression in prices.

A detailed analysis of business cycles from the end of the eighteenth century to the last quarter of the nineteenth century is not possible here, but a word about them is essential for an understanding of economic growth and for an appreciation of some of the social and political history of the times. One of the last fluctuations of the old type of depression resulting primarily from poor crops, which in turn were caused by bad weather conditions, began in France in 1787. Exceptionally disastrous harvests in 1787 and 1788 raised prices suddenly; in July, 1789, they reached the highest level of the entire century. Economic conditions improved in 1791 and 1792, but then political tampering with the economy became so extensive, foreign and domestic strife was so great, and crops were again so poor that business activity was retarded during the Terror (1793–1794). In England the fall of exports was so large that gold was drained away until the Bank of England had to suspend specie payments (1797). Subsequently the Continental blockade worked so much havoc that there were crises in both France and England. So bad did things get in France that Napoleon lost much of the support which he had previously enjoyed in the business community; in England industrial production was so slack and industrial wages so low that there were serious riots (Luddite Riots of 1811–1812). In 1815 economic activity lagged because of the unsettled political situation and the brief renewal of war which ended with the battle of Waterloo in Belgium.

Following the restoration of peace, business conditions improved somewhat, but poor crops in Western Europe in 1817 made food prices high, those in England going up with those in France. Concomitantly English manufacturers were having difficulty moving all of their output and Continental producers were having trouble meeting the competition of the English. In both places there were unemployment and wage cuts. Consequently the years 1818–1819 were depressed, with the latter being marked by the Peterloo Massacre at St. Peter's Fields at Manchester, when the Yeomanry Guard charged a workingmen's mass meeting. Even in the United States business suffered largely because of a decline in European demand for cotton and other New World products. Subsequently, business activity increased, but English speculation in South American trade and American cotton and an accompanying expansion of industry led to a crisis in 1825–1826 and to a mild recession on the Continent and in America.

In 1830, business on the Continent was somewhat disturbed by revolutions, but the building of new plant in Europe and speculation in America, both in Westward expansion and in commercial crops, made money tight. Thus when President Andrew Jackson issued his Specie Circular in 1836, requiring that all public lands be paid for in specie, the bubble of good times burst in the panic of 1837. Recovery soon followed, however, with the railway building boom of the 1840s, but this in turn came to an end in 1847–1848. Industrial prices had risen extraordinarily high because of the increased demand and agricultural prices had gone up dramatically with the poor crops and the Irish potato famine of 1846.

When stable political conditions were reestablished following the revolutions of 1848, business began to expand once more. Railway building was resumed and there was a great expansion of the ferrous-metal industry. Prices went up, and so, too, did wages and the costs of production until finally businessmen began to lose faith in the future and started to restrict their activity. In 1857 there were many bank failures, a fall in the price of stocks, a decline in commodity prices, unemployment, and in the United States a series of failures among railroad companies.

Recovery from the Panic of 1857 was rapid because of the further expansion of railways, the introduction of Bessemer converters, the building of iron steam vessels, and a series of wars.[23] This movement came to an end in 1866, just after the conclusion of the war in America, when new supplies of cotton in the world market brought the price of cotton down so suddenly that an important English bank, Overend, Guerney and Company, failed.

Again revival set in with railway construction going forward, with the opening of the Suez Canal, with the introduction of the Siemens-Martin process of making steel, with a building boom in Germany, and with an expansion in ocean shipping. By 1873 prices reached a higher level than at any time in the previous half-century; wages and profits had risen fast, and capital had become dear. This time a recession was triggered by the failure of the American bank of Jay Cooke and Company (1873), which had overextended itself in railways and which enjoyed such a good reputation that a newsboy was arrested in New York for crying, "Read all about it. Failure of Jay Cooke." In the crisis several European banks had to close their doors; stock market securities collapsed, and prices, especially those of agricultural products, fell drastically.

This time recovery was slow, but some improvement had been made by 1882, when the failure of a French bank, the Union Générale, tightened the money market. Subsequently an improvement in business was registered, but a new setback occurred in 1889 and 1890 with the breaking of the Panama Canal Company scandal (1889) and the near failure of Baring Brothers (1890).[24] Not until 1896, when prices began to go upward in a new secular trend, was business said to be good again. In 1903–1904 money was exceedingly tight and a "rich man's panic" oc-

[23] These included the War of Italian Unification, the Austro-Prussian War, and the American Civil War.

[24] The depression hit America in 1893.

curred; 1907–1908 saw another stringency of funds, although the pace of business did not slacken much. There was expansion to 1913–1914, when the entire operation of the business cycle was disturbed by war.

In the face of this new phenomenon, governments did not stand idly by, waiting for what many held to be a "self-adjusting economy" to right itself. From early in the nineteenth century, states, usually through their central banks, endeavored to curb excessive speculation by raising the discount or rediscount rate in the hope that higher interest rates would curb business expansion. Conversely, when times were bad, the banks forced interest rates down and lent more liberally in order to encourage expansion. Such measures were not, however, particularly effective, for they were not always timed correctly and did not have enough leverage to influence business policy. Hence they were supplemented in given instances with efforts to extend or contract the amount of money in circulation by the issuing or purchase of government bonds, by public works projects of which the Freycinet Plan in France (1879) was one of the first, by attempts to bolster up faltering institutions, as in the case of Baring Brothers, and by colonial expansion, which in the long run, it was hoped, would provide a necessary outlet for European goods, capital, and people. Yet, neither an understanding of nor control over business fluctuations was realized, as the Western world was to learn to its sorrow in the 1930s.

Table 18. Reference Dates and Duration of Business Cycles in the United States
(Quarterly reference dates)

Peak	Trough	Peak	Trough
	4Q 1854	4Q 1902	3Q 1904
2Q 1857	4Q 1858	2Q 1907	2Q 1908
3Q 1860	3Q 1861	1Q 1910	4Q 1911
1Q 1865	1Q 1868	1Q 1913	4Q 1914
2Q 1869	4Q 1870	3Q 1918	2Q 1919
3Q 1873	1Q 1879	1Q 1920	3Q 1921
1Q 1882	2Q 1885	2Q 1923	3Q 1924
2Q 1887	1Q 1888	3Q 1926	4Q 1927
3Q 1890	2Q 1891	2Q 1929	2Q 1933
1Q 1893	2Q 1894	2Q 1937	2Q 1938
4Q 1895	2Q 1897	1Q 1945	4Q 1945
3Q 1899	4Q 1900	4Q 1943	4Q 1949

New Risks and Insurance

Fluctuations in business activity were not, however, the only new risks which emanated from the economy. As men became more and more dependent on money to satisfy human needs rather than upon the produce of their own labors and of their own means of production, relations among individuals became more and more impersonal. Those paternalistic attitudes which had been adopted by the lord toward his serfs or by the guildmaster toward his journeymen and apprentices disappeared with the payment of wages, the ownership of capital goods by entrepreneurs, and the organizaton of production by large units. Workers, especially urban ones, and small businessmen and their dependents came to rely almost exclusively on current earnings for existence. Savings were too small to carry these people over more than short periods and they had few opportunities[25] for alternative employment. If the head of a family died, dependents could seldom expect anything from his former employer. If some member of a family became unemployable because of injury, disease, or old age—and dependents from these causes became more numerous as the average age of populations became greater and work became more dangerous—dependents fell as almost a dead economic weight on the family. In an agricultural society such persons might frequently be put to performing easy or unskilled tasks. They might be fed by putting a "little more water in the soup," and they might be housed in a loft or stable. In cities such expedients were, however, impossible. Even in bourgeois families, current earnings were necessary, for although there might be some savings to live on, they were usually not enough to last very long if the standard of living to which the family had become accustomed were to be maintained.

To meet the essentially new exigencies of economic existence, efforts were made to share the risks at first through private efforts and later through governmental intervention. At the outset, workers created mutual-aid societies whose members agreed to help those among them who were stricken with misfortune; the more well-to-do developed life insurance and annuity arrangements to ward off the effects of the worst hazards—death and old age. Then later on, labor began to clamor for state-sponsored insurance that was initiated in Germany in 1883.[26]

The most fruitful principle for meeting the new risks was that of insurance. It was based on the following conditions: that several persons have an interest of some kind that is susceptible of pecuniary estimation, that these persons would incur a loss if that interest were destroyed or impaired by the occurrence of designated perils, that an insurer assume from the above-mentioned persons the risk of loss, that such assumption be part of a general arrangement to distribute actual losses among a

---

[25] In the United States in 1944, nearly one-third of all families effected no savings; in 1957 only 13 per cent of Old Age and Survivors Insurance (governmental "Old Age" insurance) beneficiaries had assets of 5,000 dollars or over.

[26] See the discussion of Bismarck's policies below.

large number of persons bearing similar risks, and that as a consideration of the insurer's assumption of risk, the insureds make a ratable contribution, known as a premium, to a general fund from which losses are paid.

Insurance, as has been seen,[27] was used particularly in shipping in the Late Middle Ages. Subsequently, it was extended to cover the lives of masters of ships for single voyages. The closely allied arrangement of buying an annuity developed in the seventeenth century. Then in the eighteenth century, life insurance companies began to be founded, especially in Scotland and England, the first important one being the Society for Equitable Assurances on Lives and Survivorships (1762). Thence, life insurance spread to other parts of Western culture, the first company in France being founded in 1819, the first in Germany in 1827, and the first in America to continue in operation to the present day in 1843. By 1885 the amount of life insurance per capita in the United States amounted to 41 dollars. In 1942 it was 989 dollars.

This insurance just mentioned was taken primarily by the well-to-do, and efforts of the working classes to get similar relief through mutual-aid societies was at best only moderately successful. Because of this situation, workers began a drive for state "social insurance." Their requests were at last heeded in Germany where Bismarck, who was anxious to take the wind out of the sails of the Socialists, was ready to ingratiate himself with the workers. In 1883 he instituted sickness insurance; in 1884 he introduced workmen's compensation laws, and in 1889 he founded an Old Age and Security Insurance scheme—the "security" here being against disability caused by certain diseases like tuberculosis.

These laws, although diverging somewhat from the principles of private insurance, minimized losses through sharing risks. Contributions to the funds from which benefits were paid were made not only by those who stood to benefit in case of loss, that is, by the insureds, but also by employers and the government. Furthermore, whereas workmen's compensation placed liability on employers for injuries to workers which occurred in the course of employment, employers covered their risk of loss by paying premiums to private insurers. Gradually society was developing a means of assuming responsibility for the unfortunate—a method that subsequently was to be greatly extended.

[27] See further discussion below.

CHAPTER 17

The New Economy Comes of Age—
1875 to 1914

The Continuation of Earlier Trends

By 1875 the main features of the new economy in Western culture had taken shape. Economic improvement per capita of the population had become a strong and generally accepted ideology. Greater amounts of goods per unit of human endeavor were steadily being turned out by the more extensive use of machines, by the use of mechanical power, and by a more intensive division of labor. Greater amounts of materials had become available for human use in the Western world not only by increasing the production of growing things but also by exploiting the resources of the earth's crust and by drawing on reserves from a very large portion of the globe on an unprecedented scale. Greater amounts of capital were becoming available for creating more producer's goods. And man was so increasing his knowledge of the physical world that a greater control of that world seemed certain. To an ever-increasing extent consumers relied on the market for the satisfaction of their numerous wants rather than on a diversified production of their own. They used money as a medium of exchange to get what they desired, and they came to realize that money was an important factor in regulating relations among human beings. Lastly, ownership of the means of production, especially in industry, came to be concentrated to a greater degree than formerly in the hands of investors, whereas workers came to rely for their livelihood more and more on current wages rather than on the sale of the output of their own production.

After 1875 and at least up until World War I all these new aspects of Western culture's economy continued to develop and to have wide repercussions in society. Economic growth remained at a phenomenally high level; for example, the national income of Germany about trebled in these nearly forty years and the per capita income of those in work about doubled in both Germany and the United States. Inasmuch as most of the progress was realized in industry, in commerce, and in service trades, all of which tended to be concentrated in urban areas, populations became steadily more urbanized.[1] Machines were made more efficient and power became more mobile with the development of electricity and the gasoline motor. New sources of minerals were discovered, and new uses were constantly found for the stored up treasures of the earth. Improved transportation, especially with more railways, the efficient steam vessel, and the automobile, made possible the tapping of supplies hitherto considered inaccessible, the extension of the market to people in remote regions, and an increase in the division of labor. Agricultural output was augmented by the use of better strains of plants and breeds of animals, the employment of more commercial fertilizers, better utilization of the land, and most importantly of all by the bringing into cultivation vast new tracts of land in the New World, in Australia, in New Zealand, and in South Africa. Financial institutions came to play more crucial roles in amassing capital for investment in enterprise. The business cycle, generated by the system itself, seemed to have become an integral part of the new economy. Lastly, population climbed steadily from 1875 to 1914, that of Europe increasing by about one-third and that of the United States more than doubling. Birth rates began to decline; death rates went down; the mean age of the population went up; and the expectation of life at birth was increased.[2]

Moreover, in the period 1875 to 1914, certain new developments took place which set off this span of years as distinctive. One of the most important of these new departures had to do with the spread of the new economy to other parts of Western culture. At the beginning of the Industrial Revolution, as we have seen, change took place primarily in a triangle with apexes in England, Belgium, and northern France, but then it spread to New England and the Middle Atlantic states of the

---

[1] In Germany 36.1 per cent of the population lived in cities of 2,500 or more in 1871; in 1910, 60 per cent lived in such centers.

[2] The expectation of life at birth of white males in Massachusetts rose from forty years in 1875 to fifty years in 1914.

United States, to Germany, to Bohemia, to Austria, and to northern Italy. Only in selected industries, as in the textiles for which there was a steady local demand, and in mining and lumbering, for the exploitation of natural resources, was there extensive mechanization of industry beyond these areas. Thus in Europe, Germany, France, the United Kingdom, Italy, Belgium, and Sweden accounted for 83 per cent of all manufacturing production in 1870 and for 74 per cent as late as 1913.[3] Similarly, in the United States, the New England, Middle Atlantic, and East North Central states accounted for about 75 per cent of all value added by manufacture in 1913.

This concentration of industry in Western Europe and in the northeastern United States resulted in great regional inequalities in wellbeing, for the very good reason that the real product (value of goods produced) per man-hour in industry and trade was about twice what it was in agriculture. Hence, people in the so-called economically backward area strove to develop industry, if, indeed, they were motivated to improve their material status. Thus it was that Americans threw themselves with such abandon into industry, that Germany put so much of its energies into industrial development from 1870 to 1914, and that certain areas on the periphery of Western culture, like Russia, and a few completely outside it, like Japan, endeavored to mechanize their production. Inasmuch as such efforts were not without success, manufacturing grew at a faster pace than world trade[4] and the older industrialized nations of Europe had their percentages of world manufacturing reduced, which indicated that their potentials for growth were relatively not so great as those of certain of the less-industrialized areas of the world.

Accompanying these changes there was a great accentuation on nationalism in Western culture. Various people, drawn together by cultural ties, by historical traditions, and by economic interests, who for the most part spoke the same language or closely related dialects, and who usually inhabited contiguous territories, came to feel that they constituted a distinct group or nationality. They believed that they had the mission to glorify, develop, and perpetuate the elements which bound them together, that they could do this successfully only if they constituted independent, sovereign states, and that to attain their finest hour they would have to achieve some semblance of material well-being.

As at least a partial consequence of nationalism, national states began

[3] Derived from League of Nations, *Industrialization and World Trade* (League of Nations, 1946), p. 13. See also Francis Delaisi, *Les Deux Europes* (Paris: Payot, 1929).

[4] In the period 1876–1880 to 1913 world manufacturing grew fourfold, whereas world trade in primary products did not quite triple. *Industrialization and World Trade*, p. 14.

to pursue economic policies which were admittedly selfish and their nationals began to spin theories to justify such action. The ultimate aim of national economics seemed to be to make the state, if large, as economically self-sufficient as possible, or at least to develop the national economy to the limit of its potentialities. The main instrument for realizing these ends seemed to be protective tariffs, although some states were willing to grant subsidies to promising industries and some were ready to acquire colonies to supplement the potential of the homeland. In fact, the "new imperialism" of the 1875–1914 period was motivated by a curious mixture of nationalism and desire for expansion. It became particularly violent during the "long depression in prices" from 1873 to 1896.

Table 19. Percentage Distribution of World Manufacturing Production

Period	United States	Germany	United Kingdom	France	Russia	Italy	Canada
1870	23.3	13.2	31.8	10.3	3.7	2.4	1.0
1913	35.8	15.7	14.0	6.4	5.5	2.7	2.3
1936–1938	32.2	10.7	9.2	4.5	18.5	2.7	2.0

Period	Belgium	Sweden	Finland	Japan	India	Other countries	World
1870	2.9	0.4			11.0		100.0
1913	2.1	1.0	0.3	1.2	1.1	11.9	100.0
1936–1938	1.3	1.3	0.5	3.5	1.4	12.2	100.0

SOURCE: *Industrialization and Foreign Trade* (League of Nations, 1945), p. 13.

Africa was in these years partitioned and inroads were made into Asia, for colonialism was regarded as a cure for Europe's economic ills.

Lastly, in the period from 1875 to 1914, the impact of the new economy on society became clearer and more pronounced. The occupational distribution of populations in the more highly industrialized countries, like Great Britain, indicated that a larger percentage of the population was engaged in industry and services, which meant, given the structure of these two branches of the economy, that a larger proportion of the population was being hired for wages. Concomitantly there was a considerable concentration of wealth, as indicated in Table 21, although whether or not this was greater than in days of a predominantly agricultural economy is debatable. Lastly, working conditions became the object of social criticism, for although they may have been no worse than they had been in handicraft shops, they came more sharply to the attention of the public because of the concentration of work in factories.

The sharper delineation of economic interest groups led both to partisan theorizing about the way the new economy functioned and to the formulation of programs for realizing the cherished goals of those concerned. Thus employers tended to rely upon the evolutionary doctrine of the "survival of the fittest," upon the contention that all persons who contributed to production complemented each other and formed a *solidarity* in which interests were common, and upon ideas explaining how the economy worked and what must be done to make it work better.

Workers, or those who spoke in their behalf, had a variety of explanations to account for their position and of recommendations for the improvement of their lot. Certainly the theory in favor of the workers

Table 20. Occupational Distribution in Great Britain

Occupations	Distribution of working population, per cent			Distribution of income, per cent			Relative incomes per capita		
	1871	1911	1931	1868	1911	1930	1868	1911	1930
Agriculture	21.2	11.5	6.1	23.0	9.8	3.8	1.08	0.85	0.62
Mining	39.4	6.5	5.6	41.6	5.0	3.8	1.06	0.77	0.68
Manufacture		33.7	32.4		27.4	33.0		0.81	1.02
Domestic service	12.0	11.5	8.1	5.0	5.2	4.6	0.42	0.45	0.57
Railways	27.4	3.1	3.5	30.4	5.0	4.9	1.11	1.61	1.40
Building		2.4	5.1		1.9	2.7		0.79	0.53
Other		31.3	39.2		45.7	47.2		1.46	1.21

which caused the most stir was that of Karl Marx. He contended that the value of a product is determined by the labor which goes into it, for even capital was considered to be the result of previously performed labor. Goods are, however, actually sold for more than labor is paid for producing them, and hence the difference falls into the hands of capitalists. This is the surplus-labor theory of value. Consequently the rich get richer and the poor become poorer. Eventually, so Marx reasoned, conditions will become so bad that workers will, out of desperation, seize control of society by force. A dictatorship of the proletariat would then be established, a classless society would be created, and private property would be restricted to goods of individual use.

Whether or not workers believed in this theory, most of them were of the opinion that they could improve their lot by having more voice in the conduct of public affairs. Therefore they agitated for and got the franchise. They founded political parties to further their interests or tried to impose their views on existing organizations. Favorable legislation was passed establishing minimum wage standards, providing free education, and confirming the right to organize and to strike.

That workers were worse off than they had been was, however, highly questionable. Despite crowding in cities, employment in factories, and unemployment, whether resulting from business depressions, technological change, or seasonal requirements for labor, much evidence can be advanced to show that workers were partaking in the general improvement of material well-being. Real wages in the United Kingdom went up

Table 21. Distribution of Wealth in Great Britain, 1911–1913

(Persons twenty-five years and over; contemporary value of pound)

Wealth, in pounds	Persons per group		Capital per group	
	Number, in hundred thousands	Percentage of whole	Amount, in millions	Percentage
Total	18,745	100.0	6,008	100.0
100 or less	16,218	88.37	400	10.3
100–1,000	638	8.7	624	10.0
1,000–5,000	379	2.1	963	15.7
5,000–10,000	77	0.4	598	9.7
10,000–25,000	54	0.3	875	14.0
25,000–100,000	25	0.1	1,170	18.7
Over 100,000	5	0.03	1,378	21.6

roughly some 20 per cent per worker from 1876 to 1914. And expectation of life at birth, although it varied somewhat by economic classes, showed improvements throughout the spectrum of society.

Further Industrial Change

In the expansion of industry during the years between 1875 and 1914 so many important innovations were made that designating the most strategic is exceedingly difficult. Yet there is little doubt that among the very important changes was the introduction of ways of making steel which permitted an enormous expansion in the output of this product as well as a dramatic reduction in price.[5] In 1870, the United States produced only 100,000 long tons of steel compared with 1 million long tons of wrought iron; in 1890 this country turned out 10,200,000 long tons of steel to 3,000,000 long tons of wrought iron. Moreover, the price of steel rails in Britain went down from about £42 a ton in the late 1850s to

[5] The Bessemer (1856), Siemens-Martin (1867), and Thomas-Gilchrist (1879) methods contained the fundamental changes in manufacturing procedure.

£6 10s. in 1881, and to £3 15s. in 1895. Steel was the building metal *par excellence.* It was employed ever more widely as different kinds of steel were produced to meet specific needs. Among the most important of the new types of steels was tool steel, which was hard enough to cut most other metals. The first steels of this kind were produced by Robert F. Musket (1811–1891), who got high carbon steel by adding spiegeleisen, a pig iron rich in manganese, to the iron in a Bessemer converter after the "blow." The most successful tool steel was, however, produced by an American, Frederick Winslow Taylor (1856–1915). Taylor, who was also the father of scientific management, was able in about 1906 to produce a steel alloy containing chromium and tungsten, which allowed the tripling and even quadrupling of cutting speeds and the working of metals to much finer tolerances.

Steel also was used more extensively for a myriad of products from cutlery and band saws to improved railway rails and armor plate. It was

The Mesabi (view of the Hull-Rust-Mahoning open pit iron ore mine looking east from the edge of Mahoning toward the Hull-Rust mine and North Hibbing). The largest iron ore mine in the world, this pit has a total area of 1,275 acres, is 3 miles long, varies in width from ½ to 1 mile, and has a maximum depth of 435 feet. There are 55 miles of track in the pit. Development of the mine started in 1895. (*Reproduced with the permission of the Standard Oil Company of New Jersey.*)

also employed in the building of bridges, whether they were of arches, like the James B. Eads bridge across the Mississippi at St. Louis (1874),[6] were suspended from cables, like the Brooklyn Bridge (1883), or were built on cantilevers, like the Firth of Forth Bridge (1869). Steel was employed to build the skeletons of skyscrapers, the first of which was the Home Insurance Company of Chicago (1885);[7] it was used as reenforcement for concrete and gave this material such great tensile strength that

Table 22. Production of Steel
(Millions of tons)

Country	1870	1913
United States	.04	34.4
United Kingdom	.24	8.5
France	.09	5.1
Belgium		2.6
Luxemburg		1.4
Germany	.14	20.5
Austria	.02	2.9
Russia	.01	4.6
Italy		1.0
Sweden	.01	0.6

in 1911 the Tiber at Rome was bridged by a single arch made of it.[8] Steel or cast iron was used in facing shields which permitted the digging

[6] In the building of this bridge the arches were put in place by the use of temporary cantilevers. A caisson was employed to permit workers to excavate so that the piers would rest on bedrock. It was in this work that the discovery was made of how to work under high atmospheric pressure without suffering harmful results.

[7] High buildings required elevators. The first ones had been hydraulic with a plunger which reached into the earth as far as the elevator went up. The first passenger-carrying cable elevator with automatic brakes was developed by Elisha G. Otis (1853, 1857).

[8] Cement was first produced by the Englishman James Parker in 1796, who burned lumps of clay in kilns and ground the residue to powder. This was called Roman cement. Developmental work on this product was conducted by Louis Vicat (1786–1861) in France and by Johann John (1782–1847) in Prussia, who termed their stuff natural cement. This product was used on the Erie Canal and began to be made locally for construction work. The name portland cement was adopted because the finished product resembled a stone quarried on the Isle of Portland in the English Channel. Cement came into wide use for construction in the 1870s, when its price was brought down. It was particularly useful in the construction of aqueducts to provide better water for rapidly growing cities and for sewers, which were built on a large scale after the middle of the nineteenth century, for it was realized that many diseases, notably cholera, came from contaminated water. Louis Pasteur published his famous paper on bacteria in 1857, and Robert Koch established the science of bacteriology in the 1880s.

Steel. This photograph from the Fairless Works near Morrisville, Pennsylvania, represents hot metal being transferred from a blast furnace, where it has been separated from the impurites in the ore, to an open hearth furnace, where it will be further refined to get the desired quality of steel. The enormous ladle, which is being emptied, is supported by a 200-ton overhead crane. (*Courtesy of the United States Steel Corporation.*)

of subaqueous tunnels, like the Hudson and Manhattan Tube under the North River in New York (1904). Furthermore, cheap steel revolutionized the use of tools. It made possible great feats of drilling into the earth's crust in search of new riches.[9] It rendered the axles of vehicles stronger; it made builders' hardware from nails to locks more practicable. Finally, steel permitted the transportation of liquids via pipe lines, the first one being 6 miles long.

Crucial as cheap steel was to economic development, however, a wider use of other building metals was of utmost importance to industrial expansion. After steel, the first of these metals was copper. It had the advantage of forming important alloys, as with tin to form bronze and with zinc to form brass. It was worked easily; it would not rust, and it was a good conductor of heat, hence its use in cooking utensils. But the great advantage of copper was its excellence as a conductor of electricity; copper production grew by leaps and bounds after the development of that important source of power, more than quadrupling from 1880 to 1913.[10]

Of the other building metals, lead ranked first for a long time. It was used for water pipes, for paints, and later on for storage batteries and cable coverings.[11] Then came zinc, which was used for paints and for covering steel to make it rust-resistant.[12] In third place by the early

[9] The first petroleum well in the United States was drilled at Titusville, Pennsylvania, in 1859. It went down 69½ feet and produced about ten barrels a day.

[10] Although the important English copper mines were exhausted by the middle of the nineteenth century, an increase in world output was made possible by bringing into production the famous Rio Tinto mines in Spain, the mines of Arizona, Utah, and Montana in the United States, and those of Chile and the Belgian Congo and by improving the technology for reclaiming the metal by use of the flotation method, by the introduction of the reverberatory furnace to make "blister copper," and by refining by electrolysis. Reserves of copper are not great and exhaustion of supply is a real threat, but copper is not consumed to a very large extent in use and thus can be reused.

Here it may be well to note that there are two principal methods of ore concentration—the physical method and the flotation method. In the former, water is made to flow over the ore and the metal having a higher specific gravity than the waste remains behind. In the latter, which was perfected during the latter half of the nineteenth century, finely washed ore is mixed with water to which oil has been added. The metal particles attach themselves to the oil and rise to the top. This method was so much more effective than the former that is was used in nearly all nonferrous metals industries and was employed to work over "tailings" (waste heaps) of earlier undertakings.

[11] Lead is found primarily in North America and Australia, although it is widely scattered throughout the world.

[12] Zinc is produced chiefly in the United States, Canada, Mexico, Germany, Italy, and Australia.

twentieth century came aluminum, which had been discovered by Friedrich Wöhler in 1827. Its extraordinary lightness, its heat-conducting properties, and its resistance to the weather made it popular for cooking utensils, airplane construction, and paint.[13] In fourth place came tin, used for the ubiquitous tin can, which was developed following the discovery of the method to tin iron in the period from 1871 to 1890; and then came nickel, manganese, tungsten, and chromium, which were used primarily in alloys with iron.[14]

Table 23. World Total Primary Production of Copper
(In percentages)

Years	North America	South America	Europe	Asia	Africa
1801–1850	5.16	17.34	63.21	13.12	
1851–1900	37.29	21.04	29.70	4.89	2.01
1901–1925	65.77	11.07	10.23	5.78	3.03
1926–1929	49.49	19.15	11.26	5.78	13.46

Third among the categories of innovations which contributed to industrial growth should be placed achievements in mechanical engineering. Among them were the automatic lathe in which several tools were automatically brought to bear in succession upon the work and the multispindle lathe in which the piece being worked is passed on automatically from one operation to another. Then bearings with special oiling devices and ball and roller bearings were introduced which lowered the starting effort from as much as 830 pounds to 0.9 pounds. The clutch became a practical instrument for engaging a stationary piece of machinery with a moving one, which eliminated the dangerous practice of slipping belts on and off pulleys and allowed mechanical power plants to activate heavier loads. Spinning was improved by the yielding bolster (1878), which allowed an increase in revolutions of the spindle from 5,000 to 20,000 per minute. Looms were made more efficient by the development between 1881 and 1885 of a mechanism for the automatic changing of bobbins and for stopping the machine when a thread broke. Here was a forerunner of the "automation" of the post-World War II era.

On every hand mechanical devices appeared to make human labor

[13] The chief reserves of bauxite, whence aluminum is obtained, were in the United States, in the Guianas, in Hungary, and in China.

[14] As these metals came to be used more widely, methods for working them became ever more efficient. The carborundum wheel, made possible by the electric furnace in the 1890s, permitted rapid grinding; oxyacetylene welding and cutting, also developed in the 1890s, and electric welding, invented in 1889, permitted the easy joining and cutting of ferrous products.

Linotype Machine. This machine set type from molten metal in "slugs" on an entire line. The operator touched keys on the keyboard, much as one would on a typewriter. A more advanced model of this machine is used today in setting most type. Compare this machine with the manner of setting type suggested on page 95. (*Courtesy of the Mergenthaler Linotype Company.*)

more productive and more accurate. The typewriter was made more practical in 1868 and the adding machine in 1888. The stem-winding watch, that eliminated the elusive winding key, was patented in 1848. A sewing machine for shoes came onto the market after the 1850s and made possible a greater division of labor in the boot and shoe industry.

Printing was speeded by the invention of the monotype machine which perforated paper by the pressing of keys and which set type from the perforated spool, by the Mergenthaler linotype machine, about 1885, which made possible the mechanical setting of type in line-length slugs, and by the development in the 1880s of rotary presses with a capacity for printing nearly 100,000 copies of eight pages per hour. The communications industry was improved by Alexander Graham Bell's invention of the telephone in 1876, by the printing telegraph (1856), by Michael Pupin's method of extending the range of telephony by placing induction coils at intervals along the line, and by Guglielmo Marconi's invention of the radio in 1896. And the munitions industry was revolutionized by a multitude of innovations—the rifling of cannon (1859), breech-loading cannon (following 1860), the machine gun (invented by R. J. Gatling in 1862), the needle gun in which the charge was set off by a needle that perforated the shell (1866), the hammer and lock, breech-loaded rifle (1860s), and rifles with magazines (1880).

In a great many of the new industrial processes to which reference has been made, chemistry played such an important role that it is not amiss to speak of a chemical revolution. Indeed, throughout the period under discussion better cultivation of crops, converting natural products to useful goods, and finding substitutes for products in short supply depended largely upon a knowledge of chemistry. This knowledge was greatly increased after Dimitri I. Mendelieff (1834–1907) in Russia and Lothar Meyer (1830–1895) in Germany formulated the periodic law based on atomic weights (1869).

Immense progress was made in producing soda, the most generally used of the alkalies, and of the most widely employed acid, sulfuric. As we have already seen, the production of soda was first augmented by devising a method for getting it from common salt instead of the ashes of plants, but costs of manufacture were reduced after 1863 owing to the invention by Ernest Solvay, a Belgian, of a new way of processing salt and toward the close of the nineteenth century by the development of the electrolytic process.[15] So important did common salt become that its use was a barometer for the state of development of the chemical industry in any area.

[15] This process had the advantage of producing large quantities of chlorine that was in demand for bleaching and papermaking.

Sulfuric acid, which is used in nearly every heavy chemical industry— in the preparation of fertilizers, in papermaking, in explosives manufacture, and in rubber—is made by combining sulfur dioxide with air and water. Until about the middle of the nineteenth century sulfur came mostly from Sicily, but some dent was made in this regional monopoly by the use of pyrites, of which Spain had a large supply, and was completely broken by the opening of sulfur wells in Louisiana in 1908 and in Texas at a somewhat later date.

Of the other basic chemicals, nitrates, potassium, and phosphates were the most important. All of them attained economic importance as fertilizers following Justus von Liebig's discovery of the chemical composition of plants (1840). Moreover, nitrates, essential to the growing explosives industry, became of strategic importance to economic growth after the discovery (1857) of a way of using sodium nitrate in explosives instead of potassium nitrate, which was in short supply, and following Alfred Nobel's success in overcoming the dangerous aspects of using nitroglycerine to make dynamite (1863) and in combining nitroglycerine and guncotton to make smokeless powder (1887). For most of the period under survey potassium was mined at Stassfurt, Germany, and in Alsace. Phosphate rock was obtained from North Africa, especially Tunis, from Florida, and from smelting phosphoric iron ores, and nitrates were had from Chile and Peru, although on the eve of World War I, they began to be obtained from the air by the fixation process, invented by a German chemist, Fritz Haber (1868–1934).

The ramifications of the chemical revolution were almost infinite. They touched a host of common goods, like friction matches (1833), safety matches (1855), photography (Louis Daguerre had the first practical success with his daguerrotypes in 1839), photoengraving (1860), and motion pictures (Thomas A. Edison, 1893).[16] They included the founding of an entirely new and great industry, rubber, which was made possible by Charles Goodyear's discovery of a way of vulcanizing rubber by the use of sulfur (patented 1844)[17] and by the amassing of great quantities of latex from the tropics, especially from the Belgian Congo and the East Indies. They embraced the decomposition of coal tar to get dyes (synthetic alizarin 1869, indigo 1880, Congo red 1884, sulfur black 1894), to produce synthetic medicines (from aspirin to camphor), and to make available perfumes, germicides, insecticides, artificial flavors,

[16] Edison showed his first pictures in illuminated slot machines. Images were first projected on a screen by an Englishman, R. V. Hall (1895).
[17] In 1914 the rubber industry ranked twenty-seventh in the United States in terms of value added by manufacture. By 1856, the market offered a host of rubber articles: rubber boots, rubber carriage tires, and rubber sheets.

resins, and tanning materials. They even extended to the discovery of radium by Pierre and Marie Curie in 1910 and to the realization of the possibility of changing one element into another.

The economic advantages to be derived from chemistry were so obvious that the leading states of Western culture vied with one another to solve new riddles or to obtain as rapidly as possible solutions to problems discovered by others. In the first half of the nineteenth century leadership in chemistry was seized from France by England, but in the last quarter of the century Germany, thanks in part to the absence of a patent law, assumed a position of primacy which it maintained until well after World War I. At all events, the wizardry of chemistry was throughout this period almost an exclusive monopoly of Western culture, and this gave the West a great economic and power advantage over the rest of the world.

Table 24. Production of Selected Chemicals in 1913
(In thousands of metric tons)

Country	Salt	Sulfuric acid	Nitrates	Phos- phates	Potas- sium
United States	4,364	4,743	647 (sulfate of ammonia)	3,883	56
Germany	2,077	1,704	1,700 (sulfate of ammonia)		1,788
Chile	20		2,016 (nitrate of lime)		
France	1,282	1,000	155	180	531
United Kingdom	2,284	924	301		

New Sources of Power

Using chemical processes to wrest ever-greater quantities of economic goods from nature and the employment of ever more machines required the employment of constantly increasing amounts of energy. The overwhelming proportion of the energy required was produced by coal, although water power, petroleum, and natural gas became of some importance. Consequently those areas that produced coal in large quantities or could acquire this "black gold" by water transportation at low cost had a distinct industrial advantage over all other regions. Coal had, indeed, such a strategic importance in the location of industry that every great coal-mining area, like the western Pennsylvania–Ohio or the Indiana–Illinois regions of the United States, the Ruhr Basin in Germany, the

Walloon provinces in Belgium, the north of France, and later the Donets Basin in Russia, became great industrial centers.

Because coal was extensively used and expenditures for it constituted such an important percentage of final costs, efforts were made early to extract it more economically and to burn it more efficiently. Mining was improved by better pumping and ventilating machinery, by the use of mechanical elevators, by greater use of mechanical transportation both below and above ground, by pneumatic drills, by better and safer explosives, by the coal loader (1903), by conveyor belts (just prior to

Table 25. Relative Importance of Sources of Heat Energy in the World
(In percentages)

Area	Year	Coal and lignite	Oil	Natural gas	Firewood	Water power
World	1913	74.1	4.5	1.4	17.6	2.4
World	1948	54.8	24.6	7.3	7.2	6.1
United States	1889	87.0	4.5	6.5		2.0
United States	1948	46.1	30.0	11.5		12.4

Table 26. Production of Coal
(In millions of metric tons)

Year	World	Bel-gium	France	Germany	United Kingdom	United States	Russia
1871	230	13.7	12.9	29.3	117.4	42.5	
1880	330	16.9	18.8	47.0	147.0	64.8	
1913	1,214.4	22.8	40.8	190.1	292.0	571.1	
1955	1,504.1	29.9	55.3	131.8*	225.1	447.5	276.1

* West Germany

1904), and by the safety lamp. The use of coal was, for its part, made efficient by more extensive processing of coal before it was finally consumed, by improvements in smelting techniques, and by advances in coal-using equipment.

The chief chemical manipulation of coal was "coking," that is, removing all impurities from it by combustion and leaving only carbon. This was done first in "beehive" ovens, but when coal tar became industrially important new types of ovens were constructed to recover more by-products. The first of these was the Selmet-Savoy oven (1880s), but it was soon replaced by the more efficient Koppers oven, first built in 1898 in the Ruhr. Similarly, although coal had been processed to produce gas, which was widely used to light homes, factories, and public thorough-fares,[18] the manufacture and use of gas were greatly extended.[19]

In power production, feeding the fire was made easier by mechanical stokers (early twentieth century). Combustion was bettered by new designs of furnaces to handle small or powdered coal, and more heat was captured by improvements in the arrangements of the tubes in boilers. Furthermore, the compound and triple-expansion steam engines, although known in principle in the first half of the nineteenth century, began to effect phenomenal savings in fuel and incidentally to make steam power feasible for long sea voyages (circa 1870). Lastly, still greater efficiency of steam was obtained by Sir Charles Parsons' development of the turbine (1884) in which steam acted first upon a large vane wheel and then passed through slots in the casing to work another vane wheel, and so on until its expansive power was largely spent.

Table 27. World Coal Resources by Continent, 1956
(In billions of metric tons)

Continent	Total
North America	495
Europe	700
Asia	1,130
Africa	50
Australia	140
Central and South America	30

Important as coal became in providing for the insatiable appetite of industrial economy, it received significant support from both water power and petroleum. Falling water assumed a new position in the power field with the development of new devices to transform its energy into mechanical motion. Pelton wheels, used for high pressures and small heads, were perfected to a point where 85 per cent of the energy of the falling water was captured; and water turbines, efficient for handling low pressures with large volumes of water, were improved and widely adopted. For its part, petroleum began to assume a position of importance with the invention of the internal combustion engine, perfected by N. A. Otto of Cologne in the late 1860s, by Gottlieb Daimler in 1883, and by

[18] The Bunsen burner, invented in 1855, mixed gas and air to get a better combustion. The Welsbach mantle, an incandescent mantle that glowed when heated with gas, was in use after 1890.

[19] Only about 20 per cent of the heat energy of coal was turned into useful work by the normal boiler and reciprocating steam engine in 1875. The method of making producer gas from coal dust, invented by Ludwig Mond in England in 1889, which gave by-products of coal tar and cheap gas, greatly augmented this percentage.

Rudolph Diesel in 1892.[20] Although petroleum had began to be important as a result of technological changes in lighting, it came into its own as a source of mechanical energy.[21] In fact, petroleum production jumped from almost nothing in 1850 to 5,730,000 barrels in 1870 and to 407,544,000 barrels in 1913, with most of the output coming from the United States and from Russian Caspian wells.

Although both the steam engine and the internal combustion engine gave considerable mobility to mechanical power and freed industry from locating at water power sites, there was an active demand for still greater mobility of power. Some means was needed to make it available to everyone, both young and old, for performing a myriad of tasks from lighting lamps and running sewing machines to drilling teeth and propelling railway trains. Fortunately electricity provided what was required.

In the eighteenth century numerous experiments had been made with electricity and in 1800 Alessandro Volta (1745–1827) had actually made an electric battery. The practical value of electricity was not foreseen, however, until Michael Faraday changed an electric current to motion (1821) and showed that an electric current could be generated by revolving a copper coil in a magnetic field. It was not until 1867 that Werner Siemens made public his invention of a dynamo,[22] not until 1879 that electricity was used to drive the first locomotive in Berlin and that Thomas A. Edison made public his first carbon filament lamp,[23] not until 1882 that the current was turned on for the lighting system in New York, not until 1883 that Thomas A. Edison brought the generator to its essential modern form by the use of carbon brushes, and not until 1897–

[20] Diesel's engine used cheaper and heavier oil for fuel and got the material fired not by an electric spark, as in the gasoline engine, but by compression. All of the heavier distillates have a flash point that is determined by heat and compression.

The Diesel engine came to be widely used as a stationary engine because of its efficiency, whereas the gasoline motor, because of its lightness, was adopted usually in vehicles where it had to transport itself.

[21] The lamp with wick and chimney (invented 1784) was a great success, but fuel for it, whether lard or whale oil, became so dear that a search was made for a cheaper substitute. This quest led to petroleum. Kerosene, made from the simple distillation of petroleum, turned out to be just what the lighting industry wanted, whereas oil obtained in the process of refining proved valuable for lubricating the points of friction in machines, thus replacing all kinds of oiling devices, that ranged from slabs of suet to cans of dripping lard.

[22] At approximately this time electric motors were announced independently by Sir Charles Wheatstone and S. A. Varley, a classic example of the way social needs bring forth inventive responses.

[23] Sir Humphry Davy had invented the arc light in 1809, which was used after 1850 for lighting public places. The great disadvantage of the arc light was that it required frequent servicing because the carbon poles between which the current arced burned out.

An Early Electrical Dynamo (1879). This is the "Long-waisted May Anne." It was the first dynamo with an efficiency of over 50 per cent—its rating was 90 per cent. The blocks of metal constitute a magnet, and magnetism is provided by the tall piles. The coil of wire woven around a core of iron, which revolves within the magnetic field, is seen between the two pieces of iron. The brushes on the commutator are visible; on the far side is the flat pulley to which a flat belt may be attached. (*Courtesy of the Edison Laboratory National Monument.*)

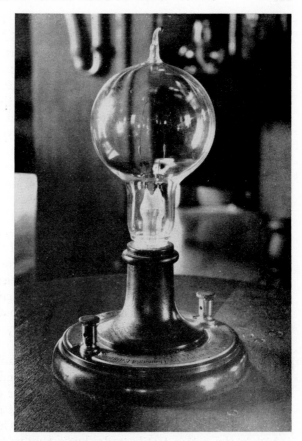

The First Light Bulb. This photograph shows Edison's incandescent electric light. A wire which glows from resistance to electricity when a current is passed through is fitted in a vacuum in a glass bulb. The absence of air prevents the wire from burning. (*Courtesy of the Edison Laboratory National Monument.*)

1898 that Niagara generating plants were put in operation. Even then problems of transmitting this form of energy were extraordinarily vexing. They were not overcome until the transformer was invented, high voltages of alternating current were employed, and much of the direct-current generating plant was scrapped.[24]

In spite of all handicaps the electrical industry grew rapidly after 1900, generating capacity in the United States attaining about 10 million kilowatthours in 1913. Great electrical equipment companies, like Siemens-Halske and the Allgemeine Electrizitäts Gesellschaft in Germany, the Thomson-Houston Company in France, the General Electric Company

[24] Not until the 1890s was transmission up to 200 miles practicable and not until this distance was spanned was it possible to build large-scale grids to take advantage of different-sized loads at different times of the day and at different seasons of the year. Successful high-power transmission was chiefly the work of Marcel Duprez (1882) and of Sebastian Ferranti (1889).

in the United States, and the British General Electric Company and Metropolitan-Vickers in Great Britain, came into being.[25] Constantly new uses were found for electricity, as in electrolysis, electric furnaces, X rays, and fluoroscopes.[26] And electric motors began to revolutionize factory production by being built into machines, to make possible the decentralization of some specialized industries that did not have large transportation costs in relation to their price, like the shirt and blouse trades, and to provide clean urban rapid transit systems. Electricity was, indeed, the great boon of the age.

With all of these innovations in the field of power continual attention was given to how work could be organized for more efficient production. In general, in this period a high correlation was found, on the one hand, between optimum production and, on the other, maximum-sized establishments, amounts of horsepower per worker, and capital investment per worker. In Germany in 1882, 55.1 per cent of the gainfully employed were in establishments of five or less, 18.6 in groups between 6 and 50, and 26.3 in those engaging more than 50, whereas in 1907 these respective percentages were 29.5, 25, and 45.4. In France, the amount of horsepower per establishment increased five times from 1852 to 1912. And in the United States the amount of capital per wage earner about doubled from 1879 to 1913.[27]

The productivity of individual workers in industry, which doubled in the United States from 1870 to 1909–1911, depended, however, not only on the amount of mechanical power per worker or on the machines at his disposal, but also on the extent to which tasks were divided and subdivided in making standardized products. This had long been apparent in the cotton textile trade, but a new and more conscious effort in this direction was made after 1895. In that year the father of scientific management, Frederick Winslow Taylor, published a famous paper on "A Piece Rate System," in which he advocated payments for accomplishing parts of jobs that would reward the particularly efficient and penalize inept or lazy workers. Moreover, he prepared time and motion studies which would show how jobs could be broken down into their essential elements in order to increase output and avoid accidents.

At the same time and connected with Taylor's program, experiments were conducted with the moving assembly line. In the manufacture of watches and sewing machines, the practice had been to bring parts together in one place and for one worker or small team of workers to put

[25] In 1913 Germany made 34 per cent of the world's electrical equipment and the United States, 19 per cent.

[26] The X ray was the invention of W. C. Röntgen in 1896.

[27] See Colin Clark, *Conditions of Economic Progress*, p. 486.

them together to form the finished product. In 1913, Henry Ford decided to try a moving assembly with the product "growing" as workers, stationed along the endless chain or belt, performed some specialized task. His trials demonstrated that the time required to assemble an automobile chassis could thus be lowered from 12½ to 1½ hours; the extension of this idea made possible in large part a reduction in the retail price of the car from $950 to $290. This price permitted in turn the tapping of a mass market and an increase in the output of Ford cars to 250,000 per year on the eve of World War I.

Agricultural Change, 1875–1913

The enormous expansion in the production of industrial goods was accompanied, as we have seen, by a 30 per cent increase in Europe's population and by a doubling of the population of the United States from 1873 to 1913. This rapid growth in the number of human beings necessitated a proportionate augmentation in the supply of foodstuffs available for consumption, if existing diets were to be maintained. Moreover, the fact that the expectation of life at birth improved by some 20 per cent in a nation like France, that workers had higher real wages and hence had more to spend on food,[28] and that the stature of American schoolboys increased very markedly,[29] suggest that diets were improved both quantitatively and qualitatively. Not only did the supply of foodstuffs increase, but a shift took place toward a greater intake of the so-called protective foods—those high in proteins and vitamins. Direct evidence shows that in America 2⅕ times more money was spent on food per capita in the decade 1904–1913 than in the decade 1869–1878 (at 1929 prices), that the average Frenchman consumed 25 per cent more wheat, nearly 100 per cent more wine, and three and one-half times more sugar in the decade 1900–1910 than in the decade 1850–1860, that more milk was drunk when rapid transportation was available, that more citrus fruits were eaten when they could be carried long distances, and that more meat was consumed when it could be kept under refrigeration in transit.

How these increased quantities and new types of foodstuffs became available to members of Western culture is one of the amazing aspects

[28] The percentage of national income spent on food has, however, declined in accordance with a "law," propounded by Christian Engel about a century ago. His law is that the smaller the family income, the greater the proportion of the income spent on food. See M. K. Bennett, *The World's Food* (New York: Harper, 1954), pp. 62–63.

[29] The evidence indicates that the stature of Boston schoolboys increased by 2 inches from 1876 to 1926.

of recent economic growth and one that touches human welfare to the quick. The explanation is to be found, in part, in increases in agricultural production in the industrialized nations of Western culture, in part, in the bringing into cultivation of great areas, like the American and Canadian West, Australia, and the Argentine; in part, in shifts in the nature of agricultural production; and in part, in getting foodstuffs from many agricultural areas, outside Western culture in return for industrial products. In many instances, however, new techniques of production, new methods of carrying and conserving, and new forms of specialized production played important roles in the change.

The smallest increases in agricultural production came from industrialized regions. Thus the volume of agricultural production in France went up only some 5 per cent from 1868–1872 to the period 1910–1913, with the major growth being in potatoes, sugar beets, and milk, whereas the volume in England actually declined.[30] On the other hand, the greatest increases were registered in countries overseas where new lands were brought into cultivation. Thus, in the United States, where the amount of farm land more than doubled from 1860 to 1913, the income realized from agriculture, adjusted for price changes, went up by over four times in the same period, while not dissimilar achievements were registered in Australia, New Zealand, the Argentine, and Canada. Consequently the older industrialized areas of Western Europe and of the Eastern seaboard of the United States became great importers of foodstuffs. World trade in primary products increased three times from 1876–1888 to 1913; by 1935 highly industrialized countries were taking four-fifths of the exports of nonindustrialized countries.

The growing dependence of industrialized countries on nonindustrialized countries for food had a direct effect on agricultural production. Within Western Europe there was a trend toward ever more *intensive* agriculture and toward specialization in the production of those goods in which producers had a comparative advantage. Thus dairying, poultry raising, the growing of fresh vegetables and sugar beets, and the raising of hogs developed, whereas grain growing, sheep raising, and wine production fell off unless these crops were protected by high tariffs. In overseas areas there was a trend toward extensive agriculture with the growing of grains and the raising of livestock on ranches. In Russia and the Danubian states, a concentration on the growing of grains continued, with these regions accounting in 1914 for 40 per cent of world wheat exports, as compared with 50 per cent of wheat exports produced by Canada, the United States, Australia, Argentina, and India.[31]

[30] Clark, *op. cit.*, pp. 212, 216.
[31] By 1928 these percentages had changed to 5 per cent and 94 per cent, respectively.

These regional specializations were made possible not only, as we have seen, by more rapid transportation facilities and by the development of a market demand in industrial districts, but also by changes in population-land ratios and in agricultural techniques. One may say, concerning the former, that when the pressure of population on land was great, that is, when the ratio of labor to land resources was high, productive units and holdings tended to be small, agriculture tended to be intensive, and the farmer tended to devote some of his energies to other employment. Such was the case of industrialized Europe in the nineteenth century and of much of Eastern Europe and of the Eastern coastal states of the United States in the twentieth century. A shift to small holdings and to intensive agriculture became the object of social reform. It was advocated by those who wanted to preserve "rural virtues" and to furnish that resistance to extreme demands for social and political change usually found on the family farm. The shift was economically justified in that it provided more food for the agricultural population by increasing output per unit of land, but it required new capital. This was furnished, in part, by governmental banks, in part by cooperatives, and in part by local bankers and merchants.

Where labor was scarce in relation to land resources, where land was especially suited for large-scale operations, or where no ready market existed for the products of intensive agriculture, productive units tended to be large. Under such conditions a great deal of machinery was used, capital investment per worker was high, and crops were grown that required little labor in relation to their value. In general, output per man-hour grew more rapidly under this system of extensive agriculture than under intensive farming, about doubling in the United States from 1870 to 1914.[32] In America, and also in France, national income from agriculture, figured on a man-hour basis, was about half what it was in industry.

Under both intensive and extensive systems of farming, however, output per cultivated acre increased considerably, although greater improvement in this regard was made under intensive farming than under extensive. In Germany, for example, production of wheat per acre increased nearly 50 per cent from 1878–1879 to 1901–1910; whereas in the United States it went up by some 8 per cent.[33] European grain growers could

[32] To be sure there was also progress in intensive agriculture. In France, for example, output per man-hour in farming increased some 23 per cent from 1870 to 1914, but that output was only about half that of the United States. See Harold Barger and Hans H. Landsberg, *American Agriculture 1899–1939* (New York: National Bureau of Economic Research, 1942); Folke Dovring, *Land and Labor in Europe 1900–1950* (The Hague: Nijhoff, 1956); and Clark, *op. cit.*, p. 216.

[33] The highest grain yields per acre were attained in countries like Denmark and the Netherlands where cultivation was especially intensive and opportunities for working marginal land were limited.

not compete with those on vast overseas farms, nor could European or Eastern American sheep raisers match the low costs attained on ranges of the American West and of Australia and New Zealand where the sheep did most of the work of raising themselves.

The extent of technological advances in farming from 1870 to 1914 may be suggested by a mass of data. In the first place, world production of nitrates, about three-fourths of which were used for fertilizer, increased from insignificant amounts in 1850 to nearly 900,000 metric tons in 1913; potash output rose to 1,348,000 metric tons, and that of super-phosphates to 16,251,213 metric tons. In Germany, the number of mowing machines on farms of 100 hectares or more went from 1,493 in 1882 to 137,624 in 1907; the number of horses, used both for transport and to haul farm machinery, increased by 25 per cent from 1860 to 1907. Hardier types of plants made possible the cultivation of grain crops in more hostile climates (Marquis wheat, for example, allowed the cultivation of wheat in the Prairie provinces of Canada). Better livestock was generally employed (the yield of milk per cow about doubled in Denmark from 1870–1880 to 1911–1913).

Trade, Transportation, and Tariffs

As has been repeatedly emphasized in preceding pages, increases in quantities of both agricultural and industrial goods would not have been possible if there had not been great specialization in production both by areas and by individuals. Furthermore, this specialization—this division of labor—would, in turn, not have been possible had there not been an enormous expansion of transportation and exchange facilities and a consequent growth of trade. Indeed, the extensive market is one of the most distinctive characteristics of the economy which Western culture developed in the nineteenth century.

In the growth of trade, railways and ocean shipping played particularly crucial roles. Railway building, which had done so much to stimulate economic activity in the second and third quarters of the nineteenth century, was continued until the earlier industrialized regions had dense networks, and overseas lands had lines which reached across vast unsettled or semisettled areas, across the United States and Canada, down the length of Africa from Cairo to the Cape, from "Berlin to Bagdad," and to remote districts of South America and Australia. So universal was the recognition that railways were necessary for economic growth and also for military operations that states proved ready to provide the necessary capital for construction if private financiers would not or could not do so. Especially in areas such as Russia and South America where economic growth was retarded, railways had to be financed by public bodies; and even in some Western European states, notably in Germany, railways were nationalized in order to get faster construction or more efficient operation.

Some idea of how extensive railway carrying became can be gleaned from the facts that in the United States railway mileage was increased from 94,665 miles in 1876 to 379,508 miles in 1913, that passenger miles went up from 12 billion in 1890 to 35 billion in 1913, and that ton-miles jumped from 76,207 million in 1890 to 301,730 million in 1913, that is, to 3,017 ton-miles per capita of the population. In Germany, the railway network grew from 17,360 miles in 1875 to 37,820 miles in 1910; and frieght carried one mile reached 34,906 million tons or 503 tons per capita at the latter date.

Table 28. Percentage Shares of World Trade, 1840–1938

Year	United Kingdom	United States	Germany	France
1840	32	8.0		10.0
1913	17	15.0	12.0	7.0
1938	13	10.7	9.2	4.7

Increase in shipping also developed rapidly, especially when iron and steel were used in the construction of hulls (after 1879), when triple and quadruple expansion steam engines began to be employed (1881 and 1894), and when the screw propeller began to replace side paddle wheels (after 1860). In the United Kingdom steam tonnage increased from 168,000 net tons in 1850 to 10,443,000 net tons in 1910, whereas sail tonnage declined from 3,000,000 net tons in 1890 to 850,000 net tons in 1913. In 1914 the leading carrying nations of the world had over 20,500,000 net tons of steam vessels, 96 per cent of which belonged to Western culture.

Such developments help account for the fact that world trade increased about threefold from 1876–1880 to 1913; and the trade of heavily industrialized nations, especially small ones which thus had to rely heavily on exchanges with others, increased enormously. Thus the per capita foreign trade of the Netherlands went up from 80 dollars in 1851–1853 to 243 dollars in 1929, that of Great Britain from 54 to 219 dollars, and that of Russia from 4 to 5.7 dollars. In some cases, as in Britain, where in 1914 25 per cent of all manufactured goods were exported, foreign trade was essential for existence. And even in other nations, like the

Table 29. Geographical Distribution of Foreign Investments in 1914
(Currencies, 1914 values)

British

Millions of pounds

Within the Empire:

Canada and Newfoundland	514.9
Australia and New Zealand	416.4
South Africa	370.2
India and Ceylon	378.8
Other colonies	99.7
Total	1,780.0

Outside the Empire:

United States	754.6
Argentine	319.6
Brazil	148.0
Mexico	99.0
Other Latin-American investments	190.0
Russia	110.0
Spain	19.0
Italy	12.5
France	8.0
Germany	6.4
Rest of Europe	62.7
Egypt	44.9
Turkey	24.0
China	43.9
Japan	62.8
Rest of foreign world	77.9
Grand total	3,763.3

French

Billions of francs

Russia	11.3
Turkey	3.3
Spain and Portugal	3.9
Austria-Hungary	2.2
Balkan states	2.5
Italy	1.3
Switzerland, Belgium, and Netherlands	1.5
Rest of Europe	1.5
French colonies	4.0
Egypt, Suez, and South Africa	3.3
United States, Canada, and Australia	2.0
Latin America	6.0
Asia	2.2
Total	45.0

Table 29. Geographical Distribution of Foreign Investments in 1914 (*Continued*)

German	
	Billions of marks
Austria-Hungary	3.0
Russia	1.8
Balkan countries	1.7
Turkey	1.8
France and Great Britain	1.3
Spain and Portugal	1.7
Rest of Europe	1.2
Africa (including German colonies)	2.0
Asia (including German colonies)	1.0
United States and Canada	3.7
Latin America	3.8
Other areas	0.5
Total	23.5

United States, where exports constituted some 10 per cent of production, a sudden decline in foreign trade could upset the total economy.

With the spread of new ways of producing goods throughout Western Europe and to other parts of the world, there were shifts in the shares of trade accounted for by individual nations.

In the conduct of trade, the countries of Western Europe which became industrialized earlier developed an excess of imports over exports, but earnings on investments abroad, on shipping, banking, and insurance services, on emigrant remittances, and on the tourist trade were such that most of these nations had plus balances in their total trade and payment accounts. Hence they had moneys to invest abroad—and invest they did. These investments usually provided capital for the more rapidly expanding economies of the world and hence contributed to the economic development of production in economically underdeveloped areas. In so far as this production competed directly with production in the areas earlier industrialized, it tended to weaken the relatively strong economic position of these regions, as exemplified in the previously mentioned shifts in percentage shares of world trade.

In foreign lending, political as well as economic considerations played a role; the French, for example, made heavy investments in Russia for the construction of strategic railways toward the West. Furthermore, an apparent need for expanding Europe's markets—a need driven home by the falling off of world trade in manufactured goods in relation to world trade in primary products between 1880 and 1896—convinced many

Relative Price Movements and Trade. A is the quantum index for world trade in manufactured goods as a percentage of that in primary goods. B_1 is the price index for manufactured goods as a percentage of that for primary goods. B_2 is the same as B_1, using the arithmetic average of the British import-prices indices for foodstuffs and raw materials as representative of primary goods.

persons of the desirability of developing backward economies so that they would buy more goods from industrialized areas.

In the opinion of many, economically backward areas could be developed most rapidly if they came under the political domination of an advanced economy. This belief was responsible, in part, for the new wave of imperialism in the years 1873–1914. In this period Africa was partitioned by the Great Powers, inroads were made into Asia,[34] and the United States acquired the Panama Canal Zone. Whether or not colonies were paying propositions has been hotly debated, for large capital investments were in many instances going to bring returns, if any, in the very distant future. Noncolonial powers, without making expenditures for conquests, could buy colonial products at the same prices as colonial powers;

[34] Earlier in the nineteenth century, Great Britain had acquired the Cape Colony and Ceylon (1815), had taken New Zealand (1840), Hong Kong (1842), and Natal (1843), and had added to its holdings in Australia. France, in its efforts to create a new empire in place of the one lost in the eighteenth century and during the Napoleonic Wars, took Algiers in 1830 and conquered the surrounding country (1847), established itself in Cochin China (1858–1867), and tried, unsuccessfully, to get a foothold in Mexico (1862). The United States, in spite of its Monroe Doctrine (1823), which held that the Western Hemisphere was no longer open for European colonization, pushed its own expansion westward and took disputed areas from Mexico (1848).

and anticolonial feeling in the colonies (and later nationalism) threatened the continuance of political control. The imperialism of Western culture "paid" in the sense of making available resources and markets which allowed its members to increase their economic well-being—to get economic goods at lower prices than would otherwise have been possible.

At times nineteenth-century imperialism was crude, if not cruel, whether undertaken by armed forces or by economic penetrators, but at the same time it had the effect that other imperialisms in the past had had, of spreading the economic ways of the more highly developed culture to the less highly developed. It gave the backward areas technologies and ideas which would allow them eventually to compete with or strike back at their erstwhile rulers.

Whereas the industrialized nations had favorable balances which they could use to build up the rest of the world, the less economically developed nations became so indebted that they needed large excesses of exports over imports to meet their obligations. Thus the United States, which imported more than it exported when it was growing up, began in the last quarter of the nineteenth century to "pay back" what it had borrowed by exporting more than it imported.

All foreign debts were not met in this way, however, for borrowers sometimes simply defaulted on their obligations and the lenders got nothing for their pains. In other cases, debtors paid in a currency which did not have the same purchasing power as that which they had borrowed, or they bought up their own securities when the prices of their obligations had fallen far below par. The largest of such defaults came after World War I, when, for example, the U.S.S.R. repudiated the debts of the Czarist regime, when inflation, especially the hyperinflation in Germany, permitted the settling of foreign debts at a great discount, and when many foreign securities seemed like such poor investments that their prices fell to unconscionable lows. Such reductions of foreign debt were significant enough to make it probable that the earnings on most foreign portfolios, in spite of their higher interest rates, were in the long run considerably less than on loans made at home.

For the most part, however, the governments of lending nations encouraged investments abroad as a means of winning friends, of increasing their nation's prestige, of getting access to sources of raw materials, or of winning markets, and gave little thought to the probability that they were strengthening potential enemies. Their policies regarding merchandise trade were, however, radically different from those pertaining to lending, if, indeed, they were not diametrically opposed to them. Most nations of Western culture believed that they should be economically strong, both for defense and for economic well-being; economic strength required high productivity of industrial goods, and economic expansion required protection of the home market. Furthermore, in most states some segment of the economy, frequently agriculture, was suffering enough from foreign competition to create an interest group that demanded protection. Finally, the long depression in prices from 1873 to 1896 and the accompanying economic stresses convinced many that governmental machinery should be used to cushion the shock of sudden changes emanating from the operation of the free market economy. Thus a combination of economic nationalism, of vested interests, and of state paternalism led to an attack, as we have seen, on the low-tariff policies adopted in the United States in 1833 and in Europe in 1860.

Protectionism had the general effect of hindering the division of labor, although customs barriers were not insurmountable; hence for the entire economy of the world, it was undesirable. Furthermore, in some cases protection led to higher domestic prices for goods than those obtaining in the free world market, but in large economies, like the American, competition among domestic producers was at that time usually sufficient to prevent such results. Protectionism is also said to have contributed to the formation of monopolies at home and to dumping abroad, such effects having been particularly marked in Germany. On the other hand, tariffs helped to keep production of individual nations diversified, which may have been an asset in time of war, and it eased the shock of change, which was becoming more violent in the forty years before 1914.

Some exponents of free trade have argued that because tariffs curbed trade and because trade served as a substitute for the migration of people to areas of greater food supply, tariffs contributed to the great migration of Europeans between the years 1850 and 1930, when some 40 million persons moved overseas. Undoubtedly this argument is somewhat spurious, for Europe's trade grew faster than its population. Emigration on a large scale began in a period of low rates, and until 1895 the largest number of emigrants came from free-trade England. Whatever the truth regarding this issue, however, the fact remains that in this period what was undoubtedly the greatest migration of all time took place—a migration that meant a diffusion of Western culture to many parts of the earth, especially to the New World, to Australia, and to New Zealand.

PART FIVE

Crises in the Economy of
Western Culture—1914 to 1957

CHAPTER 18

International, Economic,

and Social Strains and Stresses

The Nature of the Crisis in Western Culture

Magnificent as was Western culture's economic achievement in the century prior to 1914, a substantial portion of what had been built up in the nineteenth century was to be dissipated in the first half of the twentieth. Western culture became embroiled in two major "world wars," which, from the point of the culture itself were "civil wars." These internecine conflicts destroyed inestimable amounts of wealth and greatly lessened the volume of goods and services which might otherwise have gone to support creative activity in the arts, toward establishing a greater control over the physical universe, and toward permitting more orderly and just relations among men. In fact, there were those prophets of doom who thought that the wars among nation-states of Europe would undo the West, much as wars among the city-states of Greece had undone Greece.

In the second place, Western culture suffered from the fact that its economic system, prodigious as it had been in achieving economic growth, displayed a tendency to generate forces within itself which lessened its effectiveness. In 1920–1921 there was a minor economic depression, but from 1929 to 1936 there was a major one. Industrial production

403

in Europe, excluding the U.S.S.R., declined by 30 per cent from 1929 to 1932. In the United States national income fell by some 50 per cent from 1929 to 1933 and did not regain its predepression level until World War II. Unemployment was rife, suffering was great, and tensions among interest groups stretched to the breaking point. Indeed, the great depression of the 1930s aroused doubts as to the intrinsic value of the capitalist system, made apparent the absolute necessity of taking measures to prevent a repetition of such a calamity, and led in some quarters, notably in Italy and Germany, to changes that boded ill for civilization, as the vast majority of the West understood it.

In the third place, the development of the West's economy had resulted in such changes in the relative economic and political position of interest groups that new theories had been spun to rationalize the place of each and deep-seated animosities had been created among them. Economic power had definitely passed from hereditary landowners and from Churchmen to those who owned or directed great industrial, commercial, or financial enterprises, and political power within national states had shifted in the same direction. Concomitantly, many wageworkers had come to feel that they were being exploited, or at least that they were not being given adequate consideration in the operation of the free-market economy. As a result, many of them adopted an attitude that was either hostile to or highly critical of their employers and to some extent of modern capitalism. They organized both trade unions and political parties in order to "slug it out" with employer groups. Furthermore, these "new groups" were in at least partial conflict with others which represented some ideology of an earlier time, whether it was a royal house, a social "caste," a sectional institution, like slavery in the United States, or an established church. The structure of the new society was, indeed, complex and full of stresses and strains.

In the fourth place, the West seemed to be in crisis because of shifts in the location of power both within its own area and in the entire world. For a multitude of reasons the economic center of Western culture shifted from Western Europe to the English-speaking portions of North America and this shift created a separate set of tensions. The Old World was loath to recognize, much less admit, its relative loss of status; the New was not altogether willing or prepared to assume the responsibilities which went with becoming the most powerful area on earth. The Old World was not quite willing to effect the changes which were indicated, if it were to avoid conflicts which all feared would deliver it its *coup de grâce*, and not quite ready to cooperate closely with the New, now the center of power.

The fact that while Western culture was in crisis other cultures were increasing their power and their hostility to the West added to the West's predicament. In a very short time, the U.S.S.R. created both an economic and military potential which was adequate to make the West fear for its safety. Some colonial areas sought independence from European over-lords, for they had acquired the doctrine of nationalism from the West, learned some of the West's techniques of making war, and realized that the West was greatly weakened by war and social dissension. Finally, what boded particularly ill for the West was the fact that several other cultures, of which the Russian was the leader, seemed to be encroaching on the West or the West's "spheres of influence." Dangerous as such a threat was, it seemingly had the effect of forcing the West to pull itself together, to recognize its weaknesses, and to do something about them.

World War I

The first major evidence that the West was beginning to decline from its pinnacle of power was World War I. This conflict was estimated to have cost, including both losses and current wartime expenditures, 603,570,000,000 dollars—this at a time when the national income of the United States was around 50 billion dollars. It occasioned the mobilization of 65 million men between 1914 and 1918; of these, 9 million were killed, 5 million reported missing, 7 million permanently disabled, and 15 million more or less seriously wounded.

That Western culture should have become involved in such a holo-caust is one of the tragedies of modern times and one that requires solemn reflection. The war was so apocalyptic that one may ask with reason why such civilized humans as Westerners considered themselves to be should ever have become involved in it. Although this query has elicited millions of words of explanation and certainly millions of hours of investigation, a summary answer may be put simply. Tensions among national states had become acute, as suggested above, for the very con-cept of nationalism, implying as it did a sense of superiority and a special mission of the nationality, created rivalries among nations. These rivalries led to the adoption of hostile policies—policies which included matters economic. Nations which had close commercial relations and mutually profited from economic exchanges lined up against each other, in part, because of a desire to gain some advantage or to prevent some advantage being taken of them.

Yet, tensions arising from economic forces certainly did not precipitate the conflict. The crucial decision was taken, or blundered into, because certain leaders with the power to unleash the dogs of war became convinced that there was no other way adequately to safeguard their nation's prestige or to bring their nation its much-wanted glory.[1]

In 1914, leaders on both sides were convinced that the war would be short and that a quick victory would therefore redound to their glory and benefit. They never dreamed that the war would cause so much destruction nor that it would threaten the very foundations of Western culture. Their pride and their certainty about the future course of events led them to ignore one of the fundamental tenets of civilization—the creation of orderly relations among human beings according to known and just rules of behavior.

At the outset, World War I was a war of movement with great mass armies marching and countermarching in an effort to wipe out the enemy, but by December of 1914 the forces on the Western Front, where the ultimate decision was to be reached, had dug in and a war of position ensued. Thenceforth the conflict was to a large extent one of economic potentials.[2] In this contest the Allies tried to deprive the Central Powers of overseas imports and of overseas markets by means of a maritime blockade, while the Central Powers endeavored to achieve the same results by means of submarine warfare against Allied shipping, and ultimately against all shipping to Allied nations. Both sides created governmental control of their economies for the purpose of concentrating all energies upon the war. And both engaged in a considerable amount of economic cooperation in order to mobilize all the materials necessary for war and to use them in the most effective way possible.

The Allied blockade of the Central Powers was drawn very tightly.[3]

[1] Undoubtedly certain events arouse political leaders as individuals to fighting anger. Yet it should not be deduced from this that man is a fighting animal and has a biological need to fight, or that wars are consequently inevitable. Leaders, in taking hostile steps toward others, could rely on the power of nationalism to provide them popular support, but they usually forgot that the same force was operative among their potential enemies. It should be added, that popular support came also from a desire for excitement and from emotionalism rather than from sheer nationalistic pugnacity. See *The Nature of Conflict. Studies on the Sociological Aspects of International Tensions* (Paris: UNESCO, 1957).

[2] On the Eastern Front and in the Balkans the war continued to be a war of movement. The defeat of Russia by the Central Powers was a hard blow to the Allied cause, but it was not decisive. Similarly, the front in the Balkans was fairly fluid and sapped the strength of the Central Powers, but Allied victories there were also not decisive.

[3] France forbade the importation of enemy goods on September 27, 1914, and the exportation of all goods to the enemy on April 4, 1915. Stopping neutral trade with the Central Powers was difficult. The Declaration of Paris (1856) had laid down the rule of international law that neutral flags covered enemy goods, except contraband, that a blockade must be effective, and that neutral goods, except contraband, were not liable to seizure. The Declaration of London (1909) specified that a

Not only was German and Austrian shipping driven off the seas, but all possible land routes were blocked, contraband lists were extended until they included even food, and embargoes were placed on many commodities going to neutral countries adjacent to the Central Powers for fear that the goods would leak through to the enemy. The Allies invoked the doctrine of "continuous voyage," under which contraband goods billed for a neutral country were declared as destined to go to the enemy. In addition, firms suspected of trading with the enemy were black-listed, and trade with neutral countries bordering on enemy lands was limited to shipments to trusted merchants.

Such measures were not without effect, especially after the tightening of the system in March, 1915. German imports fell to about two-thirds of their 1913 level. Shortages of food were so great in Germany that in the winter of 1917 turnips became such a staple in the human diet that the year was dubbed the *Rübenjahr*. Rubber stocks became so depleted that at the end of the war many motor trucks were rolling on steel tires; fats needed in explosives were so short that housewives were requested to strain their dish water to capture whatever grease it might contain; and petroleum products both for lubrication and for internal combustion engines were at the last almost nonexistent.

On the other hand, the Central Powers' war on Allied commerce was also effective. On February 4, 1915, Germany declared that the waters around the British Isles were a war zone, that enemy vessels would be sunk in this area without warning, and that neutral ships should keep clear of it. Subsequently many merchantmen were sunk, including the British *Lusitania*, May 7, 1915, with several Americans on board. But to make the U-boat campaign more effective Germany announced, January 31, 1917, that it would begin an unrestricted and ruthless war on shipping. By the autumn of 1917 the Allies had lost 11,000,000 out of a total of 25,000,000 gross tons which they had had in April, 1915; Great Britain lost during the entire war 7,760,000 gross tons out of a total of 19,000,000. New ship construction was unable to keep pace with such losses and stocks of certain goods fell perilously low. Indeed, in March, 1917, England had a wheat stock sufficient to meet consumption demands for only eight weeks.[4]

---

blockade must not extend beyond the ports and coasts of an enemy country, that is, could not be conducted on the high seas. Great Britain, Germany, and Austria-Hungary were not signatories of this rule, but the latter two states agreed to it during the war because it was to their advantage to do so.

[4] Mention should also be made of the fact that the Central Powers blockaded Russia by controlling the Baltic Sea and by having their ally, Turkey, close the Straits. Russian imports declined to about two-fifths of their prewar value.

Shortages thus created in the economies of the belligerents, as well as the very nature of the war itself, led the participants to engage in governmental economic planning and in controlling economic activity. Prior to 1914 little thought had been given to such war measures, except as regarded transportation, the mobilization of men, and the production of war matériel, for military men thought in terms of short wars. Hence national economic planning, which was to become so important in later years, came into being piecemeal during the war.

This movement was begun by Walter Rathenau, a German industrialist, who early in the conflict became convinced that there would be severe shortages of strategic raw materials. He founded the *Kriegs-Rohstoff Abteilung* (War Raw Materials Department), which tried not only to increase the production of those goods in short supply, but also to develop substitutes for materials which could not be obtained abroad, to control the allocation of goods, and subsequently to determine the very uses to which these materials should be put. In other countries there were

Making Shell Casings in World War I. This photograph shows the interior of Woolwich Arsenal, England, in World War I. Women have largely replaced men at the lathes. Note the overhead shafts and the flat belts. By World War II shell cases could be made on automatic lathes. (*Courtesy of the Imperial War Museum and British Information Services.*)

similar bodies, sometimes composed of trade associations, sometimes consisting of representatives of government, of employers, and of employees, as in the case of the British Control Boards, and sometimes limited to governmental officials.

Also shortages of labor resulting from having so many men under arms forced states to create controls over manpower. One of the first things which governments did was to make military service more selective, that is, to take men for military duty who could be best spared from an economic point of view. They had learned during the early phases of the war that to draft men irrespective of their special skills might result in a reduction in the production of the sinews of war and that men at the front were of little value if their firepower was limited because of matériel shortages.[5] Women, retired men, and youths of premilitary age were enticed to accept productive work.[6] France and Britain imported colonial workers. The German government had the power under the National Service Law of December 5, 1916, to order all men between the ages of seventeen and sixty to work at prescribed tasks. All belligerents drew workers from neighboring countries by offers of high wages.

Furthermore, problems of food supply, which were particularly serious, owing to the fact that all the major belligerents except Russia and the United States were food-importing countries, caused still further governmental intervention. Food control boards were created, food prices were regulated, and some foods were rationed either by limiting the amounts available to individuals or by forbidding the sale of a given product except on specified days.

In the case of the Allies, shortages of food were so great that they did much to effect Interallied economic cooperation. Early in the war England and France learned that in their anxiety to buy food abroad they were bidding up prices to their mutual disadvantage; later they realized that with shipping in such short supply they would have to pool their tonnages if they were to feed their people. Accordingly combined Anglo-French boards were created for making joint purchases, an Interallied Wheat Executive was set up in November, 1916, and the all-important Allied Maritime Transport Council for the allocation of tonnage to meet the most urgent needs was established (November, 1917). Here was a form of international economic cooperation which was to be extended to almost all of Western culture in the economic reconstruction after World War II.

Also problems of war finance pushed governments deeper into eco-

[5] Germany and France withdrew skilled machinists from the army in 1915, for example, and Great Britain, shipyard workers and stevedores in 1916.

[6] France had 29 per cent more women in industry in July, 1917, than in 1914.

nomic planning, into controls, and into Interallied cooperation. All belligerents levied new taxes, many of which were to have some effect other than the mere raising of revenue and thus constituted an interesting example of functional finance. Accordingly, excess profit taxes were designed to curb war profiteering; luxury taxes were aimed to prevent productive energies from being diverted from essentials; and consumers' taxes were used to curb the consumption of goods in short supply or to discourage the manufacture of goods that detracted from war production. Finally, all belligerents had recourse to new rates to get more revenue. France and Russia adopted the income tax. France introduced a tax on business transactions (turnover tax), and Great Britain levied customs duties. France doubled its tax revenues from 1914 to 1918, and Great Britain increased its threefold.

Heroic as such measures were, however, they were not sufficient to cope with the enormous demands of the maw of Mars. Consequently, all states had to resort to borrowing. If treasury securities were held by private individuals, borrowing had no great economic consequences. But if they were held by banks, especially central banks, they became the base, the reserve, for increasing the money supply or for the extension of credit. Thus they had an inflationary effect. As a matter of fact, prices rose considerably during the war in all belligerent countries. Thus in Germany, the amount of money in circulation increased some five times and prices about doubled. Among the Allies, however, the situation was somewhat relieved by considerable Interallied borrowing, the more financially able lending to the hardest pressed.[7] When hostilities had ended, about 15 per cent of the Allied costs of the war had been met by Interallied loans. The United States had lent other Allies $7,077,100,-000; Great Britain was a creditor for $7,014,500,000; and France had assisted others to the extent of $2,237,600,000. Such pooling of resources explains, in part, why the exchange rates of Allied currencies remained at about their prewar ratios until after the conflict (the French franc in terms of the dollar declined from only 5.18 at par to 5.45 in December, 1918).

At the end of the war the economic strength of the Allies was apparent on the fronts as well as in banking houses. The enormous resources of the United States and of the British Empire, and the ability of the Allies to draw upon the reserves of the entire world because of their domination of the seas tipped the scales against the Central Powers. The Germans became aware of the predicament into which they were getting

[7] These "loans" were in effect bookkeeping arrangements representing delayed payments for deliveries of goods. They were not funds that permitted a free choice of acquiring goods in the world's markets.

themselves and made an all-out effort to stave off disaster by throwing their weight after a long build-up against the Allies in March, 1918. This desperate effort carried them to the Marne, but not beyond. Henceforth, they were literally crushed by a superior force—a force determined by a greater economic potential.

The Economic Consequences of the War

In an economic sense, however, the difference between victor and vanquished in the fall of 1918 was not very great. Losses in men and goods had been immense on both sides. For four years, the belligerents had devoted their energies to destruction, with the result that an important part of Europe's capital equipment had been destroyed or worn out.

Of perhaps even greater significance for the long run than the ruining of physical plant and the diversion of energies from construction to destruction was the fact that the war had resulted in innumerable economic dislocations. New tensions had grown up between employers and employees. Some resources had been so exhausted that shifts in the location of production were necessary; industries had been started to meet the needs of war which were not viable in peacetime. Patterns of international trade and payments had been so drastically altered that the traditional flows of goods and methods of making payments had become impossible.

Immediately after the conflict—when social structures were weakened by the displacement of peoples, when rapid demobilization of armies, with no provisions for the employing of ex-soldiers, was taking place, when patriotic fervor relaxed, and when there were great uncertainties about the future—leaders of the lower classes in several places attempted to seize control of political power. In Russia, they succeeded in overthrowing the Czarist regime (October, 1917) and setting up a communist state. In Hungary, they created a very short-lived communist dictatorship under Bela Kun (1919). In Italy, workers occupied factories and a few large estates (1920). Existing regimes were done away with in Germany, Austria, Bulgaria, and Turkey. In France, Great Britain, and the United States there were numerous strikes. In Central and Eastern Europe there were demands for land reform which envisaged the breaking up of large estates. Such troubles contributed directly to the continuation of low production, which in Europe was some 23 to 30 per cent less than it had been in 1913, and to the economic depression of 1920–1921.

To make matters worse, some wartime economic expansion required agonizing readjustment. Great munition plants had to be retooled as arms were beaten into plowshares. Allied shipyards, which had striven so valiantly to keep pace with sinkings, had to be cut back, and untold amounts of war matériel from gas masks to airplane motors had to be dumped. Moreover, the production of many basic commodities, like copper and wheat, had been so greatly increased that prices for them fell greatly and remained low throughout the 1920s.[8]

Difficult as were the readjustments to meet peacetime conditions and enormous as was the task of reconstruction, a return to the production levels of 1913 was effected with amazing rapidity. In France, which was one of the worst-ravaged nations, the index of industrial production attained its prewar figure in 1924 and the index of agricultural production reached its prewar position by 1925. In fact by 1926, all leading European countries, including the U.S.S.R., had gotten back, so far as output was concerned, to what they had achieved in 1913. This was a remarkable tribute to the recuperative powers of modern technology.

A return to the *status quo ante* was not, however, effected with such dispatch in all branches of economic activity. Especial difficulty was encountered, as has already been said, in the field of international trade and payments, or more precisely in that delicate structure of multilateral movements of goods, payments, and investments whereby the accounts of nations were settled. For one thing, the "workshop of the world" nations had lost some of their markets during the war and had difficulty in regaining them. British exports in 1921 were half what they had been in 1913 (at 1913 prices), whereas United States manufacturing production was 22 per cent and Japanese was 76 per cent greater in 1920 than in 1913. For another thing, Western European nations had to replenish their stocks of imported industrial raw materials before they could get back into full production, and they had to bring in large quantities of foodstuffs to make up for the deficiencies caused by war. Furthermore, these same nations had reduced earnings from shipping services, from earnings on foreign investments, and from banking and insurance services. As late as 1928 the ten most highly industrialized countries of Western Europe had a bare plus balance in current trade and payments.

The international trade and payments situation was finally made worse by still other disturbing factors. For a time the terms of trade, that is, the relationship of prices for imports compared with prices for exports, were unfavorable to Western Europe, so that Western Europe had to export more goods to pay for a given amount of exports than it had before the war. The creation of new states and hence of new tariff boundaries impeded the flow of goods in established patterns of production and distri-

---

[8] In the United States the acreage planted to wheat increased 25 per cent from 1914 to 1919, for example. Much of this increase was in the Southwest on land that was to be partially ruined by erosion during the droughts of the 1920s.

bution. The fear of political instability hindered the making of international loans. Curbs on immigration, like the American act of 1921,[9] created maladjustments in the supply of labor. And as though these difficulties were not enough, the entire international trade and payments picture was distorted by reparations and war debts.

Reparations and War Debts

At the conclusion of the war, the European victors wanted Germany to pay all Allied war damages and all the Allied costs of the war. The United States, however, took the position that the payment of war damages would be all that Germany could manage if she were to be returned to full membership in the economy of Western Europe. Inasmuch as such a difference of opinion existed and there was no possibility of drawing up a bill for war damages, the fixing of the amount of reparations was left to a special commission which was to submit its figure by May, 1921. In the meantime, Germany was to pay the equivalent of 5 billion dollars in commodities, securities, and gold to cover the costs of the armies of occupation.[10] Furthermore, it was to surrender part of its merchant marine, to build 200,000 tons of shipping per year for five years for the Allies, to deliver a certain amount of livestock, railway equipment, and coal, and to give the Allies most-favored-nation treatment for five years.[11]

The reparations bill which was submitted in 1921 called for the payment of 33 billion dollars, or four times what American experts at Paris had thought to be feasible. This sum was to be paid over thirty years in fixed installments of gold marks plus 26 per cent of the proceeds of German exports and plus reparations in deliveries of physical goods—the so-called reparations in kind. Here was a burden so great that the German budget, then almost in balance, was faced with a large deficit. Germany began to issue paper money on a vast scale in order to meet governmental expenses; the German mark began to fall in international exchange, and Germany was soon the victim of a runaway inflation.

Before the end of 1921 Germany informed the Reparations Commission that it could not meet its 1922 installments. Payments went into

[9] This law set quotas on the number of immigrants to be admitted to the United States in any one year. Each country was allowed a number based on 3 per cent of its nationals living in the United States in 1910, although people of some countries were actually excluded. This law favored immigration from Northern Europe and limited it from Southern and Central Europe.

[10] Dollars are given at current value. Any of the sums mentioned which might be in excess of the costs of occupation were to be credited toward reparations.

[11] Incidentally, the blockade of Germany was to be maintained until the peace treaty was signed, a stipulation which was a very bitter pill for Germany.

default, and the French and Belgians occupied the Ruhr (1923) to force collections. When this effort proved unsuccessful in the face of Germany's passive resistance, the Allies appointed a new reparations commission, chaired by an American banker, Charles G. Dawes, to try to bring some order out of the existing chaos. From the first the Dawes Commission was handicapped, because it was not empowered to alter the total bill. It did produce a plan, however, that reduced annual payments to sums considered to be within Germany's capacity to pay, extended the period over which reparations would be collected, and suggested sources of revenue for these payments.[12]

The Dawes Plan had no built-in magic, however; in essence there was only a suggestion for the prolonging of the agony. When Germany again had trouble meeting payments, a new commission was appointed, with another American, Owen D. Young, as chairman. The Young Plan of 1929 provided for both a reduction in annual payments and a lowering of the total bill, but it went into operation just as the economy was going into a tailspin. Under the stresses of the depression, a continuation of the reparations comedy was out of the question. In 1932 the parties involved signed the Lausanne Agreement that to all intents and purposes put an end to the reparations issue.[13]

Closely related to reparations as a major influence upon international trade, current payments, and capital movements were Interallied war debts. These obligations were contracted, as we have seen, during the war, but they were increased immediately after the Armistice by the sale of war stocks and the granting of further loans for immediate relief and reconstruction. Thus in 1922 the United States was a net creditor on war debts for some $10,000,000,000, Great Britain for $4,500,000,000, and France for $3,500,000,000. Britain and France wanted to distinguish between pre-Armistice and post-Armistice obligations on the ground that the former should be considered as part of a common war effort. The United States, however, insisted on collection, for it accepted the view expressed in President Coolidge's "They hired the money, didn't they?" Accordingly, Great Britain and France granted large concessions to their debtors and acknowledged loss of the aid given to Russia, but the United States tried to collect, making adjustments only upon interest charges and periods of payment. Because of this American policy, France and Britain insisted as long as they could on the payment of reparations and they finally agreed to abrogate their claims on Germany only on condition that they were no longer responsible for war debts.

In the payment of any obligation, a debtor nation must have things of

[12] It also proposed the withdrawal of France and Belgium from the Ruhr.

[13] Reparations from the other Central Powers were treated in the same way as those with Germany, but they were not a major problem, because they were not very large.

value and must be able to transfer these things to its creditor. A government usually obtains whatever it uses for payments by taxing its people or by borrowing both at home and abroad. The transfers may be in the form of gold and silver, foreign moneys, securities, merchandise, and services. In any case, however, the creditors must be willing to receive what the debtor has to give.

Immediately after the war, Germany was able to amass a certain amount of precious metals, foreign securities, foreign moneys, and stocks of goods to send to claimants on reparations account. At that time, too, when everything was in short supply, the Allies were willing to receive what was offered. Up to the Dawes Plan the Allies received on reparations account some 8,500,000,000 dollars, including a considerable amount in kind, although estimates of the total figure have varied widely. By 1924, however, Germany had little more in the way of gold and silver, foreign securities, or foreign moneys to transfer. The only way that it could get them was by exporting more goods and services than it imported or by borrowing abroad. The reparations claimants did not want the Germans to get any of their markets,[14] nor were they so willing as they had been to be paid directly in kind. In fact, they grumbled because German shipyards were building ships on reparations account while their own lay idle and British coal miners complained that German coal deliveries on reparations account to Italy were hurting their exports. Consequently, actual deliveries of goods, which had played an important role in the Dawes Plan schedule of payments, were cut drastically in the Young Plan. Then, what was of particular significance for the reparations problem was that Germany had a deficit in its foreign trade and payments from 1924 to 1930 of 8,250,000,000 dollars. Yet it paid in this period some 2,620,000,000 dollars.

Payment of war debts presented the same problems as did payment of reparations. Easily transferable values were in short supply, and each creditor was reluctant to receive goods which would compete with its own products. Yet, here, too, payments were made, the United States Treasury receiving from all debtors some 2,735,000,000 dollars in spite of the fact that those payers had unfavorable balances in current trade and payments with the United States. From Table 30, page 416, one may easily see the extent of reparations and war debt accounts from 1924 to 1931.

How reparations and war debts were paid in view of the over-all deficit in the trade and payment accounts of the payers is an interesting question. The answer is to be found in the fact that during the period

[14] France rejected a proposal by Louis Loucheur whereby Germany would have reconstructed the devastated regions. Both French capital and labor wanted this business and work for themselves.

Table 30. Total Receipts and Payments of Principal Countries on Reparations and War Debt Accounts, July 1, 1924–June 30, 1931
(In millions of dollars, current value)

| Country | Receipts from | | Payments to | | | Net position |
	Germany	All principal debtors	United States	Great Britain	Total	Excess receipts (+), payments (−)
Great Britain	564.9	881.3	1,122.1		1,122.1	−240.8
France	1,426.0	1,426.0	220.8	197.1	417.9	+1,008.1
Italy	203.2	203.2	33.0	107.1	140.1	+ 63.1
Belgium	182.2	182.2	39.8	12.2	52.0	+130.2

under consideration the United States, and to a lesser extent, Great Britain, France, Switzerland, and the Netherlands made capital loans to Germany. Germany in turn paid her creditors by means of the funds thus put at its disposal. As the claimants on reparations account were paid, they reduced their war debts. The upshot of the story was that Germany paid in reparations from the beginning of the Dawes Plan about three-fifths of what it borrowed abroad and reinvested the other two-fifths for its own account outside its frontiers. The recipients of reparations passed on to the United States to reduce their war debts about half of what they received from Germany. Finally, American private investors wound up holding German securities of doubtful value. From 1914 to 1930 the United States shifted from being a net debtor for 3 billion dollars to that of being a net creditor for 11 billion dollars, in addition to being a creditor for unpaid war debts.

Inflationary Movements in the Post-World War I Period

Reparations and war debts were responsible for badly distorting the postwar pattern of multilateral trade and payment—a distortion which would have been infinitely worse if it had not been for American loans abroad—but international trade and capital transfers were further complicated by currency inflations. Uneven rates of inflation of various currencies resulted in great discrepancies between exchange rates and prices, consequently heavy buying in areas where exchange and price advantages were to be found, and sudden flights of "hot money" from a monetary area with a weak currency to another with a strong currency, that is, one that was not in danger of becoming depreciated.

The extraordinary movement of the 1920s had its origins in the war, when governmental expenditures so greatly exceeded receipts from taxation and borrowing from individuals. What governments did to keep their bills paid was to give "promises to pay" to banks of issue. The banks, in turn, increased the supply of money with these "promises to pay" as reserves. With more money in circulation without a corresponding increase of goods for sale or of savings, prices were bid up, as can be seen in the accompanying chart.

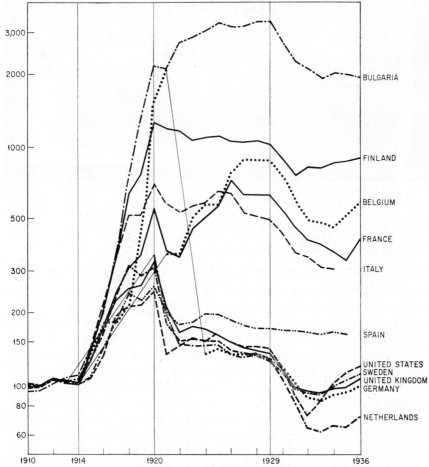

Wholesale Prices, in National Currency, of Forty Basic Commodities in European Countries and the United States, 1910 to 1936.

The most extreme inflation was that in Germany. At the end of the war, money in circulation there was five times what it had been in 1914. The public debt was up twenty times; prices had about doubled, and reparations put a tremendous burden on the public treasury. The exchange rate for the dollar, which had been about 4 marks to the dollar in 1914 went to 14.8 marks to the dollar in May, 1921, to 62.6 marks in November, and eventually to some 62 billion marks on October 30, 1923.

German Inflation Money. This bank note is for 2 billion marks. Before such notes could be printed, the face value of existing notes was raised by stamping new values on them. Even so, an ordinary businessman had to carry bundles of money in large billfolds or brief cases in order to have enough to carry on even small transactions. (*From the Moneys of the World Collection of the Chase Manhattan Bank of New York. Used with permission.*)

Prices soared, although they lagged behind exchange rates, until the mark became virtually worthless. In fact, the mortgage indebtedness within Germany of the preinflationary period became less in terms of paper marks than one glass of beer. Debts, including those represented by bonds and mortgages, were thus wiped out, but so, too, were insurance policies, savings accounts, and all forms of wealth the value of which was determined by the value of the currency.[15] Order was only reestablished when a new bank of issue, the Rentenbank, was created—a bank that used as "reserves" large agricultural holdings and business properties pledged for the purpose by their owners. This was a temporary arrangement to provide the country with a usable medium of exchange and measure of value pending the accumulation of more traditional reserves for a new Reichsbank.[16]

France, for its part, emerged from the war with a monetary problem not unlike Germany's. Although it did not have reparations to pay, it did have war debts to settle and devastated areas to reconstruct. In the ac-

[15] Some of these obligations, like life insurance policies, were subsequently "revalued," for insurance companies had properties, like real estate, that did not lose value during the hyperinflation.

[16] The new Rentenmark was declared equal to approximately 24 cents. The new money held this rate and German prices conformed to it.

complishment of the latter task it spent money lavishly on the assumption that reparations would cover all the bills. When this blithe expectation proved illusory, the supply of money was increased more rapidly to meet expenditures than was the supply of goods, and prices went up. As the French realized what was taking place, some of them sent capital abroad, changing their francs ("hot money") into apparently more stable dollars, Swiss francs, pounds sterling, or Dutch florins—a process which weakened the franc in foreign exchange. By 1926 the French franc, which had been worth about 20 cents in 1914 was bringing only .0389 cents in New York. In the extremity Henri Poincaré, who was to become known as the "savior of the franc," made a herculean effort to bring the French budget into balance, slowed up the flight from the franc, forced some of the "hot money" back to France, and finally stabilized the franc at .0392 cents.

One of the curious phases of inflation was that prices did not rise at the same rate that a currency in the process of being inflated lost value in exchange for hard currencies. Thus, in the interval between the time a currency fell in terms of another money and the time national prices had risen to the level of international prices at the new rate of exchange, goods in the inflationary country were cheap for the citizens of countries with stable currencies. For this reason, American tourists flocked to France in the 1920s because they could travel there very cheaply, and many French goods had a strong competitive position for a time in the Swiss market. Consequently inflation gave a shot-in-the-arm to exports— a spurt which could not be maintained—because of a price advantage in which the exporting country did not get full value for its goods. In the domestic economy that was experiencing inflation, investments usually slumped. Concentration of plant increased as those with stores of hard currencies abroad repatriated their moneys to buy up properties at low prices;[17] and many small businessmen and small savers lost heavily. It is probable that inflation so weakened the lower middle class economically and so discouraged it that its members were willing to listen to the proposals of extreme remedies offered to cure the ills of society—to the arguments for Socialism or for Fascism. Indeed, this class was less effective than it had been in bridging the gap between the very wealthy and the wageworkers. Thus, inflation had important social and political consequences, as well as being a disturbing factor in trade and payments. In its mild form it may have contributed to economic growth by "forcing" a certain amount of capital into investment, but in its extreme form it was certainly a deterrent to economic growth.

[17] The enormous holdings of Hugo Stinnes, which are said to have employed at their peak some 600,000 workers, were built up in this way.

CHAPTER 19

Economic Growth and Economic Depression

Economic Expansion in the Interbellum Period

In spite of distortions in the system of multilateral trade and payments, in spite of inflations, and in spite of wartime destruction of life and property, the first half of the interbellum period was one of economic expansion in Western culture.

Table 31. Indicators of Economic Growth

Unit	Europe						United States					
	1880	1913	1920	1929	1937	1950	1880	1913	1920	1929	1937	1950
Population (in millions)	247	340	338	365	387	391	50	97	106	122	129	151
Production of five grains (millions of metric tons)	85	117			115	106	68	105			92	139
Industrial production index (1938 = 100)	27	71	55	91	102	124	15	70	85	126	130	225

Yet the rate of economic growth in Europe (excluding the U.S.S.R.) was less than what it had been from 1880 to 1913 and decidedly less in the United States than what it had been. Moreover, some production was to replace what had been destroyed or worn out during the war and hence could not be considered as much of an increment to the stock of human goods of 1913. Nevertheless output per employed worker went up; the number of hours worked per year went down; and Western man had more leisure to devote to other interests than the sheer making of a living.[1] Moreover, there were more people to partake of the leisure,[2] with the greatest growth being registered in Southern and Eastern Europe and in the United States. Finally, populations were getting older, with the result that a larger percentage of populations were within the productive ages of 15 to 65.[3]

In the interwar period the greatest strides in production per man-hour were made in industry and services rather than in agriculture. As can be seen from Table 32, productivity per man-hour in agriculture was only about half what it was in industry, and in industry it was less than in the service trades.

Table 32. Real Product per Man-hour
(In dollars at 1926–1934 prices)

Year and Country	Agriculture	Manufacturing	Services and small-scale manufacturing
United States:			
1909–11	.181	0.402	0.782
1939–41	.282	1.070	1.241
Great Britian:			
1904–10	.145	0.176	0.411
1937	.200	0.353	0.669

SOURCE: Clark, *Conditions of Economic Progress*, pp. 316–317.

Various explanations have been offered to account for these differences. It has been said that farmers have "hidden" incomes, as from family gardens and housing, and "psychic" income, like fresh air, a variety of jobs, and time out of the working day for partaking of "rural pleasures." Nevertheless, it seems that prices paid for industrial goods and services indicated that those in these branches of the economy were in a stronger position in society to get more per unit of human input than those in agriculture.

[1] The average annual rate of industrial growth as a percentage, 1913 to 1936–1938, of output per man in Western Europe was 1 per cent and of output per working hour was 1.8 per cent.
In the United States the rate of growth in the same period was 1.3 per cent per man and 4.4 per cent per working hour.
[2] During World War I the population of Europe fell some two million.
[3] There were not yet enough unproductive aged to constitute a serious economic burden.

Table 33. Percentage Distribution of Gainful Workers by Occupational Divisions in the United States

Year	Agri-culture	Forestry and fisheries	Mining	Manufacturing and mechanical industries	Con-struction	Trans-portation and com-munication	Trade	Public service (not included elsewhere)	Profes-sional services	Domestic and person-al service
1850	63.6	0.4	1.1	16.3		0.5	4.0		12.2	9.7
1860	58.9	0.4	1.6	18.3		0.7	4.0		12.4	8.8
1870	53.0	0.5	1.4	20.5		4.2	6.8	0.7	2.6	9.6
1880	49.4	0.6	1.7	22.1		4.8	7.9	0.8	3.2	9.7
1890	42.6	0.8	1.9	23.7		6.0	8.8	0.9	3.8	10.1
1900	37.5	0.7	2.4	24.8		6.7	10.6	1.0	4.1	10.1
1910	31.0	0.6	2.6	28.5		7.1	9.7	1.2	4.6	8.0
1920	27.0	0.6	2.6	30.3		7.3	10.1	1.7	5.1	10.1
1930	21.4	0.5	2.0	28.9		7.9	12.5	1.8	6.7	
1940*	16.8	0.3	2.08	22.4	6.58	7.78	13.4			
1950*	14.5		1.75	28.8	4.48	7.77	18.44			

* Revised headings.

422

Table 33. Percentage Distribution of Gainful Workers by Occupational Divisions in the United States (*Continued*)

Year	Clerical occupations	Finance and real estate	Educational service	Other prof. service	Domestic service	Personal service	Government not elsewhere classified	Not allocated
1850								
1860								
1870	0.6							
1880	0.9							
1890	2.0							
1900	2.5							
1910	4.6							
1920	7.3							
1930	8.2							
1940*		2.9	3.15	4.35	4.89	5.81	3.17	
1950*		3.51		9.23			11.45	6.19

* Revised headings.

Under the given price conditions which existed, it is not surprising that the occupational distribution of the population continued to show percentagewise a drift away from agriculture to industry and the services. In Europe (excluding the U.S.S.R.) there was an increase from 1913 to 1940 of 40 per cent in the number of workers employed outside agriculture. In the United States, the trends away from agriculture and toward the services were very striking. The occupational distribution of the population in America, as illustrated in Table 33, when considered along with productivity per occupation (Table 32), provides further evidence of the extraordinary results which can be achieved by an extreme division of labor.

Increases in the division of labor were made possible primarily by an extension of the market economy, by an expansion in the use of money as a medium of exchange, by improvements in transportation made possible by the motor truck, the motor car, and high-tension electrical transmission lines, and by a greater specialization of skills as work became more technical. Sales of goods through stores increased at a faster rate than income and population. The number of ton-miles carried by Amer-

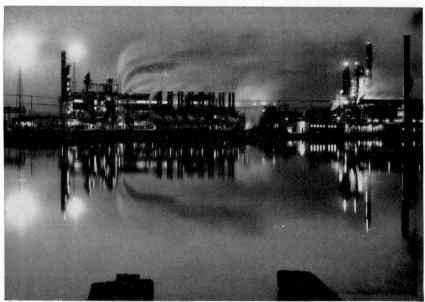

Petroleum Refining. An ethylene plant, one of many units in a large petroleum refinery in Texas. This picture shows the highly intricate and at the same time colossal equipment of modern plants. Operations in refineries are usually continuous. They are frequently located so as to permit transportation of their manufactured products by tanker or barge. (*Courtesy of the Gulf Oil Corporation.*)

ican railroads went up from 301.7 billion in 1913 to 740.5 billion in 1944 under the pressure of war, that carried by motor truck increased from almost nothing in 1913 to 48.5 billion in 1940, that of inland waterways (including the Great Lakes) rose to 117.3 billion in 1940, and that by pipelines to 71.3 billion in 1940. The amount of electricity generated in the United States increased from 24.7 billion kilowatthours in 1912 to 146.5 billion kilowatthours in 1937, and to 279.5 billion kilowatthours in 1944, which meant that large amounts of power were available in many more localities than ever before. Finally, the increasing specialization of tasks in the United States finds confirmation in the fall of the proportion of common laborers (other than farm laborers) in the total working population from 14.6 per cent in 1920 to 10.7 per cent in 1940, in the growth of technical education, and in the increased numbers going to school, especially to advanced educational institutions.[4]

New Industrial Technology

Accompanying the ever more extensive division of labor in the realization of greater productivity per man was the development of a technology based upon the tried and proved principle of using more machines to perform human tasks, the driving of these machines by mechanical power, the standardization of products, the "rationalization of production" along lines prescribed by scientific management, and the development of processes for rendering useful to man ever-increasing amounts of inorganic substances.

Among the new machines which now came into general use were rotary kilns in the cement industry, continuous rolling mills in steelmaking, and the electrical furnace for making various products where the elimination of impurities resulting from the combination of coke was desirable. Among new products that contributed to economic growth were airplanes, which greatly facilitated travel and the transportation of goods high in value and low in weight,[5] radios, which not only created an entirely new and vast industry but also opened a new era in mass communications, and business machines, which made the record keeping imposed by the extreme division of labor both more accurate and more efficient.

[4] In the United States the number of university students per thousand of the population went up from 4.21 in 1913 to 7.88 in 1930, and in France it rose from 1.040 in 1910 to 1.881 in 1932. In Italy in 1954 there are actually more students enrolled in "technical schools" than in the traditional secondary schools.

[5] Revenue miles flown in the United States' domestic traffic went up from 4,318,087 in 1926, to 110,101,039 in 1940, to 208,969,279 in 1945, and to 687,614,000 in 1955.

Production was further increased by a whole series of new processes, many of which were made possible by a greater use of chemical research. Thus in the refining of petroleum, it became possible to obtain a larger percentage of the commercially desirable gasoline by cracking, that is, by heating the raw material under pressure in the presence of a catalyst. Nitrogen in large quantities began to be obtained from the atmosphere by fixation, wood pulp was bleached by new and more economical methods, aluminum was refined by lower-cost procedures, and rayon-making processes were continually improved. The invention of plastics gave mankind an entirely new product that was to find employment in a great array of things from clothing fibers to automobile bodies. The development of mechanical (chemical) refrigeration allowed greater concentration and a greater division of labor in the production and distribution of fresh vegetables and meats. And new methods of low-cost packaging produced profound changes in marketing, especially in foods, where the self-service supermarket forecast the store of the future.

Increases in production resulting from rationalization were to be found on every hand. Sometimes the steps taken were to eliminate unprofitable enterprises, as in the British coal-mining industry in which an official Coal Mines Reorganization Committee was created (1930) to shut down uneconomical mines. Sometimes rationalization operated to step up production by the use of the moving assembly line, by a better layout of work to reduce human movements, and by a more extensive use of power tools. In coal mining a greater employment of the conveyor belt, the cutting machines, compressed air, and electric transportation about doubled the output per man-hour in the United States from 1914 to 1940. Sometimes rationalization took the form of introducing material-saving methods rather than laborsaving devices, as in the use of coal, where more and more coal was processed before being burned. In the Ruhr, by 1938 about 85 per cent of all coal was coked. Furnaces were constructed so that they could be fed by mechanical stokers or by blowing coal dust into them; fuel economies were so extensive that the amount of coal needed to produce 1 kilowatthour of electricity in central stations in America fell from 7.05 pounds in 1899 to 1.25 pounds in 1946. At times rationalization meant making such innovations as the placing of diesel engines in ships to save space and the inconvenience of soot. At other times it meant introducing friction-reducing devices, like roller bearings in existing machines. Sometimes it meant rearranging work so that there would be a continuous flow from start to finish.

Lastly, production was considerably increased by the standardization of products—a step that was necessary to realize the advantage of mass production. All too frequently custom had resulted in the continuation of various types of goods that served no useful purpose and satisfied no style demand. Thus in German coal mining 100 different models of picks had been in use before World War I and some of them had been produced by handicraft methods, whereas only three different types had any functional purpose and these three could be produced on a large scale and at a great reduction in cost. The standardization of automobiles by such far-seeing entrepreneurs as Henry Ford in America and André Citroën in France contributed much to making the automobile an article of mass consumption. A reduction in the number of types of coal cars in Germany from 175 to 3 effected an enormous saving. Standardization of sizes gave a fillip to the ready-made clothing industry. Standardized products generally made possible the chain department store, which greatly reduced the costs of distribution.

Changes in Agricultural Production between the Wars

The great strides forward in industrial production were not matched in Western culture by advances in agriculture. In Europe, agricultural production at the end of the interwar period was only some 20 to 30 per cent greater than in the 1909–1913 period, and in the United States, it was only some 30 to 38 per cent greater. Increases in output per worker were greater in industry than in agriculture in Britain, the former having risen 200 per cent from the eve of World War I to the eve of World War II and the latter only 20 per cent. Even in the United States, where farmers did particularly well compared with other countries, production per worker in agriculture went up only some 40 per cent from 1910 to 1935.

The chief reason for the relatively small growth in agricultural production per worker was lack of mechanization of operations. This lack may be explained by the very nature of farm tasks, many of which do not lend themselves readily or completely to mechanical performance. Furthermore, mechanization required capital investment which was beyond the means of small farms and which could never be amortized by farms on marginal lands. Finally, in the interbellum period the fact that agricultural prices fell much lower than industrial prices and that profits in agriculture were low tended to discourage risk capital from doing much to modernize farms.[6]

---

[6] In the United States the "parity ratio," that is, the ratio of what farmers received for their produce divided by what they paid for goods purchased (1910–1914 = 100), fell to 55 in 1932 and did not exceed 100 until well into World War II. In Germany, the index of wholesale prices for agricultural goods dropped from 100 in 1924 to 60 in 1932, while that for agricultural machinery never went below 86.

In spite of all these difficulties some mechanization did take place in agriculture. Electricity was widely installed on farms and used to perform many tasks in addition to lighting. More sanitary methods were employed in handling milk. On-the-farm refrigeration made possible the better handling of other perishable products. Field machines were more widely used, and the tractor effected a veritable agricultural revolution. The introduction of a field power plant meant the use of whole series of subsidiary machines, like plows, harrows, seeders, cultivators, and harvesters, and large enough farms to permit a full use of the equipment to produce a profit.[7] The extent of the tractor revolution may be seen in Table 34.

Table 34. Tractors in Europe and the United States

Area	Number of tractors, in thousands			Hectares of land per tractor		
	1930	1939	1951	1930	1939	1951
Europe	130	270	963	1,277	615	171
United States	1,020*	1,597*	3,800	217*	138*	53

* Including Canada.

Furthermore, agricultural output was increased by a greater use of commercial fertilizers, by better strains of plants, and by better breeds of and better feed for livestock. World production of potash (K_2O content) (excluding the U.S.S.R.) increased from 2,320,000 metric tons in 1936 to 6,300,000 in 1956, that of phosphate rock went up from 9,087,000 metric tons in 1936 to 24,900,000 in 1956, and that of nitrogen fertilizers rose from 2,400,000 metric tons in 1938 to 6,300,000 in 1956. Seedsmen marketed carefully prepared and selected seeds, including hybrid seeds, which provided hardier, healthier, and more productive plants. A 10 per cent increase in corn production in the United States from 1938–1940 to 1945 was attributed to hybrid seed alone; yields of all crops showed some increase except in those places where there was a great increase in marginal land under cultivation. Lastly, animal geneticists discovered that certain animals could produce offspring with special characteristics, such as laying more and larger eggs, producing a large quantity of milk, or of having bigger cuts of desired meat. And by an ingenious method of record keeping they were able to determine what animals should be bred. One hybrid breed of poultry produced 17 per cent more eggs than its

[7] Cooperatives might buy machinery for the use of their members. Individuals with equipment might do custom work for others, or governments might set up tractor stations for collective farms, but none of these systems proved particularly successful.

parents and one herd of cows increased its milk production by 20 per cent in twenty years with no change in feed.

In spite of a certain success in increasing yields of crops and of animals, farmers were badgered by a multitude of problems in the interbellum period. In the first place, measures to augment production required capital outlays that farmers frequently met by borrowing. Then, with the fall in agricultural prices and with the changed relationship between the prices which they charged for what they sold and those which they paid for what they bought, their predicament became grave. In Germany, the interest burden borne by farmers increased 236 per cent from 1924 to 1932, and in the relatively good year of 1928 debt payments and taxes are said to have taken 69 per cent of farmers' income. In the United States 27.8 of every thousand farms with mortgages had their mortgages foreclosed in 1924. Such conditions led in most places to governmental price-fixing arrangements, to subsidies to farmers, to tariff protection, and to governmental loans for farming. In the United States the government guaranteed prices on designated goods, beginning in 1933, in order to maintain a given level of parity;[8] in Great Britain, a traditional fortress of free trade, high tariff rates were levied on basic agricultural imports.

In the second place, agriculture was upset by shifts in diets and changes in the patterns of international trade. From the period 1910–1913 to the period 1934–1938, when the population of Europe increased 13 per cent, the consumption of wheat and rye per capital of the population fell by 9 per cent. Because people ate more animal products, fruits, and vegetables, most of which could be produced advantageously in areas of intensive agriculture, grain-growing areas were put under a handicap. Their salvation lay in mechanization and large-scale operations. Then to make matters worse, the greater decline of agricultural prices than of industrial prices placed nations that specialized in agricultural exports at a disadvantage. Thus the net exports of five major grains from the United States and Canada fell by two-thirds from 1925–1929 to 1934–1938 and those from Russia fell from 10,500,000 metric tons in 1909–1913 to 1,200,000 in 1935–1938. Denmark, an agricultural exporting nation, experienced a decline in its exports from an index of 149 in 1929 (1913 = 100) to 81 in 1933. Britain, an industrial exporting nation, saw its index of finished goods exports fall from 163 in 1929 (1913 = 100) to 124 in 1933.

Part of the difficulty of international trade in agricultural products could be accounted for by government agricultural policies, for many nations embarked on definite plans to increase their self-sufficiency in foodstuffs. They not only adopted high tariffs, but also regulated imports

[8] See p. 439, n. 19.

by quotas and currency controls, engaged in land reclamation projects,[9] and granted subventions of various types in order to stimulate the kind of production desired. Such programs usually resulted, however, in high-cost products, prices of wheat in Berlin and Paris being about twice what they were in Liverpool or the United States in 1935, and they did not lead to complete self-sufficiency, as can be seen in Table 35.

Table 35. Self-sufficiency in Foodstuffs, 1937

Country	Per cent of total consumption produced at home
Great Britain	25
Netherlands	67
Germany (1934 boundaries)	83
France	83
Italy	95
U.S.S.R.	101
United States	95

Furthermore, in order to take care of a certain number of the unemployed and to retard the rural exodus, most states favored small farms and the breaking up of large estates. Nevertheless, the drift of population from the countryside to the city continued and production on small farms remained high-cost except for crops which required a great amount of labor in relation to the value of the product. Thus poultry farming, dairying, truck farming, and small-fruit growing might be conducted successfully on small farms, but not grain growing, sheep raising, or beef-cattle grazing. From an economic point of view, it seemed desirable that governmental agricultural policies should be flexible enough to aim for greater general economic output per capita and not simply temporary supports for high-cost producers. At least, this seemed desirable so long as world production of food was sufficient to meet people's needs, so long as this food could be distributed by multilateral trade, and so long as alternate ways for more effective use of labor and capital existed.

The Great Depression of the 1930s: Its Nature

Despite growth in agricultural production, industrial expansion, and the remarkable economic recovery after World War I, undoubtedly the

[9] In the Netherlands, for example, a dike was built across the mouth of the Zuider Zee. In Italy, drainage projects like that in the Pontine Marshes, and irrigation systems like that in the Puglia Plain, added appreciable amounts of arable. In the United Kingdom, the amount of arable was increased by 40 per cent from 1934–1938 to 1948–1952, chiefly by taking land from pastures and forests. In the United States, a contrary movement was under way, that is, an effort was made to reduce arable so that crops which could not be exported would not be grown.

The Depression of the Thirties in the United States. The depression was so devasting that the unemployed had recourse to all kinds of expedients. One was selling apples, which were overproduced, on the streets of large cities. The vendors here look as though they had been accustomed to better things. (*World Wide Photos.*)

single most important event of the interbellum period was the deep economic depression of the 1930s. It disclosed with glaring lucidity a failure of Western man so to organize his economy that moments of "boom and bust" would be eliminated. It gave great impetus to state intervention in economic affairs, or put negatively, to a marked decrease in the free operation of economic forces. It gave a fillip to the creation of the "welfare state"—to a recognition that political entities should be responsible for the material well-being of their citizens—and to state participation in economic activity, to state ownership, operation, and control. It created, or drew so taut, social and economic tensions within states that to some segments of society regimes based on force seemed eminently desirable to preserve "order." And it augmented rivalries among states, as indicated by the coining of such catch phrases as the "have not" versus the "have" nations, and it thus contributed directly to World War II.

Economic depressions, as one phase of the business cycle, were obviously not new in Western culture, but the one of the 1930s was exceptional because of its impact on all parts of the West and because of its extreme severity. Although the downward movement of the curve of business activity was first manifested in the United States, declines soon set in in every economy of Western culture. Real national income fell in the United States from 100 in 1925–1929 to a low of 68 in 1931, which was comparable to the decline in national income in France during World War I. It declined in Gemany to 80 in 1932; in France it went down to 91 in 1936. Unemployment in the United States rose from 429,000 in 1929 to nearly 12,000,000 in 1933 out of a total labor force of 48,000,000. For all of Western Europe unemployment rose from 3,500,000 in the period 1921–1925 to a seasonal peak of 15,000,000 at the end of 1932. In the extreme case of Germany, at the latter date 43 per cent of the labor force was without work. In the United States bankruptcies increased by a third from 1929 to 1932. Wholesale prices fell from 95.3 in 1929 (1926 = 100) to 64.8 in 1932; the index of industrial production declined from 311 in 1929 to 192 in 1933, and the index of investments fell from a high of 178 in 1929 (1920 = 100) to 50 in 1933. World trade declined by more than 20 per cent from 1920–1929 to 1931–1935.

Although the factors which contributed to the steep fall in business activity were exceedingly numerous and their interrelationships extremely complex, it is possible to indicate some of the main forces that led to the disaster. In the first place, production of some goods, like the grains, copper, and cotton in the United States and of war matériel in all belligerent countries, was greatly expanded during the first world conflagration, but the effective demand for these goods, at least where they were being produced, fell off drastically after 1918 and adjustments in the immediate postwar depression of 1921 to the new situation were not adequate.

In the second place, rapid expansion of plant took place in the "torrid twenties," as Western Europe bent its energies on reconstruction and the United States developed its industry to meet demands that could not for the time being be satisfied by Europe. In the third place, reparations, war debts, inflation, and subsequent stabilization, frequently at exchange rates that were unrealistic in terms of prices, upset both international and domestic trade and subsequently had an effect upon production. And in the fourth place, a stock market boom in the United States carried the index of 421 common stocks from 100 in 1926 to 225 in September, 1929, while speculators borrowed money at 10 per cent in order to buy stocks that at current earnings would have paid them only 2 per cent at existing prices.

Although under these circumstances wages and wholesale prices of most commodities remained freely steady and agricultural prices were decidedly weak, rates at which entrepreneurs borrowed money to expand business activity became higher; the general costs of doing business rose to a point at which entrepreneurs hesitated to go more deeply into debt to increase the output of goods which they feared would not be absorbed by the market. In fact, buyer resistance began to be apparent in several lines and some inventories became excessive after 1926. Then in September, 1929, the "bubble" on the New York Stock Exchange burst. Between September 3 and November 13 share values on the Exchange fell by 30 billion dollars[10] and by June, 1932, had reached an index of 34 (1926 = 100). This decline turned the earlier optimism of businessmen regarding the future of business activity into rank pessimism, if not into panic. It induced lenders, especially banks, to restrict their loans and to demand repayment whenever possible, but some, like the *Creditanstalt* in Austria,[11] did not act soon enough and failed, bringing down with them many of their creditors. Bank failures and restrictions on credit set up a chain reaction which forced many businessmen to close their doors and thus to turn their workers into unemployed.

What governments should do in the face of such a large-scale economic breakdown was not clear, although it soon was only too apparent that they had to do something. They could not rely on the free operation of the system to make the necessary readjustments in a short enough period of time to prevent social unrest and perhaps the overthrow of existing political and economic regimes. All states of Western culture soon adopted the position that political intervention in economic matters was essential—that they had a responsibility for the welfare of their citizens, which is a basic tenet of the "welfare state," and that they must, by whatever means they had at their disposal, get their economies to running properly once again.

Moreover, it was abundantly clear that the economic problems of the day would not be attacked on an international basis for the good of all, but that they would be dealt with by individual nations taking unilateral action. Thus economic difficulties tended to worsen international economic relations and they aggravated political tensions among states. In fact, they contributed much to the situation in which World War II erupted.

Just how far states should go in establishing controls of their economies and what administrative machinery should be created to give economic direction were practical issues throughout the 1930s. There were those, especially the Communists and some Socialists, who believed that the system of private capitalism had outlived its usefulness and that in its place should be created a system in which the state would own and manage the means of production and distribution for the well-being of all. Then there were those, the Fascists, who held that the interests of the state were superior to the interests of the individual, that economic policies could best be formulated by representatives of interest groups—employers, employees, and state officials—organized for each major in-

[10] They had gone up 51 billion dollars in the twenty months preceding September.

[11] This bank had been founded by the Rothschilds in 1855. It was large and hitherto had been successful.

dustry, and that, although the institution of private property should be preserved, the state should aid, control, or seize properties in order to increase its economic and military strength. Lastly, there were those who thought that the economic situation could be saved without any structural changes, but by temporary governmental assistance to private concerns, especially by loans, tax relief, and limiting supplies of goods going to market.

The proposals made by Communists were not adopted in any part of Western culture. Property owners were generally opposed to them and nonpropertied, salaried workers were not generally convinced of their efficacy. They seemed to run counter to a well-established respect for private initiative and they had, as practiced by the only state which followed them, the Union of Soviet Socialist Republics, become entangled with concepts of dictatorship. In Russia not only had the state taken over the chief means of producing and distributing goods and services, but it had concentrated on the development of basic industries necessary for the production of more machines and the sinews of war rather than on the production of goods to satisfy human wants. Moreover, the Communist Party, which numbered only 2 million out of a total population of 170 million in 1936, and Joseph Stalin, who dominated the Party from 1925 until his death in 1953, determined policy, enforced it relentlessly, and permitted only members of the bureaucracy to enjoy a really high standard of living. Many Socialists were of the opinion that the millennium of which they dreamed should come by gradual reform and they were willing to make compromises with their plans for reaching their ultimate goal by accepting immediately and peacefully attained advantages. Indeed, during the depression of the thirties Western European Socialism shifted from the rigidities of Marxian logic and Marxian ultimates to a kind of reformism based on economic planning and the welfare state.

Changes proposed by Fascists were not so drastic as those advanced by Communists and had the support of persons already in high authority in certain countries of the West. The model to which these supporters of authoritarianism, statism, and corporatism looked was that of Italy, where the Fascists of Benito Mussolini had seized power in 1922 to prevent, so they claimed, the triumph of international Socialism and where they had created under the stress of labor difficulties and retarded economic development a corporate state.[12]

[12] Society was organized into "corporations," that is, bodies representing employers, employees, and the Fascist Party for the major categories of economic activity. By 1934 there were twenty-two such bodies. They were to handle labor disputes, plan the activity of their division of the economy, and provide representatives to the legislative body of the nation. Fundamental decisions were, however, made by political leaders.

The state where dictatorship along Fascist lines was most completely established was Germany. There National Socialists under Adolf Hitler came to power in 1933. All labor unions were done away with as in Italy, and were replaced by the state-controlled Labor Front. Property owners were organized according to their calling into the Estate of Trade and Industry, the Estate of Transportation, the Estate of Agriculture; artists, teachers, professional men, and journalists became members of the Chamber of Culture. In fact, however, the entire economy was run by the dictatorship, with Hermann Göring as the chief economic potentate after February, 1938.

In other states, where the traditions of representative government and the right of individuals to life, liberty, and property prevailed, such extreme attempts at political control of the economy were not made. Yet in these states there was considerable agitation for reforms either in the direction of state socialism or of authoritarianism and there were many new policies adopted which deviated widely from liberal political and economic theory and practice.

The Great Depression: The Remedies

Whatever political expedient was used to meet the existing crisis, economic measures in various countries had a considerable degree of similarity. To meet credit stringencies occasioned by the collapse of stock prices and by the calling in of loans by banks, most states declared brief debt moratoria, had their central banks extend credit, created specialized lending agencies to assist the hardest-pressed branches of their economies, devalued their currencies in an effort to raise prices, to reduce the burden of debt, and to encourage exports,[13] and limited imports by raising customs duties or by adopting import quotas.

In the United States, for example, all banks were temporarily closed in March, 1933, when Franklin D. Roosevelt was inaugurated President and they were only gradually reopened as they could show evidence of being able to meet their obligations.[14] Furthermore, more power was given to the Federal Reserve System in order to regulate the flow of credit and presumably thereby to exercise control over business activity.

[13] Higher prices meant, for example, that if a farmer raising pigs got 12 instead of 6 cents a pound for his porkers, he could pay off whatever debt he had with half the number of pigs than at the lower price.

Devaluation was expected to give temporary encouragement to exports in that prices would not go up so fast as exchange rates. Some states, especially Germany, attempted to stimulate exports by giving special exchange rates for the purchase of German goods and by making bilateral barter agreements.

[14] Federal Deposit Insurance was instituted by the Glass-Steagall bill on June 16, 1933. It insured deposits up to 5,000 dollars.

TVA's Kentucky Dam. TVA was an antidepression effort, as well as a project to reduce danger from floods, to improve inland navigation, and to develop the economy of an underdeveloped area. This dam is located on the Tennessee River near its mouth in Kentucky. It creates a reservoir 184 miles long. By regulating the flow of the Tennessee at the dam, crests on the Ohio and Mississippi can be lowered 4 feet. The dam makes possible generating capacity of 160,000 kilowatts. (*Courtesy of the Tennessee Valley Authority.*)

In France, the number of governmentally appointed representatives of the Board of Regents of the Bank of France was increased (1936) in order to insure the adoption of more socially desirable credit policies; in Belgium the bank reform of 1935 aimed at greater liquidity for banks, better managements, and a control of the money flow to influence the course of business activity. Devaluations of currencies were effected. In 1933–1934, the United States reduced the dollar in terms of gold by about 41 per cent. England left the gold standard in 1931 and subsequently devalued by 30 per cent. France devalued in 1936 and again in 1938 and the Netherlands and several other nations in 1936.[15]

In the United States immediate relief was given to the unemployed by creating the Civilian Conservation Corps (1933) for reforestation, flood, prevention, and soil erosion control, by launching a public works program (Public Works Administration, 1933), by setting up a Works Progress Administration (1935) for the employment of intellectuals and

[15] A World Economic Conference was held in London in June, 1933, but it failed to bring order into the chaos of money. In 1937, the United Kingdom, the United States, and France made a Tripartite Agreement to keep steady the relationship of the dollar, pound, and franc.

Land Reclamation in the Zuider Zee, the Netherlands. This photograph shows part of the Northeast Polder of the Zuider Zee, which only a few years ago was under the sea. The salt has been leached out of the soil, the land has been allocated to farmers, and production has begun on the "family farm" basis of organization. (*Courtesy of the Netherlands Information Service.*)

artists as well as manual laborers, and by beginning work on such great projects as the Tennessee Valley Authority and large dams in the West.[16]

In Europe, unemployment insurance schemes helped alleviate the plight of workers, especially in Great Britain where 63 per cent of the gainfully employed were covered and where public moneys were used to continue payments beyond existing reserves. In most states, however, public works projects were resorted to as unemployment continued to be a serious threat to social and political order. In Italy, considerable numbers of men were used on draining swamps and building roads. In Germany, many men were absorbed by the remilitarization of the country. In the Netherlands, workers found jobs in conjunction with the reclamation of the Zuider Zee. And in France, they were employed in building the Maginot Line, a heavily fortified military line facing Ger-

[16] Also set up were the Federal Emergency Relief Administration (May, 1933) to supplement direct relief provided by individual states and the Civil Works Administration in the winter of 1933–1934 to provide temporary employment on public works.

many from the Swiss border to the Ardennes, or in constructing such dams as the Genissiat on the Upper Rhone River.

Of greater long-range significance was the tendency for states to buy securities of ailing business concerns or to lend them so much money that governments acquired a direct voice in business management. In the United States the Reconstruction Finance Corporation with resources of 4 billion dollars was established (1932) by the government to make loans to business concerns. In Italy, the Institute for Reconstruction of Industry (IRI) was set up (1933) to give financial assistance to Italian industries— an action which was so enormous that by 1937 the state had an interest in 40 per cent of all Italian corporations. In France, the government lent money to all its important shipping companies, to civil aviation concerns, to railways, and to banks. Great Britain made loans to complete the construction of the *Queen Mary*. Austria guaranteed to cover the obligations of the *Creditanstalt*. Germany financed such projects as the hydrogenation of coal in order to have a national supply of gasoline.

In almost all countries agriculture received very special treatment, because of the particularly disastrous financial plight of farmers, because of a desire to maintain a large farm population for sentimental, social, and political reasons, and in part, because of a hope to attain greater national self-sufficiency in foodstuffs. In the United Kingdom, prices for the major grains were guaranteed beginning with the Wheat Act of 1932, and agricultural production was given protection of high tariffs and quotas, a policy which not only definitely broke Britain's low-tariff tradition but which also made possible a granting of preferential treatment to goods coming into the United Kingdom.[17]

Denmark endeavored to alter its agricultural production, reducing what it had exported and increasing what it had imported. Thus it brought down the number of pigs from 5 to 3 million by rationing the number which could be sold. It diminished the number of cattle by purchasing and slaughtering females with funds obtained by a tax on slaughtering, and it increased the output of beet sugar until the country was self-sufficient. France gave subsidies to winegrowers for pulling up vines, discouraged the production of low-grade wines, limited the percentage of flour that might be obtained from wheat, and supported the prices of various agricultural products. Like the United Kingdom, the Netherlands gave up free trade by protecting its agriculture and, like Denmark, tried to shift production to meet domestic needs. And Germany expanded output, temporarily required farm laborers to remain in farming, and protected small holdings by the Inherited Freehold Act (1933)

---

[17] This system was inaugurated by the Ottawa Agreements in 1932. Hitherto members of the empire could give preferences to English-made goods, but the United Kingdom could offer no substantial tariff advantages in return.

Contour Planting. This photograph shows tomato plants "contour" planted, on ground that was "contour" plowed and that is being "contour" irrigated. Water is brought to the ditches by a simple wooden V trough. The contour system helps to prevent erosion from water. (*Courtesy of the U.S. Department of Agriculture.*)

—a law which forbade owners from mortgaging their holdings, from selling portions of their farms, from breaking them up at inheritance, or from restricting production on pain of forfeiting their titles.

In the United States, where the market was glutted with staples and where prices had fallen to a ridiculously low level, President Roosevelt's New Deal aimed at bringing production more nearly into line with demand and at raising prices by placing a tax on processors, as was being done in England,[18] in order to get funds which could be used to compensate farmers who voluntarily reduced production. This restrictive policy raised a hue and cry as little pigs were done away with and big land companies got huge payments for *not* raising crops. But it was persisted in, for when the Supreme Court declared (1936) the enabling law to be unconstitutional on the ground that it infringed states' rights, Congress immediately passed the Soil Conservation and Domestic Allotments Act which provided for payments from funds voted by Congress to farmers for diverting acreage from overproduced crops to soil-conserving crops and for adopting soil-building practices.[19] Finally, the New Deal en-

[18] For example, 30 cents a bushel was charged on wheat milled.

[19] The new Agricultural Adjustment Act (1938) aimed particularly at supporting prices. Loans could be made to farmers for storing surpluses in years of high output. Marketing quotas were established if two-thirds of the producers of a crop in a district agreed. Parity payments were made to producers of some crops if the relationship

deavored to lighten the financial burden on farms (about 40 per cent of them were mortgaged) by creating the Farm Credit Administration, which made loans totaling 1,200,000,000 dollars from 1933 to 1936, and to reduce "agricultural slums" by resettling farmers who were living on submarginal soils to better lands.

In addition to all these efforts to deal with the depression, the states of Western culture took steps to bring some order into labor relations. In Italy[20] and Germany, strikes and lockouts were outlawed and labor contracts were virtually forced by the state upon governmentally sponsored organizations of employers and employees. In France, the doctrine of collective bargaining, that is, of contracts between business concerns and trade unions for entire industries, was accepted by the Matignon Accords (1936)[21] and compulsory arbitration was attempted. And in the United States, the National Recovery Act (1933) required labor codes (contracts) in all major plants, thus practically forcing the formation of labor unions, and the Wagner Labor Relations Act (1935), passed when the NRA was found to be unconstitutional,[22] strengthened the bargaining position of labor.

All the various measures which were taken to cope with the depression involved a certain amount of economic planning and made apparent the necessity of "plans" if states were going to continue to intervene so extensively in their economies. Already economic planning had been given a considerable impetus in Soviet Russia, where exceptional economic progress was called for by successive five-year plans;[23] planning had been widely publicized in both Fascist Italy and Nazi Germany, where it was inherent in the corporate state system. Even in many countries, like France, where the existing system remained intact, a step toward planning was taken by the creation of advisory economic councils. These bodies represented labor, capital, consumers, and the state and were

---

between farm and industrial prices fell 75 per cent below the average of prices in the period 1910–1914.

Furthermore, the Commodity Credit Corporation (1933) did some purchasing of commodities to regulate the market. It played its most important role, however, during and after World War II.

[20] In Italy in 1926.

[21] Matignon is the name of the palace of the Premier where the agreement was signed.

[22] On the ground that Congress could not delegate legislative powers to the President.

[23] They were drafted by the "Gosplan," a planning bureau established in 1921, which was, in fact, a committee of the Council of Peoples' Commissars. It should be added that over-all planning was practically forced on the U.S.S.R. by its system of state socialism.

created for the purpose of studying national economic issues and of making recommendations to the legislative and executive branches of government.[24] The concept of economic planning was thus well established before 1939, although it was only after World War II that it became a real fetish.

To the factors which thus contributed toward extending the state's role in economic life should be added two more—preparation for war and subsequently war itself. Up to the present time, war has been the single greatest economic activity of national states. Expenditures for national defense more than doubled in the United Kingdom, France, and the U.S.S.R. from 1937 to 1939, and probably the increases in Germany and Italy were even larger. In these states expenditures for defense appear to have averaged more than half of all expenditures immediately before World War II.

These large amounts of public funds were obtained partly by taxation, partly by borrowing, and partly by the issuing of paper money. Tax rates were pushed up, especially on income taxes. New taxes, like sales taxes and taxes on bachelors, were introduced, and a few capital levies, for example in Italy, were attempted. Taxes were raised to a point where in 1937–1938 they took 28 per cent of national income in France and 23 per cent in the United Kingdom.

Borrowing was also increased so that in many states the public debt exceeded national income, that of France being 71 per cent in excess and that of the United Kingdom, 63 per cent. And in nearly all countries state treasuries got advances in currency from banks of issue in return for promises to pay, or otherwise got moneys from the fiduciary system. An increase in the supply of money was thus effected without any increase in the production of goods—and this increase meant in the long run an increase in prices.

Thus in the period between the two World Wars the national state became an economic Leviathan, completely dwarfing the primarily political monster described by Thomas Hobbes in the seventeenth century. It tried to keep relatively orderly relations between capital and labor. It effected "savings" by taxing, borrowing, or extending credit to take the place of or to supplement private savings and investment when these were considered wanting. It endeavored to direct the distribution of goods both in domestic and foreign trade. And it moved in the direction of planning the entire economic life of its citizens. Such was the economy of Western culture when World War II broke upon it.

---

[24] Trade unionists in France had been particularly active in the campaign in favor of planning. The Conféderation Générale de Travail proposed a planning body immediately after World War I.

CHAPTER 20

The Economics of World War II

World War I and World War II Compared

In many ways World War II was similar to World War I. Like its predecessor, it developed out of rivalries within the national state system —and these rivalries in both instances became crystallized into hostile blocs of Great Powers. Also like its forerunner, World War II was at the outset essentially a conflict among states in Western culture and thus from the point of view of the culture was a "civil" war. Furthermore, World War II, like World War I, devolved into a war of attrition between two great economic potentials, which led to a new extension of state control over economic life. And like its precursor, World War II was enormously destructive. In fact, by one estimate, the total cost of the war, including destruction, amounted to 3,000,000,000,000 dollars. Expenditures for war materials alone came to 1,154,000,000,000 dollars. This was at least seven times the cost of World War I and World War I had set a record in this respect. Casualties, both military and civilian, were said to have been 22,060,000 dead and 34,400,000 wounded. Millions more suffered malnutrition. Over 30,000,000 people in Europe were displaced by the conflict; and all ordinary economic relationships were gravely dislocated. World War II was a large edition of World War I. It was, indeed, a "total war."

In spite of similarities, however, there were certain differences between the two great World Wars of the first half of the twentieth century. In the first place, the Axis powers represented a set of ideologies which were more foreign to the basic tenets of Western culture than anything that Germany alone had stood for in World War I—the subordination of the individual to the state, a brazen duplicity in international relations without any regard for law or honesty,[1] and a disrespect for what the West called "human rights," life, liberty, and freedom of thought and of expression. In the second place, World War II germinated in the depression of the 1930s when several states without great natural resources (Italy and Japan) or without overseas empires (Germany) considered themselves to be deprived of what should be theirs and adopted an avowed policy of territorial aggrandisement in the belief that thereby they would achieve economic growth.[2] And in the third place, there was in World War II evidence of rivalries among great cultures, for Japan was actually an enemy of the West, and the U.S.S.R., although it fought, after being attacked, with the defenders of the Western tradition, was suspicious of its Allies to the point of being hostile to them, did little to aid their military operations, and consistently planned to take every possible advantage of them.

That there should have been a second World War after the experience with the first and in light of the basic ideologies of Western culture is, to say the least, amazing; and it is clear that the war did not elicit the popular enthusiasm that was observable in the first one. That it did occur can be attributed very largely to the fact that such leaders as Benito Mussolini and Adolf Hitler, who attained positions of great power, did not represent the traditional ideologies of the West. As dictators they were able to wield power without the ordinary restraints placed upon political leaders and they did enough for certain groups in society so that they had loyal supporters. Even so, the dictators undoubtedly expected to get what they wanted by bluff. At least in a speech broadcast in October, 1933, Hitler said,

The history of the last one hundred years should in its changing course have taught France and Germany that essential and enduring changes are no longer

[1] When Hitler informed his generals of his plans for attacking Poland, he said, "No one will ask the victor whether or not he told the truth. In starting the war it is not right that matters, but victory."

[2] In his book *Mein Kampf*, Hitler had written: "We have finished with the pre-World War I policy of colonies and trade and are going over to a land policy of the future." He was also fearful of Russia. "The political testament of Germany must always be never to tolerate the establishment of two continental powers in Europe." He was also much impressed by concepts of *Geopolitik*, as generated by a Swede named Kjellén and developed by a German, Karl Haushofer. He stated very frankly, "If the Urals with their incalcuable wealth of raw materials, the rich forests of Siberia, and the unending wheatfields of the Ukraine lay within Germany, under National Socialist leadership this country would swim in plenty."

to be gained by sacrifice of blood. . . . No one could demand that millions of men in the flower of youth should be annihilated for the sake of a readjustment of indefinite scope of our present frontiers. [And then a little later he added] I am not crazy enough to want a war. The German people have but one wish—to be happy in their own way and to be left in peace.

But the dictators carried their bluffs, if such they were, to a point where retreat was impossible without a greater loss of face than they were willing to accept.

The Military Issues

Although World War II began formally by Germany's attack on Poland, September 1, 1939, forerunners of the conflict had been clearly in evidence since 1931. Late in that year Japan attacked China in Manchuria; subsequently it attempted a conquest of the entire nation. In 1936, Germany began the remilitarization of the Rhineland contrary to the terms of the Versailles Treaty. Mussolini conquered Ethiopia. Germany and Italy sent forces to fight for General Franco in Spain, while the U.S.S.R. sent troops there to assist the Republicans. In 1938 Germany annexed Austria and, following the Munich conference, took the Sudetenland from Czechoslovakia. In 1939, Germany annexed Bohemia and Moravia and set up Slovakia as a protectorate, while Ruthenia was occupied by Hungarian troops. Germany seized Memel and a part of Lithuania. Italy anexed Albania, and Germany signed with Russia the famous Nonagression Pact. By this agreement the signatories pledged to refrain from aggressive action toward each other for ten years; both carved out spheres of influence, the Russian being east of a line running from the west of Latvia and to the west of Bessarabia and the Germans being west of that line.

With Germany's invasion of Poland, events in Eastern Europe moved with lightning rapidity. Not only was the military operation a veritable Blitzkrieg (Warsaw capitulated on September 27), but Russia invaded Poland to "protect its frontiers," virtually established its dominion over Estonia, Latvia, and Lithuania, and launched a war against Finland that continued until March, 1940. On the Western Front, however, action was initially almost nonexistent and so the war there, in contrast to that in the East, was dubbed a *Sitzkrieg* (Sit-down-war). The calm on the Western Front was, however, simply a lull before the storm. From April 9, 1940, to June 17, 1940, Germany overran Denmark, Norway, the Netherlands, Belgium, and France in quick succession. Italy, thinking that a final decision in the fighting had been reached, declared war on France and Great Britain. Hitler then turned his military force on Britain and brought Rumania, Hungary, and Bulgaria into line, while Italy attacked Yugoslavia and Greece—an effort that was not brought to a successful conclusion until Germany lent a hand (April, 1941).

In the meantime, Germany's air attack on Britain had not been equally successful. Although the raids did cause great damage, German air losses were enormous (2,375 planes up to the end of October, 1940) and the Royal Air Force had managed to give the Germans a taste of their own medicine—and it was bitter stuff. Nor had Germany's submarine campaign been overwhelmingly effective, for although many ships were sunk (twenty-nine Allied ships went to the bottom in one week in March, 1941), many ships were getting through. Moreover, President Franklin D. Roosevelt decided in the crisis to transfer a million tons of merchant shipping to Britain along with fifty overage destroyers.

From the Allied point of view, however, the most hopeful prospect for the future came from the fact that the Germans made the colossal blunder of invading Russia (June 22, 1941) and the Japanese, who were allied with Germany, had the folly to attack Pearl Harbor (December 7, 1941), thus bringing the United States into the war[3]—a situation which Hitler had recognized in *Mein Kampf* as having been disastrous to Germany in World War I and to be avoided at all costs. Undoubtedly he thought that the war in the West was actually over and that Russia, an "uncooperative ally," should be dealt with before it became militarily any stronger. Germany's invasion of Russia, in spite of the fact that it led to the conquest in five months of an area three times that of the home country, sapped Germany's strength in manpower and matériel. Moreover, the United States provided the Allies with men and goods which were eventually to overwhelm the Axis Powers.[4]

The War of Economic Potentials

By December, 1941, therefore, the Blitzkrieg-Sitzkrieg aspect of World War II was over and the struggle became one between opposing economic potentials, as had World War I after November, 1914. Some idea of the magnitudes of the opponents can be seen from Table 36. The Axis was aware of the preponderance in favor of the Allies; hence its strategy

[3] Germany by now was also involved against Yugoslavia and Greece and in Libya against Britain.

[4] Even before the attack on Pearl Harbor the United States was giving aid to the Allies. Although the Neutrality Act of 1935 required the placing of an embargo on arms to belligerents, it was gradually repealed. The United States sent munitions on a "cash and carry" basis to Britain and France (beginning November 4, 1939). Congress passed the Lend-Lease Act to send arms to the Allies in March, 1941, and it permitted American ships to enter the war zones (November, 1941).

dictated an early, final decision. The Allies' plans, on the contrary, called for a holding operation pending a build-up of matériel and the training of fighting personnel—and then the delivery of a mighty blow.

The "war of economic potentials" had four distinct aspects. In the first place, it led to the "total mobilization" of the manpower and economic

Table 36. Opposing Economic Potentials in World War II

Country	National income, millions of dollars at 1925–1934 prices	Percentage of world manufactures, 1936–1938	Population
United Nations:			
United States	66,203	32.2	131,669,000
United Kingdom	21,854	9.2	46,046,000
U.S.S.R.	17,230	18.5	170,467,000
China	?	?	450,000,000
Australia	2,543		6,630,000
Canada	5,084	2	11,507,000
New Zealand	691		1,574,000
India	?		382,000,000
Axis Powers and Axis-occupied countries:			
Germany	17,580	10.7	79,375,000
Italy	5,320	2.7	42,919,000
Japan	8,171	3.5	73,114,000
Austria	1,613		*
Czechoslovakia	2,680		14,729,000
Poland	3,428		32,107,000
Hungary	1,205		14,683,000
Rumania	1,471		13,493,000
France	12,480		41,183,000
Belgium	2,033		8,092,000
Netherlands	2,624		7,936,000
Denmark	1,008		3,844,000
Norway	607		2,814,000
Yugoslavia	1,352		13,934,000

* Included in Germany.

resources of each of the belligerents, to greater governmental controls of the various economies, and to more complete economic planning than had existed either in World War I or in the depression of the thirties. In the second place, it made urgent the reduction of the enemy's productive capacity by every possible means, especially by airplane and rocket bombings. The bombings in turn led to a policy of total destruction and this policy gave the last part of the war its most distinctive characteristic, that of a *Vernichtungskrieg*. Thirdly, it led the Axis to milk its conquered countries dry, and the Allies, because of their control of most of the seas, to draw upon the entire nonbelligerent world for supplies. And fourthly, it meant that because the Allies had to deliver goods and men overseas to fighting fronts that the Axis powers could try to prevent such deliveries by submarine and air attacks on shipping—a repetition of the naval character of World War I.

The economic controls and plans which the belligerents established resembled those of World War I, but they were more rigorous and more inclusive. Rationing of consumers' goods, especially foodstuffs, was practiced everywhere. In Europe, where food was usually imported, shortages were so great that the calorie intake of individuals was determined by one's nationality, one's age, and the extent of one's muscular output.

Table 37. Calories in Normal Consumer's Rations per Day

Country	1941	1942	1943	1944
Germany	1990	1750	1980	1930
Italy	1010	950	990	1065
Belgium	1360	1365	1320	1555
France	1365	1115	1080	1115
Poland	845	1070	855	1200

Such extraordinary curbs were placed on fats, in great demand for explosives, that at one time British miners were entitled to one small cake of soap per month. Moreover, men of military age became liable for military service or other work. Every effort was made to use manpower effectively and to augment the labor force. In the United States the number of civilian workers was increased, even though some 11 million men were under arms, by the employment of retired persons, women, and young people who normally would have been in school. Production was directed more and more toward war ends by governmental allocation of raw materials and workers, by the careful placing of governmental orders, by tax arrangements, by price fixing, by the directing of governmental investments, and by publicity. Finally, over-all plans were laid down by governments for quantities and qualities of things needed for the prosecution of the war.

Under such controls and plans remarkable results were achieved. The United States increased its production of merchant ships from 342,000 deadweight tons in 1939 to 19,238,000 tons in 1943.[5] It stepped up aircraft output from 12,804 in 1940 to 49,761 in 1945. And in addition to all

[5] During the war the United States built a total tonnage equal to some two-thirds of the world's merchant tonnage of 1939.

the war matériel it turned out, it was able to produce more civilian goods than it had prior to the conflict. Although the U.S.S.R. lost to the Germans territory accounting for 63 per cent of its coal production, 57 per cent of its steel, and 40 per cent of its arable, it built up a new industrial area in the Urals and beyond the Volga. As a result its industrial output at the end of the war was down only 8 per cent compared with that of 1939. Similarly, Japan's index of manufacturing production went from 100 in 1937 to 153 in 1944; Germany increased its coal and lignite production by 30 per cent from 1937–38 to 1943–44. In spite of such accomplishments, however, many mistakes in planning were inevitably made because of constant changes in estimates of the way the fighting was going, in types of equipment required, and in production facilities. The greatest blunder was undoubtedly perpetrated by Hitler, who ordered cutbacks in schedules of production in September, 1941, because he thought the war had been won. The resulting disorder was so extensive that a veritable crisis in German military supplies occurred in 1942.

In addition to establishing rigorous economic controls within their economies, the belligerents did their utmost to draw upon the resources of others and to pool supplies so that their stores would be used most effectively. In the case of the Axis powers, such policies meant a harsh exploitation of conquered areas and a veritable dictation by Germany and Japan of how materials should be distributed. After the defeat of France, for example, Germany seized railway rolling stock, rubber, stockpiles of gasoline, and nonferrous metals, required the payment of large indemnities which were used to purchase French goods out of current production and to acquire title to plants, established a favorable exchange rate for the mark so that Germans would be induced to purchase French goods, and set up a "clearing account" in Berlin where sums owed France were allowed to accumulate. Furthermore, the Germans required the conquered areas to send them forced labor to such an extent that at the end of the war about one in every three workers in Germany was of this category. Lastly, Germany inaugurated its long-range plan for the Continent—a plan in which Germany was to be a great industrial center and its satellites were to supply her with foodstuffs and raw materials. In this way Germany aimed to keep her potential enemies in a perpetual state of economic subordination.[6]

In the case of the Allies, or of the United Nations, as they came to be

[6] Japan's long-range plan for the East was not unlike Germany's. Japan exploited the "Co-Prosperity Sphere," that is, the areas which it had conquered, and intended to draw from the "outer zone" raw materials and foodstuffs and to process them in the "inner zone," Japan, Korea, Manchuria, and North China.

called, Interallied cooperation became the watchword of the hour. Military action and matériel needs were determined in large part by the Anglo-American Combined Chiefs of Staff in Washington (created February, 1942) which collaborated with Russia and China by means of Allied Military Missions in Moscow and Chungking. Similarly, economic cooperation was effected by the Combined Shipping Adjustment Board (January, 1942) in Washington, the Combined Raw Materials Board, the Combined Food Board, and the Combined Production and Resources Board. Then to avoid a postwar Allied war debt problem, a decision was reached to "lend-lease" materials among the Allies. Thus, the United States furnished its Allies up to July 1, 1945 with goods at a cost of 47,286,000,000 dollars, with the United Kingdom and the U.S.S.R. receiving nearly equal amounts, and obtained in reverse lend-lease goods and services valued at 7,912,000,000 dollars. Finally, the United Nations purchased heavily in the free markets of the world. The United States increased its imports at current prices by 80 per cent. The United Kingdom spent so much of its foreign investments that it became a debtor to a host of countries, including India, with which it had had for years a creditor position.

That the United Nations were able to draw on the resources of a large part of the earth and were able to maintain such a large volume of production accounts in a high degree for their final victory. Yet their superiority in matériel, especially as evidenced by firepower at the fronts, was for a long time in jeopardy. American mass-production methods required a long time to get under way and shipping losses were enormous. In fact, in 1942 25 per cent of the ships on the run to Murmansk to carry supplies to Russia were sunk and the loss of Allied and neutral shipping in 1942 was 8,338,000 gross tons.[7] Only when convoys were given adequate air protection from "baby flattops" after May, 1943, did the submarine threat seem to be met. In desperation the Germans launched against Britain (June, 1944) their famous rocket bombs, but these missiles were not accurate enough either to reduce drastically Britain's production or to destroy the vast depots of matériel ready for the trans-Channel invasion of the Continent (June 6, 1944).

Threatening as were German measures to curb Allied deliveries to war fronts and effective as was the Japanese war in drawing American supplies from Europe to the Allies' "second front," retaliatory measures of the United Nations were eventually overpowering. Not only did the Allies establish blockades of their opponents and black-list firms which dealt with Axis powers, but they launched great air attacks against their

[7] The total loss of Allied and neutral shipping up to June 13, 1945 was 21,141,000 gross tons, or about one-third of the world's prewar tonnage.

LOCALITIES WITH MINERAL EXTRACTION

☐ COAL
○ PETROLEUM
△ SEDIMENTARY NON-METALLICS
▲ PRECIOUS METALS & GEMS
● BASE METALS
✕ IRON
+ FERRO-ALLOYS
■ IGNEOUS & METAMORPHIC NON-METALS

World Resources.

REGIONS OF COMMERCIAL LUMBERING & FISHING

REGIONS OF PRIMARY COMMERCIAL FOREST PRODUCTION, & REGIONS WITHIN THE RANGE OF PRESENT COMMERCIAL OPERATIONS

FOREST BEYOND THE RANGE OF PRESENT COMMERCIAL OPERATIONS

PRIMARY COMMERCIAL FISHERIES: SHORE ESTUARINE, & HIGH SEA

SECONDARY COMMERCIAL FISHERIES

LOCAL FISHERIES USING MOSTLY PRIMITIVE EQUIPMENT WITHOUT MODERN PROCESSING

World Resources.

Effects of Aerial Bombing in World War II. The devasting effects of strategic bombing are vividly portrayed in this picture. This town in Germany was completely obliterated. (*World Wide Photos.*)

enemies. They threw Germany and Italy out of North Africa and invaded the Italian Peninsula. Later, they knocked Japan out of the war by dropping the first nuclear bombs.

The air forces of the Allies in the West flew nearly one and a half million bomber sorties to the Continent and dropped over two and a half million tons of bombs. At first both the British and American air forces tried daylight "pin-point" bombing, but soon, because of heavy losses, gave up this tactic for saturation bombing. Consequently whole areas were laid waste. In August, 1943, an attack on Hamburg destroyed one-third of all dwellings and killed between 60,000 and 100,000 civilians.[8]

Target priorities in this great air war changed with military exigencies. Early in 1943 special attention was given to submarine building yards and aircraft factories. In May, 1944, oil plants became an objective of first consideration, and in September, 1944, transportation was bombed heav-

---

[8] Air raiders also took their toll of Axis shipping in the Baltic, North, and Mediterranean Seas, the Royal Air Force bagging 750,000 tons in the first half of 1942.

ily in order to prevent the massing of men and matériel to meet the invaders who had landed in Normandy in June. How effective was this strategic bombing has been the object of considerable controversy, but no one who visited the Continent, especially Germany, after the cessation of hostilities could help but be appalled by the extent of the destruction. In the case of oil plants, every major establishment was hit by July, 1944, and the production of aviation gasoline fell from 175,000 tons in April, 1944, to 5,000 tons in September. In the case of transportation, freight carloadings declined from 900,000 cars a week in August, 1944, to 214,000 cars during the week of March 3, 1945, coal traffic was practically stopped by February, 1945, and the movement of troops by rail became extremely slow and cumbersome.

In the Pacific, bombings of the Japanese homeland were begun in earnest with the conquest of Okinawa (April–June, 1945), for thereby the United States got a base within easy striking distance of the central Japanese Islands. Air attack reached its climax with the use of the first nuclear weapons. The atom bomb which hit Hiroshima was said to have killed 80,000 out of a population of 245,000, to have seriously injured another 80,000, and to have destroyed 60 per cent of all buildings; the bomb dropped on Nagasaki killed 40,000, injured an equal number, and so demoralized the entire nation that the Japanese government decided at once to sue for peace.

In addition to the havoc wrought by strategic air and rocket attacks, there was the destruction by the more traditional weapons of land forces. All resistance points were heavily shelled and reduced to shambles, as at Cassino, Salerno, Anzio, and Pisa in Italy, at Cherbourg and Sedan in France, and at Saarbrucken and Aachen in Germany.

Thus the productive capacity of the Axis powers and their occupied areas was reduced at the very time when Germany's overextended lines were demanding ever greater deliveries of goods and when workers on the home front were so driven that they needed more nourishment than they were getting to maintain their energies and more goods to keep up their morale. Through destroying the economies of their enemies and through increasing their own production of goods, as well as by victories in the field, did the United Nations win the war.

The Economic Consequences of the War

The destruction which has just been mentioned was one of the most obvious economic results of the second great war of the twentieth century. Desolation was the hallmark of the fighting, but in addition much capital equipment which remained standing had run down because of poor maintenance practices. Furthermore, Europe's stock of raw materials had become so exhausted and the long "pipelines" of supply had become so empty that some time and much capital were needed to fill them again. Finally, agricultural land that had not been laid waste had been overcropped and deprived of its usual supplies of commercial fertilizers, and livestock populations had been depleted because of the pressure for food. Thus it is not surprising that both the industrial and agricultural production of the European nations had greatly decreased, whereas that of the overseas areas, which were sources of supply, as in the case of the United States and Canada, had grown at a rapid rate. To be sure some capital investment had been made in Europe during

Table 38. Indices of Production

Country	Industry (1953 = 100)			Wheat production (1934–1938 = 100)
	1938	1946	1948	1947
Germany, West	78		41	48
Italy	62		62	63
Austria	59		54	
Japan	88	24	38	
France	71	60	81	40
Belgium	71	63	87	
United Kingdom	71	72	83	
United States	36	67	78	191
U.S.S.R.	30	29	45	
Canada	41	69	79	129

the war, but for the most part it was very spotty. Thus there was little expansion in materials-producing industries, like steel, in consumers' goods industries generally, in housing, or in transport, with the result that there were bottlenecks in these lines in the first years of reconstruction. What European economic expansion there was was limited largely to motive-power industries, especially in the smaller countries, and to the machine tool industries, notably in Germany.[9]

In the United States, on the other hand, the expansion of basic industries, such as synthetic rubber, nitrogen, potash, magnesium, copper, salt, steel, and coal, not to mention agriculture, was very great. This was because the United States was the "economic arsenal" of the United Na-

[9] Motive power increased 23 per cent in the Netherlands from 1939 to 1945 and by 35 per cent in Denmark. Expansion of the machine tool industry in Germany amounted to 75 per cent from 1938 to 1943.

tions; to fulfill its military task it had to expand plant and produce what it had formerly imported. Thus at the end of the war the United States, and to a lesser extent Canada and Australia, had productive capacity for the things which the whole world was demanding.

Destruction, undermaintenance of plant, uneven economic investment, and a great movement of expansion in the United States made Europe's position at the conclusion of hostilities difficult enough to discourage the most optimistic. Yet Europe's condition was made worse by heavy public debts, by new waves of inflation, by an almost complete breakdown of the system of multilateral trade and payments, by unfavorable terms of trade, by territorial changes, by reparations demands, and, as we shall see in the next chapter, by social and political disturbances.

Europe's public finance problems, which had been grave at the end of the depression of the 1930s, became much more serious as a result of heavy war expenditures. When a nation's very survival is at stake, public expenditures are increased with almost reckless abandon, for "penny-pinching" policies have no place under the circumstances. Thus, the United Kingdom augmented its expenditures from 1,147 million pounds in 1938–1939 to 6,190 million in 1944–1945; Germany increased its expenses nearly eleven times, and other belligerents extended theirs in comparable proportions. Efforts were made to obtain a part of the sums spent from individuals and corporations either by taxation or borrowing in order to reduce the purchasing power of those who were buyers of consumers' goods, especially luxuries, and to curb the holdings of those who might take excess profits. This policy was particularly pushed in the United Kingdom where the income tax was about doubled, with very heavy surtaxes on large incomes, where tax revenues were increased three and a half times, and where taxes covered about 25 per cent of war expenditures.

As in World War I, however, belligerents in World War II went to their banks of issue for funds to meet their bills, giving these banks their "IOU's" as security. With the new reserves thus furnished them, the banks of issue increased the amount of money in circulation or the amount of credit available to individuals in commercial bank deposits. In the period from 1938 to 1945 these amounts ranged from four times for money in circulation and three times for deposit money in the United Kingdom to nearly twenty times for money and seventeen times for deposit money in Italy. Inasmuch as national income did not increase in similar proportions, the "income velocity of money," that is, the rate of turnover of money against final income went up but little. Consequently the foundation was laid for a large increase in prices—an increase which came for the most part after the cessation of hostilities.

Equally calamitous was the international situation in trade and payments. Western Europe had liquidated so much of its external investments that whereas its earnings on these holdings in 1938 had equaled 32 per cent of its exports, in 1950–1951 earnings on investments amounted to only 9 per cent of what it sold to the rest of the world. Furthermore, Europe had accumulated new debts abroad, which required a 7 per cent increase in the 1938 volume of exports in order to provide for repayment. Prices of what Europe sold the rest of the world had not risen so much as those foodstuffs and raw materials which it imported (the disadvantage was about 15 per cent in 1946). Earnings from shipping were down because of the loss of ships, and earnings from banking and insurance had also fallen, although to a less degree. In fact, Western Europe

Table 39. Wholesale Prices
(1953 = 100)

Country	1938	1945	1950
Germany	46		85
Italy	2	39	93
France	4	14	78
United Kingdom	31	52	97
United States	46	62	94
Belgium	24	80*	93

* 1946.

as a whole had to increase its exports by 80 per cent over 1938 in order to pay for the same value of imports of that year.

The difficulties of achieving this increase were particularly burdensome because of shifts in production, trade, and payments. Industrialization in much of the non-European world meant that Europe had greater difficulty than formerly in selling its wares abroad, and some of its suppliers of foodstuffs, like the Argentine, were not able to furnish the same quantites as earlier because of shifts in agriculture. Some areas, like Eastern Europe, were unable or unwilling to maintain exports to Western Europe of materials, like petroleum. And some regions, like India, which were trying to industrialize, wanted heavy capital goods that could be obtained most readily from the United States.

For these various reasons Europe turned its own purchases more and more to the United States, although it had difficulty in selling its goods there because of American industrialization, mass production at low costs, and protective tariffs. To make matters worse, the United States had begun to produce materials that, before the war it had bought in areas with which Europe had an excess of exports over imports and where Europe had thus been able to be paid in dollars. All of these changes resulted in a situation in which Europe bought more than formerly from the dollar area and the United States spent fewer dollars abroad in regions where Europe's trading position was strong. Thus Europe had a "dollar shortage," that is, a deficit in trade and payments with the dollar area. Because of this deficit Europe had to control its imports and could not permit the free convertibility or exchange of its moneys for other currencies. Consequently a serious handicap was put upon multilateral trade and payments both in the world and within Europe itself. Western culture was thus deprived of a system that had played a significant role in its economic growth.

During the course of the war the Allies began to make plans to mitigate these difficulties in capital equipment, in trade, in payments, and in convertibility of moneys. In 1944 their representatives met at Bretton Woods, New Hampshire, to create two financial agencies which could provide credit for rebuilding what had been destroyed, for developing economically backward areas, and for stabilizing exchange rates. These agencies were the International Bank for Reconstruction and Development with a capital of 9,100,000,000 dollars and the International Monetary Fund with a capital of 8,000,000,000 dollars. Furthermore, the American draft for the projected United Nations provided for an Economic and Social Council that was to sponsor an International Trade Organization which would liberalize trade and thereby, perhaps, reduce international tensions.

Territorial Changes, Reparations, and War Debts

At the conclusion of World War II the victors did not rush headlong into the making of formal peace treaties, as they had after World War I, for there was some feeling that a more reasonable and viable settlement would be possible after emotions had subsided during a "cooling-off period." Moreover, there had been enough differences between the U.S.S.R. and its Allies to induce the conquerors to postpone final decisions, that is, to keep the situation fluid, so that they might strengthen their respective positions or by procrastination save face if their views did not prevail. Yet, despite delay in negotiating a peace treaty with the major enemy, certain issues had to be resolved and what appeared to be temporary arrangements became in effect definitive settlements. Decisions regarding boundaries are a case in point, for they became in essence permanent and permitted a subsequent creation of spheres of influence. Inasmuch as trade between such spheres came to almost a standstill, territorial arrangements had an important bearing on the subsequent development of Europe and, indeed, of the whole world.

In the case of Germany, decisions were reached piecemeal well before victory was attained. They began with the Moscow Conference in October, 1943, when the foreign ministers of the United States, the United Kingdom, and the U.S.S.R. decided that a European Consultative Commission should be created to determine policies regarding the military occupation of Germany.[10] It was this Commission which fixed the limits of the zones of occupation in Germany and thus drew the crucial line between the sphere dominated by Russia and that dominated by the the major Allies. Essentially, this meant that Russia was going to be able to control the entire region eastward from the western line of their occupation zone; the Allied dream of a *cordon sanitaire*, consisting of Poland, Czechoslovakia, Hungary, and Rumania, on the European boundaries of Russia was shattered. Moreover, Russia's position in Eastern Europe was strengthened at the Yalta Conference (February, 1945) and at the Potsdam Conference (July, 1945). At the former it was agreed that the eastern boundary of Poland should be the "Curzon Line," which gave Russia a part of prewar Poland, and at the latter, that the western boundary of Poland was to be a line from the Baltic Sea west of Swinemünde and thence along the Oder and Neisse Rivers to Czechoslovakia and that the western boundary of Russia was to be a line running from the Bay of Danzig north to Braunsberg to a meeting place at the frontiers of Lithuania, East Prussia, and Poland. Thus Russia not only increased its territory by 273,947 square miles and its population by nearly 25 million, but also attained a strategic position from which to bring pressure upon Poland, Czechoslovakia, Hungary, Rumania, Bulgaria, and Yugoslavia, states which were to become Russian satellites.

At the Potsdam Conference, futhermore, the United States, the U.S.S.R., and the United Kingdom decided that peace settlements with Italy, Rumania, Bulgaria, and Finland should be drafted by a Council of Ministers, made up of the foreign ministers of the U.S.S.R., the United Kingdom, the United States, China, and France.[11] Nevertheless, a conference was assembled at Paris, July 29, 1946, at which the "Big Four"

[10] France was admitted to the Commission in November, 1944. Incidentally, it should be noted that there was no question about the return of Alsace and Lorraine to France.

[11] Subsequently the powers took the position that only those nations which had signed surrender terms with one of the defeated powers should participate in the drafting of the treaties. Thus the peace treaty with Italy was to be drafted by Britain, the Soviet Union, the United States, and France; those with Rumania, Bulgaria, and Hungary, by Britain, the U.S.S.R., and the United States; and that with Finland, by Britain and the U.S.S.R.

(the United States, the U.S.S.R., the United Kingdom, and France) met with the "Little Seventeen" in order to make recommendations to the Council of Ministers regarding the final settlements.[12] In the discussions at this meeting the rivalry between the U.S.S.R. and the West became abundantly clear. Russia made every effort to win advantages for itself and its actual or potential satellites; the West consistently attempted to thwart such moves and to get favorable terms for its friends. In the treaties which were ultimately drafted and were signed at Paris, February 10, 1947, Yugoslavia was given Fiume and a considerable part of the Istrian Peninsula; Trieste was internationalized—a change that was to upset trade in this area and to disturb Italian-Yugoslav relations until Trieste, reduced in size, was returned to Italy (1954). Furthermore, Italy had to give up its colonies, which were to be granted ultimate independence, and to surrender the Dodecanese Islands to Greece. Hungary lost territory in southern Slovakia to Czechoslovakia and had to cede northern Transylvania to Rumania.[13] Bulgaria surrendered land which had been acquired with Nazi support from Yugoslavia. Rumania had to give up Bessarabia and Bukovina to Russia. Finland had to cede the province of Petsamo. The Saar was incorporated in the economy of France.[14] Then in a subsequent treaty with Japan, signed September 4, 1951,[15] Russia was given the southern part of Sakhalin Island and the Kurile Islands, which had been promised her at Yalta.[16]

Quite as important as the territorial changes effected by these treaties, so far as the subsequent economic development of Europe was concerned, were the clauses pertaining to reparations. The United States took the position that after the experience with reparations following World War I, it would be foolhardy to demand payments out of current production from the defeated states. It pointed out that, after the shortages of the immediate postwar period had been made up, special interests in each recipient country would be unwilling to receive goods and services and that there would be a general desire to have the vanquished powers resume their economic activity. Russia, on the other hand, insisted on reparations, for payments to a communist economy would not impinge on the interests of individuals and Russian losses had been so

---

[12] The defeated states could submit their views concerning issues at stake and proposed terms.

[13] Hungary was reduced to its size of post-World War I. Approximately 3 million Magyars were in the regions taken from Hungary after World War II.

[14] The Saar was politically united with West Germany in 1956, but France was given a few economic concessions.

[15] The U.S.S.R., Poland, and Czechoslovakia did not appear at the signing.

[16] A treaty was signed with Austria, May 15, 1955.

great that amends had to be made, even if of an avowedly punitive character.[17]

The reparations issue was raised at Yalta when the conflicting stands of the U.S.S.R. and the West became clearly evident. At that time Stalin demanded 20 billion dollars, half of which would go to Russia, to be paid over a twenty-year period. To this request Churchill and Roosevelt were flatly hostile, yet it was clear that some concessions had to be made and a compromise effected. This middle ground was reached at Potsdam. There the negotiating powers agreed upon the general principle that the war potential of Germany should be held in check by prohibiting the production of arms, ammunition, aircraft, and seagoing vessels and by limiting the output of steel, chemicals, and certain machines, but Germany should be left "enough resources to enable the German people to subsist without external assistance." From these propositions, the victors went on to establish a formula which the United States and Britain hoped would dispose of the reparations issue with dispatch and which Russia apparently believed was the best that it could get. It provided that the reparations claims of the U.S.S.R., out of which Polish claims would be covered, were to be met (1) by the dismantling and removal to the Soviet Union of certain German plants in the Russian Zone of occupation, (2) by removal of 15 per cent of "such usable and complete industrial capital equipment . . . as is unnecessary for German peace economy . . . from the Western Zones of Germany, in exchange for an equivalent value of food, coal, potash, zinc, and so forth, as may be agreed upon," (3) by removals of 10 per cent of industrial capital equipment from the Western Zones of occupation without payment, and (4) by an appropriate share of German foreign assets. Claims of the Western Powers were to be met by removals of plant from the Western Zones of occupation in Germany and from German foreign assets.[18] A reparations conference, held in Paris in 1945, established a schedule for the division of reparations and an Inter-Allied Reparations Agency was created, with its seat in Brussels, actually to parcel out the booty. Finally, the Allied Control Council, composed of each commander-in-chief of the four occupying powers in Germany, was charged with overseeing the dismantling of plant.

Although these arrangements took care of the major phase of reparations, the Russians also insisted on payments from their lesser enemies.

---

[17] This position won support from those who wanted to curb Germany economically for an indefinite period. In America, Henry Morgenthau was the chief exponent of this position.

[18] Russia was given complete control over German assets in Finland, Bulgaria, Hungary, Rumania, and eastern Austria.

Thus in the treaty with Italy provision was made for reparations in the amount of 360 million dollars, of which 100 million was to go to the U.S.S.R., 125 million to Yugoslavia, 105 million to Greece, 25 million to Ethiopia, and 5 million to Albania. Furthermore, Hungary was made to pay 300 million to the U.S.S.R. and 100 million jointly to Yugoslavia and Czechoslovakia; Bulgaria, 45 million to Greece and 25 million to Yugoslavia; and Rumania and Finland were each asked to pay 300 million to the Soviet Union over eight years.[19] In comparison with the enormous bills presented after World War I, these sums seemed small. Yet, they were enough to keep animosities aroused, although they were not enough to be a major disturbing factor in the postwar period.

Similarly, too, sufficient foresight was exercised to avoid in the aftermath of World War II a repetition of the complicated and irritating issues of war debts. The American "lend-lease" formula meant in essence that no charge would be made for war goods sent to the Allies, principally the United Kingdom and the U.S.S.R.; and the other members of the coalition adopted similar stands. What debts were contracted, especially with the United States and Canada, by European nations were for relief and rehabilitation, but even after the conflict, as we shall see, the United States soon switched from lending to giving in order to help restore the economies of Western culture.

[19] The U.S.S.R. reduced in 1948 the sums demanded of Finland, Rumania, and Hungary by $73,500,000 each. Russia got, however, as her price for making a treaty of peace with Austria 10,000 tons of oil per year for ten years and $154,000,-000 in goods to be delivered within six years.

CHAPTER 21

Economic Recovery and Expansion

Chief Characteristics of the Postwar Period

On the morrow of World War II the economic future of Western culture did not look bright. Not only were there the destruction, commercial dislocations, and public-debt burdens already discussed, but there were also tensions among groups within society, especially those between Communists and supporters of the existing economic organization. And there were fears that demobilizing vast armies and beating swords into plowshares would bring, as they had so many times in the previous hundred and fifty years, a postwar economic depression.

Yet, in spite of valid grounds for dire forebodings one of the chief characteristics of the history of Western culture after World War II was rapid economic recovery. As can be seen in Table 40, Europe surpassed its prewar level of national income by 1949, and nearly every country went on to raise its income by from 34 to 78 per cent of its prewar figure in 1954–1955. American expansion was almost as dramatic as had been the depression of the 1930s. Furthermore, despite an increase in population economic growth was sufficient to result in an increase over prewar amounts in national income per capita and in national income per man-hour.

Remarkable as was this recovery, Western Europe did not regain its *relative* prewar position either in Western culture or vis-à-vis the whole world. It had lost ground, especially to the United States and Canada, and a great economic power had risen on its eastern boundaries. Although Europe, excluding the U.S.S.R., had nearly twice the population of the United States in 1950, it produced only about equal amounts of coal and steel and lesser amounts of electricity, sulfuric acid, and grain. In sum, the national income of the United States exceeded the national income of all Western European states combined; industrial output per capita in the United States was over twice the Western European average. Furthermore, Europe's share of world export trade shrank from some 50 per cent prior to World War I to about 35 per cent for the years 1948–1950.[1]

The realization of the relative economic decline of Western Europe and of the immensity of the task of reconstruction inclined most states

Table 40. Indicators of Economic Expansion

Country	Gross domestic product at constant prices (1938 = 100)			Income per capita (1953 = 100)		
	1949	1952	1955	1949	1952	1955
France	112	128	149	87	98	111
Western Germany	100	137	178	72	94	117
Italy	101	123	150	81	94	111
Belgium	109	123	135	88	100	106
United Kingdom	113	119	134	91	97	107
United States	174	188	219	85	98	102

to engage in one or another form of economic planning. In some countries, as for example the United Kingdom and Norway, important segments of the economy where nationalized; and thus the state as entrepreneur could determine what decisions to take to achieve desired ends. In others, as in France and the Netherlands, economic development was planned by an official agency and was executed in collaboration with private interests. In still other nations, reliance for governmental control of the economy was placed primarily in traditional administrative departments and in the central banks. Indeed, the latter exerted an extraordinary influence by adopting policies to restrict or to extend credit to those parts of the economy which the state wanted to contract or to expand. Moreover, all governments aided economic growth by direct loans, tax policies, and "forced savings"; and all accepted the principle that the welfare of the individual is a fundamental responsibility of the

[1] Ingvar Svennilson, *Growth and Stagnation in the European Economy* (Geneva: United Nations, 1954), p. 169.

state, some even sanctifying this doctrine by inserting it in their constitutions.

Moreover, economic recovery was tempered by the fact that communism became a great force in the world. In all the states of Western

Output per Man-hour and Man-hours Worked in Industry in 1951.

culture, more or less important groups preached the overthrow of the capitalist system and were egged on by the Russians to put their homilies to the test. Consequently, a bloc of Western states formed an alliance against Russia. Thus a new situation was created in international relations. Instead of four or five Great Powers, which by shifting their allegiances could upset existing balances of power, there were two colossi, the U.S.S.R. and the United States, allied with states that did not have the strength to alter the basic alignment by a change of sides. These two blocs adopted such hostile attitudes towards each other that trade between them came nearly to a standstill, but each of the alliances endeavored to increase its economic potential by closer intrabloc economic ties.

Disruptive as such an alignment of hostile forces was to economic development, it was probably of less immediate importance to economic recovery and growth than the breakdown of the multilateral system of trade and payments. For reasons suggested in the last chapter, Western

Europe could not earn sufficient dollars with which to buy goods necessary for a rapid recovery. The retardation of growth made the threat of
communism more ominous. To minimize this threat and thus the expansion of Russian influence and power, the United States came to the
assistance of Western European states. In 1947 it inaugurated the

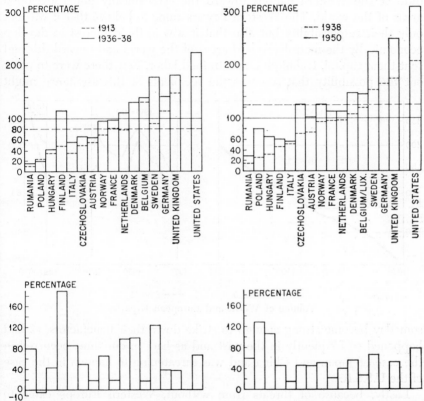

Industrial Trends in European Countries and the United States, 1913 to 1950. The
chart at the top left indicates the increase per country in the manufacturing output
per capita as a percentage of the European average for 1936–1938. The chart at the
bottom left represents the percentage change in total industrial output from 1913 to
1936–1938 and hence reflects industrial growth in relation to population growth. The
chart at the top right shows the increase in industrial output per capita as a percentage of European industrial average in 1938. At the lower right the chart shows the
percentage increase in total output from 1938 to 1950 and thus brings out the rapid
industrialization of the formerly less industrialized areas. Note: The data for Austria,
Czechoslovakia, and the United States refer to the year 1937 instead of 1938. (*Like
many of the charts in this section, these diagrams were adapted from the United
Nations publications, especially Ingvar Svennilson, Growth and Stagnation in the
European Economy, Geneva: United Nations, 1954, and the annual Economic Survey
of Europe.*)

Marshall Plan whereby it made huge gifts to its friends in Europe and subsequently in the rest of the world. By such action a new network of international debts was avoided and the alliance of powers against Russia was greatly strengthened.

Furthermore, economic recovery took place against a change in attitude of the Western nations toward the economically underdeveloped areas of the world. The Western Powers came to believe that it was not only their responsibility but also that it was in their interest to develop economically the more backward areas of the world and toward this end sent them capital, techniques, and trained labor. Few there were to point out the possibility that some of the recipients of this assistance might

——— WORLD   − − − EUROPE

Volume of World and European Exports.

someday become strong enough to strike down their benefactors, as had happened so frequently in the past and as had, in our time, occurred in the case of Japan and China and was threatening to happen in the case of the U.S.S.R.

Lastly, because of threats from without, Western Europe came to realize that it could not risk any more internecine wars and continue to exist, and that it had to become more of a political and economic unit if it were to defend itself. The strides taken to this end were little short of remarkable. It was a major characteristic of the post-World War II period that entire cultures were drawing more closely together politically in order to protect or to advance fundamental ideologies, and in this effort the West was by no means a laggard.

Recovery and Expansion

From early in World War II all belligerents gave earnest thought to the economic phases of the aftermath. As we have seen, Germany had its plan to become the industrial heartland of an agrarian continent and Japan, its dream of being the center of a "Co-Prosperity Sphere," but all countries had some concept of what their economic place in "the brave new world" should be. Each of the various governments-in-exile began to draw up blueprints for its country—plans that ranged from wishful thinking, as in the case of the Polish government, to the actual buying of goods for postwar delivery, as in the case of the Belgian. One of the governments to go furthest in this planning was that of the Free French under General De Gaulle at Algiers. There the Committee of National Liberation had an Economic Committee which not only drafted schedules of needs for lend-lease and other forms of Allied aid, but also gave thought to the future. It was, indeed, out of this group that came the Plan of Modernization and Equipment, which was developed under the leadership of Jean Monnet. Even in the United States there was an organization of businessmen, the Committee on Economic Development under the leadership of Paul Hoffman, the future director of the Economic Cooperation Administration, which made plans to effect an orderly economic transition from war to peace.

Although the schemes for recovery and methods of implementation varied by country, considerable agreement existed on the main steps to be taken. Every nation realized that there had to be a large investment in segments of the economy producing basic commodities, the Monnet Plan, by way of example, calling for special developments in coal mining, electrical production, ferrous metals, cement, agricultural machinery, and domestic transportation. Also, each realized that a larger share of national income than before the war would have to be saved and invested to attain the desired goals and that consequently the people of Western Europe must for a time do without the amount of consumers' goods they might like. Finally, each recognized that there would have to be a "will to recovery," if the targets which were set up were to be hit—a will that would accept hardships in the expectation that eventually Western Europe could again attain its economic and cultural place in the sun and some semblance, at least, of its former political and military prestige.

There was less agreement, however, on the means by which the necessary investments could be effected and by which people might be convinced of the wisdom of present sacrifices for future gain. In several countries, but notably in Great Britain and France, there was a demand for the nationalization of industries, for, by having the state become the owner and manager of properties, investments could be made directly from government funds and the benefits of industry could be assured, so it was contended, to the collectivity. In both countries nationalization became a political necessity. In France, the Council of Resistance had

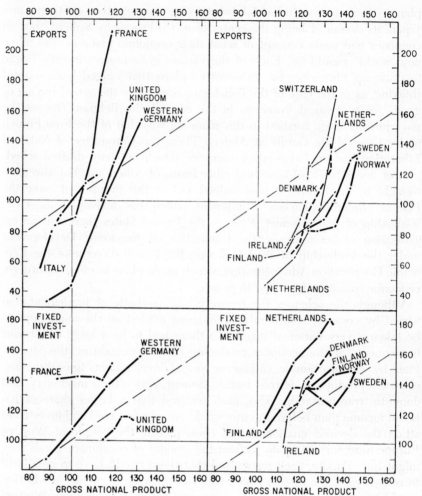

Relationship between Gross National Product and Exports, and Investment at Constant Prices.

taken a strong stand for nationalization during the war to get Communist support and the Provisional Government of De Gaulle similarly needed left-wing backing. Consequently, the French nationalized their coal mines, electricity and gas, the Bank of France, the major commercial banks and insurance companies, the Renault automobile workers, and Air France.[2] In Great Britain the Labor Party came to power in 1945 and

[2] The railways had in essence already been nationalized, although compensation had not been completed.

proceeded to nationalize the Bank of England, the coal industry, gas, electricity, and telephone services, inland transportation, and the steel industry.[3] Thus about 20 per cent of British industry was nationalized, a somewhat larger proportion in France, and considerable amounts in Norway, Sweden, and Italy.

Even though most other countries of Western culture did not nationalize industry to the same extent as those already mentioned, governments in most places tried to encourage more investments in producers' goods by allowing their central banks to extend exceptional credits to other banks, by permitting special tax deductions for such investments, and by making loans through state financial agencies. Investment became a higher proportion of national income than before the war, as can be seen in the accompanying charts, and larger percentages of investment came from governments rather than from private persons, 30 per cent of all investments in France from 1947 to 1951 coming from governmental sources. As might well have been expected, investments tended to go into those branches of economic activity where there was the greatest need, as in dwellings to replace what had been destroyed and to accommodate growing populations, where there was the greatest output per unit of input, as in manufacturing, mining, and services rather than in agriculture, and where the contribution to national income was large, as in the case of shipping in Norway.

Besides endeavoring to encourage greater savings for investment, nearly all countries of the West engaged in massive campaigns to preach the doctrine of "productivity." The fundamental argument presented was extremely simple and easily understood by the masses of both employers and employees. It was that economic well-being is a highly desirable condition and that to achieve it more goods must be produced per unit of input. This meant that employers should do everything they could to produce efficiently and that workers could not expect greater economic benefits if they did not do their share. Here was a theory which was, on the one hand, to stimulate employers to get better equipment, to arrange their plants for more efficient production, and to try to establish better relations with their workers in their own interests (personnel management) and, on the other hand, was to convince workers that there was no future for them in adopting an attitude, based on the Marxian theory, that they were inevitably going to be exploited by their employers. "Productivity" gave concrete expression to Western culture's basic tenet that one of the marks of civilization is a high level of material well-being because it permits not only freedom from want but also allows the enjoy-

[3] British steel was nationalized in 1949 and denationalized in 1953.

Table 41. Composition of Gross Investment in Fixed Capital

Country and currency	Year	Total fixed investment at current prices*	Percentages of total investment									
			By branch of the economy							By type of investment	
			Agriculture, forestry and fishing†	Mining and public utilities	Manufacturing‡	Transport and communications§	Dwellings	Public services‖	Other investment	Buildings and works	Equipment, vehicles, etc.
Belgium[a] (in billion francs)	1948	42.9	3	10	16	40	17	12	2		
	1949	47.5	3	8	18	31	25	13	2		
	1950	55.9	4	7	17	30	24	16	2		
	1951	54.3	5	9	17	28	24	15	2		
Denmark[b] (in billion kroner)	1948	2.10	8	5	17	12	23	9	26		
	1949	2.70	8	6	16	12	19	8	31		
	1950	3.30	7	5	13	12	18	8	37		
	1951	3.75	9	5	13	11	17	8	37		
France[a,c] (in thousand billion francs)	1949	1.51	8	14		13	18	9		48	52
	1950	1.60	9	15		10	19	8			
	1951	2.08	9	12		10	22	8			
Western Germany (in billion Deutschmarks)	1949	15.1	10	12	27	13	21	8	9	42	58
	1950	18.3	8	13	27	13	24	8	7	43	57
	1951	22.9	8	14	28	13	23	7	7	44	56
Greece (in thousand billion drachmas)	1948	2.22	7	16		35	32	3	7	63	37
	1949	3.08	12	15		24	31	4	14	62	38
	1950	5.17	10	19		24	31	4	12	61	39
	1951	4.54	13	33		15	30	2	7	61	39
Italy (in thousand billion lire)	1948	1.17	10	39		24	22		5		
	1949	1.32	11	39		19	26		5		
	1950	1.44	7	40		19	29		5		
	1951	1.72	9	41		16	28		6		

470

Percentages of total investment

Country and currency	Year	Total fixed investment at current prices*	By branch of the economy							By type of investment	
			Agriculture, forestry and fishing†	Mining and public utilities	Manufacturing‡	Transport and communications§	Dwellings	Public services‖	Other investment	Buildings and works	Equipment, vehicles, etc.
Netherlands (in billion guilders)	1948	3.18	7	7	23	26	15	14	8	40	60
	1949	3.59	6	6	25	23	17	15	8	44	56
	1950	4.04	6	7	28	21	16	13	9	42	58
	1951	4.47	6	11	24	22	15	12	10	42	58
Norway a (in billion kroner)	1948	4.62	12	6	20	32	16	8	6	48	52
	1949	5.23	12	6	20	32	15	8	7	47	53
	1950	5.48	12	7	19	32	15	9	6	47	53
	1951	5.90	13	8	18	28	16	9	8	47	53
Sweden (in billion kronor)	1948	4.60	8	9	27	18	23	13	2	58	42
	1949	4.52	8	9	28	14	26	13	2	58	42
	1950	5.26	8	8	28	17	25	12	2	54	46
	1951	6.37	7	7	28	19	24	13	2		
United Kingdom (in billion pounds)	1948	1.47	6	11	27	16	24	6	10	44	56
	1949	1.60	6	13	28	16	20	6	11	43	57
	1950	1.70	5	14	30	14	19	7	11	42	58
	1951	1.86	5	14	33	13	18	7	10	41	59

* Expenditure on repair and upkeep is not included in gross investment except in France, Italy, and Norway. Expenditure for military purposes is excluded throughout.
† Excluding changes in livestock.
‡ Including mining other than coal mining.
§ Excluding roads.
‖ Including roads.
a Investment in coal mining includes miners' dwellings.
b The percentages for transport and communications comprise public transport and shipping.
c Agriculture includes the food industry.
d Mining and public utilities refer to electricity only. Fishing (including whaling) accounted for 5 per cent of total investment in 1948 and 4 per cent in other years.
SOURCE: *Economic Survey of Europe since the War* (Geneva: United Nations, 1953), p. 61.

471

Table 42. Share of Sectors in Commodity Output, Prewar to 1955, at Constant Prices

Country	Year	Commodity sectors as a percentage of total commodity output				
		Agriculture	Mining and quarrying	Manufacturing	Electricity, gas, water	Construction
United Kingdom	1937	9.3	8.9	63.7	2.5	15.6
	1949	11.2	6.9	66.9	3.8	11.2
	1955	9.6	5.6	70.6	4.3	9.9
Belgium	1936–38	16.1	12.9	60.3	2.9	7.8
	1948	13.8	11.0	61.9	4.2	9.1
	1954	15.3	9.9	61.2	4.2	9.4
Luxembourg	1937–38	19.6	9.3	55.9	1.7	13.5
	1949	18.4	6.5	61.7	1.9	11.5
	1955	18.2	7.9	58.0	2.5	13.4
Western Germany	1936	21.8	6.5	60.1	2.4	9.2
	1950	19.3	6.2	60.7	4.1	9.7
	1955	14.6	5.1	66.1	4.3	9.9
Sweden	1950	21.0	66.8			12.2
Netherlands	1950	24.6	3.7	58.6	3.0	10.1
Norway	1938	36.5	3.5	45.4	2.4	12.2
	1949	27.3	2.3	50.9	3.7	15.8
	1955	22.5	2.4	54.0	4.0	17.1
Austria	1951	24.5	60.6		4.6	10.3
	1955	25.1	60.2		5.6	9.1
France	1938	34.8	4.6	52.6	1.9	6.1
	1950	31.0	4.4	52.5	2.7	9.4
	1954	30.2	4.4	52.6	2.9	9.9
Denmark	1938	37.8	0.2	51.0	1.9	9.1
	1950	36.6	0.3	50.0	2.8	10.3
	1954	35.5	0.2	49.3	3.5	11.5
Finland	1938	52.6	0.4	36.7	2.0	8.3
	1950	37.6	0.5	45.7	2.3	13.9
	1955	32.5	0.6	51.2	3.0	12.7
Italy	1938	48.6	1.3	43.5	2.4	4.2
	1950	43.5	1.1	47.4	3.5	4.5
	1955	36.1	1.8	50.8	3.6	7.7
Ireland	1950	55.5	44.5			
Portugal	1951	48.1	1.2	48.8	1.9	†
Greece	1938	65.6	34.4			
	1949	61.4	0.6	31.2	1.2	5.6
	1955	56.1	1.9	33.8	1.7	6.5
Spain	1951	59.1	2.5	32.7	1.6	4.1
Turkey	1938	79.8	1.5	13.4	0.3	5.0
	1950	75.5	2.0	16.5	0.6	5.4
	1955	73.3	2.6	18.0	1.0	5.1

† Included in manufacturing.

SOURCE: *Economic Survey of Europe* (Geneva: United Nations, 1957), Chap. 7, p. 13.

Table 43. Relative Output per Head by Sector in a Year between 1948 and 1951
(1.00 = national average)

Country	Commodity output		Services		Industry†		Agriculture		Mining and quarrying		Manufacturing	
	A‡	B‡	A	B	A	B	A	B	A	B	A	B
United Kingdom		0.97		1.03		0.96		1.13		0.92		0.95
Belgium	0.80	0.80	1.35	1.34	0.84	0.86	0.59	0.55	0.97	1.00	0.80	0.82
Luxembourg	0.90	0.87	1.19	1.26	1.04	1.17	0.55	0.40	1.16	1.32	1.07	1.20
Western Germany	1.00	0.95	1.00	1.10	1.07	1.20	0.79	0.51	1.22*	1.38*	1.14	1.28
Netherlands		1.00		1.00		1.03		0.92		1.43		1.04
Norway		0.92		1.13		1.24		0.55		2.17		1.25
Austria	1.04		0.92			1.23	0.70				1.26	
France		0.88		1.25		1.16		0.57		1.30		1.21
Denmark	0.97	0.94	1.04	1.09	1.01	1.09	0.92	0.76			1.02	1.10
Sweden	1.02	1.02	0.97	0.97	1.20	1.21	0.66	0.65			1.29	1.26
Finland	0.93	0.87	1.18	1.38	1.19	1.40	0.68	0.54	0.75*	1.00*	1.15	1.36
Italy	0.91	0.89	1.23	1.31	1.10	1.17	0.75	0.68			1.26	1.34
Ireland	0.93		1.11			0.93	0.93				0.93	
Portugal	0.94	0.91	1.15	1.25	1.31	1.41	0.72	0.66	1.00	1.00	1.32	1.43
Greece		0.85		1.39		1.22		0.69		1.33		1.20
Spain		0.93		1.19		1.12		0.83				1.26
Turkey		0.76		2.49		2.61		0.61		3.25		2.26

Country	Electricity, gas, water		Construction		Transport and communications		Trade		Other services	
	A	B	A	B	A	B	A	B	A	B
United Kingdom		1.33		0.92		0.97		1.19		0.98
Belgium	2.62	2.62	0.77	0.79	0.93	0.94	1.17	1.13	1.62	1.62
Luxembourg	1.57	1.83	0.84	0.96						
Western Germany			0.70	0.79	1.24	1.44	0.95	1.01	0.94	1.04
Netherlands		2.00		0.81				1.02		1.05
Norway		2.33		1.03		1.42		1.43		0.88
Austria	3.56		0.86		0.85		1.07		0.89	
France		2.29		0.80		1.41		1.23		1.22
Denmark	2.67	2.67	0.85	0.92	1.05	1.18	1.30	1.26	0.87	0.95
Sweden			0.96	0.96	1.05	1.06			0.77	0.77
Finland	2.50	3.00	1.25	1.47	1.09	1.30	1.40	1.59	1.07	1.26
Italy	4.60	4.60	0.38	0.40	1.44	1.44			1.19	1.26
Ireland								1.24		1.04
Portugal					1.24	1.35	1.06	1.15	1.17	1.27
Greece		2.25		1.29		1.25		1.58		1.34
Spain		2.20		0.53		0.87		1.31		1.22
Turkey				4.37		2.14		3.37		2.42

* The figures express the ratio of the percentage distribution of output to the percentage distribution of employment and show the intersector differences in output per head relatively to the national average.
† Total commodity output less agriculture.
‡ A (excluding unpaid female family helpers), B (including unpaid family helpers).
SOURCE: *Economic Survey of Europe* (Geneva: United Nations, 1957), Chap. 7 p. 23.

Modern Cotton Spinning. The progress in the art of making thread has been enormous over the last two hundred years. This picture might be compared with those showing spinning in Ancient Greece (page 23) and on the Hargreaves jenny. The principles have not, however, changed much. The twist is provided by rollers (center of the picture) and by a revolving spindle. (*Courtesy of Burlington Industries.*)

ment of the "finer things of life." Some idea of how much people cherished these "finer things" was indicated by enormously increased registrations in institutions of higher learning.[4]

Economic recovery was also stimulated by the fact that initially there was great demand for almost all goods not only because equipment had been worn out and inventory used up during the war, but also because an increase in population of 4.1 per cent in Europe from 1940 to 1950

[4] Enrollment in colleges and universities in the United States went up from 1,100,000 in 1930 to 2,500,000 in 1954.

and of 15 per cent in the United States in the same period resulted in greater needs. Furthermore, recovery immediately after the cessation of hostilities was spurred on because much productive capacity which had been unused as a consequence of the lack of raw materials to process was put back into operation and because there were ample supplies of labor to man these plants. Lastly, expansion was aided by a strong world demand, in spite of difficulties in international trade and payments, for the kind of goods which Europe could sell abroad—a demand stimulated by the efforts of backward areas to develop economically.

Many factors of economic growth were thus concomitantly favorable in both the United States and Europe in the postwar period, but some elements in the situation were less buoyant. For one thing, recovery in different countries was uneven. Germany, for example, lagged far behind others until its currency reform of 1948, which did much to restore confidence, and then lunged forward frenetically. For another, few new domestic natural resources were discovered[5] and some existing supplies, notably coal, had been used to a point where their recovery was high cost. In fact, Western Europe had several shortages, and imported coal from Poland, and even from America, at high transportation costs.

Then, too, business cycle phenomena were by no means absent, although two curious variations on the ordinary theme took place in the postwar era. Neither recessions nor booms took complete control of all the economies of Western culture at once. In fact, it seemed that whenever a recession threatened in Europe, there was expansion in the United States and that each time there was danger of a recession in the United States, there was an expansion in Europe. Moreover, every time a recession seemed imminent, something happened to change the course of events. Thus, when the European import program threatened to stall and to curb expansion, American aid through the Marshall Plan restored confidence and effective demand. Then, when anti-inflationary measures were beginning to retard recovery in 1949, devaluations of currencies had a countering effect, and in 1950 the war in Korea was a stimulus to expansion. When recessionary factors began to appear in 1951 and 1952, they turned out to be a mild readjustment following the Korean War boom; and in 1953 there was a resumption of expansion. Then after this resumption there was retardation again in 1955 and 1956. In this last period there was clearly manifested what had been going on throughout the postwar period—an increase in prices, a satisfying of demand for some goods, and an augmentation of interest rates, of wages, and generally of the costs of doing business. Thus businessmen tended to be

[5] The chief exceptions were natural gas in Italy, Germany, and France, and some coal in Alsace.

cautious about the future and to refrain from an extension of plant, which augured poorly for a continuation of prosperity. In fact, in Europe there was a definite slowing down in the rate of expansion in 1955, especially in the United Kingdom and in the textile trades, and in 1957 and 1958 a marked recession set in in the United States. Observers wondered if again a countervailing force would appear to correct the balance of activity.

Lastly, there seems to have been a maldistribution of labor and, in spite of the doctrine of productivity, several important strikes and lockouts occurred. Italy, with its economically backward south, had some two million steadily classified as unemployed in the postwar era and Western

Table 44. Private Consumption Expenditures, 1954
(In per cent)

Country	Food	Tobacco, beverages	Clothing	Rent	Fuel, light	Household	Health	Transportation	Recreation	Other
Belgium	32	9	10	14	4	11	5	7	5	3
Germany, West	33	16	14	8	4	9	4	6	6	
Italy	47	11	12	2	3	5	3	7	8	2
Sweden	31	9	14	9	5	9	3	11	8	
United Kingdom	31	16	11	9	4	11	2	8	5	3
United States	27	6	9	13	3	11	6	13	5	7

Germany, with its large number of immigrant refugees,[6] had from 1,000,000 to 1,500,000 unemployed from 1949 to 1955. On the other hand, France, Belgium, Luxembourg, Sweden, Switzerland, and Austria were, according to a survey made in 1948, drastically in need of more workers and were having to lengthen the working week and to "stretch out" work.[7] Strikes in France in 1947 and 1948, which included the coal strike when maintenance men left their posts and the mines were flooded, resulted in the loss of nearly 7,000,000 man-days of labor; strikes in the United Kingdom in 1955 caused the loss of 3,781,000 man-days, and in the United States in 1952 strikes caused the loss of 59,100,000 man-days. These cessations of work occurred, incidentally, in spite of the fact that labor's share of national income was generally larger than before the war[8] and that family expenditures for both Europe and America clearly indicated higher standards of living.

[6] Western Germany received about 400,000 refugees a year. It had a population of about 47,700,000.

[7] The "stretch out" is simply the practice of giving a worker more machines to tend.

[8] *Economic Survey of Europe, 1956* (Geneva: United Nations, 1957), Chap. 8, p. 26.

Inflation, Deflation, and Monetary Reform

While recovery in production was taking place, all countries of Western Europe were wrestling with monetary problems. Their chief effort was to prevent rapid increases in prices without curbing economic activity. Also, they wanted to establish some reasonably stable relationship between the stock of goods and money in circulation. The realization of these goals was not easy, for goods were in short supply in relation to effective demand. Farmers and black-market operators, who were making large profits, bought consumers' goods rather than long-term securities. Governments spent beyond their receipts in order to get essential services, like transportation, reestablished. And people were so convinced that prices would go up that they turned their money into goods before it lost purchasing power.

Policies adopted by different countries in the face of inflationary threats varied considerably. Nearly all maintained price controls for a time, but except in rare instances, as in Britain, such efforts were only moderately effective. Some, like Belgium (1944) and Germany (1948), attempted "currency reforms," which consisted in making everyone exchange old money for new. Such an exchange frightened war profiteers from transferring all of their monetary wealth into new money[9] and permitted governments to reduce purchasing power by releasing the new money owed in installments over several months. Others, like France and Italy, let prices rise, which was politically the easiest thing to do. And still others, like the United Kingdom and the members of the sterling bloc—countries which had their moneys tied by official exchange rates to the pound sterling—held prices down as best they could and then devalued (1949), that is, reduced the gold content of their currency unit in order to bring their prices, figured at official exchange rates to the dollar, into line with world prices.

As can be seen from Table 45, the fall in the purchasing power of money was particularly dramatic in France, Western Germany,[10] and Italy, the price rise in France having been 2,500 per cent from 1938 to 1955 and that in Italy, 5,000 per cent. In the United Kingdom, Belgium, and the Netherlands, the rise was about 300 per cent. In the United States it was a little over 100 per cent.

In all of these countries, the change in prices had the usual effect of diminishing the savings of lower-middle–class people, who invested what

[9] If they did, they might then be investigated and prosecuted for profiteering or for evading taxes.

[10] Note that Table 45 gives no index for the postwar period in Germany before the monetary reform of 1948. The rise was so high that no reliable index is available.

they could put aside in bonds, savings accounts, and life insurance. It allowed those who produced goods for the market to strengthen their economic positions;[11] it penalized those who received salaries which were not easily raised, and at least for short periods, it hurt those who were paid money wages. From a social point of view inflation tended to weaken the middle class and to sow discontent among workers, but by and large it did not strengthen arguments for radical political platforms, as it had after World War I. Following World War II, inflation provided confirmation of the contentions of those who were preaching productivity, that is, the necessity of bringing the stock of goods into a

Table 45. Indices of Wholesale Prices and Exchange Rates

Country	Wholesale prices (1953 = 100)				Exchange rates (U.S. cents per unit of national currency)			
	1938	1945	1950	1955	1938	1948	Sept.–Dec., 1949	1955
United States	46	62	94	101				
United Kingdom	31	52	80	104	489.0	403.0	280.0	280.0
France	4	14	78	98	2.86	0.3238	0.2864	0.2857
Germany, West	46		85	101	40.16	0.02	23.81	23.81
Italy	2	39	93	101	5.263	0.1739	0.16	0.16
Switzerland	47	97	95	101	22.87	23.17	23.16	23.34
Belgium	24	80	93	101	3.38	2.282	2.00	2.00
Netherlands	27	48*	87	102	54.95	37.70	26.32	26.32

* December, 1946.

more stable relation with the supply and rate of circulation of money. It is probable that the price rise after 1949, mild as it was, acted as a buoyant factor in the economy of Western culture. It was hoped that the buoyancy would be maintained and not lead to a depression.

International Trade and Payments

Although recovery in production was realized with amazing rapidity after World War II[12] and runaway inflationary movements were brought

[11] This was the case if the prices of their goods held up in relation to costs of production and in relation to the prices of other goods. Prices of staple farm goods did not maintain their relative high position, especially after 1951.

[12] It should always be borne in mind that much of postwar production had to go to replace what had been destroyed during the conflict and that, if there had been no war, there would probably have been economic growth beyond the productive

under control within five years of the end of the fighting, dislocations in international trade and payments persisted with annoying tenacity. As we have seen, Western Europe's needs for imports were very great and its ability to export in the immediate postwar period was very limited.

The problem of foreign trade and payments had been anticipated during the war and the United States stepped into the breach by helping to provide relief through UNRRA (United Nations Relief and Rehabilitation Administration) and by granting loans to its former allies. In fact, from the end of the war to August 15, 1947, the United States provided assistance totaling 8,000,000,000 dollars, distributed as follows: the United Kingdom, 4,400,000,000; France, 1,920,000,000; the Netherlands, 413,000,000; Italy, 325,000,000; and the remainder to other states, including Poland and Czechoslovakia. Furthermore, in the same period Canada opened a line of credit to the United Kingdom in the sum of 1,250,000,000 dollars and the Bank for Reconstruction and Development and the Monetary Fund advanced 540,000,000.

Unfortunately these huge amounts were soon depleted and the credit of Western Europe nearly exhausted. Yet, it was generally believed that, if foreign goods did not continue to flow to Europe, social and political disturbances would occur and that any profound upheaval might result in the establishment of Communist regimes throughout Western Europe. Such an eventuality was abhorrent to the traditionally dominant political groups in Europe and the United States, and they both sought a way out of the predicament.

At a crucial moment, George C. Marshall, American Secretary of State, stepped into the breach. In a now famous speech, delivered June 5, 1947, he stated,

> Europe's requirements for the next three or four years of foreign food and other essential products—principally from America—are so much greater than her present ability to pay that she must have additional help or face economic, social, and political deterioration of a very grave character. . . .
>
> Before, however, the United States can proceed much further in its efforts to alleviate the situation and help start the European world on its way to recovery, there must be some agreement among the countries of Europe as to requirements of the situation and the part these countries themselves will take in order to give proper effect to whatever action might be taken by this government.

With great alacrity the British and French issued invitations to all European countries except Spain and the U.S.S.R. to a conference in

---

levels of 1938. The rapid recovery achieved after both World Wars should not give the impression that wars can be fought with economic impunity.

Paris to draft a report which could be presented to Secretary Marshall.[13] On September 22, 1947, the conference submitted its findings to Washington and American funds were made immediately available. The "Marshall Plan" became a reality.

The Plan provided for the creation of an Organization of European Economic Cooperation with headquarters in Paris, which had the duty of estimating requirements, of serving as a clearinghouse for national economic plans so that member nations would not work at cross-purposes, and of dividing American aid among the various members. Thus the OEEC practically forced its members to engage in some degree of economic planning and to integrate their plans. In order to estimate needs and have an objective measure for distributing aid, OEEC decided that deficits in trade and payments, particularly dollar deficits, be used.

Actual Marshall Plan assistance was in the form of credits which participating governments could spend on imports. Individual businesses which purchased approved imports paid their governments for them in domestic currency and these sums went into the so-called counterpart funds. These counterpart funds were then used within the recipient countries for purposes approved by the receiving country and by members of American missions to these states.[14] Accordingly, not only did American aid help pay for imports, but proceeds from the sale of goods were funneled into projects for monetary stabilization and economic development.

The Marshall Plan was "programmed" to last five years, at the end of which time it was expected that Western Europe would be on its feet so far as trade and payments were concerned.[15] For various reasons, however, this goal was not attained. Some countries, instead of conscientiously trying to eliminate their trade and payments deficits, pursued easy credit policies toward importers on the theory that the greater their foreign deficits the larger would be their share of American aid. Furthermore, a business recession in the United States in 1949 led to a falling off of American purchases from Europe;[16] the Korean War resulted in purchases which forced up the prices of many raw materials which Europe

---

[13] In attendance were representatives of the United Kingdom, France, Austria, Belgium, Denmark, Greece, Iceland, Ireland, Italy, Luxembourg, the Netherlands, Norway, Portugal, Sweden, Switzerland—the sixteen states which ultimately agreed to join a movement of economic collaboration to which West Germany was added later. The U.S.S.R. forbade its satellites to attend for fear that they would be detached from her.

[14] These were the ECA missions (Economic Cooperation Administration).

[15] Amounts of American aid were to be progressively decreased in the last years of the Plan.

[16] This contributed to the devaluation of currencies by sterling bloc countries in 1949, as explained above.

imported and hence made Europe's money deficit greater than it had been. The growing hostility between the U.S.S.R., on one side, and the United States and its friends,[17] on the other, caused the United States to be all the more anxious to preserve Western Europe from communism of the Russian kind.[18]

On account of these conditions, American aid was continued. In 1949, President Truman announced his "Point Four Program" for the development of economically backward areas both for their own material better-

Table 46. Distribution of American Aid, 1945–1957
(In billions of dollars)

Area	Amount
American republics	1.5
Near East and Africa	5.5
Asia	13.1
Western Europe:	36.2
Austria	1.0
Belgium and Luxembourg	.719
Denmark	.282
Finland	.070
France	5.5
Iceland	.033
Ireland	.145
Italy	2.8
Netherlands	1.0
Norway	.294
Portugal	.070
Spain	.187
Sweden	.107
United Kingdom	6.8
Western Germany	3.9
Yugoslavia	.795

ment and for providing more raw materials and larger markets for Western culture's economy.[19] In 1951, the United States passed its Mutual Security Act[20] for military assistance to friendly nations and for

[17] The North Atlantic Treaty Organization (NATO) was formed in 1949 for collective defense. It included the United States, France, Denmark, Portugal, Iceland, Italy, the Netherlands, and Norway. Greece and Turkey were added in 1951. The Federal German Republic became a member in 1954. A joint military command was established at Supreme Headquarters of the Atlantic Powers in Europe (SHAPE).

[18] The Communist coup in Czechoslovakia took place in 1948. The Korean War broke out June 25, 1950, and Communists became involved in both that war and the one in Indochina.

[19] The United Nations undertook a similar program.

[20] This had been preceded by the Mutual Defense Assistance program of 1949.

the purchase from them of military equipment for American forces abroad.[21] Consequently American aid was more, although not exclusively, for defense rather than for economic reconstruction and it was extended to other than European nations, large sums going to the Middle and Far East.[22] In the greatest giveaway program of all time the United States made available to foreign peoples from 1945 to 1957 56,100,000,000 dollars, which was the equivalent of one-fifth of the country's national income in 1950. Of this amount, 37,400,000,000 dollars were for economic assistance and the remainder for military purposes.

There is no question but what this aid from America did much to restore multilateral trade and payments. The index of world trade

Table 47. Balance of Payments of Western Europe with the United States in the First Nine Months of Years Indicated
(In millions of current dollars)

Type of payment	Period		
	1954	1955	1956
Exports to United States	+1,456	+1,695	+2,133
Imports from United States	−2,365	−3,112	−3,721
Trade balance	− 909	−1,417	−1,588
Services (net)	+ 209	+ 182	+ 223
United States military expenditures abroad	+1,068	+1,238	+1,298
	+ 368	+ 3	− 67
Private donations and capital movements	+ 223	+ 244	+ 775
United States Government grants and credits	+ 573	+ 767	+ 496
Errors and omissions	+ 32	− 108	− 312
Change in gold and dollar reserves	+1,196	+ 906	+ 892

(1953 = 100) went from 70 in 1948 to 113 in 1955; that of Western Europe rose from 45 to 127, and that of North America from 83 to 100. The recovery of Western Europe's export trade was particularly significant, for in the case of this area there was a high correlation between exports, investments, and economic growth.

Yet, in spite of a return to some semblance of orderly international trade, Western Europe's dollar gap continued to be a serious problem.

---

[21] These were the so-called offshore procurement items.

[22] The Eisenhower Doctrine, enunciated in January, 1957, was to give military and economic assistance to any nation or group of nations in the Middle East which requested help against overt aggression from any nation controlled by international communism.

To establish a close enough balance in international accounts to obviate a continuation of American aid, it was necessary to increase Western European exports to the United States or to third markets which had a plus balance with the United States, and hence an ability to pay for their purchases in dollars, or to increase American investments abroad. Such profound "structural changes," that is, large, deep-rooted alterations in the economy resulting from very basic factors, could not, however, be realized easily, for America had in general low-cost production and after its experience following World War I did not look with favor on foreign investments. Yet, the United States appeared to be willing to make gifts to the rest of the world in the interest of curbing communism, of restoring multilateral trade, and of creating greater economic equality in the world. Nevertheless, the dollar gap was a continuing problem.

Although the restoration of a system of multilateral trade and payments was of prime importance after World War II and although the main obstacle to such a restoration was the dollar gap, there were in addition many national impediments to international trade, such as tariffs, import quotas, and exchange controls. Theorists frowned upon these impediments to trade, for the general advantages of an international division of labor were widely recognized. In line with this thinking several states proposed after World War II that an International Trade Organization be established as an agency of the United Nations, like the Bank for Reconstruction and Development, in order to give continuing attention to the freeing of trade. As a result of this proposal a General Agreement on Tariffs and Trade (GATT) was negotiated at Geneva in 1947 and a charter for an International Trade Organization was drafted at Havana in 1948. These documents envisioned a liberalization of international trade by a general abolition of import quotas and exchange controls and an eventual reduction in tariff rates. For various reasons the ITO did not come into actual existence—as of 1958—but delegates of the several countries which had signed "GATT" continued to meet, to preach reform, and to make suggestions as to the appropriate steps to be taken toward freeing trade. The Havana Charter was a considerably watered-down version of the document which had been proposed by the United States and consequently was not submitted by President Truman to the Congress of the United States.

The reasons for hesitation in the application of the principles of freer trade were multitudinous. Although European nations were striving to regain their prewar positions, they did not consider themselves strong enough to open their markets to all comers; economically underdeveloped countries wanted and in many cases needed protection for their infant

Table 48. Estimated International Transactions

(In billions

United States imports and payments abroad

Private:

Commercial imports and United States expenditures on travel, transportation, and services abroad... $15.4

Gross new private United States investment abroad (including investments from cash earnings abroad)............................... 3.7

Net personal and charitable remittances abroad................... .5

Cash earnings of foreign investments in private sector of United States
economy (net income plus depreciation and depletion charges).... .8

Subtotal, private expenditures.................................... $20.4

United States Government:

Mutual Security Programs (gross basis):

Military grants... $ 3.9

Nonmilitary grants... .5

Nonmilitary loans... .2

Subtotal, Mutual Security Programs....................... $ 4.6

Other nonmilitary grants (e. g., from Public Law 480 proceeds)..... .3

Other nonmilitary loans and investments (e. g., from the Export-Im-
port Bank and Public Law 480 proceeds)..................... .3

Net increase in holdings of short-term claims against foreigners (principally Public Law 480 proceeds)............................ .4

Subtotal, all foreign assistance programs..................... $ 5.6

Expenditures abroad by United States military forces (excluding
counterpart)... $ 2.1

Expenditures abroad by United States civilian agencies (excluding
counterpart)... .2

Subtotal, collective security expenditures abroad.............. $ 7.9

Interest payments on public debt held by foreigners.............. $ .1

Pension and other transfer payments........................... .1

Net gold purchases... .1

Subtotal, United States Government expenditures abroad........... $ 8.3

Total, private and governmental expenditures abroad.................... $28.7

* Revised balance of payments basis; adapted from Department of Commerce figures.

industries. Furthermore, there was fear that freedom to purchase goods abroad would result in such an outflow of national currency as to lead to inflation with its rise in prices and eventual devaluation, an eventuality abhorred by many. And there was also hesitation to permit the freedom of trade because of the unequal distribution of resources, restrictions on the movement of labor, and the lack of freedom in the investment of capital abroad. In spite of such hesitations, however, some reduction of rates occurred in the United States (in 1950, they were 25 per cent less than those in force in 1932 and averaged 7.7 per cent ad valorem on all imported goods) and there was great liberalization of trade in Western Europe, compared with the prewar period, as we are about to see in more detail.

of the United States, Fiscal Year 1956*
of dollars)

United States exports and receipts from abroad

Private:

Commercial exports and foreigners' expenditures on travel, transportation, and services in United States.......................... $18.6

New foreign investment in private sector of United States economy (including investments from cash earnings in the United States).. 1.1

Cash earnings of United States private investments abroad (net income plus depreciation and depletion charges)................ 4.2

Subtotal, private receipts....................................... $23.9

United States Government:

Net increase in foreign holdings of United States Government securities... $ 1.2

Loan repayments........................... 5

Income from loans and investments abroad...................... .3

Export of military goods and services.......................... 2.4

Export of nonmilitary services (e. g., the services of civilian Government experts)....................................... .3

Subtotal, United States Government receipts...................... $ 4.7

Errors and omissions... .1

Total, private and governmental receipts from abroad.................. $28.7

The Economic Integration of Europe

As Western Europe began to realize that its economic, political, and military position in the world had been greatly weakened, it began an earnest search for an explanation of the decline. It was obvious that the world wars were in part responsible for what had befallen the West and that to prevent a repetition of such folly it was necessary greatly to improve relations among the nations of the Continent. Moreover, it was thought that an improvement of these relations could be effected by minimizing economic rivalries and tensions and that this minimizing could be achieved if Western Europe operated more as an economic unit than as a number of independent pieces. Furthermore, there was general agreement that Western Europe should strengthen itself economically and that this was feasible given the area's resources, manpower, capital savings, and techniques. It was necessary, so it was thought, to increase production per capita. One important way of doing so was to create a larger market for European goods—a market that would allow producers to reduce the unit cost of their products by allowing them to increase volume. This doctrine of a larger market, although probably overstated, was preached with conviction by American leaders in the Economic Co-operation Administration,[23] was widely advocated by professional economists,[24] and became an obsession with certain European statesmen, like Robert Schuman of France.[25]

For these reasons efforts were made to realize customs unions of a few states, for negotiating arrangements to abolish the worst impediments to trade, and for machinery to deal with obvious causes of tension. Thus, Belgium, Luxembourg, and the Netherlands formed a customs union known as Benelux and the Scandinavian states set up the Nordic Council (1955) to propose reforms to member nations. The various states of Western Europe created the Council for Europe (1949) to which members of parliaments could come to discuss problems of common interest and to draft recommendations for legislation.[26] The North Atlantic Treaty Organization was established, following the signing of the Atlantic Pact (1949), to defend Western Europe against Russia. The Organization for European Economic Cooperation came into being, as we have seen, not only to divide American aid but also to exchange ideas regarding steps which had to be taken to foster economic growth throughout Europe.

Although attention was focused at first on the freeing of trade among Western European states, it was soon obvious that a unified market could not be established without envisioning "integration" of several kinds. Accordingly it was argued that in order to have freedom of move-

---

[23] See *Ninth Report of the E.C.A.* (Washington: Government Printing Office, 1950), p. 35.

[24] See, for example, Francois Perroux, *Europe sans rivages* (Paris: Presses Universitaires, 1954).

[25] For some time the smaller countries of Europe had favored freer trade within Europe because of their dependence on foreign markets. After World War II, the larger countries began to look with more favor on a European customs union, because their proportion of intra-European trade had declined more than that of small countries. The United Kingdom, however, hesitated to participate actively in plans for Western European tariff unification for fear that it would lose its preferential position with members of the British Commonwealth.

[26] An attempt was made to create an European Defense Community (1952), that is, a common European military establishment. It did not materialize because the French, the original sponsors of the project, failed to ratify the enabling act.

ment of goods there would have to be freedom of movement of manpower and of capital and that there would have to be also a general equalizing of social security systems, of tax burdens, and of economic levels. Thus there developed a movement toward European economic integration—a movement that for the long run seemed to have much in its favor.

In the short run, however, there were several obstacles in the way of integration. For one thing, it ran smack into nationalism, which had been one of the greatest forces in Western culture in the preceding century and a half and which still had great potency. For another, the integration movement had to face up to the real difficulties involved in bringing together areas with such enormous economic differences as those of southern Italy and northern France. Discrepancies in income per capita, in population growth, and in unemployment made the more highly developed regions believe that they would be forced to assume heavy burdens for peoples over whom they had no political authority. In fact, a kind of circular reasoning developed by which integration was demanded to minimize economic inequalities and in which economic inequalities themselves made integration difficult.

So far as the freedom of movement of labor within Western Europe was concerned very little was accomplished. Immigrants from countries with large unemployment and low incomes per capita were welcomed elsewhere only to do work which was heavy, dangerous, or unpleasant and to meet seasonal or other temporary needs. In such cases, working permits of foreigners were always canceled when an oversupply of labor developed—a practice which inevitably dampened the enthusiasm of others from seeking work abroad. Nor were there many opportunities for people from Southern Europe to migrate to overseas parts of Western culture where economic expansion was taking place.

Again, little progress was made in allowing investment capital to move freely from country to country. Fear of inflation led most states to adopt policies to prevent flights of funds to avoid devaluation; national plans for economic expansion necessitated the use at home of whatever investment capital was available. Although immediately after World War II a few intra-European loans were made to aid reconstruction, after 1947 no appreciable lending was carried on within Europe except by Switzerland.[27] American private lending to Europe was extremely limited, and although the use of "counterpart funds" in a way was a substitute for lending, the indefinite continuation of the "great American giveaway" could hardly be imagined.

Hence, the economic integration of Europe centered mostly on the

[27] See *Intra-European Investments* (Paris: OEEC, 1951).

liberalization of trade. To this end some regional customs arrangements were made, as we have seen; machinery for facilitating the balancing of commercial accounts was erected, and free trade in coal and steel was established. Benelux became a reality in 1948, although some quantitative restrictions were maintained during a transitional period. As was expected, intra-Benelux trade increased, Belgian-Luxembourg exports to the Netherlands having risen from 11.6 per cent of all Belgian-Luxembourg exports in the period 1936–1938 to 14.9 per cent for the year 1952, whereas Netherlandish exports to Belgium-Luxembourg rose from 10.8 per cent of all Netherlandish exports in the period 1936–1938 to 14.9 per cent in 1952. The chief difficulties were different costs of production, different wage levels, and different monetary and financial policies in the cooperating countries. Labor and capital were free to move from one country to another, but in actuality there was very little migration of either.

Despite the modest accomplishments of Benelux, the idea of customs unions continued to flourish. In 1957, a treaty creating a European Economic Community was signed by Belgium, France, Western Germany, Italy, Luxembourg, and the Netherlands. This document provided for the gradual establishment over a twelve-year period of the free flow of goods, capital, and labor among the participating powers. It provided further for the administration of the Community by a Council representing the governments of the treaty countries, for a Readaptation Fund which would bear 50 per cent of the cost of retraining and relocating workers and of reconverting plants, for a European Investment Bank with a capital of 1 billion dollars, and for an Investment Fund of 600 million dollars for overseas territories of member states. By December, 1957, this treaty had been ratified by all the powers concerned.

Perhaps the greatest boon to intra-European commerce was, however, the European Payments Union. From its inception the Organization for European Economic Cooperation attempted to facilitate the multilateral settling of intra-European commercial accounts and after some unsuccessful starts (1948) established the EPU in 1950. The Union provided for the fixing of "quotas" between each country and the Union. Up to the limit of its quota a country could pay its debits to the Union in its own currency, but beyond that amount it had to pay in gold and dollars. Again, beyond certain limits, a country had to receive payments for its credits in currencies of member states. Thus there were incentives for debtor countries to increase their exports or to decrease their imports and for creditor countries not to exceed given amounts.

In general, the EPU was a success. It had as members all the major countries of Western Europe, including the United Kingdom, and thus covered a large proportion of the trade of the world. Furthermore, it succeeded in progressively removing most of the quantitative trade restrictions in Europe so that, in 1956, 80 per cent of European trade was free of them. Finally, it managed actually to settle accounts on a multilateral basis. Certainly, it contributed to an expansion of intra-European trade by some 90 per cent between 1948 and 1951. On the other hand, the system resulted in certain rigidities, because when one country had a large and continuing credit, as was the case with Germany in the middle 1950s, or a large and continuing deficit, as was the case of France at the same time, the Union tried to establish a balance by permitting the reimposition of trade restrictions. Without the Union, however, the situation would undoubtedly have been much worse than it was.

Obviously the European Payments Union was not designed to accomplish more than a very limited task of settling international accounts and the ends of economic integration called for much more. It was thought by some that the most realistic approach to economic integration was to achieve it on a commodity basis. Thus there was created in 1951 the European Steel and Coal Community—an outgrowth of a plan proposed by Robert Schuman of France. This institution exercises sovereignty over the coal and steel industries of Belgium, France, West Germany, Italy, Luxembourg, and the Netherlands, that is, its decisions regarding coal and steel are binding on member states. Inasmuch as the Community was designed as a step toward political integration and inasmuch as it had to operate in its limited sphere much like a government, it was endowed with typical governmental institutions; a Council of Ministers to decide on major policies, an Assembly elected by member parliaments to serve in an advisory capacity, a Court of Justice to settle disputes and to rule on questions of treaty violations, and a High Authority to serve as executive. The Treaty of the ESCC provided for free trade in coal and steel among member states, for joint research, and for the abolition of cartels. Furthermore, a small percentage of sales of coal and steel is paid to the Community to cover its expenses and to provide funds for investments in the industries.

The Community appeared in the first years of its existence to be a success. It tended to force the less efficient plants to modernize, and it made investment loans from its funds to improve inefficient plants. It contributed to the stabilization of prices. It took measures to harmonize supply and demand.[28]

[28] Up to December 31, 1953, receipts from regular levies amounted to 34,400,000 dollars, of which 47 per cent came from German firms, 23 per cent from French, 11 from Belgian, 7 from the Saar, 5 from Italy, 3 from Luxembourg, and 4 from the Netherlands. Belgium and Italy received most of the investments which were made.

A Modern American Shopping Center. This photograph shows a shopping center in the midst of a post-World War II suburban housing development. Such centers have been built to give automobiles easy access to retail outlets. This permits the shopper to bring his purchases home at once. This is necessary for perishables and desirable for soft goods, for during the week, in many cases, no one is home to receive deliveries. In this area 5,000 cars can park at one time. (*Courtesy of Levitt and Sons.*)

Perhaps, however, this experiment in placing authority over an industry in a supranational body was not a fair test of integration, for coal and steel industries involved only some 3 per cent of the labor forces of the participating countries; the need for freedom of movement of capital funds was mitigated somewhat by the use of Marshall Plan counterpart funds, and coal and steel industries had already cooperated on an international level to a considerable extent. Enthusiasts for economic integration looked at the ESCC, however, as a harbinger of better things and suggested that similar communities be established in a great variety of sectors from agricultural products (the Green Pool), inland transportation,[29] heavy chemicals, and nuclear energy. Only in this last field, however, was real progress made. There a treaty was negotiated among the same powers involved in the European Economic Community treaty and in the ESCC—a treaty which provided for pooling of resources and for the common development of nuclear energy. "Euratom," the name given the new body, was to be administered by a nuclear energy commission which would have a monopoly of all refined fissionable materials, that

[29] The Inland Transport of the United Nations' Economic Commission for Europe made many suggestions for international collaboration in this industry.

is, it would control both the production, importation, and allocation of fissionable materials. As of December, 1957, all participants had ratified the treaty designed to make "Euratom" a reality.

The End of Economics Is Human Welfare

In the study of economic history which we have been making together, the emphasis placed on economic development should not obscure the

Real National Income per Capita in Selected Countries, 1913 to 1950.

fact that the end of economic activity is to increase the material well-being of individuals. In fact, the measurement which we have used throughout this study to determine economic growth has been national income per capita of the population. In Western culture it is assumed to be desirable that this income be distributed with some degree of equity, that is, that the gap between the very rich and the very poor be narrowed. Therefore, as we come to the end of our study of the post-World War II period it is appropriate that we consider briefly personal income distribution and how that distribution has been made more equitable by social security systems and by taxation.

In spite of wars and depressions there was generally in Western culture an increase in real income per capita during the first four decades

Table 49. Percentage Distribution of Total Income before Taxes and after Taxes

Before Taxes

Groups by size of income (lowest to highest by deciles)	United Kingdom 1938	United Kingdom 1955	Germany Pre-War 1933	Germany West 1950	Netherlands 1938	Netherlands 1950	Denmark 1939	Denmark 1952	Sweden 1935	Sweden 1954	United States 1929-38	United States 1939-48
1			1	1		1.3		1.4		2.0		
2			2	3		2.9	7.6	6.9		3.6		
3	33.2		4	4		4.0			16.0	5.0		
4		32.7	4	4.5	28.5	5.6	17.6	5.4		6.2		
5			7	7.5		7.2		7.0		7.8	75.2	80.6
6			8.5	9.0		8.5		8.8	6.7	9.3		
7	7.5	23.6	9.5	11.0	8.3	9.8	9.0	10.6	9.0	10.6		
8	9.3		11.0	12.0	10.7	11.7	12.3	29.2	12.2	12.7		
9	12.0	14.4	14.0	14.0	13.8	14.0	15.9		16.6	15.5		
10	38.0	29.3	39.0	34.0	38.7	35.0	37.6	30.7	39.5	27.3		
Highest 5 %											24.8	19.4

After Taxes

Groups by size of income (lowest to highest by deciles)	United Kingdom 1938	United Kingdom 1955	Germany Pre-War 1933	Germany West 1950	Netherlands 1938	Netherlands 1950	Denmark 1939	Denmark 1952	Sweden 1935	Sweden 1954	United States 1929-38	United States 1939-48
1							1.4	1.7				
2		12.0			7.3*	4.8	2.7	7.5	9.9	3.5		
3							4.4			4.4		
4	35.7					10.4		5.8		6.1		
5		23.8			20.8	17.0	18.5	7.5	6.0	8.0	75.9	83.6
6								9.2	7.5	9.7		
7	8.0				21.9	10.5	9.3	11.0	9.5	11.5		
8	22.7	24.8				12.3	12.5	29.8	13.0	13.7		
9		14.9			15.5	15.0	16.2		17.2	16.1		
10	33.6	24.5			34.5	30.0	35.0	27.5	36.9	27.0		
Highest 5 %											24.1	16.4

* Data in this column for 1946.
SOURCE: *Economic Survey of Europe in 1956* (Geneva: United Nations, 1957) Chap. IX, pp. 6, 22; Simon Kuznets and Raymond Goldsmith, *Income and Wealth of the United States* (Cambridge: Bowes and Bowes, 1952), p. 142.

after World War I. As can be seen in the accompanying chart, the greatest increases were achieved where there was no great destruction from war.

After World War II, moreover, Western culture achieved some reduction in the inequality of income distribution. At least in six countries for which information is available, the lower 60 per cent of the income earners increased their earnings and the highest 10 per cent had their share reduced, the chief losses here coming from income from property.

Whether or not the changes in income distribution reflected structural change in the economy or were simply a function of full employment and prosperity is debatable. Nevertheless, it is clear that income taxes smoothed out income inequalities to a considerable extent.

Furthermore, social security systems were so greatly extended that they brought up the distributive shares of the lower income groups. In most Western European countries extensive health insurance, with generous medical benefits, was added to the usual sickness, invalidity, old age,

Table 50. Expectation of Life at Birth

Country	Period	Males	Females
United States	1954	69.6	69.6
United Kingdom	1954	67.58	73.05
West Germany	1949–1954	64.6	68.5
France	1950–1951	63.6	69.3
Netherlands	1950–1952	70.6	72.9
Italy	1935–1937		57.49

maternity, death, and unemployment benefits. And in several places, notably in France and Italy, a system of family allowances was introduced whereby a worker's wage was increased according to the number of children he had. In the United States payments under social insurance and related programs totaled 12,606,000,000 dollars in 1955; in France, social security benefits of all kinds were estimated to constitute nearly 30 per cent of the French worker's total wage.

At all events, a degree of economic well-being was reached so that in the more advanced countries a considerable proportion of expenditures was for the finer things of life and living standards were so raised that there was a marked extension of the expectation of life at birth.

The great socioeconomic problems for the future of the West are clearly whether prevailing standards of income per capita can be maintained or raised, whether a large part of personal expenditures will be for "civilizing activity," and whether the economic and military position of the West can be kept at levels adequate to cope with threats of force from without. These are issues which will test the leadership of the future.

Bibliography

The following bibliography is designed to assist both the student and teacher in pursuing the many subjects treated in this volume. It is, however, not conceived as an exhaustive guide to the entire literature of the economic history of Western civilization, but rather as an adjunct to the text. It is considered to be adequate for all levels of university students from undergraduates to graduates. Books that have particularly useful bibliographies are marked with an asterisk.

Bibliographical Guides

There is no specialized bibliographical guide to all economic history. A most useful aid to locating bibliographies is Constance M. Winchell, *Guide to Reference Books*, 7th ed., Chicago: American Library Association, 1951. The forthcoming *Guide to Historical Literature*, prepared by a committee of the American Historical Association, will contain references of use to economic historians. There is also A. Grandin, *Bibliographie générale des sciences juridiques, politiques, économiques et sociales de 1800 à 1925–1926*, Paris: Sirey, 1926 (3 vols.).

There are several national bibliographies like F. C. Dahlmann and G. Waitz, *Quellenkunde der deutschen Geschichte*, Leipzig: K. F. Koehler, 1931, some of which contain much economic material. See also Judith B. Williams, *A Guide to the Printed Materials for English Social and Economic History*, New York: Columbia University Press, 1926 (2 vols.).

Encyclopedias

Most relevant to the work of the economic historian is *The Encyclopaedia of the Social Sciences*,* New York: Macmillan, 1930–1935 (15 vols.), but many of its articles are out of date and the entire work should be revised. See also

Ludwig Elster, Adolf Weber, and Friedrich Wieser, *Handwörterbuch der Staatswissenschaft,* Iena: Fischer, 1923–1928 (8 vols.), and R. H. I. Palgrave, *Dictionary of Political Economy,* London: Macmillan, 1925.

Historical Atlases

Historical atlases are usually oriented toward political history, but many of them contain maps illustrating economic history. See especially William R. Shepherd, *Historical Atlas,* New York: Barnes & Noble, 1956; Robert R. Palmer, *Atlas of World History,* Chicago: Rand McNally 1957; and Edward Whiting Fox, *Atlas of European History,* New York: Oxford University Press, 1957. For the United States, see Charles O. Paullin, *Atlas of the Historical Geography of the United States,* New York: American Geographical Society, 1932, and Clifford L. and Elizabeth H. Lord, *Historical Atlas of the United States,* New York: Holt, 1953. The student of economic history will find useful for place names *The Columbia-Lippincott Gazetteer of the World,* New York: Columbia University Press, 1952.

Statistical Compilations

Collections of quantitative data are available in yearbooks of all the major countries of Western civilization, such as the *Statistical Abstract of the United States,* the *Statistical Abstract for the United Kingdom,* the *Annuaire statistique* (France), *Annuario statistico* (Italy), and the *Statistisches Jahrbuch* (Germany). In some cases the statistical agencies which issue these volumes have published important historical compilations, like the *Annuaire statistique* for 1946, Paris: Imprimerie Nationale, 1947, and the *Historical Statistics of the United States, 1789–1945,* Washington: Government Printing Office, 1949.

The United Nations Organization has continued the policy of the League of Nations in publishing the very important *Statistical Yearbook* with international data. The various specialized agencies, like the International Labor Office, the Food and Agricultural Organization, and the International Bank all issue separate statistical publications.

Economic Geographies

Economic geographies and studies of world resource patterns are published frequently as new information is amassed. An excellent study of resources is Erich W. Zimmermann, *World Resources and Industries,* New York: Harper, 1951. See also W. S. and E. S. Woytinsky, *World Population and Production,* New York: Twentieth Century Fund, 1953. Another important study of this character, which has also some forecasts, is J. Frederic Dewhurst, *America's Needs and Resources,* New York: Twentieth Century Fund, 1955. The same author is preparing a similar study for Europe, *Europe's Needs and Resources,* to be published by the Twentieth Century Fund, probably in 1960.

The Nature of History, Economics, and Economic History

The literature concerning the nature of history is abundant. For the philosophy of history one may consult with profit W. H. Walsh, *An Introduction to Philosophy of History,** London: Hutchinson's University Library, 1951. For a history of history see, Herbert Butterfield, *Man on his Past*, Cambridge: Cambridge University Press, 1955. For a statement on history in relation to other social sciences, see *The Social Sciences in Historical Study*, New York: Social Science Research Council, 1954; Fritz Stern, *The Varieties of History*, New York: Meridian Books, 1956; and Mirra Komarovsky, *Common Frontiers of the Social Sciences*, Glencoe, Ill.: The Free Press, 1957.

For an introduction to economics, see a general elementary text like Paul A. Samuelson, *Economics: An Introductory Analysis*, New York: McGraw-Hill, 1958. For an appreciation of current trends in economics, see *A Survey of Contemporary Economics*, Philadelphia: American Economic Association, 1948–1952 (2 vols.).

For the history of economic theory, consult Charles Gide and Charles Rist, *A History of Economic Doctrines from the Times of the Physiocrats to the Present Day,** Boston: Heath, 1948; Eric Roll, *A History of Economic Thought*, Englewood Cliffs, N.J.: Prentice-Hall, 1956; and Joseph Dorfman, *The Economic Mind in American Civilization,** New York: Viking, 1946–1949 (3 vols.).

Regarding economic history, the student will find much food for thought in Frederic C. Lane and Jelle C. Riemersma, *Enterprise and Secular Change: Readings in Economic History*, Homewood, Ill., Richard R. Irwin, 1953; Karl F. Helleiner, *Readings in European Economic History*, Toronto: University of Toronto Press, 1946; and E. M. Carus-Wilson, *Essays in Economic History*, London: E. Arnold, 1954.

Histories of Technology and Science

Inasmuch as works dealing with specific periods or individual machines will be cited later in chapter bibliographies, only general works are listed here. A good introduction to the theory of technological development is S. C. Gilfillan, *The Sociology of Invention*, Chicago: Follett, 1935. Also useful are William F. Ogburn, *Social Change*, New York: Viking, 1952, and John Jewkes, *The Sources of Invention*, New York: St. Martin's Press, 1958.

Among histories of technology, see the comprehensive work by Charles Singer et al., *A History of Technology,** New York: Oxford University Press, 1956–   , to be completed in five volumes. Among other good studies are Maurice Daumas, *Histoire générale des techniques*, Paris: Presses Universitaires, in press (3 vols.); A. P. Usher, *History of Mechanical Inventions*, New York, McGraw-Hill, 1929; S. Lilley, *Men, Machines, and History,** London: Cobbett Press, 1948; Arthur F. M. Fleming and Harold J. Brocklehurst, *A History of Engineering*, London: A. & C. Black, 1925; *Van Nostrand's Scientific*

498

Encyclopedia, Princeton, N.J.: Van Nostrand, 1958; Richard S. Kirby, *Engineering in History,* New York: McGraw-Hill, 1926.

As an introduction to the history of science one might well turn to Herbert Butterfield, *The Origins of Modern Science,* New York: Macmillan, 1957; A. R. Hall, *The Scientific Revolution, 1500–1800,* Boston: Beacon Press, 1956; and René Taton (Ed.), *Histoire générale des sciences,* Paris: Presses Universitaires, 1957 (3 vols. planned).

See also J. D. Bernal, *Science and Industry in the Nineteenth Century,* London: Routledge, 1953.

History of Population

Alexander M. Carr-Saunders, *World Population; Past Growth and Present Trends,* New York: Oxford University Press, 1936; Marcel Reinhard, *Histoire de la population mondiale de 1700 à 1800,* Paris: Domat-Montchrestien, 1949; W. F. Willcox, *Introduction to the Vital Statistics of the United States,* Washington: Government Printing Office, 1933, W. F. Wilcox (Ed.), *International Migrations,* New York: National Bureau of Economic Research, 1929–1931 (2 vols.); Louis Dublin, Alfred Lotka, and M. Spiegelman, *Length of Life,* New York: Ronald, 1949; and Brinley Thomas, *Migrations and Economic Growth,* Cambridge: Cambridge University Press, 1954.

History of Money and Banking

An excellent introduction to the history of money and banking is Carlo M. Cipolla, *Money, Prices, and Civilization in the Mediterranean World: Fifth to Seventeenth Century,* Princeton, N.J.: Princeton University Press, 1956. Interesting general views of money and its role in economic growth are A. Dopsch, *Naturalwirtschaft und Geldwirtschaft in der Weltgeschichte,* Vienna: Seidel, 1930, and Marc Bloch, *Esquisse d'une histoire monétaire de l'Europe,* Paris: Colin, 1954. More theoretical works are Dennis H. Robertson, *Money,* New York: Pitman, 1948, and R. G. Hawtrey, *Currency and Credit,* New York: Longmans, 1950.

A. E. Feaveryear, *The Pound Sterling,* New York: Oxford University Press, 1931, is an exceedingly interesting account of a currency from its very beginnings to a recent date. Another study of this kind, but with a more legalistic emphasis is Arthur Nussbaum, *The History of the Dollar,* New York: Columbia University Press, 1957.

For an introduction to the history of banking one would do well to consider John H. Clapham, *The Bank of England,* Cambridge: Cambridge University Press, 1945 (2 vols.), and J. G. Van Dillen (Ed.), *History of the Principal Public Banks,* The Hague: Nijhoff, 1934.

General Economic Histories

Economic histories embracing the entire area of Western culture are extremely rare. Usually, economic histories are restricted to some geographical area or to a limited period of time. Of the more general works, see the multivolume *The Cambridge Economic History*,* Cambridge: University Press, 1942–   , which was begun under the editorship of John H. Clapham and Eileen Power and is being continued under the direction of M. M. Postan and H. J. Habbakuk. For the United States, the most comprehensive work is *The Economic History of the United States*, New York: Rinehart, 1945–   .

These may be mentioned among the many efforts at synthesis: Shepard B. Clough and Charles W. Cole, *Economic History of Europe*, 3d ed., Boston: Heath, 1952; Herbert Heaton, *Economic History of Europe*, New York: Harper, 1948; Werner Sombart, *Der moderne Kapitalismus*, Munich: Duncker & Humboldt, 1921–1928 (3 vols. in 6); Max Weber, *General Economic History*, Glencoe, Ill.: Free Press, 1950; J. Kulischer, *Allgemeine Wirtschaftsgeschichte des Mittelalters und der Neuzeit*, Berlin: Rütten and Loening, 1954; and Gino Luzzatto, *Storia economica dell' età moderna e contemporanea fino al 1950*, Padua: Cedam, 1952 (2 vols.).

Economic History Reviews

Many historical reviews carry articles pertaining to economic affairs, but these are the chief specialized journals: *The Journal of Economic History* (United States), *The Economic History Review* (English), *Annales* and *Revue d'histoire économique et sociale* (France), *Vierteljahrschrift für Sozial und Wirtschaftsgeschichte* (Germany), *Economia e storia* (Italy), *Scandinavian Economic History Review* (Copenhagen), and *International Review of Social History* (Amsterdam). *Historical Abstracts* is a guide to economic historical articles in scholarly journals.

National Economic Histories

Many of the works in economic history have been conceived as national histories for the very good reason that since the discipline of economic history has grown to importance the national state has played a large role in forming economic policy and in determining the economic experience of individuals. Some of these national histories are listed here; others will be noted in the bibliographies of individual chapters.

The most extensive economic history of Britain is John H. Clapham, *An Economic History of Modern Britain*,* London: Cambridge University Press, 1950–1952 (3 vols.). It covers the period since 1820. For a briefer version, see John H. Clapham, *A Concise History of Britain from the Earliest Times to 1750*, Cambridge: Cambridge University Press, 1949, and its companion, W. H. B. Court, *A Concise Economic History of Britain from 1750 to Recent Times*, Cambridge: Cambridge University Press, 1954. Consult also Ephraim Lipson, *The Economic History of England*, London: A. & C. Black, 1937–1943 (3 vols.).

The leading economic history of France is that by Henri Sée, *Histoire économique de la France*,* Paris: Colin, 1948–1951 (2 vols.). For Germany, consult Friedrich Lütge, *Deutsche Sozial- und Wirtschaftsgeschichte*, Berlin: Springer, 1952; August Sartorius von Waltershausen, *Deutsche Wirtschaftsgeschichte, 1815–1914*, Iena: Fischer, 1923; and Gustav Stolper, *German Economy, 1870–1940*, New York: Reynal & Hitchcock, 1940. For Belgium, see Henri Pirenne, *Histoire de Belgique*,* Brussels: Lamertin, 1908–32 (7 vols.), and B. S. Chlepner, *Cent ans d'histoire sociale en Belgique*, Brussels: Institut Solvay, 1956. For the Netherlands, the student will find useful Ernst Baasch, *Holländische Wirtschaftsgeschichte*, Iena: Fischer, 1927; and *10 Jaar Economisch Leven in Nederland*, The Hague: Nijhoff, 1955.

For Italy, see Gino Luzzatto, *Storia economica d'Italia*, Rome: Leonardo, 1949, vol. I (vol. II, in preparation). See also Alfred Doren, *Storia economica dell'Italia nel medio evo*, Padua: Cedam, 1939.

For Spain, J. Vicens Vives (Ed.), *Historia social y economica de España y America*, Barcellona: Teide, 1957–58 (4 vols.); and Manuel Colmeiro. *Historia de la economia politica en España*, Madrid: Lopez, 1863.

For Sweden, see Eli F. Heckscher, *An Economic History of Sweden*, Cambridge, Mass.: Harvard University Press, 1954, and G. A. Montgomery, *The Rise of Modern Industry in Sweden*, Stockholm: Almquist and Wiksell, 1939.

For Austria: K. H. Werner et al., *Hundert Jahre oesterreichischer Wirtschaftsentwicklung, 1848–1948*, Vienna: Springer, 1949; Johann Slokar, *Geschichte der oesterreichischen Industrie und ihrer Foederung unter Kaiser Franz I*, Vienna: Tempsky, 1914; and Fritz Klenner, *Die oesterreichischen Gewerkschaften*, Vienna: Gewerkschaftsbund, 1951 (2 vols.).

For Bohemia: Artur Salz, *Geschichte der boehmischen Industrie der Neuzeit*, Munich: Duncker and Humblot, 1913, and Frederick Hertz, *Economic Problems of the Danubian States*, London: Gollancz, 1947.

Among the many good economic histories of the United States, one may consult with profit Edward C. Kirkland, *A History of American Life*,* New York: Appleton-Century-Crofts, 1951; Harold Williamson (Ed.), *Growth of the American Economy*,* Englewood Cliffs, N.J.: Prentice-Hall, 1951; and Shepard B. Clough, *The American Way*,* New York: Crowell, 1953.

For a general economic history of Canada: W. T. Easterbrook and Hugh G. T. Aitken, *Canadian Economic History*,* Toronto: Macmillan, 1956: O. J. Firestone, *Canada's Economic Development, 1867–1952*, paper prepared for the International Association for Research in Income and Wealth, 1953.

For the economic history of the Argentine see Luis R. Gondra, *Historia economica de la Republica Argentina*, Buenos Aires: Sudamerica, 1943, and Ricardo M. Ortiz, *Historia economica de la Argentina*, Buenos Aires: Raigal, 1955 (2 vols.).

For Brazil: Caio Prado Junior, *Historia economica do Brazil*, São Paulo: Editora Brasiliense, 1945, and Roberto C. Simonsen, *Historia economica do Brazil, 1500–1820*, São Paulo: Editora Nacional, 1937.

For Peru: Emilio Romero, *Historia economica del Peru*, Buenos Aires: Sudamerica, 1949.

For South Africa: H. M. Robertson, *South Africa*, Durham, N. C.: Duke University Press, 1957.

Chapter 1. Civilization, Culture, and Economic Growth

For an introduction to these subjects the student would do well to consult Shepard B. Clough, *The Rise and Fall of Civilization*,* New York: Columbia University Press, 1957, where I have developed my ideas more fully than I have been able to in the present volume. In order to understand the anthropologist's views on civilization and culture and their relation to economics, see Alfred L. Kroeber, *Configurations of Culture Growth*, Berkeley, Calif.: University of California Press, 1944; Clyde Kluckhohn, *Mirror for Man*, New York: McGraw-Hill, 1949; and Pitrim A. Sorokin, *Social Philosophies of an Age of Crisis*, Boston: Beacon Press, 1950. To learn how the sociologist sees the way that men living in society function, consult Robert M. MacIver, *Society: Its Structure and Changes*, New York: Rinehart, 1949. Special theories of the rise and fall of civilization will be found in W. M. Flinders Petrie, *The Revolutions of Civilization*, New York: Harper, 1911, and Ellsworth Huntington, *Man and Civilization*, New York: Wiley, 1945.

From the abundant literature on the subject of economic growth, one may consult with profit, for theory: W. Arthur Lewis, *The Theory of Economic Growth*, London: G. Allen, 1955, and for more substantive accounts, Simon Kuznets, *National Income and its Composition*, New York: National Bureau of Economic Research, 1941; Colin Clark, *Conditions of Economic Progress*,* London: Macmillan, 1957; *National and Per Capita Incomes: Seventy Countries*, New York: United Nations, 1949; *Measures for the Economic Development of Underdeveloped Countries*, New York: United Nations, 1951; and Charles P. Kindleberger, *Economic Development*, New York: McGraw-Hill, 1958.

Chapter 2. Economic Achievements in the Ancient World

Excellent surveys of the entire period are to be found in Gordon Childe, *Man Makes Himself*,* London: Watts, 1936, and *What Happened in History*, Baltimore, Md.: Penguin, 1946. For primitive techniques, see F. M. Feldhaus, *Technik der Vorzeit*, Leizig: Engelmann, 1914. Among the standard works on the economic history of the Ancient period, one should note M. I. Rostovseff, *A History of the Ancient World*, New York: Oxford University Press, 1928, and by the same author, *The Social and Economic History of the Hellenistic World*, New York: Oxford University Press, 1941 (3 vols.), and *The Social and Economic History of the Roman Empire*,* New York: Oxford University Press, 1957 (2 vols.). Also, Tenny Frank, *An Economic History of Ancient Rome*, Baltimore, Md.: Johns Hopkins Press, 1933–1940 (5 vols.); Jules Toutain, *The Economic Life of the Ancient World*, New York: Knopf, 1930; E. M. Heichelheim, *An Ancient Economic History*, Leiden: Sijthoff, 1958, (3 vols.); Jack Finegan, *Light from the Ancient Past*, Princeton, N.J.: Princeton University Press, 1946; H. Michell, *The Economics of Ancient Greece*, New York: Macmillan, 1957; S. R. K. Glanville (Ed.), *The Legacy of Egypt*, New York: Oxford University Press, 1942; A. H. M. Jones, *Cities of the Eastern Roman Provinces,* New York: Oxford University Press, 1937; and Moses Finley, *Land and Credit in Ancient Athens,* New Brunswick, N.J.: Rutgers University Press, 1951.

Chapters 3 and 4. The Middle Ages

In addition to the more general works cited above, the more advanced student may want to push his studies into special phases of medieval life. One of the most stimulating scholars in this field has been Henri Pirenne, although some of his theories about development out of the "Dark Ages" have been questioned. Nevertheless, one will find useful Henri Pirenne, *Economic and Social History of Medieval Europe,* New York: Harcourt, Brace, 1937, and *Medieval Cities: Their Origin and the Revival of Trade,* New York: Doubleday, 1956. Another stimulating scholar is A. Dopsch. Consult his works, *The Economic and Social Foundations of European Civilization,* London: Paul, Trench, Trubner, 1937, and *Herrschaft und Bauer in der deutschen Kaizerzeit,* Iena: Fischer, 1939. One will also find many insights in A. Sapori, *Studi di storia economica medievale,* Florence: Sansoni, 1946, and H. Aubin, *Vom Altertum zum Mittelalter,** Munich: Münchener Verlag, 1949.

As an introduction to the agricultural economy on the Continent, one might begin by reading Marc Bloch, *Les Caractères originaux de l'histoire rurale française,* Paris: Colin, 1952, and G. Lizerand, *Le Régime rural de l'ancienne France,* Paris: Presses Universitaires, 1942. For England, consult C. S. Orwin, *The Open Fields,* New York: Oxford University Press, 1938; H. S. Bennett, *Life on an English Manor: A Study of Peasant Conditions, 1150–1450,* Cambridge: Cambridge University Press, 1937; and N. Neilson, *Medieval Agrarian Economy,* New York: Holt, 1936.

On the subject of feudalism, one may turn with profit to F. L. Ganshof, *Feudalism,** New York: Longmans, 1952; J. W. Thompson, *Economic and Social History of the Middle Ages,* Chicago: University of Chicago Press, 1928; and Rushton Coulborn, *Feudalism in History,* Princeton, N.J.: Princeton University Press, 1956. In connection with agriculture, one should look at G. Gibault, *Histoire des légumes,* Paris: Librairie Horticole, 1912; and H. E. Jacob, *Histoire du pain depuis 6000 ans,* Paris: Seuil, 1958.

The literature on industrial production is limited. See G. G. Coulton, *The Medieval Village,* Cambridge: Cambridge University Press, 1925, and E. Coornaert, *Les Corporations en France avant 1789,* Paris: Gallimard, 1941. On the other hand, literature on trade is extensive: E. Power and M. Postan (Eds.), *Studies in English Trade in the Fifteenth Century,* London: Routledge, 1933; Robert S. Lopez and Irving W. Raymond, *Medieval Trade in the Mediterranean World,* New York: Columbia University Press, 1955: Eugene H. Byrne, *Genoese Shipping in the Twelfth and Thirteenth Centuries,* Cambridge, Mass.: Harvard University Press, 1930; W. Heyd, *Histoire du commerce du Levant,* Leipzig: Harrassowitz, 1923 (2 vols.); Emile Levasseur, *Histoire du commerce de la France,* Paris: Rousseau, 1911–1912 (2 vols.); J. E. Tyler, *The*

Alpine Passes, Oxford: Blackwell, 1930; and A. Segré, *Storia del commercio,* Turin: Lattes, 1923 (2 vols.).

Money and banking have also been extensively investigated. Philip Grierson, *Numismatics and History,* London: Privately Printed, 1951, and Carlo Cipolla, *Money, Prices, and Civilization** (referred to earlier under the History of Money and Banking) are good introductions to money. Regarding lending, see W. E. Lunt, *Papal Revenues in the Middle Ages,* New York: Columbia University Press, 1934 (2 vols.); B. N. Nelson, *The Idea of Usury,* Princeton, N.J.: Princeton University Press, 1950; Raymond de Roover, *The Medici Bank,* New York: New York University Press, 1948; A. P. Usher, *The Early History of Deposit Banking in Mediterranean Europe,* Cambridge, Mass.: Harvard University Press, 1943; G. Mickwitz, *Geld und Wirtschaft im römischen Reich des 4ten Jahrhunderts,* Helsinki: Centraltryckeri, 1932; and J. G. van Dillen (Ed.), *History of the Principal Public Banks,* The Hague: Nijhoff, 1934. See also William Beveridge, *Prices and Wages in England from the Twelfth to the Nineteenth Century,* London: Longmans, 1939.

For transportation, see F. L. Lane, *Venetian Ships and Shipbuilders of the Renaissance,* Baltimore, Md.: Johns Hopkins Press, 1934; Archibald Lewis, *Naval Power and Trade in the Mediterranean, 500–1100 A.D.,* Princeton, N.J.: Princeton University Press, 1951; Lefebvre des Noëttes, *La Force motrice animale à travers les âges,* Paris: Berger-Levrault, 1924; and L. F. Salzman, *English Trade in the Middle Ages,* New York: Oxford University Press, 1931.

Some idea of crafts may be had from Martin S. Briggs, *A. Short History of the Building Crafts,* New York: Oxford University Press, 1925; H. Stein, *Les Architects des cathédrales gothiques,* Paris: Laurens, 1909; E. Power, *The Wool Trade in English Medieval History,* New York: Oxford University Press, 1942; and Emile Levasseur, *Histoire des classes ouvrières,* Paris: Rousseau, 1900–1904 (4 vols.). On slavery, see Charles Verlinden, *L'Esclavage dans l'Europe médiévale,* Bruges: De Tempel, 1955– . Some idea of public health may be had from Emile Levasseur, *La Population française,* Paris: Rousseau, 1889–1892 (3 vols.); G. G. Coulton, *The Black Death,* London: Benn, 1929; Charles Mullett, *The Bubonic Plague,* Lexington, Ky.: University of Kentucky Press, 1956; and Josiah Russell, *British Medieval Population,* Albuquerque, N.M.: University of New Mexico Press, 1948.

On medieval science, see Lynn Thorndike, *History of Magic and Experimental Science,* New York: Columbia University Press, 1923– (8 vols.).

Chapter 7. European Discoveries and Expansion, 1500–1700

Among the more general works, the following will provide a good introduction to the discoveries: P. Sykes, *History of Exploration,** London: Routledge, 1950; L. Outhwaite, *Unrolling the Map,* New York: Reynal & Hitchcock, 1935; A. P. Newton, *The Great Age of Discovery,* London: University of London Press, 1932; J. N. L. Baker, *A History of Geographical Discovery and Exploration,* London: Harrap, 1937; Lloyd A. Brown, *The Story of Maps,* Boston:

Little, Brown, 1949; and Charles E. Nowell, *The Great Discoveries*, Ithaca, N.Y.: Cornell University Press, 1954.

Nearly all the explorers have been extensively treated in monographs. These are some of the more enlightening: L. Olschki, *Marco Polo's Precursors*, Baltimore, Md.: Johns Hopkins Press, 1943; Henry H. Hart, *Venetian Adventurer: The Life and Times of Marco Polo*, Stanford, Calif.: Stanford University Press, 1943; E. Prestage, *The Portuguese Pioneers*, London: Macmillan, 1933; C. R. Beazley, *Prince Henry the Navigator*, London: Putnam, 1923; K. G. Jayne, *Vasco da Gama and His Successors*, London: Methuen, 1910; Frederick J. Pohl, *Amerigo Vespucci, Pilot Major*, New York: Columbia University Press, 1944; C. M. Parr, *So Noble a Captain* [Magellan], New York: Crowell, 1953; Samuel E. Morison, *Admiral of the Ocean Sea: A Life of Christopher Columbus*, Boston: Little, Brown, 1942; and J. B. Brebner, *The Explorers of North America, 1492–1806*, New York: Doubleday, 1955.

Hard upon the discoveries and explorations came trade and the first settlements. See C. H. Haring, *The Spanish Empire in America*, New York: Oxford University Press, 1947; R. B. Merriman, *The Rise of the Spanish Empire in the Old World and the New*, New York: Macmillan, 1922–1934 (4 vols.); C. H. Haring, *Trade and Navigation between Spain and the Indies in the Time of the Hapsburgs*, Cambridge, Mass.: Harvard University Press, 1918; Herbert E. Boulton, *The Spanish Borderlands*, New Haven, Conn.: Yale University Press, 1921; Edward G. Bourne, *Spain in America, 1450–1580*, New York: Harper, 1904; L. B. Simpson, *The Encomienda in New Spain*, Berkeley, Calif.: University of California Press, 1950; and J. A. Williamson, *Maritime Enterprise, 1485–1558*,* New York: Oxford University Press, 1913.

Chapter 8. Economic Consequences of European Overseas Expansion

One of the major consequences of the expansion of Europe to America was the acquisition by Europe of great amounts of precious metals. These tended to decrease the purchasing power of money, a fact reflected in price rises. These increases have been investigated by an International Scientific Committee for the Study of Prices. Among their publications are Earl J. Hamilton, *American Treasure and the Price Revolution in Spain, 1501–1650*, Cambridge, Mass.: Harvard University Press, 1934; Henri Hauser (Ed.), *Recherches et documents sur l'histoire des prix en France de 1500 à 1800*, Paris: Les Presses Modernes, 1936; M. J. Elsas, *Umriss einer Geschichte der Preise und Löhne in Deutschland*, Leyden: Sijthoff, 1936; William Beveridge, *Prices and Wages in England from the Twelfth to the Nineteenth Century*, London: Longmans, 1939; and N. W. Posthumus, *Inquiry into the History of Prices in Holland*, Leyden: Brill, 1946. Similar studies are being carried on in Belgium by Charles Verlinden and Paul Harsin. In Italy prices in the more recent period are being collected by a group of scholars among whom are Carlo Cipolla, Domenico Demarco, Giuseppe Parenti, et al. Their findings are being published in *Archivio dell'unificazione italiana*, Rome: I.R.I., 1955–   .

The impact of the new discoveries on trade was, of course, very considerable.

The shift in the center of trade is discussed in L. B. Packard, *The Commercial Revolution, 1400–1776*, New York: Holt, 1927; J. H. Parry, *Europe and a Wider World*, London: Hutchinson's University Library, 1949. See also J. Lacour-Gayet, *Histoire de commerce*, Paris: SPID, 1950–1955 (6 vols.).

For an understanding of the impact of the European market on newly opened areas, see A. Kammerer, *Les Guerres du poivre: les Portuguais dans l'océan indien et la mer rouge au XVIe siècle*, Cairo: Royal Geographical Society of Egypt, 1935 (2 vols.); C. M. Andrews, *The Colonial Period of American History*, New Haven, Conn.: Yale University Press, 1934–1938 (4 vols.); R. H. Fisher, *The Russian Fur Trade, 1550–1700*, Berkeley, Calif.: University of California Press, 1943; H. A. Innis, *The Cod Fisheries*, Toronto: University of Toronto Press, 1954; B. H. M. Vlekke, *Nusantra: A History of the East Indian Archipelago*, Cambridge, Mass.: Harvard University Press, 1943; G. M. Wrong, *The Rise and Fall of New France*, New York: Macmillan, 1928 (2 vols.).

The influence of overseas areas on Europe was also very great. On this subject consult such works as J. B. Botsford, *English Society in the Eighteenth Century as Influenced from Overseas*, New York: Macmillan, 1934; J. E. Gillespie, *The Influence of Overseas Expansion on England to 1700*, New York: Columbia University Press, 1920; and J. Klein, *The Mesta: A Study in Spanish Economic History, 1273–1836*, Cambridge, Mass.: Harvard University Press, 1920. See also E. Vaille, *Histoire générale des postes francaises*, Paris: Presses Universitaires 1947–1955 (6 vols.).

Overseas expansion had much to do with the development of capitalism and hence with interest taking. See R. H. Tawney, *Religion and the Rise of Capitalism*, New York: New American Library, 1954; and E. Troeltsch, *The Social Teaching of the Christian Churches*, New York: Macmillan, 1931 (2 vols.). See, too, the bibliography for chap. 10. Expansion also had an impact on business organization and the formation of joint-stock companies. See D. Hannay, *The Great Chartered Companies*, London: Williams & Norgate, 1926; W. R. Scott, *The Constitution and Finance of English, Scottish, and Irish Joint-stock Companies to 1720*, Cambridge: Cambridge University Press, 1910–1912 (3 vols.); and Armand Dubois, *The English Business Company after the Bubble Act, 1720–1800*, New York: Commonwealth Fund, 1938; H. Lévy-Bruhl, *Histoire juridique des sociétés de commerce de France aux XVIIe et XVIIIe siècle*, Paris: Domat-Montchrestien, 1938; and S. van Brakel, *De Hollandsche Handelscompagniën der zeventiende Eeuw*, The Hague: Nijhoff, 1908.

Chapter 9. Science, Technology, and the Early Industrial Revolution, 1500– 1700

The development of the physical sciences was to have a great influence upon techniques and subsequent industrial processes. For the beginnings of science in the modern period one may use, in addition to histories of science mentioned earlier: J. B. Conant, *An Understanding of Science: An Historical Approach*, New York: New American Library, 1952; J. Jeans, *The Growth of Physical Science*, Cambridge: Cambridge University Press, 1951; G. N.

Clark, *Science and Social Welfare in the Age of Newton*, New York: Oxford University Press, 1937; and George Sarton, *Introduction to the History of Science*, Baltimore, Md.: Williams & Wilkins, 1950–1953 (3 vols.).

Some idea of the relationship between science and technology in this period may be had from Edward McCurdy, *Leonardo da Vinci's Notebooks*, New York: Reynal & Hitchcock, 1939; and Georgius Agricola, *De Re Metallica*, (H. C. and L. H. Hoover, Trans.) London: The Mining Magazine, 1912. See also, A. Castiglioni, *A History of Medicine*, New York: Knopf, 1947, and Richard Shryock, *The Development of Modern Medicine*, New York: Knopf, 1947.

One of the pioneers in stressing an "early" industrial revolution in England is John U. Nef. See his *The Rise of the British Coal Industry*,* London: Routledge, 1932 (2 vols.); *La Naissance de la civilisation industrielle et le monde contemporain*, Paris: Colin, 1954; and *Industry and Government in France and England, 1540–1640*, Ithaca, N.Y.: Great Seal Books, 1957. See also B. Gille, *Les origines de la grande industrie métallurgique en France*, Paris: Domat, 1947; Freda Diamond, *The Story of Glass*, New York: Harcourt, Brace, 1957; and William T. O'Dea, *The Social History of Lighting*, London: Routledge, 1958.

Chapter 10. Establishing the Capitalist System

The literature on the beginnings of capitalism is extensive. A good introduction to the subject is Henri Sée, *Modern Capitalism*, New York: Adelphi, 1928. See also, Jacob Strieder, *Zur Genesis der moderne Kapitalismus*, Munich: Duncker, 1935; Henri Hauser, *Les Débuts du capitalisme moderne*, Paris: Alcan, 1930; and John A. Hobson, *The Evolution of Modern Capitalism*, New York: Scribner, 1926.

On the so-called capitalist spirit, see A. Fanfani, *Le origine dello spirito capitalistico in Italia*, Milan: Vita e Pensiero, 1933, and Max Weber, *The Protestant Ethic and the Spirit of Capitalism*, New York: Scribner, 1952.

Examples of business leaders in the period of early capitalism are to be found in V. Klarwill, *The Fugger News Letters*, New York: Putnam, 1926 (2 vols.); Richard Ehrenberg, *Capital and Finance in the Age of the Renaissance*, New York: Harcourt, Brace, 1928; and Y. Renouard, *Les Hommes d'affaires italiens du moyen âge*, Paris: Colin, 1949.

The development of capitalism is reflected in the growth of economic theory and capitalistic institutions. For the former, see Paul Harsin, *Les Doctrines monétaires et financières en France de XVIe au XVIIIe siècle*, Paris: Alcan, 1928, and Charles Rist, *Histoire des doctrines relatives au crédit et à la monnaie depuis John Law jusqu' à nos jours*, Paris: Sirey, 1951. For the latter, see, for example, C. F. Trenerry, *The Origin and Early History of Insurance*, London: P. S. King, 1926, and Terence O'Donnell, *History of Life Insurance in its Formative Years*, Chicago: American Conservation Co., 1936. Also C. E. Labrousse, *Esquisse du mouvement des prix et des revenus en France au XVIIIe siècle*, Paris: Dalloz, 1933 (2 vols.), and by the same author, *La Crise de l'économie française à la fin de l'ancien regime*, Paris: Presses Universitaires, 1944. On early panics, see Ernst H. Krelage, *Bloemenspeculatie in Nederland: De Tulpomanie van 1636–1637 en de Hyacintenhandel, 1720–1736*, Amsterdam: Van Kampen and Son, 1942; and Paul Harsin (Ed.), *Oeuvres complètes de John Law*, Paris: Sirey, 1934 (3 vols.).

Chapter 11. Mercantilism

The most penetrating study of mercantilism in recent times is Eli Heckscher, *Mercantilism*,° London: G. Allen, 1934 (2 vols.), although it has the defect of not giving consideration to Portuguese and Spanish policies. Another important study is Charles W. Cole, *Colbert and a Century of French Mercantilism*, New York: Columbia University Press, 1939 (2 vols.). It may be supplemented by his *French Mercantilist Doctrines before Colbert*, New York: Richard R. Smith, 1931, and his *French Mercantilism*, New York: Columbia University Press, 1943. A short statement of the problem will be found in chap. 1 of Shepard B. Clough, *France: 1789–1939. A Study in National Economics*,° New York: Scribner, 1939. Also G. Schmoller, *The Mercantile System and Its Historical Significance*, New York: P. Smith, 1931, and A. W. Horrocks, *A Short History of Mercantilism*, London: Methuen, 1925. For policies in Spain, see Earl J. Hamilton, *Money, Prices, and Wages in Valencia, Aragon, and Navarre, 1351–1500*, Cambridge, Mass.: Harvard, 1936, and by the same author, *War and Prices in Spain (1651–1800)*, Cambridge, Mass.: Harvard University Press, 1947; F. Braudel, *La Méditerranée et le monde méditerranéen à l'époque de Philippe II*, Paris: Colin, 1949; and R. S. Smith, *The Spanish Guild Merchant: A History of the Consulado, 1250–1700*, Durham, N.C.: Duke University Press, 1940.

For English policy, see L. H. Harper, *The English Navigation Laws*,° New York: Columbia University Press, 1939; E. S. Furniss, *The Position of the Laborer in a System of Nationalism*, New York: Houghton, Mifflin, 1920; Robert L. Schuyler, *The Fall of the Old Colonial System: A Study in British Free Trade, 1770–1870*, New York: Oxford, University Press, 1945; George Louis Beer, *The Old Colonial System, 1660–1754*, New York: P. Smith, 1912–1933 (2 vols.); M. G. Lawson, *Fur: A Study in English Mercantilism, 1700–1775*, Toronto: University of Toronto Press, 1943; K. E. Knorr, *British Colonial Theories, 1570–1850*, Toronto: University of Toronto Press, 1944. An insight into French colonial policy will be found in S. L. Mims, *Colbert's West India Policy*, New Haven, Conn.: Yale University Press, 1912.

For the story of the change in theory, see E. A. J. Johnson, *Predecessors of Adam Smith*, Englewood Cliffs, N.J.: Prentice-Hall, 1937.

Chapters 12 and 13. The Industrial Revolution

The best introduction to the Industrial Revolution is undoubtedly the small volume by T. S. Ashton, *The Industrial Revolution, 1760–1830*,° New York: Oxford University Press, 1948, but see also his *An Economic History of England: The Eighteenth Century*, New York: Barnes & Noble, 1955. An older but still useful and fuller study is that by Paul Mantoux, *The Industrial Revolution* in the Eighteenth Century. An Outline of the Beginnings of the Modern Factory System in England, New York: Harcourt, Brace, 1927. One should read G. N. Clark, The Idea of the Industrial Revolution, Glasgow: Jackson, 1953, as a corrective against exaggeration.

Studies of individual countries are enlightening on the factors which contributed to industrial change and to the whole problem of industrial diffusion both within a country and as between countries. See, J. H. Clapham, An Economic History of Modern Britain,* Cambridge: Cambridge University Press, 1936–1938 (3 vols.); W. W. Rostow, British Economy of the XIXth Century, New York: Oxford University Press, 1948; and Arthur D. Gayer, W. W. Rostow, and Anna J. Schwartz, The Growth and Fluctuation of the British Economy, 1790–1850, New York: Oxford University Press, 1953 (2 vols.). For France, see Arthur Louis Dunham, The Industrial Revolution in France, New York: Exposition Press, 1955. For Belgium, see B. S. Chelpner, Cent ans d'histoire, sociale en Belgique, Brussels: Institut de Sociologie Solvay, 1956, and F. Baudhuin, Histoire économique de la Belgique, 1914–1939, Brussels: Bruylant, 1946 (2 vols.). The United States is dealt with in Victor S. Clark, History of Manufacturers in the United States, New York: P. Smith, 1949, and C. W. Wright, Economic History of the United States,* New York: McGraw-Hill, 1949. For Germany, see M. Baumont, La Grosse industrie allemande, Paris: Doin, 1928, and Pierre Benaerts, Les Origines de la grande industrie allemande, Paris: Turot, 1933. Switzerland is treated in W. E. Rappard, La Révolution industrielle et les origines de la protection légale du travail en Suisse, Berne: Staempfli, 1914. For Italy, see Rodolfo Morandi, Storia della grande industria in Italia, Bari: Laterza, 1931.

Specifically on the diffusion of industry, one should consult Shepard B. Clough, "The Diffusion of Industry in the Last Century and a Half," Studi in onore di Armando Sapori, Milan: Cisalpino, 1957; Charles Ballot, L'Introduction du machinisme dans l'industrie française, Paris: Rieder, 1923; W. O. Henderson, Britain and Industrial Europe, 1750–1870, Liverpool: Liverpool University Press, 1954; the excellent work by Theodore Hodges, The Iron King of Liège: John Cockerill, unpublished dissertation at Columbia University, 1957; and E. Eyre (Ed.), European Civilization, vol. V, Economic History of Europe since the Reformation, New York: Oxford University Press, 1937.

Among the specialized works on technology for this period, see R. J. Forbes, Man the Maker: A History of Technology and Engineering, New York: Schuman, 1950; Siegfried Giedion, Mechanization Takes Command: A Contribution to Anonymous History, New York: Oxford University Press, 1948; and Jean Fourastié, Machinisme et bien-être, Paris: Editions de Minuit, 1953.

There are good studies of many of the industries in which rapid change was taking place. Among others, see Herbert Heaton, Yorkshire Woollen and Worsted Industries, New York: Oxford University Press, 1920; Erich Roll, An Early Experiment in Industrial Organization: A History of the Firm of Boulton and Watt, 1775–1805, New York: Longmans, 1930; F. X. Van Houtte, L'Evolution de l'industrie textile en Belgique et dans le monde de 1800 à 1939, Louvain: Institut de Recherches Economiques et Sociales, 1949; A. P.

Wadsworth and Julia deL. Mann, *The Cotton Trade and Industrial Lanca-shire, 1600–1780,* Manchester: Manchester University Press, 1931; W. H. B. Court, *The Rise of the Midlands Industries (1600–1838),* New York: Oxford University Press, 1938; W. C. Scoville, *Capitalism and French Glass Making (1640–1789),* Berkeley, Calif.: University of California Press, 1950; G. Unwin, *Samuel Oldknow and the Arkwrights,* New York: Longmans, 1924; Odette Viennet, *Napoléon et l'industrie française: La Crise de 1810–1811,* Paris: Plon, 1947; and William Woodruff, *The British Rubber Industry,* Liverpool: Liverpool University Press, 1958.

In addition one might consult W. Schlote, *British Overseas Trade from 1700 to the 1930s,* Oxford: Blackwell, 1952; John U. Nef, *War and Human Progress,* Cambridge, Mass.: Harvard, 1950; P. Lebrun, *L'Industrie de la laine à Verviers pendant le XVIIIe siècle et le début du XIXe,* Liége: Université de Liége, 1949; Edmund E. Day and Woodlief Thomas, *The Growth of Manu-factures, 1899–1923,* Washington, D.C.: Government Printing Office, 1928; Solomon Fabricant, *Output of Manufacturing Industries, 1899–1937,* New York: National Bureau of Economic Research, 1940; and H. D. Fong, *Triumph of the Factory System in England,* Tientsin: Chihli, 1930.

Chapter 14. The Agricultural Revolution

A good introduction to agricultural history may be found in N. S. B. Gras, *A History of Agriculture in Europe and America,* New York: Crofts, 1940, and Lord Ernle, *English Farming, Past and Present,* New York: Long-mans, 1936.

On the subject of landholding, see Georges Lefebvre, *La Révolution fran-çaise,* Paris: Presses Universitaires, 1951; J. Blum, *Noble Landowners and Agriculture in Austria (1818–1848),* Baltimore, Md.: Johns Hopkins Press, 1948; F. Lütge, *Die mitteldeutsche Grundherrschaft,* Iena: Fischer, 1934; C. S. Orwin, *The Open Fields,* New York: Oxford University Press, 1954; and J. D. Chambers, "Enclosure and Labour Supply in the Industrial Revolution," *Economic History Review,* ser. 2, vol. 5, no. 3.

For agricultural techniques and policy: E. Parmalee Prentice, *American Dairy Cattle, Their Past and Future,* New York: Harper, 1942; H. Hertel, *A Short Survey of Agriculture in Denmark,* Copenhagen: Bianco Luno, 1925; M. Augé-Laribé, *La Politique agricole de la France de 1880 à 1940,* Paris: Presses Universitaires, 1950; and Harold Barger and Hans H. Landsberg, *American Agriculture, 1899–1939,* New York: National Bureau of Economic Research, 1942, chap. 15.

In addition to the works on trade already cited, one should look at such general studies as E. Levasseur, *Histoire du commerce de la France de 1789 à nos jours,* Paris: Rousseau, 1912 (2 vols.); and the League of Nations pub-lications: *Europe's Trade,* Geneva: League of Nations, 1941; the *Network of World Trade,* Geneva: League of Nations, 1942; and *Industrialization and Foreign Trade,* Princeton, N.J.: League of Nations, 1945.

On roads and railroads see H. Cavaillès, *La Route française, son histoire, sa fonction*, Paris: Colin, 1946; Ch. Dollfus and E. de Geoffroy, *Histoire de la locomotion terrestre*, Paris: L'Illustration, 1935–1936 (2 vols.); L. Génicot, *Histoire des routes belges depuis 1704*, Brussels: Office de Publicité, 1948; Edward C. Kirkland, *Men, Cities, and Transportation: A Study in New England History, 1820–1900*, Cambridge, Mass.: Harvard University Press, 1948 (2 vols.) C. E. R. Sherrington, *A Hundred Years of Inland Transportation (1830–1933)*, London: Duckworth, 1934: *100 Jahre deutsche Eisenbahn*, Berlin: Reichsverkehrsministerium, 1937; and Kimon A. Doukas, *The French Railways and the State*, New York: Columbia University Press, 1945. See also, Harold Barger, *The Transportation Industries, 1889–1946*, New York: National Bureau of Economic Research, 1951; and William N. Leonard, *Railroad Consolidation under the Transportation Act of 1920,** New York: Columbia University Press, 1946.

The literature on water carrying is abundant. For an introduction to the subject one might begin with C. E. Fayle, *A Short History of the World's Shipping*, London: Allen and Unwin, 1933; A. W. Kirkaldy, *British Shipping; Its History, Organization, and Importance*, London: Paul, 1914; G. S. Graham, *Empire of the North Atlantic*, Toronto: Toronto University Press, 1950; or David Budlong Tyler, *Steam Conquers the Atlantic,** New York: Appleton-Century, 1939. On French shipping, Charles de la Roncière, *Histoire de la marine française*, Paris: Plon, Nourrit, 1899–1932 (6 vols.); and J. Godechot, *Histoire de l'Atlantique*, Paris: Bordas, 1947. For German shipping, W. Vogel and G. Schmölders, *Die Deutschen als Seefahrer*, Hamburg: Hoffman and Campe, 1949. See also, S. C. Gilfillan, *Inventing the Ship*, Chicago: Follett, 1935; the excellent book by Paul William Bamford, *Forests and French Sea Power, 1660–1789,** Toronto: Toronto University Press, 1956; Robert G. Albion, *Forests and Sea Power: The Timber Problem of the Royal Navy, 1632–1862*, Cambridge, Mass.: Harvard, 1926; John G. B. Hutchins, *The American Maritime Industries and Public Policy, 1789–1914*, Cambridge, Mass.: Harvard, 1941; and Louis C. Hunter, *Steamboats on the Western Rivers,** Cambridge, Mass.: Harvard University Press, 1949.

The importance of national postal services in communications is described in L. Kalmus, *Weltgeschichte der Post, mit besonderer Berucksichtigung des deutschen Sprachgebiets*, Göttingen: Verlag für Militär- und Fachliteratur, 1938.

Concerning commercial policy, see Aldo de Maddalena, *La politica commerciale estera degli Stati Uniti dal 1789 al 1812*, Milan: Cisalpino, 1953; Percy Ashley, *Modern Tariff History*, London: Murray, 1920; Eli Heckscher, *The Continental System*, New York: Oxford University Press, 1923; and W. O. Henderson, *The Zollverein,** Cambridge: Cambridge University Press, 1939.

Chapter 16. Revolutions in Investing, Business Organization, and Finance

The role of finance capitalism is explained in G. W. Edwards, *The Evolution of Finance Capitalism*, New York: Longmans, 1938, and from a Marxist point of view, in Maurice Dobbs, *Studies in the Development of Capitalism,** New York: International Publishers, 1947.

For the new types of banking see E. C. Corti, *The Rise of the House of Rothschild,* New York: Cosmopolitan, 1928; Ralph W. Hidy, *The House of Baring,* Cambridge, Mass.: Harvard University Press, 1949; A. Liesse, *Evolution of Credit and Banks in France from the Founding of the Bank of France to the Present Time,* Washington, D.C.: Government Printing Office, 1909; J. Riesser, *The German Great Banks and their Concentration,* Washington, D.C.: Government Printing Office, 1911; and W. Gerloff and W. Neumark, *Handbuch der Finanzwissenschaft,* Tübingen: Mohr, 1952–1956 (2 vols.).

For studies of central banks, see John H. Clapham, *The Bank of England,* previously cited; Gabriel Ramon, *Histoire de la Banque de France,* Paris: Grasset, 1929; B. S. Chelpner, *La Banque de Belgique,* Brussels: Lamertin, 1926–1930 (2 vols.); Esther R. Taus, *Central Banking Functions of the United States' Treasury, 1789–1941,* New York: Columbia University Press, 1943; and *Banking Studies,* Washington: Board of Governors of Federal Reserve System, 1941.

On stock exchanges and corporations: F. W. Hirst, *The Stock Exchange: A Short History of Investments and Speculation,* London: Butterworth, 1932; George Heberton Evans, *British Corporation Finance, 1775–1850: A Study of Preference Shares,* Baltimore, Md.: Johns Hopkins Press, 1936; and B. C. Hunt, *The Development of the Business Corporation in England, 1800–1867,* Cambridge, Mass.: Harvard, 1936. On the concentration of business, see F. Cheney, *Cartels, Combines, and Trusts,* Washington, D.C.: Library of Congress, 1944; R. Lewinsohn, *Trusts et cartels dans l'économie mondiale,* Paris: Médicis, 1950; Adolph A. Berle, Jr. and Gardiner C. Means, *The Modern Corporation and Private Property,* New York: Macmillan, 1932; R. Liefmann, *Cartels, Concerns, and Trusts,* New York: Dutton, 1932; and with different emphasis, Thomas C. Cochran and William Miller, *The Age of Enterprise,* New York: Macmillan, 1951.

On foreign investments, see L. H. Jenks, *The Migration of British Capital to 1875,* New York: Knopf, 1938; Harry D. White, *The French International Accounts, 1880–1913,* Cambridge, Mass.: Harvard University Press, 1933; Benjamin Haggott Beckhart et al., *The New York Money Market,* New York: Columbia University Press, 1931–1932 (4 vols.); and Herbert Feis, *Europe, the World's Banker,* New Haven, Conn.: Yale University Press, 1930.

On certain monetary problems, see Seymour Harris, *The Assignats,* Cambridge, Mass.: Harvard University Press, 1930; A. Nicolle, *Comment la France a payé après Waterloo,* Paris: Boccard, 1929; and W. A. Shaw, *The History of Currency, 1252–1894,* London: Wilsons & Milne, 1896.

For the history of business cycles, consult A. F. Burns and Wesley C. Mitchell, *Measuring the Business Cycle,** New York: National Bureau of Economic Research, 1946; Wesley C. Mitchell, *What Happens during Business Cycles,* New York: National Bureau of Economic Research, 1951; and Willard L. Thorp, *Business Annals,* New York: National Bureau of Economic Research, 1926.

On the subject of insurance in this period: C. W. Wright and C. E. Fayle, *A History of Lloyd's*, London: Macmillan, 1928; J. Halperin, *Les Assurances en suisse et dans le monde*, Neuchâtel: Baconnière, 1946; and Shepard B. Clough, *A Century of Life Insurance*,* New York: Columbia University Press, 1946.

As an introduction to the study of the history of modern public finance, one might read Sidney Ratner, *A Political and Social History of Federal Taxation, 1789–1913*, New York: Norton, 1942, and consult Marcel Marion, *Histoire financière de la France depuis 1715*, Paris: Rousseau, 1914–1931 (6 vols.).

Chapter 17. The New Economy Comes of Age

Inasmuch as this chapter deals primarily with the continuation of earlier trends, many of the works already cited are pertinent for the material covered.

On the "new imperialism" one will find useful Parker T. Moon, *Imperialism and World Politics*, New York: Macmillan, 1955. See also, A. Viallate, *Economic Imperialism and International Relations during the Last Fifty Years*, New York: Macmillan, 1923; P. E. Schramm, *Deutschland und Uberzee*, Brunswick: Westermann, 1950; and J. S. Bartstra, *Geschiedenis van het Moderne Imperialisme*. Haarlem: Bohn, 1958.

Enlightening books on the trade policies of the period are E. O. Golob, *The Méline Tariff: French Agriculture and Nationalist Economic Policy*,* New York: Columbia University Press, 1944; Wilhelm Röpke, *German Commercial Policy*, New York: Longmans, 1934; and B. H. Brown, *The Tariff Reform Movement in Great Britain, 1881–1895*,* New York: Columbia University Press, 1943.

On the Ruhr-Lorraine complex, see G. Greer, *The Ruhr-Lorraine*, New York: Macmillan, 1925, and Krupp, *A Century's History of the Krupp Works, 1812–1912*, Essen: Krupp, 1912. See also A. B. Parsons (Ed.), *Seventy-five Years of Progress in the Mineral Industry, 1871–1946*, New York: American Institute of Mining and Metallurgical Engineers, 1947.

The literature on the workingman's problems becomes abundant for this period. See John R. Commons et al., *History of Labor in the United States*, New York: Macmillan, 1918–1935 (4 vols.); G. D. H. Cole, *A Short History of the British Working Class Movement*, London: G. Allen, 1948; A. L. Bowley, *Wages and Income in the United Kingdom since 1860*, Cambridge: Cambridge University Press, 1937; which might be preceded by Elizabeth W. Gilboy, *Wages in Eighteenth Century England*, Cambridge, Mass.: Harvard University Press, 1934; Edouard Dolléans, *Histoire du mouvement ouvrier*, Paris: Colin, 1948 (2 vols.); Paul Louis, *Histoire du mouvement syndical en France*, Paris: Valois, 1947–1948 (2 vols.); J. Kucznski, *Labour Conditions in Western Europe, 1820–1935*, New York: International Publishers, 1937; and Leo Wolman, *Ebb and Flow in Trade Unionism*, New York: National Bureau of Economic Research, 1936.

On various kinds of trade unionism, see J. B. Duroselle, *Les Débuts du Catholicisme social en France*, Paris: Presses Universitaires, 1951; Parker T.

Moon, *The Labor Problem and the Social Catholic Movement in France*, New York: Macmillan, 1921; Jean Villain, *L'Enseignement social de l'Eglise*, Paris: Spès, 1953; E. Halévy, *Histoire du socialisme européen*, Paris: Gallimard, 1948; F. Mehring, *Geschichte der deutschen Sozialdemokratie*, Stuttgart: Dietz, 1909 (4 vols.); and Michael P. Fogarty, *Christian Democracy in Western Europe, 1820–1953,** Notre Dame, Ind.: Notre Dame University Press, 1957.

Chapter 18. International, Economic, and Social Stresses

By far the most comprehensive history of any war is James T. Shotwell (Ed.), *The Social and Economic History of the War* (World War I), New York: Carnegie Endowment for International Peace, published during the 1930s, in approximately 150 volumes. Among these, the following deserve special mention: Michael T. Florinsky, *The End of the Russian Empire* (1931); L. Grebler and W. Winkler, *The Effects of the War on Germany and Austria-Hungary* (1940); F. W. Hirst, *Consequences of the War to Great Britain* (1934); P. Renouvin, *The Forms of War Government in France* (1927); J. A. Salter, *Allied Shipping Control* (1921); Henri Pirenne, *La Belgique et la guerre mondiale* (1929); Luigi Einaudi, *La condotta economica e gli effetti sociali della guerra italiana* (1933).

For the crisis in the West, see A. A. Berle, *The Twentieth-Century Capitalist Revolution*, New York: Harcourt, Brace, 1955.

On the reparations question, see Philip M. Burnett, *Reparations at the Paris Peace Conference*, New York: Columbia University Press, 1940 (2 vols.); B. M. Baruch, *The Making of the Reparations and Economic Sections of the Treaty*, New York: Harper, 1920; and J. M. Keynes, *The Economic Consequences of the Peace*, New York: Harcourt, Brace, 1920.

On inflation following the war, the best works regarding German experience are F. D. Graham, *Exchange, Prices, and Production in Hyper-Inflation: Germany, 1920–1923,** Princeton, N.J.: Princeton University Press, 1930, and Constantino Bresciani Turroni, *The Economics of Inflation*, London: G. Allen, 1937. For France, see Martin Wolfe, *The French Franc between the Wars, 1919–1939,** New York: Columbia University Press, 1951; Pierre Dieterlen and Charles Rist, *The Monetary Problem of France*, New York: King's Crown Press, 1948; and *The Course and Control of Inflation*, Princeton, N.J.: League of Nations, 1946.

On war debts, see Harold G. Moulton and Leo Pasvolsky, *War Debts and World Prosperity*, Washington, D.C.: The Brookings Institution, 1932.

There are several works on the reconstruction after World War I. See William Ogburn and William Jaffe, *The Economic Development of Post-War France*, New York: Columbia University Press, 1929; G. C. Allen, *British Industries and Their Organization*, New York: Longmans, 1951; and R. A. Brady, *The Rationalization Movement in German Industry*, Berkeley, Calif.: University of California Press, 1933.

Chapter 19. Economic Growth and Economic Depression

C. W. Guillebaud, *The Economic Recovery of Germany, from 1933 to the Incorporation of Austria in March, 1938,* London: Macmillan, 1939; Louis R. Franck, *Les Etapes de l'économie fasciste italienne,* Paris: La Librairie Sociale et Economique, 1939; G. Stolper, *German Economy, 1870–1940,* New York: Reynal & Hitchcock, 1940; F. C. Benham, *Great Britain under Protection,* New York: Macmillan, 1941; and David E. Lilienthal, *T.V.A.: Democracy on the March,* New York: Harper, 1953.

These offer interesting studies of business leadership: R. A. Brady, *Business as a System of Power,* New York: Columbia University Press, 1943; Allan Nevins, *John D. Rockefeller,* New York: Scribner, 1940 (2 vols.); Allan Nevins, *Ford: The Times, the Man, the Company,* New York: Scribner, 1954; and *Ford, Expansion and Challenge, 1915–1933,* New York: Scribner, 1957.

On the great depression of the 1930s: H. V. Hodson, *Slump and Recovery, 1929–1937,* New York: Oxford University Press, 1938; W. K. Galbraith, *The Great Crash,* Boston: Houghton, Mifflin, 1955; M. J. Bonn, *The Crumbling of Empire: The Disintegration of World Economy,* London: G. Allen, 1938.

For this period see also, F. A. Haight, *A History of French Commercial Policy,* New York: Macmillan, 1941; Lamartine Yates, *Food Production in Western Europe,* New York: Longmans, 1940; K. E. Poole, *German Financial Policies, 1932–1939,* Cambridge, Mass.: Harvard University Press, 1939; and Lionel Robbins, *The Economic Causes of War,* London: J. Cape, 1939.

Chapters 20 and 21. The Economics of World War II and Postwar Economic Recovery and Expansion

Most of the belligerents in World War II prepared some kind of economic studies of their experiences. One of the best of this type is W. K. Hancock and M. M. Gowing, *British War Economy,* London: H. M. Stationery Office, 1949. See also, L. Baudin, *Esquisse de l'économie française sous l'occupation allemande,* Paris: Médicis, 1945; and the publications of many Federal agencies of the United States, especially the Office of Price Administration. The impact of strategic bombing is interestingly portrayed in *The Effects of Strategic Bombing on the German War Economy,* Washington, D.C.: U.S. Air Force, 1945.

The effect of the war on American agriculture is competently treated in Walter W. Wilcox, *The Farmer in the Second World War,* Ames, Iowa: Iowa State College Press, 1947. An excellent study of wartime migrations in Eugene M. Kulischer, *Europe on the Move: War and Population Changes (1917–1947),* New York: Columbia University Press, 1948; and Francis E. Merrill, *Social Problems on the Home Front,** New York: Harper, 1948. The story of relief is excellently described in George Woodbridge, *UNRRA, The History of the United Nations Relief and Rehabilitation Administration,* New York: Columbia University Press, 1950 (3 vols.). Also Karl Brandt, *Manage-*

ment of Agriculture and Food in the German-occupied and Other Areas of Fortress Europe, Stanford, Calif.: Stanford University Press, 1953.

Certain important studies were made after the war to guide the constitutional assemblies or new governments in various states. Among these the Italian is extremely useful to the economic historian: *Rapporto delle commissione economica*, Rome: Instituto Poligrafico dello Stato, 1947 (4 vols.). Of a similar kind were the reports of the *Commissariat au Plan* [Monnet Plan], Paris: 16 rue Martignac, annually since the war. For Germany, *Wirtschaft und Statistik;* for the United Kingdom, *Economic Survey;* and for Italy, *Review of the Economic Conditions in Italy*, published by the Banco di Roma, a ten-year summary of which was published in 1956.

Special studies exist for most countries. For Germany, see the excellent study by Henry C. Wallich, *Mainsprings of the German Revival*, New Haven, Conn.: Yale University Press, 1955; and André Piettre, *L'Economie allemande contemporaine, 1945–1952*, Paris: Génin, 1952. For France, Edward M. Earle (Ed.), *Modern France: Problems of the Third and Fourth Republics*, Princeton, N.J.: Princeton University Press, 1951; and *La France Economique*, which is an annual survey of the economy of France, published by the *Revue d'Economie Politique*. For the United Kingdom, see A. C. Pigou, *Aspects of British Economic History, 1918–1925*, London: Macmillan, 1947; Pauline Gregg, *Social and Economic History of Britain, 1760–1950*, London: Harrap, 1950; and Keith Hutchison, *The Decline and Fall of British Capitalism*, New York: Scribner, 1950. For the United States, Shepard B. Clough, *The American Way* (cited under National Economic Histories above); and J. K. Galbraith, *American Capitalism: The Concept of Countervailing Power*, Boston: Houghton, Mifflin, 1952. For Latin America, Paul Prebisch, *The Economic Development of Latin America and Its Principal Problems*, New York: United Nations, 1950.

On the subject of inflation, see A. J. Brown, *The Great Inflation, 1939–1951*, New York: Oxford University Press, 1955.

On the economics of the peace, Redvers Opie et al., *The Search for Peace Settlements*, Washington: Brookings Institution, 1951; also René Albrecht-Carrié, *A Diplomatic History of Europe*, New York: Harper, 1958.

For the broad view of Europe's economy since World War II, see Ingvar Svennilson, *Growth and Stagnation in the European Economy*, Geneva: United Nations, 1954. On the economic integration of Europe, see François Perroux, *L'Europe sans rivages*, Paris: Presses Universitaires, 1954. Concerning the world economy, consult Gunnar Myrdal, *An International Economy—Problems and Prospects*, New York: Harper, 1956.

To get a picture of recent developments in agriculture, consult Folke Dovring, *Land and Labour in Europe*, The Hague: Nijhoff, 1956; and on food M. K. Bennett, *The World's Food*, New York: Harper, 1954. See also, Murray R. Benedict, *Farm Policies of the United States, 1790–1950: A Study of their Origins and Development*, New York: The Twentieth Century Fund, 1953.

On the impact of technology on production, see Jean Fourastié and A. Laleuf, *Révolution à l'Ouest*, Paris: Presses Universitaires, 1957.

For capital in underdeveloped countries, see Ragnar Nurkse, *Problems of Capital Formation in Under-developed Countries,* Oxford: Blackwell, 1953; and P. T. Bauer and B. S. Young, *The Economics of Under-developed Countries,* Cambridge: Cambridge University Press, 1957.

A new interest has been shown since World War II in interest groups and their contribution to the formation of economic policy. See, Joseph Henry Foth, *Trade Associations: Their Service to Industry,* New York: Ronald, 1930; George W. Stocking and Myron W. Watkins, *Monopoly and Free Enterprise,* New York: Twentieth Century Fund, 1951; Henry W. Ehrmann, *French Labor from Popular Front to Liberation,** New York: Oxford University Press, 1947; and by the same author, *Organized Business in France,** Princeton, N.J.: Princeton University Press, 1957; Val Lorwin, *The French Labor Movement,** Cambridge, Mass.: Harvard University Press, 1955; Jean Meyaud, *Les groupes de pression,* Paris: Colin, 1958; and Günter Triesch, *Die Macht der Funktionäre,* Düsseldorf: Karl Rauch, 1956.

Many of the publications of the United Nations are excellent. Some of the series make it possible to keep abreast of developments. See especially *World Economic Survey; Economic Survey of Europe; Economic Survey of Latin America; Economic Survey of Asia and the Far East.* See also the publications of the Food and Agriculture Organization, Rome; and of the International Labor Office, Geneva.

Author Index

Subject Index